THE WISDOM OF

THE LITTMAN LIBRARY OF JEWISH CIVILIZATION

Dedicated to the memory of
LOUIS THOMAS SIDNEY LITTMAN
who founded the Littman Library for the love of God
and as an act of charity in memory of his father
JOSEPH AARON LITTMAN
יהא זכרם ברוך

Get wisdom, get understanding:
Forsake her not and she shall preserve thee
PROV. 4:5

The Littman Library of Jewish Civilization is a registered UK charity
Registered charity no. 1000784

THE WISDOM OF THE
ZOHAR

*

AN ANTHOLOGY OF TEXTS
VOLUME I

Systematically arranged and rendered into Hebrew by
FISCHEL LACHOWER AND ISAIAH TISHBY

With extensive introductions and explanations by
ISAIAH TISHBY

English translation by
DAVID GOLDSTEIN

Oxford · Portland, Oregon
The Littman Library of Jewish Civilization

The Littman Library of Jewish Civilization
Chief Executive Officer: Ludo Craddock
Managing Editor: Connie Webber

PO Box 645, Oxford OX2 0UJ, UK
www.littman.co.uk

———

Published in the United States and Canada by
The Littman Library of Jewish Civilization
c/o ISBS, 920 NE 58th Avenue, Suite 300
Portland, Oregon 97213-3786

The Hebrew version, Mishnat ha-Zohar, ws published by
Mosad Bialik, Jerusalem 1949 (Volume I), 1961 (Volume II)

First published in hardback 1989
First published in paperback 1991
Paperback reprinted 1994, 2002, 2008

British Library Cataloguing in Publication Data

[Zohar. English Selections]
The Wisdom of the Zohar: an anthology of texts.
(The Littman library of Jewish civilization)
I. Cabala
I. Lachower, Fischel__II. Tishby, Isaiah__III. Series
296.1_6__BM525. A52

ISBN 978-1-874774-28-0

Library of Congress Cataloging-in-Publication Data

Zohar. English. Selections.
The wisdom of the Zohar
(The Littman library of Jewish civilization)
Translation of : Mishnat ha-Zohar.
Includes bibliographies and indexes.
1. Cabala.__2. Zohar.
I. Lachower, Yeruham Fischel, 1883–1947.
II. Tishby, Isaiah, 1908–1992.__Goldstein, David, 1933–1987
IV. Title.__V. Series.
BM525.A52G65__1987__296.1_6__86-31253

ISBN 978-1-874774-28-0

Cover design by Pete Russell, Faringdon, Oxon.
Printed in Great Britain on acid-free paper by Alden HenDi Witney, Oxfordshire OX29 0YG

CONTENTS

VI Printed Editions, Manuscripts, Translations, and
   Commentaries

PRELIMINARIES: EVENTS AND PERSONALITIES

PART I THE GODHEAD

Section I *En-Sof* and the World of Emanation

Introduction

Section III *Shekhinah*

Introduction

VOLUME II

PART II THE OTHER SIDE

PART III CREATION

PART IV THE DOCTRINE OF MAN

Section I The Three Souls

VOLUME III

PART V SACRED WORSHIP

PART VI PRACTICAL LIFE

Section I Morality

Section II Conjugal Life

A SPECIAL PREFACE TO THE TRANSLATOR'S INTRODUCTION

The editors of the Littman Library take particular pride in presenting *The Wisdom of the Zohar* to the public. It is a work combining much wisdom, scholarship, and poetic vision—echoed in this gifted translation by Rabbi Dr. David Goldstein. We record with much sadness that David Goldstein died shortly after completing this work, and that Louis Littman, founder and guiding genius of the Littman Library, died only a few months later, not long after he had read the galley proofs from his hospital bed. This book is the first to be published in the Littman Library after his death, and as such it is a fitting tribute to him as a lover of wisdom whose contribution to Jewish learning will continue to instruct generations to come.

The literary and scholarly merit of David Goldstein's translation of *Mishnat ha-Zohar* won recognition even before it was published. The manuscript was submitted in 1987 for the George Webber Prize, offered annually by the Oxford Centre for Postgraduate Hebrew Studies for excellence in translation from Hebrew into English; shortly before his death, Dr. Goldstein learned that his work, as published here, had been awarded the Prize. David Goldstein's earlier work for the Littman Library series, entitled *Hebrew Poems from Spain*, had also received a literary award and had become a best seller; and his translation of the *Ashkenazi Haggadah* had won the silver medal at the Leipzig BookFair.

David Goldstein's whole life was devoted to scholarship, through his work as Curator of Hebrew Manuscripts and Printed Books at the British Library, as a lecturer at the Leo Baeck College, as a rabbi at the Liberal Jewish Synagogue before he joined the British Library, and as a participant in many other scholarly institutions and organizations. His colleagues respected and loved him for his integrity, quiet humour, and deep concern for everyone he encountered. His wife Berenice and his three sons supported him with their love and constant support. It is our hope that the reception this text will receive will be a source of comfort to them.

Louis Littman chose David Goldstein as one of the first editors of this series, and discussed many of his publication projects with him. As in other fields, one saw here the ability of Louis Littman's first-class mind to attract the most suitable persons for a task which was so important to him and to his family. Louis Littman had read law at Cambridge and had practised for some years as a solicitor. Eventually, he found himself involved in far-reaching enterprises, including large-scale farming. Countless demands were made upon his time. Nevertheless, he not only developed the very concept of the Littman Library of Jewish Civilization, which he dedicated to the memory of his father, but he also attended to every detail of this complex enterprise. In particular, he searched for texts which deserved publication but were considered by publishers not to be viable commercially. Louis Littman was convinced that the classic texts should be presented to new readers, and that the works of contemporary scholars should also be supported. He read *The Wisdom of the Zohar* with great care, the same care which he gave to every text published in this series. He had high standards, and he worked closely with the editor of every text because he looked upon books as a basic part of his life. When he felt death approaching he enlisted the help of his family to ensure the continuation of this series—help which had indeed surrounded and supported him for many years. Publication of his book is evidence that Louis Littman's vision will continue to be realized in accordance with his wishes.

I felt deeply humbled that Louis Littman selected me to continue David Goldstein's work as editor. In that role, I join the other editors: Rabbi Dr. Louis Jacobs, who checked and supplemented the index to this work prepared by Mrs. Lilian Rubin, and Dr. Vivian D. Lipman. As editors we shall continue to follow the guidelines that Louis Littman established, and we shall always remember both him and David Goldstein in the work which lies ahead of us. May this book be an abiding memorial to them both.

ALBERT H. FRIEDLANDER

London
Adar 5748/March 1988

TRANSLATOR'S INTRODUCTION

This translation of the *Mishnat ha-Zohar* was motivated by a desire to bring to those readers who could not master the original an insight into the teachings of the Zohar.

In my student days I tried to read the Zohar with the help of the English translation by H. Sperling and M. Simon (London, 1931). But I found that the translation itself needed constant explanation, and I did not get very far. In Professor Tishby's notes and introductions in his *Mishnat ha-Zohar* I discovered for the first time a key to an understanding of the Zohar—to its historical and literary background and its complex symbolism. I felt that others would want to share this discovery. To go back to the major work of kabbalah in this way is particularly important in our time, because there has been a veritable plethora of pseudo-Jewish mysticism published in the last thirty years, emanating mainly from writers who let their imaginations run riot, with very little knowledge of the authentic material.

I am grateful to Professor Tishby, who has guided me with many suggestions for improvement, especially in the early years of my work on the translation, when guidance was particularly important.

The Hebrew original was published by Mosad Bialik in Jerusalem in 1949. Volume I (4th edn., 1982) extended to Part III (*Creation*), and Volume II (1961) contained the rest of the anthology. I have translated the actual texts of the Zohar from the Aramaic original, accepting Tishby's variant readings, and turning to his Hebrew version at all times for clarification.

Following Tishby's procedure I have been as literal as possible in my approach. The language of the Zohar is extremely concise, often to the point of obscurity. This conciseness is reflected in the translation, but the reader will be able to find his way to the full meaning by reading the bracketed additions and by consulting the notes. The work of translation bristles with difficulties. One of the most intractable was the choice of gender for pronouns. For example, *Tiferet* is of the feminine gender, but it refers to a male element in the sefirotic system. It has not been possible for me to be entirely consistent. I have used *he*, *she*, or *it* according to context, which itself often depends on the genders used in the specific scriptural verse that forms the basis for the mystical interpretation.

References to the Bible are to the Hebrew original, which differs occasionally in chapter and verse division from Christian translations. The translations from the Bible are mine, and frequently differ radically from traditional renderings when this is demanded by the context of the Zohar's interpretation. I have drawn attention in the notes to the more traditional versions when this seemed desirable.

The *Mishnat ha-Zohar* did not contain a subject index or a bibliography, since Tishby expected to publish a third volume. I have therefore added the former and a list of works cited, together with a select bibliography of works published since the *Mishnat ha-Zohar* appeared. I have supplemented the original index of translated passages from the Zohar by including references to the passages that occur in translation in the introductions and notes. I have also added an index of references to the Bible. These indexes were prepared by Lilian Rubin, to whom I am very grateful.

Some additional explanatory remarks were necessary for an English-speaking reader. These I have added in square brackets in the notes. Round and square brackets in the body of the text are Tishby's own, unless followed by *Trans.*

When a quotation from the Zohar in the introductions and notes also occurs in the anthology, I have drawn attention to it by referring to the relevant section and the number of the passage in that section, for example: (*The Tabernacle and the Temple*, 2). Numbers in brackets in the introductions refer to passages translated in the immediately following section of the Zohar.

Where Tishby quotes sources available in English translation, I give the latter instead of, or in addition to, the original works cited.

I am extremely grateful to Mrs. K. Perlo, who typed the greater part of this difficult manuscript with great accuracy and attention to detail.

J. Abelson in his introduction to the Sperling/Simon English translation says that such a work "needs not only learning but much moral courage as well." I would add *physical strength!* This has been an immense labour. During it I have been fascinated and uplifted, and also, I must admit, occasionally dispirited. I now have an overriding sense of gratitude that I have been granted the opportunity to complete this work. I have received much help during the past twelve years. I am indebted to Mr. L. T. S. Littman, who has shown a personal interest in the work of translation from the very beginning. I am particularly grateful to my wife and family, who have lived very patiently with "the brown book"—a name given to the *Mishnat ha-Zohar* by my youngest son when a child, and one that has remained fixed in my memory ever since.

DAVID GOLDSTEIN

London, 1983

NOTE

The forms of names are generally taken from the *Encyclopedia Judaica*, 1972. Hence, for example, Margaliot, not Margulies. The transliteration system also follows the *Encyclopedia Judaica*. Ḥ is to be pronounced like *ch* in *loch*, and ẓ like *ts* in *tsar*. I have not, however, followed the system slavishly where I thought it unnecessary. Hence Hayyim, not Ḥayyim; Yohai, not Yoḥai.

ABBREVIATIONS USED IN THE NOTES

B.T.	Babylonian Talmud
HUCA	*Hebrew Union College Annual*
JJS	*Journal of Jewish Studies*
JQR	*Jewish Quarterly Review*
J.T.	Jerusalem Talmud
MGWJ	*Monatsschrift für Geschichte und Wissenschaft des Judentums*
REJ	*Revue des études juives*

PREFACE TO HEBREW VOLUME I

FIRST EDITION

The Zohar is one of the richest items in the treasury of the Jewish spirit. It has served many generations as a guide through life's complexities, and as a source of inspiration for visionaries and initiates, who immersed themselves in its mysteries. Ordinary people too have derived light and strength from its secret symbolism. But ever since the Age of Enlightenment (the *Haskalah* period), which erected a barrier between the individual Jew and many of the sources that nourished the Jewish spirit in the past, the Zohar has been relegated to a little corner and cherished by only a few restricted groups, remnants of the later kabbalists. Even during the Jewish national revival, which has stimulated research into the ancient heritage and prompted the rediscovery of forgotten resources, and when Jewish mysticism has exerted a deep fascination, the pages of the Zohar itself have remained comparatively unknown and have not been placed before the Hebrew reader in an acceptable form. Because of its strange Aramaic style and the depth and obscurity of its contents, the Zohar remains beyond the scope of Jews to-day and they cannot come to grips with it. Hillel Zeitlin planned to publish a Hebrew translation of the whole Zohar with an extensive commentary, but it did not come to fruition. Only the translation of the introduction was published, after Zeitlin's death.[1]

The *Mishnat ha-Zohar*, which was originally conceived by F. Lachower and S. A. Horodetzky, and which Lachower helped to prepare up to the day of his death, is intended to open up these hidden riches for the Hebrew reader. It comprises an extensive anthology drawn from all sections of the Zohar, including the *Zohar Ḥadash* and the *Tikkunei ha-Zohar*, in Hebrew translation, with introductions, notes, and textual variants. The aim is to present the teachings of the Zohar and its literary character in an ordered and concentrated form. This has meant dismantling the original structure, which was based on the cycle of readings from the Torah without any continuity of subject matter, and putting the selected passages in a new systematic order.

The first volume, now offered to the public, contains "Preliminaries" (*Events and Personalities*), and three parts (*The Godhead, The Other Side, Creation*), each of which is divided into sections. The preliminaries are intended to accustom the reader to the literary and imaginative atmosphere of the Zohar before he penetrates its actual mystical doctrines. Most of the selections in this part present the personalities of the Zohar, the circle of "companions" and their association with Rabbi Simeon ben Yohai, who is the leader and focus of their activities. At the end of the preliminaries there are a number of passages that deal with the remarkable characters (Rav Hamnuna Sava, Sava de-Mish-patim, and Yanuka) who meet the "companions" on their travels and reveal to them the mysteries of the Torah. The three parts on theory that follow contain most of the important passages on *En-Sof*, the world of emanation, the *Shekhinah* and the control of the worlds, *sitra aḥra* (the other side) and the activity of his powers, the creation of the world, the mysteries of the Chariot and the angels, and nature. The Zohar's teaching about man both in this world and in the next, about his relationship with God through the religious life, and about Israel and the other nations of the world from their beginnings until the end of days will form the second volume, which will also contain indexes and a bibliography.[2]

It goes without saying that any anthology, however complete and systematically arranged, cannot take the place of the original work. And, looked at from this point of view, the *Mishnat ha-Zohar* is only a beginning. A Hebrew translation of the whole Zohar, based on critical foundations, is an enormous scholarly task still awaiting fulfillment. Perhaps in our present state of research the time is not yet ripe, since a detailed philological attempt to establish the original Aramaic text is still a desideratum. Nevertheless, the want of absolute perfection need not affect the limited goal that we have set ourselves, which is to enable the reader to gain firsthand contact with the Zohar. In fact, a translation of the complete Zohar that followed the order of the original would be unlikely to achieve this aim, because of the constant repetition and lack of continuity of thought that are among the work's chief characteristics.

In arranging this selection we have tried as best we could to avoid the failings that are a feature of so many anthologies. We have particularly resisted the temptation to include small fragments, to shorten pieces, or to jump from one passage to another, which is nothing less than to emasculate the original. In general, therefore, we have chosen complete sections, large or small, even though they might contain material not strictly relevant to the theme. Consequently, there are a number of long pieces given in their entirety, each one of which occupies several pages of the original; for example, most of the *Sava de-Mishpatim* (Zohar II, 94b–99b), *Yanuka* in the *parashah Balak* (II, 186a–192a), and the *Hekhalot* in the *parashah Bereshit* (I, 41a–45b).

In the translation we have taken the first steps toward correcting errors and establishing the original text. The translation of the Zohar on the Torah follows the Vilna edition (1882), which has been compared with the first editions (Mantua, 1558–60, and Cremona, 1558) and the Constantinople edition (1736–37). That of the *Zohar Ḥadash* follows the Venice edition (1658), emended in the light of the Salonika edition (1597). The translation of the *Tikkunei ha-Zohar* follows the Amsterdam edition (1768), emended on the basis of the Mantua (1558) edition.[3] In many passages we have emended the text on the basis of quotations in the writings of the most important commentators, and in the light of the textual variants in Rabbi Abraham Azulai's *Or ha-Levanah*. This latter contains many important emendations from manuscripts, and it is a most valuable source for establishing the correct text, but only the section on Genesis has been published so far.[4] We have made a number of small emendations of our own, without authority from the sources. In the list of textual variants at the end of the book[5] we have noted only those which directly affect the Hebrew translation. It should be unnecessary to add that the text of the *Mishnat ha-Zohar*, which is not based on an examination of manuscripts nor on a detailed comparison of different sources, is not intended to be critically authoritative. This is a separate and enormous task that has yet to be realized.

Great pains have been taken to make the translation as accurate as possible. We have therefore faithfully represented the specific peculiarities in the linguistic style, where they were not due to a corrupt text. Only in those places

where the original is so elliptic or obscure that additional matter is required
have we inserted words or phrases of our own, and these are in square brackets.
Very common mistakes, such as changes in gender or number, which
undoubtedly arose from linguistic carelessness or scribal error, have been
corrected in the translation without a note. There are occasions where the text is
not sufficiently clear or where use is made of garbled or made-up expressions,
these being very common in the Zohar. Here we have had to resort to
interpretation, in full knowledge that other translations are possible.

On the question of style we came up against great difficulties that could not
easily be resolved. The Zohar is written in Aramaic, on the model of the
Talmud and the midrashim. But there are in addition unmistakable signs that
the style was influenced by the Aramaic translations (*targumim*) of the Bible, and
there are also linguistic features common to medieval literature. These latter
are sometimes so prevalent that in many places the Zohar seems like a work
written by thirteenth-century kabbalists or homilists in an artificial Aramaic
garb. This mixture of different linguistic layers sets the translator the difficult
problem of deciding which Hebrew style he should choose for his work. He
ought to be able to get some guidance from the Hebrew sections of the *Midrash
ha-Ne'elam* and from the Hebrew version of quotations from the Zohar that
appear in the writings of Rabbi Moses de Leon. But these two sources only
complicate the problem, because the *Midrash ha-Ne'elam* tends toward a
traditional rabbinic style, while Moses de Leon's language is generally
medieval in character. Moreover, the Zohar itself contains many stylistic
differences, largely dictated by the subject matter. We decided, therefore, to
allow ourselves some flexibility. In sentence construction and idiom we have
tried to approximate the translation to the rabbinic style, with the addition of a
few medieval features. In choice of vocabulary, however, we did not settle for
one particular style. We have used the whole range of Hebrew, including in a
few places modern words where necessary.

Commentaries to the Zohar have multiplied over the years, and they now
form an extensive literature of their own. However, there is hardly a single
commentary that a reader unfamiliar with the original sources can use to help
him understand the literal meaning of the text. On the contrary, most of the
commentators tried to read their own ideas into the Zohar and thus obscured
the very passages they were trying to elucidate. The notes in the *Mishnat ha-
Zohar* attempt to satisfy a long-felt need. They are intended to explain the
mysteries of the Zohar in a clear and concise fashion, as near as possible to the
literal meaning of the text. The notes are presented to the reader without any
discussion or references to supporting sources, except in a few places where this
was absolutely necessary. The sefirotic symbols are explained wherever they
occur. The rabbinic sources used by the Zohar itself are indicated in the margin
wherever such a source is specifically mentioned in the text by the use of a
phrase such as "It is taught (*tanya*)."[6] Most of the notes are not original but are
drawn from, or based on the more important commentaries. Those used most
frequently are: Rabbi Simeon Ibn Labi, *Ketem Paz*; Rabbi Moses Cordovero,
Pardes Rimmonim; Rabbi Abraham Galante, *Zohorei Ḥamah*; Rabbi Abraham
Azulai, *Or ha-Ḥamah*; Rabbi Zvi Hirsch Horowitz, *Ispaklarya ha-Me'irah*; Rabbi
Solomon Buzaglo, *Mikdash Melekh*; Rabbi Elijah, the Gaon of Vilna, *Yahel Or*.

Each section has its own separate introduction, except for the preliminaries. The ideological content of the latter is explained in other introductions, while the personalities mentioned there are discussed in the general introduction, especially in the part dealing with the narrative framework. Each introduction gives a specialized explanation of the suject matter of the relevant section that follows, and the problems raised. The Zohar's attitude to a particular topic is discussed at length and related to its source material both within and outside the area of kabbalistic literature. The explanations given in the introduction complement the notes that are appended to the translated passages of the Zohar. For example, the notes briefly identify the symbols of the *sefirot* wherever they occur, but an explanation of the whole sefirotic system and the way in which the *sefirot* are related to one another is found in the introduction to the section *Sefirot*.

The general introduction to the Zohar and to Zohar research deals with the structure of the book and its influence, and with the history of research into its authorship and composition. It is meant to offer a comprehensive survey of the role of the Zohar in the development of Judaism, a full account of the long controversy concerning the historical and literary questions about its composition, and a presentation of the latest scholarly conclusions. All the main arguments from every side are described in detail with supporting quotations. It is hoped that, by putting the arguments of those who believe in the Zohar's antiquity side by side with the results of detailed scholarly investigation, we can put an end once and for all to the futile debates that on the basis of pure hypothesis try to overturn the findings of true, objective, scientific research.

This first volume of the *Mishnat ha-Zohar* is the result of five years' concentrated work. F. Lachower translated some of the passages and I translated others. But we each revised the other's work in order to make the style as consistent as possible. I made the final arrangement of the selection in consultation with Lachower, who also read the notes and the introductions to the sections *En-Sof*, *Sefirot*, and *Shekhinah*, and made useful suggestions. His untimely death prevented him from cooperating in the other parts of the book and in the preparation of Volume Two.

My thanks are due to Mosad Bialik for bearing the great expense of producing this book and for its attractive format, and to the Jewish National and University Library, from which I derived great help. Last but not least I must acknowledge especially the help of my teacher, Prof. Gershom Scholem. My introductions are based in many instances on his important studies, and he himself helped me with advice and notes in the preparation of the general introduction, particularly in the section dealing with Zohar manuscripts.

I. TISHBY

Jerusalem, 1949

PREFACE TO HEBREW VOLUME II

Twelve years have passed since the appearance of *Mishnat ha-Zohar*, Volume I.
F. Lachower, who cooperated in translating the passages from the Zohar in that
volume and also in its final arrangement, died before it was printed. I have
consequently taken it upon myself to prepare the translations for this second
volume, which was meant to complete the whole work. I hoped at first to finish
this volume within a few years, but as I went on I thought it best to widen its
scope considerably. It is not only that the selections from the Zohar, the notes,
and the introductions are split into two volumes in addition to the first, as
mentioned in the preface to the second edition of Volume I (1957), but that this
second volume has become larger than expected, amounting to nearly eight
hundred printed pages. This has entailed a great deal of unforeseen additional
work and has delayed the appearance of Volume II.

This expansion affects every part of the book: the scope of selection, the notes,
and the introductions. The arrangement of the anthology and the method of
translation follow the lines laid down in the preface to Volume I, which were
determined in conjunction with Lachower. But I thought it essential to discuss
the subjects chosen in more detail, and to illustrate them more fully in the
translated selections. (The translations, quotations, and references from the
Zohar follow the Vilna edition as in Volume I, but selections from the *Zohar
Hadash* are now cited from the Munkács edition [1911], while those from the
Tikkunei ha-Zohar follow the Jerusalem edition [1948], edited by R. Margaliot,
because these texts are better than those used in Volume I.) In the preparation
of the notes I have also kept to the procedure of Volume I, but after further
thought and in response to requests by readers I came to the conclusion that I
had been over-brief in places where I should have been more expansive and as a
result I left some things unexplained. In this volume I have therefore expanded
the notes somewhat.

With regard to the introductions to the individual sections, whose purpose is
to explain the ideas in the Zohar and the problems connected with them in a
systematic and detailed way, I have introduced several changes that have made
them much longer. In the first place, in several of the introductions I have when
required described in some detail the Jewish attitudes of earlier times—in the
aggadic literature, in philosophy, and in pre-Zoharic kabbalah—to topics
discussed in the Zohar, in order to present them in their historico-philosophical
setting. Second, I have greatly increased the notes on these topics, occasionally
sketching the development of the Zohar's ideas and their influence on later
kabbalistic and ethical literature. I have also dealt at greater length with the
attitudes of the Zohar itself, wherever possible coming to a definite conclusion
about them, and in this connection I have quoted more extensively from the
text, including a great deal of material that does not appear in the anthology
proper.

I found that some topics were dealt with in a specific, individual manner in parts of the literature outside the main body of the Zohar. I have discussed these cases separately, as, for example, in "The Doctrine of the Soul in the *Midrash ha-Ne'elam*" and "Attitudes toward the Torah in the *Raya Mehemna* and the *Tikkunei ha-Zohar.*" In other subjects too I have discussed differences in approach between one section and another. In this way clear pointers to the ideological unity of the works appended to the Zohar have been established.

The three parts of this volume (*The Doctrine of Man, Sacred Worship, Practical Life*), divided into thirteen sections, present and explain the Zohar's ideas about the nature of man, his preterrestrial existence, his life in the physical world, body and soul, and the good and evil inclinations; about the relationship between man and God through act and spiritual intention (*kavvanah*), sacrificial worship and prayer, the study of the Torah and performance of the commandments, observances on Sabbaths, Festivals and weekdays, and sin and repentance; and about the moral requirements, dealing with individual ethical matters, family life, and the relationship between man and his fellow. Most of these topics have not hitherto been discussed in Zohar studies, and the few that scholars have dealt with, like the doctrine of the soul and the attitude to the Torah, still leave room for further research.

Volume III, which is due to be completed in three parts—*Tradition, Exile and Redemption*, and *Reward and Punishment*—will throw light on the attitudes of the Zohar to general and Jewish history, and on personal and national eschatology. There will be at the end a subject index, as well as a list of textual variants and of passages quoted from the Zohar such as have appeared in Volumes I and II.[7]

I hope and pray that I shall be able to complete this work before long and so fulfill my intention of opening the doors of the Zohar to the Hebrew-reading public and shedding light on the mystical paths in Jewish thought.

I wish to thank: the staffs of the Jewish National and University Library, Jerusalem, and the Bodleian Library, Oxford, whose books and manuscripts were of enormous value to me in the preparation of this work, and also all the other libraries outside Israel whose manuscripts I used in photocopy; the management and staff of Mosad Bialik, who worked with great devotion and patience for a number of years in preparing the book for the press; my pupil and devoted helper, Joseph Dan, who arranged the index of passages from the Zohar, and who prepared the introductions and the list of textual variants for the press; Israel Yeivin, who exerted great effort and skill in standardizing the text and in proof-reading; the owners and employees of Merkaz printers for their meticulous printing; my wife, Esther, whose continuous support helped me to overcome a number of difficulties and who encouraged me to complete this work.

I. TISHBY

Jerusalem, 1961

NOTES

1. [In *Metsudah* (London, 1943), 1: 36–82. Reprinted in H. Zeitlin, "Be-fardes ha-ḥasidut," *Ketavim*, (Tel-Aviv, 1960), pp. 229–79.]
2. [As the reader will see, this goal has been only partly realized.]

3. [On the recommendation of Prof. Tishby I have changed the references both to the *Zohar Ḥadash* and to the *Tikkunei ha-Zohar* to the Jerusalem 1948 editions (second printings, 1978).]
4. [Przemyśl, 1899.]
5. [I have not included this list since it is clearly too technical for a reader unfamiliar with the Hebrew or its Aramaic original.]
6. [In my translation these references have been incorporated in the notes.]
7. [The planned third volume has not been realized.]

GENERAL INTRODUCTION

I. THE STRUCTURE AND LITERARY FORM
OF THE ZOHAR

a. The Various Sections

The Zohar was for centuries commonly known as the Holy Zohar, and recognized as the work of the *tanna* Rabbi Simeon ben Yohai. But in reality it is not a single unified work, but a great literary anthology consisting of sections from various sources. Bibliographically speaking, the Zoharic literature comprises three books, which in the published editions[1] are divided into five parts: The Zohar on the Torah—Genesis and Exodus being in separate parts, and the rest of the Pentateuch in another part; *Tikkunei ha-Zohar*[2] (Arrangements of the Zohar); and *Zohar Ḥadash*[3] (The New Zohar). These books, apart from the *Tikkunei ha-Zohar*, are not unified works, but composed of various sections, some of which are listed in printed books and manuscripts as separate works, with even their own individual titles, while others are completely integrated into the basic text without any exterior identification.

The various sections of Zoharic literature contained in the three books are as follows:

(i) *The Zohar on the Torah*. This is the real core of the Zohar, arranged in three parts according to the order of the scriptural readings (*parashiyot*). The *Zohar Ḥadash* also contains several passages that belong here.[4] The Zohar proper is preceded by a preface (*Hakdamah*).[5] This main core consists chiefly of a mystical *midrash* on the *parashiyot* of the Torah, in the form of either short comments or more extensive disquisitions. But many of the pieces are merely aggadic in character without any obvious mystical qualities. This *midrash* does not cover all the *parashiyot* of the Torah. Many *parashiyot* of Numbers and Deuteronomy are not dealt with at all in the main text of the Zohar, and some receive only isolated comments. In most of the *parashiyot* the number of verses interpreted is very small indeed, and sometimes the interpretations impinge on the subject matter of the section in only a loose or minor way. Preceding the interpretations of the verses of each *parashah* are *Petiḥot* (forewords)—that is to say, homilies based on verses from different parts of the Bible, mostly from Psalms—whose purpose it is to introduce the subject matter of the *parashah*, on the model of the *Petiḥot* in the well-known aggadic midrashim; and in many cases the *Petiḥot* constitute the core of the exposition. Generally speaking, statements are ascribed to the rabbis of the Talmud, and especially to Rabbi Simeon ben Yohai and the members of his circle mentioned in the Zohar, but there are also a considerable number of anonymous interpretations. There are many homilies that take the form of dialogues or arguments between the rabbis, set in the framework of stories about their travels, their meetings on various occasions, and their assemblies for the study of mystical teaching. Set pieces of this kind are sometimes very short, and concentrate on one particular point, but sometimes they extend over several pages and the arguments touch on many subjects. There are also a number of legends and anecdotes that have no interpretative content at all. The subject matter covered in the sections of the Zohar on the Torah is extremely varied and encompasses the whole area of the kabbalah. This part, together with all the others except the *Midrash ha-Ne'elam*, is written in Aramaic.

(ii) *The Zohar on the Song of Songs*[6] consists of profound mystical interpretations of the opening verses of the Song of Songs. This section is structurally similar to the Zohar on the Torah.

(iii) *Midrash ha-Ne'elam* (lit., the Concealed Midrash) *on the Torah*. This is a mystical midrash parallel to the main body of the Zohar, but appertaining only to the early *parashiyot* of Genesis,[7] the *parashah* of *Shemot*,[8] and a few fragments from other *parashiyot*.[9] This section also contains anonymous expositions, rabbinic statements, and homilies in anecdotal form, as well as a large number of stories. But there are obvious differences, both in form and content, between this section and the one described above. Its outer structure is more like that of the older midrashim than the main body of the Zohar. Most of the homilies in it, which are either anonymous or attributed to different rabbis, are presented in the form of short statements, and not in long and involved expositions that are without precedent in the aggadic midrashim. Far more rabbis are mentioned in this section than in the main part of the Zohar, and there are hardly any personal connections among them, whereas nearly all the rabbis mentioned in the Zohar are portrayed as members of the circle of Rabbi Simeon ben Yohai. When we turn to the content we find that the *Midrash ha-Ne'elam* is concerned with a narrower range of specific subjects, such as creation, the soul, the afterlife, and the messianic age, while the mysteries of the divine and "the other side" (the world of evil), which are central to the Zohar proper, are alluded to only briefly, so that the basic principles of kabbalistic teaching are not to be found in this section. The way in which scriptural verses are interpreted is also quite different. Instead of revelations of the mysteries that are hidden in the language of the scriptural text, we find allegorical allusions: for example, the patriarchal narratives are interpreted as allegories of the fate of the soul in both this world and the next. The language of the *Midrash ha-Ne'elam* is partly Hebrew and partly Aramaic, and sometimes the two languages are mixed together in the same sentence.

(iv) *Midrash ha-Ne'elam on the Song of Songs*[10] contains only a few comments. There is a beginning, but no continuation.

(v) *Midrash ha-Ne'elam on Ruth*[11] is complete, and is similar in both form and content to the *Midrash ha-Ne'elam* on the Torah.

(vi) *Midrash ha-Ne'elam on Lamentations*[12] consists of a few comments on the beginning of the book arranged in the form of a verbal interchange between the Palestinian and the Babylonian rabbis.

(vii) *Sitrei Torah* (Secrets of the Torah) contains statements and fragments on some of the *parashiyot* of Genesis.[13] Most of them are anonymous, but some are ascribed to particular rabbis and occur within a narrative context. Some of the statements in this section are close in form and content to the style of the *Midrash ha-Ne'elam*; that is to say, some of the scriptural verses are interpreted allegorically as referring to the soul. But other passages do actually deal with the deeper mysteries of the Godhead, and also, here and there, with "the other side."

(viii) *Matnitin* and *Tosefta*[14] consist of scores of short and fragmented pieces scattered throughout many of the *parashiyot*, and even insterted in particular sections of the Zohar, like *Sitrei Torah* and *Raza de-Razin*, under the heading *Matnitin* (Aramaic for *Mishnah*) or *Tosefta* (Addition to the *Mishnah*). All of these pieces are anonymous, and have distinctive literary characteristics of their own. Most of them begin by exhorting the sages not to be negligent, but to arouse themselves and undertake mystical studies. These exhortations are couched in a very high-flown style, and the meaning is often impenetrably obscure, as, for example, "The highest bonds of the custodians of that side are we, with open eyes and open ears,"[15] and "The desire of a good deed is to tie knots of faith, a supreme voice aroused from heaven to earth."[16] They constitute a kind of divine voice that comes from heaven and issues a proclamation to the world in order to give the mystics new heart. A few fragments contain nothing apart from the exhortation, while other pieces contain the principles of mystic teaching in a condensed form, particularly the theory of emanation. The short expositions sometimes conclude with a transition to the subject matter of the *parashah*, thus forming a kind of introduction to statements in the main body of the Zohar. It would appear that the title, *Matnitin*, refers to this, in that these pieces constitute a kind of mystical *Mishnah*, the *gemara* to which is provided by the Zohar.

(ix) *Sava de-Mishpatim* (The Old Man of *Mishpatim*)[17] is a lengthy narrative composition whose central figure is a wonderful old man who appears to the rabbis on a journey in the shape of a poor ass-driver. At the beginning of their conversation he poses some astonishing questions and seems to the rabbis to be a complete ignoramus, but subsequently it becomes clear that he is a most learned mystic, Rav Yeva Sava, and he reveals hidden mysteries to the rabbis. The chief subject is the disclosure of the secrets of the soul contained in the legislation in the Torah concerning slaves. This section comprises the main part of the Zohar to the *parashah Mishpatim*, but it is known in kabbalistic literature as a separate work with the title *Sava de-Mishpatim*.

(x) *Yanuka* (The child)[18] is a string of homilies on various subjects set in the context of a story about a child, the son of Rav Hamnuna Sava, whom the rabbis meet in his mother's house, where they have come to stay. To their great surprise he shows himself to be a mystic, far wiser than they. This section is also incorporated into the main body of the Zohar, in the *parashah Balak*, but it has only a tenuous connection with the verses of this biblical portion,[19] and in kabbalistic literature it is considered to be a separate unit.

(xi) *Rav Metivta* (The Head of the Academy)[20] is a description of the journeys and the visions of Rabbi Simeon ben Yohai and his disciples in the Garden of Eden, and the mysteries they heard there from the head of the celestial academy, principally concerning the life to come. This work is incorporated in the main body of the Zohar in the *parashah Shelaḥ*, because the people of the wilderness appear in one of the visions and the decree that they should perish in the wilderness occurs in this particular *parashah*.

(xii) *Sifra di-Zeniuta* (The Book of Concealment)[21] is an anonymous interpretation of the *parashah Bereshit*, consisting of laconic allusions and written in a fragmented and obscure style. This short work is one of the most important sections of the Zoharic literature. In its six pages are embodied the basic principles of the whole kabbalistic doctrine set out in a very condensed form. Its main subject is the mystery of the Godhead. The work is divided into five chapters. It has no relevance whatsoever to the *parashah Terumah*, to which it is attached as an appendix, and in the Cremona edition it is placed in the *parashah Bereshit*.

(xiii) *Idra Rabba* (Great Assembly)[22] is a large work that explains and develops the ideas embodied in the *Sifra di-Zeniuta*. Statements from the *Sifra di-Zeniuta* are quoted explicitly several times. Discussion of these ideas takes place at a gathering of the disciples, with Rabbi Simeon ben Yohai at their head, with a view to revealing some of the mysteries whose meaning had previously been withheld. Rabbi Simeon ben Yohai opens the proceedings, and then the participants, on being invited, rise one by one to deliver their mystical discourses. Rabbi Simeon assesses them and develops the ideas. The different discourses combine to form an extensive interpretation of the mystery of the Godhead, using parts of the human body as symbols. The assembly comes to an end with the death of three rabbis through excessive ecstasy. This section is appended to the *parashah Naso*, which includes the laws relating to the Nazirite, because the mystery of hair[23] is here central to the image of primordial man.

(xiv) *Idra Zuta* (Small Assembly)[24] describes the last gathering of Rabbi Simeon ben Yohai and his followers before his death. The revered master delivers a long discourse to his disciples that is mainly a summary of the mysteries revealed in the *Idra Rabba*. At the most exalted spiritual point Rabbi Simeon's soul departs, on the word *ḥayyim* (life). His death and funeral are described at the end. This section is appended to the *parashah Ha'azinu*, as a conclusion to the Zohar.

(xv) *Idra de-Ve Mashkana* (Assembly of the Tabernacle).[25] This concerns a meeting of Rabbi Simeon ben Yohai with three of his followers, in which they explain mystically some verses from the biblical account of the Tabernacle. It deals principally with the mysteries of prayer. In the version we have, this section is incorporated into the main part of the Zohar on the *parashah Terumah*.

(xvi) *Hekhalot* (Palaces) is a description of the seven palaces in the celestial Garden of Eden, where souls luxuriate during their ascent, which follows their devotion in prayer or their departure from the world. This section was composed in two versions.[26] The second is much larger than the first, but they are basically identical in content. The second version is followed by a description of the seven palaces of uncleanness,[27] where the wicked are judged. These works are all anonymous, but they begin with "Rabbi Simeon said. . . ." They have no connection with the *parashiyot* of which they form a part.

(xvii) *Raza de-Razin* (The Secret of Secrets)[28] is a systematic treatment of physiognomy and chiromancy. A second parallel version is embodied in the main body of the Zohar on the *parashah Yitro*.[29] The two versions are separate treatments of the same subject, differing from one another at several points even with regard to content. They were apportioned to the *parashah Yitro*, because in it Jethro advises Moses: "you shall seek able men out of all the people" (Exodus 18: 21), and this verse is interpreted as referring to the selection of men by examination of signs on the face and lines on the hands. In the first version, entitled *Raza de-Razin*, there is no mention of any rabbi except at the beginning, where the words are transmitted in the name of Rabbi Simeon beh Yohai, while the second version is put in the usual context of conversations between Rabbi Simeon ben Yohai and his pupils.

(xviii) *Sitrei Otiot* (Secrets of the Letters)[30] is a discourse by Rabbi Simeon ben Yohai on the secrets of the Godhead that are concealed in the letters of the alphabet, particularly in the letters of the tetragrammaton, *YHVH*.

(xix) *Ma'amar Kav ha-Middah* (The Standard of Measure)[31] elucidates the mystery of the divine unity by interpreting the verse "Hear, O Israel, the Lord, our God, the Lord is One" (Deuteronomy 6: 4). At the beginning the names of Rabbi Simeon and Rabbi Eleazar are mentioned.

(xx) [The Commentary on Ezekiel's Chariot][32] is an untitled interpretation of the verses concerning the vision of Ezekiel. The piece is introduced as a discourse by Rabbi Eleazar in the presence of Rabbi Simeon ben Yohai.

(xxi) *Raya Mehemna* (The Faithful Shepherd) is a mystical work on the reasons for the commandments. Parts of it are scattered over a number of *parashiyot*,[33] depending on the relevant verses, but it is clear that originally all the pieces were joined together without relevance to the order of the scriptural verses. It exists in manuscripts as a separate work, copied independently. The central figure here is Moses himself, who received the commandments at Sinai, and the title, "The Faithful Shepherd," refers to him. He appears to the mystics and reveals to them the hidden reasons for the commandments.

(xxii) *Tikkunei ha-Zohar* (Arrangements of the Zohar) is a complete book on its own, containing seventy pieces called *tikkunim*. At the end are appended additional *tikkunim*, found in another manuscript, and the *Zohar Hadash*[34] also contains several *tikkunim* taken from manuscripts. The book opens with a special preface. Each *tikkun* begins as an interpretation of the word *bereshit* (In the beginning), and continues by interpreting verses from the *parashah Bereshit*. This section is similar in form and content to the *Raya Mehemna*, and their specific character will be discussed below.

(xxiii) Two pieces of the *Raya Mehemna* and *Tikkunei ha-Zohar* type without any particular title are found in the *Zohar Hadash*,[35] and in the Zohar itself,[36] but they are written in the style of the preceding. The piece in the *Zohar Hadash* is a parallel work to the *Raza de-Razin*.

The existence of various distinct sections in the Zoharic literature raises the question whether they were all written by the same author or whether they represent the work of many hands. This is one of the central problems of Zoharic scholarship and it will be dealt with in its proper place in the following chapters. Suffice it now to note that there are clear internal links between most of the sections. The *Sifra di-Zeniuta*,[37] the *Idra Rabba*,[38] and the *Idra de-Ve Mashkanah*[39] are quoted by name. In the *Raya Mehemna* the main body of the Zohar is referred to as *hibura kedama'ah* (the first book),[40] and several statements and stories in the Zohar itself and in other sections recur in the *Raya Mehemna* and the *Tikunei ha-Zohar*, with expansions and additional interpretations. In other sections too we find cross-references in the form of *okimana* (we have explained), *okemuha* (they have explained it), *itamar* (it has been said, elucidated), and so on, or without any particular indication. The opening of the

Idra Zuta, for example, alludes quite clearly to the story about Rabbi Simeon ben Yohai's illness, which is found in the *Midrash ha-Ne'elam*.[41] These links, which prove that the different sections are not completely independent of one another, do not, of course, solve the question of the unity of authorship.

Another question, which is also bound up with problems of critical scholarship but which can nevertheless be discussed now in a general fashion, concerns the original extent of the Zohar or of the Zoharic literature. From the brief analysis given above of the different sections in the Zohar, it is clear that those parts which follow the order of the *parashiyot* of the Torah or the verses of other biblical books—that is, the main body of the Zohar, the *Midrash ha-Ne'elam*, and the *Sitrei Torah*—are not complete in the version we now have. So the question arises: did these works leave the pen of their authors, or author, in a fuller and more complete form (which means that the missing parts subsequently perished or disappeared), or were they always fragmentary and incomplete?

Among the kabbalists themselves the accepted view was that the original scope of the Zohar was very much wider than the book we now have. In the *Shalshelet ha-Kabbalah*[42] we read: "I have heard orally that the size of this book was so great that if it was all put together only a camel could carry it." And Rabbi Solomon Delmedigo, the kabbalist philosopher known as *Yashar* of Candia, adduces evidence "from trustworthy informants" that there was in the Heidelberg library a manuscript of the Zohar on the twenty-four books of the Bible: "*Yashar* said: I have heard from trustworthy informants that when the Spaniards plundered the city of Heidelberg in 1620 they took from *Bet Eked ha-Ro'im*, i.e., the Academy, several thousand books in every language, among which were a number of holy books written on parchment. Also there was the Zohar on all the twenty-four books, an enormous load, and some of them were sent to a cardinal in Rome, and some were taken by the Duke of Bavaria, while others were dispatched to Spain."[43]

These traditions are obviously nothing but legends and exaggerations, and we cannot rely upon their accuracy. In the manuscripts and books of the early kabbalists, which quote extracts from the Zohar before its appearance in print, there are no references or pointers whatsoever to the existence of such a fully comprehensive version. But on the other hand, we may say with certainty that the manuscripts that the printers used did not contain all the pieces that belong to the Zoharic literature. The large collection of important passages that were assembled from manuscripts in the sixteenth century and printed as the *Zohar Hadash* provide conclusive evidence of this. At a few points in the *Zohar Hadash* passages are cited which complete pieces that in the Zohar on the Torah are in a fragmentary state. From the extant manuscripts and books of the early kabbalists, particularly from the fourteenth century,[44] we can extract a certain number of additional pieces that even the *Zohar Hadash* does not contain. Rabbi Moses Cordovero mentions the Zohar to the Book of Esther,[45] and Gershom Scholem[46] has published from a Cambridge manuscript portions of the *Midrash ha-Ne'elam* to the *parashah Bereshit*, in a particular version hitherto unknown.

From these facts we may deduce that, at least at the time of its appearance—at the end of the thirteenth century, as will be shown below—the structure of the Zohar did not differ basically from the text that we have today, although we may suppose that it did contain some pieces that have not come down to us. This conclusion does not in itself establish that the version we have represents the original structure of the Zohar as the author wrote it. The answer to this question depends on whether the Zohar was composed long before its actual appearance or not; in other words, it is bound up with the problem of the antiquity or the later date of the Zohar. I shall deal in some detail with this problem in the succeeding pages.

b. The Characteristics of the Zohar

The above description of the various sections that make up the totality of the Zohar has already provided an outline of its basic character, and this serves to establish the nature of the whole work: it is a homiletical exegesis. The ideas in the Zohar are not presented systematically as kabbalistic teaching, but they emerge by way of commentary and discourse. This homiletical, exegetical character predominates even in those sections like the *Idrot* and the *Hekhalot*, which from their contents one might well single out as an exposition or a concentrated systematic description of a specific topic.

Neither the exegesis nor the homiletical content of the Zohar is restricted to the Bible, although this forms its outer framework. It covers all manifestations of the Jewish spirit. Legal topics, aggadic themes, liturgical matters—all receive their mystical interpretation and exposition. By means of this mystical homiletical style the author of the Zohar moves skillfully from Bible to Mishnah, and from Mishnah to *aggadah* and prayer, weaving them together, and reflecting them as a single entity in the mirror of kabbalah. From this point of view the Zohar is a closely packed treasury of Jewish values in their totality.

However, there are many drawbacks resulting from this lack of system, in part attributable to the book's exegetical, homiletical character. Different topics are jumbled together and subjects that have practically nothing to do with one another are set side by side without any internal connection between them. At many points we jump from one subject to another, without any logical transition or rational continuity. These defects are more noticeable in the *Raya Mehemna* and the *Tikkunei ha-Zohar*, where most passages are no more than combinations of fragmentary and disparate allusions, connected solely through association, and dependent on different biblical verses. In these sections there are signs of a basic defect in the actual thought structure. But in the other sections too, most of the ideas are presented piecemeal, without any comprehensive or exhaustive elucidation at one particular point, and several important problems, such as prophecy and providence, are not treated rationally at all. This characteristic of the Zohar's style seriously obscures its ideas, which in content too are not crystal clear, and this is one of the reasons why the Zohar strikes the reader as an impenetrable and mysterious work.

The use of symbolic imagery instead of rational terminology in the expression of ideas, which is a characteristic feature of practically every section of the Zohar, deepens the opaqueness of the work and makes it even more difficult to understand. Many passages simply consist of a kind of mosaic of varied images that appear to have no connection with each other, either of logic or of subject matter. But, in actual fact, such connections do exist, and are quite clear once the key to the symbolism is understood. However, since the meaning of the symbols changes frequently according to the way in which they are combined and the place they occupy in the disposition of ideas, it is extremely difficult to grasp their actual nature and perceive their inner significance. Consequently, unless one is skilled in the secrets of the Torah and familiar with the cryptic language of symbolism, one is apt to see Zoharic writings as absurd conglomerations of words and images.

But on the other hand, the failing of the Zohar in lack of system and clarity is compensated for by its vitality and its very varied and many-sided character. Systematic thinking, which holds a measure up to human emotions and living phenomena and subjects everything to an examination based on its own particular standard, is able to fix and define the crucial basic principles of philosophy. But the mass of feelings and opinions that crowd and trouble the human soul amid the perplexities of life are disqualified in its judgment and relegated to an area outside its purview because they do not fit into the framework of its refined system. In this process of refining and purifying, pearls of thought are arranged in a systematic order and are ground and polished, but the very pulse of life is thereby removed, because they are uprooted and taken away from the source of their nourishment and growth among the actual thought processes. This kind of thing even affects the attempts at systematization to be found in kabbalistic literature. In contrast to this, the Zohar is a book that deals with real life. The life of the Jew with its spiritual turbulence is reflected here just as it is, with its lights and its shades, and there is hardly a single corner of existence not touched upon somehow within its pages. On the one side we have an investigation into the wondrous mysteries of the soul and the divine, and on the other, popular beliefs and ideas concerning necromancy and evil spirits; here we find visions of redemption and calculations of the end of time, and elsewhere the search for advice in, and a solution to, the complex relationships between man and his fellow and between husband and wife. These and similarly varied themes are all lumped together, and even interwoven with each other, in the pages of the Zohar. The trivia of confused and obscure reflections, and the overwhelming doubts and hesitations of the naked human spirit, that is to say, those primitive areas of thought and contemplation which cannot be included in an ordered system because of their insignificance or because they fall outside the categories of speculative expression and logical thinking—these are the very elements which come to the fore in the words of the Zohar. The dark and turbid nature of the Zohar, in both its form and content, reflects the darkness and turbidity of life itself, which in its increasing ferment is bound to throw up dross and waste matter.

The vitality of the Zohar is heightened by its peculiar literary qualities. There is no single unified style. On the contrary, it is characterized by successive ups and downs, from the lofty and eloquent heights of pathos to the plains of deliberate and measured exposition, from a poetic and metaphorical style to a colorless and poverty-stricken stammering. All depends on the area of life or the state of mind to be expressed. The way in which the discourses are set against the background of events and conversations involving the rabbis, which permits the expression of arguments and counter-arguments and of opposing views, also adds an element of vitality. It is not my purpose here to decide whether the narrative background has a historical foundation or not. This problem will be treated later when we come to Zohar criticism. But whatever the answer, the quality of the description of the characters, the events, and the disputations introduces movement and life, and produces a vivid and colorful work of imagination.

c. The Narrative Framework

In the *aggadot* of the Talmud and the midrashim, we find many stories about the deeds of the rabbis and events in their lives. The authors of the *aggadah* noted down any information or report that would highlight the vivid personalities and moral excellence of their revered masters, and they even praised them in a hyperbolic way by using imaginary descriptions. But in the Zohar we come across something completely new. Here the various stories are centered on one limited group, and especially on the character of the head of the group, Rabbi Simeon ben Yohai, and together they make up a broad and unique narrative background that serves as a framework for most of the book's subject matter. In some of the sections, notably the *Midrash ha-Ne'elam* on the one side, and the *Raya Mehemna* and the *Tikkunei ha-Zohar* on the other, there are significant variations in this narrative framework compared with the rest of the book. I shall treat separately the three forms in which the stories in the Zohar are presented.

(i) The Main Body of the Zohar and the Other Narrative Sections

Rabbi Simeon ben Yohai, the renowned sage from the school of Rabbi Akiva, is portrayed in the *aggadot* of the Talmud and the midrashim as a supremely righteous man, during whose life a rainbow never appeared.[47] That is to say, his own merits protected his generation, and there was no need for the sign of the rainbow, which is a reminder of God's promise not to bring the Flood upon the world again. A revelation of Elijah, the abrogation of heavenly decrees, and great miracles are all associated with him.[48] A specific trait in his character was his exaggerated confidence in his own personal greatness, which finds expression in these remarkable words of self-praise: "I can save the whole world, from the day I was born to the present day, from Judgment; and if my son Eleazar were with me, I could save the world from the Creation to the present day; and if Jotham ben Uzziah were with us, from the Creation to the end of the world. . . . I saw the sons on high and they were few in number; but if there were a thousand, my son and I would be two of them; and if there were a hundred, my son and I would be two of them; and if there were two, they would be my son and I."[49] The crucial event in his life, which undoubtedly left its mark on his character, was his concealment in a cave, together with his son Eleazar, for thirteen years, when he was forced to flee from the Romans. Many miracles are associated in the *aggadah* with both his stay in the cave and his emergence from it.[50]

These personal traits are also found in the portrayal of Rabbi Simeon ben Yohai in the Zohar. In fact, they receive far greater emphasis and are described in the most glowing colors. Here he appears as a righteous and saintly man of unique caliber. The heavenly angels, and even God Himself, take heed of his words and obey him, and his whole generation shelters under his protection. His life is a chain of miracles; signs and wonders accompany him wherever he goes; and the prophet Elijah, other holy spirits, and the souls of the righteous reveal themselves to him at every step. Here too he eulogizes himself in the most extravagant manner, and in one passage he puts himself above Moses; "I call to witness the highest heavens, and the highest holy earth that I now see what no man has seen since Moses ascended Mt. Sinai for the second time. I see my face shining like the powerful light of the sun. . . . And further still, I know that my face is shining, while Moses did not know, nor did he look."[51] His stay in the cave and his leaving it are described at greater length with the addition of miracles that are not found in the *aggadah*. But this event does not occupy a central position, and it is mentioned in only a few places in the other stories.

However, the principal characteristic of Rabbi Simeon ben Yohai as he is portrayed in the Zohar is his tremendous knowledge of the secrets of the Torah and his power to reveal them—a trait completely lacking in the other sources. In the new interpretations of the Torah that are transmitted in his name there is no evidence of any schooling in mysticism,[52] although his teacher, Rabbi Akiva, was known as one of the masters of the secrets of Creation and the Chariot, and it is related of him that he was one of the four sages who entered *Pardes*, and that only he entered in peace and departed in peace.[53] But according to the stories in the Zohar all the fine qualities we see in Rabbi Simeon ben Yohai are no more than natural concomitants of his greatness in the field of mysticism. He is portrayed as the expert in mysteries, to whom all secret paths are made plain by means of revelations from heaven, and the circle of his fellow disciples, thirsting for knowledge of the hidden world, sits in the dust at his feet in order to receive instruction from his lips. Knowledge of the unknown is the magic wand whose power enables him to rule over the upper and lower worlds.

The established members of the circle, bound to one another by very strong personal ties and appearing very frequently together, either in Rabbi Simeon's presence or on their own, are nine rabbis, all named at the beginning of the *Idra Rabba*:[54] Rabbi Eleazar, Rabbi Abba, Rabbi Judah, Rabbi Jose bar Jacob,[55] Rabbi Isaac, Rabbi Hezekiah bar Rav, Rabbi Hiyya, Rabbi Jose, and Rabbi Yesa. Rabbi Eleazar and Rabbi Abba are the leaders of the group and the confidants of Rabbi Simeon ben Yohai. These sages, who go under the name of ḥavraya (companions), meet with various incidents, particularly during their tour of the cities and villages of the Holy Land. The most important places, mentioned frequently in the accounts of their travels, are Tiberias, Sepphoris, Usha, Caesarea, and Lydda. From the stories in the Zohar it would appear that Tiberias was considered to be the place where Rabbi Simeon had his home. Sometimes Rabbi Simeon himself would travel with them, stopping on the way with his companions on the hillside and in the fields and woods, expounding the secrets of the Torah. But sometimes a number of rabbis would go off on their own, and at the end of their journey they would return to their master's house and give him their impressions of their travels, telling him of the new interpretations of Torah they had discovered, of the experiences they had had, and of the questions and problems that had puzzled them. In the eyes of his disciples Rabbi Simeon ben Yohai was a kind of oracle. He settled all their difficulties, solved the problems and enigmas that troubled them, and through his words and actions enveloped them in the holy spirit.

In addition to the members of this circle there were other rabbis who came into contact with them. Most of them are subsidiary characters who do not have an important role to play in the narrative of the Zohar. But there are a few who have a crucial importance and who are surrounded by a halo of sublime sanctity: Rabbi Pinhas ben Yair, Rav Hamnuna Sava, and Rav Yeva Sava.[56] Rabbi Pinhas, thought in the Zohar to be the father-in-law of Rabbi Simeon ben Yohai, is portrayed as a pious and holy old man, a master of secrets, and a miracle worker, almost on a par with Rabbi Simeon himself. Whenever he appears in the group he creates an atmosphere of solemn exaltation that is accompanied by rapturous visions and a particular feeling of great awe. His departure from the world preceded that of Rabbi Simeon ben Yohai, and during the last assembly before Rabbi Simeon's death his disciples trembled when it became known that the soul of Rabbi Pinhas had come from the "true" world to join the gathering.[57] Rav Hamnuna Sava and Rav Yeva Sava are remarkable men who meet the traveling companions in the guise of poor and apparently ignorant ass-drivers and it is only during their conversation with them that their wisdom and holiness become evident. In the descriptions of these meetings it would appear that they are not really alive, but that their souls have left the Garden of Eden and have donned corporeal form in order to reveal secrets of the Torah. However, at the end of the *Idra Rabba*,[58] we are told that the prophet Elijah was not present at the assembly, because at that time he had to help Rav Hamnuna Sava and his companions to escape from their imprisonment in the castle of the king. During the companions' conversation stories are told of the deeds and customs of these wonderful men, and in several places passages dealing with mystical teaching are quoted from "the book of Rav Hamnuna Sava" and "the book of Rav Yeva Sava." Rav Hamnuna's son also meets the rabbis, while he is still young, and he astounds them with his great wisdom and with celestial revelations.[59]

There are, in addition to these famous people, other old men and children, who appear anonymously but who later turn out to be righteous men in disguise and wonderful scholars of mystical lore. These characters are introduced in order to stress the high quality of that whole generation. The disciples are full of praise for their generation, in which ordinary poor old men and tender children at the very beginning of their studies are replete with knowledge and understanding of the mysteries of the world because of the greatness of Rabbi Simeon ben Yohai who dwelt among them. No other generation was like it, and none ever will be until the end of days. We often hear the companions lamenting the fact that with the death of Rabbi Simeon the light of Torah and wisdom would be stored away and darkness would descend upon the world.[60]

The two assemblies, described in the *Idra Rabba* and the *Idra Zuta*, are the central events in the narratives of the Zohar. In the *Idra Rabba* the whole group comes together in perfect cohesion and reaches the highest point in revelation of the mysteries, while the *Idra Zuta* is the apotheosis of Rabbi Simeon ben Yohai as he departs from the world. At his death the disciples are overcome by a feeling of bereavement and loneliness, and the despair that engulfs them at this time accompanies them for the rest of their lives. After Rabbi Simeon's death, the talk of the companions when they meet turns to the terrible loss that cannot be remedied, and to their deep sense of desolation. A few are fortunate enough to see their revered teacher in a dream, or to be linked in an ecstatic vision with his soul in Eden.[61] But their real consolation is to recall the memories they have of his wisdom and his greatness, and to study the mysteries that they heard from his lips.

(ii) The *Midrash ha-Ne'elam*

Rabbi Simeon ben Yohai and his circle appear in this section within the framework that obtains in the main body of the Zohar, but here the group is not so concentrated, and also stories are introduced concerning many scholars who have no connection at all with the circle of Rabbi Simeon. These additional characters are in part individual people who are not connected with each other in any one school, and the stories of their deeds are not part of a continuous whole. Each narrative is a separate entity in itself. However, in a large number of stories, a few central characters recur consistently, and their circumstances are described as if they belonged to a kind of circle or circles parallel to the group of Rabbi Simeon ben Yohai. In one series of such stories the central figure is Rabbi Eliezer ben Hyrcanus, known also as "the great Rabbi Eliezer," and with him is his pupil, Rabbi Akiva. A smaller group of stories has Rabbi Eleazar ben Arakh at the head of a mystical school. These men were disciples of Rabban Johanan ben Zakkai, preceding Rabbi Simeon ben Yohai by two generations, and they are not mentioned in the Zohar proper. Unlike Rabbi Simeon, they are known in aggadic literature as mystical characters and as students of the mysteries.

(iii) The *Raya Mehemna* and the *Tikkunei ha-Zohar*

In these sections we find once again a circle of scholars with Rabbi Simeon ben Yohai at their head, but the scene of the stories is different. Instead of travels and events on earth, most of the action takes place in heaven, in the celestial schools of the Garden of Eden. Rabbi Simeon, who is generally called here "the holy luminary" (*bozina kadisha*),[62] together with his companions, meet and talk with a band of spirits who are not of this world. At their head stands Moses, "the faithful shepherd." In this band of holy spirits are to be found the patriarchs, the prophet Elijah, the souls of unnamed righteous men, the Messiah, angels, and even God Himself. Sometimes a wonderful old man suddenly appears, or a talking shadow, and so on. At many points Rabbi Simeon and his circle seem to have left the world themselves, and to have found their home in the world of souls, but in other passages they are undoubtedly people of flesh and blood, and sometimes the heavenly and the terrestrial scenes have become confused. In the Zohar proper and in the *Midrash ha-Ne'elam* we also find descriptions of the visits that Rabbi Simeon and other scholars paid to the heavenly academies, but such events are rare visions there, while in these sections, and particularly in the *Raya Mehemna*, the heavenly academy is the normal scene of the action.

II. THE PUBLICATION AND INFLUENCE OF THE ZOHAR

a. The Testimony of Rabbi Isaac of Acre

The composition, publication, and dissemination of the Zohar are shrouded in mystery, and were it not for a single fragmentary piece of evidence, preserved and published in the *Sefer Yuḥasin* of Rabbi Abraham Zacuto, we should be really groping in the dark. This evidence is taken from a work by Rabbi Isaac of Acre, a well-known kabbalist who lived in Acre, and who, after the conquest of that city by the Muslims in 1291, left for Spain. It contains important facts and information that throw light on the circumstances of the Zohar's publication and also tell us of the different opinions that contemporaries held about its composition. The testimony of Rabbi Isaac of Acre, which is the only historical evidence on these matters, has been frequently quoted in studies on the Zohar, but because of its supreme importance I think it necessary to publish it again here in full.[63]

"In the month of Adar, Rabbi Isaac of Acre wrote that Acre had been destroyed in the year fifty [-one] (i.e., 1291), and that the pious of Israel had been slaughtered there with the four statutory kinds of death.[64] In 1305 this Rabbi Isaac of Acre was in Navarre, in Estella,[65] having escaped from Acre, and in the same 1305 he came to Toledo. And I found the diary of Rabbi Isaac of Acre, the man who wrote a kabbalistic work in 1331 and in whose time Acre was destroyed and all its inhabitants captured, in the time of Nachmanides' grandson, and the son of Rabbi David ben Abraham, the son of Maimonides. He (i.e., Rabbi Isaac) went to Spain to find out how the book of the Zohar, which Rabbi Simeon and his son, Rabbi Eleazar, composed in the cave, came to exist in his time (happy are those who have merited its truth: in its light may they see light)—'its truth' because part of it has been forged. And he said that he had been taught that one should believe whatever was written in Aramaic, for those were the words of Rabbi Simeon, but as to what was written in Hebrew, they were not his words, but the words of the forger; for the real book was written entirely in Aramaic [lit., "in the Jerusalem tongue"]. This is what he says: And since I saw that its words were wonderful, drawn from the celestial source, the fountain that pours forth without being itself replenished (blessed be His glorious kingdom for ever and ever), I pursued it and asked the scholars who possessed some of its great words of wisdom whence had come these wonderful mysteries that had been transmitted orally and not written down, and that were now plain to all who could read. And I did not find their answers to my question very convincing. Some said one thing and some said another. Some said in answer to my question that the faithful rabbi Nachmanides had sent it (i.e., the Zohar) from the land of Israel to Catalonia, to his son, and the wind had brought it to Aragon, and others say to Alicante, and it had fallen into the hands of the sage Rabbi Moses de Leon, who is also described as Moses de Guadalajara. Some say that Rabbi Simeon ben Yohai did not write the book at all, but that this Rabbi Moses knew the Holy Name and through its power wrote these wonderful words, and in order to sell them for a good price, for much silver and gold, he ascribed them to our great ancestors saying: I have transcribed for you these words from the book composed by Rabbi Simeon ben Yohai and his son, Rabbi Eleazar. When I came to Spain I went to Valladolid, where the king was, and I found Rabbi Moses there, and he liked me and spoke with me, and swore: 'may God do so to me, and more also, if there is not at this moment in my house, where I live in Avila, the ancient book written by Rabbi Simeon ben Yohai, and when you come to see me there I shall show it to you.' Rabbi Moses left me after this and went to Arévalo on his way home to Avila, but he fell ill in Arévalo and died there. When I heard the news I was furious, and resumed my journey and came to Avila. There I found a great and venerable scholar named Rabbi David de Pancorbo,[66] and we got on well together and I adjured him, saying: 'Do you know the mysteries of the Zohar, about which people are divided, some saying one thing, and some another? Rabbi Moses swore an oath to me, but did not complete his promise before he died, so that I do not know whose authority to rely on, and whose words to believe.' And he said: 'Know for sure that it is clear to me without a doubt that the Zohar was never in Rabbi Moses' possession, and in fact has never existed. But Rabbi Moses was a master of the Holy Name, and whatever he wrote in this book he wrote through its power. And now, listen how it is that I know all this. Rabbi Moses was a great spendthrift and would part with his money very easily. One day his house would be full of the silver and gold given to him by the wealthy who learned the great mysteries that he would present to them written down through the power of the Holy Name, and the next day the money would all be gone, so that he has now left his wife and his daughter naked, overcome with hunger and thirst, and in utter destitution. Now, when the news reached us that he had died in Arévalo, I went to call on a prominent wealthy man who lived in this city, by the name of Rabbi Joseph de Avila. And I said to him: If you do as I advise, you will be able to obtain the book of the Zohar, whose value surpasses both crystal and gold. I suggested that this Rabbi Joseph should summon his wife and tell her to send a servant with a present for the wife of Rabbi Moses. And this she did. And on the next day he said to her: Now go to the house of Rabbi Moses' wife and say as follows: I should very much like my son to marry your daughter, and then you will never lack bread to eat or clothes to wear. And I require nothing at all from you except the book of the Zohar from which your husband used to copy extracts for people. You shall say this [continued Rabbi Joseph] to both the mother and the daughter separately, and listen carefully to what each one says to see if their replies tally. And she did as she was asked. And Rabbi Moses' wife replied to Rabbi Joseph's wife on oath, saying: May God do so to me and more also if my husband ever possessed such a book. But he wrote what he did out of his own head and heart, and knowledge and mind. And when I saw him writing without any material before him I used to say to him: Why do you tell everybody that you are copying from a book, when you have no book, and you write out of your own head? Would it not be better for you to say that the work was your own brainchild, because then you would get more credit? And he would reply: If I told them my secret and that what I wrote was my own invention, they would pay no heed to my words, and would not give me a penny for them, because they would say that I had made it all up. But, as it is, when they hear that I am copying extracts for them from the

Zohar that was written under the influence of the Holy Spirit by Rabbi Simeon ben Yohai, they pay a lot of money for them, as you can see yourself. After this, Rabbi Joseph's wife spoke with Rabbi Moses' daughter and told her exactly what she had told her mother, that she wished her to marry her son and in return to give her mother food and clothing. And the daughter answered just as the mother did—neither more nor less. Can you want more convincing proof?'

"When I heard what he had to say I was astounded and amazed and I really believed then that there never had been a book, but that he had written pieces for other people through the power of the Holy Name. Then I left Avila and came to Talavera, and discovered there a great and remarkable scholar, a benevolent and good-hearted man, whose name was Rabbi Joseph Halevi, son of the kabbalist Rabbi Todros, and I questioned him about this book. And he said to me in reply: 'Take it for a fact that the Zohar that Rabbi Simeon ben Yohai wrote was in the possession of Rabbi Moses, and he copied from it and gave the copies to whoever he wished. And now see the important test to which I subjected Rabbi Moses to see whether he copied from an ancient book, or whether he wrote with the power of the Holy Name. This was the test. A long time after he had written for me a number of lengthy extracts from the Zohar, I hid one of them, and told him that I had lost it, and asked him to make me another copy. He said to me: Show me the end of the text that preceded it and the beginning of the text that followed it, and I shall then copy the whole section that you have lost. And this I did. A few days later he gave me the recopied text, and I compared it with the first, and I saw that there was no difference between them: nothing added, and nothing missing, no discrepancy in either subject matter or wording. But it was all of a piece, as if one text had been copied from the other. Can there be a more stringent test than this, or stronger proof?'

"Then I left Talavera and came to Toledo, and I continued to make inquiries about this book among the scholars and their pupils, and I again found them divided, some saying one thing and some another. And when I told them of Rabbi Joseph's test, just mentioned, they said it did not prove anything, because one could say that before he gave a text to someone, which he wrote through the power of the Holy Name, he would make a fair copy of it for himself, and this would always be with him, and he would keep on copying it, as if he were transcribing from an ancient work. However, there was one new element, because some students told me that they had seen an old man by the name of Rabbi Jacob, a reliable pupil of Rabbi Moses, who loved him like his own soul, and this man called heaven and earth to witness that the book of the Zohar that Rabbi Simeon ben Yohai had written . . . (I have not found the conclusion of this passage in the book)."[67]

When we come to analyze the content and weigh the truth of this evidence, we have to distinguish two areas: the direct evidence of Rabbi Isaac of Acre, that is, his own story of the things that he himself saw and heard, and the indirect evidence, that is, the information that was communicated to him. The direct evidence concerns mainly the publication of the Zohar, while the indirect evidence contains information about its authorship.

The direct evidence may be summarized in the following way: (i) The Zohar was first published in Spain at about the time of Rabbi Isaac of Acre's arrival there, that is, at the end of the thirteenth century; (ii) the book was published by

Moses de Leon as a copy of a manuscript in his possession, which, according to
him, contained an ancient work written by Rabbi Simeon ben Yohai and his
contemporaries; (iii) the copy was disseminated text by text and not in the form
of a complete book; (iv) among the scholars in Spain there were divergent views
concerning the nature of the book: some believed in its ancient origins and
accepted the tradition that Nachmanides had sent the manuscript to Spain
from Israel, while others suspected Rabbi Moses de Leon of having written the
book himself through the power of the Holy Name,[68] or of having maliciously
forged the book in order thereby to gain some material profit.

The indirect evidence tells us that (i) the wife of Rabbi Moses de Leon
testified that her husband had written the book "out of his own head and heart,
and knowledge, and mind" without any manuscript in front of him; (ii) Rabbi
Moses de Leon himself confessed to his wife that he had attributed his own work
to earlier scholars, because if he had published it in his own name he would have
got nothing for it, "but, as it is, when they hear that I am copying extracts for
them from the book of the Zohar that was written under the influence of the
Holy Spirit by Rabbi Simeon ben Yohai, they pay a lot of money for them, as
you can see yourself."

This evidence, which is an open and clear confession on the part of the
defendant, has been the main point of dispute in Zohar scholarship. On the one
hand, it can be taken as absolute proof of the late date of the book. But on the
other, it is regarded as inadmissible and completely untrustworthy by those
who maintain an earlier date. And indeed there are reasonable grounds for
doubting its accuracy. Rabbi Isaac of Acre heard the story from a man who
himself got to know of it in a roundabout way. It involves several hands with
two women at the center—the wives of Rabbi Joseph de Avila and of Rabbi
Moses de Leon. With this kind of evidence one may suppose that it was not
transmitted in its original form, but was either expanded or contracted, and
perhaps among the intermediaries there were those who harbored some grudge
against Rabbi Moses de Leon and wanted to spread scandal about him. The
cynical tone of his conversation with his wife supports this view. One could also
cite the evidence of Rabbi Jacob, a pupil of Moses de Leon, to support one's
doubts concerning his own confession. This evidence is brought in at the end of
the document and, although it is incomplete, it is possible to deduce from the
fragmentary opening—"This man called heaven and earth to witness that the
book of the Zohar, which Rabbi Simeon ben Yohai had written"—that Rabbi
Jacob was citing evidence to disprove the contention that Rabbi Moses de Leon
had written the Zohar. And although we do not know what his proofs were, and
we cannot possibly examine them, nevertheless there is some indication that his
evidence or other factors succeeded in convincing Rabbi Isaac of Acre that the
Zohar was an early work, because in his *Me'irat Enayim*, extant in manuscript,
he quotes several pasages from the Zohar under the name of *Midrash
Yerushalmi*.[69] These doubts do not completely invalidate the evidence, but they
certanly weaken it, and it cannot be relied upon unless it can be verified by
other arguments.

However, several of those who contested the evidence went too far, and
sought to destroy its reliability completely. The publisher of the *Sefer Yuḥasin*
already strikes a negative note in his comment in the first edition: "Samuel

Sholem says, You see with your own eyes the folly of those who speak arrogantly against the righteous; they do not know or understand. Words that are the secret of the world they turn into wormwood, and the words of the sealed book they consider invalid, setting its words at naught. Their proofs and their contentions are all vanity and there is no profit in them."[70] Others have quite openly stated that the testimony is forged and was not the work of Rabbi Isaac of Acre. So, for example, writes the kabbalist Rabbi Isaac Itzik Ḥaver, who came to the defense of the Zohar's antiquity: "What is really against our accepting this conversation as evidence is that there is no authoritative signature to the words found in the *Sefer Yuḥasin*, and perhaps someone in error as an opponent of the wisdom [of kabbalah] interpolated these words in the *Sefer Yuḥasin* (or in place of what the author of the *Sefer ha-Yuḥasin* found), and it is perhaps for this reason that the passage was omitted in later editions."[71] There is no foundation for this view. The authenticity of the testimony and the reliability of the details in the direct evidence can be definitely proved, as will be shown below. There is no doubt about that at all.

b. Verification of the Evidence

(i) Persons Mentioned in the Testimony

Six men are mentioned by name in the *Sefer Yuḥasin*: Rabbi Isaac of Acre, whose evidence it is, Rabbi Moses de Leon, Rabbi David de Pancorbo, Rabbi Joseph de Avila, Rabbi Joseph Halevi, and Rabbi Jacob. All these men, with the exception of Rabbi David de Pancorbo, are known from other sources, and several important matters related of them in the evidence can be confirmed from outside knowledge.

Rabbi Isaac of Acre is known as a celebrated kabbalist in Spain in the fourteenth century. He is frequently quoted throughout kabbalistic literature, and several of his books are extant in manuscript. The most important fact for our purpose is that the source of the evidence, called in the *Sefer Yuḥasin* "his book of days," that is, a kind of diary, existed in manuscript in the Baron Guenzburg Library in St. Petersburg, according to the description of it given by Shneur Sachs.[72] But it is not clear from what Sachs says whether the Guenzburg manuscript contained the evidence about the Zohar, and, unfortunately, the manuscript has disappeared in the meantime, so that it cannot be examined. Nevertheless the fact that such a book did exist, and was not merely a fabrication, goes a long way toward supporting the authenticity of the evidence.

We have very little biographical information about Moses de Leon, but a large number of his works on kabbalah are extant in manuscript, and two of them have been printed.[73] In the introductions to these books, the time and place of their composition are noted. The dates extend from 1286 to 1293, and in the books that were composed up to 1292 it is stated that they were written in Guadalajara. This confirms the evidence in the *Sefer Yuḥasin* that he was known as Moses de Guadalajara. Only one detail is known of his life before 1286—that in 1264 a manuscript copy of *The Guide for the Perplexed* in Hebrew translation was made for "the scholar Rabbi Moses de Leon."[74] The date of his death is disputed. According to Rabbi Isaac of Acre he died in 1305, but there is another tradition that he died in 1293.[75] However, there is some indication that the true date was 1305, because we know from a manuscript of Moses de Leon's *Sefer Maskiot Kesef* that it was written after 1293. The writings of Moses de Leon definitely show that, at the very least, he played an important role in the publication of the Zohar, because they are full of Zoharic idioms, some in Aramaic, but mostly in a Hebrew version, and this at a time when the Zohar was not yet available to the public, as will be shown below.[76]

The name of Rabbi Joseph de Avila, who is described in the *Sefer Yuhasin* as "a prominent wealthy man who lived in this city," has been discovered by Y. Baer in Spanish documents, in which he is mentioned as being a farmer of taxes in 1285, and as a householder in Avila in 1303.[77]

Rabbi Joseph Halevi, "son of the kabbalist Rabbi Todros", who obtained texts of the Zohar from Moses de Leon, is Rabbi Joseph Abulafia, whose name is well-known from different sources. His father, Rabbi Todros, served in the Toledo rabbinate, and was an important kabbalist and distinguished leader. Moses de Leon's personal connections with Joseph Abulafia are substantiated beyond doubt by the fact that Moses dedicated two of his books to him, the *Sefer ha-Rimmon* and the *Sefer Shekel ha-Kodesh*.

Rabbi Jacob, "reliable pupil of Rabbi Moses," is apparently the pupil of the same name for whom Moses de Leon composed his *Sefer ha-Nefesh ha-Hakhamah*.

(ii) Various Accounts of the Publication of the Zohar

There are several accounts, some of which are traditions independent of Rabbi Isaac of Acre's evidence, and other stories told by the kabbalists, which also indicate that the Zohar appeared only late, around the time of Rabbi Moses de Leon.

Rabbi Judah Hayyat, a kabbalist who was one of the Jews expelled from Spain, writes in the preface to his *Minhat Yehudah*, a commentary on the *Sefer Ma'arekhet ha-Elohut*: "How happy we are, how good is our portion, in that we are fortunate enough to possess the Zohar, which our predecessors did not have, although their little fingers were thicker than our loins, such men as Rav Hai Gaon, and Rav Sheshet Gaon, and Rabbi Eliezer of Worms, and Ramban, and Rashba, and Ravad. All these were scholars of mystical wisdom, but they did not taste its honey, because it was not revealed in their time." Rabbi Elijah Delmedigo writes in the *Sefer Behinat ha-Dat*,[78] composed in 1491, while quoting arguments against the antiquity of the Zohar: "and they also maintain that this book only appeared among our people about 300 years ago."[79] Rabbi Abraham Zacuto states,[80] without any reference to Rabbi Isaac of Acre's information: "This book appeared after Ramban and the Rosh, who did not see it."

Rabbi Hayyim Joseph David Azulai, in his *Sefer Shem ha-Gedolim*, under the heading "Zohar," quotes a story from "an ancient manuscript," which is of great interest for the way in which historical fact is reflected in the stories, concerning the appearance of the Zohar, that evolved in kabbalistic circles. He says: "I have seen something written by the Rav, Rabbi Abraham Rovigo. follows: I found in a very ancient manuscript of the Zohar owned by my teacher, Rabbi Moses Zacuto (may his light shine), the following: I have found it written in truth that the chief kabbalist, Rabbi Nehunya ben ha-Kaneh, wrote the *Sefer ha-Bahir*, and that, after him, Rabbi Simeon ben Yohai composed the Zohar, and included in it a number of works, such as the *Tikkunim*. And after the death of Rabbi Simeon ben Yohai and Rabbi Eleazar, and all that generation, the wisdom of the kabbalah perished, until the Lord prompted a certain king from the East to command that a certain place should be dug up in order to find treasure. And there a box was found containing the book of the Zohar, and the king summoned the wise men of the nations of the world, including those of Christendom, but they came and looked at the book and said to him: 'Our lord king, a sage has written this book, and it is very profound, and we do not understand it.' He said: 'Is there not in the whole world a Jew who can understand it?' 'There is,' they replied, 'in the city of Toledo.' So the king sent the books with his men to Toledo. And when the scholars of Toledo saw it, they rejoiced greatly, and sent many gifts to the king. That is how the kabbalah appeared in Israel. Here ends the passage that I found written by the rabbi aforementioned." Here we have a legendary account of a historical fact—that the Zohar appeared at a late date in Castille.

Another story, which originated in Morocco, approximates less closely to historical truth, since it states that the Zohar was first revealed in North Africa. But even here it is acknowledged that it was hidden away and concealed until a later period. This story is quoted by Rabbi Abraham Azulai in the preface to his commentary to the Zohar:[81] "They said that the book of the Zohar was hidden in Meron in a cave, and an Ishmaelite found it there and sold it to some merchants in Upper Galilee. A few pages from it came into the possession of a scholar from the West, and he went to investigate, and collected together every page from every merchant. He also searched in the rubbish heaps and discovered that merchants were wrapping and selling spices in them. However, it emanated mainly from one of the cities of the West called Todja, and perhaps this western scholar had taken it to the city where he lived."

A unique kind of evidence, which is extremely important for other reasons, is to be found in the Zohar itself, in the *Raya Mehemna* and the *Tikkunim*. A great deal is said in these sections, particularly in the *Tikkunei ha-Zohar*, about the composition of the Zohar by Rabbi Simeon ben Yohai and his companions, and about its revelation in the final generation, in the days of the Messiah. " 'And they who are wise shall shine as the brightness (*zohar*) of the firmament' (Daniel 12: 3). 'They who are wise' are Rabbi Simeon and his companions. 'Shine'— when they began to compose this work, permission was given to them and to Elijah with them, and to all the souls of the academies to descend among them . . . and (the celestial power) gave permission to the ten *sefirot* to reveal hidden secrets to them, but not to divulge them publicly until the generation of the Messiah-king."[82] "Rabbi Simeon ben Yohai said: 'It is true that the Holy One, blessed be He, has agreed that the upper and the lower worlds should be with us in this book. Happy is the generation in which this is revealed; and all this will be renewed by the hand of Moses, at the end of days, in the final generation.' "[83] The problem of whether these words are prophetic or whether they were written with the advantage of hindsight does not concern us here. Whichever way we look at it, we find in these and similar statements an allusion to the fact that the Zohar was to be hidden away and then revealed at the end of time. And since most of the calculations of the "end of days" in the Zohar fix the time of redemption at the beginning of the sixth millennium, we may deduce that these statements contain an announcement of the revelation of the Zohar at almost the exact time that it did in fact appear, according to the evidence of Rabbi Isaac of Acre.

(iii) Quotations from the Zohar

An important method of fixing the date of the appearance of the Zohar is to examine the quotations that have been made from the book. This examination shows that in the early kabbalistic literature there is no reference at all to the existence of the Zohar, and that the first quotations make their appearance only toward the end of the thirteenth century. In the *Sefer Meshal ha-Kadmoni* by Rabbi Isaac ibn Avi Sahulah, which he wrote in 1281, two passages are quoted that are found in their present form in a manuscript of the Zohar.[84] In the same author's commentary to the Song of Songs, written in 1284 and extant in manuscript, there are eight examples that have their origin in the Zohar.[85] At about the same time[86] Rabbi Todros Abulafia wrote his *Sefer Ozar ha-Kavod*, which contains two quotations from the Zohar.[87] Rabbenu Bahya ben Asher's commentary to the Torah, written in 1291, contains two examples in the form of actual quotations,[88] but elsewhere in his commentary as well as in his other writings one can see the impress of passages from the Zohar. The renowned kabbalist, Rabbi Joseph Gikatilla, who was working at the end of the thirteenth and the beginning of the fourteenth centuries, and who was the author of the *Sefer Sha'arei Orah* and other works on kabbalah, has, without directly quoting from it, the influence of the Zohar clearly stamped on several of his books, and particularly on the *Sha'arei Orah*.

All these authors lived in Spain and were contemporaries of Moses de Leon, and there is reason to believe that he had personal connections with three of them. Rabbi Isaac ibn Avi Sahulah lived in Guadalajara, where Moses de Leon also stayed. Rabbi Todros Abulafia's son, Rabbi Joseph, was on friendly terms with Rabbi Moses de Leon, as I have already shown,[89] and we may deduce that his father also knew him and was in close touch with him. Rabbi Joseph Gikatilla also lived in Castille, and although we have no biographical information concerning any personal contacts between them, it is obvious, when their writings are compared, that both he and Rabbi Moses de Leon belonged to the same circle and that they undoubtedly met.[90]

The quotations dealt with so far are introduced by a clause such as "I have seen in a midrash." Rabbi Bahya uses the phrase "the midrash of Rabbi Simeon ben Yohai." The small number of quotations and the manner in which they are quoted show that the authors involved had seen only fragments of individual sections of the Zohar. And this therefore confirms the conclusion that emerges from Rabbi Isaac of Acre's evidence, that the Zohar was published piecemeal. This conclusion will receive additional confirmation when we go on to examine the later and more extensive quotations that emanate from the beginning of the fourteenth century.

The first kabbalist to quote frequently and at length from the Zohar was Italian, Rabbi Menahem Recanati.[91] Hundreds of quotations occur in his writings,[92] especially in his commentary to the Torah, which appears to have been written in the first decade of the fourteenth century. However, an examination of these quotations shows that he had seen only a small part of the Zoharic literature. A significant number of his quotations are taken from the *Idra Rabba*. Rabbi David ben Judah the Pious, a grandson apparently of Nachmanides, who lived in Spain and was active almost contemporaneously with Moses de Leon, quotes in his as yet unprinted writings, and particularly in his *Sefer Mar'ot Zov'ot*, a large collection of statements from the Zohar, all of them in a Hebrew translation. But he had not seen the Zohar in its entirety either, in the version we have.[93] The most frequently quoted section is the *Midrash ha-Ne'elam*. Rabbi Shem Tov ibn Gaon, one of Rabbi Solomon ben Adret's students, composed a responsum on the mystery of the *sefirot*, which has come down to us in a fragmented form, and in it he tries to elucidate some passages from the Zohar, especially from the *Idra Rabba* and the *Idra Zuta*.[94] His early writings do not contain any statements from the Zohar at all, and one might consequently deduce that he did not know of the Zohar's existence. Except for the passages from the *Idrot*, he quotes only intermittently, and then mainly from the *Midrash ha-Ne'elam*. So, despite the fact that the full text of his responsum has not come down to us, and that the matter dealt with concentrates on one particular topic, we may still conclude from the quotations that he had seen only individual sections of the Zohar. Broader in scope and much nearer the full version we now have are the Zohar passages in the *Livnat ha-Sapir*,[95] which was written in the 1320s and attributed in error to Rabbi David ben Judah the Pious.[96] Only the Genesis portion of the book has been printed, but it did apparently cover the whole of the Pentateuch, and the Leviticus section is still extant in a British Library manuscript. And so it is impossible to establish whether the author knew all the sections of the complete Zohar. But even if we assume that he did, this would not contradict the fact that the Zohar appeared a section at a time. It would only show at the most that by the time the author wrote a complete edition had appeared.

However, even this supposition is very doubtful, because from various other sources we may conclude that the sections of the Zohar had not been collected together before the expulsion from Spain, perhaps not even before the actual printing of the Zohar. We find clear evidence of this in the introduction that Rabbi Judah Hayyat wrote to his commentary on the *Sefer Ma'arekhet ha-Elohut*: "And I, Judah, the son of the pious and perfect sage, Rabbi Jacob Hayyat, peace be upon him, tasted a little honey when I was in Spain, and my eyes were enlightened. And I determined to seek out and search for wisdom, and I went from strength to strength in order to collect whatever could be found of the aforementioned book, and I gathered a little here and a little there until I had most of what there was. And I believe with complete certainty that this was a reward for all the hardships that I suffered during the expulsion from Spain." Ideas in the Zohar are quoted by hearsay in the responsa attributed to Rabbi Joseph Gikatilla, which were written about the end of the fourteenth century.[97] In the *Sefer Akedat Yizhak* by Rabbi Isaac ibn Arama, a philosophical homilist active in Spain in the second half of the fifteenth century, there are a considerable number of quotations from the Zohar, but it is obvious that he had not seen the book in its entirety, because he writes,[98] "Many people have told me that in the *Midrash ha-Ne'elam* there is the following passage: 'Therefore the

children of Israel do not eat the sinew of the thigh-vein, etc. (Genesis 32: 33).
The (Hebrew word) *et* is used here in order to include the 9th of Av.'[99] They
were puzzled by this and did not understand it. And I was asked about it, and I
was also perplexed for a time, and then a suitable explanation suddenly
occurred to me. And I said that if this passage did in fact exist then it was
extremely fine, and the explanation was as follows. . . ." The Zohar manuscripts
that have come down to us, which were written before the book was printed, do
not contain the complete work.[100] And it is quite clear from the statements of
the editors and correctors in the introductions to the early printed editions that
even they did not have complete manuscripts. This, for example, is what the
corrector writes in the introduction to the Mantua edition, "We know what it
was like in the past, that only very few[101] were able to bring the blessing of this
book into their homes, and even they did not have the complete benefit of the
five books." The title pages of the printed editions also show that several
sections were collected from different manuscripts.

(iv) Titles Given to the Zohar

In the years following its appearance, the Zohar was quoted under different
names. The multiplicity and character of these titles tell us something about the
manner in which the book first appeared, and how it was disseminated. And
they serve to strengthen the conclusions that we have already reached in the
discussion of the matter so far.

The name *Zohar* is mentioned, as we have already seen,[102] in the book itself in
the *Raya Mehemna* and the *Tikkunei ha-Zohar*. And it would seem, at first glance,
that one could not have more definite proof that this was the normal, basic
name by which the book was known from the moment that it appeared. But this
supposition, so obvious and acceptable in itself, is not confirmed by the facts,
because in many important sources the name *Zohar* is not mentioned at all. This
extraordinary situation needs explaining and we can solve the problem only by
supposing that the authors of these sources did not know of the sections that
make explicit mention of the name of the book. And indeed we can see that this
is so from our examination of the quotations, because passages from the *Raya
Mehemna* and the *Tikkunei ha-Zohar* are quoted only at a later stage, a long time
after the first appearance of the Zohar. Moreover, there is reason to think, from
the text of the passages that mention the name *Zohar*, that the author meant to
apply it only to those particular sections. On the other hand, we know without
question that by the beginning of the fourteenth century the main body of the
book was known by this name. It is mentioned, for example, in the story told by
Rabbi Isaac of Acre, and passages from the book are quoted by this name in the
writings of Rabbi Menahem Recanati.[103] In Recanati's *Sefer Ta'amei ha-Mizvot*
the title is cited in two forms: *Sefer ha-Zohar ha-Gadol* (The Great Zohar) and
Sefer ha-Zohar ha-Mufla (The Exalted Zohar). But these specific designations are
not used indiscriminately. The *Zohar ha-Gadol* refers to the *Idra Rabba*, while the
title *Ha-Zohar ha-Mufla* is applied to the various sections of the Zohar on the
Torah.

The earliest quotations in the writings of Rabbi Isaac ibn Avi Sahulah and
Rabbi Todros Abulafia are introduced simply as midrash or *haggadah* or
rabbinic sayings, which shows that the passages they had did not form part of a

larger work with its own individual title. In the writings of Moses de Leon, the source of the Zoharic passages is designated by a host of names of a general and imprecise character, such as *Midrashot ha-Penimiyim* (Esoteric Discourses), *Me'orot Olam* (Luminaries of the World), *Or Yisrael* (Light of Israel), *Sitrei Torah* (Secrets of the Torah), *Sitrei ha-Yihud* (Secrets of the Divine Unity), and so on,[104] without any definite title.

Rabbi Isaac ibn Avi Sahulah and Rabbi Moses de Leon also use the name *Yerushalmi* or *Midrash Yerushalmi*, and this occurs in other sources as well.[105] But this should not be seen as a specific title because other books, like the *Sefer ha-Bahir*, and various midrashim, are also referred to as *Yerushalmi*.

An extremely common name was *Midrasho shel Rabbi Shimeon ben Yohai* or *Midrash Rabbi Shimeon ben Yohai*. It is first mentioned by Rabbi Bahya ben Asher, and occurs subsequently in a number of works, even as late as the sixteenth century.[106] Similar titles are *Sifrei Rabbi Shimeon ben Yohai, Idrei de-Rabbi Shimeon ben Yohai* (*Idra Rabba*), *Zavvatei de-Rabbi Shimeon ben Yohai* (*Idra Zuta*) in the responsum of Rabbi Shem Tov ibn Gaon, and *Mekhilta de-Rabbi Shimeon ben Yohai* in the *Sefer ha-Gevul* by Rabbi David ben Judah the Pious.

In the *Sefer Menorat ha-Ma'or*[107] by Rabbi Israel al-Nakawah, who was martyred in Toledo in 1391, there are about forty quotations from the Zohar, most of them in a Hebrew translation, and they are ascribed to a *Midrash Yehi Or*. This title is also mentioned in the *Sefer Yuhasin*,[108] although it is possible that the author took it from *Menorat ha-Ma'or*. It is likely that the origin of this name goes back to a manuscript the author had that began with the verse *yehi or* ("Let there be light").

The name *Midrash ha-Ne'elam*, which in our text belongs to a particular section, is quoted as the title of the whole work in the *Sefer Livnat ha-Sapir*, and also in the *Sefer Akedat Yizhak*. In the same way, some passages are quoted, by Rabbi Judah Hayyat for example, under the name of a certain section, like the *Idra Rabba*, that do not actually belong to that particular part.

These facts—both the anonymity on the one hand, and, on the other, the haphazard multiplicity of names and titles—demonstrate that the form of the book had not been finally settled, nor its scope definitely determined, before it was printed. The diversity of nomenclature is another proof that the book did not originally appear as a single unit, but as a succession of individual texts, with the titles changing according to the different ways in which the various sections were put together in the manuscripts.

c. The Sanctity of the Zohar

The aura of supreme sanctity, which for many generations has given the Zohar such eminence in Jewish literature, was not associated with it until some centuries after its first appearance. It was the product of a long historical development. When it first appeared, and for some time afterward, the book was known and disseminated only among the kabbalists, whose influence was limited at that time to small groups. Beyond the confines of the kabbalah, in rabbinic and philosophical literature, the appearance of the Zohar made no impression. It is mentioned only comparatively later and then in only a few works, such as the *Responsa* of Rabbi Simeon ben Zemah Duran, the *Sefer ha-Ikkarim*, the *Sefer Akedat Yizḥak* and the writings of Rabbi Isaac Abarbanel. Rabbi Joseph Albo, the author of *Sefer ha-Ikkarim*,[109] writes: "I felt compelled to write this because I have seen people making errors in this matter, and reading the Zohar and other writings of the kabbalists in a non kabbalistic way, but with their own individual interpretations, in order to demonstrate the depth of their own wisdom. And they have penetrated beyond the prescribed boundaries and set their minds to matters upon which it is forbidden to deliberate."

The kabbalists treated the Zohar, generally speaking, as an ancient book. This is evident from the names, *Midrasho shel Rabbi Shimeon ben Yoḥai*, and *Midrash Yerushalmi*; and it is also quoted by such names as *Ma'aseh Bereshit le-Ḥakhmei ha-Mishnah* (The Creation according to the Sages of the Mishnah).[110] However, there are signs that not all of them thought of it as particularly holy, and it is possible that some of them refused to accept the narrative framework as historical fact. Rabbi Joseph ibn Wakkar, who wrote a book in Arabic on the kabbalah in 1340, writes,[111] "There are many mistakes in the Zohar and one should beware of them to avoid falling into error." Several kabbalists tried in different ways to imitate the Zohar.[112] The author of the *Livnat ha-Sapir* copied the Aramaic idiom. He quotes passages from the Zohar in their original form, but he also for the most part uses Zoharic Aramaic for his own additional interpretations and comments, and it is sometimes difficult to distinguish between the original quotation and the additional material. Rabbi David ben Judah the Pious did the opposite. He translates passages from the Zohar into Hebrew, quoting them usually in their original form and attributing them to rabbis mentioned in the Zohar, but he does not divulge their literary source, and he also introduces comments of his own and quotations from other kabbalists into the customary Zoharic framework. A piece by Rabbi Azriel of Gerona is quoted as "Rabbi Hiyya began: God, the God of the spirits of all flesh . . .," and an extract from the *Sefer Sha'ar ha-Razim* by Rabbi Todros Abulafia starts: "Rabbi Simeon began: The heavens declare the glory of God."[113] This is just a simple pseudepigraphic pastime that consists of putting together different passages, some translated, some transcribed, and some original, without any imaginative creative ability. Rabbi David's little game makes one feel that he could not have taken too seriously traditions recorded in the Zohar in the name of early rabbis, to whom he was prepared to ascribe statements by thirteenth-century kabbalists.

The most original and successful imitations were the *Sefer ha-Peliah*[114] and the *Sefer ha-Kaneh*.[115] The anonymous author attributed his books to members of an ancient family, descendants of Rabbi Nehunya ben ha-Kaneh, who lived in the Holy Land and received revelations of the mysteries in the heavenly academy. From the point of view of content this author was not very original either, but collected and put together various passages from the storehouse of kabbalistic literature, particularly in the *Sefer ha-Peliah*.[116] There are not many quotations from the Zohar, and they appear in a Hebrew translation.[117] The literary form of encounter and dialogue in the heavenly academy is an imitation of the celestial background of the *Raya Mehemna* and the *Tikkunei ha-Zohar*. Imitations of another kind are to be found in the *Sefer Brit Menuḥah*,[118] attributed to Rabbi Abraham of Granada. The preface to the book contains an account of the chain of mystical tradition, and Rabbi Simeon is mentioned as the linch pin of esoteric development: "Before it came into the hands of Rabbi Simeon, and since his death, it has remained hidden and concealed, apart from other scholars, like the *geonim*, who perceived a little of it, and understood as much as they were able." The book contains six pieces in Aramaic and two in Hebrew in the name of Rabbi Simeon ben Yohai, who is also called simply *he-ḥakham* (the sage). But not a single one of these pieces can be traced to the Zohar, and it is clear from their content that they were composed by the author of the book himself as additional support for his arguments. The name *Zohar* is not mentioned at all.

All the above imitations show without a doubt that their authors did not yet have that attitude of reverential awe which characterized the approach to the Zohar of later generations.

The "canonization" of the Zohar and its wider influence were consequent upon the expulsion from Spain, which shook the very foundations of Judaism. The decline of Spanish Jewry was accompanied by a decline in rationalistic philosophy with its tendency to universalism, whereas the esoteric doctrine of the kabbalah, which had become more and more intermingled with Jewish apocalyptic and expressed the yearning for national redemption, was regarded as the last hope for the spiritual salvation of a desolated people. This historico-spiritual transformation, which brought the kabbalah out of a closed circle of mystical initiates into the wider world and also into the homes of the Jewish masses, raised the Zohar to a most exalted position, where it was surrounded by an aura of antiquity and a wondrous light. In the Zohar the mysteries of existence and of the divine were already combined with accounts of the messianic days and calculations of the end of time, and so its subject matter was fully suited to the spiritual condition of a shattered generation, who were anxious to find an answer to the perplexing terrors of exile and longed to hear the steps of the Messiah approaching.

The printing of the Zohar in the middle of the sixteenth century gave an exterior impulse to the spread of the book and helped to bring its influence to bear on wider circles. This influence reached its peak in the revival of the kabbalah in Safed, and particularly in the kabbalah of Rabbi Isaac Luria, where the intermingling of mystical and apocalyptic ideas reached their culmination. In kabbalistic literature, after the expulsion from Spain, and particularly in the Safed and subsequent periods, the Zohar was taken to be the preeminent source of mystical doctrine, and all the new mystical ideas were made dependent on it by way of interpretation. At the same time, popular consciousness was full of stories from the Zohar—the arguments and statements in it concerning the soul, the Torah, the commandments and prayers, sin and punishment, the messianic days, and the life of the world to come—that were channeled to them by ethical writings, which became a kind of popular branch of kabbalistic teaching. In this way the Zohar was able to achieve the highest possible status. It gained a place in the national consciousness as a canonical text, third only to the Bible and the Talmud. The Talmud and the Zohar were regarded as two aspects, the revealed and the concealed, of the divine revelation embodied in the books of Scripture. And, from the point of view of sanctity, the Zohar was placed in an even higher position than the Talmud. The mysteries of the Zohar were regarded as the soul of the Torah, while the laws of the Talmud formed the Torah's body. Just as the soul was more important than the body, so the Zohar was more important than the Talmud.

The holy status of the Zohar as representing the kabbalah among large sectors of Jewry, and its superiority in sanctity over the Talmud, demonstrate the victory of the mystical view of the nature of Torah and kabbalah, and of the latter's relationship to halakhic literature—a view that spread before the Expulsion in the confined circles of the initiates, and was openly expressed even in the Zohar itself.

However, this very image of soul and body contains within itself a limitation in the authority of the Zohar and the kabbalah. Soul and body are interdependent, and only when they are joined together and fulfill their respective roles in complete harmony do they constitute the whole man. In the same way, the Zohar and the Talmud, or the hidden and the revealed, cannot survive or fulfill their tasks separately without a mutual reciprocity, since the teaching of Judaism as a whole depends on both of them. And even after the "canonization" of the Zohar, it was never allowed to deprive the Talmud of absolute authority in the regulation of the practical affairs of life. The laws that were either directly or indirectly stated in the Zohar[119] were not accepted if they were found to be in opposition to clear Talmudic legal decision. Rabbi Solomon Luria (*Maharshal*), the renowned legalist who also studied kabbalah, was vehemently opposed to the practice of following the Zohar in the matter of laying *tefillin*, which he considered to be contrary to the halakhah. He writes:[120] "You ask me concerning my practice of putting on the *tefillin* of the hand—whether one should do it in a sitting or a standing position, since you have seen many of the most particular of men putting it on in a sitting position. Know, my friend, that new men have recently appeared, purporting to belong to the kabbalists and to the mystical schools. But men of weak vision cannot look at the light of the Zohar, and do not know its entrance or its exit, or its meaning. But they say they have found this in the books of Rabbi Simeon ben Yohai. Know, my friend, that to my knowledge none of my masters or my holy forebears, who served the greatest scholars in the world, acted in this way, but only in accordance with the words of the Talmud and the legal authorities. And if Rabbi Simeon ben Yohai were standing before us, and tried with all his might to change the practice of our ancestors, we would pay no heed to him, because in the majority of cases his legal opinion is not followed. . . . And so, my friend, do not follow them. Do not meddle with the mysteries of those who dare to come out with such new ideas. They think they know and understand the innermost secrets of the Torah. If only they knew what was plainly revealed (i.e., the halakhah)!"

The basis for the opposition shown here, that the law does not follow Rabbi Simeon ben Yohai, occurs in other discussions concerning the laws in the Zohar, but this formal reason is not the crux of the matter. The real grounds for opposition depend on the clear recognition that the area of both the Zohar and the Talmud is strictly limited, and that the hidden is not allowed to impinge upon the province of the revealed. The principle is enunciated in the *Sefer Yuḥasin*[121]: "This has already been agreed in Israel; that whatever does not conflict with the Talmud, and is not explained in the Talmud, but is to be found explained there (in the Zohar)—this we may accept," and this statement fixes the limit of the Zohar's authority in matters of halakhah. Rabbi Menahem Azariah of Fano, a famous Italian kabbalist who was also distinguished in the halakhah, was greatly incensed by the opinion of Luria that I have just quoted, and wrote:[122] "Rabbi Solomon Luria was rich in knowledge, for his fount [of wisdom] overflowed, but in his responsum no. 98 his lips spoke boastfully and disdainfully against these discourses, and he was indeed impoverished at that moment, and all his words here are completely vain, for they overstepped the limit of speculation, and transgressed the bounds of good conduct. It is not fit for a sage or scholar to reply to them, or even to pay heed to them." Nevertheless, even this renowned kabbalist acknowledged the limit of the Zohar's authority when compared with the Talmud. He writes in the same responsum:[123] "Whenever the gemara can be interpreted in different ways, and one of them is clarified by the Zohar, then we should turn our minds to it, and act according to its instruction . . . and if the Zohar disagrees with any one of the commentators or the geonim, but is supported by the language of the gemara, then the interpretation of the Zohar takes precedence over everything else."

The most forthright example of the accepted view of this matter is the position of Rabbi Joseph Karo, the author of the Shulhan Arukh, a renowned authority in both kabbalah and halakhah. In the Shulhan Arukh he cites only a few laws from the Zohar, and as a general rule he points out that these are stricter or preventive measures, or only characteristic of the specially pious, and not generally accepted practices.[124] In his commentary to the Tur Orah Hayyim[125] he states quite clearly that the laws of the Zohar have no authority when they are opposed to the decisions of the halakhah: "I do not know why (the author of the Sefer ha-Agur) was surprised at this (that the legal authorities conflicted with the Zohar on the question of the blessing over the tefillin) more than at several other laws. We find that Rabbi Simeon ben Yohai writes in the Zohar the opposite of the conclusion reached by the Talmud, whereas the legalists write down only the Talmudic conclusion. And the reason is that even if they had known the opinions of Rabbi Simeon ben Yohai they would not have heeded them if he disagreed with the Talmud." This concept, which recognizes the authority and the eminence of both the Talmud and the Zohar jointly, and sees them as two complementary revelations of Israel's Torah, became dominant, after the expulsion from Spain, in well-rounded normative Judaism, which preserved traditional values with great fidelity. But beyond it, either within the Jewish fold or outside it, this unity was broken, and attempts were made to drive a wedge between the Talmud and the Zohar.[126]

The earliest attempt to separate the two and to set up the Zohar as a hostile rival to the Talmud was made in Christian mysticism,[127] which grew and flourished in the Renaissance period in Italy and Germany, and subsequently spread to other countries in Europe, surviving on into the eighteenth century. The leaders of this movement believed that the principles of Christianity were contained in kabbalistic teaching, and in the Zohar as its earliest literary manifestation. The Zohar was thought in these circles to be sacred, a book that reflected the pure spiritual image of Judaism, which in their view was identical with true Christianity without the distortions of the Talmud. This view gave rise to the fact that, at the very time that the Talmud was ordered to be burned, permission was given for the printing of the Zohar with the help of Christian scholars.[128]

Within Judaism itself this division appeared in the Sabbatean movement. This messianic movement, which was based mainly on kabbalistic doctrines, adopted the Zohar as its banner from its very inception, but at the peak of its development, before the apostasy of Shabbetai Zvi, it still stood on the joint foundation of the Zohar and the Talmud, or of kabbalah and halakhah. But during its sectarian period, which continued long after the apostasy crisis, a tendency toward extreme heresy gradually gained the upper hand. It rebelled against the Talmud, threw off the "yoke" of the practical commandments, and established Judaism on the basis of the mysteries of the Zohar and the kabbalah, as against the Talmud and the halakhah. This antinomian spiritualist tendency reached its full expression and tragic conclusion in the Frankist branch of Sabbateanism. The members of the sect in Poland, who became Jacob Frank's disciples, gave themselves two characteristic names: "champions of the Zohar" and "opponents of the Talmud." Their disputes with the rabbis hinged on the status of the Zohar, contrasted with the Talmud. In the first oral disputation, which took place in Kamenetz in 1757, the Frankists formulated, among others, two principles of faith. One emphasized the truth of the Zohar and of the mysteries of the Torah in general. The second declared the Talmud to be a book of lies and distortions: "II. The Torah of Moses and his prophecy, and the words of all the early prophets, and the other books of our ancestors, are all closed and sealed. They are like a woman whose face is covered. Whoever wishes to admire her beauty must first reveal her face.[129] III. Our ancestors interpreted the Torah, and the *Shas*[130] was created in the holy tongue, and this is the Talmud, and it contains falsehoods and fictions that are opposed to the Lord and His Torah."[131] At the end of the disputation the Talmud was ordered to be burned, on the initiative of the Frankists. The absolute rift between the Zohar and the Talmud can be seen most clearly in the grotesque demand, included among the conditions of their apostasy submitted by the Frankists, that "they should be allowed to retain the books of the Zohar, and the other works of the kabbalists."[132]

The rift occurred in the opposite direction in the *Haskalah* (Enlightenment) movement in Germany and Eastern Europe. The *maskilim* tried to degrade the Zohar and to expel it as a foreign growth from the Jewish domain. On the other hand, the Talmud did not suit their frame of mind either, and disappeared completely from their midst as the movement developed. However, at the beginning of the Englightenment period they still kept faith with rabbinic writings, and even afterward, when they had thrown off the yoke of the commandments, they still regarded the Talmud and the halakhah in general as a legitimate manifestation of the Jewish spirit. On the other hand, they saw the Zohar and kabbalah as an invalid doctrine and a misshapen faith, contaminating pure monotheistic Judaism.

A distant echo of the *Haskalah's* attitude to the Zohar can be heard in the fierce controversy that broke out comparatively recently in the Yemen, which divided Yemenite Jewry into two camps.[133] Rabbi Yiḥya al-Kafiḥ, a scholar in Sa'ana, the capital of the Yemen, who was influenced by European *Haskalah* literature, waged a fierce battle against "the perverse" in his community, "who hated wisdom and knowledge," and founded a Yemenite *Haskalah* movement known by the name *Darda*. Various matters, including religious, educational, and social ideas, were involved in the controversy, but the attitude to the Zohar and to kabbalah was the central issue in the literary polemic that ensued.[134] Al-Kafiḥ embarked on a far-reaching critique of the Zohar, describing it as a foreign work that had infiltrated basic idolatrous ideas into the fabric of Judaism. He wrote:[135] "The author of the Zohar took the ideas [of the idolators] and sought to introduce them into the faith of our holy Torah, and falsely called himself Rabbi Simeon ben Yohai, the *tanna*, maintaining that the Holy One, blessed be He, called by him *Atika Kadisha* [the holy, ancient one], had revealed Himself to him, showing him hidden secrets. . . . And when this philosopher realized that the Mishnah and the two Talmudim and the true rabbinic midrashim opposed him with their belief in the unity of God, he tried to invalidate them, and scorned and scoffed at them, and at all those who studied them. . . . And he promised that Israel would never merit redemption until they ceased their practice of studying the Mishnah and the Talmud, and studied instead his new Torah, full of idolatrous pictures and images, monstrous faces and diverse copulations. God forbid that any Jew should believe that the *tanna* Rabbi Simeon ben Yohai or any other of our rabbis shared such beliefs . . . for it is the aim of our holy Torah to keep us away from the belief in idols, whether physical or spiritual, and to teach us 'that the Lord, He is God, there is none else beside Him.' " Here we have, finally, the most extreme and most penetrating expression of this feeling of separation between the Zohar on the one hand and the Talmud and true Judaism on the other.

However, all this agitation was not able to expel the sanctity of the Zohar from the religious consciousness of the people. Nevertheless, as a consequence of the Sabbatean crisis which resulted in a proclamation in Poland forbidding the study of the Zohar to any below the age of thirty,[136] students of the Zohar declined in number, and the kabbalah became once more, particularly in the East, a secret doctrine confined to restricted circles. But its numinous effect on the people as a whole did not diminish. On the contrary, the farther it receded from the grasp of knowledge and understanding, the more sacred it appeared to be. The book became more exalted and awe-inspiring, sealed with seven seals, and because of its supreme sanctity any investigation of lofty mysteries was sure to be a perilous exercise. Instead of studying the Zohar, people simply uttered phrases from it without any understanding of their meaning, in the belief "that, even if one does not understand, the language is precious for the soul."[137] For this purpose the Zohar was printed several times in square characters and with vocalization.

The sanctity of the Zohar found a powerful champion in hasidism, the widespread popular movement that arose and expanded at exactly the same time as the *Haskalah* movement was trying desperately to humiliate the Zohar and to destroy the unity of kabbalah and halakhah. In hasidism the strong connection between the Zohar and the Talmud, depicted as soul and body, was elevated to a new plane, with greater emphasis on the holiness of the Zohar. The Baal Shem Tov (the *Besht*) always carried the Zohar in his bosom, and through its power was able to perform miracles and foretell the future. When he was asked in astonishment how he was able to trace the steps of a man who had

disappeared simply by looking at the Zohar, he said in reply: "Does not the
light that the Holy One, blessed be He, made in the six days of creation enable a
man to see from one end of the world to the other, and is it not stored up for the
righteous in the time to come? And where is it stored? In the Torah. Therefore,
when I open the Zohar I can see the entire world."[138] The closeness of the
Maggid of Mezeritsch to the Besht is portrayed as being closely bound up with
the study of the Zohar: "The Besht said to him, 'Before you go tell me something
from the Zohar.' The Maggid agreed and did so. When he had finished, the
Besht said to him, 'A good explanation, but your teaching is like a body without
a soul.' The Besht then began to explain the passage in the Zohar himself. His
words were so full of joy that the Maggid saw the Besht rise in the air on his
couch and fly. At that point the great Maggid was bound to the Besht."[139]
However, rational investigation of the Zohar and kabbalistic literature was not
very common in hasidic circles, and, even among the *zaddikim*, there were
comparatively few who were distinguished for their basic knowledge and deep
understanding of mysticism, or who even composed important commentaries
on the Zohar. As for the rest of the *zaddikim* and the hasidic community in
general, they invested the Zohar with supreme sanctity, and saw in it the
absolute foundation of real Judaism. This view of the Zohar as the cornerstone
of Jewish belief is expressed in the pointed and laconic words attributed
traditionally to one of the founders of hasidism, Rabbi Pinhas of Koretz,[140]
"[Rabbi Pinhas] glorified and thanked God that He had not created him before
the appearance of the Zohar, for the Zohar 'has preserved me for Judaism.' "

III. THE HISTORY OF ZOHAR SCHOLARSHIP

a. Early Criticism

Criticism of the Zohar began at the very moment that the book appeared, at the
end of the thirteenth century. The arguments in scholarly quarters in Spain as
to whether the book emanated from Rabbi Simeon ben Yohai and his pupils, or
whether it was the work of their own contemporary, Rabbi Moses de Leon,
echoes of which are transmitted through the evidence of Rabbi Isaac of Acre,
may be seen as the beginning of that critical controversy which flared up again
much later in polemical literature and has continued indeed for many years
down to our own day. From the critical point of view, we should take particular
note of one point in Rabbi Isaac of Acre's investigation:[141] "And he (i.e., Isaac
of Acre) said that he had been taught that one should believe whatever was
written in Aramaic, for those were the words of Rabbi Simeon, but, as to what
was written in Hebrew, they were not his words but the words of the forger; for
the real book was written entirely in Aramaic." We gather from this that a
differentiation was made between those parts written in Aramaic, "the
Jerusalem tongue," and those written in Hebrew, which refer no doubt to the
passages in our *Midrash ha-Ne'elam*, and not to sections that have disappeared,
as some scholars have supposed. Consequently, when the Zohar first appeared
Aramaic was regarded as an indication of antiquity, while Hebrew was thought
to indicate more recent work, and so the *Midrash ha-Ne'elam*, or at least most of

it, was ruled to be unauthentic. This is an important distinction, because it reveals some kind of a beginning of a Zohar critique, from the point of view of language and style.

From the earliest appearance of the Zohar to the end of the fifteenth century there is no sign of a literary critique, but we can be sure beyond doubt that many philosophers and talmudists did not accept the Zohar as an ancient work, although they did not have sufficiently high regard for it to study it and disprove its antiquity. We find a clear indication of this in the *Sefer Beḥinat ha-Dat* by Rabbi Elijah Delmedigo, which was written in 1491, and which contains the earliest formulations of a number of important critical arguments. First of all, the author speaks against the kabbalah in geneal, and makes the point that "most of the followers of the Talmud, and also those who follow the plain meaning, and the philosophers, who are of our people, are strictly opposed to these [kabbalists]."[142] He then enumerates his arguments against the antiquity of the Zohar: "The opponents of this view maintain that what the adherents of the kabbalah say, namely that they are the words of Rabbi Simeon ben Yohai in a book called the Book of the Zohar, is not true. And this is evident for a number of reasons. Firstly, if Rabbi Simeon had composed it, a *baraitha* or an *aggadah* from it would have been mentioned in the Talmud, as is the case with the *Sifre* and other talmudical books, but we do not find such a mention. Furthermore, the men whose names are mentioned in this book lived many years after Rabbi Simeon ben Yohai, as is evident to whoever looks at these names and then looks at the Talmud. And, if this is so, then the author of this book could not possibly have been Rabbi Simeon ben Yohai. Furthermore, the book only appeared among our people about 300 years ago. Furthermore, if Rabbi Simeon was the father of the kabbalists, and really knew the mysteries and the allusions in the laws, the halakhah would have followed his opinion, but such is not the case."[143] It is obvious that these arguments are not the author's alone, but a summary of the arguments that were current in the circles of "the followers of the Talmud, and also those who follow the plain meaning, and the philosophers."

This critical attitude appeared again in the middle of the sixteenth century in connection with the controversy about the printing of the Zohar. Many scholars opposed this printing for a variety of reasons. Their arguments are known to us only from the counterarguments in the approbations and the prefaces of the first editions,[144] and from these it is clear that a number of those who were opposed to the printing had expressed grave doubts as to the book's antiquity. In the afterword of the *Tikkunei ha-Zohar* the following argument is cited: "Whence has come the book of the Zohar whose whereabouts up till now have been unknown, and whose name was not mentioned in the academies of the French and Spanish rabbis? And who knows whether at the present time there are not among us those pure of heart, of innocent thought and of blameless mind, who have fabricated on their own these statements and midrashim?" The strange suspicion that the Zohar might have been written just before it was printed shows the lack of knowledge that affected even scholarly circles concerning the book and the date of its appearance.

The *Sefer Beḥinat ha-Dat* was not printed during the lifetime of the author, but more than a hundred years after it was written, in 1629, by a relative of the author's, Joseph Solomon Rofe of Candia. He added his own reply, in defense of the kabbalah and the Zohar, entitled *Mazref la-Ḥokhmah*. Joseph Solomon Rofe attempts in his book to destroy the arguments of Rabbi Elijah Delmedigo, one by one, and he cites proofs for the antiquity of the Zohar and extols the wisdom of the kabbalah. This book is the earliest defense of the antiquity of the kabbalah and the Zohar, but the intention of the defense is somewhat suspect, and it is possible that the author concealed his real opinion. While countering the arguments put forward by the opponents of the kabbalah he raises new points, referring, for example, to the evidence of Rabbi Isaac of Acre in the *Sefer Yuḥasin*,[145] and drawing attention to strange and surprising matters to be found in the Zohar.[146] And even though on the face of it he refutes and destroys all the arguments, his solutions do not really match up to the difficulties and one still remains somewhat perplexed.

The relationship of Joseph Solomon Rofe of Candia to the kabbalah and the Zohar is extremely obscure and complex. He is known, on the one hand, as the author of kabbalistic works, and as so fervent a proponent of Lurianic kabbalah that he has been considered practically a disciple of Isaac Luria. But, on the other hand, a letter has been attributed to him, by the name of *Mikhtav Aḥuz*,[147] that pours scorn and ridicule upon the literature and teachings of the kabbalah, and also makes a mockery of the attribution of the Zohar to Rabbi Simeon ben Yohai. The author writes:[148] "They say that the Zohar was written by (the *tanna*) Rabbi Simeon ben Yohai. But traditions are mentioned there that emanate from later *amoraim* who came several centuries after him. Who is foolish enough to come this way, without his eyes growing dim! For the stone shall cry out of the wall, and the beam out of the timber shall answer it.[149] Unless they say that he was a prophet and had seen the book of Adam with the names and stories of the sages, and knowledge of all that was to come, no wisdom, counsel, or understanding can substantiate these lies. It is a dirge for the kabbalists and has become a lamentation." Here we have what would appear to be an amazing contradiction. But in the *Sefer Mazref la-Ḥokhmah* the author himself indicates that when he defends the kabbalah and the Zohar he does not really reveal his innermost thoughts. This is what he says:[150] "Behold, I write here against the philosophers, and come to the aid of the Lord, to act as spokesman for the wisdom of kabbalah, for thus have I been commanded by one of the mighty princes of Judah whose heart has now turned toward the words of the kabbalists. And since I am bound to him by the cords of his love I have left my own studies in order to fulfill his exalted desire. And if tomorrow another spirit comes upon him and he yearns for philosophy, and asks me to extol and exalt it and give it a place among princes, I will equip myself speedily and gird up my loins like a warrior to protect the philosopher. One great principle I would recommend to you: do not imagine that you can fathom writers' opinions from their books, for God alone knows the secrets of the heart . . . and there is no teacher or father who can tell his pupil or his child everything that is in his heart concerning matters of this kind, without sacrificing the truth." It is difficult to decide, on reading these words, whether to place Joseph Solomon Rofe of Candia among the defenders of the Zohar or among its critics and opponents. And it may be that Rabbi Judah Aryeh Modena, the pungent critic of the kabbalah and the Zohar, was right to cite the writings of Joseph Solomon Rofe in support of his own critique.[151]

b. Christian Kabbalah and Rabbi Judah Aryeh Modena

The doctrines of the kabbalah attracted the attention of Christian circles in the early Renaissance period. By the end of the fifteenth century several texts had been translated into Latin, and keen and serious interest was aroused that led to the formation of an actual movement. The orientation toward the ancient world, and the desire to discover the truth in all areas of human culture beyond the framework of Christianity, prompted Christian scholars to examine Jewish sources, and they began to study the Hebrew language and Jewish literature. The kabbalah was, for various reasons, that part of Jewish literature which was nearest to the spirit of the age. The Platonic revival and the pursuit of mystical experience and knowledge of the occult[152] were important elements in this swing toward the kabbalah. But the main reason derives from the principles of the Christian faith, for the truth sought by even the men of the Renaissance was pure Christian truth, and they were happy to find any religious-cultural manifestation that in their view confirmed the truth of Christianity. As a result of this surge of interest, the Zohar entered the sphere of Christian scholastic speculation, and its influence began to impregnate European culture.

Two famous humanists stand out as the leaders of this movement: Pico della Mirandola in Italy, and Johannes Reuchlin in Germany. One of Pico's Jewish teachers was Rabbi Elijah Delmedigo, an opponent of the kabbalah, but the mysteries of the kabbalah were revealed to him by his kabbalist teacher, Rabbi Johanan Alemanno. Pico collected various manuscripts of kabbalistic literature, among them a manuscript of the Zohar. His study of the kabbalah was based mainly on the commentary to the Torah written by Rabbi Menahem Recanati, which contained a large number of quotations from the Zohar. In 1486 Pico formulated 900 fundamental principles of religion, drawn from various sources, among them 47 principles of kabbalah, and 72 conclusions that he himself had drawn from these principles. This eclectic work was intended to disclose and combine the truths contained in different religions and systems of thought, and Pico submitted it for oral disputation, but the disputation did not take place, and the ecclesiastical authorities charged him with heresy. One of the things that aroused a storm against him was his view that no knowledge was more likely to prove the divinity of Jesus than that of magic and kabbalah.[153] Reuchlin wrote two books in dialogue form on kabbalistic matters.[154] His prime sources were the writings of Rabbi Joseph Gikatilla. He also tried to discover a basis for the fundamental teachings of Christianity in the doctrines of kabbalah.[155] Besides these two scholars and their disciples, there were several Jewish apostates active in the creation of a Christian kabbalah. The most important of these was Paulus Riccius, who summarized the principles of kabbalah in a systematic way in 1510, and translated the *Sefer Sha'arei Orah* into Latin.[156]

Christian kabbalah generally gained in strength, but knowledge of real kabbalistic source material was extremely scanty until the end of the seventeenth century, when Knorr von Rosenroth's book[157] appeared, which contained a large collection of translations from kabbalistic literature, including important sections of the Zohar. Apart from the *Sefer Yezirah* and the *Sefer Sha'arei Orah*, which had appeared in Latin translation, and the passages quoted by the leaders of the movement, Christian kabbalists relied mainly on two christianizing forgeries: *Iggeret ha-Sodot*, attributed to Rabbi Nehunya ben ha-Kaneh, and *Galya Raza*, attributed to Rabbi Judah ha-Nasi, the work of apostates from the end of the fifteenth century.[158] However, a translation of parts of the Zohar had been made in the sixteenth century by Postel,[159] but it was not published and remained generally unknown. Only individual quotations from the Zohar appear here and there. But, despite this, we find academic expositions and arguments in the seventeenth century concerning the date of composition of the Zohar, particularly among scholars in philology. In the process of arguing about the antiquity or the late date of the vowel-points, Capellus and Buxtorf the Younger touched upon the problem of the dates of the *Sefer ha-Bahir* and the Zohar, in which vowel-points are mentioned. Capellus considered the books to be late, whereas Buxtorf tried to prove their antiquity and in this way to confirm his view that the vowel-points were ancient.[160] Morin published a book in 1669 that contains critical views on the dates of the *Sefer ha-Bahir* and the Zohar.[161]

However, the accepted view in all Christian kabbalistic circles placed a very strong emphasis on the antiquity of the Zohar. This was because only if the Zohar proved to be an early work could it substantiate their claim that kabbalistic doctrine reflected basic Christian principles incorporated in early Jewish belief. The idea of the Zohar as a Jewish-Christian book received its extreme expression in the view that its author, Rabbi Simeon ben Yohai, was actually an adherent of the Christian faith.[162] Missionary pressures, particularly among the apostates, also had a bearing on the way in which the Zohar was regarded as an early work. The missionaries tried to demonstrate to the Jews the truth of Christianity on the basis of a sacred book written by the rabbis of the Talmud, and so persuade them to change their religion.[163]

The tendency of the kabbalah toward heresy and the way in which the Zohar was used to strengthen Christian belief made Jewish scholars very wary and suspicious of publishing the Zohar. We learn from what the editor says in the preface to the Mantua edition of the Zohar that those who were opposed to printing it drew attention to the risk of heresy involved in the general dissemination of the Zohar. He writes apologetically: "We have regarded it as almost a reward, and the streams of loss are running dry,[164] for there is no basis for this falsehood. But there is a spirit in man, and if he belongs to the unclean side, he will in any case tend towards evil conduct, while the pure of hand will increase the strength of his faith, fear, and wisdom; and sorrow and sighing shall flee away. . . . Desist now, we beg of you, for it is not good to spread slander concerning the perfect Torah of the Lord, by saying that destruction can come of it. . . . And even if we admit that some individuals might be misled by it, and their hearts be affected by impurity, this has no bearing on the matter, for we are not concerned with fools or the wicked, nor with their corruption or their amendment. Let the wicked eat his fill and die.[165] The Lord will deal well with the good and with the upright in heart. . . . And the fools will transgress and be punished, and their loins will always totter in the snare of the husks' habitations, and of an unclean spirit, and they will be caught in an evil trap, and thorns will vanish from the vineyard." Here we have a kind of acknowledgment that there are grounds for suspecting that a study of the Zohar might give an additional impetus to depravity, but the author of the preface maintains that this harmful influence will affect only those who are already wicked and corrupt, and therefore one should not worry about them "and thorns will vanish from the vineyard."

The danger of Christian heresy was one of the most important factors that led to the writing of the first book wholly dedicated to criticism of the kabbalah and the Zohar, the *Sefer Ari Nohem* (the Roaring Lion) by Rabbi Judah Aryeh (Leon) Modena, written in 1639. Modena, who served in the rabbinate as a member of the *bet din* in Venice, came into close contact with Christian circles, and one of the most prominent figures among the Christian kabbalists, Gaffarelli, was one of his pupils. Through his contact with Christian scholars he had occasion to dispute with them, and also with apostates among them, about questions of religious faith, and he saw the great harm that had befallen Judaism because of their reliance on the kabbalah as a true doctrine, and on the Zohar as an authentic early Jewish work. At the end of the *Sefer Ari Nohem* he stresses this point as being an important reason for his defection from the kabbalah. He writes:[166] "One of the reasons why I have refrained from the study of this is my experience, from my youth onward, of the arguments of apostates, and of how the principles and tendencies [of the Zohar] match theirs. . . . I know that you have among your Christian books a certain work written by Pico della Mirandola, who was the first Christian to study the kabbalah, which they started to read in his days. I have seen among his writings certain principles that he upheld and published in Rome, of which 47 were begotten by Hebrew kabbalists, and 72 derived from the kabbalah although produced from his own thoughts. And when several of their eminent scholars opposed him, saying that this was a new theology and belief in it heretical, he took pains to demonstrate to them that all its methods and principles constituted the basic truths of their own faith: the trinity, the incarnation, the virgin birth, the name *Jesus*, original sin that caused the death of the soul and the death of the messiah, and so on. . . . And I have already told you what was said before in Israel by the apostate Michael of Foligno (may his bones be ground to dust), the father of the *zodiato* [suddetto?—Trans.], the great preacher to the lords of Bologna, concerning the Zohar that was printed in that year, and this is sufficient for him who understands. And, after that, Giovanni of Quilini and others wrote about the kabbalah and it spread among them, as the sloping beam that supports the roof of their religion." It is clear that it was Christian kabbalah and its effects that impelled Modena to turn his attention to a critical study of the Zohar.

The *Sefer Ari Nohem* was written for his pupil Rabbi Joseph Hamitz, who was a fanatical kabbalist and tried to change his teacher's mind. The book also contains his arguments with his son-in-law, Rabbi Jacob Halevi, who wrote a book on the kabbalah, and criticized his father-in-law with the utmost severity, both orally and in writing.[167] Modena made stringent criticisms of the whole kabbalah, and condemned it as a reservoir of false beliefs and heretical opinions, but his most powerful ammunition was reserved for his criticism of the Zohar. However, his critique is somewhat superficial, because his investigation lacks the finer points of detail. Nevertheless, he notes and draws attention to several new matters, in addition to Rabbi Elijah Delmedigo's specific criticisms,

which were later to serve as important principles of Zohar scholarship. Most of
Rabbi Isaac of Acre's testimony is quoted verbatim in his book, and the
confession of Rabbi Moses de Leon, as transmitted by his wife, is accepted by
him as completely true.[168] He therefore proclaims quite decisively that the
Zohar "is a new and not a traditional work, not written by Rabbi Simeon ben
Yohai, or by any of his disciples, but a product of one of the later rabbis, written
not more than 350 years ago."[169] In addition to external proof from the *Sefer
Yuḥasin*, Modena also adduces evidence of a late date from the Zohar itself, such
as the confusion in chronology, the inclusion of prayers from a later period, the
Aramaic, the way in which the homilies are constructed in the Castilian
rabbinic style,[170] and so on. Modena convicts the whole Zohar of being a late
forgery without any valid content, apart from the literary-homiletical aspect, in
which he sees some value. He writes:[171] "However, the book itself (as you have
often heard me say) is lovable, precious, praiseworthy, and glorious, nobler in
its scholarly methods, covering the literal, homiletical, and allegorical
meanings, than any other work of commentary on the Torah. It is all
constructed in a fine, beautiful, and orderly way, and its sweet style and the way
in which the stories are interwoven into the fabric of the book cannot be
paralleled. It arouses the sleeping, awakes the slumbering, and inspires the
reader to serve the Lord."

Modena was a powerful combatant both in spirit and in his writings, but he
did not wish to engage in actual conflict, or to publicize his daring ideas. And so
his *Sefer Ari Nohem*, together with other of his polemical writings, remained
hidden in his archives and did not see the light of day during his lifetime. But
from the letters that deal with the controversy surrounding Rabbi Moses
Hayyim Luzzatto, it is clear that the book was circulated in manuscript, and
Luzzatto's dialogue, known as *Ḥoker u-Mekubbal*, was written as an answer to its
charges.[172] However, there is no mention of this in Luzzatto's work; the
problem of the Zohar is not discussed at all and the details of Modena's
criticisms are not touched upon. The book is a general defense of kabbalistic
doctrine. But his teacher, Rabbi Isaiah Bassan, says quite explicitly[173] that the
dialogue was written against Modena, and from what he says we gather that the
Sefer Ari Nohem, which he calls *Sha'agat Aryeh*, made some impression, "and all
the insolent and evil-doers gain support from it." He also quotes the letter of the
kabbalist Rabbi Aviad Sar-shalom Basilea from Mantua, in which he writes, "I
have read [Luzzatto's] answers to the *Ari Nohem*, and we find his answers really
valuable. . . . I cannot understand the motive of those who persecute this sinless
man. And I did not expect so much passion to be shown for this evil and bitter
work of the aforesaid 'roaring lion' (*ari nohem*) who said that the Zohar was a
book of lies and that the true wisdom [of kabbalah] was completely worthless
and deceitful."

Rabbi Aviad Sar-shalom endeavored himself to counter the criticisms of the
opponents of the kabbalah in the *Sefer Emunat Ḥakhamim*[174] (Mantua, 1730).
His defense is aimed mainly at criticisms that he had heard in conversations and
arguments, and the *Sefer Ari Nohem* is not mentioned at all. But from the subject
matter of the criticisms we can see that at least some of them were taken from
Modena's book, which the author's opponents had certainly read. He devotes
only two chapters (25 and 26) to the problem of the Zohar, but they contain

several important matters. The author gives a summary of Rabbi Isaac of Acre's testimony,[175] which he did not see in the *Sefer Yuḥasin* but had only heard about, and he throws some doubt on its reliability: "Behold, all the sages of Israel follow the Zohar . . . and on the other side we have some philosopher who has no faith in the secrets of the Torah, and who does not understand its words, and whose opinion has no weight either way . . . and he follows what was written, by we know not who, about a man, whose name is unknown to us, who said that a certain woman told him such-and-such, and that Rabbi Moses swore that it was not true. And, on his own evidence, he ignored Rabbi Moses' oath, and followed this woman. And by the God of heaven and earth, who will judge in flaming fire whoever slanders the oral law, even if Rabbi Moses had sworn that he had written the book, everyone who reads it and understands its words will know his statement to be utterly false." Evidently the author did not know that this testimony emanated from the famous kabbalist Rabbi Isaac of Acre. Several criticisms of the Zohar impelled him to admit that the book was edited after the death of Rabbi Simeon ben Yohai and his pupils, and that it also contained some later additional material.

The *Sefer Ari Nohem* was not printed until the *Haskalah* period.[176] Soon after it appeared it was attacked by the kabbalist Rabbi Isaac Itzik Ḥaver, of the school of the Gaon of Vilna, in his *Sefer Magen ve-Ẓinah*.[177] The author deals mainly with the question of the Zohar and replies in detail to the criticisms of Leon Aryeh Modena as well as to those of others. Several of his answers are interesting and valuable even from the scientific point of view, but the great majority are but the apologetical statements of a fanatical believer and have no basis in either logic or fact. For example, he cites as a proof for the antiquity of the Zohar the fact that certain parts of it remained a mystery until their true explanation was revealed to Rabbi Isaac Luria by the prophet Elijah, and therefore it could not possibly have been written by a later kabbalist in the thirteenth century.[178] He also quotes as authoritative the story of Rabbi Hayyim of Volozhin, which he heard from his teacher, the Gaon of Vilna, that when he used to lecture on the secrets of the Torah, Rabbi Simeon ben Yohai would sit on his right and Rabbi Isaac Luria would sit on his left, "and since he revealed awesome matters and the secrets of the Chariot in the presence of Rabbi Simeon ben Yohai and Rabbi Isaac Luria, and not before any of the other early sages of Israel, it is clear that they are the true masters, and we must acknowledge that the author of the holy Zohar, and the first to reveal the secrets of the Master of creation in writing, was in truth Rabbi Simeon ben Yohai."[179]

The author was grief-stricken when he saw the growing power of the *Haskalah* movement, and the destructive influence of the *Sefer Ari Nohem*, which not only led to the denial of the Zohar's antiquity, but was also used by the *maskilim* to refute the validity of the whole tradition. He exclaims with great bitterness:[180] "Which man, whose heart has been touched by the fear of the Lord, by love of the Torah, and of the saintly and pious ones of the Lord, the pure in heart, can restrain himself from shaking the earth and all that it contains, when he sees that (Modena's) vanities, mockeries, and blasphemies have been brought to the printing press by the accursed, wicked men of our generation. . . . They have publicized his words throughout the world, sharing them with Jacob, and scattering them in Israel. We have seen with our eyes and heard with our ears

gross blasphemies emanating from empty ignoramuses, youths who are devoid
of Torah, wisdom, and faith. They roll this corrupt book off their tongues, and
speak with enmity of the Lord and His anointed. Even with regard to the
existence and providence of God they have fallen into the net of doubt, and
some of them deny it completely. Alas for the generation in whose days such
things could arise! Therefore, I promised to demonstrate that this mocking
wrecker of a rabbi has perpetrated falsehood in his soul, and done evil to his
people, and has made great breaches in the holy Torah by means of this book,
may its name be extinguished and blotted out from the world, so that it ceases to
be a stumbling block to the House of Israel! For our eyes can see now how
widespread this defilement has become in Israel, that through this miserable
little book several poor innocent souls have been trapped in the snare of heresy,
as they clasp this book to their breasts, as if it were handed down at Sinai, and
Torah and truth had been confided to him alone, and as if (God forbid!) our
ancestors' heritage were false. And they go from one evil to the next, saying that
even the Talmud and the midrashim were made up by worthless prattlers, and
then they say the words of the prophets are nonsense, until they come to the
Torah saying that this also is made up, comparing one thing to another with
their own kind of logical deduction: just as it has been shown that 'the science of
truth,' which was hitherto thought to be valid until it was torn to pieces by 'the
lion' (Leon Modena), is false, so all, in the same way, consists of fabricated lies
and falsehoods, and there is no truth in it." It is clear from this protest that the
Sefer Ari Nohem had found its real home in the period of the Enlightenment, and
the Italian rabbi's criticism of the Zohar in the seventeenth century had become
in the nineteenth a weapon used by the *maskilim* of Germany and Eastern
Europe against tradition and religion.

c. The Sabbatean Movement and Rabbi Jacob Emden

The influence of the Zohar, as already noted,[181] reached its peak in the
Sabbatean movement with all its ramifications. This holy book, the teaching
and knowledge of which had been transmitted only to the privileged few, was
now common property, and even women and children talked of it. Rabbi
Moses Hagiz, one of the most fanatical opponents and denouncers of
Sabbateanism, complained bitterly of the way in which the Zohar was taught to
large audiences, even in a vernacular translation, in some of the great
communities of Europe at the beginning of the eighteenth century.[182] He
writes:[183] "Whereas in times past one would not find, even among the elders
and men of renown, one from a city and two from a family who would carry the
Zohar in their hand, now we have every reckless, empty-headed boy carrying
the Zohar out among the people and boasting in the town that he knows how to
interpret, and translate it from one language to another, and he will sit and read
it to women and children in the vernacular. And I never cease to be astonished
that the great men of our generation do not stop them, particularly in a certain
large city, full of scholars and scribes, whose name, out of respect, I shall not
mention, for it is great in the sight of both God and man. From it the Torah goes
forth to Israel continually, and all the great teachers have come from there, and
yet [I am amazed] that they allow people to study this holy book of the Zohar

openly in the schools among all kinds of men, and, to top it all, in the vernacular." From this it is clear that even after the decline of Sabbateanism, when the "believers" were compelled to go into hiding and act secretly, it nevertheless left its mark on the people in terms of the unrestricted dissemination of the Zohar. Rabbi Ezekiel Landau, the famous rabbi of Prague, also complained about the increased preoccupation with the Zohar and other works of kabbalah, which relegated the study of Talmud and the *poskim* to a backwater: "How incensed I am against those who busy themselves with the Zohar and kabbalistic books in public! They remove the yoke of the revealed Torah from their necks, and talk and mutter about the Zohar, and are able to master neither, so that the Torah becomes neglected in Israel. And this is not all, for in our time the followers of the sect of Shabbetai Zvi, may his bones be ground to dust, have increased in number, and we ought therefore to limit the study of the Zohar and books of kabbalah."[184]

Prague was the center of Frankist Jewry until the beginning of the nineteenth century, and members of the sect continued to study the Zohar there quite openly even at this late date, after the shameful collapse of Frankism through conversion and after the death of Jacob Frank himself, and despite the influence that Western Enlightenment began to have on the Jewish community. Rabbi Eleazar Fleckeles, the *dayan* in Prague, writes in 1790:[185] "I shall give you definite signs. . . . those who are not skilled in the *Shas* and the *poskim*, and study *aggadot* and the Zohar . . . this shall be unclean to you, the lizard according to its kind[186]—and those too with whom women sit and study." According to Fleckeles, the root of the evil was that they studied esoteric subjects instead of the halakhah: "The root of all this corruption is that they do not study the *gemara* and the *Shulkhan Arukh*, but the aggadic midrashim and passages from the Zohar instead, in order to shore up their vain and worthless building."[187] A similar picture is presented by the anonymous *maskil* who, in the same year, described the situation of the sect in Prague. He speaks in particular of the members of one of the leading families: "And if they are men of wisdom and understanding they study Zohar and lay their hands upon the writings of Isaac Luria. Their whole preoccupation, both men and women, is with kabbalistic books, and every day they set aside regularly one or two hours for the study of secret matters. And the mundane discourse of these women is not like the mundane discourse of other women, for the spirit of the Zohar and kabbalah rests upon them, and words of kabbalah are common in their mouths."[188]

Study of the Zohar in Sabbatean circles was no mere intellectual exercise intended to provide knowledge of the mysteries. A practical messianic purpose was also involved in it. According to a belief common in kabbalistic literature, the public revelation of the secrets of kabbalah was a sign of the messianic age, and it was indeed possible to bring the end nearer through such a revelation. This belief is quite explicit in the Zohar, and it is related there specifically to the secrets contained within the book itself. But the Sabbateans and the Frankists were not content, even in their study of the Zohar, to hasten redemption. They turned it inside out in their attempt to find support for all kinds of heretical opinions that arose and flourished in the life of the sect. The necessity for, and the religious role of, apostasy on the part of the messiah, and indeed of the Jewish masses, the denial of the authority of the practical *mizvot*, the condoning of licentious practices, and their transformation into religious duties, the deification of the messiah, and the belief in the incarnation of God in the body of the messiah, the trinitarian doctrine of the Frankists, and the other Sabbatean and Christianlike beliefs—authority for all these was discovered in passages from the Zohar.[189] One of the consequences of this use of the Zohar as a source for misguided exposition was that the Zohar itself became tainted in the eyes of the opponents of the Sabbatean movement, and this was the main reason why Rabbi Jacob Emden wrote his book *Mitpaḥat Sefarim* (Altona, 1768),[190] the foundation of Zohar criticism.

Emden's life was dedicated to the fight against Sabbateanism, which he regarded as an obnoxious plague that would destroy Judaism utterly. There were social and personal reasons too behind his attack, but the chief and central factor, which directed his energies so continuously and so obstinately, without pause or digression, was his perception of the evil hidden in every ramification of this great messianic movement, and his unyielding determination to do all in his power to root it out. Emden's fanatical determination to battle against Sabbateanism knew no bounds. He uncovered the secrets of the sect with great diligence, examined and reexamined every suspicious phenomenon, and exhorted his fellow rabbis to issue bans and excommunications. His bitter attacks were aimed unmercifully at every individual who was suspected of being in league, or merely in sympathy, with the sectarians. The Sabbateans had adopted the practice of inserting allusions to their secret thoughts and feelings in their literary works, particularly in the field of kabbalah. So Emden made a speciality of analyzing these secret allusions, and developed in consequence an extremely sharp critical faculty that could detect the merest whiff of Sabbatean heresy. Many books that were to all appearances quite normal were condemned as heretical by Emden, and although he suspected perfectly acceptable books by mistake, his judgment was usually accurate.

However, Emden encountered in this campaign a powerful ally of Sabbateanism that he found extremely difficult to combat. This ally was the holy Zohar, attributed to Rabbi Simeon ben Yohai and his disciples. The Sabbateans prided themselves on the words of the Zohar, and taunted their enemies with the authority of such a trustworthy and sacred source. The Sabbateans' attitude to the Zohar compelled Emden to turn his attention to an investigation of the book's sanctity and antiquity, and with his sharp eye he immediately saw many points, in addition to those known already, that aroused a suspicion of forgery. If Emden had been a man like Modena, a not-too-serious free-thinker who was not wholeheartedly committed to Judaism anyway and was positively antagonistic to kabbalah his task would have been simple and straightforward. He would merely have had to issue a denunciation, as was his wont with suspect books, and so disqualify the Zohar. But Emden's position here was complex and difficult, because he firmly believed in the truth of kabbalah as an ancient tradition that contained divine revelations about the mysteries of the true Jewish faith, and affirmation of the Zohar's sanctity was deeply imbedded in his soul. Emden was a true kabbalist, and he underwent a severe internal struggle when faced with the task of undermining the authority of this the holiest of kabbalistic books. He says himself that, forty years before writing the *Mitpaḥat Sefarim*, doubts had arisen in his mind concerning the antiquity of the Zohar, and he had kept them to himself, but the necessity of combating Sabbateanism had turned the scales, and he was now compelled to formulate and publish his views. He writes:[191] "I am truly grieved that no man perceived this and similar matters before I arose, unworthy as I am to speak. God forbid that I should rejoice that others have left me an opportunity to excel, for, in truth, I do all this against my will, as I have said. (For this reason I have never questioned the matter openly, but it remained enclosed within the chambers of my heart for forty years. I restrained my spirit , and did not wish to reveal it, until now when the Preserver of truth has constrained me. I am afraid that a later generation will prove the cleanness of a reptile[192] from the teachings of the Zohar, as they have already begun to do. . . .) I would much rather that this matter was revealed by the hand of someone other than myself, so that I should not have to reap the consequences, for I have decided to do this only as a result of great compulsion, extreme necessity, and the circumstances of the time, for I see that the hand of those who clasp the Torah is weakening . . . and our faith is in great danger—not one of all the children she has reared goes to help her—and so truth will vanish, and heresy grow stronger." At the beginning of the book he heaps praise on the kabbalah, and apologizes profusely for being compelled to raise his hand against the holy Zohar: "Why should I start a controversy and be, God forbid, an opponent of the holy Zohar? What profit would I gain from such a sin? Is not this the work of a great man? It has not oppressed me, or consumed me, or confounded me. On the contrary, it enlightens my eyes in the fear of the Lord, and it is my source for the secrets of Torah. The reproaches of those who reproach Thee have fallen upon me, as with a crushing in my bones, and my adversaries taunt me, saying to me all day 'Where is your God?' 'Zeal for the Lord has done this,' and so on; so much so that I cannot survive while the profanation of the great Name remains shut up within my bones."[193] He shows that he considered the matter very carefully, and tried as hard as possible to protect the sanctity of the Zohar: "Now, I said to myself, the Zohar is not better than the brass serpent that Moses, peace be upon him, made, so that by its means one might look towards God; and when King Hezekiah saw that it would prove to be a stumbling block to future generations, who would look merely upon the physical shape of the serpent, he decided to crush it in pieces, in order to gain favor from the Lord, and his action was approved. Far be it from me to do away unmercifully with even a small section of it, or even a word or a letter that one can possibly retain, for the book is holy, and so is its author, whoever he was, since there can be no doubt that he has strengthened our knowledge of the principles of our sacred Torah."[194]

However, once he had taken on the task of making a critical evaluation of the Zohar, he pursued it with great fidelity. He did not stop at citing the evidence of Rabbi Isaac of Acre, but examined the work from every angle, and by using his historical acumen tested its accuracy by relating it to the circumstances of its age. But even this was not sufficient. He did not simply rely on the views of his predecessors, but subjected all the books of the Zohar, page by page, to the most detailed critique, and drew up a list of some three hundred separate arguments against the antiquity of the Zohar. His reasons, which mostly follow in order the pages of the Zohar, touch upon practically every aspect of internal criticism: the personalities in the Zohar, its language, its sources, the historical allusions, and so on. From this point of view, all that modern scholars had to do was to classify the arguments, establish them on a more solid scientific foundation, and widen their scope with additional material. Emden also distinguished the various sections, noted the individual characteristics of each one, and tried to determine the date of their composition. And although on this particular subject his views, like those of most scholars, are a little vague, nevertheless a number of his theories and insights are still valid today. The conclusions he came to divested Rabbi Simeon ben Yohai and his disciples completely of the authorship of the Zohar, down to the smallest part. However, this categorical opinion of his was rarely expressed openly. For example, we find: "Indeed, my heart is divided over this, and I cannot really believe that even part [of the Zohar itself] consists of the words of the *tanna* known in the whole Talmud as Rabbi Simeon ben Yohai, as we have already said, for, whichever way we look at it, the basic passages in it concerning the secrets of the Torah, and those that seem to be the most reliable, and the most likely to have been attributed to him, are in fact set down in the names of Rav Hamnuna, and Rav Yeva Sava. . . . And there can be no doubt that Rav Hamnuna and Rav Yeva were both *amoraim*."[195] With regard to particular sections, the *Raya Mehemna, Tikkunei ha-Zohar*, and the *Midrash ha-Ne'elam*, he states quite openly that they are the work of later kabbalists, Rabbi Moses de Leon, or contemporaries of his.[196]

On only one point, on the problem of pseudepigraphy, does he take care not to draw the logical conclusions; and he tries to find a way of disposing of the charge of forgery, since this would cast an aspersion on the sacred character of the whole book. With regard to these sections, which he realized dated from the thirteenth century, he was forced to admit that their author put his words in the mouths of earlier rabbis, but he removed the sting from his criticism by saying that the author "thought that it was more praiseworthy to attribute [his words] to a great tree."[197] As far as the major part of the Zohar was concerned, which he believed was written at the end of the amoraic or in the gaonic period, he arrived at a more complicated solution. He tried here to avoid the conclusion that the transmission of the material through Rabbi Simeon ben Yohai and other rabbis was all made up, and so he says: "Out of necessity, and purely by guesswork, I would say that the Rabbi Simeon ben Yohai of the Zohar was someone else from a later age, and that he also had a son called Rabbi Eleazar, and that we are dealing here with a similar case to that of the two Joseph ben Simeons. . . .[198] It is better to believe this than to suppose that there were two Rav Hamnunas, and also two Rav Yevas, and that they were Babylonians of a different generation living before Rabbi Simeon ben Yohai in a much earlier tannaitic period, for this would involve a great many difficulties, and it is better to choose the way that involves less trouble."[199] After this we have another view: "Perhaps the Rabbi Simeon ben Yohai of the Zohar and his son, Rabbi Eleazar, were transmigrations or sparks of the souls of the *tannaim* who had these names." These amazing suggestions, which do not give any impression at all of real conviction, demonstrate the tremendous confusion and also the inner conflicts that Emden experienced when faced with the contradiction between the truth of his own critical analysis and the stature of the Zohar as a sacred book.

About fifty years after its publication Emden's book provoked a literary reaction. Rabbi Moses Kunitz, rabbi of Ofen in Hungary, came out with his *Sefer Ben Yohai* (Vienna, 1815) in order to disprove Emden's charges.[200] The first six chapters of the *Sefer Ben Yohai* are devoted to establishing the author's original method of presenting the character of Rabbi Simeon ben Yohai as it appears in talmudic literature. Kunitz tries to differentiate between two periods in the life of Rabbi Simeon ben Yohai: the period before he hid himself in the cave, when he had not reached a position of very great eminence and his opinion was not decisive in matters of law, and the period after his sojourn in the cave, when he was at the height of his powers and the law always followed his opinion. In the first period he is simply called in the Talmud Rabbi Simeon, whereas in the second period his father's name was also added. These distinctions, which were very shakily based on forced dialectical arguments, were meant to show that the Rabbi Simeon ben Yohai of the Zohar, the father of kabbalah, was identical with the talmudic rabbi during the second period of his life, and so Kunitz attempted to dispel the doubts that arose from a comparison of the portrayal of Rabbi Simeon in the Zohar with that in the Talmud. These six chapters are a kind of introduction to the seventh, called *Ma'anot u-Mitpahot*. This chapter contains long and detailed rebuttals to practically every charge that Emden made. The answers are couched in very strong language and based on a large amount of important source material, and it would seem at first sight that Kunitz succeeds in weakening and even destroying the critical arguments, and in restoring confidence in the antiquity of the Zohar. But in actual fact most of the answers are nothing more than brilliant examples of pilpulistic skill, held together by a slender web of intentional distortions.

Solomon Judah Rappaport demonstrated the real character of *Sefer Ben Yohai* in a small tract called *Nahalat Yehudah* (Lemberg, 1873), which was printed after his death. The tract consists of his marginal notes, which end at answer no. 123. Rappaport demolishes the criticisms of the *Sefer Ben Yohai* one by one, shows how completely worthless they are in content, and proves conclusively how Kunitz misused his sources. Many of Emden's crucial arguments had been completely ignored, and most of his statements had been quoted in a mutilated and distorted way that destroyed their cogency. He had adopted the same approach to earlier sources and to the writings of the medieval rabbis, which he had used to strengthen his arguments. With a few decisive words Rappaport shows that Kunitz's nonsense has no effect whatsoever on Emden's basic criticisms.

d. Zohar Scholarship in the Enlightenment Period

Scholars of the Enlightenment (*Haskalah*) period, apart from one or two whom I shall treat separately, regarded the kabbalah as a black stain on the fabric of pure Judaism, which in their view was a belief in the unity of God, seen in the light of rational thought and intellectual inquiry. Their fierce opposition to kabbalah, full of contempt and disdain, led them to belittle its importance in the history of the religious and spiritual experience of the Jewish people, and they either passed over it in complete silence, or touched upon it in only a tangential way. They were attracted, for this very reason, by the critical scholarly approach to the Zohar that had already been initiated by Modena and Emden. Several scholars were concerned with preparing the *Sefer Ari Nohem* for the press, embellishing it with their own notes and heaping florid praise upon it as a superb document that had come to the defense of the honor of Judaism.[201] One of these scholars, Isaac Samuel Reggio (known as *Yashar*) of Gorizia, went so far as to say in his preface that it was because of the guilt incurred by the idolatry of kabbalah that the burden of exile was so prolonged. He exclaims with some emotion:[202] "Son of man, take this book as a lion that will roar out their abominations before them, and will acquaint your people with their sin, and the children of Israel with their iniquities. You shall set it before them so that they will be humiliated and ashamed of what they have done, and perhaps they will return from their evil ways, and it will be well with them. And I arose, as I had been commanded, and printed this valuable book, which has hitherto remained in manuscript, for I fight the author's battle. And I join my hand with his in the pursuit and apprehension of all the vain, seducing oracles that destroy the vineyard of the Lord of Hosts. I shall smite them and they shall rise no more. I shall scatter them like chaff before the wind. I shall not rest, for our pure faith's sake, until its righteousness goes forth as a shining light, and I make it a thing of praise in the earth." Even Rabbi Jacob Emden, who was personally opposed, both by nature and by inclination, to *haskalah*, was honored and praised by the *maskilim*. His greatest sins, like his attack on the *Guide for the Perplexed*—he could not bring himself to believe that such a "heretical" book could have been written by Maimonides[203]—were forgiven him in appreciation of his critique of the Zohar.

Most of the scholars who manifested undisputed "enlightened" tendencies did not examine the Zohar very deeply. They relied mainly on their predecessors, adding remarks and notes here and there that demonstrated the late date of the book, and expressing their negative attitude in only a general way. However, one of the most powerful men in the group, the renowned historian Heinrich Graetz, entered into the very thick of things. In a special section of his work[204] he explained and clarified the various arguments, added arguments and views of his own, and summarized the whole problem by formulating his critical conclusions with the utmost clarity and precision. Graetz's attitude to the Zohar represents the spirit of Enlightenment in its fullest and most extreme form. In his strong antipathy to kabbalah he portrays the Zohar as a compendium of falsehoods, perverse imaginings, and puerile beliefs, and its author, Rabbi Moses de Leon, as a wretched prattler, a forger, and a conscienceless deceiver. Graetz held the Zohar responsible for the spiritual decline and the blight of ignorance that characterized Judaism, in his view, from the end of the Middle Ages to the Enlightenment period. The Zohar had poisoned the mind and immersed it in a drunken stupor; it had stultified the intellect and blunted the edge of the healthy and wholesome senses. In short, the Zohar was a monstrous example of degeneration in the spirit of Judaism. Graetz sometimes used their relationship to the Zohar as a standard by which to evaluate people in Jewish history. Any show of enthusiasm or sympathy for the Zohar was regarded by Graetz as a personal failing, and the individual was valued accordingly. It is no use, of course, looking for balanced objectivity in this kind of approach. Nevertheless, we should bear in mind that Graetz's hostility to the Zohar was not entirely unproductive. It led Zohar research into several important new areas.

Samuel David Luzzatto (known as *Shadal*) also wrote against the Zohar with considerable disdain and hostility, particularly in his book entitled *An Argument concerning the Wisdom of the Kabbalah, the Antiquity of the Zohar, and the Antiquity of the Vowel-points and Accents* (Gorizia, 1852).[205] But the reasons behind his opposition to the Zohar were different from those which activated the mainstream *maskilim* and which reached their full and final expression in the writings of Heinrich Graetz. Luzzatto's position in the *Haskalah* movement was unique, and this uniqueness can be seen in his attitude toward the kabbalah and the Zohar. He adopted a conservative-rabbinic standpoint in his conception of Judaism, and opposed rationalistic tendencies. For him the outstanding figures in Jewish tradition were the literalists, men of simple religious sensibility and perfect faith. He was so convinced that the theological speculations of the philosophers could be harmful to Judaism that he even dared to launch a critical attack on Maimonides himself, who was the person most honored by the *Haskalah* period. The sin of the kabbalists in his view was that "they did more evil than the philosophers" in dispensing with the plain meaning of the Torah and perverting true faith. He writes:[206] "What I really meant to say was this, that the Zohar has tended to wean the sages of Israel away from the study of the actual Torah, that is, the literal meaning, which would show them by process of deep linguistic study how many heaps of laws depend on every word, and every letter; and it has led them to waste their time and their minds on dreams and nonsense, and matters that are without substance, like *gematriot*[207] and *rashei tevot*[208] and other things. . . . And the second thing that the Zohar has done is to remove the yoke of the fear of Heaven from the necks of the sages of Israel, so that they no longer care for their Maker's honor, but ask and answer questions, and write and print books about what is above and what is below, what was before, and what will be afterward. They speak haughtily, with pride and arrogance, against almighty God—how He created His world, how He conducts it, how He contracted Himself in order to create it, and how He caused worlds to emanate from His own essence . . . and similar matters. Anyone who believes in God feels the hair on his skin bristle when he reads of such things."

The *Vikuah* was written in 1827, twenty-five years before it was published. It is arranged as a dialogue between the author and a Polish scholar who has come to stay with him. The traveler attacks the kabbalah, and denies the antiquity of the Zohar, which the author tries to defend but fails in his attempt. Luzzatto, in an "addendum" at the end of the book,[209] notes that the conversations with the Polish scholar are fictional, but the decision to publish the *Vikuah* was in fact prompted by a conversation he had with "a certain student of Polish origin" who had seen one of his students with a copy of the book and urged him to publish it "because he was sure that it would be of great benefit to our people, and particularly to those in his country, where there were tens of thousands of pseudo-pietists who were profaning the honor of the people and the honor of the Torah with their nonsense and their evil deeds." This means that it was the growth of hasidic influence, which had made the Zohar so popular in Eastern Europe, that moved the author to publish the book that he had written in his youth. The central pivot of the *Vikuaḥ* is Luzzatto's proof that the vowel-points and accents are of late origin. The denial of their antiquity affected the antiquity of the Zohar as well, because it interprets many times the mysteries associated with them. In other matters too—particularly in establishing the linguistic character of the Zohar and detecting late elements in its eschatological calculations—Luzzatto advanced scientific research.

A number of books and pamphlets were written[210] to counter Luzzatto's arguments, but only one of them, the *Sefer Ta'am Leshad* (Livorno, 1863) by Elijah Benamozegh is of any value from the point of view of Zohar scholarship. This book is also written in dialogue form. The author weighs his words well in scholarly fashion, bases his arguments on an examination of the sources, and so seeks to prove that the Zohar was edited on the basis of trustworthy traditions, both written and oral, that had been handed down from one generation to another, traces of which can also be seen in the literature that preceded the publication of the Zohar. He treats at some length the reasons for the late appearance of the Zohar and for its restricted circulation in the early period. An original and interesting idea, particularly for his time, is to be found in one of his replies to the criticism that the Zohar was never generally accepted by the Jews, as the Talmud was: "From the very beginning of our existence on earth we have been a unique nation in the world, for we are not simply a religious sect or a group of believers like the Muslims or the Christians, for God who created us did not make us a religious sect or a company of believers, but a nation and a unique people in the world, adorned with specific national laws and practices, and particular and separate from the rest of mankind through our genealogy, our customs, our birthplace, and our language, in the past, in the present, and in the future. From this it follows that, since our permanent and accepted character was political and we had grown accustomed to it because we had for so many generations constituted ourselves as a nation in our own land, our ancestral inheritance, anything that was not obviously or remotely relevant to this political character seemed foreign to us, and this was so both when we were a united people and even after the Lord had tossed us from nation to nation and from kingdom to kingdom."[211] His attempt to prove the antiquity of the Zohar failed like all other similar attempts, as we shall discover in the chapters dealing with the critical arguments and their conclusions. But nevertheless, Benamozegh raises many interesting points in the course of his discussion.

A whole array of scholars embarked upon fundamental research into the problem we are dealing with. Most of them accepted the premises of the *Haskalah* movement, but they did not hold with the extreme rationalistic viewpoint, and revealed a more or less objective scholarly attitude in their discussions of kabbalah and the Zohar. These scholars examined and elucidated the arguments of their predecessors, but they also paved new ways in Zohar research.

The first of this group was Rabbi Eliakim Hamilzahagi from Brod, the author of *Sefer Raviah* (Ofen, 1837), which contains critical notes on Zunz and Rappaport. This particular scholar, who claims to have written some seventy books[212] in addition to his published volume, concentrated his whole attention on kabbalah and the Zohar. There were among his writings a number of ambitious undertakings, such as a Hebrew translation with explanatory notes of the Zohar. Of his many books only two have so far been discovered: the *Sefer Zohorei Raviah*,[213] which is an introduction to the Zohar, and a fragment from the *Sefer Ozar Raviah*. In the printed *Sefer Raviah*[214] the author touches indirectly on the problems of kabbalistic literature and the Zohar, and his comments there, which are confined to one or two points only and are often expressed in a very laconic and allusive way, are clarified and developed considerably in the *Sefer Zohorei Raviah*, which was written after the publication of the first book. Milzahagi himself points out that he approaches research into kabbalah and the Zohar and into the relationship between philosophy and kabbalah, in an impartial objective way, without championing one side or the other. He writes:[215] "And since I have to write down the different opinions of every side, the discerning man will easily understand this, and not accuse me of supporting or sympathizing with one side or the other. Not at all. I am merely like a painter who sees both pretty, pleasant shapes, and fearful, terrifying shapes, and depicts them together on the same piece of paper . . . and all to realize the painter's desired goal, not that they affect him either for good or ill."

Milzahagi pursued his researches with great skill, and with a deep understanding of the Zohar and of kabbalistic literature in general. In the *Sefer Zohorei Raviah* he summarized Emden's arguments and subjected them to a critical examination, and he also wrote a specific book entitled *Hassagot al Sefer Ben Yohai*. But his main originality lies in his own basic research, which is presented in a systematic and comprehensive way.[216] He analyzed and classified the various sections of the Zohar and fixed their literary structure. He closely examined the language of the Zohar and wrote a book explaining its strange and foreign words. He compared and elucidated the textual variants in the Mantua and Cremona editions, as well as the repetitions in the Zohar. He drew up a detailed list of the rabbis mentioned in the Zohar, with an index and a note of their various roles. On the basis of these critical criteria, and others besides, such as an examination of the use of mystical symbols and ideas with a view to determining the date of composition, Milzahagi came to the conclusion that the Zohar was made up of various layers, some early and some late, that were written and joined together over a long period of time. This conclusion is presented as an original hypothesis concerning the way in which the Zohar developed and finally reached the form that has come down to us. His writings also deal with the way the Zohar spread, exercising an influence on different areas of Jewish religious history and experience.

Adolphe Franck's book[217] on the kabbalah closely approximates the general conclusions of Milzahagi but is very different in scholarly method. Since Milzahagi's introduction to the Zohar, like his other works, was not printed, Franck's book must be regarded as the first nineteenth-century work of Jewish scholarship specifically devoted to the doctrines and literature of the kabbalah, and of the Zohar in particular. The author, who was a French Jewish scholar, remained outside the circle of the Jewish *Haskalah* movement and the scientific study of Judaism in Germany, but Jellinek's translation of his book,[218] which appeared a year after its publication in French, brought it into their orbit. Franck's book is divided into three parts. The first part deals with the literary problems connected with kabbalistic writings, and the third chapter of this part is devoted to the question of the Zohar. The second part contains an explanation of the system of kabbalistic thought, based in particular on an analysis of statements in the Zohar. The third part discusses the relationships between the doctrine of the kabbalah and other systems of thought in order to establish its original sources. This examination and this comparison of ideas resulted in the view that the sole origin of kabbalah was to be found in Persian religion. This conclusion, which comes at the end of the book, set the pattern for the author's investigation of the composition and date of the Zohar as well. And his considered view is that particular sections were written on the basis of reliable traditions handed down in the name of Rabbi Simeon ben Yohai and his disciples, and that even older traditions are included there. Franck's book, particularly in the way it expounds kabbalistic ideas, contains a great deal of material that is still of value, although there are a considerable number of mistakes in it.[219] Its basic fault derives from the fact that the author could not deal competently with the Zohar in the original and had to rely mainly on the incomplete Latin translation, and this has a particularly adverse effect on his examination of the literary problems. Franck does not produce any original scholarship on the structure of the Zohar or on any other internal criteria. He is content on this point to quote the main arguments of Jewish and Christian scholars, and to examine and evaluate their ideas, especially with regard to the content of Zoharic statements that had already been studied by others, and in connection with the relationship of Zoharic ideas to outside sources.

Landauer, whose research work on the Zohar was published in 1845,[220] after his death, took a completely different line. He claimed to have made a remarkable discovery that solved the problem of the authorship of the Zohar. From his study of the manuscripts of the works of Rabbi Abraham Abulafia, the ecstatic kabbalist who appeared as prophet and messiah in the second half of the thirteenth century, Landauer came to the conclusion that Abulafia himself was the author of the Zohar. Landauer's work was wholly devoted to proving this theory. On the one side, he tried to undermine the truth of Rabbi Isaac of Acre's evidence, according to which the author of the Zohar was Rabbi Moses de Leon; and on the other, he cited many instances of the strong connection that existed between the Zohar and the writings of Abulafia, both in form and in content. Also the fact that many long passages from the Zohar are quoted for the first time in the books of the Italian kabbalist, Rabbi Menahem Recanati, was used by Landauer to support his thesis, since Italy was the scene of Abulafia's main activities. What first prompted Landauer, as he himself says, to attribute the Zohar to Abulafia, was his realization that the Zohar contained ideas that were very close to certain fundamentals of Christian belief. Hence, in his earlier book[221] he upheld the antiquity of the Zohar, and accepted the view, current in Christian kabbalistic circles, that the Zohar had embedded within it ancient Jewish beliefs upon which Christianity was founded—for he could not have believed it possible that a thirteenth century kabbalist had embraced Jewish-Christian beliefs, and read them into the verses of Scripture in a mystical way. But when he discovered a Christianizing tendency in the writings of Abulafia, this obstacle was removed and he was able to posit a late date for the Zohar, since there was so much other evidence to support it. In its conclusions Landauer's work is absolutely baseless. Not one of his proofs can stand up to critical inquiry, and his whole theory is just a castle in the sky. In actual fact, both the doctrine and the character of Rabbi Abraham Abulafia are completely opposed to the teachings of the Zohar, and to the picture of the author or authors that emerges from its pages. Nevertheless, his book is based on original research, and constitutes a serious effort to achieve scientific truth.

The weaknesses in Landauer's arguments became apparent as soon as his studies were published, and his viewpoint suffered accordingly. Critical research returned to the view that the author of the Zohar was Rabbi Moses de Leon, and the most important student of kabbalah in the *Haskalah* movement, Aaron (Adolph) Jellinek, sought new ways of supporting this view. The most original thing he did was to compare Moses de Leon's *Sefer ha-Nefesh ha-Ḥakhamah*, and other statements attributed to him in kabbalistic literature, with passages from the Zohar. This comparison showed that practically all Moses' ideas, expressed in Hebrew in the *Sefer ha-Nefesh ha-Ḥakhamah*, were to be found with varying degrees of exactitude in Aramaic, in the Zohar. And a number of passages from the Zohar are quoted by him in the name of early unknown sources. Jellinek regarded this as absolute proof that Rabbi Moses de Leon was, at the very least, one of the authors of the Zohar.[222] Jellinek also subjected the evidence of Rabbi Isaac of Acre to a meticulous analysis, and demonstrated, on the basis of the facts mentioned in it, how reliable it was.[223] Of course, Jellinek did not content himself with external arguments. He began to reexamine from a critical viewpoint the subject matter of the Zohar itself, and he discovered several new points that indicated its late date, including the influence of some thirteenth-century kabbalistic books on certain ideas and expressions in the Zohar.[224] However, Jellinek's work in this area was but a humble beginning. But its original flavor, and the scientific seriousness with which he approached his study of the manuscripts in order to show the hidden connections between the Zohar and earlier kabbalah, made his work extremely important. It was through Jellinek that Graetz came to his view of the Zohar, for he relied a good deal on Jellinek's researches, but their respective attitudes to kabbalah and to the Zohar were quite different. Jellinek emphasized several times how necessary it was to study kabbalah without any preconceived ideas, and he wrote on one occasion[225] that his intention was "to arouse greater interest in an area that is of such importance to the history of philosophy and theology—a fact that many scholars have not realized, let alone understood. In the ranks of the kabbalists there were men who, in depth of thought and intellectual fertility, were superior to that great band of rationalists who belonged to the school of Maimonides."

Ignatz Stern is the last scholar to be discussed in this survey. In the introduction to his study that appeared in successive parts (1858–1862),[226] he too followed the line of most of the students of the Zohar, and stressed his intention of approaching the study of the problem from an objective, scientific viewpoint. Stern's work was the most detailed and most meticulous analysis ever undertaken of the Zohar, and for this reason is of value even today. The author scrutinizes every section, practically page by page, except for the *Zohar Ḥadash* and the *Tikkunei ha-Zohar*, and deals with both the linguistic and literary characteristics and the specific ideological content of every important statement. In his analysis, and in arriving at his conclusions, Stern used a method very similar to that of biblical source-criticism. The result was such an amazing breakdown of the unity of the Zohar that, according to him, each section, and even separate statements, were composed of different layers and later additions. In order to fix a chronology for this, Stern established a number of criteria which he then considered to be authentic and reliable standards. His study proved to be the most interesting scientific attempt to demonstrate the antiquity of certain sections of the Zohar.

A book of a quite different order is that by Rabbi David Luria,[227] an important Polish scholar who set out to uphold the antiquity of the Zohar. This book, which was published after the author's death, preceded several of the works already dealt with, but its particular character necessitates separate and individual treatment. Luria tried in an original way to disprove the theory that Rabbi Moses de Leon was the author of the Zohar, and to show in a convincing fashion that the book was an ancient work and belonged to Rabbi Simeon ben Yohai and his school. The main method he used to show that Rabbi Moses de Leon was not the author of the Zohar was exactly the same one that Jellinek used to show that he was! He compared the *Sefer ha-Nefesh ha-Hakhamah* and other pieces attributed to Rabbi Moses de Leon with statements from the Zohar. Luria discovered that, on the one hand, there were substantial contradictions between Moses de Leon's kabbalah and Zoharic doctrine, and that, on the other, Rabbi Moses had misunderstood passages from the Zohar that he had quoted in his own writings. So, on the basis of these facts, Luria came to the definite conclusion that Moses de Leon could not have written the Zohar. His second argument was that passages from the Zohar are quoted by Moses de Leon's predecessors and contemporaries as having emanated from early authorities. His chief originality here was his discovery of Zoharic idioms in one of the collections of gaonic responsa. In addition to this he adduced "some evidence that the Zohar was written before the completion of the Talmud" (section 3) and "some theories that passages from the Zohar were written at the time of Rabbi Simeon ben Yohai and his pupils" (section 4), and at the end of his book he tries to disprove the arguments of those scholars who depended on the language of the Zohar as proof of its late date. The proofs and theories that he produced in order to justify the tradition that the Zohar was written by Rabbi Simeon ben Yohai and his followers are extremely weak, and are merely apologetic, savoring occasionally of the *Sefer Ben Yohai*. But his arguments against the attribution of authorship to Rabbi Moses de Leon made a strong impression and were apparently regarded as pretty solid. Even the "scientific" scholars treated them seriously when they first appeared. But on further investigation it became clear that Luria had based himself unknowingly on a very shaky foundation, because the expressions in the gaonic responsa have been shown to be unauthentic, and the statements by Rabbi Moses de Leon, which do in fact show important contradictions to the Zohar, are taken from the *Sefer ha-Shem*, which was attributed to Rabbi Moses de Leon in error.[228] The first scholar to refute Luria's theories was Graetz, who, because of his fanatical support for the late date of the Zohar, criticized him more harshly than was really warranted.

e. Later Studies of the Zohar

In more recent times, after the close of the *Haskalah* period at the end of the nineteenth century, many books and studies have appeared, written by both Jews and non-Jews, on the problem of the composition of the Zohar,[229] but none of them, apart from two that will be dealt with separately, is really important for the history of the study of the literary-historical aspects of the Zohar. Lines of basic research in various directions, which were instituted in the *Haskalah* period by such men as Milzahagi, Landauer, Jellinek, Graetz, and Stern, were neither continued nor developed until very recent times. Most of the scholars who worked on the Zohar trod well-worn paths, and their labors consisted mainly in recasting a well-known view of the matter in a new form, or in combining the basic principles of different views. And those who did try to be original based their originality not on a systematic examination of the sources, but on the most extraordinary hypotheses, most of which were the products of academic fancy and imagination. Even a scholar like David Neumark—who immersed himself in the Zohar and despite all his errors did discover and clarify several important basic ideas there—when he came to the question of the authorship of the Zohar, repeated Jellinek's view exactly, and added the strange idea that the Zohar was based on the *Sefer Ma'arekhet ha-Elohut*, an anonymous work written apparently in the school of Rabbi Solomon ben Adret, and that the selection of Rabbi Simeon ben Yohai as the central character of the Zohar was prompted in the main by the eminence accorded him in that book.[230]

An original note, not in critical research but in general approach to the Zohar, was sounded by the academic side of the new Hebrew literature that grew out of *Haskalah* and was nourished by the resurgence of the nationalistic spirit. The romantic infatuation with the nation's past and with the sacred values of Israel's history, which at times was mixed with mystical-religious yearnings for spiritual exaltation and for a holiness that would bathe everyday life in its splendor, restored the Zohar, the supreme work of Jewish mysticism, to the highest position of awe and sanctity. Writers and poets uncovered hidden treasures of poetry and great beauty in mystical literature, particularly in the Zohar and in the writings of the *hasidim*, and this attitude resulted in a poetic-romantic approach even to the academic problem of the Zohar's antiquity. Just as the most radical scholars of the *Haskalah* movement tried to denigrate the glory of kabbalah by denying the antiquity of the Zohar, so the romantics attempted to exalt its status by refuting those critical views which posited a late date for the Zohar.

The most striking representative of this tendency is Hillel Zeitlin, who sought to revive the spirit of kabbalah and hasidism through actual self-identification. Most of his writings on areas of Jewish mysticism are rapturous hymns of praise, and the same spirit of religiopoetic enthusiasm informs those articles which appear to be works of critical scholarship: *Kadmut ha-Mistorin be-Yisrael*[231] and *Mafteah le-Sefer ha-Zohar*.[232] In these articles, especially in the *Mafteah*, Zeitlin takes issue with previous students of the Zohar and tries to destroy their arguments and to demonstrate the antiquity of the book, at least as an ancient tradition. But from the scholastic point of view there is not much originality or

substance in his opinions, which are not based on a study of the sources. He
stakes his claims on the proofs offered by Rabbi David Luria—the contradictions between the writings of Rabbi Moses de Leon on the one hand, and the
Zohar and Zoharic expressions in the gaonic responsa on the other. And these
he accepted as decisive evidence. With regard to these contradictions, Zeitlin
added several new points[233] on the basis of Rabbi Moses de Leon's *Sefer Shekel
ha-Kodesh* (London, 1911), which was not known to Rabbi David Luria. But
even these contradictions, which involve mainly the question of *En-Sof*, *Keter*,
and the order of the worlds, are really only superficial. On the basis of this
slender evidence Zeitlin constructs a theory of the process of transmission of the
Zoharic tradition, and of the role of Rabbi Moses de Leon as redactor of the
texts that came into his possession.[234]

However, Zeitlin's scientific discussion of the matter is subsidiary to his
spiritual approach, which really determines his whole position. At one point he
defines quite clearly the object of his intentions, by contrasting them with the
tendencies of the *maskilim*, upon which he considered modern Zohar scholarship
to be based. He writes: "As we became liberated from the hostility of the
maskilim so there grew and flourished in the hearts of all the worthy members of
our people the realization that the Zohar was not merely a book of kabbalah,
but a titanic and miraculous creation, a great national manifestation from one
point of view, and a great divine manifestation from another. If you read
carefully the studies of later Jewish scholars you will find many passages where
they not only accord the Zohar the most fulsome praise, but they actually
regard it with reverence and sanctity."[235] This view of the Zohar as a
miraculous work, a national or divine revelation, which must be approached
only in sacred awe, is the chief element in Zeitlin's position, as it is in fact
presented in the rapturous beginning of the *Mafteah*:[236] "What is the Zohar? It
is the exalted divine soul, which suddenly came down to earth from the world of
emanation in order to reveal itself to the eyes of mankind in millions of lights
and shades, hues and colors. The Holy One, blessed be He, took one precious
stone from His crown, and threw it down to the ground, where it shattered in
pieces, sowing thousands upon thousands of lights, rejoicing, delighting, and
exulting in its myriads of hues, which came from eternity in order to lighten all
the dark corners, and to satisfy all who thirst and yearn for the light, and in
order to warm and revive all who have been slain by the ice of science, the
darkness of ignorance, the blindness and heaviness of nature, and the evil,
harshness, and cruelty of humanity." Try to find in all this some logical train of
thought, an elucidation of historical fact and circumstance, a detailed
examination of the language of the Zohar, and of the other points relevant to its
date and composition! Zeitlin, and those who follow him in thought and feeling,
deserve our gratitude for having retrieved the sparks of the Zohar's mysteries
and for making them shine again in new literary forms, but from a scientific
point of view their work represents a major retrogressive step. They removed
the problem of the Zohar's composition from the plane of reality to the dark
regions of the mysterious, beyond the grasp of the human intellect, accessible
only to those who have been uplifted by the divine.

Zohar scholarship reached a turning-point with the researches of Gershom
Scholem, who finally turned the scales in favor of an all-embracing systematic

interpretation based on a firm, scientific, critical foundation. Scholem was the first scholar to approach the whole area of kabbalah research fully equipped with an accurate scientific apparatus, and he transformed it into a well-defined operation, to be conducted in both method and judgment with all the weight of objective scholarly argument. His studies, which cover the subject from all sides—bibliographical, literary, philological, historical and ideological—are completely free from the burden of blind hatred typical of the *Haskalah* and also from the weight of exaggerated romantic adoration. Objective scholarship, which began to flower in the *Haskalah* period, came to full fruition in these studies, on the new soil of national regeneration. Scholem recognized in kabbalah a vital spiritual factor in Jewish history, but he did not approach it with a preconceived idea of its value or its historical import. It was judged and evaluated in a critical way as the results of his research on the sources became apparent. The question of the Zohar, both from the literary and the ideological point of view, occupied a central position in his research from the start, and in painstaking fashion he arrived at a penetrating explanation of the basic problems involved. His approach to the question of the authorship of the Zohar is characterized by the fact that he made a clear distinction between establishing the method and date of composition of the book, and evaluating its worth. He did not consider that the pseudepigraphic character of the book was detrimental to its intrinsic value.

In his study of the literary problem of the Zohar, Scholem did not proceed directly to a solution, but grappled laboriously with all the tangential aspects until he reached a definite conclusion. In his first essay[237] he set out to challenge the accepted critical view that Rabbi Moses de Leon had written the Zohar, and he tried to prove, by analyzing the main arguments and adducing new evidence, that the main body of the work antedated Rabbi Moses de Leon. This essay, as he explicitly states at the end,[238] was intended to be a prolegomenon to a scientific justification of this view based on the theories propounded there: "Consequently, the whole question of the development of the Zohar, its order and presentation, and its actual connection with Rabbi Moses de Leon, needs to be raised again. However, in order to provide a definite answer to these questions and say how the Zohar was created and arranged, whether Moses de Leon rearranged midrashic sources emanating from an earlier time, we know not when, or whether he added material of his own in the process of this rearrangement, and how the literary remains of earlier generations came into the possession of Rabbi Moses and of those Castilian kabbalists who preceded him—an answer to all these problems depends on a new and systematic study, without any preconceptions, of the development of the kabbalah as a whole, on a detailed study of the language and content of the Zohar, and on new knowledge of many sources that are still inaccessible to us." Scholem followed the path that he had marked out for himself—"a new and systematic study, without any preconceptions, of the development of the kabbalah as a whole . . . a detailed study of the language and content of the Zohar"—but the results that emerged from this course of action were completely different from what was expected. His hope of discovering a solid foundation for the antiquity of the Zohar suffered one setback after another, and he was gradually compelled to revise his earlier theories. In place of the anticipated conclusion, his studies led him to

confirm the view that the main sections of the Zohar were written by Rabbi
Moses de Leon, and that there was no section that antedated him. The results of
his studies drew him much nearer to Graetz's position, who had been the first to
aim a critical blow at the Zohar, but Graetz's views, for which he had only a
slender justification, were now extensively and decisively substantiated
by Scholem, who was able to draw upon new knowledge and fresh source
material.

One of the important areas in which Scholem pursued new avenues of
research was the language of the Zohar. Several scholars before Scholem had
used the structure and form of the language of the Zohar in order to establish
the date of its composition, but they did not go beyond chance impressions and
collecting isolated examples without any fundamental and systematic investigation. Hence their conclusions did not have the weight of authority. Scholem
in his work managed to get away from this kind of approach, and set about
compiling a complete dictionary of the language of the Zohar that would
contain every word and idiom and would explain their usage in the different
sections of the book. This comprehensive study proved without doubt that, in
the first place, the main body of the Zohar was a unified whole, and that,
second, its composition was of late date, for it demonstrated that all the sections
had a single linguistic shape and that this shape was full of late expressions and
forms that originated in the language of medieval scholars.

This study of the Zohar's language, which included a determination of the
meaning and usage of mystical terminology and symbolism, paved the way for
Scholem's investigation of areas beyond the field of linguistics, into the
relationship, both in terminology and thought, between the Zohar and earlier
kabbalistic literature. Scholem studied those works of kabbalah that were
already known, and also unearthed and published several important texts that
had hitherto been confined to manuscripts.[239] On the basis of these researches
Scholem was able to fix the place of the Zohar within the development of
kabbalah. In this field, in which work had been done to a slight extent by
Jellinek, Scholem came to the conclusion that the symbolism and the ideas of
the Zohar were based on trends in thirteenth-century kabbalah.

As to the relationship between the Zohar and the writings of Rabbi Moses de
Leon, several earlier scholars had dealt with it to some extent on the basis of
printed texts, while Jellinek and Graetz had also glanced at manuscript copies
of some of Moses de Leon's books. But Scholem embarked on a much wider
study and examined all the writings of his that we possess. In his researches he
compared the language and content of these texts with the Zohar, noted and
enumerated quotations from the Zohar to be found in them, and built up a
portrait of Rabbi Moses de Leon. In this way Scholem was able to establish a
firm foundation for solving the problem of whether Rabbi Moses de Leon had
written the Zohar or not.

Apart from these far-reaching studies Scholem also devoted himself to a
clarification of other matters connected with Zohar research, for example, the
structure of the book, its literary forms, its historical background, and its
influence on kabbalistic literature, and he made many original contributions in
these fields. Of the fruits of his research only a certain amount has so far been
published: a number of specialized studies, the works of kabbalists who were

active at about the same time as Rabbi Moses de Leon, and a clear summary of the results of his labors.[240] The Zohar dictionary still remains in manuscript form; Rabbi Moses de Leon's works, which Scholem began to prepare for publication when he first started his studies, have still not managed to see the light in a scientific, critical edition; and an elucidation of the complex relationships between the Zohar and earlier kabbalistic literature is still at an elementary stage. In these and similar areas Scholem left room for himself and for other scholars to make a name for themselves in Zohar research, but there is no doubt that Scholem's critical conclusions have finally put an end to the great controversy about the composition and authorship of the Zohar that raged for so many years among students of Judaism.

IV. ZOHAR CRITICISM[241]

a. Indecisive Arguments

There are a number of matters that were central to Zohar criticism in the early stages but that are hardly mentioned by later scholars because the arguments are equally weighted on both sides and from a scientific point of view it is impossible to decide between them. Also the subject matter of these arguments, which were, as we shall see, based mainly on the undisputed authority of halakhic and aggadic tradition, was not so crucial for modern critical scholarship. Nevertheless, we ought to deal with them because of the important role they played in the development of Zohar criticism; their omission would leave it incomplete.

Faulty Quotation from the Bible

A fair proportion of Emden's arguments deal with scriptural verses that are quoted by the Zohar either in an incorrect form or in a wrong connection. And there are many cases where these mistakes constitute the actual basis for the interpretation given by the Zohar. I give here a few examples of these mistakes, which are extremely numerous. (1) In the Zohar,[242] Psalm 46: 9 is quoted as "Come, behold the works of God (*Elohim*), who has made desolations in the earth," and this is interpreted as a reference to the destructive acts of the attribute of Judgment, signified by the name *Elohim*. But the verse actually uses the name "Lord" (*YHVH*), which signifies Mercy, and the author of the Zohar seems to have confused it with Psalm 66: 5, "Come, and see the works of God (*Elohim*). He is terrible in His acts towards the children of men." (2) In connection with Genesis 22: 24 the Zohar[243] writes, "Ishmael's mother bore Tahash, and he was descended on Abraham's side." But the verse actually states that Tahash was the son of Nahor and his concubine, Reumah. (3) 1 Kings 7: 25, "and all their hind parts were inward," refers explicitly to oxen, but in the Zohar[244] it is interpreted as referring to "the mystery of man," in actual contrast to animals. (4) 2 Kings 3: 15, "And it came to pass, when the minstrel played, that the hand of the Lord came upon him," refers to Elisha, but in the Zohar[245] it is introduced with "like David, of whom it is said. . . ."

Those who supported the antiquity of the Zohar, especially Kunitz and

Milzahagi, replied to these arguments by saying that variants in scriptural quotations also occur in the Talmud and the midrashim, sometimes intentionally for the sake of abbreviation, and the like, and sometimes because the early rabbis did in fact have a text different from the traditional one. In the *Sefer Zohorei Raviah* Milzahagi presents a detailed study, showing that several of the variant readings in the Zohar have a basis in early texts. The quotation of scriptural verses out of context for the purpose of interpretation also occurs from time to time in the homilies of the rabbis.

Aggadot

Emden based some of his criticism of the Zohar on a large number of *aggadot* in it, which either contradicted *aggadot* familiar from rabbinic writings or were questionable in content. Here are some examples: (1) It is written in the Zohar[246] that "the palm-tree bears fruit after seventy years," while in the *gemara*[247] it is of the carobtree that we read "that it takes seventy years, from the time it is planted, for the fruits to ripen." And they said of the palm that its fruit ripened after twelve months. (2) According to the Zohar[248] "the Torah is more splendid at night than during the day," which is in contradiction with the *gemara*,[249] which states that daytime is more appropriate for study, and that the night was created only for sleep. (3) The Zohar[250] states that Gehazi has a share in the world to come, while in the *gemara*[251] he is numbered among those who have no share in the world to come. (4) As a certain proof that the author of the Zohar misunderstood rabbinic statements, Emden cites the following:[252] "Whoever calls his companion 'wicked' is taken down to Gehinnom and they take possession of his jaws (translating *li-lehayav*)." But this is a mistranslation of the *gemara*:[253] "Whoever calls his companion...'wicked' can have his livelihood (*le-hayyav*) removed."

This criticism is easily countered by citing the well-known statement that "one does not question *aggadah*." We find contradictory and questionable *aggadot* in ancient and reliable sources as well, and difficulties similar to those which occur with the *aggadot* of the Zohar arise there too.

Halakhah

One of the earliest arguments, already mentioned by Rabbi Elijah Delmedigo as a common criticism, derives from the fact that, generally speaking, in the talmudic legal controversies with his adversary, Rabbi Judah, Rabbi Simeon ben Yohai's opinion is not accepted. Now if Rabbi Simeon ben Yohai had really been the recipient of secrets from heaven one would have assumed that his legal opinion would always have been decisive.

The usual reply to this argument was that law and the mysteries of kabbalah were two distinct disciplines and they should not be confused. This distinction between halakhah and kabbalah was justified by reference to the famous controversy between Rabbi Eliezer and Rabbi Joshua, in which Rabbi Eliezer tried to prove his point of view by means of miracles, and even a voice from heaven proclaimed that he was right, but Rabbi Joshua still maintained his view, saying that the Torah "was not in heaven," and his view was accepted as authoritative.[254] Rabbi Moses Kunitz tried to solve the problem in a more original and more complicated way. He attempted to prove that Rabbi Simeon ben Yohai's legal opinion was rejected only during the period that preceded his sojourn in the cave, but once he had emerged from the cave all his halakhic views were accepted as binding. The Rabbi Simeon ben Yohai of the Zohar, which was written in the cave, reflects the eminent sage of this second period. Kunitz's new theory, however, has no foundation whatsoever.

A similar problem arose with regard to the laws mentioned in the Zohar. Many of the laws, cited and interpreted mystically in the Zohar, contradict rabbinic statements in the Talmud and the actual halakhic decisions themselves. Here are some examples: (1) The Zohar says:[255] "In actual fact, an oath (shevuah) applies only to what is substantial, and a vow (neder) applies even to what is insubstantial, and this is already explained in the Mishnah." But the gemara says exactly the opposite:[256] "Oaths are more stringent than vows, because oaths may apply to what is both substantial and insubstantial, which is not the case with vows." (2) According to the Zohar,[257] "The Omer was a meal-offering of unsifted barley-meal," but the Mishnah explicitly states[258] that it was only the suspected adulteress's meal-offering that was of unsifted meal, while the Omer offering was of sifted meal. (3) The Zohar notes[259] in connection with a Hebrew slave that "slaves are exempt from the yoke of Heaven, and are thus exempt from fulfilling the commandments." But according to the Talmud,[260] it is only a Canaanite slave who, like a woman, is exempted from fulfilling certain commandments, and not a Hebrew slave at all. (4) On the basis of Leviticus 1: 5, "And he shall kill the bullock," the Zohar maintains[261] "that someone else should slaughter, and not the priest, for, according to the law a priest is forbidden [to slaughter]." But the Talmud[262] interprets this verse to mean that slaughtering by someone else is valid, but it is far better for the slaughtering to be done by a priest. From these and similar examples scholars have deduced that the author of the Zohar was unskilled in legal matters, and that he made mistakes as to authoritative legal decisions.[263]

In several cases attempts were made by the defenders of the Zohar to reconcile the laws in it with the actual halakhah. But in general, they simply maintained that since Rabbi Simeon ben Yohai was a *tanna* he had every right to disagree with the sages of the Talmud.

The Writing Down of the Oral Law

According to tradition it was forbidden to commit the oral law to writing. Only when it was "time to do something for the Lord,"[264] to prevent the Jewish people from forgetting the Torah did they allow it to be written down. This tradition led to the argument that the Zohar could not have been written by Rabbi Simeon ben Yohai and his disciples.[265] It was no good maintaining that the Zohar was also transmitted orally and written down subsequently, because it is explicitly stated at the beginning of the *Idra Zuta*[266] that Rabbi Simeon ben Yohai told Rabbi Abba to put down his words in writing. The prohibition of writing down the oral law was also cited in the dispute about the printing of the Zohar as an argument against the proposal to print.[267]

The defenders of the Zohar replied to this[268] that the prohibition related solely to halakhic matters, but *aggadot*, and particularly the secrets of the Torah, were allowed to be committed to writing. Indeed, we hear very early of the existence of *megillot setarim* (scrolls of mysteries). And even if we were to admit that the prohibition applied to both the secret and the revealed Torah, we could still say that the secrets of the Torah could also be written down when the time came "to do something for the Lord."

Generally speaking, the answers were sufficiently cogent to remove the sting from these criticisms. But on closer perusal it becomes obvious that in many cases there are real mistakes in the Zohar's quotations from the Scriptures, the *aggadot* and the *halakhot*, and some of these must have resulted from quoting from memory. However, the whole subject is not too important for the problem of the composition of the Zohar. The scholars who were really involved with these arguments placed a highly exaggerated value on the earlier, compared with the later generations, an estimate very widespread in Jewish tradition, as expressed in the famous dicta: "The hearts of the early scholars were as wide as the entrance to the portico, and the hearts of the later scholars were only as wide as the door of the Temple, and ours are only as wide as the eye of the finest needle";[269] "If the early scholars were sons of angels, we are sons of men; and if they were sons of men, we are like mules."[270] And therefore they saw these errors as sure signs of a late date. This estimate, of course, cannot stand up to critical examination. The early rabbis were just as likely to err and make mistakes as the later rabbis, and the mistakes in themselves cannot tell us anything about the date of composition of the Zohar. We can, however, say this, that the worst of the errors could not have been committed by scholars as great as Rabbi Simeon ben Yohai and his companions. If indeed it could be proved that the texts of the biblical verses, *aggadot*, and laws in the Zohar were taken from later sources, then they would have some serious scientific value. However, this belongs to another field of study, research into the sources of the Zohar, which is one of the foundations of the scientific critique, and I shall deal with it at greater length in what follows.

b. The Foundations of Zohar Criticism

In addition to these indecisive arguments, which do not really affect a critical view of the Zohar, there are a large number of criticisms, ranging from the earliest period of research down to our own time, that are both substantial and valid, and these constitute the foundations of the scientific approach. The defenders of the Zohar's antiquity have tried to undermine these arguments, but all their counter arguments depend on forced and quibbling interpretations that cannot stand up to critical scrutiny. However, in order to present a complete picture of the situation, I shall quote some of the counter arguments side by side with the basic criticisms, and the reader can choose for himself.

Personalities in the Zohar

The contradictions and the chronological inexactitudes, which appear in connection with the rabbis mentioned in the Zohar, are the most obvious indications of its pseudepigraphic character. These were remarked upon at a very early stage even in kabbalistic circles and by those who were very close to them. In certain sections, like the *Midrash ha-Ne'elam*, the *Raya Mehemna*, and the *Tikkunei ha-Zohar*, these contradictions are perfectly obvious for everyone to see, while in the main body of the Zohar and in other sections only a little probing is necessary to bring them to light in considerable numbers. Among the scholars mentioned in the *Midrash ha-Ne'elam*, the earliest *tannaim* and the latest *amoraim* are put together, even as members of the same band of scholars. When Rabbi Simeon ben Yohai and his disciples assemble before Moses, in the *Raya Mehemna* and the *Tikkunei ha-Zohar*, "*tannaim* and *amoraim*" are simply mentioned together several times.[271] These terms, as well as "*rabbi, rav, rabban, and rabba*," and even "*geonim*," are given a mystical interpretation.[272] We find two examples of similar interpretations in other sections.[273]

Chronological contradictions and mistakes in nomenclature occur even in regard to Rabbi Simeon ben Yohai's own family. In the Zohar[274] Rabbi Pinhas ben Yair is described as Rabbi Simeon's father-in-law, who died before he did, and whose soul came down from Heaven and was present when Rabbi Simeon's soul departed.[275] According to the Talmud,[276] however, Rabbi Pinhas was Rabbi Simeon's son-in-law, and had personal contact with the mature Rabbi Judah ha-Nasi, who had been a student of Rabbi Simeon's.[277] Many stories in the Zohar refer to Rabbi Jose ben Simeon ben Lekunya as the father-in-law of Rabbi Simeon ben Yohai's son, Rabbi Eleazar. He is described as a wealthy and hospitable man, in whose house the sages often used to meet. There is an error in the Zohar's account of the name. In other sources we find references to Rabbi Simeon ben Jose ben Lekunya, introduced sometimes as Rabbi Eleazar's wife's brother[278] and sometimes as his father-in-law.[279]

There are also several doubtful names among the eight "companions," who formed Rabbi Simeon ben Yohai's inner circle and were his personal confidants, and it can definitely be stated that one or two of them could not possibly have been members of Rabbi Simeon's entourage. Only two of them, Rabbi Judah and Rabbi Jose, are known as his companions, while it is said[280] of Rabbi Isaac that he studied in his school. The prominent *tanna* called Rabbi Abba, who in the Zohar is one of the leading figures in the group, is otherwise completely unknown. The earliest figure who could possibly be identified with Rabbi Abba is the famous *amora*, Rav, who name was Abba Arika, and this identification is in fact made in kabbalistic literature. Rav went up to Palestine from Babylon and studied in the school of Rabbi Judah ha-Nasi, that is to say, he was a pupil of Rabbi Simeon ben Yohai's pupil, and was born, as far as we can calculate, about the same time as Rabbi Simeon died. Rabbi Hiyya was Rav's uncle and teacher, and he too was one of those students of Rabbi Judah ha-Nasi who came originally from Babylon. He is indeed mentioned in the Zohar as one of the younger companions,[281] and at one point he is said to have been a child at Rabbi Eleazar's wedding feast.[282] If this was so then he could have been, from the point of view of age, one of Rabbi Simeon's group. But it is these very details that contradict the known facts, because he left Babylon with his children[283] when he was senior both in years and in Torah. There is an even greater time lag between Rabbi Simeon ben Yohai and Rabbi Hezekiah bar Rav and Rabbi Yesa. This Rabbi Hezekiah is not known from any other source, but his father's name shows, in any event, that he belonged to the amoraic period. The Talmud does mention[284] a Hezekiah who was the son of Rav's daughter, and this could possibly have been the origin of the name in the Zohar. Rabbi Yesa (also spelled Yessa, Yessah, etc.) is a name given in the Jerusalem Talmud to the *amora* Rav Asi, a pupil of Rabbi Johanan. It is said of him[285] that he fasted for eighty days so that he might be accorded a revelation and see Rabbi Hiyya Rabba. It was this scholar, who lived and worked in the fifth generation after Rabbi Simeon, that the Zohar apparently had in mind.[286] More astonishing still is the information that Rabbi Hezekiah and Rabbi Yesa both died after the assembly of the *Idra Rabba*,[287] that is to say, before the death of Rabbi Simeon ben Yohai. Rabbi Jose bar Jacob, who according to the Zohar died together with Rabbi Hezekiah and Rabbi Yesa, is not known as a scholar of any prominence in the sources. There are three men of this name in the Talmud and the midrashim, one[288] exactly as we have it here, and two with the addition of the grandfather's names (Rabbi Jose son of Rabbi Jacob bar Idi,[289] and Rabbi Jose son of Rabbi Jacob bar Zabdi[290]). All three were *amoraim*.

A similar chronological confusion occurs with the two most remarkable characters in the Zohar stories, Rav Hamnuna Sava and Rav Yeva Sava. Rav Hamnuna's dating is inconsistent even within the Zohar itself.[291] At no point does he appear alive in the circle of "the companions," but his soul reveals itself to them on their travels and is also present at the death of Rabbi Simeon ben Yohai. In the story about *Yanuka* (the child) we learn that several scholars lodged in the house of his widow and met his little boy there. On the other hand, however, it appears from the conclusion of the *Idra Rabba* that he was still alive at the time of that assembly. Rabbi Simeon ben Yohai derives considerable authority from "the book of Rav Hamnuna Sava" and "the *aggada* of the school of Rav Hamnuna Sava," and quotes a large number of statements from them on mystical topics. If we try to harmonize these various pieces of information we must perforce say that Rav Hamnuna Sava was an older contemporary of Rabbi Simeon ben Yohai, and perhaps his teacher in esoteric wisdom, and that he died at the very beginning of Rabbi Simeon's mystical activity. But even this forced hypothesis cannot be reconciled with the most extraordinary statement[292] that refers to Rav Hamnuna as a scholar who lived in the Temple period and who used to be consulted by pilgrims. In the Talmud, however, Rav Hamnuna Sava is a Babylonian *amora*, who appears among the students of Rav[293] and even transmits traditions in the name of Rav's disciples.[294] There is likewise a contradiction in chronology with regard to Rav Yeva Sava. He is also depicted in the Zohar as a wondrous character who, during his lifetime or after his death, appeared to the scholars on a journey in the guise of a poor ass-driver.[295] His ideas on mystical subjects are also quoted in the name of "the book of Rav Yeva Sava" and "the *aggada* of the school of Rav Yeva Sava." In contradistinction to this, he is referred to in the Talmud[296] as a Babylonian *amora*, and one of the pupils of Rav.

A very large number of *amoraim* are mentioned in the Zohar, and there is no need for our particular purpose to dwell on most of them. It will be sufficient to extract just a few characteristic examples. Two stories concerning Rabbi Eleazar ben Arakh will serve to highlight the absurd confusion in the *Midrash ha-Ne'elam* in matters of chronology. In one story[297] Rabbi Ze'eira goes to visit Rabbi Eleazar ben Arakh. During their conversation Rabbi Eleazar reminds Rabbi Ze'eira of an interpretation that he had heard from Rabbi Bo that he had subsequently forgotten. Rabbi Eleazar ben Arakh lived around the time of the destruction of the Temple and was one of Rabban Johanan ben Zakkai's disciples, while both the Rabbi Ze'eiras known to us were Babylonian *amoraim*, and the more distinguished of them, who went up to Palestine from Babylon, studied at the feet of one of Rav's disciples.[298] Thus we find that about two hundred years separate Rabbi Eleazar ben Arakh from Rabbi Ze'eira! Another story[299] relates that Rabbi Dostai was preparing to go to visit Rabbi Eleazar ben Arakh, and that Rabbi Haggai wanted to accompany him. However, Rabbi Dostai would not accede to this request until Rabbi Haggai had proved his competence in mystical matters. When they arrived at Rabbi Eleazar's, he tested both of them, and then took them into his inner chamber, and during his conversation with them explained to them an exposition by Rabbi Isaac. Several *tannaim* are known by the name of Rabbi Dostai, some of them quite early, but the earliest *tanna* called Rabbi Isaac was contemporaneous with Rabbi Simeon ben Yohai. Rabbi Haggai is mentioned in the main body of the Zohar and in the *Sitrei Torah*.[300] He is depicted as a scholar who was sent from Babylon to study with Rabbi Simeon ben Yohai, but because of his deep humility he concealed his own knowledge, and the "companions" thought he had no understanding of the Torah. This portrayal shows quite clearly that the reference was to the scholar from the Talmud,[301] but he was an *amora*, a disciple of Rav Huna.[302] Let us, finally, take a brief look at Rabbi Simlai and Rabbi Rehumai. Rabbi Simlai is cited in the Zohar[303] as a doctor of the soul, who in the age of the "companions" used to persuade the wicked to repent. The reference is undoubtedly to the great preacher who was a Palestinian *amora* and a pupil and servant of Rabbi Judah II the Patriarch, the grandson of Rabbi Judah ha-Nasi.[304] Rabbi Rehumai is referred to as an older companion of Rabbi Simeon ben Yohai.[305] This name is known only among the later Babylonian *amoraim*, after the generation of Abaye and Rabba. However, in the *Sefer ha-Bahir*, he is mentioned as one of the most important mystics, and he probably found his way into the Zohar from there.

These examples, which form only a tiny part of the chronological errors in the Zohar, show us that the traditions concerning the rabbis are fictitious and have no historical foundation. The author did not know the historical order of the generations of rabbis, and possibly he did not even worry about chronological consistency when he chose his characters for the narrative framework of the Zohar. We may therefore deduce that the personalities who are mentioned in the Zohar and nowhere else—and there are a large number of them—are not real scholars who by chance were not mentioned in earlier sources, but are in fact merely fictitious names.

Various answers have been given in response to these arguments and the conclusions that can be drawn from them. One of them really belongs to the domain of religious faith beyond the scope of academic discussion. According to this, the statements of the *amoraim* and the conversations between the *tannaim* and the *amoraim* took place in the world of souls, in the Garden of Eden, and were revealed in a miraculous way and noted down in the Zohar. This answer was fairly widespread in kabbalistic circles, in various forms. In the *Sefer Ḥemdat Yamim*,[306] for example, it is said in reply to a questioner, "The truth as I see it is that many of the things that they composed a long time after their death in the Garden of Eden have been revealed to us . . . and that most of the things that you find concerning the arguments of the *amoraim* and the *geonim* derive from the original interpretations they wrote in their last work, after their death, in the Garden of Eden."

Those kabbalists and supporters of the Zohar who were not content with metaphysical arguments tried to remove the difficulties by reconciling the presentations in the Zohar with the sources that contradicted them. On the question of the family relationship between Rabbi Simeon ben Yohai and Rabbi Pinhas ben Yair, they tried to justify the reading in the Zohar by emending the text of the *gemara*, namely, from *ḥatanei* (son-in-law) to *ḥotenei* (father-in-law),[307] or by interpreting the statement so that *ḥatanei* referred to Rabbi Simeon.[308] With regard to several of the later rabbis, such as Rav, Rav Hamnuna Sava and Rabbi Simlai,[309] they made calculations to try to show that in their youth they could have met Rabbi Simeon ben Yohai and his disciples. All these interpretations are merely attempts at artificial harmonization, and even if we were to accept them as a last resort in particular instances, they would still resolve only a small proportion of the chronological errors.

Another answer, which could be used as a more general counterargument, involves the supposition that the scholars mentioned in the Zohar are not at all identical with the later rabbis of the same name in other sources, but that they are rabbis of an earlier generation.[310] It is possible with this solution to remove all the difficulties. But we would at the same time have to accept the remarkable hypothesis that there is in the Zohar a large group of important rabbis of whom nothing is known in other sources, but whose names, and sometimes even patronymics, are identical with the names of later rabbis. And we would have to suppose, in addition, that some of these "unknown" rabbis had the same personal qualities and the same experiences as their later namesakes.

Such far-fetched theories were not accepted by even the most fervent defenders of the antiquity of the Zohar. And so they generally put forward another view, namely, that the statements by later rabbis were introduced into the Zohar several generations after it was composed, just as saboraic statements were introduced into the Talmud, and that the names of *amoraim*, who are portrayed as having had personal contact with Rabbi Simeon ben Yohai and his pupils, were either late additions or copyists' errors.[311]

This hypothesis was used not only to explain away the contradictions in chronology, but also to draw a veil over other indications of late date, such as linguistic characteristics, historical allusions, and traces of later source material, and we must examine this matter briefly without anticipating the detailed discussion that follows. In some places it is possible to prove without a doubt, by philological methods, that particular phrases, and even a number of lengthy passages,[312] did not originate with the author, or authors, of the Zohar, and we ought certainly to look at those passages which have been used to substantiate the theory that later additions were made, and I shall in fact deal with this separately in the chapter "Various Solutions."[313] However, to declare quite simply that every phrase or statement that throws doubt on the antiquity of the Zohar is a later addition is merely a way of evading a critical evaluation. And if we were in fact to adopt this argument in all seriousness with respect to all the doubtful passages in the Zohar, we should have to invalidate and scrap a large part, perhaps most, of the book. And, once the omissions and excisions had been made, only unintelligible fragments would remain in most sections of the Zohar. Samuel David Luzzatto was right when he said[314] on this point: "I do not know, and I have never heard, of a book that has had so much material added to it as the Zohar. Since we have in the Zohar so many statements that cannot possibly be attributed to the *tannaim* and the *amoraim*, no intelligent man should make difficulties for himself by believing that these matters are merely additional to the book. It would be better for him to state categorically that the whole book is a forgery."

The Topography of the Zohar

There are many places mentioned in the Zohar, especially towns and villages in Palestine that Rabbi Simeon ben Yohai and the other scholars in the Zohar either inhabited or visited. When we examine the references to, and descriptions of, these localities we find that the author drew his information about actual places from literary sources, and that occasionally, either because of a mistake in interpretation or a faulty reading, he made topographical errors, and that he even invented places that never existed.[315]

Lydda, one of the central places in the Zohar scene, was thought to be a town in Galilee, because it is cited as being in the neighborhood of Usha and Caesarea.[316] The cave in which Rabbi Simeon and his son hid themselves is referred to as being in the wilderness of Lydda,[317] whereas according to the early sources[318] it was situated in Galilee. The Sea of Kinneret, which was in the territory of Naftali, is described in the Zohar[319] as a sea in the territory of Zebulun, where they fished for the murex, from which they extracted the purple dye for the *zizit* (fringes). In the *gemara*,[320] however, they obviously thought that the Mediterranean was the source of murex. The Babylonian town Mata Mehasia is, according to the Zohar, Kfar Tarsha in Galilee, and in the story about Rabbi Aha[321] it is explained how the name was changed from Kfar Tarsha to Mata Mehasia. What prompted this fabrication was, it seems, the statement in the Talmud[322] that "Mata Mehasia cannot be categorized as either a city or a village." Kfar Kardu, cited[323] in the Zohar as a place of Jewish settlement, apparently in Palestine, never existed at all. The mountains of Ararat are in the *Targum Onkelos*[324] called *turei Kardu*, that is, the mountains of Kurdistan, and on the basis of this reference the author of the Zohar produced his Kfar Kardu. *Turei Kardu* are themselves cited in the Zohar as the mountains of Ararat,[325] but there also it would appear that they were considered to be mountains in close proximity to the Palestinian border, for the rabbis are depicted as journeying and suddenly coming upon the *turei Kardu*.

Kapotkia in the Zohar is a very clear example of a topographical error caused by a misunderstanding of the sources, coupled with some help from the author's own imagination. It is mentioned frequently, but not as the province of Cappadocia in Asia Minor but as a village in Palestine. There are a few statements[326] to the effect that the inhabitants of Kapotkia had evil qualities. This shows that the source of this fictitious village is to be found in a mistaken interpretation of a passage in the Jerusalem Talmud,[327] which talks of "the Cappadocians in Sepphoris," that is, natives of the province of Cappadocia who had come to live in Sepphoris. The author of the Zohar misunderstood this, thinking that the reference was to the inhabitants of a village near Sepphoris, and so he made up stories concerning their way of life.

In this field also apologists have attempted to cover up the facts with some very slender arguments. With regard to the Sea of Kinneret, they have tried to

prove on the basis of unreliable sources that the territory of Zebulun did in fact
extend to the shore of Kinneret, or they put forward the far-fetched theory,
based on aggadic material, that after the destruction of the Temple the murex
emigrated from the Sea of Kinneret to the Mediterranean, and that the Zohar
reflects the situation obtaining before the destruction of the Temple.[328]
Similarly, they attempted to justify the existence of a Kapotkia in Palestine by
not taking the Talmudic statement literally.[329] From a critical point of view
there is no value, obviously, in such arguments, and we must conclude from the
topographical errors in the Zohar that the author did not know Palestine and
that his descriptive accounts are drawn from literary information and from his
own fertile imagination.

The Language of the Zohar

The greater part of the Zohar is written in Aramaic, apart from the *Midrash
ha-Ne'elam*, which is written mostly in Hebrew or in a mixture of Hebrew and
Aramaic. Several scholars, especially Rabbi Judah Leon Modena,[330] regarded
the Aramaic language as an important indication of the late date of the book
and of its pseudepigraphic character. It is quite clear that the Zohar was written
for very limited scholarly circles, and that the Aramaic garb was intended to
conceal the secrets of the Torah from the ordinary people. But in the tannaitic
period it was Hebrew that was the language of the scholars, while Aramaic was
the common vernacular, and so a book dealing with mystical doctrines could
not possibly have been written at that time in Aramaic. Hence we may
conclude that the Zohar was written at a later date, when Aramaic was known
only as the language of literary source material, which none but the rabbis
could understand, and that the author, not knowing that exactly the reverse
situation obtained in the time of Rabbi Simeon ben Yohai, thought to give his
book an impression of antiquity by writing it in Aramaic.

However, the basic critical inquiry must be into the nature of the language of
the Zohar, whether Hebrew or Aramaic. The Hebrew of the *Midrash ha-Ne'elam*
is similar in its overall form to the language of the early *midrashim*, but its specific
vocabulary, idioms, and stylistic characteristics bear the imprint of medieval
Hebrew, and its midrashic manner is clearly that of a later imitation. In the
Aramaic of the other sections, apart from the *Raya Mehemna* and the *Tikkunei
ha-Zohar*, the indications of a later date are not so obvious, but linguistic analysis
and a comparison of the language of the Zohar with known Aramaic sources
show that this Aramaic is an artificial language drawn from specific literary
source material, and it contains a mixture of dialectical linguistic expressions
that never existed side by side in the living language. It contains words and
idioms that originated in medieval Hebrew and they can be seen through the
Aramaic veneer. The poverty of the vocabulary, which amounts to no more
than a few thousand words, and the many errors in word formation and syntax,
also show that we are dealing here with a late artificial language. Samuel David
Luzzatto[331] described the linguistic character of the Zohar as follows: "For, in
truth, it is not the language of the Bible, or of the Mishnah, or of Daniel and
Ezra, or of Onkelos and [Targum] Jonathan, or of the Jerusalem Targumim, or
of the Babylonian Talmud, or of the Palestinian Talmud, or of the midrashim,
or of the *geonim*, or of the commentators, or of the codifiers, or of the

philosophers; but a ridiculous language, a mixture of all the languages I have mentioned, a language that would come automatically to the lips of anyone who wanted to write in the Talmudic style without studying it sufficiently. And, in fact, I know a man who learned a tiny scrap of Talmud and then tried to write in the Talmudic style, and all he could do was write in the style of the Zohar." This description, which sees the language of the Zohar as a mixture of styles of various types and ages, is quite right, generally speaking, when applied to the linguistic characteristics of all the sections, both the Hebrew and the Aramaic. But as far as the specific nature of Zoharic Aramaic is concerned, Scholem[332] has established that it is based, in particular, on the language of the Babylonian Talmud and the Targum Onkelos, together with some syntactical elements from the Targum Yerushalmi. However, the Palestinian Talmud, which without a doubt reflects the very language of Palestine itself, had no influence at all on the language of the Zohar. The more common grammatical forms are taken from the Targum Onkelos. The author apparently thought that it was the language of this Targum that was spoken in Palestine at the time of Rabbi Simeon ben Yohai.

The most obvious signs of medieval linguistic usage in the Zohar are the philosophical terms and expressions that were firmly embedded in the world of medieval scholastic thought, and most of them originated in the Hebrew language of the twelfth and thirteenth centuries, in the translations from Arabic made by the ibn Tibbon family. Philosophical terms connected with the soul are very common, such as: *nefesh ha-sikhlit* (the intellectual soul), *nefesh ha-bahamit* (the animal soul), and *nefesh ha-mitavah* (the desiderative soul);[333] *zurah ha-medabberet* (the rational, lit. speaking, form), *zurah ha-zomahat* (the vegetative form), and *zurah ha-sikhlit* (the intellectual form);[334] *koah ha-mahazik* (the retentive faculty), *koah ha-mitorer* (the appetitive faculty), *koah ha-ta'avah* (the desiderative faculty), and *koah ha-tenuah* (the faculty of movement);[335] *moah ha-zikkaron* (the brain of memory); *moah ha-mahashavah* (the brain of thought); *moah ha-dimyon* (the brain of imagination);[336] *eyn ha-sekhel* (the eye of the intellect).[337] Of the other philosophical terms one should note these quite obvious examples: *ilah ha-ilot, sibah ha-sibot* (the cause of causes),[338] *kavod nivra* (created glory),[339] *koah* and *poal* in the Aristotelian sense of "potentiality" and "actuality,"[340] and references to the four elements (*yesodot*),[341] and to perception (*hassagah*) in the sense of intellectual perception.[342] These terms occur particularly in the *Midrash ha-Ne'elam*, the *Raya Mehemna*, and the *Tikkunei ha-Zohar*, and some of them also in the *Sitrei Torah*. But the influence of philosophical terminology can also be seen in the Aramaic garb of the main body of the Zohar and of other sections. Apart from the term *yesodot*, which is used frequently in this form, we should note the following words: *ashgahuta* (= *hashgahah*, providence), *amshak-huta* (= *hamshakhah*) in the sense of "emanation," *adbakuta* in the sense of "intellectual perception,"[343] *golma* (= *golem*, hylic matter),[344] *perishan* (= *nivda-lim* or *nifradim*) and *alma de-peruda* (*olam ha-perud*), which originate in the common philosophical terms *sekhalim nivdalim* or *nifraim* (separated intelligences) and *olam ha-nivdalim* or *olam ha-nifradim* (the world of the separated intelligences).[345] There are some words and expressions of a more general nature that are drawn from medieval vocabulary, and I shall provide a few characteristic examples that are used in all sections of the Zohar: *remez* (both the nominal and verbal forms) in the sense of "allegory," *ragish* (*muhash*, perceptible by the senses), *it'ar* (*hitorer*) in the sense of "discussing a topic," *im kol da* (*im kol zeh*, nevertheless), *kayama li-she'ilta* (*omed bi-she'elah*, problematic).

A few words show the influence of Arabic and Spanish.[346] The examples hitherto adduced are certainly not sufficient to prove that the author knew these languages fluently, but they do indicate that he must have lived in Spain. On this point Emden cites definite proof as far as the author of the *Raya Mehemna* and the *Tikkunei ha-Zohar* is concerned. It says in the *Raya Mehemna*:[347] "The *Shekhinah* is a brightness, and the fire has brightness (*ve-nogah la-esh*—Ezekiel 1: 13). Hence they call the synagogue *esh nogah*." The reference is clearly to the word *esnoga*, which is a Portuguese corruption of *synagoga*, and apparently commonly used by Castilian Jews as well.

Some instructive examples of the language of the Zohar may be found in the errors in Aramaic words and forms, and in changes in the original meanings. Conjugations of the verb are frequently confused and interchanged. The *Pe'al* is often used in the sense of the *Pa'el* or the *Afel*, for example, *le-mahadei, le-me'al, le-mazkei*, in place respectively of *le-hada'ah* (to cause someone to be glad), *le-a'ala'ah* (to introduce), *le-zaka'ah* (to accord merit). And similarly, in reverse, *le-karva, le-ashra'ah, ulifana*, in place of *le-makrev* (to approach), *le-mashrei* (to rest), *yalafna* (I or we learn). The *Itpa'al* is used transitively, for example, *le-istamara* (to keep), *le-itzana* (to feed), *le-itdabaka* (to attain, perceive). The meanings of many words are changed in the Zohar, and sometimes even their forms are incorrect. The verb *ozif* (to lend money) means in the Zohar "to accompany someone." *Tukfa* (strength) is used in the Zohar to mean "lap, bosom" as well.[348] *Tikla*, whose origin is *takla* (weight), signifies not only "a balance" but also "a sphere." *Zahuta*, which in Aramaic always means "thirst," is interchanged with the Hebrew *zahut*, and used in the sense of "clear understanding." *Tayyah*, which means simply "an Arab" in the Talmud, always signifies "a mule-driver" in the Zohar, and specifically "a Jewish mule-driver," and it even has a verbal form (*le-tay'ya*).[349] The mystical term *bozina di-kardinuta* may have two meanings: "a light of darkness" or "a strong light," that is to say, either its form or its meaning is incorrect.[350]

There is another interesting mistake in the Zohar. It says in II, 13b: "A ray (*aputa*) of fire came out and surrounded him." However, in Aramaic *aputa* does not mean "ray" but "nose" or "forehead." The author of the Zohar was trying to imitate the narrative style of the *gemara*:[351] "a ray (*zuzita*) of light went out of his forehead (*aputa*)," but his memory failed him and he changed *zuzita* to *aputa*.

The language of the Zohar has a particular characteristic in that it contains a large number of words that have no traceable source at all. A few of them are mentioned only once, but most of them occur in a large number of places and in a variety of connections. The use of these words is extremely odd. Only rarely is it possible to determine their meaning from the context, while for the most part it is difficult even to guess what the author had in mind. Generally speaking, two or three of these words are used together, and such joint usage does not help to clarify the individual words. They remain completely obscure. Here are some examples of these extraordinary combinations [in conjectural transliterated form—Trans.], taken from various sections of the Zohar: *susefita di-kemarei gav kultevei* (Zohar I, 30a), *keturei ramai di-kasturei di-hustara* (I, 62a—*Tosefta*), *mastanit sefasina gav kitrei di-nura* (I, 176b), *nefak kustefa di-gurdena* (I, 201b), *sifta betufsera kaftala'ei shekhiḥei* (I, 241b), *purkena tiska de-kinta* (II, 56a), *okhlosin ve-kuztorantim ve-kunteireisin ve-kalteiroslin di-edom* (II, 56b), *she'ala de-keitrei be-kizfa shekian* (II, 175b), *tatekuta'ei misinetan be-galpavei be-itgalaya* (II, 234b), *tihara di-tifasa gelifa be-shifasa* (II, 295b—*Idra Ẓuta*), *netalu lei be-tikra de-sikla* (II, 296b—*Idra Ẓuta*), *be-kelida di-kalditin gelifin di-amid netuzarita* (*Ẓohar Ḥadash*, 12b—*Midrash ha-Ne'elam*), *hanei keludatei de-zakfin bi-ludeteihon mayya ve-milḥa* (idem, 12c—*Midrash ha-Ne'elam*), *kuzetifa di-vodita itbar* (idem, 59c—*Midrash ha-Ne'elam*). These examples form only a small part of the large vocabulary of such words, but one can already see from these that the great majority of them begin with the letter *tet, samekh,* or, in particular, *kuf.* This very strange fact, together with the forms and usages of the words, give the impression that we have here figments of the imagination, whose main purpose was to astound and bewilder the reader. There is reason to believe that, with many of the words, the author had no definite meaning in mind. Some of the verbal acrobatics, like *susefita, kaftira, katfira, tufsera, kustorin, krofinus,* and so on, are made up by intentionally manipulating well-known words, and the others have been newly and freely coined. Several peculiar variations in the words may be laid to the account of the copyists, who quite naturally made a number of errors in transcribing such obscurities.

The artificial character of the language of the Zohar and the indications of its late date, which are confirmed by its syntactical methods and other stylistic qualities that I have not dealt with,[352] constitute a solid philological foundation for a scientific critique. The results of a linguistic investigation show quite clearly that the book was not the work of early scholars who wrote and spoke Aramaic. There is clear evidence to show that the language of the Zohar was a late imitation, which developed in the thirteenth century on the basis of a reading of specific literary sources. The author chose Aramaic because he thought it was the language of the rabbis, to whom he sought to attribute his book, and because it would have been more difficult for him to conceal the signs of a late date if he had written in Hebrew—as we can see from the Hebrew passages in the *Midrash ha-Ne'elam.* Also, as regards content, Aramaic was a far more suitable garb for the secrets of Torah. We must also add that the author had before him earlier mystical writings, like the *Sefer Shimusha Rabba*[353] and the *Aggadat Rabbi Yehoshua ben Levi,*[354] which had been written in artificial Aramaic. The intention of the author to give his book an air of antiquity and of bewildering peculiarity through the use of linguistic devices is also apparent from his invention of purely imaginary words.

These basic arguments were only partly dealt with by those who sought to answer the critics. Modena's case, that the writing of the Zohar in Aramaic showed that it was late, since in Rabbi Simeon ben Yohai's time the language used by the rabbis was Hebrew, prompted various replies, but they are all very insubstantial. They resorted, among others, to the argument that even the Book of Daniel was partly written in Aramaic, and they also adduced the proclamations of the Heavenly Voice (*bat kol*) which, according to the Talmud, were heard in the Temple in Aramaic.[355] A much more bizarre argument was that the *Sifra di-Ẓeniuta* and the *Idrot* were written in Aramaic because they were based on an Aramaic verse in Daniel, "and in consequence it was thought right to transmit the whole Zohar in this language."[356] The same writer bases himself on the hypothesis that Rabbi Abba, who according to the Zohar was Rabbi Simeon ben Yohai's scribe, was a Babylonian, and so the book was written in Aramaic, Rabbi Abba's native tongue.[357] The last refuge is the argument that the motive for writing the Zohar in Aramaic can only be understood mystically.[358]

The defenders of the Zohar's antiquity maintain, with regard to its linguistic character, that we find a mixture of styles and idioms in the early sources too, and so this particular aspect of Zoharic language is no indication of a late date. Moreover, some scholars singled out the language of the Zohar as being typically Palestinian Aramaic. Gaster,[359] who believed that the Zohar was essentially composed piecemeal in esoteric circles in Galilee, described the language of the Zohar as a corrupt, popular dialect that was spoken in Galilee, in those circles which did not adopt the Greek tongue. This dialect approximated very closely to the later language, and that is why the language of the Zohar seems so much like that of the late sources, and, particularly, the Targum to Ecclesiastes. This view is pure supposition, and is shown by the results of linguistic analysis to have no basis in fact.

To give an idea of some specific refutations, here are a few characteristic examples. Kunitz's reply[360] to the problem of philosophical terminology was that our early sages were well-versed in all the sciences and that therefore it is no surprise to find philosophical matters in the Zohar. He tried to explain the word *esnoga* as an amalgam of *ishan* and *senug*, and to interpret it as a place of obeisance.[361] Similarly, defenders attempted to explain away the literal meaning of *ilat ha-ilot* (cause of causes) in order to remove it from the area of philosophical speech.[362] And they looked to the Talmud to support the Zoharic usage of the word *tay'ya* in a sense that conflicts with its plain literal meaning.[363] As regards the peculiar and difficult words for which there is no source, Milzahagi[364] maintained that some of them have their origin in ancient Syrian, but in his extant work he gives no proof for his argument. From all that has been said it is obvious that in this field too none of the objections is strong enough to affect the critical arguments.

Historical References

The pseudepigraphic character of the Zohar and the late date of its composition are also revealed by the allusions in it to medieval historical events and situations, which the author did not worry about, either because he surrounded them with a cloak of antiquity or because he really did think that they belonged to antiquity and was thus guilty of anachronism. The most common form of camouflage was to describe these things as if foretelling the future, but the material itself shows that it was a case of prophecy after the event. Sometimes we find that the very thing cited in one place as a prophecy of the future is described elsewhere as an event that had actually taken place in the days of early imaginary rabbis.

The most striking historical factor is the relationship between the Zohar and the two religions, Christianity and Islam, that dominated the Middle Ages and were hostile to Judaism. These religions are frequently mentioned by the usual terms, Edom and Ishmael, which also designate in the Zohar the ruling nations to whom Israel was subject, that is, the Christians who ruled in Europe and the Arabs who ruled in the East. There are also a number of derogatory statements about Egypt that are meant to be anti-Islam and anti-Arab. This emerges quite clearly from the fact that the Prince of Egypt, known in the *aggadah* as Rahab, appears in the Zohar as the Prince of Ishmael as well.[365]

The Talmudic *aggadah*, in connection with the giving of the Torah, tells how "The Holy One, blessed be He, offered it to every nation and tongue, and they would not accept it, until He came to Israel, and they accepted it."[366] The Zohar, following later midrashim, presents a version that entails the offering of the Torah to Edom and Ishmael in particular.[367] The reference in the Zohar's version is quite clearly to the adherents of Christianity and Islam, and the Zohar seeks to show that, by their refusal to accept the Torah, the followers of these faiths, though claiming to be the bearers of divine revelation, do not possess God's true teaching.[368] On the other hand, the Zohar acknowledges that Christianity and Islam have something in common with Judaism. This acknowledgement is contained in the suggestion that two peoples are close to Israel in believing in the unity of God.[369] Several passages carry an echo of the religious polemics that were conducted in medieval times.[370] The polemic against Christian supremacy is most evident in the following passage:[371] "A certain ruler (*hegemona*) said to Rabbi Eleazar, 'Are you conversant with the teachings of the Jews?' 'Yes,' he replied. 'Do you not maintain,' he continued, 'that your faith and Torah are true, while our faith and Torah are false? Yet it is written (Proverbs 12: 19), "The lip of truth shall be established for ever, but a lying tongue is but for a moment." Now our domination has lasted for years and years, generation after generation, and has never been taken away from us. It has really been "established for ever". But your sovereignty lasted for only a very short time, and then was immediately taken from you, so that in you was fulfilled the scriptural verse "a lying tongue is but for a moment."' Rabbi Elezar said to him 'I see that you are learned in the Torah.' (May the man's spirit depart!) 'If the verse had said "is established for ever" then your interpretation would have been justified, but it actually says "shall be established"—in the future the lip of truth shall be established, which is now not the case, for in our time now the lip of falsehood is dominant, and the lip of truth lies in the dust. But in the time to come, when truth will stand secure, and sprout from the earth, then "the lip of truth shall be established for ever," ' etc. It is quite clear that the disputant was a Christian ecclesiastic, who referred to the Gospels as "our Torah."[372] It is related in another passage[373] that a Gentile sage put three problems to Rabbi Simeon ben Yohai: Scripture does not refer to a third rebuilding of the Temple; the distressed condition of the Jews shows how far removed they must be from God; the Jews who have been prohibited from eating *nevelah* and *terefah*[374] are weak and ill, while Gentiles are strong and healthy. These are all typical of the arguments brought against the Jews by Christians in the Middle Ages. The most important anti-Islamic passage, from the critical point of view, is the fervent outburst put in the mouth of Rabbi Eleazar ben Arakh, who exclaimed in tears:[375] "Stone, stone, sacred stone, the most exalted in the world because of the sanctity of your Master, the children of the Gentiles will in future despise you, put unclean images upon you, to defile your holy place, and all the unclean will draw near to you.[376] Alas for the world, at that time! . . . I weep because I can see that upon this stone they will place the defilement of the Gentiles, the corpses of the dead. Who would not weep? Alas for the world! Alas for that time! Alas for that generation!" The sacred stone is the foundation-stone of the Temple, and the reference must be to the Mosque of Omar[377] that was erected on it. According to the version in the Munich manuscript, it is written in the *Raya Mehemna*[378] "Jesus of Nazareth and Mahomet, who are dead dogs," instead of "idolaters," as in our version.

Arab domination in the land of Israel, and Jewish exile in Arab lands are dealt with quite clearly in the Zohar, particularly in connection with apocalyptic descriptions of the wars at the end of time, and the days of the Messiah. The land of Israel was handed over to the descendants of Ishmael in return for their observance of the rite of circumcision. "Now come and see! The angel appointed over the descendants of Ishmael stood for four hundred years[379] in supplication before the Holy One, blessed be He. He said to Him: 'Does a circumcised man have a portion in Your name?' 'Yes,' He replied. 'But Ishmael was circumcised,' he said; 'why then does he not have a share of You, like Isaac . . . ?' Alas for the time when Ishmael was born into the world, and circumcised! What did the Holy One, blessed be He, do? He removed the descendants of Ishmael from their attachment to the heavens above, and gave them a share below in the Holy Land, because of the rite of circumcision that obtains among them. And the descendants of Ishmael will rule over the Holy Land for a long time, while it is completely fruitless, in the same way as their circumcision is fruitless and imperfect. And they will prevent the children of Israel from returning to their place, until the descendants of Ishmael have been fully recompensed."[380] The passage continues with a description of the war at the end of time, and this begins with an obvious allusion to the battles that took place during the Crusades: "The descendants of Ishmael will in the future stir up fierce battles in the world, and compel the descendants of Edom to gather together against them, and they will wage war against them, on sea, on dry land, and near Jerusalem. And these (the Muslims) will rule over those (the Christians), and the Holy Land will not be handed over to the descendants of Edom." We can see from the contents of this passage that it was written after the expulsion of the Christians from the land of Israel.[381] The clearest statement concerning exile by the Muslims in the Middle Ages, which from the point of view of content is not veiled in any way, is attributed to Rabbi Judah: "'A handmaid that is heir to her mistress' (Proverbs 30: 23). This refers to Hagar who bore Ishmael, and he brought several evils upon Israel, dominating them and afflicting them with all kinds of distress, and decreeing a number of forced apostasies upon them. And to this day they rule over them, and do not allow them to follow their religion. And Israel has experienced no exile more harsh than that of Ishmael."[382] A meeting between Arabs and Jews is described in an adjoining passage. "Rabbi Joshua was on his way up to Jerusalem, and he saw an Arab who was traveling with his son. These two met a Jew. He said to his son, 'This Jew is an abomination, whom his Master has despised. Mock him, and spit on his beard seven times, for he is descended from a once lofty nation, and I know that they are in subjugation to the seventy nations.' His son went and took hold of his beard." In this account, connected with the *tanna* Rabbi Joshua, the author sought to emphasize the harshness of the servitude that the Jews experienced during the exile by the Muslims. The insults and humiliations that the Jews suffered at the hands of Christians in the Middle Ages are also quite clearly described.[383]

The calculations of the end of time in the Zohar also reveal the true date of its composition. Most of the calculations in the main body of the Zohar and in the other sections fix the beginning of the end in the years 1300–1310,[384] except for the *Raya Mehemna*, which puts the date of the coming of the Messiah around 1340.[385] Those who calculated the end of time were wont to fix the date of redemption very close to their own age. And yet we find that Rabbi Simeon ben Yohai and his disciples "postponed" the end for some 1200 years, until the very time of Rabbi Moses de Leon! The obvious solution to this enigma is that the author of the Zohar lived, and wrote the book, at the end of the thirteenth century. One passage[386] states explicitly that 1200 years of exile had already passed, and that the darkness before the dawn, that is, the period of the pangs of the Messiah, would last another 66 years. So this passage must have been written between 1268 and 1334.

There are references in many passages to the internal conditions of Spanish Jewry in the thirteenth century, and in particular to the moral situation, in, for example, the oft-repeated admonitions concerning sexual relations with Gentile women. These refer specifically to relations with female Arab servants, which were quite common in certain Spanish Jewish circles.[387] In the main body of the Zohar itself, most of the references to the internal situation are somewhat imprecise, but in the *Raya Mehemna* and the *Tikkunei ha-Zohar* we find some very detailed descriptions. These sections are full of reprimands and complaints against the wealthy and powerful members of the community, and we see here a reflection of the religious and social conditions that obtained in Spanish Jewry at that time. This area has been investigated and elucidated by the basic research of Yizhak Baer,[388] who has shown how the work of a Christian preacher, belonging to the spiritual Franciscans from the middle of the twelfth century, influenced the author of the *Raya Mehemna*.

Replies to these arguments were both few and weak, and they are not worthy of consideration from the point of view of scientific criticism. The defenders of the Zohar's antiquity maintain that the passages dealing with Christian and Arab rule, with the exile under the Muslims, and, even more so, with the calculations of the end of time, were actually spoken as prophecies concerning the future,[389] and those statements which cannot be interpreted prophetically are invalidated as later additions.[390] Apart from these more general counter-arguments, they tried in a number of particular instances to gloss over indications of a late date. For example, they argued that the two nations that were close to Israel in their belief in the unity of God were not Edom and Ishmael, that is, Christianity and Islam, but the Edom and Egypt of antiquity,[391] even though it cannot possibly be said that their belief approximated to Jewish monotheism. Others connected this "nearness" with Persia and Greece, basing themselves on other passages in the Zohar,[392] even though the latter refer quite clearly to only one nation, Greece.[393] And even if we did at a pinch concur in one particular or another, the other critical arguments would remain unanswered and are strong enough to outweigh these forced individual interpretations.

Evidence of Contemporary Practice

The religious and cultural environment in which the author of the Zohar lived and worked also left its mark on the book. The order of the liturgy and the prayers themselves, laws and customs, superstitions, matters connected with sorcery and demonology, descriptions of the Garden of Eden and of Gehinnom, medical views and linguistic knowledge—these and similar things, which are introduced in some detail or merely referred to in passing, provide indications and allusions from which it is possible to gain some support in establishing the date of the Zohar. Apart from medical and grammatical matters, and to some extent the liturgy, comparative studies of Jewish and non-Jewish culture in the Middle Ages have not yet been made in these areas, and so, in a general discussion such as this, I shall be able to use them in only a limited way. Research into the anatomical and medical knowledge of the Zohar shows that its origin is to be found in the ideas that were current in the Middle Ages, and particularly in Arabic medical literature.[394] This conclusion is particularly important with regard to those sections which have a specifically "antique" character, such as the *Sifra di-Zeniuta* and the *Idrot*, which are full of information of this kind. As far as the question of sorcery is concerned, I cannot enter into all the details of the magical practices so often depicted in the Zohar, which, according to experts in this field, reveal traces of medieval magic. But I should note the statement in the Zohar[395] that "sorcerers and magicians are diminishing in number." This does not fit in with the ancient world, but with the medieval period in Christian countries, where sorcerers were hunted down and belief in magic was beginning to wane. A number of relevant examples of medieval usage can be found in the Zohar.[396] The statement in the *Tikkunei ha-Zohar*[397] about the two pairs of *tefillin* is a conclusive example from the area of religious usage: "since those of the later generation are not proficient, they put on two pairs of *tefillin*." The origin of this practice is the dispute between Rashi and his grandson, Rabbenu Tam, over the order of the scriptural passages in the *tefillin*, and so it could not have been current earlier than the end of the twelfth century.

In the field of linguistics the principal criterion is the citation of vowel-points and accents, which came into existence in the gaonic period. These marks are mentioned or alluded to in nearly every section of the Zohar, but they occur more frequently in the Zohar to the Song of Songs, the *Raya Mehemna*, and the *Tikkunei ha-Zohar*. In many places the vowel-points and the accents are cited by name, and even their form is described.[398] The vowel-points are interpreted mystically as the seed of emanation.[399] Sometimes it is said that the vowel-points are below, inside, or above the letters.[400] The relationship between the vowel-points and the letters is compared to that between the soul and the body[401] or between the clothes and the body.[402] Many of the allusions are connected with the names of God, interpreted according to their vocalization, particularly with the tetragrammaton vocalized with the vowels of *Elohim*.[403] On several occasions the accents are mentioned and interpreted in connection with particular words in the Torah.[404] In the *Raya Mehemna* and the *Tikkunei ha-Zohar*[405] even the order of the accents is mentioned, in the Sefardi version: *zarka, makkef, shofar holekh, segolta*. The most interesting passages occur in the Zohar to the Song of Songs, where the author tries to prove that the vocalization and the accents are of ancient origin. He argues that their origin goes back to Moses at Sinai: "and they were entirely forgotten, but sages arose who had received the light of wisdom from the earlier rabbis and they put them above the letters in order that the letters might be pronounced properly."[406] It is quite clear that these words were written in full knowledge of the fact that the vocalization and the accents were of late origin, and they were intended to counter the view that they did not exist in earlier times. A polemical note is sounded even more clearly in another statement:[407] "And if you say that the vocalization was an invention of the later rabbis (tikkun sofrim), then God forbid! For even if all the prophets in the world were like Moses, who received the Torah at Mount Sinai, they would still have no right to add a single tiny vowel to a single letter, even to the smallest letter in the Torah." In the Tikkunei ha-Zohar there are references to grammarians (marei dikduk), and to the technical term tenuah gedolah (long vowel);[408] and even the Masora Magna and Parva are interpreted mystically.[409]

The elucidation of the mysteries of prayer is one of the central themes of the Zohar. These mysteries involve many prayers that were undoubtedly composed or used after the tannaitic period, or even after the completion of the Talmud. Here are a number of prayers of this type: "Blessed God, great in knowledge," from the Weekday Morning Service, and "God, Lord of all works" from the Sabbath Morning Service;[410] the sanctification "they will give You a crown,"[411] the saying of Kol Nidrei on the Eve of the Day of Atonement;[412] the order of the Avodah beginning "You have established,"[413] the additions of "Remember us unto life," and "in the Book of Life"[414] in the Amidah during the Ten Days of Penitence; the saying of penitential prayers (selihot and tahanunim) during the morning-watch (ashmoret).[415] The established order of prayer that occurs in the Zohar also shows its late date. There is reason to believe that an examination of the prayers and the order of service in the Zohar would reveal unmistakable signs of the Sefardi liturgy of the twelfth and thirteenth centuries.

The origin and date of the vocalization and the accents were a source of controversy up till recent times. Even scholars with a keen critical sense, like Rabbi Azariah dei Rossi and Moses Mendelssohn, were inclined to believe that they were of ancient origin, and even adduced proof from the Zohar.[416] And so, while there was no clear solution to the problem, there was some justification for opponents to argue that the references to vocalization and accents in the Zohar could not be used at all to fix the date of its composition.[417] However, the most recent research proves without doubt that the vocalization and the accents are late, and this conclusion puts an end to all counterarguments, demonstrating as it does that such references in the Zohar are a clear indication of its late date.

Other critical arguments concerning, for example, the citation of late prayers and medieval medical ideas, have been refuted by maintaining that the prayers in the Zohar are old,[418] and that the rabbis of the Talmud were also experts in anatomy and medicine.[419] These refutations can perhaps be justified in those few particular instances upon which these scholars base their views, but in general they are not strong enough to destroy the critical arguments concerning the matters under discussion. Kunitz's reply[420] to Emden's charge, that the reference in the Tikkunei ha-Zohar to the custom of putting on two pairs of tefillin

is an allusion to the controversy between Rashi and Rabbenu Tam, is typical of
the apologetic contortions of those who support the antiquity of the Zohar.
Kunitz proposes three ways of removing the difficulty: (1) Rabbi Simeon ben
Yohai foresaw the later controversy with the aid of the holy spirit; (2) The
controversy actually began in the tannaitic period, and, in fact, the specially
pious practice of putting on two pairs of *tefillin*, because of the uncertainty
involved, was also ancient. The later rabbis were divided concerning the
opinions of the earlier rabbis, and were trying to come to a definite decision in
the matter one way or the other; (3) The paragraph in the *Tikkunei ha-Zohar* is a
later note that accidentally got transposed into the text. Kunitz concludes:
"And so the severity of the rabbi's criticism can be with justice overcome in
these three ways, and whoever thinks about these things can choose whichever
way he likes. The criticism that at first glance seemed to be as bitter as
wormwood is finally reduced to nothing, and you need no longer worry about
it." "Whoever thinks about these things can choose," indeed, between the
well-founded arguments of the critics and the airy-fairy interpretations of the
apologists.

The Sources of the Zohar

The determination of the literary sources used in the Zohar provides much
decisive evidence concerning the late date of the book. However, in this field,
too, the critic has to negotiate a number of difficult obstacles, since most of the
quotations do not appear in their original language or their original form, but
are quite freely reworked by the author, who in many instances covered his
tracks. Nevertheless, scholars have succeeded in removing the outer covering
and have revealed the actual sources, and it is now possible to list hundreds of
quotations that are drawn from unquestionably late source material. These late
sources are extremely wide in scope. They include work from the amoraic
period up to the second half of the thirteenth century, and are extremely varied
in type: Targumim, *aggadah* and halakhah, liturgical poetry, philosophy,
biblical commentary, lexicons, codes, and both *hekhalot* and kabbalistic
literature.

The *Targum Onkelos*, which in the view of some leading scholars was written
in Babylonia, and was in any event not prepared before the amoraic period, is
mentioned several times in the main body of the Zohar and in a few other
sections, and many quotations from it are put in the mouths of *tannaim*. The
Targum of Jonathan ben Uzziel, who according to the Talmud[421] translated
the Prophets, but whose translation did not survive, later translations being
ascribed to him, is also quoted in the Zohar. Research into these quotations
shows that the author of the Zohar knew the later translations and that the titles
of the Targumim had already become confused in his mind. It says in the *Sitrei
Torah*[422] that Onkelos translated the Torah and Jonathan ben Uzziel
translated the Scriptures. The *Targum Yerushalmi* (or Palestinian Targum),
ascribed in error to Jonathan ben Uzziel, is quoted in his name in the Zohar
itself[423] and in the *Midrash ha-Ne'elam* to Ruth.[424] In the *Raya Mehemna*[425] the
Targum Jonathan to Chronicles is mentioned, and in the *Tikkunei ha-Zohar*[426]
even the *Targum Onkelos* to Chronicles is quoted, although Onkelos is known
only in connection with the Targum to the Pentateuch, and it says explicitly in
the Talmud[427] that Jonathan was not allowed to translate the Hagiographa.

An indication of the late date of the Zohar is the fact that Aramaic is referred to simply as "the language of the Targum,"[428] showing that the author lived in an age when Aramaic was known principally as the language of the translations of the Bible.

Parts of talmudic literature are quoted by their titles, such as Mishnah, Baraitha, Tosefta, Jerusalem Talmud, and Babylonian Talmud, the six orders of the Mishnah, and various separate tractates. These references are more common in the *Raya Mehemna* and the *Tikkunei ha-Zohar*. Hundreds of quotations from the *amoraim*, and from stories about their lives and actions, are interspersed through all sections of the Zohar. Here are a few examples in which amoraic statements are either ascribed to *tannaim* or quoted with specific reference to their origin in the Talmud: (1) Rabbi Hiyya said in the presence of Rabbi Simeon ben Yohai, "We have learned that a dream that is not interpreted is like a letter that is not read."[429] This was actually said by the Babylonian *amora*, Rav Hisda.[430] (2) Rabbi Eleazar said, "This is like the teaching that the Holy One, blessed be He, shed two tears into the Mediterranean Sea," and Rabbi Jose disagreed since these were the words of a necromancer "and both he and his words are deceitful."[431] This argument between two *tannaim* is about a story connected with the Babylonian *amora*, Rav Katina.[432] (3) Rabbi Hiyya said that in the arguments in the Heavenly Academy they are sometimes swayed in their decisions by interpretations of Torah originated by a rabbi on earth "and they say, 'who has proved this point? So-and-so has proved this point.' "[433] This passage is an obvious reference to the story about the death of the Babylonian *amora* Rabbah bar Nahmani.[434] (4) Rabbi Simeon ben Yohai bases himself[435] on an event in the life of Rabbi Eleazar ben Pedat,[436] who went up from Babylon to the land of Israel several generations after Rabbi Simeon's death. (5) A story about the *amora* Rabbah bar Bar Hana, a contemporary of Rabbi Eleazar ben Pedat, is cited as coming from "the *hagdarah de-vatra*[437] of Rabbah bar Bar Hana."[438] (6) The address of the late Babylonian *amora* Rabba to the inhabitants of Maḥoza[439] is quoted in this way: "And so the masters of the Mishnah interpreted it as follows: Honor your wives that you may enrich yourselves."[440]

In addition to the talmudic *aggadah*, the author of the Zohar also drew abundantly upon midrashic literature. His main sources were *Midrash Rabbah*, *Midrash Tehillim*, the *Pesiktot*, and the *Pirkei de-Rabbi Eliezer*. Of special importance from the critical point of view are the quotations from the *Pirkei de-Rabbi Eliezer*, which are to be found in practically every section of the Zohar.[441] This source is a pseudepigraphic midrash, written in the geonic period. An interesting example of the Zohar's use of late pseudepigraphic midrashim is the story of Adam and Lilith, which is introduced by the phrase "we find this in the books of the ancients (*rishonim*),"[442] and which is taken from the *Alphabet of Ben Sira*,[443] written about the tenth century.

I have already mentioned,[444] in connection with the liturgy, several poems written by the early *payyetanim* that were introduced into the prayer book and referred to in the Zohar as recognized liturgical passages. Of relevance to the date of the book's composition are two lines ("mighty men stand in the breach" and "they annul the decrees"), from the *piyyut* "Men of faith have perished," which are quoted in the *Tikkunei ha-Zohar*.[445] But particularly important for determining the date of the Zohar are the traces of Spanish poetry. Jellinek[446] drew attention to several places where he found ideas drawn from the poems of Ibn Gabirol, Judah Halevi, and Alharizi, but, since these are common concepts and images and are not quoted in the Zohar in their original poetic form, there is no philological proof here of the influence of these poems. On the other hand, there are without question several places in the Zohar, and explicitly in the *Raya Mehemna* and the *Tikkunei ha-Zohar*, where idioms from Ibn Gabirol's *Keter Malkhut* (The Kingly Crown)[447] may be discovered. The lines "But there is a Lord over them, who darkens their lights," which refer in the *Keter Malkhut* (section 12) to the eclipse of the sun, are quoted literally in connection with the mystery of the eclipse of the sun and the moon.[448] And in the words that precede these lines ("as the moon and the stars receive [light] from the sun") we can see the influence of the *Keter Malkhut* (15, 17): "[the sun] distributes light to all the stars of heaven. . . . When Thou didst appoint it to bestow light upon the stars above and below, and upon the moon." The subject matter of the well-known lines (2): "Thou art One, and the wise in heart marvel at Thy Unity, For they know what it is. Thou art One, and Thy Unity does not diminish nor increase, Is neither wanting nor superfluous. Thou art One, not like one created or enumerated, For neither plurality nor change can touch Thee, Without attribute, without name," influenced the author of the *Tikkunei ha-Zohar*, and several phrases are actually quoted, with slight modification: "Furthermore, from the point of view of [the word] 'one' she is four, and together with him thirteen, the enumerated One, but, from the point of view of the Highest above the high (i.e., *Keter* or *En-Sof*) she is one, but not like the named and enumerated one . . . and from the point of view of Lord over all there are no names . . . and from the point of view the of the Cause above the high the emission of its light is neither wanting nor superfluous . . . but as the Cause above the high, there is nothing above it that can add to or subtract from it . . . it can add to and subtract from all of them, and there is nothing that can add to or subtract from it."[449] In place of the original "created one" we have here "the named one," which suits the subject matter better. Ibn Gabirol's expression "For they know not what it is," which is based on the verse, Exodus 15: 16, about the manna, is turned in the *Tikkunei ha-Zohar* into a mystical interpretation of the verse: "It [i.e., the *Shekhinah*] is called 'what' (*mah*) from the viewpoint of *Hokhmah* . . . and it refers through this *mah* to the Cause above the high: 'for they knew not that it was *mah*.' "[450] The author of the main body of the Zohar used the same method with another expression of Ibn Gabirol's. In the *Keter Malkhut* (10) we have: "And these fourfold elements have one principle, And one origin, and thence they emerge and assume new forms, And thence they separate and become four main elements (lit., heads)." This is cited in the Zohar in the form of a mystical interpretation of Genesis 2: 10: "Come and see: the [supernal] fire, air, water and dust are all bound inextricably together, without any division, and when this dust produces subsequently [the material elements] they are not bound together like the supernal ones, as it is said: 'and from thence it was parted and became four heads.' "[451] In passages dealing with the doctrine of the Godhead and the doctrine of the soul the Zohar frequently uses the term "Soul of soul," which comes from the *Keter Malkhut* (4): "Thou livest but not through soul or spirit, For Thou art Soul of soul."[452]

Ibn Gabirol's philosophical work *Mekor Ḥayyim* (*Fons Vitae*) did not influence the Zohar directly,[453] but it is possible to discern the traces of other philosophical books. The Zohar's interpretation of *tohu va-vohu* ("waste and void") as form and matter is without any doubt based on Rabbi Abraham bar Hayya in his *Sefer Hegyon ha-Nefesh* (The Meditation of the Soul).[454] Judah Halevi's *Kuzari* had a great influence on the early kabbalists and this influence can be seen also in the teachings of the Zohar.[455] However, for present purposes, I shall content myself with just two examples where the direct literary connection is quite clearly demonstrable. The statement in the *Kuzari*[456] that "Israel among the nations is like the heart among the limbs" is quoted in that form in the Zohar:[457] "Israel among the other peoples is like the heart among the limbs." The development of this idea in the *Kuzari* through an elucidation of the simile is also repeated in the Zohar.[458] In the *Kuzari*[459] the "companion" is asked: "Do you know why Jews move to and fro when they read Hebrew?" and he replies, "they say it is because the natural heat arouses them." But this reply is refuted and another one is substituted. In the Zohar[460] the question is put to Rabbi Simeon ben Yohai by Rabbi Abba and the reply that is rejected in the *Kuzari* is cited in mystical guise as the answer of Rabbi Simeon: "The souls of Israel are hewn from the sacred flickering lamp . . . when they say a word from the Torah the light flickers and they cannot restrain themselves, but move to and fro from side to side like the light of a lamp."

The writings of Maimonides, particularly the *Sefer ha-Madda* (Book of Knowledge) from the *Mishneh Torah*, and the *Moreh Nevukhim* (The Guide for the Perplexed), had a considerable influence on the Zohar, and especially on the *Midrash ha-Ne'elam*. One of the most striking examples is the enumeration of the names of the ten companies of angels by Maimonides.[461] In the *Midrash ha-Ne'elam*[462] the names are all the same, and in the two passages in the *Raya Mehemna* and the *Tikkunei ha-Zohar*[463] the name *Keruvim* is changed to *Elim* in one and to *Shina'anim* in the other, and in the second passage the name *Malakhim* is changed to *Tarshishim*. Of particular interest is the name *Ishim*, which can only come from philosophical literature, where it is identical to the Active Intellect. In the *Sitrei Torah*[464] it is said that when the child is formed in the womb the body is constructed through the force derived from *Ishim*. This idea is taken from Maimonides:[465] "And God gives to each body a form that is suited to it by means of the tenth angel, which is the form called *Ishim*." Another example that shows the undoubted influence of Maimonides is the allegorical view taken of the legend concerning the eating of leviathan.[466] Maimonides writes:[467] "This is what is meant by the rabbinic statement that they enjoy the radiance of the Divine Presence—they know and perceive some of the truth of the Holy One, blessed be He, that they did not know when they were in corporeal form in the lower world . . . and the sages metaphorically called this goodness prepared for the righteous 'a meal.'" And in the *Midrash ha-Ne'elam* it is said:[468] "But the deserving righteous are fed until they achieve perfect perception. And there is no eating or drinking but this, and this is the meal and the eating." The descriptions of paganism in the Zohar as the worship of the hosts of heaven, bound up with necromancy and idolatry, are taken from Maimonides' accounts of the Sabaean sect in the *Moreh Nevukhim* and the *Sefer ha-Madda*.[469]

The interpretations of scriptural verses in the Zohar bear the impress of medieval exegesis. In every section we find a great number of comments taken from the well-known exegetes, either in their original form, or with slight variations, or paraphrastically.[470] I shall select as examples a few characteristic quotations from the writings of the more important commentators, Rashi, Rabbi Abraham ibn Ezra, and Rabbi David Kimchi.[471] (1) Zohar:[472] "'*Hava*' (come) always implies an invitation." Rashi:[473] "Every *havah* is an invitation." (2) Zohar:[474] "'They went out with them' (Genesis 11: 31). It should have said 'with him.' . . . But [it means that] Terah and Lot went out with Abram and Sarai." Rashi: "'They went out with them.' Terah and Abram went out with Lot and Sarai." (3) Zohar:[475] "'Put away the strange gods' (Genesis 35: 2). These are the ones they took from Shechem." Rashi: "'The strange gods' that you have from the spoil of Shechem." (4) Zohar:[476] "'Who redeems' (Genesis 48: 16). It should have said 'who redeemed.' What does 'who redeems' mean? [It means] that he is always by man's side and never leaves a righteous man." Rashi: "'The angel who redeems me'—an angel who is usually sent to me in my need." (5) Zohar:[477] "Rabbi Judah said: Since it says 'the earth was corrupt' what is the point of 'before God' (Genesis 6: 11)? The answer is that since they committed their sins openly, in the sight of all, so it was 'before God'. Rabbi Jose said: I say the opposite. At first, it was 'before God' in that they did not act openly. They acted 'before God' but not before mankind." Ibn Ezra: "Some say that 'before God' means publicly. And others say that it means that they were corrupt in private, and in hidden matters that were known to God alone." Rabbi Abraham ibn Ezra rejects both views, and in the Zohar they become the divided opinions of two *tannaim*. (6) Zohar:[478] "I am who I am, but Esau is your firstborn." Ibn Ezra gives the identical interpretation of this verse (Genesis 27: 19). (7) Zohar: "Why was it called *ziz*?[479] Beeing seen, to be looked at. Since it was there to be seen by people it was called *ziz*."[480] Ibn Ezra: "Perhaps it comes from the root *ziz*, something that can be seen." (8) Zohar:[481] "'He shall be brought to the priest' (Leviticus 13: 2). It does not say 'he shall come' but 'he shall be brought.' Whoever sees him (the leper) is obliged to bring him to the priest." Ibn Ezra: "'He shall be brought,' willingly or unwillingly, for whoever sees one of these signs [of leprosy] must compel him to come." (9) The statement in the *Idra Rabba*[482] about the position of wisdom, discernment, and knowledge (*hokhmah, binah, da'at*) in the *materiae* of the three cavities of the skull is based on Ibn Ezra.[483] (10) Zohar:[484] "Is there such a thing as a 'dismissed sea' (*yam nigrash*—Isaiah 57: 20—a literal rendering of the phrase usually translated as 'a troubled sea'). Yes, when the sea departs from its usual custom and moves without control, it is as if 'dismissed' and uprooted from its place . . . 'And its waters cast up mire and dirt.' Its waters throw out all the mire and dirt of the sea on to its shores." David Kimchi: "The interpretation of 'like a *yam nigrash*' is like the sea that is dismissed to the shore all the time . . . and when it comes to the shore its waters fetch up the mire and dirt from the sea-floor to the dry land." (11) Zohar:[485] "The end of this verse does not match the beginning, for it is written 'I chose no city' and then 'but I chose David.' What has one to do with the other? It should have said 'but I chose Jerusalem.' However, when the Holy One, blessed be He, wanted to build a city, He looked first at the leader of the prospective inhabitants of that city, and then He would build the city and bring in the people. That is why it is written 'I chose no city,' until I saw that David was going to be the shepherd of Israel." David Kimchi: " 'But I chose David.' Since it started by saying 'I chose no city' it should have continued 'but I chose Jerusalem.' But the interpretation is as follows: I did not proclaim My choice of Jerusalem until I had chosen David to lead My people Israel." (12) Zohar:[486] " 'Behold, I cannot speak' (Jeremiah 1: 6), i.e., in order to proclaim anything or reprove the world with the holy spirit." David Kimchi: "And as to his saying 'I cannot speak' this refers to words of reproof."

We can also find clear traces in the Zohar of early mystical literature, from the first centuries of the medieval period, such as the *Sefer Yezirah* and the *hekhalot* literature written by exponents of the *Ma'aseh Merkavah*. The influence of the *Sefer Yezirah* is not confined merely to technical terms like the "32 paths of wisdom," "voice," "spirit," "speech," and the "six dimensions (*shesh kezavot*)," which are the basic materials of the whole kabbalistic literary corpus, but can be seen in idioms taken directly without doubt from the *Sefer Yezirah*. For example, "[Abraham] looked, weighed and put together"[487]; "with the fingers of the hands, five against five."[488] The *Sefer Yezirah* is cited by name, and even attributed to the patriarch Abraham.[489] The influence of the *hekhalot* literature is very marked in the descriptions of the Chariot and the palaces, and in the angelology of the Zohar.[490] There are also passages where the author tries to imitate the style of the exponents of the *hekhalot*. A good example of this is the Hebrew passage in the Midrash to Ruth,[491] which begins: "Rabbi Nehunya said: A son of the exalted one spoke to me when I went up to the firmament. . . ."

The most important area of research into the sources of the Zohar concerns the influence of kabbalistic literature from the end of the twelfth century and from the thirteenth century. From a general ideological point of view one can see the position of the Zohar in the history of kabbalah as an intermingling of two main currents: the speculative kabbalah of Rabbi Isaac the Blind and the circle of his disciples in Gerona, and the gnostic kabbalah of the Castilian kabbalists led by Rabbi Isaac Hacohen and Rabbi Moses of Burgos.[492] However, to establish direct literary connections on the basis of detailed philological proof requires minute analysis, because a great deal of the material recurs in different sources, and in the Zohar itself they usually appear in the author's own free version with many alterations and additions. There is room for much more research in this area, for only a small part of pre-Zoharic kabbalah has been investigated so far, and no systematic comparison between the Zohar and the writings of the earlier kabbalists has ever been attempted. However, even before the completion of such research, it is possible to note a considerable number of kabbalistic sources that the author of the Zohar certainly made use of. We can see the influence of the *Sefer ha-Bahir*, written in the form we have it sometime in the twelfth century, in many passages in the Zohar, particularly in the symbolism of the *sefirot*. The appearance in the Zohar of the late *amora* Rabbi Rehumai as one of the great mystical sages also demonstrates a direct connection with the *Sefer ha-Bahir*. Among the kabbalists of Gerona we must pay special attention to Nachmanides and his two companions, Rabbi Ezra and Rabbi Azriel. There is no doubt as to the influence of Nachmanides' commentaries to the Torah and to Job, and of the section on reward in his *Torat ha-Adam*. Here, for example, are a number of parallels from his commentary to the Torah, where the direct connection is obvious without any need to enter into explanations of the ideas involved. (1) Zohar:[493] "This is what He said, 'If you do [your work] well, shall it not be lifted up' (Genesis 4: 6)? What does *se'et* (lifted up) mean? It means 'superiority,' as in *yeter se'et* (Genesis 49: 3), since the firstborn always takes precedence." Nachmanides: "My view is that it means: if you do well you shall have superiority (*yeter se'et*) over your brothers, for you are the firstborn." One should note that Nachmanides designates this interpretation as his own original view, not necessarily held by other commentators. (2) Zohar:[494] "What does 'according to the cry of it' (Genesis 18: 21) mean? This is the decree of judgment which always demands justice." Nachmanides: " 'If they have done altogether according to the cry of it, which is come unto Me,' according to strict judgment they will be destroyed." (3) Zohar:[495] " 'And if you (*at*) deal thus with me' (Numbers 11: 15). It should not have said *at* (the feminine form) but *attah* (the masculine form). However, he refers to the place where death rules, and that place is feminine." The reference is to the *Shekhinah* (the Divine Presence), which is also the attribute of Justice mentioned by Nachmanides: "And the real truth is that 'if you deal thus with me' is spoken in connection with the attribute of Justice."

The commentary to the Song of Songs, written by Rabbi Ezra and printed in the name of Nachmanides, is one of the most important sources of the Zohar.[496] The following examples should be noted from the point of view of verbal identity. (1) Zohar:[497] "This is the significance of the letter *bet* (through) 'Through wisdom shall a house be built' (Proverbs 24: 3), and it is also written 'King Solomon made himself a palanquin of the wood of Lebanon' (Song of Songs 3: 9). This 'palanquin' is the ordering of the lower world from the upper world, for before the Holy One, blessed be He, created the world, His name was concealed within it . . . until He determined to create the world. Then He sketched it and built it, but did not complete it until He had wrapped Himself in a cloak of the supernal splendor of thought (i.e., Wisdom) and He created it, and brought forth great supernal cedars from the light of that supernal splendor. . . . This is why it is written 'of the wood of Lebanon', for it was from these that He made His palanquin." Rabbi Ezra:[498] " 'King Solomon made himself a palanquin of the wood of Lebanon,' that is to say, through the outpouring and luster of Wisdom he made the light to shine, and it emanated from it. This is what is meant by *Bereshit Rabbah*: 'Whence was the light created? The Holy One, blessed be He, wrapped Himself in a garment, and made its luster shine from one end of the world to the other.' The 'garment' was the preparation for Wisdom's emanation, which encompassed everything, and 'being wrapped' means that He received splendor from the outpouring . . . and of this Solomon said, 'of the wood of Lebanon'—thence came the emanation of all." (2) Zohar:[499] " 'My beloved is mine, and I am his, that feedeth among the roses' (Song of Songs 2: 16). Who made me my beloved's and who made my beloved mine? The fact that he rules his world with roses . . . Another interpretation: 'that feedeth among the roses (*shoshanim*)'—that rules his world with six years (*shesh shanim*)." Rabbi Ezra:[500] " 'My beloved is mine and I am his, that feedeth among the roses'—who rules his world with six things." (3) Zohar:[501] "Come and see, [we may deduce this] from the smell of the incense, some of whose ingredients are red and some white; for example, frankincense, which is white, and flowing myrrh, which is red, and the scent arises from both the red and the white." Rabbi Ezra:[502] " 'Myrrh and frankincense'—two things that are contrasted in appearance; one is red and the other white."

Traces of the writings of Rabbi Azriel, particularly his commentary to the liturgy, which is extant in manuscript,[503] are especially noticeable in the explanations of the purpose of particular areas, for example, the mystery of the Amen,[504] and the mystery of the various blessings.[505] One could cite a large number of conclusive parallel passages, but they would need a detailed analysis and explanation, and this is not the place for that. The source of the names of the palaces that occur in the Zohar, and their identification with the *sefirot*, is apparently Rabbi Azriel's commentary to the liturgy.[506] Rabbi Ezra's interpretation of the *aggadot*, as well as possibly that of Rabbi Azriel, had an influence on the Zohar. Here I ought to cite one passage, which is derived from Rabbi Ezra's commentary to the *aggadot*, but which can definitely be established as taken by the author of the Zohar from the expanded version of Rabbi Todros Abulafia, a contemporary of Rabbi Moses de Leon. Zohar:[507] "But the secret of the matter is that we have learned, 'Let a man always enter a distance of two doors, etc.'. . . This is an allusion to the statement of David, 'Lift up your heads, O ye gates' (Psalm 24: 7). These are *Ma'on* and *Makhon*,[508] which are in the innermost recesses at the start of the degrees (i.e., the *sefirot*) *Ḥesed* (Love) and *Paḥad* (Fear), and these are the 'doors of the world'. Therefore a man must when praying concentrate on the Holy of Holies, which is the Holy Name, and then recite his prayer. And these, the two crowns, are the two doors." Rabbi Ezra:[509] " 'A distance of two doors'—you already know that the 'two doors' are an allusion to *Ma'on* and *Me'onah*." And elsewhere[510] we have: " 'doors of the world'—he calls the crowns 'doors' because they are the beginning." Rabbi Todros:[511] "Here there is a reference to the statement of King David, peace be upon him, 'Lift up your heads, O ye gates,' which are *Ma'on* and *Makhon*, which are the innermost recesses, the beginning of the seven *sefirot*, which are the 'doors' of the world. He wished to say that a man, when praying, should concentrate on the Holy of Holies, which is the heaven of heavens." It is perfectly obvious that the passage in the Zohar is an Aramaic translation, with minor modifications, of Rabbi Todros. At one of the most important points in the Zohar's doctrine of the divine we can see the influence of the *Sefer Ginat Egoz*[512] by Rabbi Joseph Gikatilla, who was also a contemporary of Rabbi Moses de Leon.

Obviously this multiplicity of sources is not mentioned at all in the Zohar, apart from some particular or general references to rabbinic statements and a few allusions to the *Sefer Yezirah*. In contrast to this, many passages are quoted from various strange sources that never existed at all. Some bear the names of ancient biblical characters like *Sifra de-Adam Kedama'ah* (Book of Adam), *Sifra de-Ḥanokh* (Book of Enoch), *Matnita de-Bezalel* (Mishnah of Bezalel), *Sifra de-Shlomo Malka* (Book of King Solomon) or *Sifra de-Ḥokhmata de-Shlomo Malka* (Book of the Wisdom of King Solomon) or *Razei de-Atvan de Shlomo Malka* (Secrets of the Letters of King Solomon). Some are attributed to sages in the Tamud and the Zohar, such as *Sifra de-Rav Hamnuna Sava, Sifra de-Rav Yesa Sava, Matnita de-Rabbi Eleazar ben Arakh, Atvan Gelifan de-Rabbi Eleazar* (The Engraved

Letters of Rabbi Eleazar), and *Sifra de-Aggadata de-Vei Rav*. The *Sifra de-Ashmodai Malka* (Book of King Ashmodai) and similar titles are also quoted. Other sources of the same kind are cited that have no personal association, such as *Sifra de-Aggadata*, *Sifra de-Harshei* (Book of the Sorcerers), *Sifra de-Hokhmata Ila'ah di-Vnei Kedem* (Book of Heavenly Wisdom of the Sons of the East), and several passages are quoted from general sources, such as *sifrei kadmaei* (ancient books), *marei sitrei Torah* (masters of the secrets of the Torah). A few of these sources like the Book of Enoch and the Book of Wisdom of King Solomon are known by name, but the actual passages quoted in the Zohar do not come from the books we know. But, for the most part, the actual titles themselves have been invented. It is clear that the author wanted to conceal his real sources, and so fabricated imaginary works instead.

The defenders of the antiquity of the Zohar respond to these criticisms with one general counterargument, which can be couched in two ways: (1) Some tried to reverse the relationship, maintaining that it was not the Zohar that was influenced by late sources, but that the late sources drew upon the Zohar. Those who held this view openly acknowledged the fact that the Zohar did not actually appear before the end of the thirteenth century. But they argued that rabbinic circles possessed oral traditions about Zoharic teachings, or else had access to scrolls containing mysteries.[513] (2) Others maintained a more cautious position, and argued for the existence of hidden sources that influenced both the Zohar and later writings. One of the supporters of this view writes as follows about the idea in the *Kuzari* that "Israel among the nations is like the heart among the limbs," which is repeated almost word for word in the Zohar: "Judah Halevi also grasped this idea which was borrowed from the academy of the sages of truth, for the philosophers also made use of it in their own way. . . . It would appear that there was current in the academy of the homilists a saying such as: 'Israel is the heart of the world. But who is the heart of Israel?—The Holy One, blessed be He.'"[514] In connection with the verses from the *Keter Malkhut* that occur in the Zohar, he writes in astonishment, "This matter is very perplexing. For one cannot believe that the sages of truth took verses, which as they stand in the *Keter Malkhut* seem to require a literal interpretation, and then built lofty towers upon them. And even if we say that the basic material was known to the inner circles of the sages, can we also maintain that the details of the versification were known too, and were used by each as he thought fit?"[515] From a scientific standpoint the answer to this problem is quite clear. There is no reason or foundation for believing that either the stylistic idioms or the scriptural interpretations or the philosophical ideas that I have quoted, and that are found in the books of later scholars, came from ancient writings or traditions that existed in the days of the so-called ancient sages of the Zohar. On the contrary, all the evidence points clearly to the fact that their real source is in later writings. The Zohar's method of transforming lucid material into esoteric material was customary throughout kabbalistic literature, and there is no occasion for surprise here at all.

Among the more particular counterarguments should be noted the idea that amoraic statements quoted in the Zohar in the names of *tannaim* were in effect the views of *tannaim* that had been passed down from one generation to another and been repeated in the Talmud in the name of *amoraim*.[516] If we were dealing with only isolated examples, and with statements whose contents did not point to their late date, such a view could be accepted as a distinct possibility. But when we are faced with a large number of such statements in the Zohar, which for the most part are undoubtedly late, containing, for example, references to events in the lives of the *amoraim*, then this view is seen to be untenable.

Research into the sources of the Zohar, from which we can also gain a picture of the author's intellect and religious inspiration, helps us considerably in fixing the precise date of the Zohar's composition. For this purpose we have to establish the date of the latest sources of which traces can be found in the Zohar. These are Nachmanides' Commentary to the Torah, the *Sefer Ginat Egoz* by Rabbi Joseph Gikatilla, and the *Sefer Ozar ha-Kavod* by Rabbi Todros Abulafia. Nachmanides' commentary was completed around the time of his death in Israel, about 1270. The *Sefer Ginat Egoz* was written in 1274. The *Sefer Ozar ha-Kavod* was written, it would seem, about 1280. The use that the author of the Zohar makes of this book is particularly important, because it contains in itself certain passages from the *Midrash ha-Ne'elam*.[517] One might, at first glance, argue, albeit without any scientific foundation, that Rabbi Todros had cited a passage from the Zohar in a Hebrew translation. But the fact that the passage I have quoted originated in the *Commentary to the Aggadot* of Rabbi Ezra of Gerona completely destroys this idea. Consequently, from the quotation from Rabbi Todros that occurs in the Zohar we may deduce that certain sections of the Zohar were composed after the appearance of passages from the *Midrash ha-Ne'elam*. This conclusion is important not only in establishing the date of the Zohar in general, but also in fixing the order in which the separate sections were composed.

c. Evidence for the Antiquity of the Zohar

Literature in defense of the Zohar's antiquity contains some positive evidence in support of this position, apart from the attempts to undermine and destroy the critical arguments. This evidence is sparse and restricted in scope, and in fact has no substance at all, as we shall see. But it is precisely because we have accepted a scientific approach that we should describe and sift this evidence, and we shall find that it will also demonstrate the weakness of those who maintain the antiquity of the Zohar.

The most common, and, at first sight, the strongest evidence is the view that the influence of the Zohar can be discerned in early sources, and certainly in books that were written before the appearance of the Zohar at the end of the thirteenth century. Kunitz[518] drew up a detailed list in which he cited examples from the *Targum Yerushalmi*, the *geonim*, commentators to the Talmud, and many codifiers, all of which in his view showed the influence of the Zohar. Rabbi David Luria and Benamozegh also shared this view. Luria[519] relied mainly on the responsa of the *geonim*, which we have already dealt with elsewhere,[520] and Benamozegh argued[521] that several rabbinic expositions, particularly the *aggadot* of the Jerusalem Talmud, could not be understood without reference to statements in the Zohar, and that enigmatic passages in Ibn Ezra and Nachmanides, allusions in the *Kuzari*, and even Maimonides' strictures against the mystics, necessitate the view that these rabbis were familiar with at least some of the secrets of the Torah contained in the Zohar.

An examination of these arguments shows that the evidence is purely illusory. Some of it is based on literary misapprehensions, as with Luria's theory that the Zoharic references in the responsa of the *geonim* are founded on fact, or Benamozegh's view that the allusion to the *Mekhilta* of Rabbi Simeon ben Yohai, mentioned by Nachmanides, is to texts of the Zohar,[522] whereas in actual fact it refers to a halakhic midrash that has since come to light and been published. The exponents of this view were again in error when they took every mystical reference that did in fact originate in earlier times, as a sign of the Zohar's influence. However, most of their evidence is based not on error but on pure sophistry. This especially affects those matters which do have a direct connection with the Zohar, but in precisely the reverse direction from that maintained by the defenders of the Zohar's antiquity. For example, Kunitz cites laws and customs that the codifiers certainly did not take from veiled traditions in the Zohar, but that the author of the Zohar himself took from the writings of the codifiers, in order to insert them into his mystical teachings. Material of this sort is very useful because it supports the evidence for the late date of the Zohar.[523]

They attempted at several points to reverse the critical arguments and to use them as evidence for the Zohar's antiquity. The fact that the Zohar was written in Aramaic, which Modena[524] considered to be one of his strongest arguments, was taken by Franck[525] as showing that the book was written in antiquity, when Aramaic was still understood by the masses. Others[526] pointed out that the quotation of scriptural verses according to a nontraditional text, of laws in an unaccepted form, and of *aggadot* that go contrary to the common rabbinic *aggadot*,[527] demonstrates that the author of the Zohar must have been one of the early rabbis, because otherwise he would not have dared to alter the pattern that the rabbis had established. To submit evidence of this type shows considerable naiveté. If a medieval kabbalist wanted to attribute his book to the rabbis of the Talmud, he would, not surprisingly, write it in Aramaic in order to give it an aura of antiquity. The fact that at the time of Rabbi Simeon ben Yohai the rabbis wrote in Hebrew, and not in Aramaic, does not invalidate this view. Franck argued[528] that if the book had been written as an intentional forgery the author would have taken care *not* to write in Aramaic; but, on the contrary, the fact that it *is* written in Aramaic shows how ignorant the author was of historical conditions. The remaining evidence implies a very strange view of the author of the Zohar, who would have taken great care not to stray, God forbid, in any way from the fixed, received tradition. But the very essence of pseudepigraphic writing is itself a departure from received tradition, and, indeed, from historical fact. As for the text of the scriptural verses, we may assume that most of the variants are due to imprecise quotation, either because of sheer forgetfulness or because of a variant reading that the author had in his possession.[529] However, it is clear that, in general, the author of the Zohar did not mind altering earlier rabbinic statements to suit his own mystical ideas and expositions, and not even fixed halakhic legal material could curb his spirits.

Milzahagi[530] cites evidence of a more particular kind, which is based on the Zohar's failure to mention certain specific kabbalistic features. These are: the terms *kabbalah* and *sefirot*; the reference to the first *sefirah* by the name *Keter* or *Keter Elyon*; the *zazahot* as hidden forces within *En-Sof*;[531] belief in transmigration of the soul as a fixed punishment, and especially transmigration into both domestic and wild animals; *gematriot*, which regard certain letters, exceptionally, as units of tens and hundreds; and vowels and accents. His argument was that these matters are to be found in those sections which he himself acknowledged to be late, and the fact that they are not mentioned in the other sections shows that these must come from an earlier period. The facts as he presents them are for the most part correct, but the deductions he makes are without foundation. It is true that apart from the *Raya Mehemna* and the *Tikkunei ha-Zohar*, and a few passages from the *Midrash ha-Ne'elam*, there is no mention of the terms *kabbalah* and *sefirot*, nor of *azilut*, which Milzahagi failed to mention. But it would seem that the real reason for this was the author's realization that these terms in particular were really modern, and so he used other terms in their place, like *mehemanuta* (faith) instead of *kabbalah*, *kitrin* (crowns), and *dargot* (steps, degrees), and other terms[532] to indicate the *sefirot*, and *amshakhuta* instead of *azilut*, but even these were part of thirteenth-century kabbalistic vocabulary. The doctrine of the *zazahot*, mentioned in the *Tikkunei ha-Zohar*, originated in the responsa attributed to the *geonim*, and so Milzahagi tried to deduce from this that the main body of the Zohar preceded the geonic period. But the truth is that these responsa are forgeries and were written at the beginning of the thirteenth century, or, at the very earliest, at the end of the twelfth century.[533] We must say, in addition, that the whole essence of the argument is invalid from the start, because the author of the Zohar did not put every single kabbalistic doctrine into his book. He selected those ideas which suited his temperament and to which he could give his assent.[534] Therefore his treatment of the belief in transmigration does not prove anything. And we can say the same of the *gematriot*, which Milzahagi mentions, and which occur only in the *Tikkunei ha-Zohar*, for there was no obligation or necessity for every kabbalist to use them; and one could give many examples of kabbalists, both before and after Rabbi Moses de Leon, who do not mention this type of *gematria* at all. The use of the name *Keter* for the first *sefirah* can also be seen in the same light, although here Milzahagi's argument is factually incorrect as well. His theory is that the author of the Zohar refrained from using this term because in his view the *Keter Elyon* was not one of the ten *sefirot*. But even if this theory were correct it would still not constitute proof of the Zohar's antiquity. On the contrary, this very subject was one of the points at issue in thirteenth-century kabbalah, and the attachment of the Zohar's author to one particular viewpoint would establish his position in the history of kabbalah. But the fact is that the attitude of the Zohar is different. *Keter Elyon* is considered to be one of the *sefirot*, as a primeval force indeed, closely connected with *En-Sof*, as I shall explain later,[535] and the name also occurs in a number of places. Milzahagi himself cites those passages[536] in which *Keter Elyon* is discussed, but he tries to take them out of their literal context. As to the vowels and the accents, I have already shown[537] that they are objects of speculation throughout the Zohar.

Other evidence, which seems at first sight to have some scientific foundation, is based on the existence of ancient ideas in the Zohar. Christian scholars have maintained[538] that the approximation of some ideas in the Zohar, particularly in connection with its treatment of God, to the principles of Christian belief, proves its early date. This argument is based on the view that in the Middle

Ages there was no spiritual contact whatsoever between Judaism and Christianity. However, modern historical research has completely disproved this idea. On the other hand, Christianizing tendencies that they attributed to the Zohar are just nonexistent, and are merely the fruit of the Christian kabbalists' imagination. Evidence based on the Zohar's similarity to Philo[539] also belongs to this category. There is indeed a certain similarity, particularly in the allegorical method of interpreting Scripture, which is to be found especially in the *Midrash ha-Ne'elam*. But the author of the Zohar is merely following the customary medieval philosophical practice, which was apparently influenced in an indirect way by Philo. This is also true of the specifically Philonic ideas, which reached the Zohar through Neoplatonic philosophical channels. A weightier argument is that based on the Zohar's similarity to gnostic literature from the second and third centuries. Since these gnostic writings were unknown in the Middle Ages, an attempt has been made to prove from this similarity that the author of the Zohar lived at the time of the gnostic movement, or that the ideas in the Zohar antedated gnosticism and had some influence upon it.[540] The discovery of this similarity to gnosticism has an important bearing on the study of Zoharic doctrines,[541] but there is no need to conclude from it that the Zohar is a work of antiquity. On the one hand, it is quite certain that definitely gnostic ideas did develop in kabbalah without any direct literary connection with ancient gnosticism. This is abundantly clear from the striking similarity of Lurianic kabbalah to Manichaeism, which certainly cannot be attributed to any historico-literary relationship between them. On the other hand, there is no doubt that elements of ancient gnostic ideas did penetrate the world of kabbalistic thought in the twelfth and thirteenth centuries.

Finally, we must deal with the evidence that apologists have adduced in order to justify the tradition that the Zohar originated in the circle of Rabi Simeon ben Yohai and his disciples. Kunitz[542] collected a large number of statements by Rabbi Simeon ben Yohai and his pupils, from the Talmud and the midrashim, in order to show that they had some connection, remote or close, with passages in the Zohar. Most of these statements do, in fact, have some material connection with the Zohar, but they do not afford one shred of evidence that would point to the Zohar's antiquity. Obviously, among the rabbinic statements from which the author of the Zohar deduced kabbalistic mysteries were some attributed to Rabbi Simeon ben Yohai, and he even went out of his way to give them a mystical interpretation. Kaminka adopted what would seem to be a more scientific approach. First of all, he tried to show that from Rabbi Simeon ben Yohai's authentic pronouncements one could piece together a spiritual image of him as a master of esoteric doctrines.[543] But when, after even the most far-fetched and ingenious interpretations, he found it difficult to discover any justification for his thesis, he started to attribute to Rabbi Simeon ben Yohai statements by the *amora* Rabbi Johanan that had no connection with Rabbi Simeon at all. Here are two examples of the so-called mystical statements of Rabbi Simeon ben Yohai: (1) "Rabbi Simeon ben Yohai said: It is permitted to save the idolater from sin even at the cost of his life. We may deduce this from an *a fortiori* argument. If it is permitted to save someone, about to afflict injury to a person, from sin at the cost of his life, it should be even more permitted to do this in the case of injury to the Almighty."[544] Kaminka discovers in the words "injury to the Almighty" the mystical idea, common in the Zohar, that man's transgressions inflict injury on the Almighty. But Rabbi Simeon ben Yohai is talking about idolatry, which may be designated as an "injury to the Almighty" without any mystical connotation at all, whereas Kaminka implicitly attributed[545] to him the idea of "murder as an injury to the Almighty," even though Rabbi Simeon in his statement stresses the fact that murder is "injury to a person," that is, injury to man alone, in contradistinction to idolatry which is "injury to the Almighty." (2) "Rabbi Simeon ben Yohai said: Three commandments[546] were enjoined upon Israel on entering the land of Israel, but they are practiced both in the land and outside the land, and it is right that they should be practiced."[547] This obviously legalistic statement proves, according to Kaminka,[548] that Rabbi Simeon ben Yohai attributes to the commandments "a spiritual and eternal relevance," similar to the mystical concept of the commandments in the Zohar! Once he had "proved" with this kind of reasoning the general mystical tone of Rabbi Simeon's statements, Kaminka went on to quote in another article[549] specific evidence that several of the statements of Rabbi Simeon, Rabbi Eleazar, and Rabbi Johanan could not be understood without reference to the mysteries of the Zohar. In order to give some idea of this evidence I shall quote just one example: "Rabbi Johanan said in the name of Rabbi Eleazar, the son of Rabbi Simeon: Whoever wishes to preserve his property should plant an *adar* there."[550] The precise meaning of *adar* is not clear, but it is absolutely certain that it must be some kind of tree, and the word is used a few times in this sense in both Hebrew and Aramaic (*idra*).[551] In contrast to this Kaminka thinks[552] that this statement conceals a mystical idea which can be understood through the *Idrot* in the Zohar, to which the word *adar* refers!

To sum up: those who believe the Zohar to be an ancient work have not succeeded in producing a shred of proof to support their claim. The critical approach has established a large and decisive body of proof that conflicts with their rather slender evidence and provides remarkable testimony of its late date from a number of different aspects, as I have shown in some detail. Every attempt to refute or undermine the basic critical arguments has failed, and the conclusions that may be deduced from these arguments remain completely justified.

V. VARIOUS SOLUTIONS

a. Later Redaction

The critical arguments, even those which were discussed at a very early date, such as the problem of the reference to *amoraim* and the quotation of amoraic statements, are sufficiently weighty to disprove the popular belief that the whole Zohar in the form we have it today was written by Rabbi Simeon ben Yohai and his disciples. However, it is possible to maintain this "pure" belief by advancing supernatural and superrational arguments that are beyond the range of scientific enquiry. I have already touched upon this point,[553] but here is an example from Rabbi Nahum of Chernobyl:[554] "How can man be exalted

by means of the Torah? Only by coming to the hidden light, that he might see
by means of the hidden light what is to befall the world from one end to the
other . . . this means that both the present and the future are the same to
him . . . and so Rabbi Simeon ben Yohai was able to say in the Zohar what
Rabbah bar bar Hana was to say several centuries after him. Similarly Moses,
our teacher, peace be upon him, was able to see Rabbi Akiva who lived
thousands (!) of years after him. Through their learning they came to the
hidden light, where there is no distinction between present and future, for it is a
place where what is is on a par with what shall be."

But even in kabbalistic circles there were many who were not content with
this and tried to resolve the difficulties in a rational and factual way. The
solution they adopted was that the passages in the Zohar were first of all
transmitted orally, and in short disconnected manuscript texts. It was only
many generations after Rabbi Simeon ben Yohai that they were arranged in
bookform in the order of the scriptural readings; in the meantime additional
material had been included from later rabbis. In his explanation of the Zohar,
Rabbi Abraham Galante writes[555] with regard to a passage that contains a
chronological contradiction: "These are the words of the author (i.e., editor) of
the book from the geonic period, or of other scholars, who put together all the
statements written down by Rabbi Abba, who was Rabbi Simeon ben Yohai's
scribe; and they divided these statements up among the scriptural readings,
each verse in its own *parashah*, and they added the phrases such as 'Thus we have
learned,' etc. And there are many instances of this sort in the Zohar, and they
should all be explained in this way." This view is propounded in a far more
positive way by Rabbi Moses Hagiz:[556] "The truth shows that the author and
editor of the holy Zohar was indeed a very great man. The manuscripts came
into his possession, and the Heavens favoured him with the task of publishing
the mysteries of secret and exalted wisdom, and he arranged the texts in the
order of the scriptural readings. But neither Rabbi Simeon ben Yohai, God
forbid, nor Rabbi Abba put them in the order which we now have. This would
obviously be a mistake, and a stupid thing to believe,—like those who imagine
that we believe impossibilities, such as that the Talmud in the form we have it
was known to our patriarch, Abraham, a thing that has never entered the heads
of the people of the Lord 'bearing the store of seed' (Psalm 126: 6) We, praise be
to God, know the chain of transmission of the whole oral law—what was
transmitted, and how it was done. . . . Similarly, here, with this awesome
volume of the Zohar, we need not doubt that in the main the words are exactly
as they proceeded from the mouth of Rabbi Simeon ben Yohai and his
companions, and therefore whoever questions this is as if he were to question the
Divine Presence. However, it was the editor who rightly connected the texts
together as they came into his possession."

This approach was adopted by many other scholars who did research on the
Zohar and tried to prove its antiquity.[557] Sometimes they compared the
composition and redaction of the Zohar to the growth and completion of the
Talmud and of other great works in early Jewish literature. Rabbi Moses
Kunitz established a schematic parallel between the order of composition of the
sections of the Zohar on the one hand, and the Mishnah and the Jerusalem and
Babylonian Talmudim on the other. He writes:[558] "The Zohar was completed

by the disciples of [Rabbi Simeon ben Yohai's] disciples about eighty years
after his death, near to the time of the completion of the Mishnah. The *Raya
Mehemna*, the *Midrash ha-Ne'elam*, and the *Tikkunim* were completed by later
amoraim two hundred years after this, around the time of the completion of the
Jerusalem Talmud. And the *Zohar Ḥadash* was completed about a hundred
years later, that is, about three hundred years after the completion of the Zohar
itself, and that is at the time of the completion of the Babylonian Talmud. And
just as the later holy rabbis, who worked on the completion of all the sacred
books we have mentioned, were distinguished enough to add some of their own
traditions and interpretations to the words of the original authors, so here, these
scholars considered the sacred mysteries, and were also able to add their own
traditions and their own views, until the sacred books of Rabbi Simeon ben
Yohai were finally completed." Others tended to postdate the completion of the
Zohar to the Middle Ages, and there were even those who attributed the final
work of redaction to Rabbi Moses de Leon.

Those who maintain the late redaction theory try to prove thereby that the
Zohar as a whole is an ancient book that originated in the circle of Rabbi
Simeon ben Yohai. They are prepared to acknowledge a later element only
with regard to the outer literary form of the book, and to certain particular
passages. Their conclusions would completely strip the book of its pseudepigraphic character. This theory, however, cannot stand up to critical inquiry,
even in those areas which they particularly discussed in order to resolve the
dating problem, for example, the problem of the later rabbis that appear in the
book. These *amoraim* appear in the Zohar in the same environment as Rabbi
Simeon ben Yohai and their statements are put in his mouth and in the mouths
of his companions. What is more, this theory does not offer any response at all to
the other critical arguments, which have been outlined in the previous chapter
and which afford a large number of obvious indications of a late date that
cannot be accounted for simply by late editing. The truth is that this solution is
not a scientific attempt to deal with the problem, but merely an easy way of
avoiding the difficulties involved.

b. Composition over a Long Period of Time

In contrast to this unscientific solution to the problem we also find a scientific
approach, based on a serious consideration of the whole range of critical
arguments, which posits a different theory, championed by an important group
of Zohar scholars. According to this theory, the different sections of the Zohar
originated layer by layer in different ages, to be put together at a later period.
Within this generally agreed approach there are a number of differing opinions
in the group about the order in which the sections were composed, and also
about the precise date of their final redaction. I shall explain quite briefly the
main ideas.

The whole concept first found expression in the conclusions that Rabbi Jacob
Emden reached in his notes on the antiquity of the Zohar.[559] Emden
distinguished three (really four) main components of the Zoharic literature: (a)
the *Sefer ha-Zohar* itself made up of two elements; (b) the *Raya Mehemna* and the
Tikkunei ha-Zohar; (c) the *Midrash ha-Ne'elam*. In the *Sefer ha-Zohar* he designated

three sections, *Matnitin*, *Tosefta*, and the *Sitrei Torah*, as works written in the amoraic period on the basis of earlier traditions. But other sections, *Midrash ha-Zohar*, *Sifra di-Zeniuta*, the *Idrot*, *Sava*, and *Yanuka*, he considered to be the original creation of a scholar or a group of scholars from the amoraic, saboraic, or geonic periods. Either these ascribed their own opinions to Rabbi Simeon ben Yohai and his disciples, or they had the same names as the aforementioned *tannaim*, or the souls of the talmudic scholars had transmigrated to the members of this circle. The *Raya Mehemna* and the *Tikkunei ha-Zohar* were, in his view, written by a thirteenth-century Spanish kabbalist, Rabbi Moses de Leon, or the prophet from Avila, who is mentioned in the responsa[560] of Rabbi Solomon ben Adret as the author of a divinely inspired book on the secrets of the Torah. Or else they were the revelations of this prophet that were written down by Rabbi Moses de Leon. The *Midrash ha-Ne'elam* he considered to be a weak imitation of the earlier sections. In addition to this Emden suggested that each of these components contained a great deal of material added by correctors and copyists.

Milzahagi classified the various sections of the Zohar, and developed a comprehensive theory as to how they originated over a long period of time. In his view, most of the statements in the *Midrash ha-Zohar* associated with the names of Rabbi Simeon ben Yohai and the members of his circle mentioned in the *Idra Rabba* are genuinely old. These apart, only the *Sifra di-Zeniuta* and the *Idrot* can really be said to be early. The *Sifra di-Zeniuta*, which Rabbi Simeon ben Yohai himself quotes in the Zohar as an authority, was written before his time, while the *Idrot* are the explanations that Rabbi Simeon and his disciples gave of the *Sifra di-Zeniuta*. The other sections, whether anonymous like the *Matnitin* and the *Tosefta*, or introduced by the names of rabbis and presented in a narrative framework, such as the *Hekhalot*, *Sava*, and *Yanuka*, are later imitations. And this can be said with even more certainty of the *Raya Mehemna*, the *Tikkunei ha-Zohar*, and the *Midrash ha-Ne'elam*. The Zohar went through many editorial phases, which are meticulously spelled out in the *Zohorei Raviah*, until it was finally given the form in which we have it.

Franck thought[561] that the *Sifra di-Zeniuta* and the *Idrot* were ancient works that originated in their present form from Rabbi Simeon ben Yohai and his disciples. The other parts were edited at different times on the basis of traditions that emanated from Rabbi Simeon's circle, together with a good deal of additional material. Among the latter were complete sections from a later period. The complete contents of the whole Zohar were collected together and crystallized during the first to the seventh centuries.

Stern noted twelve main sections, apart from the *Tikkunei ha-Zohar* and the compositions in the *Zohar Hadash*. These were: (a) *Sifra di Zeniuta*, (b) *Idra Rabba*, (c) *Idra Zuta*, (d) *Midrash ha-Zohar*, (e) *Razin de-Razin*, (f) *Hekhalot*, (g) *Matnitin* and *Tosefta*, (h) *Raya Mehemna*, (i) *Sitrei Torah*, (j) *Midrash ha-Ne'elam*, (k) *Sava de-Mishpatim*, (l) *Yanuka* (a general title for all the narrative sections). The *Sifra di-Zeniuta* was an ancient work that apparently comprised the main themes transmitted in mystic circles. The *Idra Rabba* was written in Babylon as an explanation of the *Sifra di-Zeniuta*. The description of the assembly of Rabbi Simeon ben Yohai and his disciples is fictitious, but one may presume that the author was in possession of traditions from Rabbi Simeon's circle. The *Idra Zuta* was a redaction of ideas from the *Idra Rabba*, and it appears to have been written in the West. The *Midrash ha-Zohar* came into being and reached its present form gradually, over many generations, and it also contains ancient traditions. The form in which we have it today derives from about the end of the twelfth century. *Razin de-Razin* and the *Hekhalot* are medieval imitations of earlier sections. The remaining sections, which one could term "Zoharic apocrypha," were not written before the time of Rabbi Moses de Leon. The narrative passages, attached to the *Midrash ha-Zohar*, are the work of later editors, who were trying to enhance the midrash that had been handed down to them, and to fill in the gaps in the *parashiyot* of the Zohar.

These and similar views were based on various indications of a later or earlier date, in language and content, which seemed to separate the different sections from one another. However, most of the scholars who held these views realized themselves that here were clear signs of a thirteenth-century dating even in those sections which they considered to be early. And so they were forced to extract from them a large number of sentences and fragments and say that they were later additions. In so doing they demonstrated the weakness of their position, because these so-called additions are an integral part of the passages in which they occur, as can be seen from the examples already given in *The Foundations of Zohar Criticism*.[562] The complete fallacy of this differentiation between early and late in the Zohar is shown by the detailed results of Stern's own research. With the knife of a surgeon he cut the statements in the Zohar into small pieces, in order to discover the oldest elements. But in the process of operating he was compelled to excise material in the most haphazard way, and most of the sections that remained after surgery are mere rags and tatters. We must add to this the fact that since Stern did his research, other scholars have discovered new and unmistakable evidence of a late date, which highlights even more the artificiality of his analysis. So we find that internal indications of a late date in the Zoharic material are weighty enough to disprove the theory that any one section of the Zoharic literature was composed before the thirteenth century.

c. Composition in the Thirteenth Century

The view that the Zohar with all its various sections was a thirteenth century creation was established by studies undertaken by several scholars in the last century, especially Jellinek and Graetz, and it has been reaffirmed recently in a much more refined and authoritative way by the researches of Gershom Scholem. However, this general view still leaves a number of particular problems unresolved and these scholars have advanced different solutions to them: Is the Zohar a unified whole, that is, was it written by one particular kabbalist, or can one see in the various sections the creative product of several kabbalists? Is there any foundation for attributing the composition of the Zohar to Rabbi Moses de Leon or not? And if he was the author, what led him to write a pseudepigraphic work? What relationship is there between his Hebrew books and the Zohar, and what is the chronological order of composition of the different sections of the Zohar?

Graetz offered a straight and absolutely uncompromising solution to these questions. He accepted *in toto* the evidence relating to the composition of the Zohar contained in the diary of Rabbi Isaac of Acre, and pronounced unequivocally that the whole Zohar, without any differentiation whatsoever among the various sections, was the work of Rabbi Moses de Leon. His financial worries, and the failure of his Hebrew writings were, according to Graetz, the main reasons why he wrote the Zohar. He could not acquire wealth and honor through the books that appeared under his own name, and so he tried to obtain them by means of literary forgery and the dissemination of pseudepigraphic texts. Apart from the evidence of Rabbi Isaac of Acre, Graetz based himself mainly on the Zoharic idioms in Rabbi Moses de Leon's books. From these he deduced that his Hebrew books were written first.

The evidence from the writings of Rabbi Moses de Leon had been cited first by Jellinek, and it was he who established their chronological precedence over the Zohar. But he came to different conclusions.[563] In his view the sections of the Zohar were written by a group of kabbalists, led by Rabbi Moses de Leon. Emden's allusion[564] to the possibility that, in the composition of the *Raya Mehemna* and the *Tikkunei ha-Zohar*, there was some connection between Rabbi Moses de Leon and the prophet of Avila, prompted Jellinek to formulate a quite extraordinary theory concerning the way in which the whole Zohar was written. At first, Rabbi Moses de Leon's group tried to disseminate kabbalistic writings in Aramaic as if they were the revelations of an angel to a young man from Avila. The first such book was the *Sifra di-Zeniuta*, and this was the one that had come into the possession of Rabbi Solomon ben Adret as the book by the prophet of Avila, with the title *Sefer Pela'ot Hokhmah* (The Wonders of Wisdom). Once doubts had been cast on the veracity of these revelations, and Rabbi Solomon ben Adret had expressed his own opposition, Rabbi Moses de Leon and the members of his group turned to pseudepigraphy, and attributed their writings to Rabbi Simeon ben Yohai and his disciples. Several sections, which had already been written as prophetic revelations, were now recast and made to fit the new literary framework. An indication of the earlier form is still to be found in such phrases as "*petah hai yanuka* (this young boy began)," and the like, which occur at the beginning of a large number of passages in the Zohar. Also an allusion to the earlier name of the book, *Sefer Pela'ot Hokhmah*, is to be found in the later name *Sefer ha-Zohar ha-Mufla*, cited in the writings of Recanati. This fanciful theory, which has no foundation in fact, was accepted by some scholars as a serious scientific hypothesis.

Gershom Scholem, who covered the whole ground afresh, has proved conclusively that all the sections of the Zohar, including the *Sifra di-Zeniuta* and the *Midrash ha-Ne'elam*, thought to have been respectively the oldest and the newest parts, are one, in language and in content, and that they all bear the imprint of one and the same author. The only exceptions are the *Raya Mehemna* and the *Tikkunei ha-Zohar*, which have, from all points of view, a specific character of their own.[565] As a result of his study of the writings of Rabbi Moses de Leon, and his comparison of them with passages from the Zohar, he was able to establish that the main bulk of the Zohar was written by Rabbi Moses de Leon at the end of the thirteenth century. As for the *Raya Mehemna* and the *Tikkunei ha-Zohar*, he came to the conclusion that they were written at the beginning of the fourteenth century by an unknown Spanish kabbalist who apparently belonged to the school of Rabbi Moses de Leon. As to the question of the order in which the sections of the Zohar were written, Scholem demonstrated that it was in fact the *Midrash ha-Ne'elam* that was written first. The earliest quotations from the Zohar, which date from about 1280, are all taken from the *Midrash ha-Ne'elam*, and the internal connections between this and the other sections also prove its earlier date. The particular nature of the *Midrash ha-Ne'elam*, whose main characteristic is that it shows the strong and quite clear influence of philosophical literature, can be explained as the expression of the first stage of Rabbi Moses de Leon's spiritual development; that is to say, it makes a kind of transition from philosophical enlightenment to the gnostic-mythical kabbalah to be found in the main body of the Zohar.[566]

Looked at from a general point of view, Scholem's studies confirm the position of Graetz. His conclusions differ only with regard to the *Raya Mehemna* and the *Tikkunei ha-Zohar*. But when we come to the question of the motivation for writing the book and the evaluation of Rabbi Moses de Leon's pseudepigraphic activity, the case is quite different. Scholem rejects the hypothesis that the author of the Zohar was an underhand forger who attributed his own work to earlier rabbis for material gain, or for the sake of popular renown. This would not be in keeping with the portrait of Rabbi Moses de Leon's character that appears from his Hebrew writings.[567] Scholem, therefore, invalidates that part of Rabbi Isaac of Acre's evidence which contains the defendant's confession, transmitted by his wife, of the reasons for writing the Zohar: "If I told them my secret and that what I wrote was my own invention, they would pay no heed to my words, and would not give me a penny for them, because they would say that I had made it all up. But, as it is, when they hear that I am copying extracts for them from the Zohar that was written under the influence of the Holy Spirit by Rabbi Simeon ben Yohai, they pay a lot of money for them, as you can see yourself." One must suppose that this statement was distorted, or entirely invented, by enemies of Rabbi Moses de Leon. Pseudepigraphy, in itself, cannot simply be put down to fraudulent intentions. Many extremely important religious works have been composed in this way. Sometimes it is the author's attempt to subjugate his own desire for personal self-glorification that prompts him to remain anonymous. Sometimes pseudepigraphy is the expression of the author's deep conviction that the revelations that have been accorded him are eternally true, and so must have been known also to the early rabbis.[568] This approach leads Scholem to a completely different evaluation of the Zohar from that of Graetz. The Zohar is not a "book of lies," but a great and remarkable thirteenth century work that contains a mystical representation of the spirit of Judaism.

Scholem also uses critical philological arguments to refute Graetz's position on this subject. After comparing Rabbi Moses de Leon's books with the Zohar, he saw quite clearly that all his books, beginning with the very first one, *Sefer Shushan Edut* (1286), were full of quotations and references that showed that the author had before him a written copy of the Zohar. Jellinek and Graetz, therefore, made a big mistake when they maintained that his Hebrew books antedated the Zohar. This also undermines the argument that the Zohar was written for financial reasons after the failure of the books that had been written under Rabbi Moses de Leon's own name.[569]

In the light of these conclusions Scholem was able to establish a reasoned chronology for Rabbi Moses de Leon's literary work.[570] The *Midrash ha-Ne'elam* was written about 1280, and the other sections of the Zohar were composed between 1280 and 1286. It is difficult to fix the order of composition of the different parts, but one may suppose that the *Sifra di-Zeniuta* and the *Idrot* were among the earliest to be written. From 1286 to 1293, when his last dated book, *Sefer Mishkan ha-Edut*, was written,[571] he was engaged in writing his Hebrew works, which were mainly intended to popularize ideas in the Zohar, and to prepare the ground for its publication. The *Sefer Mishkan ha-Edut* contains open propaganda for the mysteries of the Zohar. A few extracts from parts of the Zohar appeared around 1290, but the main work of copying and dissemination was done from 1293 to 1305, the date of Rabbi Moses de Leon's death. It would appear that even after 1293 he made several alterations to passages in the Zohar while he was editing it, and perhaps he even added some material, but in general it can be said that in his last years he was not writing creatively, but only editing and publishing.

d. Unresolved Questions

The problem of the authorship of the Zohar and the time of its composition has been finally resolved by the studies of Gershom Scholem. His arguments, even though they have not been published in detail, but only summarized, show without a doubt that Rabbi Moses de Leon wrote all the sections of the Zohar, with the exception of the *Raya Mehemna* and the *Tikkunei ha-Zohar* and a number of minor additions. However, there are certain specific problems that have not been fully worked out, and need further discussion, especially the question of the chronological order of Rabbi Moses de Leon's literary work and the relationship between his Hebrew writings and the Zohar.

Scholem concluded that the life and work of Rabbi Moses de Leon can be divided into three stages: (1) a period of pseudepigraphic writing, about 1280–1286; (2) a period of Hebrew writing under his own name, 1286–1293; and (3) a period in which he edited and disseminated the pseudepigraphic texts, 1293–1305. This division gives the impression of an artificial pattern, and cannot be easily explained psychologically. We are required to accept the difficult proposition that the author wrote and completed the Zohar before writing anything else, that he then kept it for seven years, apart from a few texts that he showed to his wife and friends, and turned instead to the composition of other books; and that then, from about the age of fifty until his death, he stopped writing and devoted himself entirely to publishing his earlier works.

Scholem's explanation of this theory is that the Hebrew books were written as propaganda to prepare the way for the publication of his pseudepigraphic work, which Rabbi Moses de Leon had been keeping in reserve. But this very explanation raises a number of serious difficulties from several points of view, most of which Gershom Scholem himself discusses, in comparing the Hebrew works with the Zohar. (1) Most of the Zoharic passages in the writings of Rabbi Moses de Leon are quoted as his own original contributions, without any reference to an earlier source, and sometimes the element of originality is positively stressed, for example in his responsa texts.[572] Now this is surprising if we hold that these passages already existed in the Zohar, and that he was planning to publish them as the work of Rabbi Simeon ben Yohai and his pupils. (2) Generally speaking, those Zoharic passages which are quoted are merely sentences or small fragments forming part of a passage the whole of which is to be found in the Zohar as we have it. Sometimes these quotations are explained by the author, and these explanations are also to be found in the Zohar. It is difficult to see how this method of composition can accord with Scholem's theory. (3) A similar problem arises from the fact that the Zoharic passages, and even some of the acknowledged quotations, do not copy the Zohar exactly, but differ in both form and content in several important respects. How could the writer who wanted to disseminate these passages as the work of earlier rabbis treat them in this way? (4) Statements from the Zohar are sometimes quoted in the name of "commentators" (*mefarshim*), a term that does not in the least suit the rabbis of the Talmud. (5) Last, in a few places Rabbi Moses de Leon opposes, sometimes quite fervently, particular ideas in the Zohar. A clear example of this concerns the purification of souls in the river of fire. Rabbi Moses de Leon writes:[573] "And even though there are many diverse opinions about this subject (i.e., the nature of the celestial Gehinnom) . . . some of them are incorrect, and far from the truth, and there are other views that can never be right, views that state that the rabbinic opinion of the verse (in Daniel 7: 10) 'A fiery stream issued and came forth from before him,' is that the souls that ascend upward to be bound up in the bond of life enter this 'river of fire.' This is incorrect." Now, this opinion that Rabbi Moses de Leon refutes occurs at several points in the Zohar. Furthermore, part of a passage in the Zohar[574] in which this view is expressed is quoted by Rabbi Moses de Leon[575] as his own original idea, namely, the comparison of the soul to a garment made from the salamander. What can be the explanation of this odd relationship to passages in the Zohar, always supposing that he did already know them as passages from the Zohar?

These difficulties lead one to think that there must be another solution to this problem. Probably, by 1286, when he wrote his *Sefer Shushan Edut*, he had prepared only a few sections of his pseudepigraphic writing, but these included the *Midrash ha-Ne'elam*. Even during the period when he wrote his Hebrew books, Rabbi Moses de Leon was still working on *parashiyot* of the Zohar, which he had started earlier. Indeed, his main pseudepigraphic activity was concentrated in these years, insofar as he put into his Hebrew writings fictitious quotations under the name of "midrash", or of earlier rabbis, or of "commentators" (*mefarshim*). This is to say that even those Zoharic passages that are introduced as definite quotations were not yet all there in front of him, in their Aramaic version, under the name of Rabbi Simeon ben Yohai and his disciples. It was not until about 1293 that he began to work intensively again on his pseudepigraphy, and from that date until his death he set about finishing the sections of the Zohar, which he then began to distribute piece by piece. During this period he cast his Hebrew writings into an Aramaic mold, putting the views expressed there into the mouths of rabbis from the Talmud, and in the process he diverged at a number of points from his earlier opinions. Perhaps the interruption in his pseudepigraphic activity was caused by doubts cast on the genuineness of the *Midrash ha-Ne'elam*, as would appear from the evidence of

Rabbi Isaac of Acre.[576] It was for this reason that he subsequently changed the language and the literary form of the work.

This theory, which solves most of the difficulties mentioned above, is possibly supported by the fact that the references and allusions to a supposedly ancient book are more frequent and more definite in the *Sefer Mishkan ha-Edut*, written in 1293, than in the earlier books. Clear evidence of Rabbi Moses de Leon's tendency to quote, in his Hebrew books, passages of his own invention that have no direct connection with the Zohar can be found in the citations from a "Book of Enoch," which he quotes in several places but which are not mentioned at all in the Zohar.[577] Gershom Scholem's argument that *Sefer Orhot Hayyim*, attributed to Rabbi Eliezer the Great, was also written by Rabbi Moses de Leon[578] would strengthen the evidence that he wrote pseudepigraphic material in the Zoharic style, but outside the framework of the Zohar itself.

This theory can also help us with several other problems. (1) The fact that the *parashiyot* of the Zohar, particularly in Numbers and Deuteronomy, are not complete, gives one the impression that the work is in a fragmentary state. Scholem is forced to argue[579] that the author's interest or creative power waned before the work was finished. Our theory does not require such a forced explanation. It is simply that the composition of the Zohar was interrupted *in medias res* by the death of Rabbi Moses de Leon. (2) This also explains why we find that all the kabbalists of the fourteenth and fifteenth centuries had only a partial knowledge of the Zohar, and why there never existed a complete manuscript of the work. Even the incomplete manuscripts that we do have are put together in different ways. One must presume that Rabbi Moses de Leon himself never succeeded in putting all the sections of the Zohar together and distributing them as one complete unit. And so the kabbalists received only independent and separate texts that were then arranged in a variety of ways. (3) Rabbi Moses de Leon's writings contain Zoharic statements, including some that are actually stated to be quotations, that do not occur in the Zohar we have. Scholem's theory would have it that they did once exist in the Zohar and were later excised, while, according to our theory, we could say that these are passages that the author never put into Aramaic when he reedited his Hebrew writings. (4) The contrasts in ideas and in terminology between the *Midrash ha-Ne'elam* and the other sections of the Zohar are explained by Scholem in terms of the transition from speculative-philosophical kabbalah to mythical-gnostic kabbalah that took place in Rabbi Moses de Leon's mind. But this explanation is very questionable if we accept the view that the Hebrew books were written after the whole Zohar had been completed, because they still have this speculative character. The problem is resolved if we assume that the main body of the Zohar was not written before 1293, that is to say, that the basic spiritual turning-point occurred in the latter years of Rabbi Moses de Leon's life.

Needless to say, our theory is also of the nature of sheer supposition, and in the present state of scholarship we cannot express a definite view on these unresolved questions. The publication of Rabbi Moses de Leon's Hebrew writings in a scientific critical edition would throw a clearer light on this mysterious chapter, and would take us to the very heart of his creative genius. Now that Rabbi Moses de Leon's authorship of the Zohar has been proved, this task remains one of the most urgent prerequisites for further Zohar research.

VI. PRINTED EDITIONS, MANUSCRIPTS, TRANSLATIONS, AND COMMENTARIES

a. Printed Editions of the Zohar

The preparations for printing the Zohar, which were given an added external impetus by the decree of Pope Paul IV in 1554 that the Talmud and its commentaries should be burned, caused a bitter controversy. Many rabbis put up a fierce opposition to it, and even issued bans and excommunications. Only one of the anti-printing documents has so far been published,[580] and most of the opponents' arguments are known to us only from the counter arguments of the supporters of the project, the editors and the printers. The fundamental reasons for the opposition were based on the following considerations: (1) Kabbalah is a false doctrine, and the Zohar a late fraudulent work; (2) Study of the Zohar is bound to lead to heresy;[581] (3) One should not study kabbalistic wisdom, because of "the shortcomings of the student and the profundity of the subject"; (4) It is forbidden to reveal the secrets of the Torah to the general public; (5) The printing of the Zohar would conflict with the prohibition of writing down the oral law.[582] An additional argument was that the printing of the Zohar and other kabbalistic books at that particular time would serve to intensify the papal decree, which would be extended to include other books as well as the Talmud.[583]

The editors and the printers disregarded these warnings and relied on the decisions of various rabbis, chief among them being Rabbi Isaac Delattes, in their efforts to refute the arguments of their opponents. They looked upon the printing of the Zohar as holy work that would wean the mind away from the study of philosophical literature, which had become very popular in Italy, especially after the decree that the Talmud should be burned.[584] On the basis of statements in the Zohar itself, they believed that to publish it was to take an important step on the road to redemption.[585] Their reply to the criticism that it was forbidden to reveal the secrets of the Torah was that the Zohar was already available in manuscript, but that only the wealthy were able to obtain it, while the poor who yearned to study it did not have the wherewithal to buy a copy.[586]

A start was made with the *Tikkunei ha-Zohar*, which was printed in Mantua in 1558. In the same year they began to print the Zohar there in three volumes, and the printing of the third volume was completed in 1560. In 1559–60 the Zohar was also printed in Cremona, in one volume, in a very large format. This edition was printed in the press of a Christian, Vicenzo Conti, and one of his editors and correctors was the apostate Vittorio Eliano, the grandson of the grammarian Rabbi Elijah Baḥur. The preface to this edition contains a criticism of the Mantua edition, and the editors promise to produce a more nearly perfect piece of work. But the corrector's preface to the Mantua edition, printed at the beginning of the first volume, also contains references to the parallel edition. The corrector remarks: "We know that others will wreak havoc, and will be filled with shame, and will confuse the different readings. And this is because they have sunk in deep mire and do not know the right way." *En passant*, he makes fun of the large format: "There are those who have widened their mouths, and lengthened their tongues, for they have taken a page as big as a cedar in Lebanon." It therefore follows that as early as 1558 plans were known for printing the Zohar in Cremona.

It was Rabbi Immanuel of Benevento who established the text of the Mantua edition, and according to one of the printers, Rabbi Jacob Hacohen of Gazolo, quoted at the end of the *Tikkunei ha-Zohar*, he used ten manuscripts.[587] First of all he picked out two whose texts seemed to him to be the most reliable, as the corrector says in his preface to the Zohar: "to correct and establish the text of his version with two copies that the knowledgeable could see were good and reliable." Subsequently, he acquired a manuscript from Safed, and he used this as a basis for establishing the final text. It would seem that Rabbi Immanuel, in comparing the different manuscripts, put in some serious and responsible philological work. In general he produced just the finally selected text on its own, but in a few places he notes alternative readings. The Cremona edition was based on six copies, as stated in the preface, "two of which we used as our main guides (lit., were like eyes to us)," one from Egypt and one from Palestine. Doubtful readings were examined by experts, and if they approved the text common to most of the manuscripts, then just the single version was printed. But if they preferred a minority reading, this was also cited in "a small Spanish type." There are important and obvious differences between the two editions, both in the text and in the order of various passages. There are also several passages that occur in one edition but are missing in the other. A detailed scientific comparison has yet to be done, but generally speaking one can say that the Mantua text is the better of the two.

Of the large number[588] of printings of the Zohar only two[589] were patterned on the Cremona edition. All the remaining editions were printed on the model of the Mantua printing, page for page. However, textual emendations were made, and notes and explanations added in the margins. Also the additional passages in the Cremona edition and in the *Zohar Hadash* were appended to each volume with the heading *Hashmatot* (Omissions) and *Tosafot* (Additions). In the Amsterdam edition (1715) the *Hashmatot* are printed at the beginning, and at the end of the third volume "Indices (*Maftehot*) to the Great Zohar, the *Zohar Hadash* and the *Tikkunim*" are put in, and these were reprinted in most subsequent editions. As far as textual correction is concerned the Constantinople edition (1736–37) is of particular importance, because there the Mantua text is edited and corrected on the basis of manuscripts from the school of Isaac Luria's disciples, and it also contains supplementary material from a manuscript owned by a Rabbi Israel Benjamin. This text has been accepted and reprinted in all the latest editions.

The editions of the *Tikkunei ha-Zohar* outnumber even those of the Zohar itself. It has been printed about seventy-five times. Several editions were printed page for page like the first edition (Mantua, 1558), but many were printed in a different format, and also with textual emendations, changes in the arrangement of the material, and with the addition of other pasages, notes, and explanations. Changes in arrangement are particularly noticeable in *Tikkunim* 20, 21, and 70. Some editions also contain extensive commentaries. From the textual point of view, one should pay special attention to two editions: the Ortakoi edition (1719), which contains changes and emendations based on corrections in the hand of Rabbi Hayyim Vital in the margins of the Zohar, which were transcribed by Rabbi Hayyim Alfandari while he was in Egypt; and the Constantinople edition (1740), which was corrected by Rabbi Hayyim Yeruham ben Rabbi Jacob Vilna Yerushalmi.

The first printing of the *Zohar Ḥadash* was the Salonika edition (1597), and it was printed again in the same fashion in Cracow (1603). The text is corrupt in both editions, and neither of them contains the *Midrash ha-Ne'elam* to Ruth, which had been printed previously as a separate book.[590] The book was printed for a third time in Venice (1658), with substantial emendations and changes, with Rabbi Joseph Ḥamiz as editor, and Rabbi Moses Zacuto as corrector. In this edition the *Midrash ha-Ne'elam* to Ruth was added for the first time. The other editions were all modeled on the Venice text, with a few alterations, and with the addition of notes and explanations—except for one edition (Munkács, 1911), which was emended on the basis of manuscript corrections by kabbalists.

b. Zohar Manuscripts[591]

The situation with regard to manuscripts of the Zohar is not very satisfactory from the critical point of view. The early manuscripts, written about the time of the book's first appearance, are no longer extant, and even the latest ones that we have are not complete. Only two fragmentary copies have so far been discovered from the fourteenth century: (1) Vatican 202, which was written not later than 1350. Here we find several separate fragments of the Zohar among writings from the circle of the disciples of Rabbi Solomon ben Adret. (2) Cambridge Add. 1023, written in the second half of the fourteenth century. This manuscript is the second volume of transcripts of several *parashiyot* of the Zohar. It consists in the main of sections from the *Midrash ha-Ne'elam* together with a few *parashiyot* from the Zohar itself. It is particularly valuable because one section of the *Midrash ha-Ne'elam* appears there in a completely different version from the printed text and from that of other manuscripts.[592]

From the fifteenth century there are still only a very limited number of manuscripts, but they are more complete, particularly with regard to Genesis. However, here too there are many gaps. One should note that in several manuscripts complete sections are missing, such as the *Idra Rabba* and the *Idra Zuta, Sava de-Mishpatim, Yanuka,* and so on. The most important manuscripts from this period are: (1) Vatican 206; (2) Parma (De Rossi) 1137; (3) Parma (De Rossi) 1392, written in Italy in 1482; (4) British Library 762 [Add. 17745] (Genesis only); (5) Paris 778–779. Oxford 1564 (Genesis and Exodus) and Gaster 747 [British Library Or. 10527] were written at the end of the fifteenth or the beginning of the sixteenth century. From the first half of the sixteenth century, that is, shortly before the Zohar was printed, there are a large number of manuscripts.

It is possible to divide most of the manuscripts into three groups, according to the way in which the material is arranged, particularly in regard to the *parashah Bereshit*. (1) The order in which we have it in the printed text, which also occurs in a few manuscripts; (2) The arrangement of the *parashah* in three parallel sections, each of which contains a succession of connected interpretations on the whole *parashah* from beginning to end. The first section begins with *Be-resh hurmanuta de-malka* (15a) and continues with the text as printed until *Kelilan be-hai be-raza de-mehemanuta* (22c). It then continues with *yishrezu ha-mayim* (34a) to *ki adonai dibber* (38a). The second section begins with the passage "we have learned that every 'Solomon' that is mentioned in the Song of Songs" (29a), and continues with the text we have up to "the Lord shall be One, and His name One"(34a). It then continues with *yishrezu ha-mayim* (46b) until the end of the *parashah*. The third section contains passages from the *Midrash ha-Ne'elam* printed in the *Zohar Ḥadash*. This kind of arrangement is found in seven manuscripts. Of those mentioned above, the following belong to this category: Oxford 1564, Vatican 206, British Library 762, and Parma 1137. In some of these manuscripts we find, at the beginning of the book, before *Be-resh hurmanuta de-malka*, the lines from "And God said: Let there be light" (45b) to "and you who cleave to the Lord your God," and so on (46b), which also occur at the beginning of the *Zohar Ḥadash*. It would appear that this is the origin of the title, sometimes given to the Zohar, of *Midrash Yehi Or* (The Midrash "Let there be Light").[593] (3) A mixture of homilies from the main body of the Zohar with passages from other sections, particularly from the *Midrash ha-Ne'elam*. The whole is arranged in the order of the scriptural verses. This is without doubt a late, artificial arrangement, and yet manuscripts of this type have in the past been valued the most highly. Landauer[594] described in detail the Munich MS 217–219, and proclaimed that it was the earliest and most important manuscript for the study of the Zohar, since it contained many passages missing from the printed text. Steinschneider[595] dealt with this error and demonstrated that there were no unknown sections in the manuscript, but that passages from the *Midrash ha-Ne'elam* and other pieces had been inserted within the text of the main body of the Zohar, in order that the arrangement should follow the order of the scriptural verses. The manuscript was written in the first half of the sixteenth century. The Gaster MS 747, whose antiquity and excellence were pointed out by the owner,[596] also belongs to this group, but it has no particular critical value, as Scholem's investigations have shown. We should also note another manuscript of this type, Rome, Casanatense 2971, which was written for a distinguished ecclesiastic. The manuscript was completed in 1513.

As far as the actual text is concerned, there is not a great deal of difference between the manuscripts and the printed editions. Sometimes the printed text, particularly the Mantua text, is preferable. Also there is only a small amount of additional material in the manuscripts. The superiority of the manuscripts lies mainly in matters of orthography, paragraphing, and of the forms of difficult or unusual words. In some manuscripts there is an attempt to divide the Zohar into chapters. This division is also found in the text of passages from the *Midrash ha-Ne'elam* on the *parashah Bereshit*, which were printed in the *Zohar Ḥadash*. One should also note that several additions, which proliferated in the printed text, are missing in the manuscripts, such as passages by the author of the *Tikkunei ha-Zohar* on the *parashah Bereshit* (22a–29a), and the first pages of the *parashah Va-yehi* (211b–216a), whose nature was discussed by the kabbalists themselves. The passages on the *parashah Va-yehi* are clearly stated by the correctors of the Mantua edition to be imitative and additional.

Passages from the *Raya Mehemna* are not quoted at all in the manuscripts as appendages to the Zohar. They occur on their own as a separate work, but only in later manuscripts. There is no early manuscript, either, of the *Tikkunei ha-Zohar*. The earliest manuscripts discovered so far are Paris 786, written in 1458, and Cambridge Add. 520, from the same period.

Since the situation with regard to Zohar manuscripts is so unsatisfactory, considerable value, from the scientific point of view, must be placed on the collection of quotations from the Zohar to be found in kabbalistic books from the end of the thirteenth and the beginning of the fourteenth centuries, whether quoted anonymously or definitely ascribed to the Zohar. The most important here are the writings of Rabbi Menahem Recanati,[597] which contain about seven hundred explicit quotations, including a considerable number of lengthy passages. Other books of value in this respect are: the writings of Rabbi Bahya ben Asher, *Sefer Sha'arei Orah* by Rabbi Joseph Gikatilla, the writings of Rabbi David ben Judah the Pious, *Sefer Livnat ha-Sapir*, and the *Sefer Menorat ha-Ma'or* by Rabbi Israel al-Nakawah.[598] All these books were written before the earliest manuscripts now in our possession; hence their great value in establishing the text of the Zohar and understanding it correctly.

c. Translations of the Zohar

The need to translate the Zohar into Hebrew was felt at a very early time. The writings of Rabbi David ben Judah the Pious, from the beginning of the fourteenth century, and especially his *Sefer Mar'ot ha-Zov'ot*, contain many passages from the Zohar in a Hebrew version.[599] At the end of the *Midrash Yonah*[600] there is a large section from the *Zohar Va-yakhel* (II, 198b–199b) in Hebrew translation. The *Sefer Menorat ha-Ma'or* by Rabbi Israel al-Nak-awah,[601] who was martyred in Toledo in 1391, quotes scores of passages under the name of *Midrash Yehi Or*, which are nothing but Hebrew versions of texts from the Zohar. In Rabbi Abraham Azulai's Introduction to his *Sefer Or ha-Hamah* (Jerusalem, 1876) he says that his corrections are taken "also from a book of the Zohar translated into the holy tongue by Rabbi Israel Nakawah." From this it would appear that the latter translated the entire Zohar into Hebrew, or at least large sections of it. Scholem thinks[602] that "the Zohar in the holy tongue" mentioned in some sixteenth-century notes on the Zohar,[603] and also "the book of the Zohar translated into the holy tongue," several passages from which are quoted in British Library MS 768 [Add. 27003], both refer to Rabbi Israel al-Nakawah's translation.

In later years, from the sixteenth century onward, we find various translations both in manuscripts and in printed books. Oxford MS 1561 contains a Hebrew translation of a large proportion of passages from the Zohar, following the order of the *parashiyot*.[604] Oxford MS 1563 is an anthology that contains some passages from the Zohar in a Hebrew version, together with a textual explanation by Rabbi Samuel bar Benjamin. At the end of the manuscript there are the approbations of German and Polish rabbis, dating from 1642 to 1647. In the Vatican MS 226 a few *parashiyot* of the Zohar are quoted, including the *Sifra di-Zeniuta* as well, in a Hebrew translation that follows the printed text.[605] In several manuscripts, for example, British Library 739 [Add. 27076], 743 [Add. 16407], 769 [Or. 3655], there are Hebrew translations of individual passages. The *Sefer Mekor Hokhmah* (Prague, 1611) by

Rabbi Issachar Baer of Kremnitz is a Hebrew translation of fragments and short literalist passages arranged in order of the *parashiyot*. The *Sefer Me'ulefet Sapirim* (Constantinople, 1640) by Rabbi Solomon Algazi is a selection of pieces from the ethical passages of the Zohar, in order of subject matter, partly in an accurate Hebrew translation, and partly in a paraphrastic version. In the *Sefer Ispaklarya ha-Me'irah*[606] (Fürth, 1776) by Rabbi Zvi Hirsch Horowitz, which is an explanation of the Zohar, there is a Hebrew translation of a passage from the *Idra Rabba* (III, 135b–136a). Practically all these translations were done for readers who were unskilled in kabbalah; therefore the more difficult and profound matters are omitted. Consequently, their value for the understanding of the Zohar is not very great.

In more recent times there have been three attempts to translate the Zohar into Hebrew in a comprehensive fashion.[607] The first translator was Rabbi Eliakim Milzahagi, who says himself, in a manuscript copy[608] of *Sefer Zohorei Raviah*, that he finished translating all the sections of the Zohar, except apparently the *Tikkunei ha-Zohar* and the *Zohar Ḥadash*, and that he was preparing to print this translation together with three of his own commentaries, and with the notes entitled *Derekh Emet*. This translation, a short excerpt from which was cited as an example in the *Sefer Zohorei Raviah*,[609] never reached the printed page, and the manuscript is now lost. Hillel Zeitlin also had a plan for translating the whole Zohar, and for publishing it with an extensive commentary, but only a translation of the introduction to the Zohar was ever printed.[610] The only translation that was published in its entirety, in conformity with the translator's plans, was the one by Rabbi Judah Yudel Rosenberg.[611] The translator arranged the passages from the Zohar, unlike the original, in the order of scriptural verses from the Pentateuch, Psalms, Song of Songs, Proverbs, and Ecclesiastes. The translation was published together with the original, with a commentary entitled *Ziv ha-Zohar*. But all the difficult, more abstruse passages were omitted, and were printed only in the original Aramaic.

Of the translations into other languages we should note the following: (1) The partial Latin translation by Knorr von Rosenroth at the end of the seventeenth century.[612] Unlike most of the Hebrew translations, this translation contains in particular the more difficult and important sections, such as the *Sifra di-Zeniuta*, the *Idra Rabba*, and the *Idra Zuta*. The difficulties of both language and subject matter led naturally to many mistakes. This translation had a tremendous influence, being the main source of information about the Zohar in cultured European circles until the beginning of the twentieth century.[613] (2) The French translation by Jean de Pauly, in seven volumes, with notes and commentaries.[614] The name of the translator is fictitious, and his real identity has never been discovered. This translation includes most sections of the Zohar, but it is full of dreadful errors, and Christianizing falsifications. The translation was done in the years 1900–1903, and was then corrected by a "reliable" rabbi, but the "corrections" are also full of mistakes.[615] (3) The English translation of H. Sperling and M. Simon, which was published in five volumes.[616] The translators did their work in good faith, but their lack of knowledge of kabbalistic doctrine led them into error from time to time. Most of the separate sections are missing from the translation, and even in the *Midrash ha-Zohar* itself the translators skipped many difficult and important passages. (4) The selection of passages from the Zohar in German translation, by E. Müller.[617] The selection is arranged according to subject matter. The translation was effected with great care, but there are frequent mistakes in comprehension. The selection suffers from the fact that nearly all the passages are cut down in size. (5) The German translation of the beginning of the Zohar (I, 15a–22a) by Gershom Scholem.[618] The original text was corrected by comparing it with manuscript material. Brief explanations are inserted into the translation, in order to complete the sense. (6) Gershom Scholem also edited an anthology from the main body of the Zohar, in an English translation.[619]

d. Zohar Commentaries

The scope of Zohar interpretation is extremely wide, and there are scores[620] of commentaries, either partial or complete, in print. There are in addition a large number of unpublished commentaries still in manuscript. However, only a small proportion of them really help us to understand the literal meaning of the Zohar. The kabbalists saw the Zohar as a vast treasury containing the whole of kabbalistic wisdom, including all the new concepts that originated as it developed; and most of the commentators also attributed to the Zohar thoughts and ideas that had no place whatsoever in the mind of the original author. This is particularly true of Lurianic interpretation, which actually forms the bulk of the commentaries. Lurianic kabbalah involved a complete reversal of the principal concepts of mystical teaching, and the commentaries that were written in the spirit of Lurianic kabbalah, were, with a few exceptions, only descriptions and expositions of the new ideas within the framework of Zoharic material.

The most important commentary, one that covers the whole Zohar to the Torah, is the *Sefer Or ha-Ḥamah* (The Light of the Sun) by Rabbi Abraham Azulai.[621] Three commentaries are assembled together in this book: (1) A shortened version of the great commentary by Rabbi Moses Cordovero, entitled *Sefer Or ha-Yakar* (The Precious Light): (2) The commentary by Rabbi Hayyim Vital, which, according to Rabbi Abraham Azulai's preface, he wrote before he learned Torah from Rabbi Isaac Luria; and (3) The comments of an anonymous kabbalist that Rabbi Abraham Azulai discovered in the margins of a copy of the Zohar. This anthologizer also abridged the *Sefer Yareaḥ Yakar* by Rabbi Abraham Galante, under the title *Sefer Zohorei Ḥamah*,[622] and this also contains some notes of great value for the understanding of the Zohar. However, only the sections on Genesis and Exodus have been printed.

The *Sefer Ketem Paz* (Fine Gold),[623] the extensive and profound commentary by Rabbi Simeon Labi, is acknowledged to be of great importance. This commentary was written in Tripoli about 1550, and so antedates the printing of the Zohar. It is therefore helpful in correcting the printed text. In the approbation of the rabbis of Livorno it was described as "a commentary to the Zohar on Genesis and Exodus," but the commentary to Exodus has not been printed.

Of the commentaries that were written after the spread of Lurianic kabbalah three are noteworthy, in that they still throw light on the literal meaning of the text: (1) *Sefer Mikdash Melekh* by Rabbi Shalom Buzaglo.[624] This extensive commentary, although based on Lurianic kabbalah, does contain many explanations that are very near to the literal meaning of the Zohar. (2) *Sefer Ispaklarya ha-Me'irah*[625] by Rabbi Zvi Hirsch Horowitz, a brief commentary that does not follow in the footsteps of Lurianic kabbalah. The author's notes contain valuable textual emendations. (3) *Sefer Yahel Or* by Rabbi Elijah of Vilna,[626] whose comments elucidate many of the most obscure points in the Zohar.

Many commentaries were written only on individual sections, particularly on the *Sifra di-Zeniuta*, the *Idra Rabba*, and the *Idra Zuta*, but here too it is difficult to find reliable explanations of the text. This is also the case with commentaries on the *Tikkunei ha-Zohar*. Only a few commentaries have been written on the sections of the *Zohar Hadash*.

Apart from the commentaries, the kabbalists wrote many manuals to help one to understand the Zohar, including indexes, glossaries of difficult words, lists of textual variants, and so on. Some of these are very valuable, and here are a few examples: (1) *Sefer Mar'eh Kohen* by Rabbi Issachar Baer Hacohen of Szczebrzeszyn[627] which contains an index both of subject matter and of scriptural verses, according to the Cremona edition. The whole book was translated into Latin by Knorr von Rosenroth. (2) *Hibbur Amudei Sheva* by Rabbi Aaron Selig of Zolkiew.[628] This book is arranged in five sections. One section deals with passages in the Mantua edition that are missing from the Cremona edition, and another section deals with passages that are repeated in the Zohar, but with different readings. (3) *Maftehot ha-Zohar* (Indexes to the Zohar) by Rabbi Israel Berechiah Fontanella,[629] in two parts. The first part is an alphabetical index of subject matter, written by a kabbalist called Samuel in the sixteenth century, and revised by the editor; and the second part is an index of scriptural verses, compiled by Fontanella himself. These two indexes are very detailed and accurate, and are extremely useful for the study of the Zohar. (4) *Sefer Yesha Yah* by Rabbi Joseph ben Shraga[630] gives explanations of difficult words in the Zohar. (5) *Sefer Imrei Binah* by Rabbi Issachar Baer of Kremnitz[631] is a similar work. This is printed in the margins of many Zohar editions. (6) *Sefer Or ha-Levanah* by Rabbi Abraham Azulai[632] gives a list of textual variants from manuscripts, for the purpose of correcting mistakes in the printed text. This important book, described in the preface to the *Sefer Or ha-Hamah* as "the little lamp, which gives light to the man who walks in the pitch darkness of mistakes and textual variants, which are more common in the Zohar than in any other book," has been printed only as far as the Genesis section of the Zohar. (7) *Yalkut ha-Zohar* by Rabbi Isaiah Menahem Mendel of Lodz[633] is a compendium of extracts from the Zohar, the *Zohar Hadash*, and the *Tikkunei ha-Zohar*, arranged in alphabetical order of subject matter. It includes at the end an anthology of proverbs and stories from the Zohar.

Finally, we should note that most of the kabbalistic books, written after the expulsion from Spain, contain a large number of lengthy explanations of passages from the Zohar, and some of them have great interpretative value, even though they were not written in the form of commentaries. The most important books of this kind are: Rabbi Judah Hayyat's commentary to the *Sefer Ma'arekhet ha-Elohut*, Rabbi Meir ben Gabbai's *Sefer Avodat ha-Kodesh*, and the *Sefer Pardes Rimmonim* by Rabbi Moses Cordovero. It is sometimes possible to use these and similar books that were written before the Zohar was printed in order to establish a correct text.

In more recent times two new editions of the Zohar have appeared. One of them, prepared under the editorship of the kabbalist Rabbi Judah Leib Ashlag, has already filled twenty-one printed volumes (Jerusalem, 1945–55), and these contain the Zohar and the *Zohar Hadash*. Every passage is accompanied by a long explanation and by the editor's commentaries, entitled *Ha-Sulam* and *Mar'ot ha-Sulam*. From the second volume onward a full Hebrew translation is inserted, bit by bit, into *Ha-Sulam*. The explanations follow the Lurianic system and are of little help in clarifying the literal meaning of the text. From the scientific point of view, this edition has considerable value in the way it traces references in the accompanying textual apparatus although there are gaps in its references to source material. The other edition (Zohar, *Tikkunei ha-Zohar*, and *Zohar Hadash*), five volumes (Jerusalem–Tel-Aviv, 1940–53), was prepared by Reuben Margaliot, with the addition of notes and comments under the heading *Nizozei Zohar*. This publication follows the Vilna edition, and not only is the text uncorrected, but it actually contains serious additional errors as the result of lax proofreading. The *Nizozei Zohar* contains material of considerable value for a critical study of the Zohar, especially in the parallels it draws with the writings of medieval scholars,[634] but the author spoils everything by trying to show that these parallels point to an early date for the composition of the Zohar.

Let me conclude by noting that Agnon's *Sefer Yamim Nora'im* (Jerusalem, 1938) contains a selection of passages from the Zohar translated into Hebrew.

Notes to General Introduction

1. The printed editions of the Zohar will be considered in a later chapter. The two earliest printings of the Zohar on the Torah are Mantua, 1558–1560, and Cremona, 1559–1560. Current editions follow the Mantua printing.
2. First printed Mantua, 1558.
3. The *Zohar Hadash* was not written at a later date, as is mistakenly thought by some scholars. It is a collection of pieces and complete works from the Zoharic literature that were missing from the printed editions and assembled from manuscripts by the kabbalists of Safed. First printed Salonika, 1597.
4. Most of the passages were printed in later editions at the end of each part of the Zohar on the Torah, under the heading *Tosafot* (Addenda) or *Hashmatot* (Omissions).
5. In the Cremona edition the comments in the *Hakdamah* are not inserted as a preface at the beginning of the book but as ordinary statements in the middle of the *parashah Bereshit*.
6. *Zohar Hadash*, 61d–75b.
7. *Bereshit, Noah, Lekh Lekha* (*Zohar Hadash* 2d–26b); *Va-yera, Hayyei Sarah, Toledot* (Zohar I, 97a–140a); *Va-yeze* (*Zohar Hadash* 27b–28d).
8. Zohar II, 4a–5b, 14a–22a. In the printed texts these sections are incorporated into the main body of the Zohar.
9. *Zohar Hadash*—*Be-shallah, Aharei mot, Ki teze.*
10. *Zohar Hadash*, 60a–61d.
11. Ibid., 75a–91b.
12. Ibid., 91a–93d.

13. Zohar I, 74b–75a; 76b–77a; 78a–81b; 97a–102a; 107b–111a; 146b–149b; 151b–152a; 154b–157b; 161b–162b; II, 146a. Some passages so entitled are also incorporated in the *Zohar Ḥadash* (*Toledot, Va-yeshev, Aḥarei mot*).

14. These pieces are scattered throughout the three volumes of the Zohar on the Torah, and at a few points in the *Zohar Ḥadash*.

15. Zohar I, 62a.

16. Ibid., 161b. [The English translations given are purely hypothetical.]

17. Zohar II, 94b–114a. The opening (94a–b) belongs to the *Tikkunei ha-Zohar*. Most of the book is translated below, pp. 177–97.

18. Zohar III, 186a–192a. Translated in full below, pp. 197–223.

19. In the Cremona edition it is included in the *parashah Devarim*.

20. Zohar III, 161b–174a. The text has several lacunae.

21. Zohar II, 176b–179a.

22. Zohar III, 127b–145a. Both the opening and the conclusion are translated below, pp. 155–59.

23. [One of the vows that the Nazirite takes is to grow his hair (Numbers 6: 5).]

24. Zohar III, 287b–296b. Both the opening and the conclusion are translated below, pp. 161–65.

25. This section is referred to at the beginning of *Idra Rabba*, and according to the note in later editions it is to be found in Zohar II, 122b–123b. But Scholem has established (see *Major Trends in Jewish Mysticism*, [1941], p. 386, n. 14) that it is really ibid. 127a–146b.

26. Zohar I, 38a–45b; II, 244b–262b. The main part of the first version is translated below, pp. 597–614.

27. Ibid., 262b–268b.

28. Zohar II, 70a–75a. The continuation of this version is in *Zohar Ḥadash*, 35b–37c.

29. Zohar II, 70a–78a.

30. *Zohar Ḥadash*, 1b–7b. The subsequent additional fragments do not belong to this section.

31. *Zohar Ḥadash* on the *parashah Va-etḥanan*, 56d–58d.

32. *Zohar Ḥadash*, 37c–41b.

33. Zohar II and III. The longest and more important sections are II, 114a–121a; III, 97a–104a; 108b–112a; 121b–126a; 215a–258a; 270b–283a.

34. 93c–122b.

35. 31a–35b.

36. Zohar I, 22a–29a.

37. Zohar II, 47b, 52b, 84a, 176a–b; III, 48b, 60b; and many times in the *Idra Rabba*, and twice (III, 289a, 291a) in the *Idra Zuta*. Sometimes it is quoted as *Zeniuta de-Sifra*.

38. Zohar I, 217a; II, 61b; III, 79a, 145b, 148a, 288a; *Zohar Ḥadash*, 44b. It is always quoted as *Idra Kadisha*.

39. Zohar III, 127b.

40. Particularly at several points in the *parashah Pinḥas*.

41. This story is translated below, pp. 159–61.

42. (Venice, 1586), 31b.

43. *Mazref la-Ḥokhmah* (printed in *Ta'alumot Ḥokhmah*, Basle, 1629), 22a.

44. E.g., the writings of Rabbi Menaḥem Recanati, and Rabbi David ben Judah he-Ḥasid. See below, pp. 20–22.

45. *Sefer Or Ne'erav* (Venice, 1587), III, chap. 3, "The books, indeed, which one should cherish for the purpose of self-improvement, are the works of Rabbi Simeon ben Yohai (peace be upon him), like the Zohar, the *Tikkunim, Raya Mehemna, Shir ha-Shirim, Sava*, and *Yanuka*, and, of those which preceded him, the *Sefer Yezirah*, the *Sefer ha-Bahir*, and the Midrash to Ruth and the Midrash to Lamentations from the

Zohar, and of those which came after him, the Midrash to the Book of Esther from the Zohar." It is possible that the phrase "those which came after him" implies that the work was a later imitation.

46. "Parashah Ḥadashah min ha-Midrash ha-Ne'elam she-ba-Zohar," *Louis Ginzberg Jubilee Volume* (New York, 1946), Heb. section, pp. 425–46.

47. J.T. *Berakhot*, 9, 2.

48. See Rabbi Moses Kunitz, *Sefer Ben Yoḥai* (Vienna, 1815), chap. 3. In this book the author collects together the passages that speak in praise of Rabbi Simeon ben Yohai.

49. B.T. *Sukkah* 45b.

50. B.T. *Shabbat* 33b and elsewhere.

51. Zohar III, 132b (*Idra Rabba*). [See Exodus 34: 29.]

52. However, in the Middle Ages two apocalyptic works were written under his name, namely, *Nistarot de-Rabbi Shimon ben Yoḥai* (Jellinek's *Bet ha-Midrash*, 3: 78–82) and *Tefillat Rabbi Shimon ben Yoḥai* (ibid., 4: 117–26).

53. B.T. *Ḥagigah*, 14b.

54. See below, p. 156.

55. The name of this rabbi, who is mentioned as being one of the three rabbis who departed at the end of the assembly, is not found elsewhere.

56. Rabbi Jose ben Simeon ben Lekunya, Rabbi Eleazar's father-in-law, is also mentioned frequently, but not as a scholar. He plays the part of a host, whose house is a meeting place for scholars.

57. See below, p. 163.

58. Zohar III, 144b.

59. See below, pp. 197ff. It would appear from this story that Rav Hamnuna used to live at Kfar Sikhnin and that he died shortly before the scholars came to stay at his wife's house.

60. See below, for example, pp. 148–51.

61. See below, pp. 165–69.

62. This title is also found in the Zohar proper, but it is much less common.

63. The version quoted here is from the *Sefer Yuḥasin ha-Shalem* (ed. Filipowski, London and Edinburgh, 1857, pp. 88–89), with corrections from the Oxford MS version, which was published, with omissions, by A. Neubauer in *J.Q.R.* 4 (1892): 361–68. An imperfect text of the evidence was printed in the first edition of the *Sefer Yuḥasin* (Constantinople, 1566), and omitted in the other editions.

64. Lit., "with the four deaths of the *Bet Din*," i.e., stoning, burning, beheading, and strangling. See Mishnah *Sanhedrin* 7: 1.

65. The *Sefer Yuḥasin ha-Shalem* reads "Italy."

66. See G. Scholem, "Ha-im Ḥibber R. Mosheh de Leon et *Sefer ha-Zohar*," *Mad'ei ha-Yahadut* 1 (1926): 17, n. 7.

67. The Neubauer text reads: There are some pages missing from the book here, and therefore I have not finished what I have learned about all this.

68. The theory that the book was written through the power of the Holy Name, that is to say, that Rabbi Moses was a medium for automatic writing, removes the slur of intentional forgery.

69. See Scholem, "Ha-im Ḥibber," p. 19.

70. *Sefer Yuḥasin ha-Shalem*, p. 222.

71. *Sefer Magen ve-Zinah* (1855), 51b.

72. See Scholem, "Ha-im Ḥibber," p. 17.

73. See Jellinek, *Moses ben Schem-Tob de Leon und sein Verhältniss zum Sohar* (Leipzig, 1851), pp. 19–20, 41–45, 52–53; G. Scholem, "Ha-im Ḥibber," pp. 20–21. The printed works are: *Sefer ha-Nefesh ha-Ḥakhamah* (Basle, 1608) and *Sefer Shekel ha-Kodesh* (London, 1911).

74. See G. Scholem: *Major Trends*, p. 194.
75. See idem, "Ha-im Ḥibber," pp. 21–22.
76. See pp. 49, 54.
77. "Ha-im Ḥibber," p. 18, n. 8.
78. In Joseph Solomon Rofe of Candia, *Sefer Ta'alumot Ḥokhmah* (Basle, 1629), 5b.
79. Apparently this should read "200."
80. *Sefer Yuḥasin ha-Shalem*, p. 45.
81. *Sefer Or ha-Ḥamah* (Jerusalem, 1876), 2a.
82. *Tikkunei ha-Ẓohar*, beginning of the preface.
83. *Tikkunei ha-Ẓohar, Tikkun* 69, 110a. See also the end of *Tikkun* 6.
84. See G. Scholem, "Ha-Ẓitat ha-Rishon min *ha-Midrash ha-Ne'elam*," (*Tarbiz* 3:
    181–83); and "Parashah Ḥadashah," p. 425. Professor Y. Baer has informed me
    that in the *Sefer Meshal ha-Kadmoni* (Tel-Aviv, 1953), pp. 172–74 there is another
    quotation from the *Midrash ha-Ne'elam*. The passage begins at the end of chap. 47
    and continues until the beginning of chap. 48. The source is *Zohar Ḥadash, Midrash
    ha-Ne'elam, Lekh Lekha*, 24d. The source material has been reworked in rhymed
    prose, but the passage begins in this way: "We have found a powerful example
    given by the sages concerning an awesome sacred mystery." The same "example"
    occurs in Rabbi Moses de Leon, *Sefer ha-Nefesh ha-Ḥakhamah*, pt. 4, sig. 5, fol. 1d,
    beginning, "The rabbis said . . . " (attributed in the *Midrash ha-Ne'elam* to "Rabbi
    Pinhas"). The version in *Meshal ha-Kadmoni* approximates more both in style and
    in content to that of the *Midrash ha-Ne'elam*. See Y. Baer, *A History of the Jews in
    Christian Spain* (Heb.), 1959, pp. 508–9, where there is a detailed discussion of the
    relationship between the *Meshal ha-Kadmoni* and the *Midrash ha-Ne'elam*.
85. Scholem, "Kabbalat R. Yizḥak ben Shlomo Avi Sahulah ve-*Sefer ha-Ẓohar*," *Kiryat
    Sefer* 6: 109–18.
86. The date of Rabbi Todros's death is disputed by Graetz, Baer, and Scholem.
    Graetz (7: 204) thinks that he died at the beginning of the fourteenth century.
    According to Baer (*Dvir* 2: 314–15; *Zion* 2: 46, n. 61) the date should be 1283.
    Scholem's latest opinion is that he died in 1298 ("R. David ben Yehudah
    he-Ḥasid, Nekhed ha-Ramban," *Kiryat Sefer* 4: 317, n. 1).
87. See Scholem, "Ha-im Ḥibber," pp. 26–27. The other quotations mentioned there
    are not from the Zohar. See idem, "Ha-Ẓitat ha-Rishon," p. 183. Rabbi David
    Luria was the first to draw attention to these quotations.
88. Scholem, "Ha-im Ḥibber," p. 28. One of these quotations had already been
    studied by Rabbi Jacob Emden. See also A. Gottlieb, *Ha-Kabbalah be-Kitvei Rabbenu
    Baḥya ben Asher* (Jerusalem, 1970), pp. 167–93, 264–74.
89. See above, p. 18.
90. Scholem, *Major Trends*, pp. 194–95.
91. The time when he was active and the quotations from the Zohar to be found in his
    writings have been often discussed in connection with the study of the Zohar,
    particularly by Luria, Landauer, and Jellinek.
92. Namely, Commentary to the Torah (Venice, 1545); *Sefer Ta'amei ha-Mizvot* (Basle,
    1585); Commentary to the Liturgy (appended to the *Ta'amei ha-Mizvot*).
93. See Scholem, "R. David ben Yehudah he-Ḥasid, " pp. 302–27.
94. See Scholem, "Seridei Sifro shel R. Shem Tov ibn Gaon al Yesodot Torat
    ha-Sefirot," *Kiryat Sefer* 8–9.
95. Jerusalem, 1913.
96. See Scholem, "R. David ben Yehudah he-Ḥasid," pp. 326–27.
97. Idem, "Teshuvot ha-Meyuḥasot le-R. Yosef Gikatilla" in *Festschrift Dr. Jakob
    Freimann* (Berlin, 1937), pp. 165, 169–70.
98. *Sefer Akedat Yizḥak* (Lemberg, 1868) I, 225b (*parashah Va-yishlaḥ*).
99. It is found in Zohar I, 170b.

100. See below, pp. 99–101.
101. [Lit., "one from a city and two from a family."]
102. Above, p. 19.
103. Above, p. 20.
104. See Rabbi David Luria, *Ma'amar Kadmut Sefer ha-Zohar* (1856), 2a; Scholem, "Ha-im Hibber," pp. 23–24.
105. See Luria, op. cit., 21a–22a; Scholem, op. cit., pp. 25–26; idem, "Kabbalat R. Yizhak ben Shlomo," pp. 113–17.
106. *E.g., in the Sefer Avodat ha-Kodesh* by Rabbi Meir ibn Gabbai.
107. Ed. Enelow. See his introductions, 1: 21–22; 2: 26–28; 3: 29–34.
108. P. 45.
109. Sec. II, chap. 28.
110. Rabbi Shem Tov ibn Gaon in his responsum on the mystery of the *sefirot*.
111. See Scholem, *Major Trends*, p. 394, n. 124.
112. The earliest and most successful imitations are the *Raya Mehemna* and the *Tikkunei ha-Zohar*, which were incorporated into the Zohar itself and considered part of it. However, the determination of their status as imitative of the Zohar depends on the result of research, which will be explained below. Hence they are not dealt with at this stage.
113. See Scholem, "R. David ben Yehuda he-Hasid," pp. 313–17.
114. Koretz, 1784.
115. Poryck, 1786.
116. See Jellinek, *Bet ha-Midrash*, III, pp. xxxviii–xlv.
117. Jellinek has established that the quotations from the Zohar were taken from citations in the works of Recanati.
118. Amsterdam, 1648.
119. All the laws in the Zohar were collected and arranged according to the system of the *Shulhan Arukh* in the *Sefer Yesh Sakhar* (Prague, 1609) by Rabbi Issachar Baer of Kremnitz.
120. *She'elot u-Teshuvot Maharshal* (Lublin, 1574), no. 98.
121. *Sefer Yuhasin ha-Shalem*, p. 45.
122. *Teshuvot* (Venice), no. 108, p. 111a.
123. P. 108b.
124. See Joseph Solomon Rofe of Candia (Crete) *Sefer Mazref la-Hokhmah*, 23b–27b; M. Kunitz, *Sefer Ben Yohai, Ma'anot* 131–132.
125. *Bet Yosef*, no. 25 on the words *viyevarekh asher kiddeshanu*.
126. Indeed, in a few kabbalistic works, particularly the *Raya Mehemna* and the *Tikkunei ha-Zohar*, the *Sefer ha-Peliah* and the *Sefer ha-Kaneh*, antitalmudic tendencies are discernible, but these tendencies did not reach the stage of actual opposition, or division within orthodox kabbalah.
127. Christian mysticism and the Sabbatean movement will be considered in more detail in the next chapter.
128. See Graetz (Hebrew trans.) 7: 263–64.
129. Based on the Zohar. See below pp. 196–97.
130. [A traditional name for the Talmud, being a Hebrew abbreviation of *shishah sedarim*, "six orders" of the Mishnah.]
131. M. Balaban, *Le-Toledot ha-Tenu'ah ha-Frankit* (Tel-Aviv, 1934), 1: 135.
132. Ibid., 2: 207.
133. A detailed account of the controversy appeared in a special section of *Shevut Teman* (Tel-Aviv, 1945), pp. 166–231.
134. See *Sefer Milhamot ha-Shem* (Jerusalem, 1931) and *Sefer Da'at Elohim* (Jerusalem, 1931), both by Rabbi Yihya al-Kafih. The Yemenite kabbalists replied to his accusations in a long work entitled *Emunat Adonai* (Jerusalem, 1938).

135. Preface to *Sefer Milḥamot ha-Shem*.
136. See Balaban, 1: 126.
137. Rabbi Moses Hayyim Luzzatto in the preface to his *Sefer Kalaḥ Pitḥei Ḥokhmah*.
138. *Shivḥei ha-Besht*, ed. Horodetzky (Berlin 1922), p. 78.
139. A. Cahana, *Sefer ha-Ḥasidut* (Warsaw, 1922), p. 150.
140. M. J. Guttman, *Torat Rabbenu Pinhas mi-Koretz* (Bilgoraj, 1931), p. 26.
141. See above, p. 13.
142. *Sefer Beḥinat ha-Dat* (Basle), 5b.
143. Ibid. [See above, n. 79.]
144. However, one decision of a kabbalist rabbi, who opposed printing because of the prohibition against revealing the secrets of the Torah, was published in an article by S. Assaf, "Le-Pulmus al Hadpasat Sifrei Kabbalah," *Sinai* 5: 360–68. See also I. Tishby, "Ha-Pulmus al *Sefer ha-Zohar* ba-Me'ah ha-Shesh-esreh be-Italiah," *Perakim* 1 (Jerusalem, 1967–68): 131–82.
145. *Mazref la-Ḥokhmah*, 22a.
146. Ibid., 27b–28a.
147. The letter was published by A. Geiger in *Melo Ḥofnayim* (Berlin, 1840), Hebrew section, pp. 1–14.
148. Ibid., p. 10.
149. [Habbakuk 2: 11.]
150. *Mazref la-Ḥokhmah*, 20a–20b.
151. *Sefer Ari Nohem* (Jerusalem, 1929), pp. 8, 61, 62, 65. See also pp. 38, and 78–79.
152. The leader of this occult tendency in Christian kabbalah was Agrippa von Nettesheim in his book *De Occulta Philosophia* (1530–1533). See Scholem, "Alchemie und Kaballa," *MGWJ* (1925), p. 106; J. L. Blau, *The Christian Interpretation of the Cabala in the Renaissance* (New York, 1944), pp. 78–88.
153. See A. E. Waite, *The Holy Kabbalah* (London, 1929), pp. vii–ix, 442–52; Blau, pp. 10, 14–15, 19–26, 28; Scholem, "Zur Geschichte der Anfänge der christlichen Kabbala," *Essays Presented to Leo Baeck* (London, 1954), pp. 158–93. Professor H. Wirszubski has drawn my attention to the fact that in Jules Dukas, *Recherches sur l'histoire littéraire du quinzième siècle* (Paris, 1876), p. 57, a fragment is quoted from a Latin letter written by Rabbi Elijah Delmedigo to Pico della Mirandola, in which Delmedigo lists in Hebrew several kabbalistic works: *Sefer ha-Zohar*, *Me'irat Enayim*, *Sha'arei Orah*, Recanati, *Ma'arekheth ha-Elohut*, and a commentary to the *Sefer Yezirah*. He then goes on to discuss the theory of the *sefirot*. See idem, pp. 56–77. So we see that one of the Zohar's critics and an opponent of kabbalah furnished information about them to Pico. Wirszubski has published recently a number of important articles on the Jewish apostate known as Flavius Mithridates, who did a great deal to spread kabbalistic ideas among the Christians, mainly by translating kabbalistic writings into Latin for Pico. See in particular Wirszubski, *Flavius Mithridates, Sermo de Passione Domini* (Jerusalem, 1963).
154. *De verbo mirifico* (Basle, 1494); *De arte kabbalistica* (Hagenau, 1517).
155. See Waite, pp. 458–61; Blau, pp. 41–59.
156. Ibid., pp. xi, 433, 459; Blau, pp. 65–77. On the influence of kabbalah in the Renaissance and the development of Christian kabbalah, see the series of publications by F. Secret. Particularly important for our purpose is *Le Zohar chez les kabbalistes chrétiens de la Renaissance* (Paris, 1958).
157. *Kabbala Denudata* (Sulzbach, 1677–78; Frankfurt, 1684). See Waite, pp. 470–71, 476–79.
158. See Scholem, "Alchemie und Kabbala," pp. 107–8.
159. See Blau, pp. 14, 97.
160. Ibid., pp. 108–9.
161. See Scholem, *Bibliographia Kabbalistica*, no. 843. In the eighteenth and nineteenth

centuries many Christian scholars studied the problems of the Zohar, but this is not the place to go into details.

162. This view was expressed by Schöttgen in 1735. See Waite, p. 60, n. 1.

163. Waite, pp. 47, 82–83, 470–71.

164. [Cf. Isaiah 19: 6.]

165. [Cf. B. T. *Baba Kamma* 69a.]

166. Pp. 95–96. See also p. 9.

167. I have discovered in manuscript the piece defending the Zohar written by Rabbi Jacob Halevi, which his father-in-law, Leon Modena, disputed in the *Ari Nohem*. It is important because it helps to explain Modena's book. One should also note the *Sefer Ben David*, a short work by Modena attacking the kabbalistic belief in the transmigration of souls. This book, like the *Ari Nohem*, was apparently written for his pupil Rabbi Joseph Ḥamiẓ. I have found in manuscript some notes on this work sent to Modena in a letter, apparently a reply by the pupil for whom the work was intended. In a manuscript exchange of letters between two Italian scholar acquaintances of Modena, there is talk of bitter criticism of his disbelief in transmigration, without mentioning his name explicitly. It is also said there that Modena intended to publish a work attacking kabbalah and that one ought to frustrate this design. The work in question seems to have been the *Ari Nohem*.

168. Pp. 69–74.

169. Pp. 56–57.

170. Pp. 67–69.

171. P. 57.

172. See S. Ginzberg, *R. Mosheh Ḥayyim Luzzatto u-Vnei Doro* (Tel-Aviv, 1937), 2: 255, 268, 344.

173. Ibid., pp. 352–58.

174. Part II of Rabbi Jacob Emden's *Sefer Mitpaḥat Sefarim* (Altona, 1768) is devoted to a detailed critique of this book.

175. End of chap. 26.

176. Edited first by I. Fürst (Leipzig, 1840).

177. The book was printed in 1855 without name of author, or date and place of publication, because of the censor. Two other books were written against the *Ari Nohem*: *Eymat Mafgi'a al Ari* (Livorno, 1856) by Elijah ben Amozeg, and *Eymat Mafgi'a al ha-Ari Nohem* (Warsaw, 1888) by Rabbi Moses Sofer. The first does not deal with the problem of the Zohar, and the second is not worth discussing.

178. See *Magen ve-Ẓinah*, 27b, 45a, 52a.

179. Ibid., 45b.

180. Ibid., 25b–26a.

181. See above, p. 28.

182. Popular knowledge of kabbalah had already begun to spread among Polish Jewry by the middle of the sixteenth century, before the growth of Lurianic kabbalah. This seems evident from the statement of Rabbi Moses Isserles in the *Sefer Torat ha-Olah* (Prague, 1570) III, 4: "Many ordinary people now jump at the opportunity to learn something of kabbalah, for it is a delight to the eyes. And they are particularly keen on the writings of the later [kabbalists] whose books reveal their ideas quite plainly, especially in our own time when kabbalistic works are printed, such as the Zohar, Recanati, and *Sha'arei Orah*. Whoever reads can ponder on them, and imagine that they understand it all, although their writings will not be really understood, since there is no personal transmission from one kabbalist to another. And it is not only the intelligentsia who study kabbalah. Ordinary people, who walk in darkness and do not know their right hand from their left and cannot even understand one section of Rashi's commentary to the Bible, hasten to learn

kabbalah. . . . And they have only to see a little of it, and they start boasting and discussing it in public, but they will be called to account for it." It is also probable that the kabbalah was generally known in Prague and the surrounding area, because Isserles' remarks are copied word for word, without any reference to the source, in the preface to the *Sefer Va-yeḥal Mosheh* (Prague, 1613) by Rabbi Judah Aaron Moses Altschuler, who was a native of Prague, and rabbi of the Kromau community in Moravia.

183. *Sefer Mishnat Ḥakhamim* (Wannseebeck, 1733), no. 240. Preceding this statement he complains of those who permit the learning of Zohar and mysticism generally, even from heretics and apostates, and particularly from Sabbateans.

184. Responsa, *Noda bi-Yhudah*, I, *Yoreh De'ah*, no. 74.

185. *Kuntres Ahavat David* (Prague, 1790), 6b.

186. [Leviticus 11: 29.]

187. Op. cit., 18a. See also 25b, 27a.

188. *Siḥah bein Shnat Takas u-vein Shnat Taksa* (Prague, 1800), pp. 11–12.

189. See Balaban, *Le-Toledot ha-Tenu'ah ha-Frankit*, 1: 145–60; 2: 217, 226–29, 235–37, 238–41.

190. Quotations from the book are from the Lvov edition, 1870.

191. *Mitpaḥat Sefarim*, p. 11.

192. [Hebrew *sherez*, an allusion to Shabbetai Zvi. A reptile was an unclean animal. See Leviticus 5: 2.]

193. *Mitpaḥat Sefarim*, p. 4.

194. Ibid., p. 2. See also his apologia at the end of the book (pp. 102–5).

195. Ibid., p. 36.

196. Ibid., pp. 37–40.

197. Ibid., p. 8, and similarly on pp. 3 and 38.

198. [See Mishnah, *Baba Batra*, 10: 7.]

199. *Mitpaḥat Sefarim*, pp. 36–37.

200. Reuben Rappaport, editor of *Sefer Mitpaḥat Sefarim* (Lvov edition), also appended critical notes on Emden under the title *Ittur Sofrim*.

201. See the remarks by N. S. Libowitz in the preface and introduction to the *Sefer Ari Nohem*.

202. Ibid., pp. xxv–xxvi. The first two sentences are presented as the words of *Kol Kore* (A voice crying), which urged him to publish the book.

203. *Mitpaḥat Sefarim*, pp. 56, 64–65.

204. *Geschichte der Juden*, 7: Anhang 12. Most of A. B. Gotlober's views on the Zohar in *Toledot ha-Kabbalah ve-ha-Ḥasidut* (Zhitomir, 1870) are no more than a paraphrastic copy of Graetz's arguments.

205. *Vikuaḥ al Ḥokhmat ha-Kabbalah ve-al Kadmut Sefer ha-Zohar ve-Kadmut ha-Nekudot ve-ha-Te'amim*.

206. Ibid., pp. 122–23.

207. [*Gematria* is a method of biblical interpretation based on the numerical equivalent of the letters of a word.]

208. [Lit., "heads of words." Another method of interpretation was to take the initial letter of each word of a biblical verse, and regard the resulting word or words as of some significance.]

209. *Vikuaḥ*, p. 137.

210. *Sefer Aneh Kesil* by Rabbi Jedidiah Nissim and *Sefer Aderet Eliyahu* by Rabbi Solomon Nissim (both Livorno, 1855) are replies by kabbalists. The first consists mainly of chastisement and denunciation of heresy in the *Vikuaḥ*, while the second contains nothing of substance relevant to Zohar research. The *Sefer Ishtadlut im Shadal* (2 pts. Warsaw, 1896–97) deals only with the question of the vowel-points and the accents, and does not touch upon criticism of kabbalah and the Zohar.

211. *Ta'am Leshad*, pp. 45–46.
212. See G. Kressel, "Kitvei Elyakim Hamilzahagi," *Kiryat Sefer*, 17 (1940): 87–94.
213. This is extant in the author's autograph in the National Library in Jerusalem (Hebr. MSS 121, 4°). See G. Scholem, *Kitvei Yad . . . Kabbalah* (Jerusalem, 1930), no. 13.
214. See chaps. 5, 19, 24, and n. 4 to *hassagah* 28.
215. *Sefer Raviah*, 25b.
216. From the point of view of comprehensiveness the only drawback is that the *Tikkunei ha-Zohar* and the *Zohar Hadash* are not included within the range of his studies that are known to us.
217. *La Kabbale ou la philosophie religieuse des Hébreux* (Paris, 1843).
218. *Die Kabbala oder die Religions-Philosophie der Hebräer* (Leipzig, 1844). The book also appeared in a Hebrew version by M. Rabinsohn, *Ha-Kabbalah o ha-Philosofia ha-Datit shel ha-Yehudim* (Vilna, 1909).
219. Franck's book had several scholarly repercussions. See G. Scholem, *Bibliographia Kabbalistica*, p. 48, no. 370. The most important sequel, which both revises and supplements Franck's work, is D. H. Joel's book: *Midrash ha-Zohar, Die Religionsphilosophie des Sohar und ihr Verhältnis zur allgemeinen jüdischen Theologie* (Leipzig, 1849). However, as far as Zohar scholarship in particular is concerned, Joel has nothing original to say.
220. M. H. Landauer, "Vorläufiger Bericht in Ansehung des Sohar" *Literaturblatt des Orients* 6: 322, and subsequently.
221. *Wesen und Form des Pentateuchs* (1838).
222. This research is detailed in his book *Moses ben Schem-Tob de Leon und sein Verhältnis zum Sohar* (Leipzig, 1851).
223. *Beiträge zur Geschichte der Kabbala* (Leipzig, 1852), 2: 72–74.
224. Ibid., 1: 41–45.
225. Ibid., 2: preface.
226. *Versuch einer umständlichen Analyse des Sohar* (Ben Chananja, vols. 1–5, 1858–62).
227. *Ma'amar Kadmut Sefer ha-Zohar* (1856).
228. See G. Scholem, "Ha-im Hibber," pp. 45–52.
229. Some of the larger works are: S. Karppe, *Étude sur les origines et la nature du Zohar* (Paris, 1901); A. E. Waite, *The Secret Doctrine in Israel, a Study of the Sohar and its Connections* (London, 1913); A. Bension, *The Sohar in Moslem and Christian Spain* (London, 1932). Waite's book was subsequently included in his *The Holy Kabbalah* (London, 1929).
230. See D. Neumark, *Toledot ha-Philosophiyah be-Yisrael* (New York, 1921), 1: 204–14.
231. *Ha-Tekufah*, 5: 280–322.
232. Ibid., 6: 314–34; 7: 353–68; 9: 265–330.
233. See ibid., 6: 329–34.
234. Ibid., 7: 365–68.
235. Ibid., 6: 328. He goes on to quote in support S. A. Horodetzky and Mendele Mocher Seforim.
236. *Ha-Tekufah*, 6: 314.
237. "Ha-im Hibber R. Mosheh de Leon et *Sefer ha-Zohar*," *Mad'ei ha-Yahadut* 1 (1926): 16–29.
238. Ibid., pp. 28–29.
239. See in particular "Kabbalot R. Ya'akov ve-R. Yizhak benei R. Ya'akov ha-Kohen," *Mad'ei ha-Yahadut* 2 (1927): 163–293; and "Le-Heker Kabbalat R. Yizhak ha-Kohen," *Tarbiz* 2–5 (1931–34).
240. *Major Trends in Jewish Mysticism*, pp. 156–204.
241. This chapter contains the more important arguments that have accumulated in the critical literature. We give a number of clear examples of each type, together

with the counterarguments of its opponents. Most of the arguments are repeated
by a large number of scholars and I did not think it necessary always to indicate the
source of the material. However, in a few particular instances I do give the main
source.

242. I, 58b.
243. II, 147b.
244. II, 244b.
245. *Tikkunei ha-Zohar*, end of *Tikkun* 69, [119a].
246. III, 16a.
247. B.T. *Bekhorot* 8a.
248. III, 23a.
249. B.T. *Eruvin* 65a.
250. III, 51a.
251. B.T. *Sanhedrin* 90a.
252. II, 122a.
253. B.T. *Kiddushin* 28a.
254. B.T. *Baba Mezia* 59b.
255. II, 115b. (*Raya Mehemna*).
256. B.T. *Nedarim*, 13b.
257. III, 96b.
258. B.T. *Sotah* 14a.
259. III, 108a.
260. B.T. *Berakhot* 20a–b et seq.
261. III, 124a.
262. B.T. *Berakhot* 31b, *Yoma* 28a, *Zevahim* 32a–b.
263. See Leon Modena, *Ari Nohem*, pp. 60–65.
264. [Psalm 119: 126, later interpreted by the rabbis to refer to a time of national or
     spiritual emergency.]
265. See *Ari Nohem*, pp. 58–59, 66.
266. See below p. 162.
267. See the legal opinion of Rabbi Isaac Delattes in the Mantua edition of the Zohar.
268. Basilea, *Emunat Hakhamim*, chap. 25; Modena, *Magen ve-Zinah*, 49b; Kunitz, *Ben
     Yohai, ma'aneh* 131, p. 134.
269. B.T. *Eruvin* 53a.
270. B.T. *Shabbat* 112b.
271. Zohar II, 157b; III 243a; and many times elsewhere.
272. *Tikkunei ha-Zohar*, *Tikkun* 21, 70 and elsewhere.
273. Zohar II, 110b (*Sava*) and 257b-258a (*Hekhalot*).
274. III, 36a, 144b, 200b, 240b.
275. See below, p. 163.
276. B.T. *Shabbat* 33b.
277. See B.T. *Hullin*, 7b, and J.T. *Demai*, 1, 3.
278. B.T. *Baba Mezia*, 85a.
279. *Pesikta de-Rav Kahana*, ed. Buber, 91a–92a.
280. *Bereshit Rabbah*, 35: 4.
281. Below p. 130.
282. Below p. 577.
283. B.T. *Sukkah* 20a.
284. Ibid., 44b.
285. J.T. *Kilayim*, 9, 3.
286. It seems that at one point (Zohar, II, 125b) this Rabbi Yesa was meant to be the
     tanna, Rabbi Jose ha-Galili, Rabbi Akiva's companion, who was certainly not a
     pupil of Rabbi Simeon's. In several places there is a quotation from Rabbi Yesa

Sava and also from the *Sifra de-Rabbi Yesa Sava*, of which there is no record in the earlier sources. From one statement (III, 9a–b) it seems that he was considered to be an earlier scholar from the Temple period.

287. See below, p. 158.

288. J.T. *Berakhot* 9, 2.

289. *Bereshit Rabbah* 98: 22.

290. J.T. *Peah* 1, 5.

291. See above, p. 11. There are other references to Rav Hamnuna Kadma'ah (III, 199a) and to Rav Hamnuna Sava Kadma'ah (II, 145a, 146b).

292. Zohar II, 124a.

293. B.T. *Pesahim* 105a. Other scholars, all of them from Babylon, are also called Rav Hamnuna, but without the qualifying title of Sava.

294. B.T. *Sukkah* 42a; *Ketubot* 40a; and elsewhere. In Zohar II, 79a Rabbi Simeon ben Yohai is quoted as saying to Rabbi Jose: "Thus I learned from my father who spoke in the name of Rav Hamnuna Sava." In several places it is said that Rav Hamnuna Sava went up to Palestine from Babylon (Zohar III, 72b, and elsewhere).

295. See above, p. 11.

296. B.T. *Pesahim* 103b.

297. *Zohar Hadash* 27d–28a (*Midrash ha-Ne'elam*).

298. However, as a last desperate resort, you could solve this difficulty by saying that the reference in the Zohar is to an earlier scholar, a few of whose statements are quoted in the name of "a younger scholar (*ze'eira*) among the men of Jerusalem."

299. *Zohar Hadash* 25c–26b (*Midrash ha-Ne'elam*).

300. Zohar I, 89a (*Sitrei Torah*), III, 158a. Many statements are quoted in his name in the *Midrash ha-Ne'elam*. The story in the *Sitrei Torah* is exactly the same as the one in the *Midrash ha-Ne'elam*, with some slight stylistic variations. But Rabbi Dostai and Rabbi Eleazar ben Arakh are replaced by Rabbi Hiyya and Rabbi Eleazar (without the patronymic), and the subject matter of the expositions is different, without Rabbi Isaac's name being mentioned at all. A comparison of the two versions is very instructive from the critical point of view.

301. Cf. B.T. *Avodah Zarah* 68a.

302. See B.T. *Moed Katan* 25a.

303. III, 75b. [See below, p. 1478]

304. See B.T. *Avodah Zarah* 37a.

305. See below, pp. 154–5. Several statements are quoted in his name in the *Midrash ha-Ne'elam* to the Book of Ruth.

306. (Venice, 1763), 2: 122d.

307. *Sefer Yuhasin ha-Shalem*, p. 46.

308. *Ben Yohai, Ma'aneh* 67.

309. Ibid., nos. 57, 69.

310. Ibid., nos., 29, 57; David Luria, *Ma'amar Kadmut Sefer ha-Zohar*, 29b–30a.

311. *Mazref la-Hokhmah*, 21a–21b; *Emunat Hakhamim*, chap. 26; *Magen ve-Zinah*, 26a, 49b–50a; Solomon Nissim, *Aderet Eliyahu*, p. 21; Benamozegh, *Ta'am Leshad*, p. 57.

312. E.g., the opening pages of the *parashah Va-yehi* (Zohar I, 211b–216a).

313. Below, pp. 87–96.

314. *Vikuah al Hokhmat ha-Kabbalah*, pp. 117–18.

315. See G. Scholem, "She'elot be-Vikoret ha-Zohar mitokh Yedi'otav al Erez-Yisrael," *Zion, Me'assef* 1 (1925): 40–55; *Major Trends in Jewish Mysticism*, pp. 168–69.

316. Zohar II, 5a, 36b; I, 8a.

317. See below, p. 151. The cave of Lydda is also mentioned elsewhere in the Zohar.

318. *Kohelet Rabbah* 10: 11: "They hid in the cave at Peka," where the reference apparently is to Peki'in. The text varies in other sources, but from all of them it is clear that the cave was not far from Tiberias. See Y. Ben-Zvi, *Ha-Yishuv ha-Yehudi bi-Kfar Peki'in*, (1922), pp. 4–5.

319. II, 48b; III, 150a.

320. B.T. *Megillah* 6a.

321. Zohar I, 101a–101b (*Midrash ha-Ne'elam*). Mata Meḥasia is mentioned again (I, 72a) and here also it is apparently meant to be in Palestine. Kfar Tarsha is mentioned (I, 92b) as a place near Tiberias.

322. B.T. *Ketubot* 4a.

323. *Zohar Ḥadash*, 11b–11c (*Midrash ha-Ne'elam*). There the reference is to "the mountain of Kfar Kardu," where Rabbi Jose ben Paẓi (an unknown scholar who according to the Zohar was a Palestinian contemporary of Rabbi Abba) met a boy by the name of Ahavah, later to be the father of Rav Ada (a Babylonian *amora* and pupil of Rav). The boy's teacher in Kfar Kardu was Rabbi Alexandrai (a later Palestinian *amora*).

324. Genesis 8: 4.

325. I, 63a; III, 149a; *Zohar Ḥadash*, 49a (*Sitrei Torah*).

326. Zohar II, 38b; *Zohar Ḥadash* 24c (*Midrash ha-Ne'elam*).

327. J.T. *Shevi'it*, 9, 4. See the note of S. Klein, *Zion, Me'assef* 1, p. 56.

328. See R. Margaliot, *Niẓoẓei Zohar* (Jerusalem, 1940–46), II, 48b, no. 9.

329. Ibid., I, 69b, no. 5. Margaliot tries to conclude from B.T. *Yevamot* 25b that the Kapotkia mentioned here was a place near Lydda, but it is obvious from the phrase *Megiẓat Kapotkia* (i.e., Mazaca, later Caesarea, the capital of Cappadocia) that the reference is to the well-known province of Cappadocia.

330. *Ari Nohem*, p. 68.

331. *Vikuaḥ al Ḥohkhmat ha-Kabbalah*, pp. 113–14.

332. *Major Trends*, pp. 163–68, particularly p. 164. In his notes to this chapter, which contains a description and an exhaustive analysis of the language of the Zohar in all its aspects, Scholem quotes many examples, most of which had not been noted in the earlier critical literature. Most of the examples that I give below are also cited there.

333. Zohar I, 79b (*Sitrei Torah*), 90b–91a (*Sitrei Torah*), 109a–b (*Midrash ha-Ne'elam*); III 29b (*Raya Mehemna*), 33b (*Raya Mehemna*); *Zohar Ḥadash* 9a (*Midrash ha-Ne'elam*); and also several times in the *Midrash ha-Ne'elam* to Ruth.

334. *Zohar Ḥadash* 6d (*Midrash ha-Ne'elam*).

335. Zohar I, 109b, 128b, 137b, all from *Midrash ha-Ne'elam*.

336. III, 247b (*Raya Mehemna*). We should note parallel terms in the *Tikkunei ha-Zohar*, *Tikkun* no. 70, 126a: *nefesh ha-zikkaron, nefesh ha-maḥashavah, nefesh ha-meẓayyer*.

337. II, 116b; III, 230b (*Raya Mehemna*).

338. See the passages from the *Raya Mehemna* and the *Tikkunei ha-Zohar* in the section on *En-Sof* below.

339. *Tikkunei ha-Zohar*, preface, 5a.

340. Ibid., *Tikkun* no. 19, 40a; *Zohar Ḥadash*, 34b–34c.

341. Zohar I, 27a and often.

342. I, 126a (*Midrash ha-Ne'elam*) and often.

343. The verbs *adbak* and *itdabak* also occur often in this sense. This usage shows a misunderstanding of the original meaning in Aramaic.

344. I, 15a (*kotra be-golma*, a mist within matter).

345. See below, pp. 556–57.

346. See Scholem, *Major Trends*, p. 165.

347. Zohar III, 282a. See also *Tikkunei ha-Zohar*, preface, 7a.

348. The origin of this error is a misunderstanding of the Targum. Numbers 11: 12, "carry it in your bosom" is explained in Onkelos as "endure it in your strength (*be-tukefakh*)". The author of the Zohar thought that this was the exact literal translation.

349. Zohar II, 156a.

350. The first rendering would necessitate the reading *di-kadrinuta*. According to the second explanation, found in kabbalistic literature, the origin of the word is in the phrase in the *gemara* (B.T. *Pesaḥim* 7a, 21b) *ḥitei kurdanita*, but there the reference is to wheat from Kurdistan, which, according to Rashi, is very hard. The author of the Zohar has used the word as if it in itself meant "hardness" or "strength."

351. B.T. *Ta'anit* 25a.

352. See Scholem, *Major Trends*, pp. 163–65.

353. Scholem, *Sidrei di-Shimusha Rabba* (*Tarbiẓ*, 16 (1945): 197–203).

354. Jellinek, *Bet ha-Midrash*, 5: 43–44. Quoted first of all in Nachmanides' *Sha'ar ha-Gemul*.

355. *Magen ve-Ẓinah*, 50a–50b.

356. *Ma'amar Kadmut Sefer ha-Ẓohar*, 32a.

357. Ibid., 29b–30b.

358. *Magen ve-Ẓinah*, 50b; *Ma'amar Kadmut*, 30b–31a.

359. Hastings, *Encyclopaedia of Religion and Ethics* (1921), 12: 858–62.

360. *Ben Yoḥai, Ma'aneh* 3.

361. Ibid., *Ma'aneh* 1.

362. J. L. Zlotnik, *Ma'amarim mi-Sefer Midrash ha-Meliẓah ha-Ivrit* (Jerusalem 1939), pp. 37–39.

363. S. Poshinsky, "Le-Ḥeker Sefat ha-Zohar," *Yavneh* 2 (1940): 140–47.

364. *Ẓohorei Raviah* (MS) 3a.

365. III, 192b.

366. B.T. *Avodah Ẓarah* 2b.

367. II, 3a; III, 192a–193a. And see Steinschneider: *Polemische und apologetische Literatur* (Leipzig, 1877), pp. 317–18.

368. Consider the statement in the Zohar (III, 192a): "This verse is not clear, and one must ask: When the Holy One, blessed be He, went to Seir (Edom), to which of their prophets did He reveal Himself? and when He went to Paran (Ishmael), to which of their prophets did He reveal Himself? If you say that He revealed Himself to all of them, we do not find such a thing anywhere; but only to Israel, and by Moses."

369. Zohar I, 13a. The Zohar here follows Nachmanides (on Genesis 2: 3) as far as Islam is concerned. Of Greece also it is said (II, 237a) that "they are near to the way of faith," i.e., to the mystical religion. This approximation must be based on Neoplatonic writings, which circulated in the Middle Ages as the work of ancient Greek philosophers.

370. See Steinschneider, op. cit., pp. 360–62; Bacher, "Judaeo-Christian Polemics in the Zohar" *JQR* 3 (1891): 781–84.

371. Zohar II, 188a–188b.

372. In the *Ẓohar Ḥadash*, as well, at the end of *Va-yeze*, 28d (*Midrash ha-Ne'elam*), there is an allusion to the fact that the Christians in their doctrines destroyed true prophecy: "the air of the land of Israel makes men wise and promotes prophecy, but the descendants of Esau spoil both the air and prophecy." In the Midrash to Ruth (31c) there is a reference to the "other gods" of Ishmael and Esau, and it is said of the gods of Esau's descendants that "all the children of Israel bow down to the Holy One, blessed be He, and the god of the children of Esau bows down to them."

373. Zohar III, 220b–221a.

374. [*Nevelah* refers to animals that have not been ritually slaughtered, *terefah* to animals that are found, after slaughtering, to have organic defects.]

375. *Ẓohar Ḥadash*, 27d–28a.

376. The original says: *ve-khol mesa'abin yikrevun bakh*. The meaning seems to be that the unclean Gentiles will approach the holy place. But it is possible to interpret the phrase to refer to unclean prayers, or unclean sacrifices.

377. However, the description is not accurate, because there are no "images" or "corpses of the dead" in the Mosque of Omar. The author has fabricated idols and graves in order to highlight the uncleanness of the mosque, in accordance with his habit of adding a little something from his own imagination to his "prophetic" descriptions. It is possible that the expression *golmei mesa'abin* does not refer to idols but to bodies, and so is parallel in meaning to *pigrei mitaya*.

378. Zohar III, 282a. See Steinschneider, op. cit., p. 362.

379. These four hundred years were apparently meant to be calculated from the beginning of the fifth millenium (i.e., 240 C.E.), and this would lead us to the precise date of the conquest of the land of Israel by the Arabs in 634–638. Rabbi David Luria tried to use this date to prove, by means of apologetic hair-splitting arguments, that the passage was written as a prophecy of the future. See *Ma'amar Kadmut Sefer ha-Zohar*, 25b–26a.

380. Zohar II, 32a.

381. An echo of the Muslim-Christian wars during the Crusades can also be heard in another apocalyptic account (*Zohar Ḥadash*, end of *parashah Balak*).

382. Zohar II, 17a (*Midrash ha-Ne'elam*). See also III, 219a, 242b, 246b (*Raya Mehemna*), *Zohar Ḥadash*, 47b (*Midrash ha-Ne'elam*).

383. Zohar II, 188b.

384. Zohar I, 116b–117a, 119a; *Zohar Ḥadash*, end of *Balak*. Only one statement (*Zohar Ḥadash*, end of *Va-yeshev*, *Sitrei Torah*) fixes the beginning of the end at a later date, namely, 1540 years after the destruction of the Temple, i.e., 1608. Those scholars who thought to find this date in the *Midrash ha-Ne'elam* (I, 139b–140a) are mistaken, because the reference there is to the resurrection of the dead in 5408, i.e. 1648, but the proponent of this idea also agreed that the redemption would start at the beginning of the sixth millennium. See the *Vikuaḥ al Ḥokhmat ha-Kabbalah*, pp. 118–19; A. H. Silver, *A History of Messianic Speculation* (New York, 1927), pp. 90–92.

385. Zohar III, 249a, 252a.

386. Zohar II, 9b.

387. See Y. Baer, "Todros ben Yehudah Halevi u-Zemano," *Zion* 2 (1937): 42–44.

388. "Ha-Reka ha-Histori shel ha-*Raya Mehemna*," *Zion* 5 (1940): 1–44.

389. *Ben Yoḥai*, Ma'aneh 23; *Ma'amar Kadmut Sefer ha-Zohar*, 25b–26b.

390. See R. Margaliot, *Nizozei Zohar* on Zohar II, 17a, no. 2.

391. *Ben Yoḥai*, Ma'aneh 4. See also Solomon Judah Rappaport in *Naḥalat Yehudah*.

392. *Nizozei Zohar* (I, 13a, no. 11).

393. See above, p. 117, n. 369. One statement in the Zohar (II, 237a), apart from the reference in it to Greece's proximity to the way of faith, is an almost word-for-word quotation from the *Pesikta de-Rav Kahana*, ed. Buber, 40b. And there it is explicitly stated that the Persians were idolaters: "The Persian kings were upright, and the only fault that the Holy One, blessed be He, found in them was that they were idolaters, and this they merely inherited from their ancestors." Ishmael's nearness to God and to the true faith is also alluded to in II, 87a.

394. See K. Preis, "Die Medizin im Sohar," *MGWJ* (1928), pp. 167–84; Y. Rabin, "Ha-Refuah be-*Sefer ha-Zohar* u-ve-Sifrei Kabbalah Aḥerim," *Ha-Rofe ha-Ivri* 31 (1958): 80–90.

395. II, 172b.

396. See Bacher (*REJ* 22 (1891): 137–38; 23: 133–34). The customs cited there are: the kissing of the hand as a sign of respect (see in particular Zohar III, 296b), and the allusions to armed combat in the description of arguments on matters of Torah. The kissing of the hand is also cited in rabbinic statements as a praiseworthy custom practiced by foreigners, but not by Jews in the land of Israel.

397. *Zohar Ḥadash*, Tikkunim, 101c–101d.

398. Zohar I, 15b, 17a, 24a–24b (this belongs to the *Tikkunei ha-Zohar*); II, 158a (*Raya Mehemna*); III, 205b; *Midrash Ruth* (*Zohar Hadash* 84b), and many more. See I, 100b (*Sitrei Torah*); II, 180a.
399. Zohar I, 15b, 17a.
400. Zohar II, 184b; *Tikkunei ha-Zohar*, preface, 7a.
401. Zohar I, 15b. See Y. L. Zlotnik: *Ma'amarim mi-Sefer Midrash ha-Melizah ha-Ivrit*, pp. 33–36.
402. *Zohar Shir ha-Shirim* (*Zohar Hadash*) 73a–73b. And see also 73c.
403. Zohar II, 97b (*Sava*); III, 10b, 65a. The vocalizations of names are mentioned frequently in the Zohar to the Song of Songs, and in the *Tikkunei ha-Zohar*.
404. Zohar III, 189a, 191b (*Yanuka*), 201a, 203a, 205b.
405. Zohar I, 24b; II, 158a; III, 247b, and frequently elsewhere, particularly in the *Tikkunim* of the *Zohar Hadash*. See *Vikuah al Hokhmat ha-Kabbalah*, p. 120.
406. *Zohar Hadash*, 70b.
407. Ibid., 22d.
408. *Tikkunei ha-Zohar*, preface, 7b.
409. *Zohar Hadash, Tikkunim*, 105d. [The Masora gives an exhaustive account of the verbal peculiarities of the Hebrew Bible with a view to the preservation of the authentic text.]
410. Zohar II, 132a, 205b, 260b; III 234b (*Raya Mehemna*).
411. *Tikkunei ha-Zohar, Tikkun* no. 18, 34b; *Zohar Hadash, Tikkunim*, 100c.
412. Zohar III, 255b (*Raya Mehemna*).
413. Zohar III, 33a (*Raya Mehemna*), 63b.
414. *Tikkunei ha-Zohar, Tikkun* no. 18, 32b–33a; *Tikkun* no. 57, 91b.
415. Zohar III, 121b (*Raya Mehemna*).
416. See Milzahagi, *Sefer Raviah*, 30c–31b.
417. Milzahagi followed a different tack. He acknowledged that the vocalization and the accents were late, but argued that all the passages dealing with these things did not belong to the main body of the Zohar, but to separate sections, which he himself considered late. His analysis, however, is forced and artificial.
418. *Magen ve-Zinah*, 50a; *Ben Yohai, Ma'aneh* no. 79.
419. *Ben Yohai, Ma'aneh* no. 51; Franck, *Kabbala*, pp. 99–100.
420. *Ben Yohai, Ma'aneh* no. 121.
421. B.T. *Megillah* 3a.
422. Zohar I, 89a.
423. I, 31b. In later editions the sentence where the Targum Jonathan is mentioned is bracketed, but in the Mantua edition the quotation is introduced without qualification.
424. *Zohar Hadash*, 75d.
425. Zohar III, 257a.
426. *Tikkun* no. 13, 29a. In *Tikkun* no. 47, 83b, the same quotation is cited with a textual variant in the editions: "Onkelos or Jonathan."
427. B.T. *Megillah* 3a.
428. Zohar I, 9b, 88b–89a (*Sitrei Torah*); II, 129b, 132b–133a.
429. Zohar II, 183b.
430. B.T. *Berakhot* 55a.
431. Zohar II, 19a–19b.
432. B.T. *Berakhot* 59a.
433. Zohar III, 185b.
434. B.T. *Baba Mezia*, 86a.
435. Zohar III, 216b (*Raya Mehemna*).
436. B.T. *Ta'anit* 25a.
437. I.e., the tractate *Baba Batra* (73b).

438. *Tikkunei ha-Zohar*, preface, 2b. See Zohar III, 223b (*Raya Mehemna*).
439. B.T. *Baba Mezia* 59a.
440. *Tikkunei ha-Zohar*, *Tikkun* no. 15, 30b.
441. See Y. L. Zlotnik: *Ma'amarim mi-Sefer Midrash ha-Melizah ha-Ivrit*, pp. 54–55. The parallels cited there represent only a small part of the passages from the *Pirkei de-Rabbi Eliezer* that are either quoted or referred to in the Zohar.
442. Zohar, I, 34b.
443. *Ozar Midrashim*, ed. Y. D. Eisenstein, p. 47.
444. See above, p. 73.
445. Preface, 11b; *Zohar Hadash, Tikkunim*. 94b.
446. *Beiträge*, I, pp. 26–28.
447. See ibid., pp. 29–30, 37–38; Zlotnik, op. cit., pp. 30–32, 43–44.
448. Zohar III, 82b (*Raya Mehemna*).
449. *Zohar Hadash, Tikkunim*, 103a–103b. [The *Shekhinah* is the letter *dalet* of the word *ehad* (one). *Dalet* has the numerical equivalent of four. The remaining letters, *alef, het*, amount to nine, and these represent *Tiferet*, who comprises the nine remaining *sefirot*. Therefore, the totality of the word, when the *Shekhinah* and *Tiferet* are together, equals thirteen. See also Zohar II, 42b (*Raya Mehemna*).]
450. *Zohar Hadash, Tikkunim*, 101a.
451. Zohar II, 24b.
452. See Zlotnik, op. cit., pp. 32, 73; Scholem, "Ikvotav shel Gabirol ba-Kabbalah," *Me'assef Sofrei Erez-Yisrael* (1940), pp. 163–65.
453. See ibid., pp. 165–68.
454. See below, pp. 473, n. 65; 485.
455. See *Ta'am Leshad*, pp. 119–50. The author intended to show the influence of the kabbalah on Rabbi Judah Halevi by noting the parallels between them.
456. II, 36.
457. III, 221b.
458. Cf. III, 161a–161b. And see Zlotnik, op. cit., pp. 5–16, 68–69.
459. II, 79–80.
460. III, 218b.
461. *Hilkhot Yesodei ha-Torah*, II, 7. See R. Margaliot's essay, "Ha-Rambam ve-ha-Zohar" *Sinai* 32 (Year 16, 1953): 263–74; 33: 9–16, 128–35, 219–24, 349–54; 34 (Year 17, 1954): 227–30, 386–95. This work of considerable scope is extremely important for proving the late date of the Zohar—which is quite the opposite of the author's intention, which was to show the influence of the Zohar on Maimonides. One should note that the author is careful not to stress this intention.
462. *Zohar Hadash*, 6a.
463. Zohar II, 43a; *Zohar Hadash*, 33b (which belongs to the *Tikkunim*).
464. Zohar I, 81a.
465. Op. cit. IV, 6.
466. [By the righteous in the world to come.]
467. *Hilkhot Teshuvah*, VIII, 2–4.
468. Zohar I, 135d.
469. See Scholem, *Major Trends*, p. 173.
470. See Bacher, "L'exégèse biblique dans le Zohar," *REJ* 22 (1891): 33–46, 219–29.
471. Excerpts from Nachmanides in the Zohar will be dealt with among the quotations from kabbalistic literature.
472. II, 18a (*Midrash ha-Ne'elam*). Similarly I, 75a.
473. Genesis 11: 63; 38: 16; Exodus 1: 10.
474. I, 77b. The Zohar alters the sentence to suit its own particular interpretation. See Nachmanides' explanation of this verse.
475. I, 173a.

476. I, 230a.

477. I, 60b.

478. I, 167b.

479. [The *ziz* is the name given to the gold plate on the High Priest's miter on which was inscribed "Holy to the Lord" (Exodus 28: 36).]

480. II, 217b. The wording may lead one to believe that the Zohar here used Rashbam's interpretation: "Since it was placed on the forehead where it could be seen by people, it was called *ziz*."

481. III, 48a.

482. III, 136a.

483. Exodus 31: 3.

484. I, 74b.

485. II, 198a, on I Kings 8: 16: "I chose no city out of all the tribes of Israel to build a house, that My name might be there; but I chose David to be over My people Israel."

486. III, 133a (*Idra Rabba*).

487. Zohar I, 78a. Cf. *Sefer Yezirah* I, 2; VI, 4.

488. III, 147a (*Idra Rabba*). Cf. *Sefer Yezirah* I, 3.

489. III, 277b (*Raya Mehemna*), and several times in the *Tikkunei ha-Zohar*.

490. These influences are discussed in the introductions to the sections *The Account of the Chariot* and *Angels*.

491. *Zohar Ḥadash*, 82d–83a.

492. See Scholem, *Major Trends*, pp. 176–80.

493. I, 36b.

494. I, 106a.

495. III, 155b. See H. D. Chavel, "*Sefer ha-Zohar* ke-Makor Hashuv le-Ferush ha-Ramban al ha-Torah," *Sinai* 43 (year 21, 1958): 337–64. This article is another attempt to transpose the origin of the influence and the thing influenced, by using a common pseudoscientific apologetic method. Most of the parallels cited in the article demonstrate quite clearly the influence of Nachmanides on the Zohar, while some have no connection with the Zohar at all, and others come from works that antedate both the Zohar and Nachmanides, either in medieval literature or in the Talmud and the midrashim.

496. See Jellinek, *Beiträge* 1: 41–45. Rabbi Ezra's *Commentary to the Song of Songs* was published in a French translation in a scientific edition, together with notes and studies by G. Vajda, *Le Commentaire d'Ezra de Gérone sur la Cantique des Cantiques* (Paris, 1969).

497. I, 29a.

498. *Commentary to Song of Songs* (Altona, 1764), 5a–6a.

499. II, 20a–20b (*Midrash ha-Ne'elam*). [See below, p. 930.]

500. Op. cit. 5a.

501. II, 20b (*Midrash ha-Ne'elam*). [See below, p. 931.]

502. Op. cit., 5c.

503. See. I. Tishby, "Kitvei ha-Mekubbalim R. Ezra ve-R. Azriel mi-Gerona," *Sinai* (year 8), pp. 169–78.

504. E.g., III, 285–286a.

505. III, 270b–271b. This passage is designated as belonging to the *Raya Mehemna*, but in fact only the continuation, from the words *adhakhi sava izdaman*, belongs to that section.

506. See below, pp. 593–94.

507. III, 8b. See also 164a. [The rabbinic quotation is from B.T. *Berakhot* 8a.]

508. Two of the seven heavens (B.T. *Hagigah* 12b), meaning literally, "residence" and a "defined place."

509. I. Tishby, *Perush ha-Aggadot le-Rabbi Azriel* (Jerusalem, 1945), p. 11, according to the text quoted there in the list of variants. Cf. also p. 9.
510. Ibid., p. 11, n. 9.
511. *Sefer Ozar ha-Kavod ha-Shalem* (Warsaw, 1879), p. 9.
512. See Scholem, *Major Trends*, p. 173. Of the other literary types I may draw attention simply by name to several sources that I can demonstrate were used by the author of the Zohar: *Sefer he-Arukh*, the dictionaries of Ibn Parhon and David Kimchi, the commentary by Rabbi Shabbetai Donnolo to the *Sefer Yezirah*, and the *Tosafot* to the Talmud. See also the parallels adduced in the *Sefer Ben Yohai, Ma'aneh* no. 130.
513. *Ben Yohai, Ma'aneh* nos. 51, 110, 127, 130. *Ta'am Leshad*, pp. 40–43, 52–58.
514. Zlotnik, *Ma'amarim mi-Sefer Midrash ha-Melizah ha-Ivrit*, p. 16.
515. Ibid., pp. 32–33.
516. *Ben Yohai, Ma'aneh* nos. 16, 22, 72, 100, 101 and elsewhere; *Ma'amar Kadmut Sefer ha-Zohar*, 27a–27b.
517. See above, p. 20.
518. *Ben Yohai, Ma'aneh* no. 130.
519. *Ma'amar Kadmut Sefer ha-Zohar*, 3b–22a.
520. Above, p. 50.
521. *Ta'am Leshad*, pp. 49–58, 104–50.
522. Ibid., pp. 52–53.
523. Extremely important, from this point of view, are the notes of R. Margaliot in his *Nizozei Zohar*, despite the fact that the author tried to obscure their critical value.
524. See above, p. 64.
525. *Kabbala*, pp. 74–75.
526. *Mazref la-Hokhmah*, 21b; *Zohorei Raviah* (MS) 30b–31a; *Ma'amar Kadmut Sefer Ha-Zohar*, 22b–25a.
527. See above, p. 56.
528. *Kabbala*, pp. 75–76.
529. See above, p. 55.
530. *Zohorei Raviah* (MS) 15b–20a.
531. See Cordovero's *Pardes Rimmonim*, pt. XI.
532. See below, p. 269.
533. See Scholem, *Reshit ha-Kabbalah* (Jerusalem, 1948), pp. 172ff., and 258–59.
534. See Scholem, *Major Trends*, pp. 176–81.
535. See below, pp. 242–46.
536. Zohar III, 10b, 269a, 288b (*Idra Zuta*).
537. Above, pp. 72–73.
538. See above, pp. 33–34.
539. See C. Siegried, *Philo von Alexandria* (Jena, 1875), pp. 289–99; S. Karppe, *Etude sur les origines et la nature du Zohar*, pp. 413–19. Many exegetical and ideological parallels are cited in these two works. Franck (pp. 215–49) also points out the parallel in ideas, but in his view the Zohar was not influenced by Philo. They both drew upon ancient traditions. A new attempt to prove the antiquity of the Zohar on the basis of a supposed parallel between the *Midrash ha-Ne'elam* and the writings of Philo was made by S. Belkin in "*Ha-Midrash ha'Ne'elam* u-Mekorotav ba-Midrashim ha-Alexandriyim ha-Kedumim," *Sura* 3 (1957–58): 25–92. Zvi Werblowsky, however, refuted Belkin's view with detailed counterarguments in his "Philo and the Zohar," *JJS* 10 (1959): 25–44, 112–35.
540. See Franck, *Kabbala*, pp. 81–82, 251–60.
541. See below, pp. 235–37, 447ff. See I. Tishby, "Gnostic Doctrines in Sixteenth-century Jewish Mysticism," *JJS* 6 (1955): 146–52.
542. *Ben Yohai, Ma'aneh* 128.

543. A. Kaminka, "Ha-Rayanot ha-Sodiyim shel R. Shimon ben Yoḥai," *Sefer Klausner* (Tel-Aviv, 1937), pp. 171–80.

544. B.T. *Sanhedrin* 74a.

545. Op. cit., p. 173.

546. I.e., *orlah, kilayim,* and *ḥadash.*

547. B.T. *Kiddushin* 38a.

548. Op. cit., pp. 178–79.

549. "Le-Kadmut *Sefer ha-Zohar,*" *Sinai* 7 (1940–41): 116–19.

550. B.T. *Bezah* 15b.

551. See J. Levy, *Neuhebräisches und Chaldäisches Wörterbuch über die Talmudim und Midraschim,* s.v. *adar.*

552. Op. cit., pp. 116–17.

553. Above, pp. 61–62.

554. *Sefer Meor Enayim, Parashah Zav.*

555. *Sefer Zohorei Ḥamah* (Venice, 1655) 152b. And see *Sefer Yuḥasin ha-Shalem,* p. 45.

556. *Sefer Mishnat Ḥakhamim* (Wanseebeck, 1733), nos. 332, 334.

557. See *Emunat Ḥakhamim,* chaps. 25–26; *Magen ve-Zinnah* 49b–50a; *Ma'amar Kadmut Sefer ha-Zohar* 26b; *Ta'am Leshad* pp. 50–52.

558. Ben Yoḥai, *Ma'aneh* 129, fol. 120c.

559. See *Mitpaḥat Sefarim,* pp. 38–40.

560. I, no. 548.

561. *Kabbala,* pp. 88–98.

562. See above, pp. 58ff.

563. His evidence and main conclusions are to be found in his *Moses ben Schem-Tob de Leon.*

564. See above, p. 90.

565. See *Major Trends,* pp. 166, 168, 180.

566. Ibid. pp. 181–86.

567. Samuel David Luzzatto had already remarked (*Vikuaḥ al Ḥokhmat ha-Kabbalah,* p. 136) that after examining the books of Rabbi Moses de Leon he could find no trace of deliberate deceit.

568. Several scholars have expressed the view that the author of the Zohar had no intention of presenting his characters and his stories to the reader as historical fact, but that he was only trying to construct a literary-dramatic form. Scholem's views tend in a similar direction. But this approach seems to me to be somewhat far-fetched.

569. See Scholem, "Ha-im Hibber," *Kiryat Sefer,* 1: 22–24; *Major Trends,* pp. 186–88.

570. Scholem estimates that he was born in 1240. See *Major Trends,* p. 194.

571. One should point out that Scholem has a note that Rabbi Moses de Leon's *Sefer Maskiot Kesef,* extant in manuscript, was written after 1293. See *Major Trends,* p. 393, n. 113.

572. That is, apart from the responsa inserted in Rabbi Moses de Leon's books. See Tishby, "She'elot u-Teshuvot Rabbi Mosheh de Leon be-Inyanei Kabbalah," *Kovez al Yad,* vol. 5/15 (Jerusalem, 1951), pp. 11–38.

573. *Sefer ha-Nefesh ha-Ḥakhamah,* part III.

574. II, 211b.

575. *Sefer ha-Nefesh ha-Ḥakhamah,* part II.

576. See above p. 30. Rabbi Isaac of Acre's evidence stems, of course, from the beginning of the fourteenth century, but one assumes that the doubts he mentions arose earlier.

577. See *Major Trends,* pp. 198–99.

578. Ibid. pp. 183, 200, and 393, n. 103. Scholem elaborates in more detail on the relationship between the *Sefer Orḥot Ḥayyim,* which is also called the *Testament of*

Rabbi Eliezer the Great, and the Zohar in his article "Mekorotav shel *Ma'aseh Rabbi Gediel ha-Tinok* be-Sifrut ha-Kabbalah," *Le-Agnon Shai* (Jerusalem, 1959), pp. 293–305). A. Jellinek, who reprinted under the title *Seder Gan Eden* a work included with the *Orḥot Ḥayyim* in manuscripts and some printed editions (*Bet ha-Midrash*, III, pp. 131–40), dealt with the similarities between this work, the Zohar, and Rabbi Moses de Leon's *Mishkan ha-Edut* (ibid., pp. xxvi–xxviii), and he even quotes parallel passages (ibid., pp. 194–98). Since he concluded that the *Seder Gan Eden* was written by the author of the *Testament*, and since, in his view, the *Testament* was written before the Zohar, he tended to regard the *Seder Gan Eden* also as an early work, and as one of the Zohar's sources. On the other hand, I. Abrahams, who dealt only with the *Testament* itself, was inclined to date it later, on the basis of "the similarity between the Testament and the Zohar, a similarity well brought out by the title page of the Salonica edition of 1568 and by the notes in Leiner's Lublin edition of 1903" (*Hebrew Ethical Wills* [Philadelphia, 1926], 1: 31) As to the relationship between the *Testament* and the *Seder Gan Eden*, my own opinion is that, contrary to the views of Jellinek and Scholem, who agrees with him on this point, the two works are completely separate, both in style and content, and that they were put together later, in order to complete the description of the Garden of Eden, which, in keeping with its character, is only alluded to at the end of the *Testament*. All of Scholem's detailed evidence to show that this book belongs to the category of Zoharic literature is based solely on the *Seder Gan Eden*, and indeed as far as this text is concerned his arguments are extremely convincing. But this is not the case with the *Testament*, whose composition is, in my view, still an open question. Possibly it preceded the Zohar and influenced it, but the reverse could also be true. In any event I cannot see any reason for putting it in the context of Zoharic literature.

579. *Major Trends*, p. 185.
580. See S. Assaf, "Le-Pulmus al Hadpasat Sifrei Kabbalah," *Sinai* 5: 360–68.
581. See above, pp. 34–35.
582. See above, pp. 57–58.
583. On the controversies about the printing of the Zohar, see A. Ya'ari, *Meḥkerei Sefer* (Jerusalem, 1958), pp. 216–19; Tishby, "Ha-Pulmus al *Sefer ha-Zohar* ba-Me'ah ha-Shesh-esreh be-Italia," *Perakim* 1 (Jerusalem, 1967–68): 131–82.
584. See the corrector's preface to the Mantua printing of the Zohar; Assaf, op. cit., p. 360.
585. Rabbi Isaac Delattes, at the beginning of the Mantua edition.
586. Rabbi Moses Basola, at the beginning of the Mantua edition of the *Tikkunei ha-Zohar*.
587. He writes as follows about Rabbi Immanuel: "He gave good money to unearth from store whatever he could find of the *Sefer ha-Zohar* and the *Tikkunim*, and even at night he did not rest, but stayed with his disciples, his friends, and with those who loved him, in order to correct the text with the help of the ten copies that he had." It is not clear from this whether the ten manuscripts were of the Zohar, or of the *Tikkunei ha-Zohar*. But in the corrector's preface to the Zohar there is also a reference to "the many copies" that Rabbi Immanuel had.
588. Scholem gives a detailed list of all the printings of the Zohar, the *Zohar Ḥadash*, and the *Tikkunei ha-Zohar* in his *Bibliographia Kabbalistica*, pp. 166–82.
589. Lublin, 1623–24; Sulzbach, 1684. The Sulzbach edition contains variants of the Cremona text from the Mantua edition and also has additional notes and explanations.
590. First ed. Thiengen, 1560, under the title *Sefer Tapuḥei Zahav*.
591. The brief descriptions of manuscripts in the catalogues, which are not, generally speaking, very precise, do not tell us much about their nature or date. Professor Gershom Scholem is the only one so far to have examined them systematically. The

information presented here was communicated to me orally by him, and I here register my profound gratitude to him for allowing me to publish the material in this introduction.

592. See Scholem, "Parashah Ḥadashah min *ha-Midrash ha-Ne'elam*," *Louis Ginzberg Jubilee Volume* (New York, 1946), Heb. section, pp. 425–46. The whole section is published there.
593. See above, p. 23.
594. *Literaturblatt des Orients* (1845), pp. 341–43.
595. *Die hebräischen Handschriften der K. Hof- und Staatsbibliothek in München* (1895), pp. 98, 243–46.
596. See Hastings, *Encyclopedia of Religion and Ethics*, 12: 860.
597. See above, pp. 20–21.
598. See above, p. 23. I also deal with the *Sefer Menorat ha-Ma'or* in the next section, in connection with Zohar translations.
599. See above, pp. 21, 23.
600. See Jellinek's *Bet ha-Midrash* I, pp. xix, 102–5; Zunz, *Ha-Derashot be-Yisrael* (Jerusalem, 1947), p. 415, n. 98.
601. Ed. Enelow. See his introductions 2: 27–28; 3: 32–33.
602. Ibid., 4: 92.
603. *Derekh Emet* to the Zohar, I, 34b.
604. The translation of the *parashah Bereshit* was printed with the title *Sefer ha-Zohar ha-Shalem al ha-Torah* (Jerusalem, 1946). According to the introduction by the editor, Rabbi Obadiah Hadayah, they intended to print the other sections. The published excerpt shows that the translation is extremely fragmentary, and stylistically obscure. The editor suggests, from the colophon, that the translator was Rabbi Berechiel, but it is possible that this is only the name of the copyist. Neubauer notes in his Catalogue that the manuscript was finished by Marcheshvan 1576, but, according to the version quoted in the editor's introduction, the date was the Eve of Rosh Chodesh Kislev 1603.
605. This information I received from Professor Gershom Scholem.
606. Fol. 88c.
607. I cannot deal here with selections of aggadic material and sayings from the Zohar, and other books of this kind.
608. Fols. 2a–2b.
609. Fol. 30b.
610. *Metsudah* (London, 1943), pp. 40–82. Neither the translation nor the explanation fulfilled the hopes that Zeitlin raised. The original text was not corrected in the least, and in many places the translation is inaccurate. Nor does the style match that of the Zohar. In his explanatory notes many matters are introduced that have nothing to do with the literal meaning of the Zohar.
611. *Sefer Zohar Torah al Ḥamishah Ḥumshei Torah*, in 5 vols. The first two volumes were printed in Montreal (1924), and the last three volumes in New York (1924–25). The first volume was originally published separately (Warsaw, 1906), with the title *Sefer Sha'arei Zohar Torah*. This is a shortened edition, and arranged slightly differently. An additional volume on Psalms was published under the name *Sefer ha-Zohar ha-Kadosh* (Bilgoraj, 1929). The same title was given to the seventh volume, on Song of Songs, Proverbs, and Ecclesiastes (Bilgoraj, 1930). (From a note by J. L. Zlotnik.) Instead of clarifying the subject matter, the translator's system forced him to mix up the *parashiyot*, and to chop up the passages into small pieces. The translation itself is unreliable. Rosenberg also published *Sefer Nifle'ot ha-Zohar*, a collection of tales from the Zohar, in Hebrew and in Yiddish.
612. *Kabbala Denudata*, II (Frankfurt, 1684).
613. See above p. 33.

614. *Sepher ha-Zohar* (Paris, 1906–12).
615. See Scholem, *Bibliographia Kabbalistica*, p. 120.
616. *The Zohar* (London, 1931–34).
617. *Der Sohar* (Wien, 1932).
618. *Die Geheimnisse der Schöpfung* (Berlin, 1935).
619. *Zohar, the Book of Splendor* (New York, 1949).
620. Scholem has published a bibliographical list of the commentaries and manuals to the Zohar in his *Bibliographia Kabbalistica*, pp. 185–210.
621. Jerusalem, 1876–79. This edition, however, lacks the commentary to the Zohar on Numbers and Deuteronomy. The more complete edition is that of Przemyśl, 1896–1898.
622. Venice, 1655 (Genesis), Przemyśl, 1882 (Exodus). The Przemyśl edition of the *Or ha-Hamah* also contains notes from the *Zohorei Hamah*.
623. Livorno, 1795, in 2 vols.
624. Amsterdam, 1750, in 5 vols. It would seem from the approbations that the book first appeared in the period 1751–52. It was very popular in kabbalistic circles, and was printed nine times.
625. Fürth, 1776.
626. Vilna, 1882.
627. Cracow, 1589.
628. Cracow, 1635–36. The book is extremely scarce. There is a copy in the Jewish National and University Library in Jerusalem.
629. Venice, 1744.
630. Venice, 1637.
631. Prague, 1611.
632. Przemyśl, 1899.
633. Piotrków, 1912.
634. See above, nn. 328, 329, 390, 392, 523. See also R. Margaliot "Ha-Rambam ve-ha-Zohar," *Sinai* (1953–54).

THE WISDOM OF THE ZOHAR

PRELIMINARIES: EVENTS AND PERSONALITIES

1. THE GREATNESS OF RABBI SIMEON BEN YOHAI
(Zohar I, 155b–156a)

Rabbi Simeon went to a town where he was met by Rabbi Abba, Rabbi Hiyya, and Rabbi Jose. When he saw them he said: New interpretations of Torah are needed here.

The three of them sat down, and, as each one of them sought to leave, he began by quoting a verse from Scripture.

Rabbi Abba began by quoting: "And the Lord said to Abraham, after Lot had separated from him, Lift up your eyes and see . . ." (Genesis 13: 14).[1] Was Abraham to possess the land only as far as he could see, and no farther? How far can a man see? Three, four, five miles? And yet it says, "for the whole land that you see"! However, when he looked toward the four quarters of the globe he saw the whole land, for the four quarters of the globe comprise the entire world. Moreover, the Holy One, blessed be He, raised him up above the land of Israel and showed him how it was connected to the quarters of the globe,[2] and so he saw it in its entirety. In the same way, whoever looks upon Rabbi Simeon sees the entire world—the delight of the upper and the lower worlds.

Rabbi Hiyya began by quoting: "The land upon which you lie, to you will I give it, and to your seed" (Genesis 28: 13). Was this spot all that the Holy One, blessed be He, promised him? Only five or six feet? However, at that precise moment the Holy One, blessed be He, compressed the whole land of Israel into a space of six feet. So that particular spot contained the whole land. And just as that spot comprised the whole land, so it can be said with even more justification of Rabbi Simeon, who is the light of the whole earth, that he is equal in worth to the entire world.

Rabbi Jose began by quoting: "This time will I thank the Lord" (Genesis 29: 35).[3] Should she not have thanked the Holy One, blessed be He, for all the others she bore, and not only for this one? Judah, however, is the Throne's fourth son, and completes the Throne.[4] And so Judah alone is the perfection of the Throne, and the chief support. With how

---

[1] The biblical passage continues: ". . . from the place where you are, to the north, south, east and west; for the whole land which you see, to you will I give it, and to your seed for ever."

[2] The land of Israel was thought to be the center of the world.

[3] [Spoken by Leah when her son Judah was born.]

[4] Judah, the ancestor of King David, is a symbol of *Malkhut*, which is the fourth leg of the Throne of the Heavenly Chariot, the other three being *Hesed*, *Gevurah*, and *Tiferet*.

much more justice can this be said of Rabbi Simeon, who illumines the whole world with Torah and causes many lamps to shine.

2. THE TEACHING OF RABBI SIMEON BEN YOHAI

(Zohar II, 14a–15a. *Midrash ha-Ne'elam*)

Rabbi Hiyya the Great was going to visit the masters of the Mishnah in order to learn from them, and he came to the house of Rabbi Simeon ben Yohai. He saw a curtain[5] that divided the house. He was surprised, and said: I shall listen to a word from his mouth, from here.

He heard someone say: "Flee, my beloved, and be like a gazelle, or a young hart" (Song of Songs 8: 14).[6] The entire demand that Israel makes of the Holy One, blessed be He, is that expressed by Rabbi Simeon: Israel's desire is that the Holy One, blessed be He, should neither go away nor remove Himself, but actually to flee like a gazelle or a young hart. Why is this? Rabbi Simeon said: No other creature in the world acts like the gazelle or the young hart. When it runs away it moves very slowly and turns its head back toward the place it is leaving. And it keeps turning its head back all the time. Similarly, Israel says: Master of the universe, if we compel You to remove Yourself from us, then please flee like the gazelle or the young hart, which runs away with its head turned back toward the place it is leaving. And this is what is meant by "And yet, for all that, when they are in the land of their enemies, I will not reject them, neither will I abhor them, to destroy them utterly" (Leviticus 26: 44). Here is another interpretation: When the gazelle sleeps, it sleeps with one eye closed, and keeps watch with the other. Similarly, Israel says to the Holy One, blessed be He: Act like the gazelle, for "Behold, He that keeps Israel neither slumbers nor sleeps" (Psalm 121: 4).

Rabbi Hiyya heard this, and said: Alas, the celestial beings are studying Torah in the house, and I remain outside!

He wept.

Rabbi Simeon heard him and said: The *Shekhinah* must be outside. Who will go out?

Rabbi Eleazar, his son, said: If I am burned, it will not be with unholy fire,[7] for the *Shekhinah* is on the other side of it.[8] Let the *Shekhinah* enter and the fire be made whole.

He heard a voice that said: The pillars have not yet been erected, nor the gates set up. Here he is one of the lesser spices of Eden.[9]

---

[5] A curtain of fire.   [6] [See *Targum Jonathan* to this verse.]

[7] If I am burned with the fire of the curtain, it will be with holy fire.

[8] The *Shekhinah* is outside with Rabbi Hiyya.

[9] Rabbi Hiyya's knowledge of the mysteries was imperfect, and since he was one of the youngest members of Rabbi Simeon's circle it was not right for him to be admitted to the inner sanctum.

Rabbi Eleazar did not go out.

Rabbi Hiyya sat down, and wept, and sighed. He opened his mouth and said: "Turn, my beloved, and be like a gazelle or a young hart" (Song of Songs 2: 17).

The gate of the curtain opened. Rabbi Hiyya did not go in. Rabbi Simeon raised his eyes and said: This must mean that permission has been given to him who is outside; and we are inside.

Rabbi Simeon rose. The fire moved from his place to the place of Rabbi Hiyya.

Rabbi Simeon said: A spark of resplendent light is outside, and I am here, inside.

Rabbi Hiyya's mouth was struck dumb. When he moved inside he lowered his eyes and did not raise his head.

Rabbi Simeon said to his son, Rabbi Eleazar: Rise. Pass your hand over his mouth, for he is unaccustomed to this.

Rabbi Eleazar arose and passed his hand over Rabbi Hiyya's mouth.

Rabbi Hiyya opened his mouth and said: The eye has seen what I have never seen; what has come to pass was beyond my imagining. It is good to die in the flaming fire of pure gold, in a place where the sparks fly out on every side, each spark ascending to the three hundred and seventy chariots, and each chariot dividing into myriads upon myriads, until they come to the Ancient of Days, who sits on the throne, and the throne shudders before him into two hundred and sixty worlds, until it comes[10] to the place of the bliss of the righteous, until it is heard throughout all the firmaments, and all the upper and lower regions, all at the same time, are astounded and say: This is Rabbi Simeon ben Yohai, who shatters all things. Who can stand before him? This is Rabbi Simeon ben Yohai, whose voice, when he opens his mouth and begins to study Torah, is heeded by all the thrones, all the firmaments, and all the chariots, and all of these, who praise their master, neither open nor close [their mouths]—all of them are silent, until in all the firmaments, above and below, no sound is heard. When Rabbi Simeon completes his study of the Torah, who has seen the songs, who has seen the joy of those who praise their master? Who has seen the voices that travel through all the firmaments? They all come on account of Rabbi Simeon, and they bow and prostrate themselves before their master, exuding the odours of the spices of Eden as far as the Ancient of Days—and all this on account of Rabbi Simeon.

Rabbi Simeon opened his mouth, and said: Six levels[11] went down to Egypt with Jacob, and each one of them numbered ten thousand, and

---

[10] I.e., the spark, which is the teaching of Rabbi Simeon ben Yohai.

[11] Six companies of angels, corresponding to six *sefirot*, with *Tiferet* (i.e., Jacob) in the middle. [The word translated as "levels" is *dargin*, Heb. *ma'alot*, which can also be rendered "degrees" or "steps."]

there were six corresponding levels in Israel,[12] and six corresponding levels in the throne above, and six corresponding levels in the throne below, as it is written "There were six steps to the throne" (1 Kings 10: 19). And the verse "I make you into ten thousand as the growth of the field . . ." (Ezekiel 16: 7)[13] makes six.[14] It is written correspondingly, "And the children of Israel were fruitful, and increased, and multiplied, and grew mighty exceedingly . . ." (Exodus 1: 7)[15]. Come and see. Each one of them was multiplied by ten, and became sixty, and these are the sixty warriors[16] that surround the *Shekhinah*, and these are the sixty myriads[17] that emerged from exile with Israel, and that went into exile with Jacob.

Rabbi Hiyya said to him; Were there not seven, that became seventy?[18]

Rabbi Simeon said to him; Seventy is not relevant here. And if you should imagine that it was seven, it is written, "And there shall be six branches going out of its sides; three branches of the candlestick [on one side, and three branches of the candlestick on the other]" (Exodus 25: 32), and the branch in the middle is not counted, since it also says "[the seven lamps] shall give light in front of the candlestick" (Numbers 8: 2).[19]

While they were seated Rabbi Eleazar said to his father, Rabbi Simeon: What was the purpose of the Holy One, blessed be He, in bringing Israel down to Egypt, to exile?

Are you asking one question or two?

Two. Why exile? and why Egypt?

Rabbi Simeon said: There are two, but they are really one. Stand up, so that through you this matter may be settled on high in your name. Speak, my son, speak.

[12] The Israelites who left Egypt numbered six hundred thousand, corresponding to the six levels that went down to Egypt with Jacob.

[13] [Usually translated "I cause you to increase . . .," but the first word of the verse is *revavah*, which also means "ten thousand".]

[14] This is deduced from the continuation of the verse, where six levels are alluded to, as follows: "And you increased (1) and grew up (2), and you came (3) to excellent beauty (4); your breasts were fashioned (5), and your hair was grown (6)."

[15] The six levels are deduced from "were fruitful (1), and increased (2), and multiplied (3), and grew mighty (4) exceedingly (5); and the land was filled with them (6)." It is possible that there is an allusion here to the story that the Israelite women in Egypt used to bear six children at a time.

[16] According to Song of Songs 3: 7.

[17] [I.e. 600,000].

[18] There are seven *sefirot* from *Ḥesed* to *Malkhut*, and from them extend the seventy branches of the holy tree. And so seventy people went down to Egypt with Jacob, and these correspond to the seventy nations.

[19] One must exclude from the seven *sefirot* the *sefirah Tiferet*, around which the others are arranged, in the same way that only six of the branches of the candlestick are enumerated, even though there were seven lamps.

He began by quoting: "There are sixty queens and eighty concubines" (Song of Songs 6: 8). The "sixty queens" are the celestial warriors, derived from the power of *Gevurah*, imprisoned within the husks of the holy creature, Israel.[20] The "eighty concubines" are appointed over the husks that are beneath it.[21] And "the maidens without number" may be likened to "Is there any number to his armies?" (Job 25: 3).[22] And yet it says "My dove, my undefiled, is but one. She is the only one of her mother" (Song of Songs 6: 9). This is the holy *Shekhinah*, emerging from the protective vessels, the light of light, illuminating all, and she is called "mother".[23] This is what the Holy One, blessed be He, did on earth. He scattered all the peoples on every side, and appointed guardian angels over them, as it is written, "which the Lord your God has allotted to all the peoples" (Deuteronomy 4: 19), and He took as His own portion the Assembly of Israel, as it is written, "For the portion of the Lord is His people, Jacob the lot of His inheritance" (Deuteronomy 32: 9), and He called her "My dove, my undefiled, [who] is but one. She is the only one of her mother." This is the *Shekhinah* of His glory, which He caused to dwell among them, unique, and reserved for her alone.[24] "The daughters saw her and called her happy" (Song of Songs 6: 9); in the same way we have "Many daughters have done valiantly but you excel them all" (Proverbs 31: 29). "The queens and concubines, and they praised her" (Song of Songs 6: 9)—these are the guardian angels that were appointed for the peoples.

Furthermore, the hidden meaning of this is as follows: we have learned that "the world was created by ten sayings,"[25] and yet when you look at the matter closely you will see that there are three, and the world was created with these, namely, wisdom, understanding, and knowledge.[26] The world was created only for the sake of Israel, and when He wished the world to endure, He made Abraham with the sign of wisdom, Isaac with the sign of understanding, and Jacob with the sign of knowledge,[27] and this is why it is written "And by knowledge are the

[20] Around the sefirotic tree, whose main stock is *Tiferet*, the creature (*Ḥayyah*) called "Israel," are unclean husks, who derive influence from the tree. This influence is not conveyed to them directly, but through intermediary powers emanated from the attribute of Judgment, the *sefirah Gevurah* (Might), and these are called *gavraya* (mighty ones, warriors).

[21] The husks that lie beneath the tree.

[22] "The maidens" therefore represent the hosts of chariots and angels.

[23] The *Shekhinah*, the lenient attribute of Judgment, emerges from the powers of Judgment that are in *Binah*, which radiates brilliant light upon the *sefirot* and is called "the celestial mother."

[24] The *Shekhinah* is the lower mother, and the Assembly of Israel is related to her in the same way as the *Shekhinah* herself is related to *Binah*.

[25] *Pirkei de-Rabbi Eliezer*, III.

[26] Cf. Exodus 31: 3.

[27] Generally speaking, the level of the patriarchs in the Zohar corresponds to *Ḥesed*,

chambers filled" (Proverbs 24: 4).[28] At that precise moment the whole
world was completed, and when the twelve tribes were born to Jacob, it
was all fashioned on the celestial pattern. When the Holy One, blessed
be He, saw the great joy of the lower world that it was fashioned on the
celestial pattern, He said: Perhaps they will now mingle with the other
peoples[29] and there will be a resulting blemish in all the worlds. So what
did the Holy One, blessed be He, do? He moved them all to and fro, until
they went down to Egypt, to dwell among a stiff-necked people, who
scoffed at their laws and would not deign to marry them or mix with
them, but who regarded them as slaves. Their men despised them and
their women despised them, so that the whole was perfected with holy
seed. Meanwhile the iniquity of the other peoples was completed, as it is
written "up to that time the iniquity of the Amorites had not been
complete" (Genesis 15: 16),[30] and, when they left, they left holy and
righteous, as it is written "the tribes of the Lord, a testimony to Israel"
(Psalm 122: 4).

Rabbi Simeon came and kissed him on the head. He said to him:
Stand where you are, my son, for your moment has now come.

Rabbi Simeon sat down, and Rabbi Eleazar, his son, stood and
expounded wisdom's mysteries, and his face shone like the sun, and his
words spread abroad and moved in the firmament.

They sat for two days, and did not eat or drink, not knowing whether
it was day or night. When they left they realized that they had not eaten
anything for two days. Rabbi Simeon therefore quoted "And he was
there with the Lord forty days and forty nights; bread he did not eat . . ."
(Exodus 34: 28). If we [have had such an experience] after an hour,
what could Moses have experienced, of whom Scripture says "He was
there with the Lord forty days . . ."?

When Rabbi Hiyya came and related all this to Rabbi [Judah
ha-Nasi], he was amazed, and his father, Rabbi Simeon ben Gamaliel,
said to him; My son, Rabbi Simeon ben Yohai is a lion, and Rabbi
Eleazar, his son, is a lion. But Rabbi Simeon is not like other lions. Of
him it is written, "The lion has roared. Who will not fear?" (Amos 3: 8).
And since the worlds above tremble before him, how much more should
we? He is a man who has never had to ordain a fast for something that he

Gevurah, and Tiferet, which is also called Da'at (Knowledge). Hokhmah (Wisdom) and
Tevunah [or Binah] (Understanding) are the two upper sefirot to which Hesed and Gevurah
are connected.

[28] The construction of the world, which was created for the sake of Israel, was
completed only with the birth of Jacob, the father of the tribes, who was made with the
sign of knowledge.

[29] The peoples of Canaan.

[30] The time had come for the peoples of Canaan to be destroyed because of their
iniquity, and there was no longer any fear that the Israelites would mix with them on
their return.

really desired. But he makes a decision, and the Holy One, blessed be He, supports it. The Holy One, blessed be He, makes a decision, and he annuls it. And so we have learned:[31] What is the meaning of "ruler over man—righteous—ruler of the fear of God" (2 Samuel 23: 3)?[32] The Holy One, blessed be He, is the ruler over man, but who rules over the Holy One, blessed be He? The righteous, for He makes a decision, and the righteous annuls it.

3. THE ANGEL OF DEATH PUT TO FLIGHT
(Zohar I, 217b–218b).

Rabbi Isaac was sitting downcast one day at Rabbi Judah's door. Rabbi Judah went out and discovered him sitting downcast by his gate. He said to him; What is the matter?

He replied: I have come to you in order to ask three things of you. One is that, when you discourse on the Torah and mention some of the things that I have said, you should speak them in my name, so that my name should be mentioned. One is that you should help my son Joseph to learn Torah. And one is that you should go to my grave on each of the seven days [of mourning] and offer prayers for me.

He said: Why do you ask this?

My soul leaves me every night, and does not shine upon me in a dream, as it used to do. Furthermore, when I am praying and come to "hearkenest unto prayer,"[33] I look for my image on the wall and I do not see it. And so I tell myself that, since the image has disappeared and is no longer seen, the herald must already have gone out to issue the proclamation, for it is written, "Surely man walks as a mere image" (Psalm 39: 7)—as long as his image remains with him a "man walks," and his spirit resides within him. But when a man's image disappears and is no longer seen, then he disappears from the world.[34]

Rabbi Judah said: You could have deduced this from "our days upon earth are but a shadow" (Job 8: 9). Everything you ask I shall do. But I ask you to select a place for me by your side in that world, such as I have enjoyed in this.

Rabbi Isaac wept, and said: I beg you not to leave me during the days to come.

They went to Rabbi Simeon and found him studying Torah. Rabbi Simeon raised his eyes and saw Rabbi Isaac, and he saw the angel of

[31] B. T. *Moed Katan* 16b.

[32] [This is a word-for-word translation of the verse.]

[33] The closing words of the *Shma kolenu* (Hear our voice), one of the benedictions of the *Amidah*.

[34] A man's shadow was considered to be the appearance of the "image"—an invisible ethereal body surrounding the visible body. The "image" was thought to disappear thirty days before death.

death running and dancing in front of him. Rabbi Simeon arose, and took Rabbi Isaac by the hand, and said: I command that whoever is accustomed to enter should enter, and whoever is not accustomed to enter should not enter.

Rabbi Isaac and Rabbi Judah entered. The angel of death was bound outside. Rabbi Simeon realized that the time had not yet come,[35] for it had been set for two o'clock in the afternoon. Rabbi Simeon seated him in front of him and began to teach him Torah.

Rabbi Simeon said to Rabbi Eleazar, his son: Sit by the door, and do not speak with anyone you see. But if he wants to come in, put him under oath not to.

Rabbi Simeon said to Rabbi Isaac: Have you seen the image of your father today, or not? For we have learned: When a man is about to depart from this world, his father and his dearest friends are with him, and he sees them and recognizes them. And all those with whom he is to live on one and the same level in that world, they all assemble near him and accompany his soul to the place where it is due to reside.

He replied: So far I have not seen him.

Rabbi Simeon stood up at once and said: Master of the universe, we recognize Rabbi Isaac as being one of "the seven eyes"[36] that are here. I claim him. Give him to me.

A voice then proclaimed: The master's throne is near to the wings of Rabbi Simeon.[37] He is yours, and you shall bring him with you when you come in to reside on your throne.

Rabbi Simeon said: Agreed.

Immediately Rabbi Eleazar saw the angel of death depart, and he said: A thong of fire cannot exist[38] in the presence of Rabbi Simeon ben Yohai.

Rabbi Simeon said to his son, Rabbi Eleazar: Come in and take hold of Rabbi Isaac, for I can see that he is afraid.

Rabbi Eleazar entered and took hold of him, and Rabbi Simeon turned his face away to study the Torah.

Rabbi Isaac fell into a slumber and saw his father, who said to him: How fortunate you are in this world and the next, for among the leaves of the Tree of Life in the Garden of Eden is planted a tree that is great and powerful in both worlds, and this is Rabbi Simeon ben Yohai. And now he holds you in his branches. How fortunate you are, my son!

But, father, what is to be my situation there?

He replied: For three days they were beautifying your chamber, and

[35] For the angel of death to slay Rabbi Isaac.
[36] The seven companions that left the assembly with Rabbi Simeon. (See Zohar III, 144b).
[37] [Rabbi Isaac's proximity in spirit to Rabbi Simeon is envisaged as being part of the "wings" of Rabbi Simeon.]   [38] Punishment has no power.

had arranged for the windows to be open, so that you should have light from the four quarters of the world. And I saw where you were, and I was happy and said: How fortunate you are, except that your son is still unlearned in the Torah. And then twelve righteous companions were about to come for you, but before I left a voice arose through all the worlds: The companions standing here must adorn themselves for his sake, for Rabbi Simeon ben Yohai has made a request, and it has been granted. Furthermore, the seventy places that are adorned here belong to him, and each place has doors that open for him onto seventy worlds, and each world is open to seventy channels, and each channel is open to seventy celestial crowns, and from there paths open out to the Ancient One,[39] concealed from all, so that one might see the supernal graciousness,[40] which radiates and gives pleasure to all things, as it is said, "To behold the graciousness of the Lord, and to visit His temple early" (Psalm 27: 4). What does "to visit His temple early" mean? It is indicated by "In all My house he is trusted" (Numbers 12: 7).[41]

Father, he asked, how long have I been given in this world?

I am not permitted [to say], he replied, and man is not told. But at Rabbi Simeon's great feast[42] you will prepare his table, as it is said, "Go forth, you daughters of Zion, and gaze upon King Solomon, even upon the crown with which his mother has crowned him, on his wedding day, on the day of his heart's joy" (Song of Songs 3: 11).

Then Rabbi Isaac awoke and smiled, and his face shone. Rabbi Simeon noticed, and looked at his face.

Have you heard something new? he said.

Yes, he replied, and he told him, and he prostrated himself before Rabbi Simeon.

It is taught that from that day forth Rabbi Isaac would take his son by the hand and teach him Torah, and he never left him. When he went in to Rabbi Simeon, he would make his son sit outside, while he sat before Rabbi Simeon, and he quoted to him "O Lord, I am oppressed. Be Thou my surety" (Isaiah 38: 14).

4. MIRACLES: THE PLANTATION OF RABBI PINHAS BEN YAIR

(Zohar III, 200b–202b)

Rabbi Pinhas went to visit his daughter, Rabbi Simeon's wife, who was

---

[39] *Keter.*   [40] *Binah.*

[41] This is a reference to Moses. The house is the Divine Presence (the *Shekhinah*) and Moses is the master of the house. Here the house is also equated with the Temple. The divine influence is channeled down from *Keter*, through *Binah* and *Malkhut*, to the abode of Rabbi Isaac.

[42] On the day of Rabbi Simeon's death. When the righteous departs from this world,

ill. His companions went with him, and he rode on his donkey. As he was
going along he met two Arabs. He said to them: Do you know if any
voices have ever been heard in this field?

We do not know about the past,[43] they replied, but we do know that
in our own time some robbers, who used to attack travelers, were
crossing this field one day, and they met some Jews and were about to
attack them. But the voice of a donkey was heard in this field, a long way
away, braying twice, and a flame of fire accompanied the sound, and
burned them up; and so the Jews were saved.

Arabs, Arabs, he said, because of what you have told me you will be
saved today from other robbers, who are lying in wait for you on the
road.

Rabbi Pinhas wept and said: Master of the universe, You have
performed a miracle for my sake; those Jews were saved, and I did not
know.

He then began by quoting: "To Him who alone does great wonders,
for His mercy endures for ever" (Psalm 136: 4). How much goodness
does the Holy One, blessed be He, perform for the children of men, and
how many miracles does He prepare for them every day, and no one
knows but He alone! A man gets up in the morning, and a snake comes to
kill him. The man happens to put his foot on its head and kills it, and no
one knows of it, except the Holy One, blessed be He, alone; hence, "to
Him who alone does great wonders." A man goes on a journey, and
robbers lie in wait to kill him. Another man comes along and is taken
instead of him, and the first man is saved, and no one knows the good
that the Holy One, blessed be He, has done him, nor the miracle that He
has prepared for him, except He alone; hence, "to Him who alone does
great wonders"—He alone acts and knows. Others do not know.

He said to his companions: Friends, what I wished to know from the
Arabs, who frequent these fields, was whether they had heard the voices
of the companions studying Torah, for Rabbi Simeon and Rabbi
Eleazar, his son, and the other companions, went on before us, and knew
nothing of us. And so I asked these Arabs about them, because I know
that Rabbi Simeon's voice makes the fields and mountains tremble. But
they have shown me what I did not know.

As they went along the Arabs returned.

Old man, old man, they said, you were asking about the days of old,
and not about recent times, but today we have seen wonders upon
wonders. We saw five seated men, and an old man with them, and we
saw birds gathering together and spreading their wings over their heads.

it is a joyful moment for him, because his soul clings to the *Shekhinah*, and ascends with it
to the king's heavenly palace.

[43] Rabbi Pinhas's question was ambiguous and could refer either to the recent past or
to ancient times.

Some came and some went, but there was always shade over their heads, and the old man raised his voice and they listened.

Rabbi Pinhas said: This is what I was asking about. Arabs, Arabs, go now, and may your path be prepared before you, wherever you wish to go. Two things you have told me, and they have given me joy.

They went.

The companions said to him: How shall we know where Rabbi Simeon is staying?

He replied: Leave it to the master of my beast's footsteps, for he will direct his steps there.

He did not urge his donkey, but his donkey turned off the road for two miles, and went there. He began to bray, three times. Rabbi Pinhas dismounted and said to the companions: Let us prepare ourselves to greet the countenance of the Ancient of Days, for they come to meet us, the long countenance and the short countenance.[44]

Rabbi Simeon heard the braying of the donkey. He said to his companions: Let us arise, for the voice of the donkey that belongs to the pious old man has been aroused to greet us.

Rabbi Simeon arose, and the companions arose.

Rabbi Simeon began by quoting: "A Psalm. O sing unto the Lord a new song, for He has done marvelous things" (Psalm 98: 1). The accent on the word mizmor (Psalm) is written upright above the word. Why? This has great significance, for this mizmor[45] comes crowned with a celestial crown[46] above its head and it comes upright. Who said this song? The milch-kine[47] with the lowing sound that they made. "Sing to the Lord a new song." To whom did they say "sing"? To several chariots, several officers, several degrees, who had come there and gone out to receive the Ark, and to them they said "Sing to the Lord a new song"—in the masculine.[48] Why do we have shir here, whereas Moses said shirah (Exodus 15:1), in the feminine? Moses had simply the Ark alone[49]—this (zot) came out from exile, together with its hosts,[50] and no more; and so we have et ha-shirah ha-zot (this song) in the feminine. But

[44] Terms for the sefirot, but here referring to Rabbi Simeon ben Yohai and to his son, Rabbi Eleazar.   [45] The Shekhinah.

[46] Crowned with the influence of Tiferet, which was then joined with the Shekhinah.

[47] They brought back the Ark of the Covenant from the Philistines. The word in I Samuel 6: 12, va-yisharnah (usually translated "they took the straight way"), is here connected with shir "to sing." See B. T. Avodah Zarah 24b.

[48] [The Hebrew word for "song" occurs in both the masculine gender (shir) and the feminine (shirah).]

[49] The Ark is the symbol of the Shekhinah, the female receptacle for the tablets of the law, which symbolize Tiferet (the written Torah). The female element is called zot (this). During the exile in Egypt she alone was subjugated, without her husband, Tiferet [and it was only later, at Sinai, after Moses had sung his song at the Red Sea, that the tablets were put in the Ark.]   [50] The angels of the Shekhinah.

here both the Ark and what was concealed within it[51] came out, and because of that which is concealed within it, Scripture says *shir ḥadash* (a new song) in the masculine.

"For He has done marvelous things"—the things that He did to the Philistines and to their idols. "His right hand . . . has wrought salvation for Him." For whom? For Himself. Who is "Himself"? The *mizmor* itself, for the celestial holy spirit[52] is concealed within it. "His right hand"[53]—this is that which the old man possesses,[54] and "His right hand" supports this *mizmor* and does not allow it to fall into the hands of another. We must here reveal a certain matter. The whole time that the right hand is ready to effect a miracle it takes hold of this *mizmor* and places it before it in order to support it, as a father supports his son with his right hand across his chest, saying, "who dares to come against my son?" When he rebels against his father, then his father puts his hands on his shoulders from behind, and thrusts him into the hands of his enemies, if one can say such a thing. At first it is written "Your right hand, Lord, glorious in power" (Exodus 15: 6). In whose power? In the power of someone already known.[55] In Arabia they call a man's chest "power".[56] So this right hand is "glorious" and takes hold of "the power",[57] saying "Who dares to come against my son?" What is written after this? "He has drawn back His right hand from before the enemy" (Lamentations 2: 3). He puts his right hand upon his shoulder and pushes him[58] into the hands of his enemies. At first his right hand was in front of him across his chest to support him, and afterward on his shoulders from behind, in order to push him. And here we have "His right hand, and His holy arm, have wrought salvation for Him"—both arms support Him.[59] Those kine, who were unaccustomed to miracles except on that particular occasion, sang this song as they lowed. With how much more right does this donkey sing a song as he brays, for he belongs to the pious old man, and so is used to miracles.

You may say, friends, that no donkey has ever done such a thing since the day the world was created. But come and ponder upon the ass of Balaam the wicked, who overcame her master in everything. Has not the

[51] The tablets of the law, symbolizing the male.   [52] *Tiferet.*
[53] *Hesed*—the right arm.
[54] Apparently the reference here is to *Tiferet*, called "old man Israel," and it inclines toward the right. But it is possible that the "old man" is Rabbi Pinhas, and Rabbi Simeon wishes to point out, in passing, that he has reached the level of *Ḥesed*.
[55] The Hebrew word *ba-koaḥ* ("in power") means literally "in the power," i.e., a power already known, here a reference to the "chest" of the *Shekhinah*.
[56] There seems to be no basis in fact for this supposed Arabic usage.
[57] The "chest" of the *Shekhinah*, in order to protect it from the husks.
[58] He casts the *Shekhinah* into exile among the husks, because of the sins of Israel.
[59] The right and the left—*Hesed* and *Gevurah*. Even the left arm joins in the salvation of the *Shekhinah*, when virtues are in the ascendant, just as the right arm joins in the exiling of the *Shekhinah* when sins are in the ascendant.

donkey of Rabbi Pinhas ben Yair more justification [for acting miraculously]? Furthermore, when Balaam's ass spoke, a celestial angel was above her. And now, friends, we must reveal something. Listen. The mouth of the ass that was created on the eve of the Sabbath[60] at twilight, do you think that the mouth remained open from that time, or that the Holy One, blessed be He, imposed certain conditions[61] at that time? It was not like that. Here there is a mystery transmitted to the sages, who pay no attention to the stupidity of the heart. The "mouth of the ass," the upper level of asses on the female side,[62] is that which rested upon that particular ass and spoke from above her. When the Holy One, blessed be He, created the level called "mouth of the ass," He shut it in a cleft in the great deep,[63] and He sealed it until the time came. When the time came He opened the cleft, and it emerged and rested upon the ass, and spoke. In the same way we have "And the earth opened her mouth (et piha)" (Numbers 16: 32). The particle et[64] is to include Dumah,[65] who is the "mouth of the earth." "The mouth (et pi) of the ass" (Numbers 22: 28) includes Kamriel, who is called "the mouth of the ass." In the same way we have "the mouth of the well" (Numbers 21: 17).[66] Who is "the mouth of the well"? The level that was appointed over it below, and it is below "the mouth of the Lord."[67] And who is this? His name is Yehadriel.[68] These three mouths were created on the eve of the Sabbath at twilight. When He sanctified the Sabbath day, the mouth arose[69] that was appointed over all other mouths. And who was this? The day[70] that arose and was sanctified in all things, the one called "the mouth of the Lord." On the eve of the Sabbath at twilight the other

[60] According to Mishnah *Avot* 5: 8 "Ten things were created on the eve of the Sabbath at twilight, namely, the mouth of the earth (Numbers 16: 32); the mouth of the well (ibid., 21: 16); the mouth of the ass (ibid., 22: 28)," etc.

[61] He made a condition, at the Creation, that when the time came for a miracle to be effected, the mouth of the ass would open.

[62] The power of uncleanness appointed over asses is one of the female elements among the husks.

[63] The abode of the husks.

[64] [*Et* is simply a sign of the accusative, and may be regarded as superfluous to the text. Hence it may be considered to have an additional interpretative significance.]

[65] The prince of Gehinnom. Korach and his company went down to Gehinnom when the mouth of the earth opened.

[66] The well in the wilderness which, according to a homiletical interpretation, sang a song.

[67] The *Shekhinah*, the mouth that receives influence from the tetragrammaton, which is *Tiferet*.

[68] A holy angel who ministers to the *Shekhinah*, called "well," in contrast to Dumah and Kamriel, who are both on the unclean side.

[69] Ascended in order to join the upper *sefirot*.

[70] The *Shekhinah*, the seventh of the seven lower *sefirot*, which correspond to the seven days of Creation, is, mystically speaking, the Sabbath, and especially the eve of the Sabbath.

mouths were created, the day was sanctified, and the mouth arose that has dominion over all—"the mouth of the Lord."

In the meantime they had seen Rabbi Pinhas coming, and they went to meet him. Rabbi Pinhas came and kissed Rabbi Simeon.

He said: I have kissed the mouth of the Lord, fragrant with the spices of His garden.

They were happy together, and sat down. As soon as they had sat down, all the birds that had been providing shade flew away and dispersed. Rabbi Simeon turned his head around, and said in a thunderous voice: Birds of heaven! You have no respect for your Master's glory, which dwells here.[71]

They stopped, neither moving from their place nor coming nearer to them.

Rabbi Pinhas said: Tell them to continue on their way, for they have not been given permission to return.

Rabbi Simeon said: I know that the Holy One, blessed be He, wishes to perform a miracle for us. Birds, birds, go on your way, and tell whoever is appointed over you that he did in fact have the power,[72] but that now he does not have the power. I have removed it until the day of the rock[73] arrives, when the cloud rises between two mighty ones and they are not joined together.

The birds dispersed and went away. Then they saw that three trees had spread their branches in three directions over them, and there was a fountain of living waters in front of them. All the companions were glad, and Rabbi Pinhas and Rabbi Simeon were glad.

Rabbi Pinhas said: These birds had been put to great trouble, and we should not want animals to be troubled overmuch, for it is written "His tender mercies are over all His works" (Psalm 145: 9).

Rabbi Simeon said: I did not put them to any trouble; but if the Holy One, blessed be He, takes pity on us, we cannot refuse His gifts.

They sat beneath the tree, drank some water, and refreshed themselves there.

Rabbi Pinhas began by quoting: "A fountain of gardens, a well of living waters, and flowing streams from Lebanon" (Song of Songs 4: 15). "A fountain of gardens." Is a garden fountain the only kind of fountain there is? Are there not a number of good and precious fountains in the world? Yes, but the pleasure derived from them is not all of the same kind. The fountain that springs up in the desert, in an arid place, benefits whoever sits and drinks there. But "a fountain of gardens"—how good and precious it is! This fountain benefits plants and fruits. Whoever

---

[71] I.e., the *Shekhinah* that is present here.

[72] To serve Rabbi Simeon ben Yohai by means of the birds.

[73] When the dire day comes and Judgment rules supreme, then he will want that power restored to him.

approaches it derives pleasure from all of these—pleasure from the water, pleasure from the plants, pleasure from the fruits. This fountain is crowned with everything. It is surrounded with so many roses, so many fragrant plants. This fountain is more beautiful than other fountains, "a well of living waters." And we explain it in this way: it all refers to the Assembly of Israel.[74] It is "a fountain of gardens."

What are these "gardens"? The Holy One, blessed be He, has five gardens,[75] in which He takes great delight. And there is one fountain,[76] hidden and concealed, for them all, which waters and saturates them, and they all produce fruits and plants. There is one garden[77] below them, and this garden is protected on all sides.[78] Below this garden are other gardens[79] that produce their species of fruit. And this garden changes and becomes a fountain[80] that waters them. "A well of living waters"—if necessary it becomes a fountain, and if necessary it becomes a well. What is the difference? Pouring out water of its own accord is one thing; having its water drawn up for drinking is another.[81] "And flowing streams from Lebanon." What does "flowing" mean? These are the five sources,[82] which go out from Lebanon above,[83] and they flow; for when they become a fountain,[84] water gushes forth, and the drops flow one after the other—sweet water for which the soul yearns. In this way the Holy One, blessed be He, has performed a miracle for us in this place, through this fountain. And to this fountain I apply this verse.

He began again by quoting: "When you besiege a city for many days, fighting against it in order to capture it . . ." (Deuteronomy 20: 19). How splendid are the paths and byways of the Torah, for every word contains so many ideas, so many good things for mankind, so many jewels casting light on every side. There is no word in the Torah that

[74] I.e., the *Shekhinah*.

[75] The five *sefirot* from *Hesed* to *Yesod*, in the middle of which lies *Tiferet*, called "the Holy One, blessed be He," and if you include this one you have six. Or, possibly, "the Holy One, blessed be He" refers to the concealed God, *En-Sof*, who delights in these six *sefirot*; and they are called "five" because *Tiferet* and *Yesod* are taken together as one.

[76] *Binah*, which nourishes and sustains the lower *sefirot*.

[77] The *Shekhinah*, which is watered from above.

[78] So that the husks should not gain access to it.

[79] Worlds outside the sphere of the Godhead.

[80] The *Shekhinah*, in relation to what is above it, is a garden that receives influence, but, in relation to what is below it, it is a fountain that pours out influence.

[81] When the *Shekhinah* is seen as a fountain, influence pours from it without any help from below. But when it is seen as a well, then, because of the scarcity of merit in the world, the work of the righteous is necessary, so that through their good deeds they can draw up from it the waters of salvation and blessing.

[82] The *sefirot*, which have been previously called "five gardens" when seen in relationship to *Binah*. Here they are called "sources" and "flowing", because of their relationship to the *Shekhinah*, which is watered by them.

[83] The upper *sefirot*, particularly *Hokhmah*.

[84] To water the garden of the *Shekhinah*.

does not contain many lights that illumine every side. This verse has a literal meaning and a homiletical meaning. And it also contains heavenly wisdom that instructs him who has need of it. How happy is the lot of the man who is continually preoccupied with the Torah. What does Scripture say about the man who studies it? "His delight is in the Torah of the Lord, and in His Torah does he meditate day and night, and he shall be like a tree . . ." (Psalm 1: 2–3). What is the connection between one and the other? Whoever studies the Torah day and night will not be like a shriveled tree, but "like a tree planted by streams of water".[85] Just as a tree has roots, bark, pith, branches, leaves, flowers, and fruit—these seven parts amounting to seven [times] ten, to seventy[86]—so the words of the Torah have literal meaning, homiletical meaning, speculative allusions, *gematriot*, hidden mysteries, ineffable mysteries, one above the other, unfit and fit, unclean and clean, forbidden and permitted. The branches spread out from here on every side. He shall be like a veritable tree; and, if not, then he is not a master of wisdom.

Come and see how much the Holy One, blessed be He, loves those who study the Torah. Even when judgment hangs over the world, and permission is given to the destroyer to destroy, the Holy One, blessed be He, instructs him concerning those who study the Torah. The Holy One, blessed be He, says to him: "When you besiege a city"—because they have committed many sins before Me and been found guilty—"for many days." What is the significance of "many"? The three successive days that attest the presence of plague in a city.[87] How do we know that "many days" signifies three days? From the verse "If a woman have an issue of her blood many days" (Leviticus 15: 25). Does this really mean "many days"? No. Three successive days are called "many days." So here. "When you besiege a city many days" means the three successive days that attest the presence of plague in a city. Come, I shall give you instructions concerning the members of My household: "You shall not destroy its tree." This is the scholar who is in the city, for he is the tree of life, the tree that bears fruit. Another view is that "its tree (*ezah*)" refers to the one who gives advice (*ezah*) to the city, to save it from the judgment, and who teaches them the way that they should go. Therefore, "you shall not destroy its tree by wielding an axe against it"—by wielding judgment over it, or by wielding over it a glinting sword, a sharp sword, that kills other creatures. "For you shall eat of it."

[85] This is not therefore a promise of reward, but an obligation on the part of the true sage to bear fruit in every area of the Torah.

[86] The seven parts of the tree correspond to the seven *sefirot*, which constitute the sacred Tree of Divinity. Each one of these *sefirot* contains the ten sefirotic stages, thus making seventy parts in all, corresponding to the traditional "seventy facets" of the Torah.

[87] The plague is the work of the "destroyer," who is laying siege to the city.

Shall the destroyer eat of it? No. But "she shall eat of it," namely, the mighty Rock, from whom emerge all the sacred powerful spirits.[88] The pleasure and desire of the Holy Spirit in this world are satisfied only by the teaching of the righteous. It is he, as it were, who sustains her, and provides food for her in this world, far more than all the sacrifices put together. What does Scripture say about sacrifice? "I have eaten my honeycomb with my honey. . . . Eat, friends" (Song of Songs 5: 1). But since the day when the Temple was destroyed and the sacrifices ceased, there is nothing for the Holy One, blessed be He, but words of Torah, and the Torah that is renewed in the mouth of the righteous. And so we have "For she shall eat of it"—her only food in this world comes from him and from those like him.[89] And since she eats from him, and he feeds her, "you shall not cut it down"—take care of him; do not touch him.

"For the man is a tree of the field." This particular man is known above and below.[90] "A tree of the field"—a great and mighty tree, which is the support of "the field that the Lord has blessed" (Genesis 27: 27),[91] a tree of which that field always takes cognizance.

"To come before you in siege." This phrase relates to the beginning of the verse, where it says "You shall not destroy its tree (ezah)." The man who gives them advice (ezah) and prepares the city "to come before you in siege," also advises them to fortify themselves and to return in penitence. And he prepares weapons for them, cornets and trumpets. What does "to come before you" mean? To come before Me, and to withdraw before you—because of their fear of you.

"In siege"—where the upper and the lower beings cannot enter. And where is that? The level attained by the penitent. What is penitence? It is "siege," a mighty place, and a mighty Rock.[92] When they accept this advice, I forgive them their sins, and I welcome them gladly.

This is the commandment of the Holy One, blessed be He, concerning

---

[88] The Hebrew word *tokhal* can be translated either "you shall eat" or "she shall eat," the subject in the latter case being here "the mighty Rock," i.e., the *Shekhinah*, who is feminine. The spirits of the righteous fly out into the world from the bosom of the *Shekhinah*, who is also called here "the Holy Spirit."

[89] [Hebrew *mimmennu*, meaning "of it" in the scriptural verse, can also mean "from him."]

[90] The definite article in the biblical quotation [which is usually framed as a question] gives rise to this interpretation. "The man" is the righteous one who is praised in the upper and the lower regions.

[91] This "field" is the *Shekhinah*, which receives blessing from *Tiferet*.

[92] "Siege" (Heb. *mazzor*)—a place of narrow straits, and a name given to *Binah*, which is like a fortress, difficult to penetrate. *Binah* is repentance, to which only the truly penitent can ascend in the world to come. The righteous man exhorts the sinful inhabitants of the city to return in penitence, and thereby escape the destroyer and penetrate the celestial "siege."

"Mighty Rock," mentioned above in connection with the *Shekhinah*, here refers to *Binah*.

those who study the Torah. Therefore happy are those who study the Torah. Those who study the Torah are this world's mighty trees. See what the Holy One, blessed be He, has done. He has planted these trees. How blessed is this journey! The Holy One, blessed be He, has produced for us not just one tree but three tall trees, spreading their branches on every side. May it be the will of Heaven that these trees and this fountain be never removed from this place.

And to this day they are there, with the fountain of water, and people call them "The Plantation of Rabbi Pinhas ben Yair."

5. THE RIGHTEOUS MAN OF HIS TIME. ANNULLING THE DECREES—I

(Zohar Ḥadash, Va-yera, 26b)

"And Abraham shall surely become ..." (Genesis 18: 18). The numerical value of *yihyeh* ("shall become") is thirty.

One day Rabbi Simeon went out and saw that the world was dark and gloomy and its light sealed up.

Rabbi Eleazar said to him: Let us go and see what the Holy One, blessed be He, requires.

They went and found an angel in the form of a lofty mountain, emitting thirty flames of fire from his mouth.

Rabbi Simeon said to him: What are you trying to do?

I am trying to destroy the world, he said, because thirty righteous men do not exist in this generation; for this was the decree that the Holy One, blessed be He, enacted with Abraham—"And Abraham shall surely become," and the numerical value of "shall become" (*yihyeh*) is thirty.[93]

Rabbi Simeon said to him: Go, I beg you, to the Holy One, blessed be He, and tell Him that Ben Yoḥai exists in the world.

The angel went to the Holy One, blessed be He, and said: Master of the universe, it has been revealed to You what Ben Yoḥai said to me.

The Holy One, blessed be He, said to him: Go and destroy the world, and pay no heed to Ben Yoḥai!

Rabbi Simeon saw the angel approaching, and said: If you do not go away I shall forbid you to enter Heaven, but you shall be with Uzza and Azael.[94] And when you come into the presence of the Holy One, blessed be He, say that if there are not thirty righteous men in the world, let twenty suffice, for it is written "I shall not do it for the sake of twenty" (Genesis 18: 31). And if there are not twenty, let ten suffice, for it is written "I shall not destroy it for the sake of ten" (Genesis 18: 32). And if

[93] The continued existence of the world depends on there being thirty righteous men in it.

[94] Angels who were driven out of Heaven because they rebelled against God, and who are chained to the mountains of darkness.

there are not ten, let two suffice, namely, myself and my son, for it is written, "At the mouth of two witnesses . . . shall a *davar* be established" (Deuteronomy 19: 15), and *davar* means "world," as Scripture says "In the *davar* of the Lord, the heavens were made" (Psalm 33: 6).[95] And if there are not two, then there is at least one, and that is myself, for it is written "The righteous man is the foundation of the world" (Proverbs 10: 25).

At that moment a voice proclaimed from heaven: How happy is your portion, Rabbi Simeon, for the Holy One, blessed be He, issues a decree in the world above, and you annul it in the world below. Truly, of you is it written, "He fulfills the desire of those that fear Him," (Psalm 145: 19).

6. THE RIGHTEOUS MAN OF HIS TIME.
ANNULLING THE DECREES—II

(Zohar III, 15a)

One day [Rabbi Simeon ben Yohai] was sitting at the gateway to Lydda. He raised his eyes and saw the sun shining, but its light was blotted out three times. As the light grew dark, black and green colors appeared in the sun.

He said to his son, Rabbi Eleazar: Follow me, my son, and let us see, for a decree has certainly been proclaimed in the world above, and the Holy One, blessed be He, is trying to tell me; for whatever is decreed above is held in abeyance for thirty days, and the Holy One, blessed be He, does not act before informing the righteous, as it is said, "For the Lord God does nothing without revealing His secret to His servants, the prophets" (Amos 3: 7).

During their journey they entered a vineyard. They saw a snake moving along with its mouth open, and burning the ground in the dust. Rabbi Simeon bestirred himself and clasped the head of the snake in his hands. The snake was pacified, and closed its mouth, but he saw that its tongue was moving.

He said: Snake, snake, go and tell the supernal serpent[96] that Rabbi Simeon ben Yohai exists in the world.

It put its head in a crevice in the ground.

Rabbi Simeon said: I decree that just as the lower one returns to the crevice in the ground, so the upper one will return to the crevice in the great deep.[97]

Rabbi Simeon whispered a prayer. While they were praying they heard a voice: You who have been appointed to cut down,[98] return to

[95] [*Davar* means "word; thing; matter."]

[96] The primordial serpent is one of the main protagonists of "the other side", and the snake is his emissary below.

[97] The great deep is the abode of the husks, whence they emerge to destroy the world.

[98] The powers designated to destroy the world.

your places. The band of the violent does not dwell in the world, for Rabbi Simeon ben Yohai has overpowered it. Blessed are you, Rabbi Simeon ben Yohai, for your master takes more pleasure in your glory than in all the rest of mankind. Of Moses it is written, "And Moses entreated (va-yeḥal)" (Exodus 32: 11). This really means "he trembled".[99] But you, Rabbi Simeon, decree and the Holy One, blessed be He, fulfills your decree; whereas He decrees, and you annul His decree.

Meanwhile they noticed that the sun was shining and the blackness had disappeared.

Rabbi Simeon said: The world smells sweet.

He entered his house and interpreted: "For the Lord is righteous. He loves righteousness. The upright shall behold His face" (Psalm 11: 7). What is the meaning of "For the Lord is righteous. He loves righteousness"? It is because "their faces gaze directly."[100] What are "their faces"? The celestial countenances[101] from whom the inhabitants of the world must seek mercy in all that is required of them.

7. RABBI SIMEON BEN YOHAI AND HIS GENERATION—I

(Zohar II, 149a)

Rabbi Jose was studying the Torah, and Rabbi Isaac and Rabbi Hezekiah were with him.

Rabbi Isaac said: We see that the making of the Tabernacle was like that of heaven and earth, and the companions have so little knowledge of their mysteries that they cannot eat, or put their hands to their mouths, or swallow.[102]

Rabbi Jose said: Let us take these things up to the sacred lamp,[103] for he prepares sweet dishes,[104] like those of the holy Ancient One,[105] the mystery of all mysteries; he prepares dishes that do not need salt from another. Furthermore, we can eat and drink our fill from all the delights of the world, and still have some to spare. He fulfills the verse "So he set it before them, and they ate, and had some to spare, according to the word of the Lord" (2 Kings 4: 44).

He began by quoting: "And the Lord gave Solomon wisdom, as He promised him. And there was peace between Hiram and Solomon; and

---

[99] The translation "he trembled" is based on the verb ḥilḥel.

[100] [Another possible translation of the second half of this verse].

[101] These are the sefirot. The interpretation of the verse is as follows: God loves the righteousness of man's deeds, for through their power the sefirot can gaze directly at one another, and a stream of blessing and mercy is released upon the world.

[102] They cannot understand the inner meaning of the scriptural verses.

[103] Rabbi Simeon ben Yohai.

[104] Reveals the secrets of the Torah.

[105] Keter. Rabbi Simeon ben Yohai derives the mysteries from the highest source.

they made a league between them" (1 Kings 5: 26). This verse can be interpreted at several points. "And the Lord"—there was agreement between upper and lower. "And the Lord"—He and His court.[106] "Gave wisdom"—like someone giving a present or a gift to his friend. "As He promised him"—the perfection of wisdom in riches, peace, and power. This is the meaning of "as He promised him."[107] "And there was peace between Hiram and Solomon"—what is the significance of this? They informed one another of the hidden meanings of the words they uttered, while other men were not able to perceive or understand them. Because of this, Hiram agreed, in return, with everything that Solomon said. King Solomon realized that it was not the wish of the supreme King that wisdom should be revealed through him to such an extent that the Torah, which was sealed from the very beginning, should be disclosed, even to a generation like his, that was more nearly perfect than other generations. He had opened doors in the Torah, but they still remained closed, except to those sages who were sufficiently worthy, and they were confused about them and did not know how to speak of them. But in this generation, in which Rabbi Simeon ben Yohai lives, it is the wish of the Holy One, blessed be He, for the sake of Rabbi Simeon, that the sealed things should be revealed by him. But I am astounded how scholars of this generation can pass one single moment without standing before Rabbi Simeon in order to study Torah while Rabbi Simeon is alive in the world. Nevertheless, in this generation wisdom will not be obliterated from the world. Alas for the generations when he departs, and the sages diminish in number, and wisdom is obliterated from the world!

Rabbi Isaac said: What you say is true, for one day I was walking along with him, and he opened his mouth to speak Torah, and I saw a pillar of cloud stretching down from heaven to earth, and a light shone in the middle of the pillar. I was greatly afraid and I said: Happy is the man for whom such things can happen in this world. What is written concerning Moses? "And when all the people saw the pillar of cloud stand at the door of the tent, all the people arose and worshiped, every man at his tent door" (Exodus 33: 10). This was most fitting for Moses, the faithful prophet, supreme over all the world's prophets, and for that generation, who received the Torah at Mount Sinai and witnessed so many miracles and examples of power in Egypt and at the Red Sea. But now, in this generation, it is because of the supreme merit of Rabbi Simeon that wonders are revealed at his hands.

[106] I.e., *Tiferet* and *Malkhut*, the mystery of both the written and the oral Torah. [These two interpretations are based on the word "and," which otherwise would appear to be superfluous.]

[107] In addition to the wisdom for which Solomon asked, God also gave him riches and honor (see 1 Kings 3: 13).

8. RABBI SIMEON BEN YOHAI AND HIS GENERATION—II

(Zohar III, 79a)

Rabbi Judah taught: The generation in which Rabbi Simeon ben Yohai lived consisted entirely of righteous, pious men who were afraid of sinning, and the *Shekhinah* dwelt among them—which was not the case with other generations. Therefore, these things are explained and not concealed. In other generations it was not so. They could not reveal the contents of the supreme mysteries, for those who knew them were afraid. But when Rabbi Simeon communicated the secret of this verse,[108] the eyes of all the companions streamed with tears, and all the things that he said were revealed in their sight, as it is written, "With him do I speak mouth to mouth, openly, and not in riddles" (Numbers 12: 8).

One day Rabbi Yesa inquired,[109] and said: The egg of truth, which comes from the bird who lives in the fire, and splits into four pieces—two of them ascend, one descends, and one rests in the resting-place of the great sea.

Rabbi Abba said: You have turned the holy into the profane in the presence of Rabbi Simeon, for of him it is written, "with him do I speak mouth to mouth."

Rabbi Simeon said to him: Before the egg splits[110] you will depart from the world.

And so it was in the assembly of Rabbi Simeon.[111]

It is taught: In Rabbi Simeon's days, a man would say to his fellow: Open your mouth, and let your words cast light. After Rabbi Simeon's death, they would say: "Do not let your mouth cause your flesh to sin" (Ecclesiastes 5: 5).

It is taught: Rabbi Simeon said: If the world's inhabitants understood what was written in the Torah, they would not come and anger their Master.

9. RABBI SIMEON BEN YOHAI AND HIS GENERATION—III

(Zohar III, 79b)

Happy is the generation in which Rabbi Simeon ben Yohai lives! Blessed is its portion between the upper and the lower worlds! Scripture says of

[108] The context deals with Leviticus 18: 19, "And you shall not approach a woman during her menstrual impurity, to uncover her nakedness."

[109] He asks for a solution to the riddle, and realizes that the riddle refers to the chain of the *sefirot*.

[110] Before the mystery of the divine is revealed.

[111] Rabbi Yesa and two other companions died before the close of the assembly (see below, p. 158).

it, "Happy are you, O land, for your king is a free man" (Ecclesiastes 10: 17). What does "a free man" mean? A man who lifts his head to reveal and interpret things, and does not fear—this is a free man. He says what he pleases and does not fear. What does "your king" mean? This is Rabbi Simeon ben Yohai, the master of the Torah, the master of wisdom, for when Rabbi Abba and the companions saw Rabbi Simeon they ran after him, saying, "They shall walk after the Lord, who shall roar like a lion" (Hosea 11: 10).

10. RABBI SIMEON BEN YOHAI AND RABBI ELEAZAR IN THE CAVE

(Zohar Ḥadash, Ki tavo, 59c–60a)

Rabbi Simeon ben Yohai fled to the desert of Lydda, and lived in a cave with his son, Rabbi Eleazar. A miracle was performed for them, and a carob tree and a water source came into being for them. They ate of the carob tree, and drank of the water. Elijah, may he be remembered for good, visited them twice a day, and instructed them, and no one knew where they were.

One day the scholars in the academy were puzzled, saying: The curses in Leviticus refer to the first Temple, and the curses in Deuteronomy[112] refer to the second Temple, to the latest exile. The curses in Leviticus contain some assurances and an expression of the love of the Holy One, blessed be He, for Israel, for it is written, "And I will remember my covenant with Jacob . . . And yet, for all that, when they are in the land of their enemies [I will not reject them] . . ." (Leviticus 26: 42, 44) The curses in Deuteronomy contain no assurances, and no consolation at all, unlike the earlier curses.

And they did not understand.

Rabbi Judah ben Ilai arose and said: Alas that Ben Yohai is absent. No one knows of him, and even if one did know, one would not be permitted to say.

Rabbi Jose, the son of Rabbi Judah, awoke in the morning one day and saw the birds flying and a dove following them. He got to his feet and said: Dove, dove, faithful from the days of the Flood, image of the holy people,[113] it is right and fitting for you to go on a mission for me to Ben Yohai, wherever he is to be found.

The dove turned and alighted in front of him. He wrote a message, saying what he had to say, and the dove took it in its beak and flew away to Rabbi Simeon, and gave it to him with its wing. He looked at the message and wept, and Rabbi Eleazar, his son, with him. He said: I weep on account of my separation from the companions. And I weep on

[112] See Leviticus 26 and Deuteronomy 28.
[113] The community of Israel is compared to a dove.

account of the things that are not revealed to them. What will later generations do, when they reflect upon this?

Meanwhile, Elijah, may he be remembered for good, arrived, and saw that he was weeping. He said: I was about to go on another mission, but the Holy One, blessed be He, sent me to stay your tears. Alas! rabbi. Alas! There was no need for me to reveal these things to the righteous now, but the Holy One, blessed be He, has said to me as follows: The first curses comprise thirty-two verses, and these all correspond to the paths of the Torah.[114] The latter curses comprise fifty-three verses and these correspond to the sections of the Torah.[115] In the first exile, at the time of the first Temple, Israel transgressed the secret paths of the secret [Torah], and their sins were revealed, and their end; but their consolation and their assurance were revealed also. In the last exile, at the time of the second Temple, Israel transgressed the fifty-three sections of the revealed [Torah], but their sin is concealed, and their end is concealed, and assurances and consolations are not written down for them.

Then a wind passed by them and separated them, and Elijah went up in a chariot of fire, and Rabbi Simeon was left weeping. And he fell asleep at the entrance to the cave.

After a time, Elijah, may he be remembered for good, arrived and said: Arise, Rabbi Simeon, awake from your sleep. Blessed is your portion, for the Holy One, blessed be He, takes delight in honoring you. All the assurances and consolations of Israel are written in these curses. Think of a king who loves his son. Even though he curses him, and punishes him, he still has love in his heart for him. When he displays great anger, his mercy is immediately aroused for him. So with the Holy One, blessed be He: even though He curses, His words appear in love—He curses openly, and they are great benefits, for these curses are uttered in love. Such was not the case with the former curses, all of which were uttered in strict judgment, whereas here there is judgment and love, as with a father who has pity on his son, and who holds the lashes of the whip in his hand, and utters a loud roar and a great cry, but his strokes are soft, because of his mercy.

Of all these curses the most severe is, "Also every sickness, and every plague, which is not written in the book of this Torah, them will the Lord bring upon you, until you are destroyed" (Deuteronomy 28: 61). Here we have the father's assurances to his son in great love. It is not written *ya'aleh* ("he will bring") but *ya'lem* ("he will conceal").[116] He will

---

[114] The thirty-two paths of wisdom that make up the esoteric Torah.

[115] The *sidrot* of the Torah.

[116] [*Ya'lem* is usually translated "He will bring them." But it is here derived from a Hebrew verbal root meaning "to hide, conceal."]

subdue them and cover them in the holes[117] where they exist, so that they cannot emerge, but remain subdued and covered in their holes. "Until you are destroyed"—this will never be, to all eternity, for the Holy One, blessed be He, has sworn never to destroy Israel for all time, but that the remembrance of them shall endure for ever, as it is written, "so shall your seed and your name remain" (Isaiah 66: 22).[118] And it is also written "By My life, if heaven above can be measured" (Jeremiah 31: 36).[119] Since the oath is that the children of Israel will never be cut off, and since all the hidden and concealed diseases and plagues are not due to emerge to afflict them until the time comes for them to be cut off, this can never come to pass for ever and ever.

The end of all [the curses] and their conclusion is, "And the Lord will bring you back to Egypt in ships, by the way of which I said to you: You shall see it no more again. And you will sell yourselves there as bondmen and bondwomen, and no one shall buy you" (Deuteronomy 28: 68). Here are the assurances and the consolations that the Holy One, blessed be He, will enact for Israel at the end of days. "And the Lord will bring you back to Egypt in ships"—an assurance that He will repeat the signs and wonders which the Holy One, blessed be He, performed in Egypt in the early days, as it is said, "As in the days when you came out of the land of Egypt, will I show him marvelous things" (Micah 7: 15). "In ships" (be-oniot) here is to be taken as you explained it before: "in poverty" (be-aniut),[120] when the purse is emptied of money. In the future all the inhabitants of the world will come against Israel in ships, intending to annihilate them, but they will all drown in the sea, just as it happened in the early days, when there was great rejoicing. Here it is written "in ships", and elsewhere it is written "in the ships of their song" (Isaiah 43: 14). Just as there was singing then, so there will be singing here. "By the way of which I said to you." From the very creation of the world, the Holy One, blessed be He, did not reveal His power in the world, or the time of His favor, except in that "way": "for whereas you have seen the Egyptians" (Exodus 14: 13),[121] in the same way, and in the same fashion, shall it be done for you; for subsequently they will gather themselves together against them from all sides, and Israel will think that they are about to be destroyed and be sold to their enemies. So it is

---

[117] In the depths of the husks, the place where evils reside.

[118] The whole verse reads "as the new heavens and the new earth, which I will make, shall remain before Me, so shall your seed and your name remain."

[119] The quotation is not accurate. The whole verse reads "Thus saith the Lord: If heaven above can be measured, and the foundations of the earth searched out beneath, then will I cast off all the seed of Israel for all that they have done, saith the Lord."

[120] The two Hebrew words are similar apart from the change of one letter. The allusion is to the belief that the Messiah will come when there is widespread poverty.

[121] The full verse reads, "for whereas you have seen the Egyptians today, you shall see them again no more for ever."

written "and you will sell yourselves there." It does not say "you will be sold," but "you will sell yourselves." You will think in your own minds that you will be sold, but it will not happen, for "no one shall buy you," and no one will have power over you. All this will happen at the end of days and all depends on repentance, and all is sealed, as it is written "that you may understand everything that you do" (Deuteronomy 29: 8). Whoever has a mind should think, and understand how to return to his Master.

Rabbi Simeon said to him: Where is the redemption of Israel revealed among these curses?

Look, and examine the most evil place, and there you will find it.

He looked, examined, and found it written, "And your life will be suspended before you, and you will fear night and day, and you will not be assured of your life" (Deuteronomy 28: 66).

[He said:] Although the companions know the time [of redemption], the life [of redemption] is suspended before us, and [its timing] is a matter of doubt. This explanation is the key, and the whole matter is irrefutable.

He wrote a message at evening time, and put it in the mouth of the dove. It flew to Rabbi Jose, who had remained in his place with expectant eyes. When he saw it, he said: Dove, dove, how much more faithful you are than all the birds of heaven. He cited in its praise, "And the dove came in to him at eventide, and, behold, in her mouth an olive leaf freshly plucked" (Genesis 8: 11).

He took the message, joined the companions, and showed it to them, and when he revealed the matter to them they were astonished.

Rabbi Judah wept and said: Alas, even though we do not know it,[122] nevertheless "in the place where the tree falls, there it lies" (Ecclesiastes 11:3). Where Ben Yohai is, there are the companions with him, and they respond to him and learn from him. Ben Yohai's soul is so worthy that the Holy One, blessed be He, works wonders for him. He makes a decree, and the Holy One, blessed be He, executes it. He is destined to be the leader of the righteous who dwell in the Garden of Eden. He will encounter the face of the *Shekhinah*, and see the Holy One, blessed be He, and exult gleefully with the righteous, saying to them, "Come, let us prostrate ourselves and bow down; let us kneel before the Lord, our Maker" (Psalm 95: 6).

11. THE EMERGENCE FROM THE CAVE

(Zohar I, 11a–11b)

Rabbi Pinhas used to visit Rabbi Rehumai by the shore of Lake

---

[122] I.e., where Rabbi Simeon ben Yohai is.

Kinneret. He was a venerable man, full of days, and his eyes could no longer see.

He said to Rabbi Pinhas: I have had a trustworthy report that our companion, Yohai, has a jewel, a precious stone, and I have looked upon[123] the light emitted by this jewel, and it is like the light of the sun emerging from its sheath, illuminating the entire world. This light extends from the heavens to the earth, and will continue to illumine the whole world until the Ancient of Days[124] comes, and sits upon the throne[125] as is fitting. This light is all contained within your house,[126] and from the light contained within your house a fine, slender ray[127] has emerged, and it will go out and illumine the whole world. How blessed is your portion! Go, my son, go, and follow this jewel, which illumines the world, for the hour is now ripe for you.

He left him, and prepared to go on board a ship with two other men. He saw two birds darting low over the lake. He called to them, and said: Birds, birds, darting low over the lake, have you seen where Ben Yohai is?

He waited a little. Birds, birds, he said, Go, and come back to me.

And they flew away.

They embarked and set off across the lake. Before they had disembarked the birds returned, and in the mouth of one of them was a message that said that Ben Yohai had left the cave, together with Rabbi Eleazar, his son.

He went to him and found him transformed, for his body was covered with mould. He wept, and said: Alas, that I should see you so!

He replied: Blessed is your portion in that you have seen me so, for had you not seen me in this state, I would not be in this state.[128]

12. THE ENTRY INTO THE GREAT ASSEMBLY

(Zohar III, 127b–128a. *Idra Rabba*)

It is taught that Rabbi Simeon said to the companions: How long shall we sit by a column that has but a single base?[129] It is written, "It is time to do something for the Lord. They have frustrated Your Torah" (Psalm 119: 126). Time is short, and the creditor is impatient. A herald cries out

[123] He saw inwardly that Rabbi Simeon ben Yohai had left the cave, and his brilliance was illuminating the world.   [124] *Keter*.

[125] The "throne" is the array of the *sefirot*. The light of Rabbi Simeon ben Yohai unites the *sefirot*.

[126] According to the Zohar, Rabbi Simeon ben Yohai was Rabbi Pinhas's son-in-law, and not father-in-law as in the Talmud.

[127] Rabbi Eleazar, the son of Rabbi Simeon ben Yohai.

[128] I.e., I would not be at the high level of experience that I attained in the cave.

[129] How long shall we study Torah without knowing the hidden foundation of it in the secrets of kabbalah?

every day. But the reapers in the field[130] are few, and they are on the edges of the vineyard.[131] They do not look, nor do they know fully where they are going. Assemble, friends, at the meeting place,[132] garbed in mail, with swords and lances in your hands. Look to your equipment: counsel, wisdom, understanding, knowledge, sight, power of hands and legs. Appoint a king over you who has the power of life and death and who can utter words of truth, words that the holy ones above will heed, and that they will rejoice to hear and know.

Rabbi Simeon sat down and wept. He said: Alas, if I reveal! Alas, if I do not reveal!

The companions who were there were silent. Rabbi Abba arose and said to him: If it pleases you, master, to reveal, you know it is written, "The secret of the Lord is for those who fear Him" (Psalm 25: 14), and these companions do fear the Lord, and they have already entered the assembly of the sanctuary.[133] Some of them have entered, and some have also emerged.[134]

It is taught that the companions who were present with Rabbi Simeon were counted, and they were: his son, Rabbi Eleazar, Rabbi Abba, Rabbi Judah, Rabbi Jose bar Jacob, Rabbi Isaac, Rabbi Hezekiah bar Rav, Rabbi Hiyya, Rabbi Jose, and Rabbi Yesa. They stretched out their hands to Rabbi Simeon, and extended their fingers toward the heavens, and they went into the field among the trees and sat down.

Rabbi Simeon arose and prayed. He sat down among them and said: Put your hands in my lap.

They put out their hands, and he grasped them.[135]

He began by quoting: "Cursed be the man that makes a graven or molten image . . . the work of the hands of the craftsman, and that sets it up in secret" (Deuteronomy 27: 15).[136] And they all responded by saying, Amen.

Rabbi Simeon began by quoting "It is time to do something for the Lord." Why is it time to do something for the Lord? Because "they have

[130] A reference to the mystics.

[131] They do not penetrate the inner complexities of the kabbalah.

[132] The precise meaning of *idra* in the Zohar is not clear. But the reference is obviously to a meeting, a gathering of the companions. Here the meeting was to be in the open air, as indicated later.

[133] A meeting that studied the mystical secrets of the Temple (referred to apparently in II, 127a–146a).

[134] Some of the companions entered this assembly in peace, but were not accounted worthy enough to receive a revelation of all the secrets. But others achieved a complete perception, and these emerged in peace.

[135] He took them all in his hand, as a symbol of the mystery of the divine unity.

[136] He reminds the companions of the prohibition against ascribing corporeality to the Godhead, because he is about to speak of the mystery of God in symbols, which might appear to be corporeal.

frustrated Your Torah." What does this phrase mean? It refers to the heavenly Torah,[137] which is annulled[138] if this Name is not treated as it should be, and this alludes to the Ancient of Days.[139] It is written, "Happy are you, O Israel, who is like you?" (Deuteronomy 33: 29). And it is also written, "Who is like You, O Lord, among the mighty?" (Exodus 15: 11).[140]

He called to his son, Rabbi Eleazar, and sat him down before him, and Rabbi Abba he seated on the other side. And he said: We comprise the whole.[141] Thus far are the pillars set right.[142]

They were silent. They heard a sound and their knees knocked together. What sound was it? The sound made by the entry of the assembly of heaven.

Rabbi Simeon was glad, and said: "O Lord, I have heard the sound of You, and I am afraid" (Habbakuk 3: 2). At that time it was right to be afraid, but with us it depends on love, as it is written, "And you shall love the Lord, your God," "because the Lord loved you," and "I have loved you," and so on.[143]

Rabbi Simeon began by quoting: "He that walks about as a talebearer reveals secrets. But he that has a faithful spirit conceals a thing" (Proverbs 1: 13). This verse is difficult. It ought to have said, "The man that is a talebearer." What is the significance of "He that walks about"? It means that the man who is unsettled in his mind and insecure keeps whatever he hears moving about inside him, like bran in water, until he casts it out.[144] Why is this? because he does not have a stable mind. But of the man of stable mind it is written "But he that has a faithful spirit conceals a thing." "A faithful spirit" means here "a secure spirit," as in "I will fasten him as a peg in a secure place" (Isaiah 22:

---

[137] *Tiferet*, the symbol among the *sefirot* of the written Torah.

[138] If there is no proper purposive concentration (*kavvanah*) on the tetragrammaton (the name, translated "Lord"), which is specific to *Tiferet*, this leads to the annulment of the heavenly Torah. The biblical verse is interpreted thus: It is time to do something for the name "Lord." If this is not done, then they have frustrated Your Torah.

[139] The possessive in the phrase "Your Torah" refers to *Keter*, which is also called "Ancient of Days," and *Tiferet* is its Torah.

[140] These two verses also deal with *Tiferet*, which is called Israel, which in turn is the name "Lord" (the tetragrammaton), as may be deduced from the occurrence of the phrase "Who is like you" in both verses.

[141] This appears to mean that they represent *Hesed*, *Gevurah*, and *Tiferet*, which comprise the whole range of the *sefirot*, in the threefold aspect of Love, Judgment, and Mercy.

[142] The pillars of the world of the *sefirot* are arranged correctly.

[143] The three verses quoted are respectively: Deuteronomy 6: 5; 7: 8; and Malachi 1: 2. Habbakuk's vision was of God's attribute of judgment, and therefore it was associated with fear. But Rabbi Simeon's revelation was of the attribute of mercy, i.e., of love.

[144] I.e., reveals the secret.

23).[145] The thing depends on the spirit. It is written "Do not allow your mouth to cause your flesh to sin" (Ecclesiastes 5: 5), and the world endures only because of the mystery. And so, if in mundane matters there is a need for secrecy, how much more need for secrecy is there in the most mysterious affairs of the Ancient of Days, which have not been transmitted even to the angels in Heaven.

Rabbi Simeon said: I do not ask the heavens to listen, nor do I ask the earth to give ear, for we are the worlds' support.

13. THE EXIT FROM THE GREAT ASSEMBLY
(Zohar III, 144a–144b. *Idra Rabba*)

It is taught that before the companions left the assembly Rabbi Jose bar Rabbi Jacob, Rabbi Hezekiah, and Rabbi Yesa died, and the companions saw the holy angels carry them up in a litter. Rabbi Simeon said a word and the companions were pacified. He cried aloud and said: Perhaps, God forbid, it has been decreed that we should be punished, because matters have been revealed through us that had not previously been revealed since Moses stood on Mount Sinai, as it is written, "And he was there with the Lord forty days and forty nights . . ." (Exodus 34: 28). Of what worth am I if they were punished because of this?

He heard a voice: Blessed are you, Rabbi Simeon, blessed is your portion, and blessed are these companions who stand with you, for things have been revealed to you that have not been revealed to any power above. Look, it is written, "with his firstborn he shall lay its foundation, and with his youngest he shall set up its gates" (Joshua 6: 26).[146] With how much greater delight did their souls cleave to the uppermost realms when they were taken from the world.[147] Blessed is their portion, for they have ascended in complete perfection.

It is taught that during the process of revelation the upper and the lower regions trembled, and the sound traveled through two hundred and fifty worlds, for venerable matters were being revealed in the world below, and while the souls of these men were being perfumed with these words, their souls departed with a kiss, and attached themselves to the litter, and the angels of heaven carried them away to the regions above. And why just these? Because these were they who had entered, but had not emerged, on the previous occasion,[148] whereas all the others had both entered and emerged.

[145] [The relevant Hebrew word is *ne'eman*, which can mean "faithful" or "sure, secure."].

[146] The revelation of the mystery of the Godhead, which is akin to the construction of a building, imperils those who are involved with it.

[147] Therefore their death should cause no grief.

[148] This refers to "the assembly of the sanctuary," mentioned above, p. 156.

Rabbi Simeon said: How blessed is the portion of these three, and blessed is our portion in the world to come on account of this.

A voice was heard a second time, which said: "But you that cleave to the Lord, your God, are alive every one of you this day" (Deuteronomy 4: 4).

They arose and departed. Every place they looked at exuded perfume. Rabbi Simeon said: This means that the world is blessed because of us.

All their faces shone, and people could not look at them.

It is taught that ten entered and seven emerged. Rabbi Simeon was happy and Rabbi Abba was sad. Rabbi Simeon was sitting one day with Rabbi Abba. Rabbi Simeon said something and they saw those three. The angels of heaven were taking them and showing them the hidden storerooms on high, because of the honor due to them. And they brought them to the mountains of pure balsam. Rabbi Abba was consoled.

It is taught that from that day forward the companions did not leave Rabbi Simeon's house, and that when Rabbi Simeon was revealing secrets, only they were present with him. And Rabbi Simeon used to say of them: We seven are the eyes of the Lord, as it is written, "these seven, the eyes of the Lord" (Zechariah 4: 10).[149] Of us is this said.

Rabbi Abba said: We are six lamps[150] that derive their light from the seventh. You are the seventh over all, for the six cannot survive without the seventh. Everything depends on the seventh.

Rabbi Judah called him "Sabbath," because the [other] six [days] receive blessing from it, for it is written "Sabbath to the Lord" and it is also written "Holy to the Lord."[151] Just as the Sabbath is holy to the Lord, so Rabbi Simeon, the Sabbath, is holy to the Lord.

14. THE ILLNESS OF RABBI SIMEON BEN YOHAI

(Zohar Ḥadash, Bereshit, 18d–19a. Midrash ha-Ne'elam)

Our rabbis taught that when Rabbi Simeon ben Yohai became ill he was visited by Rabbi Pinhas, Rabbi Hiyya, and Rabbi Abbahu.

They said to him: Can a man who is the pillar of the world be near to death?

He said: It is not the heavenly court that is concerned with my case. I know that I am beyond the jurisdiction of any angel or judge in heaven, for I am not like other men. But the Holy One, blessed be He, not His

[149] They represent the seven sefirot from Ḥesed to Malkhut, which direct and supervise the world, and, as such, are "the eyes of the Lord."

[150] Corresponding to the six sefirot from Ḥesed to Yesod, that receive influence from Binah, which is the seventh from the bottom, and Rabbi Simeon corresponds to Binah.

[151] Exodus 20: 10; 16: 23. The latter verse reads more fully "a holy Sabbath to the Lord."

court, judges my case. This is similar to the plea that David made to Him, "Judge me, O God, and plead my cause" (Psalm 43: 1). And Solomon also said likewise, "That He may execute justice for His servant"(1 Kings 8: 59)—He Himself, and no one else. And we have learned that when a man is on his deathbed the heavenly court examines his case. Some of them are inclined to acquit him, and they point out his merits. Others are inclined to convict him, and they point out his guilt, and the defendant does not emerge from the case as he would wish. But whoever is judged by the supreme King, who has dominion over all, is fortunate, and in a trial of this kind man must inevitably be successful. Why is this? We have learned that the attributes of the supreme King are always inclined toward acquittal, and He is entirely merciful,[152] and He has the power to forgive iniquities and transgressions, as it is written, "For with You there is forgiveness" (Psalm 130: 4)—and not with anyone else. Therefore I asked Him to judge my case, so that I might enter the world to come through the thirteen doors,[153] which only the patriarchs have passed through, with no one to prevent me; and, furthermore, so that I might not have to seek permission [from the doorkeepers].

Rabbi Simeon said something, and his visitors realized that he was no longer present. They were astounded, and none of them could utter a single word because of the deep fear that had fallen upon them. While they were sitting there, perfumes from many spices wafted over them, and they began to regain their courage, and at last they saw Rabbi Simeon talking, but they did not see anyone else except him.

After a while Rabbi Simeon said to them: Did you see anything?

No, said Rabbi Pinhas, but we were all astounded that we could not see you for a long time in your sickroom. And when we did see you, perfumes from the spices of the Garden of Eden wafted over us, and we heard your voice speaking, but we do not know with whom you were talking.

And you heard no other words, except mine?

No, they replied.

You are not sufficiently worthy to see the countenance of the Ancient of Days. Let me tell you something, he continued. I am surprised that Rabbi Pinhas did not see anything, for I saw him just now, in that world, below my son, Rabbi Eleazar. And they have now sent for me from above, and shown me the place of the righteous in the world to come. And the only place that satisfied me was one near Ahija, the Shilonite, and so I chose my place, and went there, together with three hundred righteous souls. Above them was Adam, who sat by me and spoke with me, and asked that his sin should not be revealed to the whole world,

---

[152] [Lit. "He is entirely the side of mercy."]
[153] A reference apparently to the thirteen attributes of mercy.

apart from what the Torah says of it, and that it should remain concealed with the tree of the Garden of Eden.[154] But I told him that the companions had already revealed it. And he said: Whatever the companions have revealed among themselves is good and proper, but not to the rest of mankind.

What is the reason for this? The Holy One, blessed be He, is concerned for His own honor, and does not wish to publicize [Adam's] sin, except in respect of the tree from which he ate. But the Holy One, blessed be He, revealed it to me, by the Holy Spirit, and to the companions, so that they might discuss it among themselves, but not to the younger companions or to those who are still to come into the world, This is something that is not known to everyone, and they err thereby; not because of the sin that he committed, but because of the honor of the supreme name,[155] which people do not treat with sufficient care, and it is written, "this is My name for ever" (Exodus 3: 15), and they will begin to ask unnecessary questions. This is referred to in "lest they break through to the Lord, to gaze, and many of them fall" (Exodus 19: 21), which we interpret as follows: the companion that teaches the sacred name to all will fall and be more tightly trapped by that sin than they, as it is written "and many (rav) of them fall," that is, the Rav will fall, and be trapped by that sin.

Rabbi Eleazar, his son, approached him, and said: Father, what was my position there?

He replied: Blessed is your portion, my son. A long time will elapse, and you will not be buried next to me.[156] But in that world I have selected a place for me and a place for you.

Blessed are the righteous, who in the future will praise the Master of the universe, like the angels who minister to Him, as it is written, "Surely the righteous shall give thanks to Your name; the upright shall dwell in Your presence" (Psalm 140: 14).

15. REVELATION OF MYSTERIES BEFORE HIS DEPARTURE

(Zohar III, 287b–288a. Idra Ẓuta)

It is taught that on the very day that Rabbi Simeon was to depart from the world and he was busy arranging his affairs, the companions gathered in Rabbi Simeon's house. Rabbi Eleazar, his son, Rabbi Abba,

[154] The description of Adam's sin as eating the fruit of the Tree of Knowledge really conceals his true sin. The Tree of Knowledge is a symbol of the *Shekhinah*, whose perfection depends on her complete union with the upper *sefirot*, and particularly with her companion, *Tiferet*, which is the Tree of Life. Adam's sin consisted in the fact that he considered the *Shekhinah* to be a separate force on its own, and so he removed her from the array of the *sefirot*, thus destroying the divine unity.

[155] The *Shekhinah*, which was harmed by Adam's sin.

[156] See B. T. *Baba Mezia* 84b.

and the other companions were there with him, and the house was full. Rabbi Simeon raised his eyes and saw that the house had become full.

Rabbi Simeon wept and said: On a previous occasion when I was ill, Rabbi Pinhas ben Yair was with me, and the companions waited for me until I had selected my place.[157] And when I returned, fire surrounded me increasingly, so that no man could enter without permission. But now I see that it has ceased, and the house is full.

While they were seated there, Rabbi Simeon opened his eyes, and saw what he saw, and fire enveloped the house. They all left, except Rabbi Eleazar, his son, and Rabbi Abba. The other companions stayed outside.

Rabbi Simeon said to Rabbi Eleazar, his son: Go and see if Rabbi Isaac is there, because I have given a pledge to him.[158] Tell him to arrange his affairs and sit by me. Blessed is his portion.[159]

Rabbi Simeon arose and smiled, and was happy. He said: Where are the companions?

Rabbi Eleazar arose, and brought them in, and they sat down before him.

Rabbi Simeon raised his hands, and prayed, and was happy, and said: Let those companions who were at the assembly[160] present themselves here.

They all left, except Rabbi Eleazar, his son, Rabbi Abba, Rabbi Judah, Rabbi Jose, and Rabbi Hiyya. In the meantime Rabbi Isaac had entered. Rabbi Simeon said to him: How pleasant is your portion! How much joy is to be added to your life today!

Rabbi Abba sat behind his back, and Rabbi Eleazar sat in front of him.

Rabbi Simeon said: Now is a propitious hour, and I am seeking to enter the world to come without shame. There are sacred matters that have not been revealed up till now and that I wish to reveal in the presence of the *Shekhinah*, so that it should not be said that I departed from the world with my work incomplete. Until now they have been concealed in my heart, so that I might enter the world to come with them. And so I give you your duties: Rabbi Abba will write them down, Rabbi Eleazar, my son, will explain them, and the other companions will meditate silently upon them.

Rabbi Abba rose from behind his back, and Rabbi Eleazar, his son, sat in front of him.

[157] In the Garden of Eden. See above, p. 160.
[158] When the angel of death tried to kill him. See above, pp. 135–37.
[159] Because he is about to depart from the world together with Rabbi Simeon ben Yohai.
[160] The great assembly. See above pp. 156, 158.

He said to him: Arise, my son, for, behold, another sits in that place.[161]

Rabbi Eleazar rose. Rabbi Simeon wrapped himself in his cloak and sat down.

He began by quoting: "The dead do not praise the Lord, nor do any that descend to silence (*Dumah*)" (Psalm 115: 17). "The dead do not praise the Lord." This is certainly true of those who are called "dead,"[162] for the Holy One, blessed be He, is called "living," and He dwells among those who are called "living,"[163] and not with those who are called "dead." And at the end of the verse it is written, "nor do any who descend to *Dumah*." And all those who descend to *Dumah*[164] will remain in Gehinnom, unlike those who are called "living," in whose glory the Holy One, blessed be He, takes pleasure.

Rabbi Simeon said: How different is this moment from the assembly, for at the assembly the Holy One, blessed be He, was present with His chariots, but now, see, the Holy One, blessed be He, has come here with the righteous from the Garden of Eden. And this did not happen at the assembly. The Holy One, blessed be He, is more concerned with their reputation than with His own, as it is written of Jeroboam. He used to offer incense to and worship idols, but the Holy One, blessed be He, was patient with him, until he raised his hand against Iddo the prophet, and then his hand withered, as it is written, "and his hand dried up" (1 Kings 13: 4)—not because he worshiped idols, but because he raised his hand against Iddo the prophet. And now the Holy One, blessed be He, is concerned with our reputation, and they have all come with Him.

He said: Look, Rav Hamnuna Sava is here, surrounded by seventy righteous men, marked with crowns,[165] each one of them reflecting light from the shining countenance of the Holy, Ancient One, the most mysterious of mysteries; and he has come to listen with joy to the words that I utter.

While he was seated, he said: Look, Rabbi Pinhas ben Yair is here. Prepare a place for him.

The companions who were there trembled. They rose and moved further away into the house and sat down, but Rabbi Eleazar and Rabbi Abba remained with Rabbi Simeon.

Rabbi Simeon said: When we were in the assembly, all the companions used to speak [Torah], and I joined in with them. But now I speak on my own, and they all listen to my words, the upper and the lower worlds. Blessed is my portion on this day!

[161] One of the righteous, who had come from the Garden of Eden.
[162] The wicked.
[163] The righteous.
[164] The prince of Gehinnom.
[165] Spiritual crowns were engraved on them.

16. THE DEPARTURE OF RABBI SIMEON BEN YOHAI

(Zohar III, 296b. *Idra Zuta*)

Rabbi Abba said: The holy light[166] had not finished saying "life,"[167] when his words were hushed. I was writing as if there were more to write, but I heard nothing. And I did not raise my head, for the light was strong, and I could not look at it. Then I became afraid. I heard a voice calling, "Length of days, and years of life [and peace will they add to you]" (Proverbs 3: 2). I heard another voice saying "He asked life from You. [You gave it to him, even length of days for ever and ever]" (Psalm 21: 5). All that day the fire did not leave the house, and no one could get near it. They were unable, because the light and the fire surrounded it the whole day. I threw myself upon the ground and groaned. When the fire had gone I saw that the holy light, the holy of holies, had departed from the world. He was lying on his right side, wrapped in his cloak, and his face was laughing. Rabbi Eleazar, his son, rose, took his hands and kissed them, and I licked the dust beneath his feet. The companions wanted to mourn, but they could not speak. The companions began to weep, and Rabbi Eleazar, his son, fell three times, and he could not open his mouth.

And then he began to speak: Father, father, they were three, and they have become one.[168] Now the creatures will move away,[169] the birds are flying and sinking into the clefts of the great sea, and the companions are all drinking blood.[170]

Rabbi Hiyya got to his feet, and said: Up till now the holy light has taken care of us. Now we can do nothing but attend to his honor.

Rabbi Eleazar and Rabbi Abba rose, and put him in a litter.[171] Who has ever seen disarray like that of the companions? The whole house exuded perfume. They raised him on his bier, and only Rabbi Eleazar and Rabbi Abba occupied themselves with it. The powerful and mighty

[166] Rabbi Simeon ben Yohai.

[167] He had been interpreting Psalm 133: 3, "For there the Lord commanded the blessing, even life for ever."

[168] The apparent meaning of this is that of the three sages who were bound so closely together, namely, Rabbi Simeon ben Yohai, Rabbi Pinhas, his father-in-law, and Rabbi Eleazar, his son, only Rabbi Eleazar now remained.

[169] Even the animals will mourn and leave their haunts, and the birds will hide in the rocky clefts of the sea. Or perhaps the reference here is to the celestial creatures (*hayyot*) and the angels, and, if this is so, the great sea would be the *Shekhinah*, and the angels would hide beneath her wings.

[170] Their grief is so intense that it is as if they were drinking blood. Or perhaps we should translate "they were bleeding" with grief. [The concept of the mourner drinking his salt tears mixed with his own blood was common in medieval Jewish and Arabic literature.]

[171] The original is *be-tikra de-silka*, which has no Aramaic source. However, from the context, it would appear that some kind of litter is intended.

men of the town[172] came and pleaded with them, and the inhabitants of Meron cried out all together, for they were afraid that he might not be buried there. When the bier came out of the house, it went up into the air and fire flared out in front of it.

They heard a voice, saying: Come, and assemble for the feast of Rabbi Simeon. "He enters in peace. They rest on their beds" (Isaiah 57: 2).

When he was brought into the cave, they heard a voice in the cave: "This is the man that made the earth tremble, that shook kingdoms" (Isaiah 14: 16). How many accusers in the firmament are reduced to silence on this day because of you, Rabbi Simeon ben Yohai, whose Master prides Himself on you every day.

Blessed is his portion, above and below. How many secret chambers are preserved for him! Of him it is said, "Go your way to the end, and you will rest, and come into your portion at the end of days" (Daniel 12: 13).

17. AFTER THE DEATH OF RABBI SIMEON BEN YOHAI

(Zohar I, 216b–217a)

It is taught that Rabbi Jose said: From the day that Rabbi Simeon left the cave, matters were not hidden from the companions, and the celestial mysteries were radiated and revealed among them as if they had been promulgated at that very moment on Mount Sinai. When he died it was as is written "the fountains of the deep and the windows of heaven were stopped" (Genesis 8: 2), and the companions experienced things that they did not understand.

One day, for example, Rabbi Judah was sitting at the gate of Tiberias, and he saw two camels that had worked the ropes loose on their backs. One of the loads fell down, and the birds came, but before anyone could get near them they flew away. And then some other birds came, and people went over to them and threw stones at them, but they did not fly away. They shouted at them, but they still would not go away.

They heard a voice, saying: The crown of crowns is in darkness,[173] and her husband[174] is outside.[175]

While he was sitting there a man passed by, looked at them, and said: This does not fulfill the verse; "And the birds of prey came down upon the carcasses, and Abram drove them away" (Genesis 15: 11).[176]

Rabbi Judah said: I tried, but they would not fly away.

---

[172] This may refer to the scholars.
[173] The *Shekhinah* is in exile among the husks.   [174] *Tiferet*.
[175] There is no connection or union between *Tiferet* and *Malkhut*.
[176] The birds that flew down upon the spoil were a symbol of the husks' dominance over the sacred.

The man turned his head and said: This man has not yet shaved the head of his master, nor cut the hair of the consort.[177]

He ran after him for three miles, but he did not speak to him. Rabbi Judah was downcast.

One day he was sleeping beneath a tree, and he saw in a dream four wings outstretched, and Rabbi Simeon ascending above them with a Torah scroll. He did not leave one book of celestial mysteries or *aggadot*, but he took them all up with him. He took them up to the firmament. And he then saw him disappear from sight, and he could no longer be seen.

When he awoke, he said: Truly, since Rabbi Simeon died, wisdom has departed from the world. Alas for the generation that has lost the precious stone, from which the upper and the lower regions looked down, and from which they gained their support!

He presented himself to Rabbi Abba, and told him. Rabbi Abba put his hands upon his head, and wept, and said: Rabbi Simeon, the millstones with which they ground fine manna every day, and then gathered it, as it is written, "he that gathered least gathered ten heaps" (Numbers 11: 32)[178]—both the millstones and the manna have now departed, and nothing remains of them in the world, except that mentioned in the verse "take a jar, and put in it an omerful of manna, and lay it before the Lord as a keepsake" (Exodus 16: 33). And even this is not to be revealed, but is "a keepsake"—to be stored away. Who is now able to reveal mysteries, and who can have knowledge of them?

Rabbi Abba whispered to Rabbi Judah. He said to him: In truth, the man whom you saw was Elijah, and he did not wish to reveal mysteries, so that you might realize how worthy Rabbi Simeon was in his time; and so that this generation might mourn him.

He said: Alas, that we should have to weep for him.

Rabbi Judah wept over him all day, for he had met him in the holy assembly[179] of Rabbi Simeon and the other companions.

He said: Alas, that we did not depart on that day with the three[180] that did depart. Then we should not have seen how changed this generation is.

18. IN THE CELESTIAL ACADEMY

(Zohar I, 4a–4b)

Rabbi Hiyya prostrated himself upon the ground, kissed the dust,[181]

---

[177] Hair symbolizes the powers of Judgment that the righteous have to remove from the *sefirot*.   [178] This verse actually refers to the quails, not to the manna.

[179] See above, p. 156.

[180] Three companions died during the assembly. [See above, p. 158.]

[181] Where Rabbi Simeon ben Yohai lay buried.

and wept, and said: Dust, dust, how obdurate you are, how insolent you are, for all the delights of the eye waste away in you. You shatter and destroy all the pillars of the luminaries of the world. How insolent you are, for the holy light, who used to illuminate the world, the great master, the prince whose merits sustained the universe, wastes away in you. Rabbi Simeon, the light of the luminary, the light of the worlds, you have wasted away in the dust, but you survive and guide the world.[182]

He fell silent for a moment. Then he said: Dust, dust, do not be too proud, for the pillars of the world shall not be entrusted to you, and Rabbi Simeon will not waste away in you.[183]

Rabbi Hiyya arose, and went away still weeping, and Rabbi Jose was with him. From that day on he fasted, for forty days, in order that he might see Rabbi Simeon. They said to him: You are not permitted to see him. He wept, and fasted another forty days. They showed him a vision of Rabbi Simeon and his son, Rabbi Eleazar, discussing the point that Rabbi Jose had made,[184] and several thousands were listening to his words. Then he saw a number of large, celestial wings,[185] and Rabbi Simeon and Rabbi Eleazar, his son, mounted them, and they went up to the academy in the firmament, and all the wings waited for them. He noticed that on their return they shone more brightly and emitted more light than the resplendent light of the sun.

Rabbi Simeon opened his mouth and said: Let Rabbi Hiyya enter, and let him see what preparations the Holy One, blessed be He, has made, to renew the countenances of the righteous in the future world. Blessed is he who enters here without shame, and blessed is he who stands in that world[186] like a pillar, powerful in all things.

He saw himself entering, and Rabbi Eleazar, and the other pillars who were seated there rose. But he was ashamed, and withdrew, and went in and sat at the feet of Rabbi Simeon. A voice proclaimed: Cast your eyes downward, do not raise your head, and do not look. He cast his eyes downward, and saw a light shining into the far distance, and the voice spoke again and said: Hidden, concealed, celestial beings,[187] with the open eyes, those which roam throughout the world, consider and see! You slumbering beings of the lower world, with the closed pupils, awake! Turn darkness into light[188] and bitterness to sweetness before

[182] Your soul survives in the Garden of Eden, and your merit helps to guide the affairs of the world.

[183] The bodies of holy righteous men do not rot.

[184] In the preceding section (3b) Rabbi Jose had made a statement, in the name of Rabbi Simeon, on the interpretation of the mystical significance of "In the beginning He created. . . ."

[185] Wings of angels.

[186] In the world below, before the ascent of the soul.

[187] Angels, or souls of the righteous.

[188] Turn judgment into mercy.

you come here. Every day expect the light, which will shine when the king summons the hind,[189] and glorifies himself, and is called "the supreme king of the world." Whoever does not hope for this every day in that world has no place here.

He noticed in the meantime that there were several companions around the standing pillars,[190] and he saw them being transported up to the academy in the firmament. Some ascended and some descended. And above them all he saw a winged creature[191] who came and swore on oath that he had heard, behind the curtain, that every day the king remembers and summons the hind that lies in the dust, and that he then kicks impatiently at the three hundred and ninety firmaments, and they all tremble and shake before him. And he sheds tears because of this,[192] and these tears fall, boiling like fire, into the great sea. From those tears the prince of the sea is created and sustained, and he sanctifies the name of the holy king, and takes it upon himself to swallow all the waters of creation and to gather them within himself, when the nations join together against the holy people; and the waters will dry up, and they will cross on dry land.

Meanwhile he heard a voice saying: Make room, make room, for King Messiah is coming to the academy of Rabbi Simeon ben Yohai, for all the righteous men there are heads of academies, and the academies there are noted.[193] And all the companions from each academy ascend from the academy here[194] to the academy in the firmament, and the Messiah is coming to all these academies, to approve the teachings from the mouths of the sages.

At that moment the Messiah came, adorned by the heads of the academies with celestial crowns. At that moment all the companions rose, and Rabbi Simeon rose, and his light ascended to the highest point of the firmament.

He said to him: Blessed are you, Rabbi, because your teaching consists of three hundred and seventy lights, and each light has six hundred and thirteen explanations,[195] and they rise and bathe themselves in the rivers of pure balsam, and the Holy One, blessed be He, sets His seal upon the teaching from your academy, and on that from the academies of Hezekiah, King of Judah, and Ahijah the Shilonite. I have not come to set a seal upon your academy,[196] but the winged creature is here, and I know that he will enter no academy except yours.

---

[189] The king will summon the *Shekhinah*, in order to bring her out from exile, and the light of redemption will shine.   [190] The heads of the academies.   [191] Metatron.

[192] Because of the exile of the *Shekhinah*.

[193] Are known by their own particular names.

[194] In the lower Garden of Eden.

[195] Corresponding to the 613 commandments.

[196] For you do not need my approval. But I have come in order to hear from you what the winged creature told you.

At that moment Rabbi Simeon told him of the oath that the winged creature had sworn. Immediately the Messiah began to tremble, and he raised his voice, and the firmaments trembled, and the great sea trembled, and leviathan trembled, and the world seemed about to overturn. In the meantime, he saw Rabbi Hiyya sitting at the feet of Rabbi Simeon. He said: Who brought a mortal here, clothed in the garb of that world?

Rabbi Simeon said: This is Rabbi Hiyya, the light of the lamp of the Torah.

He said: Let him be gathered with his sons, and let them be members of your academy.

Rabbi Simeon said: Let him be given time.

They gave him time, and he departed shaking, his eyes streaming with tears.

19. RAV HAMNUNA SAVA

(Zohar I, 5a–7a)

Rabbi Eleazar went to see his father-in-law, Rabbi Jose, the son of Rabbi Simeon ben Lekunya, and Rabbi Abba went with him, and another man was leading the mules behind them.

Rabbi Abba said: Let us open the doors of the Torah, for the hour and the season are ripe for us to follow the usual road.

Rabbi Eleazar began by quoting: "You shall keep My Sabbaths" (Leviticus 19: 30; 26: 2). Let us look more closely. The Holy One, blessed be He, created the world with six days, and each day revealed its work, and transmitted its power on that particular day.[197] When did it reveal its work[198] and transmit its power? On the fourth day,[199] because the first three days were sealed up and not revealed. But when the fourth day came, it produced the work and the power of all of them, which are fire, water, and air. Although they are three celestial elements, they were all suspended, and their work remained unrevealed until earth revealed it. Then the skill of each one of them was known. Now you might say that this must have happened on the third day, concerning which it is written, "Let the earth put forth grass," and "the earth brought forth ..." (Genesis 1: 11f.). But, although this is written of the third day, it

---

[197] The creation of the world in six days was effected through the power of the six celestial days, i.e., the *sefirot* from *Ḥesed* onward. Each celestial day transmits its power into the specific activities of the day that corresponds to it in the process of creation.

[198] When did the potentiality concealed within the *sefirot* emerge into actuality?

[199] After the emanation of *Malkhut*, the last *sefirah*, which in the enumeration of the days is considered as the fourth day, because it is the fourth of the celestial elements, the constructive powers of creation. *Ḥesed*, *Gevurah*, and *Tiferet* correspond to fire, water, and air, and *Malkhut* corresponds to the element earth. *Malkhut* brings into actuality the potentialities of the other *sefirot*.

actually happened on the fourth, and it was included with the third day, so that it should be one whole,[200] without a division. Subsequently, on the fourth day, its work was revealed, in order to produce an artisan for each and every skill, for the fourth day is the fourth foot[201] of the celestial throne. And all the activity of all of them, whether of the earlier days or of the later days, depended on the Sabbath,[202] and of this it is written "And God gathered together [His work] on the seventh day" (Genesis 2: 2).[203] This is the Sabbath and the fourth foot of the throne. But what about the plural form in "You shall keep My Sabbaths"? This refers to both the Sabbath of Sabbath night, and the Sabbath of the day itself, which are indivisible.[204]

The mule-driver, who was leading the mules behind them, said: What is the meaning of "and fear my sanctuary"?[205]

This is the sanctification of the Sabbath.

What is this sanctification of the Sabbath?

This is the holiness that descends upon it from above.

If this is so, then you have turned the Sabbath into something that is not itself holy, but holiness rests upon it from above.

Rabbi Abba said: And so it is: "And you shall call the Sabbath a delight, and the holy of the Lord honorable" (Isaiah 48: 13). The Sabbath is mentioned separately from "the holy of the Lord."

In that case, what is "the holy of the Lord"?

The holiness that descends from above, and rests upon it.

If the holiness that descends from above is called "honorable," it would appear that the Sabbath itself ought not to be "honorable." Yet it is written "And you shall honor it" (ibid).

Rabbi Eleazar said to Rabbi Abba: Let this man be. He has some wisdom that we do not know.

They said to him: You explain it.

He began by quoting: "My Sabbaths" (et shabbetotai). The particle et includes the Sabbath limits,[206] which are two thousand cubits on every side. And the reason why it uses the plural is to include the Sabbath of

---

[200] The third day is *Tiferet* (male), to which *Malkhut* (female) is attached through the mystery of the "double-countenance" (*do-parzufim*). Therefore earth is mentioned on the third day, even though its activity took place on the fourth.

[201] These *sefirot*, the four elements, are also the four feet of the throne in the celestial chariot.

[202] *Malkhut* is also in mystical terms the Sabbath, since it is the last *sefirah*, and it comprises all the *sefirot* that are above it, including those whose activity takes place after the fourth day.

[203] Usually translated "And God finished . . . ," from the Hebrew verb *kalah*. But *kalal* means "include, comprise, gather."

[204] *Malkhut* is also called *laylah* (night), and this refers to Sabbath night, while the Sabbath day is symbolized by *Yesod*, through whose means male and female are joined.

[205] The continuation of "You shall keep My Sabbaths."

[206] The limits of holiness, beyond the world of emanation.

both the upper regions and the lower regions,[207] which are two, included and sealed together. Another Sabbath remains,[208] which was omitted and downcast. She said to Him: Master of the universe, from the moment You made me I was called "Sabbath," and every day has a night.[209] He said to her: My daughter, you are Sabbath, and I call you "Sabbath," but now I shall crown you with a more exalted crown.

He issued a proclamation that said, "You shall fear My sanctuary," and this is the Sabbath of Sabbath night, which is fear,[210] and fear dwells in it.[211] And what is that? It is that which the Holy One, blessed be He, comprises in "I am the Lord."[212]

I have learned from my father, who taught with great precision as follows: et includes the Sabbath limits. "Sabbaths" refers to the circle and square within,[213] which are two. Corresponding to these two, we have two sanctifications, which we must mention. One is the va-yekhulu, and the other is kiddush.[214] The va-yekhulu has thirty-five words, and the kiddush, which we use, has thirty-five words, making in all the seventy names[215] with which the Holy One, blessed be He, and the Assembly of Israel adorn themselves. Since both circle and square are "My Sabbaths," they are both included in shamor[216] ("keep"), as it is written, tishmoru ("you shall keep"), while the celestial Sabbath[217] is not included here in shamor, but in zakhor, for the celestial king is perfected through zakhor.[218] Consequently, he is called "the king from whom

---

[207] The upper Sabbath is Binah, which is the seventh sefirah, counting from Yesod upward. The lower Sabbath is Yesod, which is the seventh sefirah, counting from Binah downward.   [208] Malkhut.

[209] Yesod, which is "day," needs Malkhut, which is "night."

[210] Malkhut, the attribute of Judgment, that produces fear.

[211] Hokhmah (Wisdom), which is also called "fear" (Yirah), dwells in Malkhut, which is the lower Hokhmah.

[212] This phrase occurs in both the relevant verses quoted. In Malkhut the Godhead is revealed in its aspect of "I," and in this phrase it is linked with Tiferet, which is the tetragrammaton, "Lord."

[213] A new interpretation of the plural "My Sabbaths." The two Sabbaths are Yesod and Malkhut. Yesod, the male aspect, is called "circle," and it is joined in mystical union with Malkhut, called "square," the female aspect. Thus they are both comprised within the one word shabbetotai.

[214] [The va-yekhulu (and they were finished), comprising Genesis 2: 1–3, is part of the sanctification said on Sabbath eve, and this is followed by the kiddush.]

[215] According to the midrash, God has seventy names.

[216] The word shamor [used in Deuteronomy 5: 12] indicates the female, and since here both male and female are included together, tishmoru (plural) is used.

[217] Binah, which is also the celestial king. It is not included in the phrase "you shall keep My Sabbaths," but in another verse (Exodus 20: 8): "Remember (zakhor) the Sabbath day, to sanctify it."

[218] The word zakhor signifies the male (zakhar), and the main principle in the arrangement of the lower sefirot, constructed by means of Binah, is based on the male, Tiferet, which is the central pillar of the whole structure. Therefore Binah is also called zakhor.

comes peace," and his peace is *zakhor*.[219] Therefore there is no dissension in the heavenly realms. There are two kinds of peace in the world below: Jacob and Joseph. So it is written twice, "Peace, peace, to the far and the near" (Isaiah 57: 19). "To the far" refers to Jacob, and "to the near" refers to Joseph, as it is said, "From afar the Lord appeared unto me," (Jeremiah 31: 3)[220] and "His sister stood afar off" (Exodus 2: 4).[221] "And to the near," as it is written, "New [gods] that came up recently [lit., nearby]" (Deuteronomy 32: 17).[222] "From afar" is the highest point that stands in its palace.[223] And of this it is written *tishmoru*, for they are both comprised in *shamor*.[224] "And you shall fear My sanctuary" is the middle point,[225] which one should fear more than anything else, for the punishment that it inflicts is death, as it is written, "those that profane it [i.e., the Sabbath] shall surely be put to death" (Exodus 31: 14). Who are "those who profane it (*me-haleleha*)"? Whoever enters the hollow (*halal*) of the circle and the square, the place where the point resides, and damages it,[226] shall surely be put to death. So it is written, "And you shall fear." And this point is called "I," and upon it rests the supreme unknown,[227] which remains unrevealed, and this is *Yod*, *He*, *Vav*, *He*, and it is all One.

Rabbi Eleazar and Rabbi Abba dismounted and kissed him. They said: You have so much wisdom in your power, and yet you go on leading the mules behind us? Who are you?

He replied: Do not ask who I am, but let us go together and study Torah. And let each one of us say words of wisdom to illuminate the way.

They said to him: Who gave you permission to come here, and be a mule-driver?

He said: The letter *yod* waged war against the two letters *kaf* and *samekh*, to persuade them to make an alliance.[228] *Kaf* did not want to

[219] *Tiferet* and *Yesod*, two male *sefirot*, mediate and make peace between Mercy and Judgment (*Ḥesed* and *Gevurah*, and *Neẓaḥ* and *Hod*), and they are also called Jacob and Joseph.

[220] It is said of "the Lord," i.e., *Tiferet*, that He appeared "from afar."

[221] The subject is Miriam, who mystically speaking is *Malkhut*, the *sefirah* opposite *Tiferet*.

[222] Hence "near" means something new, i.e., a later stage in the process of emanation.

[223] *Hokhmah* is the highest point, the beginning of emanation, and it stands in the palace of *Binah*. From the union of the two is born the son, *Tiferet*, and so it is said of him that he is seen "from afar."

[224] This harks back to the beginning of the discourse: *Yesod* and *Malkhut* are both included in the word *tishmoru*.

[225] The womb, which is the central point of the female principle, which is also called "Zion" and the "Holy of Holies." (See Zohar III, 296a–296b).

[226] By sinning, he allows the husks to take hold of the hollow of the womb.

[227] *Tiferet*, which is hidden, in comparison with *Malkhut*.

[228] The three letters mentioned make the word *kis* (purse, money). *Yod* wanted him to be wealthy, but it was not successful. So he had to become a mule-driver.

leave its place and join, because it could not survive for one moment anywhere else. *Samekh* did not want to leave its place, for it had to support those that fall, because without *samekh* they would not be able to stand.[229] *Yod* came to me on its own, kissed me and embraced me. She wept with me, and said: What shall I do for you, my son? Look, I shall now ascend and take my fill of many good things, secret, precious letters from on high,[230] and then I shall come to you, and be your support, and I shall give you two celestial letters to keep, in addition to those that have gone, namely *yesh*:[231] the celestial *yod*, and the celestial *shin*;[232] and they will be treasuries, full of good things for you. Therefore, my son, go and be a mule-driver.

That is why I act as I do.

Rabbi Eleazar and Rabbi Abba wept for joy, and said: Come and ride, and we shall lead the mules after you.

Did I not tell you, he said, that it is the king's command, until that mule-driver comes.[233]

They said: You have not told us your name nor the place where you live.

He replied: The place where I live is fine and exalted for me. It is a tower,[234] flying in the air, great and beautiful. And these are they who dwell in the tower: the Holy One, blessed be He, and a poor man. This is where I live. But I am exiled[235] from there, and I am a mule-driver.

Rabbi Abba and Rabbi Eleazar looked at him, and his words pleased them. They were as sweet as manna and honey.

They said: If you tell us the name of your father, we shall kiss the dust of your feet.

Why? he asked. It is not my wont to use the Torah in order to exalt myself. But my father used to live in the great sea, and he was a fish[236]

[229] [*Kaf* also means "palm of the hand," or "sole of the foot." And *samekh* means "support." There is a play on these meanings here.]

[230] He would possess wisdom instead of wealth.

[231] Composed of the two letters *yod* and *shin*. *Yesh* means "substance," and is a name given to *Ḥokhmah*, which emanates from *Keter*, called *ayin* (nothing). So we have the relationship of "something from nothing." *Yesh* also represents the first letter (*yod*) of the tetragrammaton. *Shin* + *yod* signifies also the number 310, and there may be a reference here to the 310 worlds prepared for the righteous in the life to come.

[232] Possibly *Binah*.

[233] The Messiah, who will come "lowly and riding on an ass" (Zechariah 9: 9).

[234] *Yesod*. The Holy One, blessed be He, and the *Shekhinah*, which is called "poor" and "wretched" because it has no light of its own, are connected with *Yesod*. We might also say that the tower is the palace of the Messiah, and the "poor man" who lives there is the Messiah.

[235] He here gives a hint to the rabbis that he comes from the world of souls, but they do not understand the allusion.

[236] By using the word *nuna* (fish), he shows them that he is Rav Hamnuna Sava, who used to swim in the sea of the Torah. All the other rabbis were "small fry" compared to him, and they learned Torah from him. He speaks mystically of his previous existence in

that used to circumnavigate the great sea from end to end. He was so great, ancient, and honorable that he used to swallow all the other fish in the sea, and spew them out again, live and healthy, and full of all the goodness in the world. He was so strong that he could cross the sea in a single second, and he produced me like an arrow from a mighty warrior's hand. He hid me in the place that I described to you, and then he returned to his place and concealed himself in the sea.

Rabbi Eleazar considered his words, and said: You are really the son of the sacred lamp, you are really the son of Rav Hamnuna Sava, you are really the son of the light of the Torah, and yet you drive mules behind us?

They both wept together, and kissed him, and continued their journey.

They said: If it seems good to our lord, let him tell us his name.

He began[237] by quoting: "And Benaiah, the son of Jehoiada" (2 Samuel 23: 20). This verse has been interpreted, and it has been interpreted well, but the verse is meant to show us heavenly secrets of the Torah. "And Benaiah, the son of Jehoiada"—this phrase alludes to the mysteries of wisdom, a concealed subject, but the name is the decisive factor.[238] "Son of a living man"—this is the righteous man, the life of the worlds.[239] "Master of deeds"—the master of events and all the celestial powers; they all come from him. He is the Lord of Hosts, a sign among all His hosts; He is perceived[240] and supreme above all; "master of deeds." "From Kabzeel"—this great and honorable tree, supreme above all, from where does it come? From which level does it come? Scripture tells us "from Kabzeel"[241]—a level, lofty and concealed, that "the eye has not seen . . .,"[242] a level that gathers all from the supreme light, and from which all proceeds, and this is the holy palace, concealed, in which all levels are assembled and concealed.[243] And

the world, as if he were his own father, but the rabbis understand it literally and think that he is the son of Rav Hamnuna.

[237] By way of reply he starts to reveal mysteries from which they will be able to deduce his personality.

[238] Benaiah symbolizes *Yesod*, the name being construed as the son (*ben*) of *yod, he, vav*, i.e., son of the *sefirot* symbolized by these three letters, namely, *Ḥokhmah, Binah*, and *Tiferet*.

[239] [The phrase is usually rendered "son of a valiant man."] "The righteous man . . ." is the accepted symbol of *Yesod*, mystically represented by Joseph, the righteous, preserver of sexual purity, who gives life to the worlds, and sustains them.

[240] His effect and influence are discernible throughout all the celestial hosts.

[241] *Binah*, which gathers (*mekabez*) within itself influence from the supreme light, which is *Ḥokhmah*.

[242] Isaiah 64: 3. *Binah* is the mystical representation of the world to come, which is the subject of this verse.

[243] The lower *sefirot* are begotten by it, and they are assembled within it, like an embryo in its mother's womb.

through the body of this tree[244] all the worlds are sustained, and all the sacred hosts feed on it and preserve themselves. "He smote the two altar-hearths (*Ariel*) of Moab." Two sanctuaries[245] were sustained by him, and nourished by him: the first Temple and the second Temple. When he departed, the influence that descended from above ceased, and it was as if he smote them and destroyed and obliterated them, and the sacred throne fell.[246] This is what Scripture means by "And I was in the midst of the exile" (Ezekiel 1: 1)—the level called "I" was in the midst of the exile. Why? "By the river *Kevar*"[247]—by the river that used to flow, but whose waters and eddies have ceased and it does not flow as it used to do. So we have in the Scriptures "The river is drained and dry" (Job 14: 11). "Drained" refers to the first Temple and "dry" to the second Temple. And so "He smote the two altar-hearths of Moab." "Moab"—because they originated from the Father (*me-ha-ab*)[248] in heaven, and they were destroyed and obliterated because of Him,[249] and all the luminaries that illuminated Israel became dark. Furthermore, "he went down and slew the lion." Beforehand, when the river was flowing down with water, Israel lived in perfection, for they used to bring sacrifices and offerings in order to make atonement for their souls. And the image of a lion used to descend from above, and they saw it on the altar, lying down by its food, eating sacrifices like a mighty warrior, and all the dogs[250] used to hide from it and refused to go out. Sins compelled him to descend[251] to the lower levels, and he killed the lion, for he was no longer willing to give it its food; and so it was as if he killed it. "He slew the lion"—actually, "in the middle of a pit"—in the sight of the other side, the evil side. When the other side saw this it took encouragement, and dispatched a dog to eat the sacrifices. And what was the lion's name? Uriel, whose face is the face of a lion. And what was the dog's name? Baladan, who does not come into the human category,[252] but is a dog, with the face of a dog. "In the day of snow,"[253]—on the day when sins

---

[244] *Yesod.*   [245] The Temple was called "Ariel."

[246] When the Temple was destroyed the *Shekhinah* [the level called "I"] also fell from the heights and went down into exile.

[247] [*Kevar* means "once, in the past."] The reason for the exile of the *Shekhinah* was that the influence of the river, i.e., *Yesod*, that used to flow, had stopped.

[248] Before they were destroyed they received divine influence.

[249] Because He withheld influence from them.

[250] The forces of uncleanness.

[251] *Yesod* caused the influence to descend to the husks, which are "the lower levels," and prevented it from reaching the lion, an element of holiness, and in this way it "killed" the lion.

[252] The image of Man (*Adam*) is a most exalted one, and even in the scheme of the *sefirot* it appears as *Adam Elyon* (Celestial Man), *Adam Kadmon* (Primordial Man). The powers of uncleanness have no right to this image. [There is a pun here on Baladan, and *bal adam* (not man).]

[253] Water is *Hesed* (Mercy), but snow, congealed water, is a symbol of dire judgment.

take their effect, and judgment is passed in the heavenly court. Of this it is written, "She is not afraid of the snow for her household" (Proverbs 31: 21)[254]—this refers to judgment in heaven. Why? Because "all her household are clothed with scarlet," and she can withstand the fierce fire.

This is the mystical interpretation of the verse. How does it continue? "And he slew an Egyptian man, a man good to see" (2 Samuel 23: 21).[255] Here the verse informs us in a mystical fashion that whenever Israel sin he departs from them, and withholds from them every good thing and all the lights that shine upon them. "He slew an Egyptian man"—this is the light of the light[256] that shines upon Israel. Who is that? Moses, as it is written, "And they said, an Egyptian man delivered us . . ."[257] There he was born, there he grew, and there he ascended to the celestial light. "A man good to see,"[258] as it is written "visibly (mar'eh) and not by riddles" (Numbers 12: 8). "Man," as it is said, "man of God,"[259] so to speak, the consort of "the sight (mar'eh) of the glory of the Lord" (Exodus 24: 17). He was found worthy enough to sustain this level, according to his deepest desire, while he was on earth—something of which no other man was worthy.[260] "And the Egyptian had a spear in his hand." This was God's staff that was put in his hand, as it is said, "with God's staff in my hand" (Exodus 17: 9). And this was the staff that was created at twilight on the eve of the Sabbath.[261] On it was engraved the holy name with a holy incision, and with it he sinned at the rock, as it is said, "and he smote the rock twice with his staff" (Numbers 20: 11). The Holy One, blessed be He, said to him: Moses, I did not give you my staff for this. By your life, you shall not hold it in future. He immediately "went down to him with a rod"—with a dire judgment, and "plucked the spear out of the Egyptian's hand," for from that time forth it was withheld from him, and he did not hold it again ever. "And he slew him with his own spear." Because of the sin that he committed by smiting [the rock] with his staff, he died, and did not enter the holy land, and this light was withheld from Israel.

[254] The subject of this verse is "the woman of worth," who is the *Shekhinah*. According to her nature she is very near to *Gevurah* (Power, Might), which has the aspect of both snow and fire, but she does not fear the dire judgment that is part of *Gevurah*, because she receives influence from the six *sefirot* that precede her, called "the primordial years," which include *Ḥesed* and *Raḥamim*. (See Zohar I, 238b.)

[255] [Usually translated "a goodly man." Heb., *ish mar'eh*.]

[256] The light of *Tiferet* shone upon Moses, and thereby illumined Israel.

[257] Exodus 2: 19, referring to Moses.

[258] Moses, who is, mystically speaking, *Tiferet*, reached in his lifetime the level of consort of the *Shekhinah*, called *mar'eh* and *Elohim*.

[259] Deuteronomy 33: 1 (*ish Elohim*), referring to Moses.

[260] Not even Jacob, who is also *Tiferet*, for he reached this eminence only after his death.

[261] See Mishnah Avot 5: 8.

"He was honored from the thirty" (2 Samuel 23: 23).[262] These are the thirty celestial years,[263] which he drew upon and transmitted downward. As he drew upon them, he got nearer to them. "But he did not reach the three."[264] They came to him, and gave to him with a willing heart, but he did not come to them. But, although he was not numbered with them,[265] "David set him over his guard,"[266] and he was always inscribed on his heart. They were never separated. David set his heart upon him,[267] and not he upon David, since in eulogies, songs, and in love, which the moon offers to the sun, she draws him near to her, for he dwells with her. And this is the meaning of "And David set him over his guard."

Rabbi Eleazar and Rabbi Abba fell down before him. In the meanwhile they lost sight of him. They rose and looked on every side, but they did not see him. They sat down and wept, and they could not speak to one another.

After a time Rabbi Abba said: We have surely learned[268] that whenever the righteous are embarked on a journey and discuss the Torah, the righteous of that world come to them. This was surely Rav Hamnuna Sava, who came to us from that world in order to reveal these things to us, and before we could recognize him he went away and was hidden from us.

They arose and tried to goad the mules, but they would not move. They tried once more to goad the mules, but they still would not move. They became afraid and left the mules. And that spot is still called Mules' Place.

20. THE OLD MAN OF *MISHPATIM*

(Zohar II, 94b–99b)

Rabbi Hiyya and Rabbi Jose met one evening in Migdal Zur. They stayed there and were very happy in each other's company.

Rabbi Jose said: How happy I am that I have seen the face of the *Shekhinah*; for up till now, through the whole journey, I was perpetually annoyed by an old man, a mule-driver, who kept on asking me, as we

---

[262] [Usually translated "he was more honored than the thirty."]

[263] The three *sefirot*, *Hesed, Gevurah, Tiferet*, in each of which the array of the ten *sefirot* are reflected, pour out influence upon *Yesod*, who transmits it downward.

[264] The three upper *sefirot*, *Keter, Hokhmah, Binah*, brought down influence to him, but he was not able to draw near to them.

[265] *Yesod* is not counted as one of the *sefirot*. They are the source of influence, while *Yesod* is simply the channel by which it is transmitted.

[266] David is *Malkhut*, which receives the influence, and *Malkhut* is attached to *Yesod*.

[267] *Malkhut*, which is the moon, yearns for *Tiferet*, the sun. And in her love songs she attracts *Yesod* toward her.

[268] When he had gone it was revealed to them that he had come from the world of souls, and that the word *nuna* (fish) had referred to himself.

went along, "Who is the serpent[269] that flies in the air and goes on his way alone, while the ant that is carried between his teeth is at rest—he began with union and ended with separation? And who is the eagle that nests in the nonexistent tree, whose young are stolen, but not by living creatures; who were created in a place where they were not created; who descend when they ascend, and who ascend when they descend; two making one, and one making three? Who is the beautiful girl[270] that has no eyes,[271] whose body is both hidden and revealed; who goes out in the morning and is concealed during the day; who adorns herself with nonexistent adornments?" All this he would ask me on the journey, and I was annoyed. But now I have some peace; for if we had been together earlier we would have studied Torah instead of dealing with these other nonsensical matters.

Rabbi Hiyya said: This old mule-driver, do you know anything about him?

He replied: All I know is that there was no substance in what he said. If he had had any knowledge he would have begun with a quotation from the Torah, and the journey would not have been spent so fruitlessly.

Rabbi Hiyya asked: Is that mule-driver here somewhere? For sometimes among these empty heads you can find a bell of gold.

He is here, feeding his mule.

They called him, and he came to them.

He said to them: Now, two are three, and three are one.[272]

Rabbi Jose said: Did I not tell you that all that he says is worthless and stupid?

He sat down before them, and said to them: Rabbis, I have been a mule-driver for only a short time. I used not to be a mule-driver, but I have a little son, and I put him to school, for I wanted him to study Torah. And now whenever I find one of the rabbis about to embark on a journey I lead the mules after him. Today also I thought I would gain some new insight into the Torah, but I did not hear a thing.

Rabbi Jose said: Of all the things I heard you say I was perplexed by only one; either you said it out of stupidity or it is simply a waste of time.

Which was that? asked the old man.

"The beautiful girl . . ."

The old man began by quoting: "The Lord is for me; I will not fear;

[269] Commentators interpret the riddles that follow in terms of the mystical aspects of levirate marriage, which is the main subject of the whole section. But most of the meaning is obscure.

[270] This riddle is explained later (pp. 196–97) with reference to the Torah.

[271] She is hidden and sealed up.

[272] As he meets the scholars, so two become three; and the three of them are united as one in the study of the Torah.

what can man do to me? The Lord is for me as my helper . . . it is good to trust in the Lord" (Psalm 118: 6–8). How good, pleasant, precious, and exalted are words of Torah! And how can I say them in the presence of rabbis, from whose mouths I have not yet heard a single word? But it is my duty to speak, for there is no shame whatsoever in saying words of Torah in the presence of anyone.

The old man wrapped himself in his garment, and began: "And if a priest's daughter be married to a foreign man,[273] she shall not eat of that which is set apart from holy things" (Leviticus 22: 12). This verse is supported by the next verse: "If a priest's daughter be a widow, or divorced, and have no child, and returns to her father's house, as in her youth, she may eat of her father's bread, but no foreign man shall eat of it." These verses mean precisely what they say, but the words of Torah are also sealed. What wonderful words of wisdom are sealed in every word of the Torah, and they are known to the sages who understand the ways of Torah; for the Torah does not consist of dreams, transmitted through an interpreter by word of mouth. Nevertheless, one must interpret them in their own particular way. If dreams need someone to interpret them in their way, how much more do the words of Torah, the delight of the Holy King, need to be followed according to the way of truth, as it is written, "For the ways of the Lord are right . . ." (Hosea 14: 10).

Now is the time to expound. "Priest's daughter" is the celestial soul, the daughter of our father, Abraham,[274] the first proselyte. He drew this soul out of a celestial place.[275] What is the difference between "a priestly man's daughter"[276] and "a priest's daughter," where "man" is not mentioned? There is a priest who is called "a priestly man," and not a real "priest." Similarly, we have "priest", "priestly ruler," "High priest," and a priest who is not "High." "Priest," pure and simple, is greater and nobler than "priestly man." And so we have three words for "soul"[277]—neshamah, ruah, and nefesh. "A priest's daughter married to a foreign man"—this is the holy soul (neshamah), drawn from a celestial place and put into a secret place in the Tree of Life,[278] and when the breath of the celestial priest blows, and puts souls into this tree, they fly

---

[273] [Usually translated "common man." But the Hebrew word zar also means "strange, foreign," and this is necessary for the interpretation that follows.]

[274] Ḥesed.   [275] From Binah.

[276] Leviticus 21: 9, where, unlike 22: 12, the word "man" (ish) is mentioned. It would appear that "a priestly man" refers to Michael, who represents Ḥesed in the world of the angels. His daughter is the soul (nefesh), the lowest spiritual part of man, whose origin is in the world of the angels, but she is inclined to sin ("she profanes herself by playing the harlot"—the continuation of 21: 9).

[277] There are three parts to the human soul, each one of which has a specific source in the upper spheres, and a specific role in the life of man.   [278] Yesod.

from there and enter a treasury.[279] Alas for the world, when men do not know how to protect themselves, but strike up a connection with[280] the evil inclination, who is the "foreign man," and then the "priest's daughter" flies downward and discovers the building of the "foreign man." Since it is the wish of her master, she goes in there and is subjugated, and cannot rule,[281] and so does not achieve perfection in this world. And when she leaves him "she shall not eat of that which is set apart from the holy things," as do the other souls, which reach perfection in this world.

And there is something else in this verse, "a priest's daughter married to a foreign man." Wretched is the holy soul that belongs to "a foreign man," and who is attracted to a proselyte, and flies to him from the Garden of Eden, by a concealed path,[282] to a building that is constructed from an unclean foreskin. Such a soul belongs to "a foreign man."

Furthermore—and this is the most exalted mystery of all—on the pillar set aside for the scales,[283] amid the air that blows, there are scales on one side and other scales on the second side: scales of righteousness[284] on one side and scales of deceit[285] on the other. And these scales never rest, but souls ascend and descend, enter and return. And there are souls that are tormented,[286] when man rules over his fellow, as it is written, "when a man rules over another to his hurt," (Ecclesiastes 8: 9)—certainly "to his hurt," for the soul that belongs to "the other side"—the "foreign man"—is tormented by him. This is the meaning of "to his hurt," to the hurt of the "foreign man," while she "will not eat of that which is set apart from the holy things," until the Holy One, blessed be He, does what He does.[287] Scripture tells us that when "a priest's daughter is married to a foreign man" such will be the outcome. Here we

[279] The treasury of souls in the Garden of Eden. [See below, p. 701.]

[280] At the moment of intercourse they produce semen out of desire that derives from the evil inclination, and not in a spirit of holiness and purity. The body produced by this kind of union is the "building" of the evil inclination.

[281] The task of the soul is to rule over the body and the evil inclination, but the evil inclination has the upper hand in his own "building."

[282] The souls of proselytes are formed from the union of the souls of the righteous in the Garden of Eden. They fly from there, shelter beneath the wings of the *Shekhinah*, and then descend into the bodies of the proselytes.

[283] On these scales the souls are weighed, when they descend to this world and when they ascend to the future world.   [284] On the side of holiness.

[285] On the side of *sitra ahra*—the other, or evil, side.

[286] These are the souls that come to the scales when the "other side," the "man of Belial," is in the ascendant through the power of sin, and rules over the souls of men. They are then weighed in the scales of deceit, and tormented by the husks. [See below, pp. 755–57.]

[287] The tormented soul will not achieve perfect holiness until the Holy One, blessed be He, releases her from the power of the husks.

have the mystery of how the souls are tormented. This world depends entirely on the Tree of Knowledge of Good and Evil,[288] and when the inhabitants of the world conduct themselves well the scales tip toward the good side, and when they conduct themselves ill they tip toward that [other] side. And he torments and seizes all the souls that happen to be in the scales at that time, but "to his own hurt," for those souls[289] are stronger than anything on the evil side, and they destroy him. A symbol of this is the holy Ark,[290] which was seized by the Philistines, and they had control of it—but to their own hurt. In the same way, these souls are tormented by "the other side"—to his own hurt. And what becomes of these souls? We have seen in the books of the ancients that from them will emerge the pious of the nations of the world, and the scholars who are illegitimate, but who take precedence over an ignorant but renowned High Priest,[291] even though he enters the Holy of Holies.

The old man wept for a moment. The companions were astonished and said nothing.

The old man resumed by quoting: "If she is evil in the eyes of her master, who has espoused her to himself, then he shall let her be redeemed, to a foreign people . . ." (Exodus 21: 8). This section was spoken with reference to: "And if a man sell his daughter for a maidservant, she shall not go out as the menservants do. If she is evil . . ." (Exodus 21: 7). Master of the universe, who does not fear You, for You are the ruler of all the kings in the world, as it is said, "Who would not fear You, King of the nations, for it befits You . . ." (Jeremiah 10: 7)? There are many people who misunderstand this verse, although they all say it, and this verse is not correct in their mouths. For is the Holy One, blessed be He, really "King of the nations"? Surely, He is King of Israel! And thus is He called, for it is written, "When the Most High gave to the nations their inheritance . . ." (Deuteronomy 32: 8),[292] and then it is written, "For the portion of the Lord is His people." And so He is called "King of Israel". And if you say that He is also called "King of the nations," this seems to praise them for the fact that the Holy One, blessed be He, rules over them; and not as the sages say, that they were handed over to His servants and His representatives. Furthermore, there is the end of the verse, where it is written, "For among all the wise men of the nations, and in all their kingdom, there is none like You" (Jeremiah 10: 7). All this seems like praise of the other peoples, and it is a wonder

[288] *Malkhut*, which is goodness. But evil is destined to take hold of it and drag it down to the deep. Its condition depends on human conduct, which determines whether the scales shall dip toward good or evil.
[289] The sanctity contained in the souls destroys from within the husks that torment them.   [290] See 1 Samuel 5.   [291] [See B. T. *Horayot* 13a.]
[292] This verse and the next continue ". . . when He separated the children of men, He set the borders of the peoples according to the number of the children of Israel. For the portion of the Lord is His people, Jacob the lot of His inheritance."

that, because of this verse, they do not rise to the highest point of the firmament. But the Holy One, blessed be He, has blinded their eyes, and they know nothing of Him, for we say of them that they are nothing, nought and vanity, as it is written, "All the nations are as nothing before Him. They are accounted by Him as things of nought and vanity" (Isaiah 40: 17). The verse [in Jeremiah], however, makes of them a great, exalted, and honorable principle.

Rabbi Hiyya said to him: But it is also written, "God reigns over the nations" (Psalm 47: 9).

He said: I see that you follow them closely, and are using this verse in order to support them. I ought really to reply first to the questions I have raised, but since I find you in the way I shall remove you, and then I shall go on to remove all [the other obstacles]. You will notice that all the names and epithets of the Holy One, blessed be He, are expanded as is their wont, and are clothed one with the other; and they are all divided out into certain ways and paths—apart, that is, from the unique name, the most choice of all names, which He granted to the unique people, the most choice of all peoples, and that name is: *Yod, He, Vav, He,*[293] as it is written "For the portion of the Lord is His people," and it is written, "And you who did cleave to the Lord" (Deuteronomy 4: 4), to this particular name rather than to any of the other names. Of His remaining names there is one that is expanded and divided out into a number of ways and paths, and that is *Elohim*, and He assigned and shared this name among the lower regions in this world, and this name was apportioned to servants and representatives[294] who guide the other peoples, as it is said, "And God (*Elohim*) came to Balaam at night" (Numbers 22: 20), "But God (*Elohim*) came to Abimelech in a dream of the night" (Genesis 20: 3). And so with all the representatives that the Holy One, blessed be He, assigned to the other peoples—they are all included under this heading, and even idols are given this name.[295] And it is this name that rules over the nations, but this is not the name that rules over Israel. There is a unique name for the unique people, the people of Israel, the holy people. You might well retort that we should explain the verse in this way. "Who would not fear You, King of the nations?"—this is *Elohim*, the name that rules over the nations, and fear resides in him, for Judgment resides in him! But this is not so, and the verse does not refer to this; for if it were so, we should have to include idols in this category as well.[296] Now that your main support has been removed the verse is quite clear, with but a little reflection: "Who would not fear You, King of the nations?" And if you argue that "King of the

---

[293] [The tetragrammaton, usually translated "Lord."]
[294] Angels are also given the name *Elohim*.
[295] They are called "other gods" (*elohim aherim*).
[296] And we should consequently have to fear idols.

nations" refers to the Holy One, blessed be He, then you are wrong, for it means "which king of the nations would not fear You, would not be terrified of You, would not tremble before You? Which king of the nations would not fear You?" In the same way we have, "Praise the Lord, praise servants of the Lord, praise the name of the Lord" (Psalm 113: 1). Whoever hears this does not know what it means,[297] since it says "Praise the Lord" and then repeats "praise servants of the Lord"; whereas it should have been written, "Servants of the Lord, praise the name of the Lord." So here it should have been written, "Which king of the nations would not fear You?"[298] But the whole can be understood as emended.[299] "For among all the wise men of the nations, and in all their kingdom, there is none like You." What was it that became disseminated among them in their wisdom? That "there is none like You." They all admitted it. When they saw in their wisdom Your work and Your power, this matter spread among them and they said, "There is none like You." Among all the wise men of the nations, and throughout their kingdom, they said "There is none like You," and it became widespread among them.

The companions rejoiced and wept and said nothing. And he also wept, as he had at the beginning.

He began again by quoting: "She said to Abraham, Dismiss this maidservant and her son" (Genesis 21: 10).[300] The companions have argued from this that Sarah sought to rid her house of idolatry,[301] and that is why it is written, "in all that Sarah says to you, listen to her voice" (Genesis 21: 12). The verse we are dealing with states, "And if a man sells his daughter"—this is the soul during its migrations caused by the evil deeds in the world[302]—"for a maidservant"—when the time comes for "the other side," through the evil rotation of the turning balances,[303] by which she is tormented, to send her forth from there, she shall certainly "not go out as the menservants do." Who are these souls that are oppressed? There is a mystery here. These are the souls of the little babies as they suck their mothers' breasts. The Holy One, blessed be He, foresees that if they survive in the world they will give forth a foul odor, and be as bitter as vinegar. So He takes them while they are still small,

[297] In the verse "Who would not fear You . . ." it seems at first sight that "King of the nations" is the object of the verb. Here too, in the verse "Praise servants of the Lord," "servants of the Lord" seem to be the object of praise.
[298] [In the Hebrew text this can be effected simply by changing the order of the words.]
[299] I.e., this linguistic usage is quite in order, and has a parallel in Scripture.
[300] See also *Bereshit Rabbah* 53: 15.
[301] Hence "maidservant" is a name for idolatry, which is "the other side." So here we have support for the explanation given to the verse below.
[302] Sins in the world serve to strengthen "the other side," and the soul migrates to the domain of the husks. [303] The balances of deceit.

while they still smell sweetly. What does He do? He permits them to be tormented at the hands of that "maidservant," and this is Lilith; for when they are handed into her power she rejoices over that particular child and torments it,[304] and removes it from the world while it is sucking at its mother's breasts.

And if you say that these souls[305] might have performed goodness in the world,[306] that is not the case here, for it is written, "If she is evil in the eyes of her master"—so that after a time the man would degenerate because of [that soul] if he remained with her. This is the one that is tormented. The other is not tormented. Of these it is written, "And I saw all the tormented ones . . ." (Ecclesiastes 4: 1). And this is "if she is evil in the eyes of her master." "Who has espoused her to himself." *Lo* (to himself) is written here with an *alef*.[307] You might ask whether the Holy One, blessed be He, had destined "the other side"[308] for her from the moment she was created. The answer is, No. It was the movement of the balances that led ["the other side"] "to espouse her to himself," and this was not the case beforehand. "Then he shall let her be redeemed. . . ." What does this mean? The Holy One, blessed be He, redeems her,[309] as the odor rises, before it becomes foul, and takes her up to the topmost heaven, to His own academy. You might say that when she has been tormented by "the other side," He gives her, as they said,[310] to the pious among the other nations, and to the scholars who are illegitimate. But Scripture specifically states, "to sell her to a foreign people he shall have no power" (Exodus 21: 8), obviously, "since he has dealt treacherously with her," for it has tormented her[311] with the torments of the movement of the balances, and so clearly [He gives her] to Israel, but not to another. And when she leaves the balances, "she shall not go out as the menservants do," but crowned with a diadem placed proudly on her head. You might think that "the other side"[312] would place her

---

[304] The child's body is tormented, and its soul is freed and ascends to the Garden of Eden.

[305] The souls of the children that are tormented by Lilith.

[306] I.e., if they had remained alive they would have done good deeds.

[307] [And would normally mean "no, not." (This is the *ketiv*.) However, it is always taken to mean "to him, to himself," which is Hebrew *lo*, (the *kere*), with *vav* as the final letter.]

[308] I.e., that the soul was destined to be tormented by "the other side" from the very beginning of its existence. This is not so. But, because of the movement of the balances, when "the other side" dominates the world as a result of sin, it takes control of the soul that happens to be in the balance at the time.

[309] He saves the soul through the death of the child.

[310] In "the books of the ancients." See above, p. 181.

[311] Although "the other side" torments the souls, it has no power to place them in a foreign unclean body.

[312] I.e., that the soul would be perpetually in the power of "the other side," and it would place her in the body of the child.

within the child. But it is not so; for He takes her and rejoices with her, and she flies from His hand and enters that place.[313] And it visits the child, and rejoices in him, and plays with him, and yearns for the flesh. Afterward, the Holy One, blessed be He, takes his soul, and it takes the body, and after this[314] the whole comes into the power of the Holy One, blessed be He.

Let us learn more. "She shall not go out as the menservants do." What does this mean?[315] When she leaves the scales, and "the other side" rejoices, the Holy One, blessed be He, gives her a sign, and seals her with a certain ring, and He spreads His precious garment over her. What is that? The holy name, *Eloha*. This is the meaning of *be-vigdo vah*[316]—the King's precious garment is spread over her, and then she is protected, so that she should not be sold to a foreign people but only to Israel. This is the meaning of "As in the days when God (*Eloha*) protected me" (Job 29: 2). Concerning this mystery it is written here, "to sell her to a foreign people he shall have no power, with this garment on her"—while the King's precious garment is on her. Since, with His garment on her, it is written "to sell her to a foreign people he shall have no power," what power does "the other side" have over her?[317] Let us see. All the world's inhabitants are in the power of the Holy King, and all of them have a certain time in this world,[318] before He wishes to bring them up from the world. But she has no time [in this world],[319] and so it plays and is happy with them.[320]

Furthermore, man can take counsel from these verses. How many fine and lofty ideas there are in the words of Torah, and all of them are true when seen in the way of truth, and perceived by the sages who know and follow the way of truth. When the Holy One, blessed be He, sought to create the world, it was His wish that He should fashion all the souls[321] subsequently to be given to mankind. And all of them were formed in His presence in the exact image that they were later to have in the world of men. He sees each one of them and some are destined to pollute their

[313] The body of the child.
[314] At the resurrection of the dead, the body also escapes from the power of "the other side."
[315] What is the "diadem" mentioned above?
[316] Translated above as "since he has dealt treacherously with her." The phrase can also punningly mean "with His garment on her," and so this new interpretation implies that "the other side" can have no power over the soul, because the garment of the Holy One, blessed be He, is spread over her.
[317] If she is protected, what power does "the other side" have over her, once the torments are concluded?
[318] An allotted span of life.
[319] "The other side" has cut short her life in babyhood.
[320] "The other side" plays with souls of this type.
[321] All souls have their own individual existence from the very creation of the world. [See below, pp. 698–703.]

way in the world. When their time comes, the Holy One, blessed be He, summons each particular soul, and says, "Go to a certain place, and enter that man's body." She replies, "Master of the universe, I am content with the world I live in now. Let me not go to another world, where they will subjugate me[322] and I shall be defiled[323] among them." "From the day you were created," says the Holy One, blessed be He, "you were created for this, to live in that world." When the soul realizes this, she descends unwillingly, and enters that place. When the Torah, which gives the whole world counsel, saw this, she gave advice to the inhabitants of the world and said, "See how compassionately the Holy One, blessed be He, treats you. A precious jewel that belonged to Him, He has sold to you for nothing, that you might have dominion over it in this world."

"And if a man . . ."—this is the Holy One, blessed be He, "sell his daughter"—this is the holy soul, "for a maidservant,"—to be a maidservant under your domination in this world, then you are implored, when the time comes for her to leave this world, to see to it that "she shall not go out as the menservants do,"—she shall not leave defiled by iniquity, but she shall leave in freedom, clean and pure, so that her Master can rejoice in her and be exalted through her, and give her a fine reward among the sparkling lights of the Garden of Eden, as it is said "And He shall satisfy your soul with sparkling lights" (Isaiah 58: 11),[324] obviously, only if she leaves clean and pure, as she should. However, "if she is evil in the eyes of her master"—if she leaves besmirched with the mire of iniquity and does not appear before Him as she should, then woe to that body, for it will be bereft of that soul for ever.[325] For when souls ascend in purity and leave this world in cleanliness, each soul is entered in the book of the King's treasury, each of them in its own name, and [the herald] proclaims, "This is the soul of so-and-so. Let her be reserved for the body that she has left." And then it is written he "has espoused her to himself," with a *vav*.[326] But if she leaves "evil in the eyes of her master," having become defiled with sin, and with the mire of iniquity, then he "has not espoused her," with an *alef*, and the body is bereft of her, and she is not reserved for it unless her partner had made his peace [with the Holy One, blessed be He], and had returned with her in penitence while she was still in the body. In that case, "he shall let her be redeemed," as it is said, "He redeemed his soul from going into the pit" (Job 33: 28). "He shall let her be redeemed"—by the man who decides to redeem her, and return in penitence; and to both sides the Holy One,

322 In order to satisfy the needs of the body.
323 By satisfying the desires of the evil inclination.
324 [*Be-zahzahot* ("with sparkling lights") is usually translated "in drought."]
325 The soul will not return to the body at the resurrection.
326 [See above, n. 307.]

blessed be He, says "let her be redeemed" through penitence. After he has returned in penitence, he may redeem her from the path to Gehinnom. "To sell her to a foreign people he shall have no power." Who is this "foreign people"? The soul is distressed, for when she leaves the world, and man has enticed her to sin, she wishes to ascend aloft to the holy encampments, because the holy encampments are situated on the way to the Garden of Eden, and the foreign encampments are on the way to Gehinnom. If the soul is worthy there are many holy encampments prepared to accompany her and to take her into the Garden of Eden. If she is unworthy, there are many foreign encampments ready to take her along the road to Gehinnom. And these encampments consist of angels of destruction ready to take vengeance upon her, and so Scripture is there to affirm that "to sell her to a foreign people he shall have no power"—these are the angels of destruction—"when His garment is upon her"[327]—this is the protection with which the Holy One, blessed be He, invests her, so that a foreign people might have no power over her while His protection envelops her.

"And if he espouse her to his son" (Exodus 21: 9). Come and see how much care a man must take not to stray from the path in this world, for if a man is worthy in this world, and preserves his soul as he should, then he is the man in whom the Holy One, blessed be He, takes delight, and through whom He is glorified every day among His own retinue. He says, "See how the holy son that I have in that world performs such deeds, and how proper his actions are." When the soul leaves this world, innocent, clean, and pure, the Holy One, blessed be He, illumines her with many lights, and He says of her every day, "This is the soul of so-and-so, my son. May she be reserved for the body she has left." And so it is written, "If he espouse her to his son, he shall deal with her as with daughters." What is the significance of "as with daughters"? There is a mystery here for the wise. Within the mighty rock, in the hidden firmament, there is a palace called the Palace of Love. There treasures are hidden, and all the kisses of the king's[328] love are there, and the souls that are beloved of the king enter there. When the king enters the palace, where it is written "And Jacob kissed Rachel" (Genesis 29: 11),[329] and finds the holy soul there, he goes to meet her, and kisses her, and embraces her, and takes her up with him, and delights in her. This is the meaning of "he shall deal with her as with daughters,"—as a father deals with his beloved daughter, in that he kisses her, and embraces her, and presents her with gifts, so the Holy One, blessed be He, deals with the worthy soul every day, as it is written "he shall deal with her as with daughters." This is the significance of "He deals with him that waits for Him" (Isaiah 64: 3). Just as the daughter completes her deed in this

---

[327] [See above, n. 316.]   [328] The king is *Tiferet*.
[329] This signifies the Holy One, blessed be He, kissing the *Shekhinah*.

world, so the Holy One, blessed be He, completes another deed for her in the next world, as it is written, "The eye has not seen a God beside You, who deals with him that waits for Him." And here we have "he shall deal with her."[330]

The old man prostrated himself, and prayed, and wept, as he had at the beginning. He said: "If he take him another . . ." (Exodus 21: 10). What is the meaning of "another"? Will the Holy One, blessed be He, restore another soul to the righteous in this world, and not the soul that performed the will of her Maker in the world? If that is the case, then there is no assured hope at all for the righteous. What is the meaning of "If he take him another"?

The old man began by quoting: "And the dust returns to the earth as it was, and the spirit returns to God who gave it" (Ecclesiastes 12: 7). The companions have interpreted this verse in connection with the destruction of the Temple.[331] "And the dust returns to the earth as it was"—this parallels "And the Canaanite was then in the land"—"as it was." "And the spirit returns to God who gave it."[332] What is the meaning of "And the spirit returns"? This is the *Shekhinah*, which is the holy spirit, [which returned] when it saw, during the ten journeys that it made,[333] that Israel did not wish to go back in penitence to the Holy One, blessed be He, and that "the other side" had taken control of the holy land. This is how the companions interpreted it.

Let us learn together. The spirit[334] of the righteous man is adorned with an image[335] in the Garden of Eden below; and on all Sabbaths, and festivals, and New Moons, the spirits are crowned[336] and stripped[337] and ascend on high. Just as the Holy One, blessed be He, deals on high with the exalted, holy soul,[338] so He deals with the spirit that comes before Him. He says, "This is the spirit of the body of so-and-so."[339] The

[330] [In both verses *ya'aseh* ("he shall deal") is used. It also means "he shall do." Hence the reference to "deeds."]

[331] "The dust" is the serpent, the power of uncleanness, which ruled over the land of Israel at the time of the Temple's destruction. It also ruled there earlier, before Israel had conquered the land, and is called "the Canaanite," mentioned in the verse quoted, Genesis 12: 6.

[332] The *Shekhinah* left the land of Israel and returned to *Binah*, the upper *Shekhinah*, from which it had emanated.   [333] See B. T. *Rosh Hashanah* 31a.

[334] There are three parts to man's soul: *nefesh*, *ruah*, and *neshamah*. When he dies, his *nefesh* remains by the graveside; his *ruah* ("spirit" here) goes to the terrestrial Garden of Eden, and his *neshamah* ("soul" here) goes to the palaces in the celestial Garden of Eden.

[335] In the terrestrial Garden of Eden the spirit is enveloped by a spiritual garment, which is like an image of the body.

[336] With the crowns of the celestial Garden of Eden.

[337] They take off the garments that they had donned in the terrestrial Garden.

[338] The pleasures that are continuously accorded to the soul are accorded also to the spirit whenever it ascends.

[339] The body is commended because the spirit achieves its ascent through the commandments fulfilled by means of the body.

Holy One, blessed be He, immediately crowns that spirit with a number of crowns, and takes great delight in it. You might think that because of this spirit[340] the Holy One, blessed be He, would lose His concern with the soul. But it is not so, for "her food, her clothing, and her conjugal rights he shall not diminish."[341] These are the three exalted names[342] to which the verse "The eye has not seen a God beside You" refers, and they are all connected with the world to come[343] and originate there. One of them is *she'erah* (her food): the radiation of the light that illumines the secret path, the food that sustains all, and this is called *YHVH*, with the vocalization of *Elohim*.[344] If you change the order of the letters of *she'erah*, you have *asher he*,[345] connected with "from Asher—his bread shall be fat" (Genesis 49: 20), and so this too is *she'erah*. *Kesutah* (her clothing): the garment of the king, another radiation that illumines and protects her perpetually; the king's garment, which He spreads over her, is *Eloha*,[346] referred to in the phrase "with his garment upon her", and this is there continuously, never removed from her, "her clothing." And what are "her conjugal rights" (*onatah*)? This is the radiation of the world to come, which contains every thing: *Adonai Zevaot*[347] (Lord of Hosts), and this illumines all the exalted hidden lights of the Tree of Life,[348] in which conjugal rights are concealed, and from which they emerge, and all this with the desire and the pleasure of the world to come. These three things he shall not diminish, if she is worthy as she should be. But if she is not as she should be, then these three are withheld from her, in that a crown is not made for her from a single one of them. Let us learn from the phrase, "if he does not do these three things for her"—because she does not deserve them—"then she shall go out for nothing, without money (*kesef*)." She leaves him, and they push her out,

[340] During the time of the spirit's ascent the soul would lose some of her pleasures.

[341] The verse is interpreted as follows: "If he take him another"—when the Holy One, blessed be He, brings up the spirit as well to Him—"her food, her clothing, and her conjugal rights he shall not diminish"—even then the pleasures that the soul experiences will not be diminished.

[342] Namely, the tetragrammaton (*YHVH*), with the vocalization of *Elohim*; *Eloha*; and *Adonai Zevaot* (Lord of Hosts). This is explained below.

[343] With *Binah*, which is the mystical symbol of the world to come.

[344] This name is particular to *Binah*, which in essence is Mercy, and the letters of the tetragrammaton denote this aspect. However, the forces of Judgment also have their origin in *Binah*, and this is indicated by the vocalization of *Elohim*.

[345] This too is an allusion to *Binah*, the mystical representation of *asher* in the phrase "I am that I am" (*ehyeh asher ehyeh*), and *Binah* is also symbolized by the first *he* of the tetragrammaton.

[346] The name *Eloha* is compounded of *El*, the name particular to *Hesed*, and the letters *vav* and *he*, symbolizing *Tiferet* and *Malkhut*. So its essence is *Hesed* (Mercy), which spreads its wings over the soul.

[347] This name indicates *Yesod* in its relationship with *Nezah* and *Hod*, forces of sexual intercourse and procreation, which contain the mystery of *onah* ("conjugal rights").

[348] *Tiferet*, the source of influence in sexual intercourse.

"without *kesef*"—she will have no desire (*kosef*) and no pleasure at all. This is the reproof of the Torah. All good counsel depends on it, for it gives good counsel to mankind. And now let us return to earlier matters,[349] to the celestial protection that the Holy One, blessed be He, spreads over her, so that she should not belong to a foreign people, for it says that "his garment is on her," protecting her continuously.

"And if he espouse her to his son, he shall deal with her as with daughters." The old man said: "Companions, when you go to that rock[350] upon which the world depends, tell him to remember the day of snow,[351] when beans were sown of fifty-two[352] different colors, and we cited this verse, and he will tell you."

They said: Please, let him who began the discussion tell us.

He said to them: I know for sure that you are righteous men, and that it is right to tell you a word of the wise, but when you refer him to this matter he will add the finishing touch to what I tell you now. Now we must speak. Who is he that is called "son" of the Holy One, blessed be He? Let us learn. Whoever reaches the age of thirteen and over is called "son" of the Assembly of Israel.[353] And whoever has achieved the age of twenty years[354] and more is called "son" of the Holy One, blessed be He,[355] for it says "You are sons to the Lord your God," (Deuteronomy 14: 1). When David reached the age of thirteen, and was about to embark on his fourteenth year, then it was written, "The Lord said to me: You are my son; today I have begotten you" (Psalm 2: 7). What is the reason for this? Before that time he was not His son, because the celestial soul had not yet settled upon him[356] and he was still in the years of uncircumcision. And so we have "To-day I have begotten you"—on this particular day I have begotten you; I,[357] and not "the other side," as has been the case up till now, I alone. At the age of twenty, what is written concerning Solomon? "For I was a son unto my father"

---

[349] The subject of the earlier discussion concerning the spreading of the garment of the name *Eloha* over the soul, to prevent its being transmitted, by means of "the other side," to the pious among the other nations, and to the scholars who are illegitimate. See above, pp. 184–85.

[350] Rabbi Simeon ben Yohai.

[351] The day when they engaged in a polemical battle over the Torah. The reference is to 2 Samuel 23: 20, "he slew a lion in the midst of a pit, in the day of snow."

[352] This alludes to a discussion on the mystery of when man would reach the stage of being "a son" to the Holy One, blessed be He. *Ben* (son) has a numerical value of 52.

[353] The *Shekhinah*.

[354] From then on he becomes liable to punishment from Heaven for his misdeeds. See B. T. *Shabbat* 89b.

[355] *Tiferet*.

[356] Before the age of thirteen, the *neshamah*, the celestial and holiest part of the soul, does not settle upon man, and he is under the domination of the evil inclination, which derives from "the other side," called "uncircumcision."

[357] The *Shekhinah*, the *sefirah* nearest to the lower world, is revealed by its name, "I."

(Proverbs 4: 3)—unto my real father.[358] "And if he espouse her to his son"—a son aged thirteen years and over, for he has then emerged from the dominion of "the other side," which had accompanied him. What is written next?—"he shall deal with her as with daughters." What is the significance of "as with daughters"? We have learned: Every day the Holy One, blessed be He, looks upon the child held in the power of uncircumcision. He emerges from it and is taken to school, and breaks [that power]; he goes to the synagogue, and breaks it. What does the Holy One, blessed be He, do to that soul? He brings her into His own abode, and gives her presents, and many gifts, and adorns her with beautiful finery, until the time comes when He brings her to the marriage canopy[359] within the "son" aged thirteen years and upward. "If he take him another." Here we have the most profound mysteries, transmitted to the sages, but we must first mention one thing. Let us learn. On the Sabbath, as the day is sanctified, souls go out from the Tree of Life,[360] and these holy souls fly down to people below, and stay in them the whole of the Sabbath day. And when the Sabbath is over, all the souls ascend and are crowned with sacred crowns[361] on high. In the same way, the Holy One, blessed be He, prepares for Himself this man,[362] and this is the other soul, and although this soul is prepared for him,[363] the "food, clothing, and conjugal rights" are not diminished from the soul that he already had, as I have explained.

The old man wept, as he had at the beginning, and said to himself: Old man, old man, how greatly you have toiled to master these holy matters, and yet you have narrated them in a single moment! If you maintain that you should have more respect for these things, and not disclose them, it is written, "Do not withhold good from those who possess it, when it is in the power of your hand to do it" (Proverbs 3: 27).[364] What is the meaning of "Do not withhold good from those who possess it"? The Holy One, blessed be He, and the Assembly of Israel are here, because wherever words of Torah are spoken the Holy One,

[358] I.e., *Tiferet*, the divine father of the soul (*neshamah*), which is formed by the union of *Tiferet* with *Malkhut*. At the age of twenty, additional sanctity is bestowed by *Tiferet* upon the soul.

[359] This is the meaning of "as with daughters."

[360] The additional souls that rest upon Israel on the Sabbath. They originate from *Tiferet*.

[361] Crowns from the sanctity of the Sabbath, which they have drawn down from above.

[362] He draws near to Him the man who has reached the age of thirteen by providing him with the additional soul.

[363] Even though this additional soul is given to him on the Sabbath, and this is the significance of "If he take him another," the "normal" soul is not deprived of her pleasures.

[364] ["Those who possess it," lit., "its masters." The usual translation is "him to whom it is due."]

blessed be He, and the Assembly of Israel are there listening. And when they go and listen to these words, the good side is strengthened in the Tree of Knowledge of Good and Evil,[365] and ascends upward, and the Holy One, blessed be He, and the Assembly of Israel are adorned with the good, and they are then the possessors of the good. Old man, old man, you have spoken these words, and yet you do not know whether the Holy One, blessed be He, is here, or whether those who stand here are worthy enough to receive these words. Do not be afraid, old man, for you have joined battle many times with powerful men, and you have not been afraid. And should you be afraid now? Say what you have to say, for surely the Holy One, blessed be He, and the Assembly of Israel are here, and those who are here are worthy. Were it not so, you would not have encountered them, and you would not have embarked upon these matters. Say what you have to say, old man. Speak without fear.

He began by quoting: "O Lord, my God, You are very great. You are clothed with glory and majesty" (Psalm 104: 1).[366] "Lord, my God"—this is the beginning of faith,[367] the elevation of thought and the world to come, one indivisible[368] mystery. "You are great"—this is the commencement,[369] the first of the ancient days, the right side. "Very"—this is the left side.[370] "You are clothed with glory and majesty"—these are the two staves of willow.[371] Here it ends.[372] When it comes within the Tree of Life,[373] the latter hides itself, and does not wish to be one of the number, because of that "very". What is this

[365] The *Shekhinah* is called "the Tree of Knowledge of Good and Evil," since both Mercy and Power are active in her. When Judgment is in the ascendant, because of sin, the husks, which are the powers of evil, take hold of her, and are nurtured by her. But discussions of Torah encourage the growth of "the good side" in the *Shekhinah*, and with the help of the good that is in them she becomes united with her Master.

[366] [Subsequent verses are quoted in the rest of this paragraph.]

[367] The two names "Lord" and "my God" represent *Hokhmah* (thought) and *Binah* (the world to come), which are the perceptible initial aspects of the mystery of the Godhead, whereas *Keter* is beyond the reach of perception.

[368] *Hokhmah* and *Binah* are seen as father and mother, who are in uninterrupted union, whereas the union of *Tiferet* with *Malkhut* is not continuous.

[369] *Hesed*, also called *Gedulah* (Greatness), is the first of the seven lower *sefirot*, which parallel the days of creation and produce the array of divine forces necessary for the structure and operation of the world.

[370] *Gevurah*, strict Judgment, indicated by the word "very," in accordance with the midrash (*Bereshit Rabbah* 9: 5): "In the Torah of Rabbi Meir they found written, And behold it was very good, and behold it was good to die (or, death was good)." [A play on the words "very" (*me'od*) and "to die' (*mot*).] Through the power of *Gevurah* the forces of destruction and death of "the other side" are able to work.

[371] *Nezah* and *Hod*, representing the willow branches that are carried on the Feast of *Sukkot* (Tabernacles).

[372] The end of the description of the chain of the *sefirot*.

[373] When we get to *Tiferet*, which is the Tree of Life, we find that it refuses to be part of the enumeration, because it does not want to be next to "very" (*me'od*), which refers to death (*mot*).

"very"? The left side of all the branches below,[374] among which is a branch of bitterness.[375] Therefore the Tree of Life hides itself and does not wish to be included in the number, until it goes back to the beginning[376] and commends it in another way,[377] and says "who cover Yourself with light as with a garment"—this is the beginning of the light of the first day. "Who stretch out the heavens"—here the left side is included,[378] but it does not say "very", for the left is included with the right, and shines within the heavens as a whole. "Who lay the beams of your upper chambers in the waters,"—here the Tree of Life goes out in joy,[379] and the two staves of willow take root in it, for they grow in the waters of the river[380] that flows from Eden. This is the meaning of "Who lay the beams of your upper chambers in the waters."[381] What are these "upper chambers"? They are the staves of willow. And this is the significance of "that spreads out its roots by the river" and also of "There is a river, whose streams make glad the city of God." What are these "streams"? The same as "its roots." They are called "upper chambers," "roots," and "streams"—all of them are rooted in the waters of that river. "Who make the clouds Your chariot." This is Michael and Gabriel[382]—they are "the clouds." "Who walk upon the wings of the wind"—in order to bring healing to the world, and this is Raphael.[383] From then on You "make the winds Your messengers,"[384] and so on.

Old man, old man, since you know all this, declare it, and do not fear. Say what you have to say, and let the words that are in your mouth shine forth.

The companions were glad, and listened with joy to his holy words.

He said: Alas, old man! Alas, old man! What have you embarked upon? You have embarked upon the great sea. Now you must swim your way clear.

[374] The forces of Judgment that are active in the world.

[375] The "other side."

[376] Until the description begins anew with *Hesed*.

[377] Without giving a special mention to *Gevurah*, which alludes to the power of the "other side."

[378] The word "heavens" (*shamayim*) is composed of two words: "fire" (*esh*) and "water" (*mayim*), which symbolize *Gevurah* and *Hesed*. So *Gevurah* is not mentioned here as a separate power of strict Judgment, but intermingled with *Hesed*, by means of *Tiferet*, which is called "heaven."

[379] It reveals its active power in the *sefirot* that are below it.

[380] *Yesod*, which draws influence from *Tiferet*.

[381] *Tiferet* waters *Nezah* and *Hod* through the river *Yesod*. Similarly, in the next quotation from Jeremiah 17:8 the river is *Yesod*. In the third quotation from Psalm 46:5 the river (*Yesod*) makes the *Shekhinah* (the city of God) glad by union, with the cooperation of *Nezah* and *Hod* (its streams).

[382] The angels of *Hesed* and *Gevurah*.

[383] The angel of *Tiferet*.   [384] The angels of the *Shekhinah*.

"If he take him another." There are a number of revolutions[385] here that have not been revealed until now, and they are all true, as is fitting, and one should not depart even a hair's breadth from the way of truth. First, one should remark upon the following: the souls of proselytes[386] all fly from the Garden of Eden by a concealed path. When their souls, which have flown from the Garden of Eden, depart from this world, to which place do they return?[387] But we have learned:[388] whoever was first to take possession of the property of proselytes has a right to it. So here, the sacred, exalted souls[389] that the Holy One, blessed be He, has prepared in the Garden of Eden below, as we have said, all go out at appointed times[390] and ascend, in order to delight themselves in the Garden of Eden on high, and they meet the souls of proselytes.[391] Whichever one of these souls takes hold of them, has a right to them, and they garb themselves with them and ascend. And they all remain in that garb[392] and descend to the Garden[393] in that garb, because in the Garden only those can stay who are garbed[394] in the manner of those who are there. You might argue that because of this garb the souls are deprived[395] of some of the pleasure that they originally enjoyed. But it is written "If he take him another, her food, her clothing, and her conjugal rights he shall not diminish"—in the Garden[396] they remain in the clothes that they were the first to seize and to which they had a right; but when they ascend on high they strip them off,[397] because they do not remain garbed there.

The old man wept as he had at the beginning, and said to himself: Old man, old man, you have real cause to weep, you have real cause to shed tears over every word. But it is revealed before the Holy One, blessed be He, and His holy *Shekhinah*, that I speak with a willing heart, and with a

---

[385] Hidden primeval movements in the life of souls.

[386] They are formed from the union of the souls of the righteous in the Garden of Eden, and they fly from there beneath the wings of the *Shekhinah*.

[387] Since they are inferior to the souls of Israel, they cannot share the same status in the Garden of Eden. [388] B.T. *Baba Batra* 52b.

[389] On their descent to this world they stay a while in the terrestrial Garden of Eden and take their enjoyment there.

[390] On Sabbaths and festivals.

[391] Which hover near the Garden of Eden.

[392] As they ascend; but they take it off when they enter the celestial Garden of Eden, as is explained below.

[393] When they return from the celestial Garden of Eden, they descend to the terrestrial Garden of Eden, having first garbed themselves with souls of proselytes.

[394] In the terrestrial Garden of Eden all the souls are clothed in a spiritual garment, which has a corporeal appearance in this world. Therefore those souls which have the right to the soul of a proselyte can enter in this particular garb.

[395] I.e., since they have earned the right to an additional garment, they forfeit in return the pleasures prepared for them in the celestial Garden of Eden.

[396] The terrestrial Garden.

[397] And enjoy the pleasures prepared for them.

desire to worship them, since they are the possessors of every word, and adorn themselves with them.

All these holy souls descend to this world, in order that each one should dwell in its place,[398] where they are seen by mankind. And they all descend after they have been garbed with those souls,[399] as we have said, and in this way they enter the holy seed,[400] and in this garb they remain in order that they may draw upon it while they are in this world.[401] And when these garments have drawn upon the things of this world,[402] the holy souls enjoy the scent that they experience from these garments.

The Holy One, blessed be He, puts all the secret things that He does into the holy Torah, and it all exists in the Torah. The Torah reveals the secret, and then immediately clothes it in another garb, and it is hidden there and not revealed. The wise who are full of eyes, although the matter is sealed in a garment, see it through the garment. And when the matter is revealed, before it enters the garment it is seen by those with sharp eyes, and even though it is immediately concealed it is not lost from their sight. In several places the Holy One, blessed be He, gives instruction concerning the proselyte, so that the holy seed should take special care of them.[403] He then takes the hidden subject[404] from its sheath, and after it has been revealed it returns at once to its sheath and dons its garment there. When He gives instruction concerning the proselyte in all these places, He takes the subject from its sheath and it is revealed, and He says: "for you know the soul of the proselyte."[405] It then at once enters its sheath,[406] returns to its garment, and is hidden, and it continues, "for you were strangers in the land of Egypt." Scripture thinks that because it is immediately garbed no one will notice it. Through the soul of the proselyte, the holy soul gains knowledge[407] of the things of this world, and benefits from them.

The old man resumed by quoting: "And Moses entered into the midst

[398] Within the body, where they are manifested in this world.

[399] The souls of proselytes.

[400] The Jewish people.

[401] By its means they gather impressions of the world, for the soul of the proselyte has already been in the world, and is accustomed to it.

[402] I.e., have fulfilled commandments, and done good deeds.

[403] Not to oppress them.

[404] The mystical significance of this instruction—that one should protect the souls of proselytes, which serve as garments for the souls of Israel.

[405] The mystery is revealed in the words "the soul of the proselyte" in Exodus 23: 9. [The biblical Hebrew ger, used here, means "stranger," and is usually translated thus, but it came to mean "proselyte." The whole mystical interpretation depends on this.]

[406] In the continuation of the verse the mystical meaning is concealed by immediately connecting the matter with the sojourn of Israel in Egypt.

[407] And this is the true meaning of the phrase, "For you know the soul of a stranger (proselyte)."

of the cloud, and went up into the mount . . ." (Exodus 24: 18). What is this cloud? It is the same as that mentioned in "I have set My bow in the cloud" (Genesis 9: 13). We have learned that the bow took off its garments[408] and gave them to Moses, and in that garment Moses ascended the mountain, and from there he saw what he saw, and enjoyed all, as far as that place.[409]

The companions came, prostrated themselves before the old man, and wept, and said: Had we come into the world for no other purpose than to hear these words from your mouth it would have sufficed us.

The old man said: It is not for this alone that I began to speak, for an old man like me does not rattle on or raise his voice for one thing only. How confused the inhabitants of the world are in their understanding! They do not see the path of truth in the Torah, but the Torah calls to them every day in love and they will not even turn their heads. It is true, as I have said, that the Torah takes a subject from its sheath, and it is revealed for a moment and then immediately hidden; but when it is revealed from within its sheath, and then at once concealed, it is revealed only to those who know it and recognize it.

What can be compared to this?[410] It is like a girl, beautiful and gracious, and much loved, and she is kept closely confined in her palace. She has a special lover, unrecognized by any one and concealed. This lover, because of the love that he feels for her, passes by the door of her house and looks on every side, and she knows that her lover is constantly walking to and fro by the door of her house. What does she do? She opens a tiny door in the secret palace where she lives and shows her face to her love. Then she withdraws at once and is gone. None of those in her lover's vicinity sees or understands, but her lover alone knows, and his heart and soul and inner being yearn for her, and he knows that it is because of the love that she bears him that she showed herself to him for a moment, in order to awaken love in him.

So it is with the Torah. She reveals herself only to her lover. The Torah knows that the wise man walks to and fro every day by the door of her house. What does she do? She shows her face to him from the palace and signals to him, and she withdraws at once to her place and hides herself. None of those who are there knows or understands, but he alone knows, and his heart and soul and inner being yearn for her. And so the Torah is revealed, and then is hidden, and treats her lover lovingly, in order to awaken love in him.

Come and see. This is the way of the Torah. At first, when she begins to reveal herself to a man, she gives him a sign. If he understands, good.

---

[408] The bow is the *Shekhinah*, in which appear the colors of the *sefirot*. When it dwells below, it is garbed in clouds of glory.

[409] I.e., the place of the *Shekhinah*.

[410] Here follows the explanation of the riddle posed earlier. See p. 178, and n. 270.

If he does not understand, she sends to him and calls him a fool. The Torah says to the messenger that she sends to him. "Tell that fool to come here, that I might speak with him." So it is written, "Whoever is foolish, let him turn hither, he that lacks understanding . . ." (Proverbs 9: 4). He comes to her, and she begins to speak with him through the curtain that she has spread before him, in the way that best suits him, so that he can understand little by little, and this is *derash* (homiletical interpretation). Then she talks with him through a very fine veil and discusses enigmatic things, and this is *haggadah* (narration). And then when he has become accustomed to her, she reveals herself to him face to face, and speaks to him about all her hidden mysteries, and all the hidden paths, that have laid concealed in her heart from ancient times. Then he becomes a complete man, a true master of Torah, the lord of the house, for she has revealed all her mysteries to him, and she has neither hidden nor withheld anything from him.

She says to him: You saw the sign that I made to you at the beginning. These are the mysteries that were contained within it. This is what it really is.

He sees at once that one should not add to these things or subtract from them. The real meaning of the text of Scripture is then revealed, [from which] one should not add or subtract even a single letter. Therefore men ought to take note of the Torah and pursue her, and become her lovers, as I have explained.

21. THE CHILD

(Zohar III, 186a–192a)

Rabbi Isaac and Rabbi Judah were on a journey, and they came to a place called Kfar Sikhnin. They lodged with a woman who had a young son, and he used to spend the whole day at school. On this particular day he left school, went home, and saw these scholars.

His mother said to him: Come near to these famous men, and you will obtain blessings from them.

He approached them, but before he got too near he turned away again.

I do not want to get near them, he said to his mother, because they have not said the *Shema*[411] today, and I have been taught that whoever does not say the *Shema* at its proper time should be shunned the whole day long.

They heard and were astonished, and they raised their hands and blessed him.

They said: It is true; we have been preoccupied today with a

[411] [Lit. "Hear," the first word of the daily statutory Jewish prayer, taken from Deuteronomy 6: 4–9.]

bridegroom and his bride. They did not have the necessary prerequisites, and had to delay their marriage, and there was no one else to assist them. So we occupied ourselves with their affairs, and did not say the *Shema* at the proper time, for whoever is occupied with fulfilling one commandment is exempted from fulfilling another. But how did you know this, my child?

He replied: I knew it from the smell of your clothes as I came toward you.

They were filled with astonishment. They sat down, washed their hands, and began to eat. Rabbi Judah's hands were dirty, and he pronounced the blessing before washing.

The child said to them: If you are disciples of Rav Shemaiah, the Pious, you should not have pronounced the blessing with dirty hands. Whoever pronounces the blessing with dirty hands deserves to die.

The child began his discourse by quoting: "When they go into the tent of meeting, they shall wash with water, that they die not . . ." (Exodus 30: 20). We learn from this verse that whoever does not take care of this, and appears before the King with dirty hands, is punishable by death. For what reason? Because a man's hands dwell in the topmost part of the world.[412] There is one finger[413] on a man's hand that is the finger that Moses raised.[414] It is written, "And you shall make bars of acacia-wood: five for the boards of the one side of the tabernacle, and five bars for the boards of the other side of the tabernacle . . ." and then it is written, "and the middle bar among the boards shall pass from end to end" (Exodus 26: 26–28). Now you might think that this middle bar is a separate one, and not included in the five. But it is not so. The middle bar is one of the five—two on one side, two on the other, and one in the middle.[415] This is the central bar, the pillar of Jacob, the mystery of Moses. Parallel to this are the five fingers of the human hand. The middle bar in the center is larger and more important than the others, and the others depend on it. These five bars are called the five centuries, through which the Tree of Life passes.[416] And the holy covenant of circumcision[417] is effected through the five fingers of the hand. This is a secret matter that I have spoken. It is for this reason that all the priestly benedictions depend upon the fingers, and Moses spread out his hands

---

[412] They symbolize the *sefirot*.   [413] The middle finger.

[414] In the war with Amalek (Exodus 17: 11).

[415] The five bars represent the *sefirot* from *Hesed* to *Hod*, with *Tiferet* in the middle ("the middle bar"). *Tiferet* holds the balance between Mercy on the one side (*Hesed* and *Nezah*) and Judgment on the other (*Gevurah* and *Hod*). Jacob and Moses are symbolized by *Tiferet*.

[416] See *Bereshit Rabbah* 15: 7. [This tradition has it that it would take five hundred years to reach the top of the Tree of Life.] The Tree of Life is *Yesod*, which rises and draws influence from the five *sefirot*.

[417] The covenant is represented by *Yesod*.

for this purpose.[418] Since so much depends on them, it is only right that they should be clean when one uses them to bless the Holy One, blessed be He, for through them and through their representative [on high] the holy name is blessed. Therefore, since you are so wise, why have you not paid special attention to this, and followed the dictum of Rav Shemaiah, the Pious, who said: Dirt and filth are offered to "the other side," for "the other side" is nourished by dirt and filth; and so water used in washing the hands at the end is *hovah*?[419]

They were astonished, and unable to speak.

Then Rabbi Judah said: What is your father's name, my child?

The child was silent for a moment, and then went to his mother and kissed her.

Mother, he said, these scholars have asked me about my father. Shall I tell them?

Have you tested them, my child? said his mother.

I have tested them, he said, and I have found them lacking.

His mother whispered something to him, and he returned to them.

He said to them: You asked about my father. He has departed from the world, and whenever holy, pious men embark upon a journey he drives the mules behind them.[420] If you are exalted, saintly men, how is it that you have not discovered him driving the mules behind you? I summed you up at the very beginning, and now I know that I was right, for my father has only to see the mule [of a holy and pious man], and he straightway drives it along behind, in order to bear the yoke of the Torah. Now, since you are not worthy enough for my father to be your mule-driver, I shall not tell you who he is.

Rabbi Judah said to Rabbi Isaac: This child does not seem to me to be human.

They ate, and the child spoke words of Torah, and gave new interpretations of Torah.

They said: Come, let us bless [God].[421]

The child said: You have well spoken, because the holy name is not blessed through this benediction unless one first expresses one's intention to say it.

He began by quoting: "I shall bless the Lord at all times . . ." (Psalm 34: 2). What need was there for David to say "I shall bless the Lord"? David saw that it was necessary to express his intention. And he said "I shall bless," for when a man is seated at table the *Shekhinah* is present,

---

[418] In order to draw influence down from the *sefirot*.

[419] "Water before [a meal] is a commandment (*mizvah*); water afterwards is a duty (*hovah*)"—B.T. *Hullin* 105a. *Hovah* is taken here in the Aramaic sense of "sin." The water used in the later washing, which takes away the dirt, is granted to "the other side," which is the domain of sin.

[420] His soul clothes itself in human form in order to be of service to the wise.

[421] [The opening words of the grace after meals.]

and "the other side" is also present. As soon as he expresses his intention to bless the Holy One, blessed be He, the *Shekhinah* is able to prepare itself to face the realm above in order to receive blessings, and "the other side" is humiliated. And if a man does not express his intention to bless the Holy One, blessed be He, "the other side" rejoices, and shakes with mirth, for it gains a share in that blessing. You might ask why, in that case, we do not have to express an intention with the other blessings? The answer is, because there the object of the benediction itself represents the intention. Let us learn how this applies. If one says a blessing over a piece of fruit, the fruit itself represents the intention, and one says the blessing over it, and "the other side" has no share in it. Before this, when the fruit is still in the power of "the other side," one does not say a blessing over it, for it is written "it shall not be eaten,"[422] to prevent us from saying a blessing over the fruit, and to prevent "the other side" from being blessed. But when it emerges from its power it may be eaten, and a blessing is pronounced over it, and it represents in itself an expression of the intention to say a blessing. Similarly, with all the good things of the world over which blessings are said—they all represent the intention to bless, and "the other side" has no share in this blessing. You might say, In that case the cup of wine in the grace after meals also represents this intention. Why say explicitly: Come, let us bless [God]? This is because the cup of wine has already fulfilled that function when it was drunk [during the meal] and when the blessing, "He who creates the fruit of the vine," was said over it. When we come to the grace after meals we need an additional expression of intention, for the cup is now needed for the Holy One, blessed be He, and not for food. Therefore we have to express our intention verbally. You might say that "Let us bless Him of whose bounty we have eaten" is the expression of the intention, and "Blessed be He of whose bounty we have eaten" is the actual benediction. That is correct. But "Let us bless . . ." is a second expression of intention. The first expression[423] is for the cup of blessing on its own, but when this cup[424] is raised it is associated with the second expression, in the phrase "Let us bless . . .," in relation to the upper world, whence come every food and every benediction. That is why it is expressed in the third person,[425] for the upper world is hidden, and there the intention to pronounce a benediction can only be expressed on this level, with the cup of benediction.

[422] Leviticus 19: 23. The quotation refers to fruit produced by a tree during the first three years. The fruit in these three years was thought to be the province of "the other side."　[423] I.e., "Come, let us bless. . . ."

[424] The "cup of blessing" represents *Malkhut*. With it one blesses *Binah*, which is the upper world, the source of emanation.

[425] "Let us bless Him. . . ." Other blessings are in the form "We bless You, O Lord . . ." [Hebrew *nistar* means both "hidden" and the grammatical "third person."]

Rabbi Judah said: How fortunate we are, for we have never in our lifetime heard words such as these, until this moment. As I said, this [child] is not human.

He said to him: My child, angel of God, and His beloved, you interpreted the passage "And you shall make bars of acacia-wood; five for the boards of the one side of the tabernacle . . . and five bars . . . and five bars . . . and five bars for the back part toward the west."[426] Now there are many bars mentioned here, but a man has only two hands.

He said: This illustrates the saying: You can tell a man from his mouth. But since you have not understood, I shall tell you.

He began by quoting: "The wise man, his eyes are in his head" (Ecclesiastes 2: 14). Now, where would a man's eyes be if not in his head? In his body, or in his arm? Is this the way in which the wise man is distinguished from the rest of humanity? This verse must be understood in the following way. We have learned that one should not walk four cubits bareheaded.[427] Why? because the *Shekhinah* rests upon the head, and both the eyes and the words of the wise man are "in his head," that is, they are directed toward Him who rests upon his head. And when his eyes are there, he knows that the light that burns upon his head needs oil, for man's body is the wick and the light burns above it. King Solomon exclaimed: "Let your head never lack oil" (Ecclesiastes 9: 8), for the light on the head needs oil, and that is good deeds. And so it is written, "The wise man, his eyes are in his head"—and not elsewhere.

Now you are surely wise men, and the *Shekhinah* rests upon your head, and yet you could not understand the passage, "And you shall make bars . . . for the boards of the one side of the tabernacle, and five bars for the boards of the other side of the tabernacle." The verse stipulates "one" and "other."[428] It does not mention a third or a fourth. So "one" and "other" represent the two sides,[429] and it therefore calculates only with these two.

They came and kissed him.

Rabbi Judah wept and said: Blessed is your portion, Rabbi Simeon, and blessed is the generation in which, through your merit, even the little children of their master's house are tall and mighty rocks.

His mother came and said to them: Masters, only look upon my son, I pray you, with a good eye.

Blessed is your portion, they said to her, worthy woman, the most precious of all women, for the Holy One, blessed be He, has chosen your portion, and raised your banner above all the other women in the world.

[426] Exodus 26: 26–27. See above, p. 198, where the five bars are connected in the child's interpretation with the fingers of the hand.   [427] B.T. *Shabbat* 118b.

[428] [The Hebrew literally means "second."]

[429] Right and left, representing *Ḥesed* and *Gevurah*, which in mystical terms are the two arms.

The child said: I do not fear the evil eye, because I am the son of a great and noble fish[430] and fish do not fear the evil eye, for it is written "And let them swarm as a multitude in the midst of the earth."[431] What does "as a multitude" mean? It means: in order to have mastery[432] over the [evil] eye. We have learned: "The fish of the sea are covered by the waters and the evil eye has no [power over them]."[433] "As a multitude in the midst of the earth" means: among mankind that are upon the earth.

They said: My child, angel of God, there is no evil eye in us, and we do not come from the side of the evil eye. But may the Holy One, blessed be He, shelter you with His wings.

He began by quoting: "The angel who has redeemed me from all evil, may he bless [the lads; and let my name be named in them, and the name of my fathers, Abraham and Isaac; and let them swarm as a multitude in the midst of the earth]" (Genesis 48: 16). This verse was said by Jacob through the holy spirit. Since he said it through the holy spirit, then it must contain a secret of wisdom. "The angel"—he called [the Shekhinah] "angel," but he also called her by other names. Why is she called "angel" here? She is called "angel" when she is a messenger from above, and receives glorious light from the supernal mirror,[434] for then father and mother[435] bless her, and say to her, "Go, my daughter, and keep your house. Look after your house. This is what you shall do to your house: go and feed them. Go, for the world below is waiting for you. The members of your household expect food from you. You have all that is necessary to provide for them." Now you might say that there are several places where she is called "angel," without her coming to feed the worlds; and, furthermore, that she does not feed the worlds under this name, but under the name Adonai.[436] This is true, but when she is sent from the father and mother she is called "angel," and when she dwells in her place, upon the two cherubim,[437] her name is Adonai.

When the Shekhinah first appeared to Moses she was called "angel." She did not appear thus to Jacob, but in an earthly form, as it is written, "Rachel came [with the sheep of her father; for she tended them]" (Genesis 29: 9). This was the image of another Rachel,[438] as it is written, "Thus says the Lord: A voice is heard in Ramah . . . Rachel weeping for her children" (Jeremiah 31: 15). "Rachel came"—pure and simple;[439]

[430] He gives a hint here that he is the son of Rav Hamnuna Sava. Aramaic *nuna* means "fish." See above, p. 173, n. 236.

[431] Genesis 48: 16. *Ve-yidgu*, "let them swarm" is connected by the child with *dag*, "fish."   [432] Their large numbers will overpower the evil eye.

[433] B.T. *Berakhot* 20a.   [434] *Tiferet*.   [435] *Hokhmah* and *Binah*.

[436] A name peculiar to *Malkhut*.

[437] The two angels below the *Shekhinah*, who transmit the influence downward.

[438] The *Shekhinah*, weeping for her children.

[439] Without qualification, i.e., the *Shekhinah*.

"with the sheep"—with her accompanying "levels"; "of her father"—really;[440] and all of them were counted and entrusted to her care; "for she tended them"—she guided them and was put in charge of them. However, in the case of Moses it is written, "And the angel of the Lord appeared to him in a flame of fire" (Exodus 3: 2). Now you might say that Abraham was even more highly regarded, for with him "angel" is not written, but simply "And the Lord appeared to him by the terebinths of Mamre . . ." (Genesis 18: 1). There, with Abraham, it was *Adonai*[441] that appeared to him, for at that time Abraham had accepted the covenant [of circumcision], and He was revealed to him as master and ruler, something that had previously been concealed from him. And it was right for this to be so, for at that time he became associated with this particular level, and no farther, and so, through the name *Adon*, He became his master. But with Moses there was no differentiation in time, for it is written "Moses Moses" without disjunctive punctuation,[442] while "Abraham, Abraham" (Genesis 22: 11) is written with disjunctive punctuation. Abraham was at one time imperfect, and later became perfect, so there is a difference between the later Abraham and the earlier Abraham. But with Moses, as soon as he was born, a shining mirror[443] was with him, as it is written, "And she saw him, that he was good" (Exodus 2: 2), and it is also written, "And God saw the light that it was good" (Genesis 1: 4). So Moses was immediately associated with his level. That is why it says "Moses Moses" without disjunctive punctuation. Therefore, in Moses' case, she belittled herself, and it is written "the angel of the Lord." Jacob called her "angel" when he was about to depart from the world. Why? Because at that moment he took possession of her in order to rule [over her]:[444] Moses in his lifetime, Jacob after he departed from the world; Moses in body, Jacob in spirit. Blessed was the portion of Moses!

"Who has redeemed me from all evil"—[Jacob] never approached the evil side, and evil could exercise no power over him. "May he bless the lads"—Jacob was setting his house in order,[445] like a man who goes to a new house, and sets it in order and provides ornaments for it. "May he bless the lads"—these are they who are designated, appointed over the world, so that blessings may flow from them, the two cherubim. "And let my name be named in them"—he now sets his house in

---

[440] The supernal father, *Hokhmah*, from whom she receives her hosts.

[441] The tetragrammaton is actually written in the biblical text, but the revelation was really that of *Adonai*, as the tetragrammaton is pronounced.

[442] Exodus 3: 4. [Disjunctive punctuation is a vertical line in the Hebrew text between two words.]

[443] *Tiferet*, that was Moses' level.

[444] He ascended to the degree of *Tiferet*, the *Shekhinah*'s partner.

[445] He was summoning the cherubim for the *Shekhinah*; they are alluded to in the "ordering" and ornamenting of the house.

order,[446] and ascends to his level, because the conjunction occurred with Jacob; the body became attached to the necessary place, and the two arms with it. Once the lads had been blessed properly, then, immediately, "let them swarm as a multitude in the midst of the earth." Fish customarily spawn in water, and if they come out of the water on to any land they die right away. But these are not like that. They come from the great sea,[447] and when they disperse in order to procreate they do so "in the midst of the earth"—something that happens with no other fish in the world. What is written before this? "And he blessed Joseph, and said . . ." (Genesis 48: 15). But we do not find Joseph's blessings here. He blesses him later, as it is written, "Joseph is a fruitful vine" (Genesis 49: 22). But since he blesses these lads he also blesses Joseph, for they cannot receive blessing except through Joseph.[448] And because he is hidden,[449] and it is not right for him to be revealed, it is written in the third person,[450] "and let my name be named in them, and the name of my fathers"—they are blessed through the patriarchs, and from no other source. "In the midst of the land"—this is the covering[451] that conceals what is necessary.

They came and kissed him, as they had at the beginning. They said: Come, let us bless [God].[452]

Let me say the blessing, he said, for all that you have heard so far has emanated from me, and I shall fulfill in myself the verse, "He that has a good eye shall be blessed, [for he gives of his bread to the poor]."[453] Read rather "he shall bless." Why? Because "he gives of his bread to the poor." You have partaken of the bread and sustenance of my teaching.

Rabbi Abba said: My son, the beloved of the Holy One, blessed be He, surely we have learned: The host says the blessing before the meal, and the guest says the blessing after the meal.[454]

I am not the host, he said to them, and you are not my guests. I have discovered a verse that I shall implement, for surely I am the one "who has a good eye." I have spoken Torah quite voluntarily up till now, and you have partaken of my bread and sustenance.

---

[446] The earlier "ordering" was below the level of the *Shekhinah*. This one is above it, through the influence that descends to the *Shekhinah*, through union with the body and the two arms (*Tiferet*, *Hesed* and *Gevurah*), which are Jacob and his two forefathers, Abraham and Isaac.   [447] *Malkhut*.

[448] Joseph is *Yesod*, and the influence that descends to the cherubim from the *Shekhinah* reaches the *Shekhinah* through the channel of *Yesod*.

[449] They conceal the sign of the covenant, which is *Yesod*.

[450] Joseph is not mentioned in this verse. See also p. 200, and n. 425.

[451] This is an allusion to *Yesod* which, when in union, is within the *Shekhinah*, called "earth."   [452] See above, p. 199, and n. 421.

[453] Proverbs 22:9. [The child wishes to read *yevarekh* (he shall bless) instead of *yevorakh* (he shall be blessed).]

[454] B.T. *Berakhot* 46a, [where this opinion is ascribed to Rabbi Simeon ben Yohai.]

He took the cup for the blessing, and began to say grace, but his hands trembled, and he could not hold the cup. When he came to "for the land and for the food",[455] he said, "I will lift up the cup of salvation, and call upon the name of the Lord" (Psalm 116: 13), and then the cup steadied itself in his right hand, and he continued the grace. At the end he said: May it be God's will that one of these present[456] may be accorded life from the Tree of Life, upon which all life depends. And may the Holy One, blessed be He, vouch for him, and may he also find a surety below, so that he might be joined through his pledge with the Holy King.

When he had concluded grace he closed his eyes for a moment, and then he opened them. He said: Friends, may peace light upon you from the good Master, to whom all peace belongs.

They were amazed, and wept, and blessed him. They stayed there the night, and in the morning they arose and went. When they came to Rabbi Simeon ben Yohai they told him what had happened.

Rabbi Simeon was astonished, and said: He is the son of a mighty rock, and most worthy to be at a stage higher even than man can understand; he is the son of Rav Hamnuna Sava.

Rabbi Eleazar became agitated, and said: I must go and see this burning lamp.

He will not achieve fame for himself in this world, said Rabbi Simeon, for there is something of the celestial in him, and it is a mystery. A continuing light shines upon him from his father, and this mystery[457] is not current among the companions.

One day the companions were sitting together and were waging war [over matters of Torah]. There were present Rabbi Eleazar, Rabbi Abba, Rabbi Hiyya, Rabbi Jose, and other companions. They said: We find it written in Scripture "Be not at enmity with Moab, neither contend with them in battle . . ." (Deuteronomy 2: 9). This is because Ruth and Naamah[458] were later to be descended from them. But should not this have applied even more forcibly to the Midianites? Moses' wife, Zipporah, was from Midian, and Jethro, and his children, all of whom were truly righteous, came from Midian, and, furthermore, they reared Moses in Midian. And yet, the Holy One, blessed be He, said, "Take vengeance for the children of Israel on the Midianites" (Numbers 31: 2).

---

[455] [See *Authorised Daily Prayer Book*, ed. Singer (1962 ed.), p. 379.]

[456] He prays on behalf of Rabbi Isaac, for whom death had been decreed, but who was saved by the pledge of Rabbi Simeon ben Yohai. See above, pp. 135–37.

[457] How the soul of the deceased father can continue to shine upon the son.

[458] [Ruth was a Moabitess (Ruth 1: 4), and an ancestor of King David (ibid., 4: 22).] Naamah was an Ammonitess, one of King Solomon's wives, and was the mother of Rehoboam (1 Kings 14: 21), and therefore also a matriarch in the Davidic house. The Ammonites are also to be protected, according to the passage in Deuteronomy (2: 19): "Do not harass them, or contend with them."

It looks as if there is some bias here, because the Midianites have more reason to be saved than the Moabites.

Rabbi Simeon said: A man who is going to pick figs in the future is not the same as a man who has picked them in the past.

Rabbi Eleazar said to him: Even though he has already picked them, [the tree] still deserves to be praised.

The man who has not yet picked his figs, he replied, looks after the fig tree all the time, so that it should not suffer any blemish, for the sake of the figs that he will gather later on. But once he has picked his figs he leaves the fig tree, and does not look after it any more. So Moab, which was going to produce figs in the future, was protected by the Holy One, blessed be He, as it is written, "Be not at enmity with Moab." But of Midian, whose figs had already been produced and gathered, it is written, "Harass the Midianites" (Numbers 25: 17), because this fig tree was not going to bear any more fruit, and could be burned.

He began by quoting: "And Moab said to the elders of Midian . . ." (Numbers 22: 4). It was the Moabites who made the first move, and because of the figs that Moab was to bring into the world, they were saved from punishment.

Rabbi Eleazar wanted to visit his father-in-law, Rabbi Jose, the son of Rabbi Simeon ben Lekunya. Rabbi Abba and Rabbi Jose went with him. They set off, and discussed Torah throughout the journey.

Rabbi Abba said: It is written, "And the Lord said to me: Be not at enmity with Moab, neither contend with them in battle." And it is also written, "When you approach the Ammonites [do not harass them, or contend with them]." Is there any difference between these two? They seem to be treated equally. And yet we have learned[459] that when Israel approached the Moabites they were visibly equipped for battle, as if they wished to wage war against them. But in the case of the Ammonites they were all enveloped in their cloaks and no weapons of war could be seen at all. And yet the verses quoted show that they were to be treated equally!

Rabbi Eleazar said: So they are, but we have learned[460] that one daughter was barefaced and said "Moab," as it is written "And she called his name Moab."[461] Consequently, Israel confronted them in as barefaced a manner as she, when she said "Moab," [meaning] "from my father did this son come." But the younger, who said, "Ben Ammi,"[462] disguised her conduct. And so Israel disguised their conduct in relation [to the Ammonites]. They wrapped themselves in their cloaks

---

[459] Tanḥuma, Balak, 2.   [460] B.T. Baba Kamma 38b.
[461] Genesis 19: 37. [Moab and Ammon were both descended from the children that the daughters of Lot bore to their father. The older daughter did not try to conceal her incestuous conduct and called her son "Moab" meaning "from the father."]
[462] "Son of my people," Genesis 19: 38.

and presented themselves to them as real brothers. These matters have already been reconciled.

As they were going along Rabbi Eleazar remembered the child. They made a detour of about ten miles and came to the place. They were received in the house, and when they went in they found the child sitting down while a meal was being laid for him. As soon as he saw them, he approached them.

He said: Let the pious and holy ones enter. Let the pillars of the world enter. They are praised by both the upper and the lower worlds. Even the fish[463] of the great sea come on to dry land to meet them.

Rabbi Eleazar went and kissed him on the head, and then he kissed him on the mouth. Rabbi Eleazar said: The first kiss is for the fish that leave the waters and walk on dry land. The second kiss is for the eggs of the fish, which produce fine fruit in the world.

The child said: I can tell from the smell of your garments that Ammon and Moab have been contending with you. How did you escape from them? You had no weapons. For if you had, you would have walked in safety, without fear.

Rabbi Eleazar, Rabbi Abba, and the companions were filled with amazement.

Rabbi Abba said: How blessed is this journey, how blessed is our portion, that we have been enabled to see this!

They prepared the meal, as they had done earlier.

He said: Wise and holy men, do you like your sweetmeats battle-free, or do you prefer the bread of war and a meal with weapons? Would you like to bless the King[464] with all the weapons of war, for the table cannot be exalted without war?[465]

Rabbi Eleazar said: Beloved, adored, and holy child, we would prefer that. We have used all these weapons, and we know how to fight with sword, and bow, and lance, and sling-stones. But you are a child, and you have not yet seen how the mighty heroes of the world wage war.

The child laughed, and said: That is true. I have not seen it. But it is written, "Let not the man who puts on his armor boast like the man who is taking his off" (1 Kings 20: 11).

They laid the table with bread and everything else that they needed.

Rabbi Eleazar said: There is so much joy in my heart because of this child. How many new interpretations of Torah will be spoken at this table. That is why I said before that I knew that there were clappers of the bells of the holy spirit within him.

---

[463] A reference to his father, who goes out to meet righteous men on their journeys. See above, p. 202, n. 430, and p. 199, n. 420.

[464] [Say grace after meals.]

[465] The meal cannot reach an exalted stage of sanctity unless there is a "war" of words, involving new interpretations of Torah.

The child said: Whoever wants bread, let him eat it with the edge of the sword.

Rabbi Eleazar rejoiced. The child turned and approached him. He said: Since you have boasted of your own prowess, you must begin the battle. I said earlier that the battle should begin after the meal, but now, whoever wants fine bread, let him bring his weapons with him.

Rabbi Eleazar said: You should show me some of your own weapons.

The child began by quoting: "It shall be that, when you eat of the bread of the land, you shall set apart a portion for a gift (terumah)[466] to the Lord" (Numbers 15: 19). This verse refers to the wave-offering of a sheaf of barley.[467] What is this "wave-offering"? If it refers simply to the fact that the priest has to wave it aloft, what difference does it make[468] to us whether he waves it [aloft] or holds it low? But it is in actual fact essential to raise it on high.[469] And this is the force of the word terumah. And even though we explain [that terumah should be] one-fiftieth part, and so it is, yet this tenufah signifies "raising."[470] One of wisdom's secrets is here. Alas, holy and pious ones, wielders of the lance, that you did not serve Rav Shemaiah the Pious, for if you had done so you would have known the meaning of tenufah, the meaning of "wheat," the meaning of "barley."

The tenufah, about which I have spoken, may be regarded as tenu peh,[471] and its secret significance is in "Give glory to the Lord, your God" (Jeremiah 13: 16), for the celestial mouth is the glory that we should give to the Holy One, blessed be He.[472] Therefore, we must raise it aloft to show that the "mouth" that we are giving belongs to Him, for the supreme King receives praise only when Israel prepare this glory, and give glory to the King. So this tenufah is "give glory," and the verse with which I began really refers to the act of raising something.

"It shall be that when you eat of the bread of the land . . ." Is this bread really barley? No, it is not. But we bring barley as an offering

---

[466] [Terumah signifies, literally, something raised.]

[467] Actually the verse refers to the special portion of bread, or dough-offering. But it is interpreted here in connection with the "wave-sheaf," in order to explain that the wave-offering (tenufah) was actually something raised (terumah). See Leviticus 23: 17, "You shall bring out from your homes wave-loaves."

[468] The act of waving has already been described in a previous verse (Leviticus 23: 11, "And he shall wave the sheaf before the Lord"); so there is logically no need to mention the precise word, "wave-offering" (tenufah), again here.

[469] Tenufah indicates the Shekhinah, whom one must raise aloft, and she is also called terumah.

[470] See Mishnah Terumoth 4: 3. This explanation is correct, but nevertheless it also has the meaning of "being lifted up," and in this sense tenufah and terumah are one and the same.

[471] [Literally "give mouth," the Hebrew letters of which also form tenufah.]

[472] The "mouth," and the "glory" are symbols of the Shekhinah, which must be united with the Holy One, blessed be He, i.e., Tiferet.

because barley is the first crop that the earth produces. Barley (se'orah) is "the measure of he" (shiur he),[473] a known level in the measure of he. The word ḥittah (wheat) has a dagesh in the middle,[474] [to show] that the "other side" has no share of sin there. Ḥittah is the daughter[475] who endears herself to her father so that he fulfills her desire. And what is ḥittah? It contains all the twenty-two letters [of the alphabet].[476]

Rabbi Eleazar said: Although we ought to listen, we must say something here, and draw the bow.

The child said: The shield is ready to meet the arrow.

Rabbi Eleazar said: It is true that we call her "ḥittah," but we see that the letters ḥet and ṭet do not occur among the tribes,[477] but here we do have both ḥet and ṭet, and yet we call her "ḥittah."

That is indeed true, said the child, because ḥet (sin) lies very close to her.[478] The tribes do not contain these letters, because they come from the side of holiness on high, but the letters do remain close to her. But if you want to draw out your sword, you could ask: Why did the daughter take those letters? You would know the answer to this if you understood the sin of Adam, which, they said, involved wheat.[479] When this tree is victorious, the good side seizes "the other side" completely, and subjugates it. The earliest companions interpreted this word, and began at some distance [from the real meaning]: simply "wheat."[480] The later ones came and said that it was real wheat.[481] Then Isaiah came to interpret it, as it is written, "[Keep far] from ruin (meḥittah), for it shall not come near you" (Isaiah 54: 14).[482] This is why there is a dagesh in the middle so that it should not be read ḥata'ah (sin), for were it not for the dagesh it would be ḥata'ah. This change from ṭet to tav[483] spells destruction for "the other side." This is the explanation of the matter.

You, companions, who did not serve Rav Shemaiah the Pious, say

---

[473] The word se'orah is divided to make this phrase. The letter he is the Shekhinah, and shiur he alludes to the nature of the Shekhinah.

[474] The dagesh (or dot) demonstrates that one should not pronounce the word "ḥata'ah" (sin). So it does not belong to the domain of sin.   [475] The Shekhinah.

[476] Ḥittah in gematria equals 22. The Shekhinah comprises all the divine powers.

[477] The letters ḥet and ṭet [which together form the Hebrew word for sin] do not occur in the names of any of Jacob's sons.

[478] The "other side" is close to the Shekhinah, and lies in wait for her.

[479] Adam separated the Shekhinah from her "husband," and subjugated her to "the other side." This event was alluded to by the rabbis when they said that the tree from which Adam ate was "wheat" (ḥittah), which gave the domain of sin (ḥet) power over her. See B.T. Berakhot 40a.

[480] They did not reveal its secret meaning.   [481] The Shekhinah.

[482] He interpreted that this ḥittah, when it is victorious, brings ruin (meḥittah) upon the "other side."

[483] [The t sound in ḥittah is the Hebrew letter ṭet, while the t in meḥittah is the Hebrew letter tav.]

that "the other side" has no share in the five species of corn.[484] But it is not so, for "the other side" has a share in everything that rots in the ground. What share does he have? The chaff that the wind blows away, as it is written, "Not so the wicked, for they are like the chaff that the wind blows away" (Psalm 1: 4). This wind is the holy spirit, as it is written "For the wind passes over it, and it is gone . . ." (Psalm 103: 16), for the holy spirit scatters it to all the corners of the world, so that it can no longer be found. So much for the female [of "the other side"]. But what of the male? This is straw. Chaff and straw go together, and that is why they are exempted from being tithed, for there is no part of sanctity in them. The letter *he* is pure corn, without straw of chaff. The letters *het* and *tet* are male and female, the straw and the chaff, and the letter *he* is pure corn. And so the perfect species of tree is *hittah*,[485] and the tree involved in Adam's sin was *hittah*, for everything is comprised in the word *hittah*, and in its secret meaning.

Rabbi Eleazar was astonished, and the companions were astonished.

Rabbi Eleazar said: It is really so.

The child said: This is the real meaning of the verse with which we began, for barley was the first crop to come into the world, and it was intended to be food for the beast,[486] and this is the hidden meaning of the thousand hills that produce food every day for it to eat. This is called "bread of *terumah*,"[487] the food of *terumah*,[488] and it is offered at night,[489] for it is written, "And when the sun is down he shall be clean; and afterward he may eat of the holy things, because it is his bread" (Leviticus 22: 7). "Of the holy things"—this is *terumah*. "*Of* the holy things," and not holy things without qualification; for something that is unqualifiedly holy is not called *terumah*, since we have learned (Mishnah *Hagigah* 3: 1) that "greater stringency applies to holy things than to *terumah*." The Holy Land[490] was under the authority of the Holy One, blessed be He, and no alien authority[491] had access there. How could the Holy Land be examined [to see] if she had remained faithful, and was not united with any alien authority? By bringing an offering of barley, on the pattern of the suspected adulteress.[492]

[484] Wheat, barley, spelt, goatgrass, and oats. It is from these five species that one could set aside the *hallah*, or dough-offering [see Mishnah *Hallah* 1: 1.] Hence their degree of sanctity was considerable, and "the other side" could have no share in it.

[485] [Which consists of the three letters *het*, *tet*, and *he*.]

[486] An allusion to the *Shekhinah*, which is fire consuming fire, and is nourished by companies of angels, which die and are renewed every day, and these latter are the "thousand hills." See *Vayikra Rabbah*, chap. 22 (end), and Zohar I, 18b.

[487] This phrase does not occur in the Bible.

[488] *Terumah* [lit., an offering that is raised] is the *Shekhinah*.

[489] When the *Shekhinah* rules.   [490] The *Shekhinah*.   [491] "The other side."

[492] When a woman is suspected of adultery without cause, her chastity is investigated through the bringing of an offering of barley [Numbers 5: 15]. In the same way, Israel demonstrates the purity of the *Shekhinah* by bringing an offering of a barley-sheaf.

Rabbi Abba said: The blade of the sword is certainly turned against you.

I hold a shield and a buckler, said the child, to protect myself from it.

Rabbi Abba said: Is there no alien authority in the Holy Land, and has it no access there? In that case where do the chaff and the straw come from?

The child began by quoting: "And God created man in His own image . . ." (Genesis 1: 27), and it is written, "And God said to them: Be fruitful and multiply" (ibid., 1: 28). Was the procreation of children dependent on the serpent's cohabitation with Eve?[493] Or was it dependent on the sin of Israel with the Golden Calf?[494] In reality, even if the serpent had not cohabited with Eve, Adam would have begotten children, for as soon as he was created it was decreed that they should "be fruitful and multiply, and replenish the earth." And the progeny would all have been born in purity,[495] without any evil substance. Similarly, the Holy Land, before the alien authority entered, produced chaff and straw that did not come from that side,[496] and outside the land are to be found the chaff and straw of "the other side," which imitates holiness, as a monkey apes human beings.

Rabbi Eleazar and the companions came and kissed him.

It seems to me, the child said, that by these weapons of war I have earned this meal.

Indeed, you have, said Rabbi Eleazar, for you hold all the weapons in your hand, and they are all triumphant in your hand.

They came and kissed him, as they had at the beginning.

He resumed and said: "And in the vine were three branches . . ." (Genesis 40: 10). This is the vision of the mystery, but after that comes his own vision,[497] as it is written, "and Pharaoh's cup was in my hand" (ibid., 11). Now, the vision of the mystery was for Joseph's sake, in order to bring him a message that Joseph might hear and understand. We have learned that there are seven firmaments,[498] and they are seven palaces, and they are both six[499] and five,[500] and they all originate from

---

[493] The evil inclination gained a hold over Adam because of the evil substance [often regarded as sensuality or lasciviousness] with which the serpent infected Eve. Since children are formed with the aid of the evil inclination, it follows that if Adam and Eve had not sinned they would not have had children.

[494] When Israel assembled at the foot of Mt. Sinai, the evil substance derived from the serpent was removed, and until their sin with the Golden Calf they were just like Adam before he sinned. [See B.T. Shabbat 146a.]

[495] Without the aid of the evil inclination. The procreation that took place with the aid of the evil inclination was the result of Adam's sin.

[496] In the land of Israel even chaff and straw originate from the side of holiness.

[497] I.e., that of the chief butler.   [498] Seven sefirot from Hesed to Malkhut.

[499] If Malkhut is omitted.

[500] If Yesod is also omitted, by being considered together as one with Tiferet.

the wine[501] of the Holy, Ancient One, on high. Jacob brought that wine from afar,[502] and squeezed it out from the grapes of the vine.[503] Then Jacob brought the wine, which was suited to him, and rejoiced and drank, as it is written, "and he brought him wine, and he drank" (Genesis 27: 25). Here the upper and the lower are included together,[504] and so Scripture makes a special point of providing the word with two accents,[505] to indicate two movements, downward and upward. Enoch Metatron said that "he brought him wine" means that he put water in the wine,[506] for if water had not been added he would not have had the strength to drink it, and Enoch Metatron spoke wisely. And so the word *lo* has two accents, because it extends to both extremes.[507] This wine went from one level to the other,[508] and they all tasted it, until Joseph the righteous[509] also tasted it, for he is the faithful beloved, and this is the meaning of "like the best wine that glides down smoothly for my beloved" (Song of Songs 7: 10). What does "like the best wine" mean? It means that Jacob came and put water in it. This is "the best wine." And it was as Enoch Metatron said.

Rabbi Eleazar was astonished, and Rabbi Abba was astonished. They said: This wine belongs to you. You have conquered, holy angel, by means of the holy spirit.

He said to them: This vine now expects to produce fruit. "The vine" [mentioned above] is the vine that is known as sacred, for there is another vine,[510] called "a strange vine," and its grapes are not good grapes, but hard; they seize the heart and bite like a dog. These grapes are called "the degenerate plant of a strange vine" (Jeremiah 2: 21). But the first has the definite article, the celebrated vine tasted by all the holy ones, the wine of the Ancient One, good wine, the wine that Jacob mixed with water, so that whoever knew how to taste wine tasted it, and it was good for the palate. This vine, on the arrival of the wine,[511] puts forth three branches,[512] and these are the three images of the patriarchs by

[501] The influence that proceeds downward by emanation from the supreme source.

[502] From the upper *sefirot*.

[503] From the lower *sefirot*, which brings down the influence to *Malkhut*, which is called *gefen* (vine).

[504] Jacob and Isaac symbolize *Tiferet* and *Gevurah*, and they are also the "fathers" of the lower world.

[505] The word *lo* (him) in the Hebrew text has a double accent (*merka kefulah*), which is taken to indicate a double extension of influence, upward and downward. [I have paraphrased the Zohar text here.]

[506] Water is *Hesed*, and wine is *Din*. The influence of *Din* (Judgment) needs to be tempered with *Hesed* (Mercy).

[507] Toward *Hesed* and *Din*.   [508] From one *sefirah* to the other.   [509] *Yesod*.

[510] *Lilith*, who is the equivalent, on the "other side," of the *Shekhinah*.

[511] The influence from above.

[512] The three *sefirot*, *Hesed*, *Gevurah*, and *Tiferet*, cause the *Shekhinah* to put forth three tendrils, corresponding to themselves, and they stand for the three patriarchs.

whom it is sanctified. There is no sanctification without wine, and no blessing without wine, wherever rejoicing takes place.[513]

"And it was as if she were budding" (Genesis 40: 10),[514] that is, like a bride who adorns herself, and enters in love, in the joy of the wine that has been mixed with water. Straightaway "her blossom rises"; she raises up her love for her beloved, and begins to sing, and to enter in love. And then the tender grapes begin to fill out and ripen, and they become full of the good, old wine, the wine that Jacob had mixed with water. Therefore, when you say grace over a cup of wine, and you come to the words "for the land,"[515] you should put some water in it, for you should not say the blessing "Have mercy on Israel, Your people" except over wine that is mixed with water, for otherwise who would have the strength to drink it? This vision was intended for Joseph, since the matter depends on him.[516] Enoch Metatron said that "the three branches" represented the three patriarchs. But it has four![517] This is the meaning of "it was as if she were budding (foraḥat)."[518] At the moment she rose and spread her wings to fly, "her blossom" rose—and this was the fourth that remained, that rose with her and did not become separated from her. This is the significance of "And He rode upon a cherub and flew" (2 Samuel 22: 11), which means "when he flew." Similarly ke-foraḥat means "when she flew."[519] Enoch Metatron spoke wisely, and it was as he said.

Rabbi Eleazar was astonished, and Rabbi Abba was astonished. They said: Holy angel, messenger from on high, behold, the wine belongs to you, and you have conquered through the mystery of the holy spirit.

All the companions came and kissed him. Rabbi Eleazar said: Blessed is the Merciful One who sent me here.

The child said: Companions, bread and wine[520] are the mainstay of the meal. All the other foods are subsidiary to them. And it is the Torah that makes them prosper, and they belong to her. And now the Torah implores you with love, saying "Come, eat of my bread, and drink of the wine which I have mingled" (Proverbs 9: 5). Now, since the Torah invites you and begs you to do this, you should comply with her wishes.

They said: This is certainly true.

---

[513] I.e., at marriages and other joyful occasions where wine is ritually drunk.

[514] [A continuation of the verse quoted at the head of this section. The subject is "the vine," which is feminine in gender. Traditional translations are somewhat different.]

[515] This blessing concerns the Shekhinah (the vine), who is the celestial "earth."

[516] Joseph represents Yesod, which is the origin of the joy of love.

[517] Including the sefirah of Joseph.   [518] [Foraḥat also means "flying."]

[519] [The Hebrew particle ke usually means "like, as." Here it is taken to mean "as" in the sense of "when, while."]

[520] He refers here to the two expositions—of the bread of terumah, and of the wine.

They sat down, and ate, and rejoiced with him. When they had eaten, they remained at table.

He began by quoting: "And Moab said to the elders of Midian . . ." (Numbers 22: 4). It is not written that the elders of Moab spoke to the elders of Midian, but "And Moab said." The younger ones took advice from the elders,[521] and the elders complied with their request and gave them advice. What advice did they give them? Evil advice they took upon themselves. They said to Moab, "We have reared an evil growth in our midst. And who is this? Moses, their teacher; all because of a certain priest,[522] who dwelt among us, who nursed him, and brought him up in his house, and gave him his daughter in marriage. Furthermore, he gave him money, and sent him to Egypt to destroy the land, and he followed him together with his whole household. If we can uproot their teacher from the world, his whole people will be uprooted from the world." And all the wicked counsel concerning the event at Peor[523] emanated from Midian.

Come and see how everything emanated from Midian, how all their advice was aimed at Moses. It was on their advice that they hired Balaam. When they saw that Balaam could not prevail [over Israel] they decided on another evil plan, and prostituted their wives and their daughters more than Moab did, for of the Midianite women it is written, "These were for the children of Israel . . ." (Numbers 31: 16). So everything emanated from Midian. They advised their prince to prostitute his daughter, intending to catch Moses in their net. They adorned her with all kinds of charms, so that their leader might be taken, but the Holy One, blessed be He, "turns wise men backward" (Isaiah 44: 25). They expected that the leader would be taken in their net, but they did not understand. They saw, but they did not see. They saw the leader of the people fall with her, and several thousand others [of Israel], and they thought that it was Moses. They set her loose against Moses, and instructed her not to lie with anyone else. She asked them how she was to recognise him. They said, "The man before whom you see everyone standing—with him you shall lie and with no one else." When Zimri ben Salu appeared, twenty-four thousand people from the tribe of Simeon rose before him, because he was their chief. And she thought that he was Moses, and lay with him. And when all the other [Simeonites] saw this, they did what they did, and the event that happened came to pass.[524]

Everything emanated from Midian, in several ways. And for this reason the Midianites were punished. The Holy One, blessed be He, said

[521] [The younger Moabites asked advice from the elder Midianites.]
[522] Jethro [the Midianite priest, Moses' father-in-law].
[523] [See Numbers 23: 28; 25: 3 and 18.]
[524] [For the whole episode, see Numbers 25: 6–15.]

to Moses, "Avenge the children of Israel on the Midianites" (Numbers 31: 2). It is right and fitting that you should do so. But Moab I shall leave until two jewels[525] emerge from them. It will be David, the son of Jesse, who will take vengeance upon Moab, and he will wash out the pot that is full of the filth of Peor. This is the meaning of "Moab is my washpot" (Psalm 60: 1), to be sure. Before those two jewels emerged they were not punished, but when they had emerged David came and washed their filth out of the pot. So all of them were punished: Midian in the days of Moses, Moab in the days of David.

Come and see how, despite all this, the wicked Midianites did not cease their evil practices. Generations later, when they saw that Joshua had died, together with all the elders that deserved to have miracles performed at their behest, they said, "Now the time is ripe for us." What did they do? They went to Amalek, and said, "You should remember what you suffered at the hands of the Israelites, and of Moses their teacher, and Joshua his disciple—how they destroyed you from the face of the earth. Now the time has come when they have no one to protect them, whereas we shall be with you"—as it is written, "the Midianites came up, and the Amalekites, and the children of the east . . ." (Judges 6: 3), "and because of Midian the children of Israel made dens for themselves" (ibid 6: 2). No other people in the world has done as much evil as Midian. Or you could say "as Amalek" because of the zeal for the covenant, for they threatened the covenant.[526] And so the Holy One, blessed be He, directed His eternal passion against them that will never be forgotten.

They said: This is true, without any doubt.

He began by quoting: "And the Lord said to me: Be not at enmity with Moab . . ." (Deuteronomy 2: 9). "And the Lord said to me"—did we not know before that the Holy One, blessed be He, spoke with Moses, and not with anyone else? Why do we need the phrase "to me"? The Holy One, blessed be He, prohibited only Moses from harming Moab, not anyone else. He did not prohibit David. And so we have "to me." "Be not at enmity with Moab"—even in the slightest regard, for someone will be descended from them to wreak vengeance on them on behalf of Israel, namely, David, a descendant of Ruth, the Moabitess. "Neither contend with them in battle" (ibid.)—a prohibition given to Moses, but to no one else. Now you might say that the prohibition could not have extended to Joshua, and to the elders who outlived Moses. But such is not the case, for they were all members of Moses' court, and what was forbidden to Moses was forbidden to them also. Furthermore, the

[525] Ruth and Na'amah.

[526] Midian, in that they prostituted their wives, and the Amalekites in that they cut off the membra of the Israelites and threw them up in the air (*Tanḥuma*, ed. Buber, *Ki teze*, p. 41).

two beautiful jewels had not yet appeared. Ruth did not appear until the time of the judges, and she was the daughter of Eglon, King of Moab. When Eglon died by the hand of Ehud, they appointed another king. His daughter was orphaned, and she was brought up in an orphanage in the fields of Moab. Elimelech came and married her to his son. You might wonder whether Elimelech converted her there. No, he did not, but she learned all the ways of a Jewish household, the food and the drink, before she was converted. It was only afterward, when she went with Naomi, that she said "Your people shall be my people, and your God my God" (Ruth 1: 16).

Na'amah appeared among the Ammonites in the days of David. Then the holy spirit rested upon David. It said to him, "David, when I measured the whole world, and drew lots, Israel became 'the line (*hevel*) of His inheritance' " (Deuteronomy 32: 9).[527] Now I remember what Moab did to "the line of His inheritance." What is written concerning Moab? "He measured them with the line (*hevel*)" (2 Samuel 8: 2),[528]—with the very line of the inheritance of the Lord.[529] The line took hold of all those who were descended from them. It is written, "one full line" (ibid.). What was the "one full line"? That which is described in "the whole earth is full of His glory"[530] (Isaiah 6: 3). And he said "This one for life, and this one for death." And the line took hold of all those that had to be put to death. Therefore he took the line and stretched out the line, on account of what they had done to the line of the inheritance of the Lord. As for Midian, all their descendants were destroyed by Gideon, who did not preserve alive any of those who had afflicted Israel, either through the advice they gave or by some other means. The Holy One, blessed be He, retains His hatred for all those who harm Israel, and wreaks vengeance on them. But if the world is to gain some good from them in the future, He delays His anger until that particular good has come to the world. He then seeks justice and vengeance from them.

Rabbi Eleazar said: It is certainly true, and this is the explanation of the matter.

The child said: From now on, companions, prepare your own weapons of war, and draw up your battle line.

Rabbi Eleazar began by quoting: "Bless the Lord, you angels of His, mighty in strength [that fulfill His word, listening to the voice of His

---

[527] [The usual translation is "lot of His inheritance." But the rendering of *hevel* as "line" is necessary here to the context.]

[528] The complete verse reads "And [David] smote Moab, and measured them with the line, making them lie down on the ground. And he measured two lines to put to death, and one full line to keep alive."

[529] The *Shekhinah*, which is the celestial Assembly of Israel, is also called "the line (or lot) of the inheritance of the Lord," and it was through the power of the *Shekhinah* that David punished Moab.   [530] "His glory" is the *Shekhinah*.

word]" (Psalm 103: 20). King David, intending to bless the Holy One, blessed be He, summons the hosts of heaven, that is, the stars and the planets, and the other hosts, and joins his soul to them, in order to bless the Holy One, Blessed be He. This is the meaning of "Bless the Lord, all works of His, in all places of His dominion; bless the Lord, O my soul" (ibid., 22)—he concludes all the blessings with a reference to his own soul. He summons the angels on high to bless Him, as it is written "Bless the Lord, you angels of His. . . ." Before Israel came on the scene the angels on high would begin and finish the work. But when Israel came and stood at Mount Sinai and said "We will do, and we will listen" (Exodus 24: 7) they took up the work from the ministering angels, and were comprised within "His word."[531] Thenceforth, there was work in the land of Israel on one side, and among the holy angels on the other, and Israel would complete the work and bring it to perfection. Therefore, we have first "you mighty in strength that fulfill His word," and then we have "listening."[532] How blessed are Israel that take up the work from them, and through whom the work is established!

The child said: Protect yourself, and prosper with your weapons. But is this the only praiseworthy thing that Israel took?

This is the only praiseworthy thing that I have discovered, he replied.

The child said: Since your sword does not prosper—or possibly because you do not wield it properly—leave the sword to him who knows how to fight. The most praiseworthy thing, which was transmitted to the ministering angels only in association with Israel, was sanctification (*kiddush*). Blessing was transmitted to the angels on high separately, just as it was transmitted to Israel, but sanctification was not transmitted to them separately, but only in association with Israel, for they do not pronounce sanctification without Israel. You might object, and quote "And one called to the other, and he said: [Holy, holy, holy is the Lord of Hosts]" (Isaiah 6: 3). But when do they do this? Only when Israel pronounce sanctification below. As long as Israel do not pronounce sanctification below, they do not sanctify [above], because sanctification ascends from three worlds, and not from two.[533] So we have "And one called"—one—"to the other"—two—"and he said"— three. There are three worlds, and three corresponding sanctifications. And so this is a praiseworthy thing for Israel in that they have received the power to sanctify below, on their own.

Rabbi Eleazar said: This is very true. And we have already explained these matters. We have furthermore deduced that three sanctifications were transmitted to Israel below from the verse "Sanctify yourselves,

---

[531] They were then called those "that fulfill His word."

[532] [Parallel to "we will do, and we will listen"—doing precedes listening.]

[533] From the lower world, the home of Israel, from the world of the angels, and from the world of the Chariot.

and be holy, for I, the Lord, am holy" (Leviticus 11: 44).[534] "Sanctify yourselves"—one—"and be holy"—two—"for I, the Lord, am holy"—three. Here sanctification was transmitted to them.

He said: Correct, but you did not remember your lance, until I took it from your back, and put it into your hand. Remember from now on the lance that is in your hand. Return now to the place where you left off.

Rabbi Eleazar said: The matters we are dealing with concern blessing. What does "bless" mean?[535] Extend the blessings from the place whence the blessings originate until they form a lake,[536] through the extension of the outpouring. And because of the outpouring of the water into this lake, the water begins to swarm at once with fish of various kinds. What is this extension? It is "the Lord," the extension of the light that shines from the illuminating mirror,[537] extending from top to bottom. This is for the angels on high, who live in the lofty home of the celestial abode. To them it is said "Bless the Lord." But we, who dwell below, say "Bless (*et*) the Lord" (Psalm 134: 1–2), for we must draw down this *et*[538] upon us, since through it we may enter into the presence of the King, and look upon His face. And so David said, "I shall look upon Your face in righteousness" (Psalm 17: 15). Actually, by means of righteousness.[539] So the opening of prayer is "Bless (*et*) the Lord",[540] so that we might draw down upon our heads this *et*. And when we draw down this *et*, we must pray, and praise [God]. Therefore, it is forbidden for you to bless someone until you have prayed, and drawn down upon his head this *et*. For if you bless a man before this, you draw down *bamah* (high place)[541] upon his head instead of this *et*. Therefore, to the ministering angels it is said "Bless the Lord," but of us it is said "Bless the Lord" with an additional *et*.

The child said: I am now certain that your weapons of war are good. Remember them. Do not forget them. The power of the man who prepares for war is in the lance and sword. But what is the significance of "you who are mighty in strength, that fulfill His word, listening to the voice of His word"?

---

[534] This is a misquotation. "The Lord" does not appear in the original. But see Leviticus 20: 7.   [535] [In Psalm 103: 20, quoted above.]

[536] The influence that pours out from the upper *sefirot* forms a lake in the lowest *sefirah*, and from this the lower worlds are nourished. [There is a play on words here between *berakhah* (blessing) and *berekhah* (lake).]   [537] *Tiferet.*

[538] [Unlike verse 20 in Psalm 103, the expression "Bless the Lord" here contains the Hebrew particle *et*, which is merely the sign of a following accusative.] This *et* is joined, but subsidiary, to the name of God ("the Lord"), and serves to indicate the *Shekhinah.*

[539] "Righteousness" (*zedek*) is also a name for the *Shekhinah*, which is the attribute of Judgment.   [540] [The traditional Jewish summons to prayer.]

[541] The *bamah* (high place) is a place of idolatrous worship, and signifies here "the other side." Whoever blesses a man (in greeting) before he has sanctified himself through prayer, draws down upon his fellow the power of uncleanness.

Rabbi Eleazar replied: I have already said.

The child said: I am now certain that the power of your arm has weakened. This is not the time to wait, but to put one stone after the other in the sling, as it is said, "with a sling and with a stone" (1 Samuel 17: 50)—with speed, one after the other.

Rabbi Eleazar rejoiced, and Rabbi Abba and the companions rejoiced.

The child began by quoting: "I am black but comely, daughters of Jerusalem [as the tents of Kedar, as the curtains of Solomon]. Do not look upon me that I am swarthy, [that the sun has tanned me] . . ." (Song of Songs 1: 5–6). These words have already been explained. When [the *Shekhinah*] experiences great love for her beloved, she makes herself extremely small, because of the thrust of love that she cannot bear, until nothing can be seen of her but the tiniest point, which is the letter *yod*. She then envelops herself straightaway with all her hosts and her companies, and she says "I am black," because there is no white at all inside this letter, as there is with the other letters. This is the meaning of "I am black", namely "I have no room to bring you in under my wings." "As the tents of Kedar"; we have learned that this stands for the letter *yod*, which contains no white.[542] "As the curtains of Solomon"— this is the letter *vav*.[543] Therefore "Do not look upon me" means "Do not look at me at all, because I am a tiny point." What do the powerful warriors, all her hosts, do? They roar[544] like mighty lions, as it is said, "The young lions roar after their prey" (Psalm 104: 21). And because of these loud and mighty roars that the powerful warriors give vent to, like lions, the beloved hears in the realms above, and knows that his loved one is as deeply in love as he, so much so that nothing of her image or her beauty can be seen. Then, guided by the roaring voices of her powerful warriors, her much beloved leaves his palace with many gifts and many offerings, with perfumes and spices, and comes to her, and finds her black and tiny, with no image or beauty at all. He draws near to her, embraces her and kisses her, until she is gradually aroused by the perfumes and spices, and in the joy of her beloved by her side she is restored, and with her adornments, her image, and her beauty, she becomes the letter *he*, as at the beginning.[545] And this is what the mighty warriors have done for her: they have restored her to her image and her

[542] *Kedar* is derived from a Hebrew root meaning "black."

[543] Solomon is the King, *Tiferet*, symbolized by the letter *vav*, and when she is joined in sexual union with him she is "comely" (*na'avah*). [The word *vav* also means "hook", and it is used frequently in connection with the hanging of the curtains in the tabernacle. See Exodus 26: 32, etc.]

[544] They seek food and the outpouring of influence from her because she has departed from them.

[545] When she receives influence and transmits it downward, she is considered to be the last letter, *he*, in the divine tetragrammaton (*yod, he, vav, he*).

beauty. Their might and power have caused this. And of this it is written "The mighty in strength who fulfill His word"—"fulfill His word" without a doubt, for they repair this "word,"[546] and restore it to its original image. When she has been restored and rendered beautiful in her image, as at the beginning, they and all the remaining hosts stand, ready to listen to what she says, and she stands like a king among his troops. This is the undoubted meaning of "they who fulfill His word." There is a parallel to this in the world below, for when the wicked appear she envelops herself and makes herself small, until only a single point can be seen of her whole image. But when "the mighty in strength" and the truly righteous arrive, they, as it were, make this "word", and she gradually begins to shine, and is restored to her image and her beauty: the letter *he*, as at the beginning.

The companions came and kissed him. Rabbi Eleazar said: Even if the prophet Ezekiel had said this, it would have been a wonderful thing to hear.

Rabbi Eleazar took him and kissed him, as at the first.

The child said: Let me say grace.

They said: You are blessed, and it is right for you to pronounce the blessing.

He said: How holy you are, and how many blessings are prepared for you by the holy mother, since you have not prevented me from saying the blessing.

He began by quoting: "He that withholds corn, the people shall curse him. But blessing shall be upon the head of him that sells it" (Proverbs 11: 26). This verse is to be understood literally. But we have learned[547] that everyone is obliged to say the blessing of grace after meals, and if a man does not know how, then his wife or his children shall say the blessing for him. But a curse shall come upon the man who is so ignorant of the blessing that he needs his wife or his children to say the blessing for him. And if he does know, then he should train his son and hand him the cup for grace. And whoever stops him from being trained, "the people shall curse him"; "he withholds a son"[548] from blessing the Holy One, blessed be He, and from being trained in the commandments. In the phrase "the people shall curse him," we have a singular subject and a plural verb, where we might have expected both to be either in the singular or in the plural.[549] *Le'om* (people) is singular as in "and the one people shall be stronger than the other people" (Genesis 25: 23). How shall we understand this? *Le'om* is written defectively,[550] so that we can

546   The *Shekhinah*. [The Hebrew word for "fulfill" here also means "do, make, render."]   547   [See B.T. *Berakhot* 20b.]
548   [The Hebrew word for "corn" here (*bar*) is identical with the Aramaic word for "son."]
549   [I have given the general sense rather than a literal translation of this sentence.]
550   In our texts it is *not* written defectively.

interpret it as "to the holy mother (la-em)[551] shall they curse him," namely, this man who prevents his son from blessing the Holy One, blessed be He.

I am my mother's only son. Give me the cup, and I shall bless the holy King, who has summoned to my mother's house men of valor, before whom I have spoken powerful words, and over whom I have gained a victory. Therefore I shall pronounce the blessing. But before this, let the verse with which we began be properly explained. "He that withholds corn (bar), the people shall curse him"—whoever withholds his son (bar), as I have explained, they shall curse him to the mother, as it is said, "And the son of the Israelite woman cursed the name" (Leviticus 24: 11). That is, they specify him[552] to the mother in that they detail his sins to the holy mother. "But blessing shall be upon the head of him that sells it"—upon the man who trains his son to bless the Holy One, blessed be He, and brings him up in the commandments of the Torah. But the mystical meaning[553] of this is written in the mystery of the celestial realm: "What is his name, and what is his son's name, if you know?" (Proverbs 30: 4)—the customary designation,[554] that is, "The Lord of hosts is His name" (Isaiah 47: 4), and "his son's name" is Israel,[555] as it is written "Israel is My son, My firstborn" (Exodus 4: 22). Therefore all the keys of faith depend on Israel, and Israel exults in [this] and says "The Lord said to me: You are My son" (Psalm 2: 7). And so it is, to be sure, for the father and mother[556] have adorned him and blessed him with many blessings, and spoken and commanded all: Kiss the son (Psalm 2: 12), that is, kiss the hand of this son, indicating that he had been given dominion over all, so that all should serve him. "Lest he be angry" (ibid.)—for they had adorned him with justice and mercy;[557] justice for him who deserved justice, and mercy for him who deserved mercy. All the blessings from above and below were accorded this son, and became crowns for him, and whoever withholds blessings from this son, his sins are made explicit before the holy mother, before the real mother.[558] "But blessing shall be upon the head of him who sells it." Whoever says grace and invites whoever should be invited with the cup

---

[551] Malkhut, Shekhinah.

[552] [Leviticus 24: 11 is taken to mean that the son of the Israelite woman blasphemed by pronouncing the ineffable Name of God. See Targum Onkelos of this verse, and Rashi ad loc., and B.T. Sanhedrin 56a. In the same way, Proverbs 11: 26 is taken to mean that the people "pronounce" the man's sins before the "mother."]

[553] Here a more mystical interpretation is given to the verse. According to this the son is Tiferet and the mother is Binah, the upper Shekhinah.

[554] Here the name "Lord of Hosts" is assigned, exceptionally, to Binah. [See Zohar II, 79a, where "His name" is assigned to Hokhmah.]

[555] Tiferet, celestial Israel.   [556] Hokhmah and Binah.

[557] Tiferet is essentially Mercy, but Judgment is also intermingled with it.

[558] Binah.

of blessing [to say grace], shatters, and thereby humiliates, "the other side," while the side of holiness moves into the ascendant. This is the meaning of "But blessing shall be upon the head of him who shatters."[559] Just as he rises and blesses the Holy One, blessed be He, and causes "the other side" to be broken, so the Holy One, blessed be He, extends blessings upon him from above, and the power[560] called "blessing" rests upon his head. So now, friends, let us say grace.

They gave him the cup for the blessing, and he said grace, and all the companions were joyful, for since the time of Rabbi Eleazar's wedding they had not experienced such joy as on the day when they sat there. First they blessed him with great gladness and with a willing heart.

The child said: You should not depart without words of Torah, for so we have been taught.[561]

He began by quoting: "And the Lord went before them by day in a pillar of cloud [and by night in a pillar of fire, to give light to them]" (Exodus 13: 21). The cantillation sign on "And the Lord" is written above the line. Why? How beautiful and gracious the bride was, who until that time had been enslaved in exile, and who now walked with her head erect in joy, among her retinues, and with "the Lord," which has the accent above.[562] "Went before them by day." Up to this time they did not know whether this bride was going before them or not, because there is a disjunctive accent on "And the Lord." But she was there, although it was the supernal elder[563] who went before them, the master of the house, summoned[564] by the Holy One, blessed be He. And who was he? Abraham, as it is written "By day the Lord will command His lovingkindness" (Psalm 42: 9), and it is also written "If My covenant be not with day and night" (Jeremiah 33: 25),[565] the day that comprises all days,[566] the day that gives light to the other days, the day of all other days, to be sure. And so it is called yomam and not yom. Hence, "their day went before them."[567] He went before them in the day, and the bride went at night, as it is written "and by night in a pillar of fire, to give light to them." This is the bride; each of them acted as was fitting. And as for

---

[559] [Mashbir means both "selling corn" and "shattering."]

[560] The Shekhinah.   [561] B.T. Berakhot 31a.

[562] "And the Lord" represents the Shekhinah when in union with Tiferet, and so she would be erect and joyful.

[563] Ḥesed, symbolized by Abraham, the first of the six sefirot that together form the world of the male, the master of the house.   [564] Appointed for this particular task.

[565] The first verse shows that yomam (by day) is Ḥesed (lovingkindness, mercy), and the second verse implies that he is master of the house, who is united with the female (night) by means of the covenant (of circumcision).

[566] Ḥesed represents the first of the six days of creation, which includes all subsequent days. In the sefirotic realm, Ḥesed gives light to the six sefirot beneath it.

[567] [Yomam, usually rendered "by day," can also also mean "their day," i.e., the day belonging to all days, Ḥesed. And it can then be taken as the subject of the verb.]

you, my friends, may they go before you always "their day and their night."

They kissed him and blessed him as at the beginning, and then they departed.

They came to Rabbi Simeon and told him what had happened. He was astonished, and said: How worthy he is. But he will not make a name for himself. When a tiny splint flames, it flares for a moment and is then extinguished. And I have already explained the origin of this light.[568]

He began by quoting: "Mighty in the earth shall be his seed: the generation of the upright shall be blessed" (Psalm 112: 2). When a man is mighty in the earth,[569] mighty in Torah, exercising power over his evil inclination, then he is really "mighty in the earth." His light ascends and great influence extends from it, and then "the generation of the upright shall be blessed." It is actually written [defectively]—"he shall bless."

Rabbi Abba said: We have known children who have uttered the most exalted words, and who have later become leaders in the world.

He said to him: With a child who says a word or two from time to time, without full understanding, we can be assured that he will be worthy enough to teach Torah in Israel. But with this child, whose light is stable, and who has perfect understanding, it is different. Furthermore, the Holy One, blessed be He, yearns to smell the scent of this apple—blessed is his portion! Blessed are you righteous, of whom it is written "And the remnant that is escaped of the house of Judah shall again take root downward, and bear fruit upward" (2 Kings 19: 30). "Take root downward"—like his father, who has departed from the world, and takes root downward in the academy of the firmament, and bears fruit upward in the academy on high.[570] How good are both the roots and the fruit! It is not for me to accuse the Holy One, blessed be He, but were it not for the fact that He longs to smell his sweet scent, no one could prevail over him. But may it be God's will that his mother should not suffer because of him.[571]

And so it was.

22. RABBI ELIEZER THE GREAT

(Zohar I, 98a–99a; *Midrash ha-Ne'elam*)

The rabbis taught[572] that, one Sabbath eve, when Rabbi Eliezer the Great was ill, he asked his son, Hyrcanus, to sit at his right hand, and he

[568] It came from the illumination of his father's soul.

[569] This short comment prefaces the subsequent passage concerning the righteous, such as Rav Hamnuna Sava, who acquire merit not only for themselves but also for their children.

[570] The children learn there in the "department" of the Holy One, blessed be He.

[571] That he should not die during her life-time.

[572] The following is an expansion of the passage in B.T. *Sanhedrin* 68a.

began to reveal to him profound mysteries, but [his son] paid no attention to his words because he thought that his mind had begun to wander. But when he realized that his father's mind was still fully active, he learned from him one hundred and eighty-nine supernal secrets. When he reached the marble stones[573] mingled with celestial water, Eliezer wept and ceased his discourse.

Arise, my son, he said.

Why, father?

I can see that I shall soon descend from the world. Go, he continued, and tell your mother that she shall take off my *tefillin* in a celestial place.[574] And when, after my departure from the world, I come here to see them, she shall not weep, for they are near to the upper and not to the lower realms, and the human mind knows nothing of them.

While they were sitting there, the sages of the time came to visit him. He cursed them for not having come to minister to him, for we have learned:[575] Greater is the service [of the Torah] than the study of it.

But then Rabbi Akiva came.

He said to him: Akiva, Akiva! Why did you not come to look after me?

My master, he replied, I did not have the time.

He grew angry, and said: I shall be surprised if you do not suffer an unnatural death.

He cursed him, wishing that his death should be more painful than the death of the others.

Rabbi Akiva wept, and said: Master, teach me Torah.

Rabbi Eliezer began to discourse on the Chariot.[576] Fire came and enveloped both of them.

The sages said: This shows that we are not worthy or suitable enough for this.

They went to the outside door and sat there. What happened happened, and the fire departed, and he then taught him three hundred legal decisions concerning "the bright spot,"[577] and two hundred and sixteen meanings of verses from the Song of Songs, and Rabbi Akiva's eyes streamed with tears, and the fire returned as at the beginning. When he came to the verse "Support me with dainties, refresh me with apples, for I am love sick" (Song of Songs 2: 5), Rabbi Akiva could no longer bear it, and he raised his voice, weeping and moaning, and could

573 A reference to the statement of Rabbi Akiva (B.T. *Ḥagigah* 14b), when he entered *Pardes*: "When you reach the stones of pure marble, do not say, Water, water."

574 This passage is obscure both in syntax and content. In *Sanhedrin* we find that his son, Hyrcanus, wanted "to take off his *tefillin*, but he rebuked him, and he departed in disgrace." [*Tefillin* (phylacteries) are not worn on the Sabbath.]

575 B.T. *Berakhot* 7b.

576 [The first chapter of Ezekiel, one of the two most esoteric themes, the other being Creation.]

577 The laws concerning symptoms of leprosy, etc. [See Leviticus 13: 2, etc.]

not speak for fear of the *Shekhinah* that was present there. He taught him all the profundities and the celestial mysteries contained in the Song of Songs, and he made him swear not to use a single verse from it, in case the Holy One, blessed be He, should destroy the world thereby, for it was not His wish that His creatures should make use of it, owing to the great sanctity that it contained.

Rabbi Akiva then departed, lamenting, his eyes gushing water.

Alas, my master, he said, alas, my master, that the world should be orphaned of you.

All the other sages came in to him, and inquired of him, and he answered them.

Time was pressing for Rabbi Eliezer. He stretched out both his arms and laid them upon his heart. He opened his mouth and said: Alas for the world, the upper world! You are about to take back and conceal all light and illumination from the lower world. Alas for you two arms of mine! Alas for you two *Torot*,[578] which will today be consigned to oblivion from the face of the earth.

For, as Rabbi Isaac said, throughout Rabbi Eliezer's lifetime the Torah shone from his mouth as on the day when it was given on Mount Sinai.

He said: I have taught Torah, and I have uttered wisdom, and I have ministered to scholars. For if all the world's inhabitants were scribes they would not be able to write [it all] down. And my pupils fell short of my wisdom by only as much as an eyelid's cosmetic, and I [have fallen short] of my masters by only as much as can be drunk from the sea.

[He said this] only in order to grant more merit to his teachers than to himself.

They were asking him questions about the law concerning the levir's sandal,[579] until the moment when his soul departed and he said "Clean."

Rabbi Akiva was not present. At the close of the Sabbath, Rabbi Akiva found him dead. He tore his garments, and cut his flesh, until the blood dripped down over his face, and he wept and cried. He went outside, and said: Heavens! heavens! Tell the sun and the moon that a light greater than theirs has now been extinguished!

[578] The written Torah and the oral Torah. According to the text in *Sanhedrin* he referred to his arms as being two scrolls of the Torah.

[579] [See Deuteronomy 25: 9.] According to *Sanhedrin* the question concerned " the shoe on the shoemaker's last."

PART I

THE GODHEAD

SECTION I. *EN-SOF* AND THE WORLD OF EMANATION

INTRODUCTION

a. The Mystery of the Godhead

[1] Kabbalistic teaching, as it is presented in the pages of the Zohar at the end of the thirteenth century after a process of development and crystallization lasting more than a hundred years, is extremely wide-ranging, impinging on every area of existence and seeking solutions from a religio-mystical point of view to the mysteries of the world and the problems of life. At the very core and foundation of this teaching is one particular subject of investigation: the mystery of the knowledge of the Godhead. The great themes of the Creation and the Chariot, the existence and activity of the angels, the nature of the spiritual worlds, the forces of evil in the realm of Satan, the situation and destiny of Man, this world and the next, the process of history from the days of Creation until the end of time—all of these topics are no more than the boughs and branches of the mighty tree of the mystery of the Godhead. The knowledge of this mystery, which depends on man's spiritual level and on the root of his soul, is the basis of religious faith as seen by the kabbalah, and it is therefore called in the Zohar "the mystery of faith" (*raza di-mehemanuta*).

Obviously, the originality of the kabbalah does not consist in the fact that it assigns a central position to the divine. Jewish creativity in both the early and the medieval periods revolved entirely around the pivot of faith and religious experience, and in the very nature of things this kind of creativity took place under the aegis of the divine spirit. But in the matter of the Godhead the kabbalistic method is completely different, both in approach and content, from other methods in the life of the Jewish spirit.

[2] In order to highlight the special standpoint of kabbalah I can briefly describe the three basic attitudes that were at work, and that influenced the Jewish people, either in actual life or through literary channels, as the kabbalah began to develop: (a) The rabbinic approach, which found expression in halakhic literature, in the *aggadah* and ethical writings, and which served as the main foundation for popular faith, for the worship of God, and for the religious life of the time; (b) The mystical approach, which established itself in the restricted circles of those who had "descended to the Chariot," centuries before the growth of kabbalah, and whose tendencies are reflected in the writings that fall under the heading of *hekhalot* literature, and in later *midrashim*. A distant offshoot of this group may be seen in the German hasidic movement, which was active in the twelfth and thirteenth centuries, and which was led by Rabbi Judah the Pious, to whom is attributed the *Sefer Hasidim*, and by his disciple, Rabbi Eleazar ha-Rokeah of Worms; (c) The philosophical approach, with the teaching of Maimonides at its head, which spread far and wide at the beginning of the thirteenth century, affecting many different Jewish groups.

In the rabbinic approach we do not find any doctrine of the Godhead at all, in the full meaning of the term, that is, a doctrine that credits man with a systematic and clearly argued understanding of the nature of God, and of the mysteries in the divine realm. The main element in this approach is the mutual relationship between God and His creation, with Man, and particularly Israel, the people of God, at its center. According to this approach there are two sides. On the one side, there is God, Creator and Guide of the world, who gave the Torah and the commandments, who cares for His creatures, who requites man according to his deeds, and who causes His presence to rest upon Israel. On the other side, there is Man, subject to God's sovereignty, whose task it is to learn and to fulfill the Torah, and to seek a relationship with God through prayer, good deeds, and the sanctification of life. The image of God, in Himself, is described only in general and vague terms, and the Divine Being never becomes the subject of study or the object of precise knowledge.

On this point there is no fundamental difference between the rabbinic approach and the mystical trends that I have mentioned. It is true that the principal topic in the *hekhalot* literature is "the observation of the Chariot," that is to say, the ascent of the soul to the lofty heights of the world of the Chariot, and its descent from there, suffused with visions of the supreme and awesome King, seated upon His throne of glory and surrounded by His bands of angels and ministers. But this literature does not describe the nature of God. It deals rather with the awesome experience of the soul as it ascends and descends, with the perils that lie along its path, and with its rapture at the splendor of God's glory and the brilliance of His entourage. This was certainly not the place to discuss the doctrine of the Godhead; and even the relationship between God, man, and the world is not treated in a way that leads to systematic teaching or knowledge. Even in the literature of the German *ḥasidim*, which does contain from time to time traces of specific views on the nature of God, these views are subsidiary to the central and basic thrust of their writings, namely, the preparation of the soul to draw near to God through a life of piety and ascetic acts of penitence. Neither the starting point nor the goal of the German *ḥasidim* is concerned with the perception of heavenly mysteries, but with man's self-preparation for confrontation with God.[1]

[3] The standpoint of the kabbalah is quite different.[2] Its underlying motives and purpose are activated by the desire to uncover the hidden layers in the mystery of God and to penetrate the depths of the secrets of Heaven. It developed a systematic presentation of the doctrine of the Godhead, the understanding of which was set before man as an exalted task, upon which depended his success and his soul's salvation both in this world and the next. The Zohar knows no bounds in its extravagant praise of mysticism; at every opportunity it reverts to an expression of its great worth and importance. The pure soul descends from the abodes of splendor in the heavenly realms to the dark valley of this world only in order to realize, in the corporeal life, in the lowest depths of existence, that supreme perception which it enjoyed when it resided in the heights of Heaven. Knowledge of the science of mysticism is the main bridge leading to the attachment of the soul to God. And so the masters of this science are called "the sons of the palace" (*benei hekhala*), for they alone are worthy enough to enter the palace of the King and enjoy the splendor of His

glory. The Torah in its literal sense, and the whole range of the commandments, are but lower rungs in the ladder of religious values, at the top of which stands knowledge of the hidden mysteries. The Zohar denigrates with great severity those who occupy themselves with only the literal dimension of the Torah and do not strive to master the secret of the Godhead concealed within it. The narratives in the Torah are like clothes; the commandments stand for the body, while the mystical doctrine is the soul. "The fools in the world look only upon the clothes, which are the narratives of the Torah; they know no more, and do not see what is beneath the clothes. Those who know more, do not look upon the clothes, but upon the body beneath the clothes. The wise, the servants of the supreme King, those who stood at Mt. Sinai, look only upon the soul, which is the foundation of all, the real Torah."[3] Even one's portion in the world to come depends mainly on one's knowledge of mystical doctrine, and whoever neglects its study forfeits the protection of his good deeds, and will be dismissed from the chamber of the Holy One, blessed be He. "This sacred creature stands [in the second palace] as the soul ascends and comes toward it. It asks her about the mystery of the wisdom of her Master. And according to the wisdom that she has pursued and attained she is given her reward. But if she was able to attain it and did not she is driven out, and cannot enter, and remains beneath that palace covered with shame."[4]

[4] It is precisely in this area that the kabbalah seems to share common ground with its rival discipline, rationalist philosophy. The philosophers, Maimonides chief among them, considered perception of intelligibles, that is to say, certain knowledge of the separate intelligences, and matters pertaining to the Godhead, to be the highest perfection in the life of man. The attainment of this lofty stage was not merely the object of philosophical enquiry, but the very foundation for the fulfillment of one's religious duty. They, too, stressed the importance of "the secrets of the Torah," which consisted mainly in a knowledge of the higher intelligibles, and they relegated the exponents of the literal Torah and the observers of the practical commandments to a much lower stage than that occupied by those who had philosophical insight into the doctrine of the divine. Maimonides depicts the ladder of perfection among men according to their nearness to, or remoteness from, God, in terms of a king sitting in his palace, with his subjects, who seek to enter his presence, divided into various categories according to their position relative to the king's abode. Only the philosophers, those who have knowledge of divine matters, are compared to the princes who stand in the king's chamber, while of the literalists he writes: "Those who arrive at the palace, but go round about it, are those who devote themselves exlusively to the study of the practical law; they believe traditionally in true principles of faith, and learn the practical worship of God, but are not trained in philosophical treatment of the principles of Torah, and do not endeavour to establish the truth of their faith by proof."[5] Life in the world to come also depends on knowledge of the intelligibles. Only the man who develops his intellect by perceiving divine matters, and reaches the stage of "acquired intellect," will earn eternal life after death.

The points of contact between these ideas and the position held by the kabbalah are strikingly obvious, and there is reason to believe that the kabbalists drew upon the views of the philosophers. Nevertheless, an enormous distance separates kabbalah from philosophy. And I do not refer here to the great difference in content in the knowledge of the divine mystery, about which I shall speak in more detail later, but to the many differences in the kind of perception.

[5] First of all, we must deal with the question of the instrument of perception. The philosophers thought of the intellect as the means whereby one attained knowledge of divine matters—that same intellect which was at work in the acquisition of less important facts. This is because perception of divine intelligibles was no more than the highest stage in the logico-discursive knowledge process. The intellect progresses from one subject to another by a process of deduction and analogy until it comes to the acme of perception, the realm of the divine. This is not the case with kabbalah. In the Zohar the attainment of the mystery of the Godhead is confined to the holy soul, which is hewn from a divine source and is not identical with the rational intellect. In order to differentiate it from the simple intellect, this medium of perception is called, in the writings of Rabbi Moses de Leon, "the true intellect" or "the holy intellect," and, looked at in this way, it approximates both in nature and function to "the divine force" in the doctrines of Rabbi Judah Halevi. This instrument of perception does not perceive logically, but has an intuitive or visionary grasp while in a state of contemplation. This perception is obtained through the conjunction of the soul with the divine light that irradiates it.[6]

But it is not only the means of perception that is different in kabbalah. The goal is also different. For the philosophers the Godhead is simply an object of knowledge; that is to say, the motive for perceiving it is to enrich the store of acquired facts, and to endow man with intellectual perfection. But according to the kabbalah, a grasp of the mystery of the Godhead gives the kabbalists the wherewithal to influence and act in the divine realm. The kabbalist does not merely absorb a perception of the divine with receptive passivity. It becomes transmuted within him into active creative energy. As a result of this perception the divine spark, which was quenched when the soul descended into the body, is rekindled in the soul, and man becomes thereby a real partner with the Creator of the world, both in the hidden life of the world of emanation and in the direction of the lower worlds. With the grasp of the mystery of the divine, a powerful interdependent relationship is established between man and his Creator, and the power of the soul ("the impulse below") works together with the power of the divine ("the impulse above"), by a process of mutual aid. This activist purpose, which does so much to give Jewish mysticism that specific image which differentiates it from most of the mystical currents in other religions, brings into sharp relief the basic contrast between kabbalah and philosophy in their respective approaches to the perception of God.

b. *En-Sof* and the Order of the *Sefirot*

[1] However, the most original feature of kabbalistic doctrine is in the actual content of the mystery of the divine. The image of God portrayed in the descriptions of the kabbalists is absolutely different from that depicted anywhere else in Judaism. In place of the strict Lawgiver and Ruler of the *halakhah*, or the merciful Father of the *aggadah*, or the awesome King of those

who "descend to the Chariot," or the necessary Being and hidden Mover of the philosophers, all of whom are distinguished by both uniqueness and unity, we find in the kabbalah a divine image that is compound and complex, and that seems to be opposed and foreign to the Jewish spirit. It was not apparently a single God that was revealed to the kabbalists in their contemplation, but a number of different divine substances, arrayed in the order of the ten *sefirot*. But even this order did not constitute the divine in its entirety. The *sefirot* are emanated forces that originate and spread from a hidden source, called *En-Sof*. And so the multiplicity of the divine *sefirot* on the one hand, and the duality of the sefirotic order and *En-Sof* on the other, are the two basic factors in the mystery of the Godhead as presented by the kabbalah. These require analysis and clarification.

The question of the nature and functions of the *sefirot* will be discussed in the introduction to the following section. Here I shall deal only with the relationship between the *sefirot* and *En-Sof*, and specifically with the kabbalistic concept of *En-Sof* itself.

[2] Most kabbalists, including the author of the main body of the Zohar, do not regard the *sefirot* as separate entities existing outside the realm of the Godhead—that is to say, spiritual intermediary stages between God and man. They regard them rather as parts of the divine being, if one can say such a thing. They are, indeed, called "levels" or "stages," but the reference here is to inner stages within the Godhead. *En-Sof*, the hidden God, dwelling in the depths of His own being, seeks to reveal Himself, and to unloose His hidden powers. His will realizes itself through the emanation of rays from His light, which break out of their concealment and are arrayed in the order of the *sefirot*, the world of divine emanation. Subsequently, through the power of the *sefirot*, the lower, nondivine, worlds are established, in which the divine governance of the *sefirot* acts and reveals itself. Thus the *sefirot* are the self-revealing God, that is, the reflection of *En-Sof* in the mirror of revelation that is turned toward the world outside itself.

The concealment that is in *En-Sof* has a twofold character. First, its essence does not appear outside its own hidden domain, and it does not take part directly in the processes of creation or conduct of the world. Its nature is not apprehensible, and is beyond the limits of thought or perception. The second aspect of concealment is deeper than the first. It is true that in the world of the *sefirot*, and particularly in the upper realms, the immanence of *En-Sof* itself is always present (*Influence and Direction*, 11). But even the *sefirot* are unable to apprehend its nature: "All these luminaries and lights depend on it for their existence, but they are not in a position to perceive. That which knows, but does not know (i.e., *En-Sof*), is none but the Supernal Will, the secret of all secrets, *Ayin* (nothing)"(1).[7]

The absolute concealment of *En-Sof* demonstrates one of the differentiating characteristics of the kabbalistic approach to the mystery of the Godhead. Only a portion of this mystery, the part that concerns the self-revealing God, is susceptible to knowledge and perception. But as far as *En-Sof*, the hidden God, is concerned, the mystery is one of non-knowledge and non-perception. Just as the highest religious duty of man requires for its fulfillment a knowledge of his Creator, that is to say, that he should enter into the mystery of the *sefirot*, so it is also incumbent on him to recognize the limits of mystical perception and to acknowledge the concealment of *En-Sof*. The obligation of knowledge ("for he who does not know Him cannot serve Him")[8] and the obligation of recognizing non-knowledge ("restrain your mouth from speaking, and your heart from thinking, and if your heart runs let it return to its place")[9] are bound up together before the mystery of the Godhead.

[3] This concept of *En-Sof* had a number of important consequences for a religious life conducted in a kabbalistic spirit. *En-Sof* was beyond the horizon of human aspiration, and completely separated from man. The God of religious experience, to whom man turns with the devotion of prayer and the commandments, and who answers those who call upon Him, is not the hidden God, but the God who reveals Himself through the system of the *sefirot*.

But more than this, even the God who revealed Himself on Mt. Sinai, and through the medium of prophecy, is not *En-Sof* itself, but His *sefirot*, and the names of God recorded in Scripture are not in any sense to be applied to *En-Sof*, for it cannot be categorized by any name or epithet. This extreme and bold concept of the concealment of *En-Sof* is already alluded to in the *Perush Eser Sefirot* by Rabbi Azriel of Gerona,[10] one of the earliest kabbalists: "Know that *En-Sof* cannot be an object of thought, let alone of speech, even though there is an indication of it in every thing, for there is nothing beyond it. Consequently, there is no letter, no name, no writing, and no word that can comprise it." This idea is expressed in a more direct and extreme fashion in the *Sefer Ma'arekhet ha-Elohut*,[11] by an anonymous author who was, it seems, a contemporary of the author of the Zohar: "Know that the *En-Sof* that we have mentioned is not referred to in the Torah, the Prophets, or the Hagiographa, or in the words of the rabbis, but the worshipers (i.e., the kabbalists) have received a little indication of it."

Statements as unequivocal as this are not to be found in the Zohar, but we may confidently deduce from the material in general that this was the standpoint there too.[12] References to *En-Sof* are practically always accompanied by exaggerated expressions of concealment, such as, "that secret which is not perceived or known,"(1) and so on.[13] Moreover, the author of the Zohar actually fulfilled the obligation of reticence with regard to the hidden nature of *En-Sof*, and restricted his references to the hidden God to just a few allusions. This explains why in the selection here I have included only one passage from the Zohar itself in the *En-Sof* section, for the other references to *En-Sof* are not sufficient to form another extract.

[4] In the Zohar only one name is used specifically for the hidden God: *En-Sof*. This name is late. We come across it for the first time in the writings of Rabbi Isaac the Blind, the son of Rabbi Abraham ben David, and in the writings of his pupils, who were active in Provence and Spain at the end of the twelfth and the beginning of the thirteenth centuries. In the *Sefer ha-Bahir*, which preceded these kabbalists, the two words are not yet used as a proper noun, but as an adverbial phrase: "And so with thought: when you think, you will think without end (*le-en sof*) or limit."[14]

There are two elements in the term *En-Sof* that characterize the concept of the hidden God: (a) the negative element, and (b) the impersonal element. The meaning of *En-Sof* [lit., no end] is the absence of all limit or measure. It is absolutely beyond our intellectual capability to know or express in a positive way one single iota of the hidden nature of *En-Sof*, but we can, and we must, strip it of any form or quality known to us, for any known thing that is attributed to it blemishes its unparalleled and unknowable perfection, and imposes a limit on its infinity. "Know that one cannot attribute to *En-Sof* will or desire or intention or thought or speech or deed, although there is nothing beyond it, and one can say nothing of it that implies its limitation"—so writes Rabbi Azriel.[15] And in the Zohar we find: "But there are no end, no wills, no lights, no luminaries, in *En-Sof*"(1). *En-Sof* is the source of Will and Thought, which are the first two *sefirot*, but these two faculties are not to be attributed to its hidden being.

This negative approach also affected the question of personality. According to the early kabbalists and the Zohar, the real meaning of *En-Sof* is "that which has no end," which means that one should not think of the hidden God in the form of an active, creative, personal entity. The characteristic of personality should be applied only to the God who reveals Himself in the *sefirot*.

The early kabbalists did use other terms to designate the hidden God, but only one of them is comparable to *En-Sof* from the point of view of the negative and impersonal approach: "that which thought cannot grasp" (*mah she-en ha-mahashavah masseget*). Here the denial of personality is expressed quite clearly by the use of the word *mah* (what, that which). In the remaining early terminology just a slight hint of positive usage can be discerned. Some terms are intended to stress the absolute unity of the hidden God, as in "the One" (*ha-ehad*), "the perfect unity" (*ha-ahdut ha-shelemah*), "the perfection of unity" (*hashlamat ha-ahdut*), and "the symmetry of unity" (*hashva'at ha-ahdut*). Others describe the causal relationship between the hidden God and revealed existence, such as "root of roots" (*shoresh ha-shorashim*), "the first cause" (*ha-sibah ha-rishonah*), and "the cause of causes" (*sibah ha-sibot*, and *ilah ha-ilot*).

Many kabbalists of the thirteenth century dropped these terms, and in the Zohar itself they are not used at all of the hidden God. *En-Sof* was accepted as practically a unique expression. This terminological standardization, which took place before the composition of the Zohar, shows how far the extremely negative approach to the concept of the hidden God extended, even though at the very same time, as we shall see later, attempts were made to introduce a positive content into the traditional negative term. The consistent refusal to use perfectly clear terms like "first cause" or "the cause of causes" in the Zohar demonstrates that, although the hidden God is the source of all—or, in Rabbi Azriel's phrase, "there is nothing beyond it"—nevertheless, causal expressions were considered unsuitable because of its utter impenetrability.[16]

c. Dualism and Unity

[1] The absolute distinction between two areas or facets within the Godhead—the dualism of the concealed Emanator, on the one hand, and, on the other, the array of His active emanated powers in His role as Creator of the world—is a complete innovation in Judaism, and seems to be foreign to it. And we do indeed find a close parallel to this idea in the theories of Gnosis, which flourished in the early centuries of the Christian era. With their various

mythical descriptions and differing nuances of thought, the Gnostics present to us an image of God with two faces: on the one side, the unknowable, unapproachable God (*agnostos theos*), remote from any worldly existence, and indescribable except in a negative fashion; and on the other side, the *demiourgos*, God of the world, its Creator and Guide. The *demiourgos* is usually depicted as one of the powers of emanation of the hidden God, which constitute the divine *pleroma* ("fullness"). And so we must ask: what is the connection between kabbalistic doctrine and ancient pagan and Christian Gnosis? This question has two elements: (a) How near ideologically are the two doctrines? and (b) Does the approximation of ideas derive from some historical link, that is, was Gnosis the breeding ground for kabbalistic teaching?

There is no single answer to these questions. As far as the doctrine of the *sefirot* is concerned, it can be established without a doubt that there is some reflection here of a definite gnostic tendency, and that it did in fact emerge and develop from a historico-literary contact with the remnants of Gnosis, which were preserved over a period of many generations in certain Jewish circles, until they found their way to the early kabbalists, who were deeply affected by them both spiritually and intellectually. Marks of this contact, and of this process of development, can be discerned in the *Sefer ha-Bahir*, the first literary record of kabbalistic doctrine, which, in the form we have it, seems to have been written in the twelfth century.[17]

This is not the case when we come to the question of the hidden God and His relationship with the order of the *sefirot*. Here it is quite obvious that Gnostic dualism differs in both nature and purpose from the dualism that exists in kabbalistic teaching. In Gnosis separation between the unknowable God and the Creator of the world is not just a matter of concealment and revelation. They are opposed to one another like contrasted, hostile powers. The creation of this world was not an act originally planned by the divine mind as a complementary counterpart to the heavenly world above, but occurred as a result of the rebellion of *demiourgos* against the hidden God. The ruler of this world is the god of evil and judgment, who sinned against the god of goodness and mercy and erected a fortress for himself to rule over with his evil laws. The kabbalah, clearly, does not posit a dualism such as this, with two separate powers,[18] for it would be absolutely contrary to the belief in the unity of God. The main point of Gnosis, moreover, particularly in the Marcionite system, was directed against Jewish teaching, which it depicted as a corpus of wicked legislation derived from the *demiourgos*, whom it identified with the God of Israel.

From the historical point of view, too, the concept of the hidden God in kabbalah, in its crystallization as *En-Sof*, cannot be traced to Gnostic influence. In the *Sefer ha-Bahir*, for example, which does reflect Gnostic influence, not only is the term *En-Sof* lacking, but the whole idea connected with it is absent also. It would appear from the presentation in the *Sefer ha-Bahir* that the God who reveals and develops His attributes through the system of emanation does not dwell above the sefirotic tree, but actually "nests" in it and is attached to it. Similarly, there is no trace of the negative and impersonal character of the Master of the *sefirot*. On the contrary, He is usually mentioned in some personal guise, such as "the Holy One, blessed be He," or "the King," and He is portrayed as a creative and active personality. The concept of an impersonal, hidden God arose at a later stage in kabbalah, in the schools of the Spanish and Provençal kabbalists, as a result of the confrontation of Gnostic elements with Neoplatonic philosophical ideas. These kabbalists read Neoplatonic works and were influenced by them, as their own books show, and the concept of the hidden God is a result of this influence. At the very beginning of the new speculative kabbalah, *En-Sof*, which represented the God of Plotinus and his followers, was joined to the system of the *sefirot*, which was the Jewish version of the Gnostic *pleroma*, and so the kabbalistic mystery of the divine, comprising the hidden God and the revealed God, came into being.

[2] This solution to the problem of the origin of the mystery of the Godhead in kabbalah, and of the way in which it developed, raises another important question. If kabbalistic dualism was not simply the outcome of ancient Gnostic tradition, but was created by the kabbalists in the twelfth century from a combination of different elements, it follows that internal factors and contemporary religious drives must have moved them to formulate this kind of concept. But what actually were these motives? What were these promoters of a new religious awareness trying to do by complicating the theosophic concept of God that they had received from the exponents of the Gnostic tradition?

In order to answer this question we must try to understand the religious situation that prevailed in Jewry at that time, in those areas where the kabbalah was beginning to develop. Two forces with diametrically opposed religious goals clashed and struggled with one another in the Jewish spirit of that age: popular rabbinic faith and philosophical speculation. The tension between the two rival movements was most keenly felt, and most bitterly expressed, in their disagreement concerning the idea of God. The very strong desire to feel and substantiate the close relationship between man and the living God intensified the trend in popular belief toward myth, toward a vision of God mirrored in corporeal images. The philosophers saw in this tendency a profanation of the divine Name, and waged a holy war against it. They tried to cleanse and purify the concept of God of the dross of corporeality, and to stress God's complete separation from any being but His own. The recognition of His absolute transcendence, and the denial in Him of any positive attributes, became the basic principle of the philosophical doctrine of God. The battle between the followers of "the God of Abraham, whom souls yearn to taste and see" and the adherents of "the God of Aristotle, to whom one draws near through speculation" was bitterly contested among the ranks of Israel.[19]

However, the two sides in the battle refrained from developing and realizing their aims to their fullest extent, or with complete logical consistency. There were certain feelings and attitudes within accepted, traditional Judaism that were active in every Jewish soul and were regarded as fundamental, which put a brake on both popular and philosophical trends. Popular rabbinic belief was forced to restrain the demands for mythology that clamored within it, because of the ancient and unequivocal hostility that Jewish monotheism displayed toward pagan myth. Blatantly anthropomorphic descriptions, such as giving the measurements of the Creator's limbs in the mystical work, *Shiur Komah*, in which small groups of a Gnostic character indulged, were not likely to gain popular favour. On the other hand, philosophical thought also suffered serious limitations in its speculation on the nature of God. Despite their desire to divest the Godhead of any attribute or characteristic, and to hide Him from view through positing His absolute transcendence and His infinite removal from human perception or apprehension, the philosophers were unable to resist completely the demands of the living faith, based on the written and oral Torah, which tried to see in God a personal figure, the height of moral perfection, who guided the affairs of the world with justice and righteousness, who cared for His creatures, and supported them in times of sorrow. The tortuous arguments and inconsistencies of Maimonides in different parts of his theory of God show the great difficulty in which philosophical thought found itself.

When we consider these two contrary, but not fully realized, tendencies, in whose midst the kabbalistic doctrine of the Godhead took root and flourished, we can gain a better understanding of the factors and motives that lay behind it. In the two-way concept of God propounded by the kabbalists, the central religious problem of the age found a unique solution. To the dilemma that at that time split the Jewish world—the "God of Abraham" or the "God of Aristotle," the approachable living God of religion, or the remote, abstract God of philosophy—the kabbalists offered a new and staggering solution: Have both, and both of them in their full vigor, without any feeble compromise. The Creator of the world, the God of Israel, who exists in the system of the *sefirot*, the personal God, who with a keen eye supervises man's deeds and the progress of his life, who listens to prayer, and reveals Himself in the vision of the religious contemplative—this God is the complete and absolute fulfillment of the expectations of popular belief. And, at the same time, *En-Sof*, the God who is divorced from man and the world, beyond all perception, enclosed within the majesty of His own transcendental being—this God is the God of Maimonides and his followers, in all His purity, with no theological concession whatsoever. So the kabbalists turned, on the one hand, to the remnants of Gnosis, through whose images and descriptions they were able to perceive the self-revealing God, even as far as the image of *Adam Kadmon* (Primordial Man), and they drew, on the other hand, upon speculative ideas from pure Neoplatonic sources in order to express the absolute concealment of *En-Sof*.

This idea of the mystery of the Godhead in kabbalah establishes the spiritual and historical position of the early kabbalists in the conflict between philosophy and its opponents. They tended toward both sides. In their belief and their religious experience they recognized the nearness of God, and in the communion and exultation of the soul they heard the rustling of the *Shekhinah*'s wings. But their minds were open to philosophical ideas, and they acknowledged the justice of the arguments against the attribution of corporeality, which tarnished the perfection and majesty of God. In the dualism of the hidden God, and the self-revealing God, they discovered a way of satisfying both the demands of philosophical speculation and the yearnings of religious emotion.[20]

[3] However, the solution of this difficulty led the kabbalists straight into another, and provoked a fierce reaction against them in various quarters. This idea of theirs seemed to undermine the basic principle of the Jewish faith; it looked like an attack on the belief in the unity of God. Two distinct divine areas,

ten *sefirot* within the Godhead—this was dangerous heresy in the eyes of both the traditionalists and the rationalists.

In a letter of Rabbi Meir ben Simeon of Narbonne, from the first half of the thirteenth century, the kabbalists are directly arraigned of the crime of heresy because of their belief in the dualism of *En-Sof* and the *sefirot*. He contrasts their erroneous doctrine with the true concept of God, "with whom there is no other, the true One in perfect Oneness, without association or combination of *sefirot*, the first Cause, the Cause of all causes, doing great things, bringing forth something from nothing, solely by His own will . . . one should not associate anything with Him, for it is not right to associate the Creator with that which He has created, or matter with its Maker, or the emanated with the Emanator." This dualism is also actually referred to by one of the most important early kabbalists Rabbi Asher ben David, in the reproof that he addressed to the kabbalists' disciples, who allowed their opponents to misconstrue their statements, "and they imagine in their hearts that they believe in two powers, and that they thereby deny the truth of their religion."[21]

The kabbalists themselves, who sought to preserve their belief in the unity of God, and to remain within the confines of the traditional faith, were extremely concerned with this problem and tried various ways of reconciling their ideas with the principle of divine unity. The appearance of dualism and the plurality of facets within the Godhead, together with the urgent need to preserve the principle of unity, produced one of the paradoxical elements that are part of the very nature of kabbalistic teaching, and it appears in different forms throughout the whole development of kabbalah. In the Zohar, too, we can see many signs of the tension produced by this inner contradiction, especially in phrases such as "and all is one" (*ve-khula had*), which occur like a continual refrain at the end of the various imaginative excursions into the domain of the divine. There are two images that often recur, in the Zohar and elsewhere, in attempts to solve this problem.

The first solution depicts the unity of the Emanator and the emanated in the image of "a flame attached to a burning coal":[22] "Come and see: The Holy One, blessed be He, produced ten crowns, holy diadems, above, with which He crowns Himself and clothes Himself, and He is they, and they are He, like a flame attached to a burning coal, and there is no division there" (*The Forces of Uncleanness*, 2). The flame had been contained within the burning coal, and when it flared out nothing new was created; that which was hidden simply became revealed, and so from the point of view of nature and being, the flame is neither different nor separate from the burning coal. Similarly, in the case of the *sefirot* and their relationship with *En-Sof*. In the writings of the early kabbalists this idea is expressed in the succinct formulation: "The beings existed but the emanation was new," that is to say, the *sefirot*, the supernal "beings," already existed within their hidden source, and it was only their revelation, through the process of emanation, that was new. Revelation through emanation is also explained by way of the philosophical expression "emergence from potentiality into actuality": "But emanation takes place when the force, which is hidden and sealed, is revealed from potentiality into actuality."[23]

In the Zohar we find another simile on this subject, which in form is very much like that of the flame and the burning coal, but which is actually different in content: "like a lamp from which lights spread out on every side, but when we draw near to examine these lights, we find that only the lamp itself exists."[24] It would seem that the connection between the lights and the lamp is the same as that beween the flame and the burning coal, but this was not really the author's intention. Through this simile he is attempting to provide a different solution to the problem of unity and diversity within the Godhead, a solution more extreme than the first. The lights, which seem at a distance to be different rays from the flame of the lamp, do not exist at all. They are an optical illusion. Therefore, when one looks at them more closely, one sees that "only the lamp itself exists." The meaning of this simile is that the *sefirot* in themselves have no ontological reality. From the point of view of the divine essence, only the unique unity of *En-Sof* exists, and the difference between the hidden, infinite Emanator and the revealed, limited, emanated beings, and likewise the differentiation within the system of emanation itself, is nothing but a reflection of the divine in the mirror of created things, which, because of their limited nature and their lack of unity, are not sufficiently able to grasp absolute unity and infinity.[25]

However, these and similar solutions, intended to secure for kabbalah an unassailable position within the framework of ancient Jewish tradition, were not sufficient to obscure the fundamental novelty in the kabbalistic concept of the divine unity. Since the kabbalists ignored the danger of heresy, and saw no need to indulge in apologetics, they revealed their innermost thoughts without any restraint, and so we can see the definite change that had taken place in their teaching concerning belief in the unity of God. They did not inculcate an absolute, static unity, nor a firm, personal unity, but a kind of organic unification of disparate parts, a dynamic unity with an inner movement, a surge of secret life, the unity of a source together with the springs that well up from it; that is to say, the divine unity was not a permanent fixture, but a continuous process of incident and renewal.

[4] This inner process in the life of the Godhead goes by the name of *sod ha-yihud* (the mystery of unification), and it constitutes the principle aim and object of the mystical worship of God. Through devotion in prayer and the fulfillment of the commandments, man becomes an active participant in the renewal of the unity of the divine forces. The "mystery of unification" has two components: the preservation of harmonious unity within the structure of the world of the *sefirot*, and the unification of the Emanator with the world of emanation through the return of the *sefirot* to their source.[26] The "mystery of unification," particularly in its highest aspect, whose significance will be more clearly understood in what follows, helped to shield the kabbalah from the weighty accusations leveled against its doctrine of the Godhead when seen in the light of traditional expectations and man's approach to God.

We have already seen that the kabbalistic idea of the nature of *En-Sof* removes it from the area of religious life by relegating its existence to impenetrable heights that the human soul cannot possibly reach. It is the *sefirot* that constitute the goal of religious devotion, but even then not the system as a whole, but as individual objects of worship, varying with the intention of the worshiper, the nature of the result desired, and the circumstances of the act of devotion. This type of worship of God, especially in the unrefined way in which the opponents of kabbalah understood it, was bound to meet with a bitter reception everywhere. For one thing, this form of worship was not geared to the essence of God Himself, and, for another, it was directed at various "gods" who occupied a lower position than the supreme Deity; that is to say, there appeared to exist here a kind of idolatry. This view of kabbalistic worship was very clearly expressed in the already mentioned letter by Rabbi Meir ben Simeon of Narbonne: "These fools say that one should not proffer gratitude, prayer, and blessing to the primal, everlasting God, without beginning or end. Woe to their souls! What has come upon them, what do they intend by this! They have brought Israel into contempt; they have turned backward in their rebellion, and removed themselves from the Ancient One of the world . . . and why should we talk further of the ideas of these fools, whose prayers and blessings to the gods all imply that they are created and emanated, and that they have a beginning and an end . . . they say that they pray by day to one created god, and by night to another god who is above the first, but created like him, and on holy days to another."[27]

The kabbalists themselves did not ignore this problem, but tried to explain and justify their point of view. The simple answer they gave was that, even if the devotion of the worshiper could extend in a direct manner only to the realm of the *sefirot*, nevertheless, in a roundabout way, by means of the *sefirot* it did connect with *En-Sof*; and, similarly, the influence that flowed down as a result of the power of this devotion, extended from *En-Sof* down to the *sefirot*. Accordingly, the *sefirot* were like intermediate stages or intercessors between man and *En-Sof*.[28]

Another and more profound version of this solution to the problem involves close contact between man and *En-Sof*. Albeit that one directs one's devotion to specific *sefirot*, nevertheless, through a process of unification, one actually ascends to *En-Sof*. Enthusiastic devotion below causes the *sefirot* to unite with one another. As they ascend stage by stage, they are comprised into one whole, their own individual identities disappear, and they return to their hidden source.[29] The activating devotion, in which both the soul and mind of man are steeped, ascends together with the *sefirot*. In other words, the process of unification within the Godhead serves as a bridge by which man can attach himself to *En-Sof*. This is how the founders of kabbalah understood and explained the profound significance of mystical devotion. Rabbi Isaac the Blind writes: "The only way to pray is by means of finite things (i.e., the *sefirot*) [by which] man may be received, and raised in thought as far as *En-Sof*";[30] and his disciples, following him, developed the theory of devotion (*kavvanah*) in the same spirit. In the Zohar also, devotion's ascent to *En-Sof* is mentioned several times with the same implication: "The seventh palace, 'O Lord, open my lips,' is the most sublime secret, in a whisper, without a sound being heard. This is where one's intention is to direct one's devotion and raise one's desire upward to *En-Sof*."[31] And with even more stress on the connection between the ascent of the devotion and the "mystery of unification," we have: "And as his mouth and his lips move he should direct his heart and his will to rise higher and higher in order to unify all in the most sublime secret, where the resting-place is for all desires and thoughts, in the mystery that exists in *En-Sof*."[32] In this sense, it is said of *En-Sof* (*Sefirot*, 13): "It is not in number, or in thought, or in calculation, but in the devotion of the heart," that is to say, devotion comes to it through the "mystery of unification."

And so, in contrast to the extreme self-concealment of *En-Sof*, which creates a gulf between man and the hidden God, the possibility is granted, through the "mystery of unification" of bridging the gulf. Clearly, the intellect or the will cannot ascend by perception or devotion to the innermost sanctum. But through the submerging and eventual disappearance of the soul in the sea of the Godhead, through attachment to the *sefirot*, it has the possibility of contact with *En-Sof*, and of drawing light and influence from the hidden source. To put it another way, in the words of Rabbi Isaac the Blind, "the way of knowledge" is sealed, but "the way of nourishment" is open.

d. *En-Sof* and *Keter*

[1] The extreme Neoplatonic concept of *En-Sof*, which has been explained in the foregoing paragraphs, was not preserved in all its purity, nor did it remain the sole viewpoint in kabbalah. On the contrary, from the very beginning, as it grew and flourished, an opposite tendency came to the fore, which sought to remove *En-Sof* from its absolute unapproachability and to approximate it more nearly to traditional belief. This tendency reached its climax and fullest expression in the teaching of some kabbalists, for whom *En-Sof* had become transformed into a personal God who revealed Himself through the works of creation and His direction of the world, while the *sefirot* were simply the instruments for His activity.[33] However, as a rule, both these viewpoints were accommodated, and as a result of this accommodation certain ideas emerged that aimed to leave the *sefirot* within the realm of the Godhead in its aspect of the revealed God, and at the same time to diminish slightly the concealment of *En-Sof*. These ideas, traces of which can be seen even among exponents of the most extreme view, were mainly expressed in the way in which the connection was established between *En-Sof* and *Keter*.

The question of the nature and status of the first *sefirah* was subject to argument, and this produced a number of varied and complex views. The character and direction of the argument are reflected quite clearly in the two most conflicting views of the matter: (a) The process of emanation from *En-Sof* began with the appearance of the first *sefirah*, and this remained at the head of the sefirotic system as the first object of emanation; and (b) The first *sefirah* was *En-Sof* itself, and only the nine *sefirot* below it were emanated forces.[34] The reasoning behind these two views is perfectly obvious. The first view expresses the absolute remoteness of *En-Sof* from the system of the *sefirot*, and also stresses the inherent dualism there. The second view establishes a strong connection between *En-Sof* and the *sefirot*, and to a large extent divests it of its hidden quality. It is true that *Keter* is also beyond human perception, and the proponents of this view could therefore maintain the concept of the hidden God over against the image of the God who reveals Himself through the lower *sefirot*; but this type of concealment is very different from the concealment of *En-Sof* who is above all the *sefirot*. The first *sefirah* has both names and qualities. It is mentioned in Scripture, and its nature is defined as Thought or Will.

An important intermediate view holds that, while *Keter* is not identical with *En-Sof*, it is separated just the same from the system of emanation, and is not to be included among the ten *sefirot* at all. It did not begin its existence as part of the emanatory process, but is preexistent like *En-Sof*. Those who hold this view make up the number of the *sefirot* by dividing the *sefirah Hokhmah* into two,[35] the upper part, which takes the place of *Keter*, being called *Haskel*. Or else they introduce a special *sefirah*, *Da'at*, which represents both the revealed nature of *Keter* and the innermost being of *Tiferet*.[36]

The reasons for this approach need explaining. There seem to be two factors that led to its formulation. The first arose from the theological difficulties involved in the doctrine of emanation. In the nature of *En-Sof* there is no active element. It has neither will nor thought. How then could one possibly attribute to it any involvement in the process of emanation? More important than this: the emanatory process must lead to innovation and change in the being of *En-Sof*! The theory of the preexistence of *Keter* as eternal Will removes these difficulties, for emanation now becomes the work of the Will, and there is no need to attribute it to *En-Sof* itself. The second factor arises from the concealed nature of *En-Sof*. The joining of *Keter* to *En-Sof* as a preexistent entity above the realm of emanation introduces an active force, and a positive, defined concept into the world of the hidden God, and so makes a tiny breach in the wall of His concealed otherness. This approach, therefore, constitutes a kind of compromise between the two opposing viewpoints mentioned above. The Neoplatonic nature of *En-Sof* suffers no blemish as to its essence, but the pre-existence of Will within the hidden domain tempers its negative and impersonal character.[37]

[2] The problem of the relationship between *En-Sof* and *Keter* became the subject of fierce controversy in later kabbalah. The proponents of the three views described above all based their opinions on the Zohar and thought they could find support there.[38] However, in contrast to the generally eclectic character of Zoharic teaching, which, as we shall see later, applies even to the description of the nature of *En-Sof*, nevertheless, on this particular point, the book presents only one opinion. The problem is not dealt with in precise terms, but we can deduce with some certainty from its general attitude and from various allusions that the author of the Zohar does not identify *En-Sof* with *Keter*, and that, on the other hand, he does not regard *Keter* as an emanated force identical in nature with the other *sefirot*.

The differentiation between *En-Sof* and *Keter* is made quite plain throughout the book, and in a number of passages they are mentioned as two distinct entities. For example, *En-Sof* is described as a contrast to *Keter*, which is called *Ayin* (nothing): "*En-Sof* cannot be known, and does not produce end or beginning like the primal *Ayin*, which does bring forth beginning and end" (1). At another point it is stated quite clearly that above *Keter* there is the "unknowable," that is, *En-Sof*: "*Keter* is the highest above the high, beginning of all beginnings, and there is that which is above this, which is unknowable."[39] *En-Sof* makes impressions upon *Keter*, which is called *tehiru* (purity), or *avir* (air). *Bozina di-kardinuta* (the spark of blackness, or the darkened light), which constitutes the standard by which the precise nature of the emanated powers is fixed, is emanated "from the mystery of *En-Sof*" into the domain of *Keter* (*Sefirot*, 1). This process is also described in another way, but here too there is a clear distinction between *En-Sof* and *Keter*: The light that does not rest in light (*En-Sof*) reveals and produces the sparking of all the sparks (*bozina di-kardinuta*), and this activates the will of wills (*Keter*), and is concealed within it, and is not known."[40]

However, there is no reference anywhere in the Zohar to the start of *Keter*'s existence as an emergence from *En-Sof*. The first occurrence of emanation to be mentioned is usually the "sparking" of the highest point of *Hokhmah* from *Keter*. Only in a few places, such as in the passages dealing with the *bozina di-kardinuta*, do we find descriptions of processes, preceding the emanation of *Hokhmah*, occurring inside *Keter*, and even here the existence of *Keter* is taken for granted as something that was always there side by side with *En-Sof*. It is portrayed as "primal air" or "supreme purity" surrounding *En-Sof*, a kind of perpetual halo encompassing *En-Sof* before the commencement of emanation, "an envelopment of crystal light,"[41] and by its means the *sefirot* emanate "like jewels, drop by drop" (*Sefirot*, 33). *Keter* and *En-Sof* are inextricably and continuously linked together: "The first world (*Keter*) [is] that supernal world concealed from all, which cannot be seen, and cannot be known, except by Him (*En-Sof*), who is hidden within it" (*Influence and Direction*, 11). Consequently, *Keter* is called "the supreme mystery of *En-Sof*" (*Sefirot*, 17).

And so we have here the intermediate view of the early kabbalists concerning the nature of *Keter* as a preexistent entity, but at the same time separated from the essence of *En-Sof*. However, in one important respect the doctrine of the Zohar is different, for it teaches that *Keter* is to be counted as one of the ten *sefirot*.[42] The terms used for *Keter*, particularly the name *ehyeh* that is attributed to it, are included in the whole system of nomenclature of the *sefirot*. Furthermore, the Zohar does not bring in any other *sefirah* to take the place of *Keter*.[43] It is true that in most of the descriptions of the sefirotic chain, and the structure of emanation, we find *Hokhmah* at the top, with no mention of *Keter* at all. But we must not deduce from this that *Keter* is not to be numbered among the *sefirot*. Its absence only highlights its unique eminence. Whereas *Hokhmah* is called "first" and "beginning" (*sheruta*), *Keter* is designated as the origin of the beginning (*Sefirot*, 18), or in the words of Rabbi Moses de Leon: "From there (from *Keter*) came forth the point of concealment (*Hokhmah*), the first of all levels, and all the remaining mirrors, the beginning of all existence, for supernal *Keter*, may its name be blessed, is not a beginning."[44]

[3] This view gives the nature of *Keter* a peculiar characteristic. It has a place, as the first *sefirah*, in the order of emanation, but at the same time it is divorced from it and has its abode in a higher realm. From the very beginning it dwells in close proximity to *En-Sof*, and in its aspect of primal Will it acts, so to speak, as a partner of the hidden Emanator. Among the terms used for it by the Gerona kabbalists are "emanating force" and "emanating light." This means that *Keter* acts as a kind of transitional stage, which has both the characteristics of the Emanator and the marks of emanation impressed upon it.

The existence of this transitional entity tends to give the nature of *En-Sof* a positive quality, much more than the earlier kabbalistic idea, which saw it as the primal Will above the system of emanation; for here we have a real bridge between the concealment of *En-Sof* and the revelation of the forces of emanation. The essential, functional link between *En-Sof* and the first *sefirah* acts in two directions: *Keter* rises and conceals itself, and *En-Sof* experiences a movement toward revelation.

In a number of places in the Zohar there are indications of a more positive approach to *En-Sof*, in connection with the view, just described, of the relationship between *En-Sof* and *Keter*. A number of terms, such as *setima dekhol setimin*, *temira dekhol temirin* (both meaning "secret of all secrets"), and *atika de-atikin* ("the most ancient of the ancient"), and others, are applied both to *En-Sof* and to *Keter*. It is sometimes difficult to determine which one the author had in mind. A term common to both is sometimes used in a general way indicating both *En-Sof* and *Keter* together in their aspect of the emanating power.[45] Take, for example, this introduction to a description of the process of emanation: "When the secret of all secrets sought to reveal itself, it first made a single point (*Hokhmah*), and this arose to become thought" (*Sefirot*, 10). *Hokhmah* emanates from *Keter*, but it is *En-Sof* that seeks to reveal itself, and the term "secret of all secrets" includes both of them. Furthermore, the positive term *reuta* (will), which designates the nature of *Keter* in its relationship with *En-Sof*, is also used of *En-Sof* itself: "When the supernal will (*En-Sof*) . . . rests upon the will (*Keter*) that cannot ever be known or grasped" (*Sefirot*, 6).

The influence that the *En-Sof*-*Keter* relationship had upon the idea of the nature of the hidden God is expressed mainly in specific strata of the Zohar, namely, the *Idrot*, and particularly the *Idra Zuta*. These sections are characterized by their strange and remarkable anthropomorphic imagery, and they present the world of the divine in a new form, of which there is no trace in the rest of the book except for a few obvious allusions. The image of the divine is depicted in two "countenances": *Atika Kadisha* (the holy old man) called *Arikh Anpin* (long countenance), and *Ze'ir Anpin* (short countenance). The first countenance constitutes the world of absolute mercy, and the second countenance is, in contrast, the world of judgment. As far as the sefirotic system is concerned, *Atika Kadisha* represents *Keter*, while *Ze'ir Anpin* comprises the other *sefirot* from *Hokhmah* to *Malkhut*.[46] With this division into two separate areas—*Keter* on one side and the remaining *sefirot* on the other—the supreme and unique eminence of the first *sefirah* is given greater emphasis.

But this approach contains a new and important element, one crucial to our subject. *Atika Kadisha* signifies not only *Keter*, but the combined world of both *Keter* and *En-Sof*; that is to say, the realm of the hidden God and the first *sefirah* are considered as forming together one single unit. Here is a description of the make-up of *Atika Kadisha* in the form of three "heads": "Three heads are engraved, one within the other, and one above the other. One head is concealed wisdom, which covers itself and is not opened, and this concealed wisdom is head of all, the head of the remaining wisdoms; the supernal head, *Atika Kadisha*, the secret of all secrets, the head of every head; the head that is not a head—it is not known, nor can it be known, whatever exists in this head, for it is not apprehensible by wisdom or knowledge. . . . This *Atika*, the oldest of the old, the supernal crown on high, which is adorned with all the crowns and diadems—all the lights shine and flash forth from it, and it is the supernal hidden light that cannot be known. This *Atika* exists in three heads, and they are comprised in one head, which is the supernal head far above."[47] "The head that is not a head" is *En-Sof*. "The supernal head" is *Keter*. And "concealed wisdom," also called "concealed brain," is the aspect of *Hokhmah* that is in *Keter*, and from which the *sefirah* of *Hokhmah* emanates, that is, *Keter* in its aspect of the source of emanation. Consequently, in *Atika Kadisha* we have all together: *En-Sof*, or the hidden root, and two aspects of *Keter*—a preexistent and hidden being, and also a power that reveals itself through the activity of emanation.

In another passage the relationship of *Keter* to *En-Sof* is depicted from the point of view of the process of emanation: "For I have said that all the lights draw their light from the supernal light, the mystery of all mysteries, and they all constitute levels of illumination, and in the light of each level there is revealed what is revealed . . . each one shines and is held in the light that is within, and does not separate outward . . . the light that is revealed is called 'the garment of the King'; the light that is within is hidden light, in which dwells the one that is not separated, and is not revealed. And all the lights and all the luminaries draw their light from *Atika Kadisha*, the secret of all secrets, the supernal light."[48] The *sefirot* shine forth from *Keter*, called "the supernal light," and "the light that is within," and its brilliant splendor is revealed through them. This shining is internal, within the Godhead, "and does not separate outward." But even in this internal shining the revelation of the light occurs only with reference to *Keter*. *En-Sof* is not directly involved in the process of emanation, for it "is not separated, and is not revealed." Its involvement is purely incidental, through its being attached and adjacent to *Keter*.

Here we see quite clearly the ambiguity in the Zohar's view of the relationship between *En-Sof* and *Keter*. On the one hand, *Keter* is raised to the status of emanator, and *En-Sof* is removed from all emanatory activity. On the other hand, the hidden God is brought nearer to the system of emanation by being attached to the first *sefirah*, and a window is opened through which one may positively apprehend His nature through the image of *Atika Kadisha*.

e. *En-Sof* in the *Raya Mehemna* and the *Tikkunei ha-Zohar*

[1] In the later sections of the Zohar, the *Raya Mehemna* and the *Tikkunei ha-Zohar*, which were composed by another hand, the world of the divine assumes a form quite different from that portrayed in the main body of the book. Here too, it would seem, we have the duality of the hidden God and the revealed God, and the concealed nature of *En-Sof* receives considerable emphasis; indeed, its inculcation is accompanied by severe warnings: "You are the highest of the high, the secret of all secrets; You are altogether beyond the reach of thought"(4); "Woe to him who compares Him to any attribute, even to those attributes that He has" (6). The *sefirot*, including even *Keter*, are darkened when they wish to look upon *En-Sof* (3). In actual fact, however, both *En-Sof* and the *sefirot*, in these sections of the Zohar, are different in nature from the divine entities that are given these same names in the approach described above.

In contrast to the fragmentary and enigmatic allusions that we find in the main body of the Zohar, we have here many passages that contain long and systematic descriptions of the supreme God, and of His relationship to the *sefirot* and the Creation. There are important differences too in terminological usage. In place of the negative term *En-Sof* [lit., "without end"], which had its origin in kabbalistic literature, we find, more usually, the philosophical term *ilat ha-ilot* (cause of causes, i.e., First Cause),[49] which does not occur at all in the Zohar proper. The title *En-Sof* loses its basic meaning, and also its specificity. It is used quite clearly of both *Keter* and the Supreme God together,[50] and from this joint usage we may conclude that it does not signify the denial of finiteness within the hidden nature of God, but the actual unbounded influence that pours into the *sefirah* of *Keter*, that is to say, a positive infinitude at the beginning of revelation: "Thus the Cause of causes makes ten *sefirot* and calls *Keter* 'source,' and there is no limit there to the outpouring of its light, and so He calls Himself '*En-Sof*' "[51] (6).

The "cause of causes" of the *Raya Mehemna* does not dwell within the depths of itself, without any activity. It is both an active and an activating force which establishes the worlds and takes care of them. Even the creation of heaven and earth is attributed to it (4). This is a theistic-personal God, the highest active cause, the Creator, completely incorporeal and concealed as to His essence, but partially revealed through His attributes and His acts. The image of this God is well known from the writings of the philosophers, and, indeed, it is the God of Jewish speculative theology that is depicted here, in a mystical garb and colored by the kabbalistic literary style.

The real core of the concept of God held by this anonymous kabbalist is the problem of the attributes, which is the basic theological question in both Jewish and Arabic medieval philosophy: how can we possibly assign to God attributes that fragment His perfect unity, and which make His simple nature more complex by adding spiritual and even corporeal characteristics that contradict His absolute incorporeality? This problem is not clearly stated in the *Raya Mehemna*, but it can be read between the lines, and the solutions offered there are similar to those of the philosophers, not only in content, but also quite often in presentation. Obvious philosophical expressions are common with this author: "You are one, but not in number"; "You are wise, but not with a known wisdom; You understand, but not with a known understanding" (4), and so on.

These expressions are expanded in a sense that is very like the philosophical connotation from which they spring. God is denied attributes that are separate from His simple, unique essence, and all the powers and characteristics that are attributed to Him, such as wisdom, understanding, mercy, and justice, are merely indicative of His acts, which appear in His conduct of the world as revelations of wisdom, understanding, and so on; that is to say, they are "attributes of action" and not attributes of essence. "It is all to show how the world is conducted; not that You have a known righteousness that is Justice, nor a known law that is Mercy, nor any of these attributes at all" (ibid.). Even the sacred names are terms relating to action, testifying to the works of the Creator, and to His relationship to the world (5). Consequently, as to His essential nature before the creation of the world, "it is forbidden to fashion for Him a form or image in the world, not with the letter *he*, and not with the letter *yod*, and not even with the Holy Name,[52] and not with any letter or vowel-point in the world."[53]

[2] The deeds of the Creator are revealed and accomplished by means of the ten *sefirot*, which were formed in order to be used as instruments for the divine activity: "You are He who produced ten *tikkunim* (regulators), which we call ten *sefirot*, so that through them You might guide the secret worlds that are not

revealed, and the worlds that are revealed" (4). They are given the names of divine forces and attributes, not as substances that belong to the divine realm, but simply as vessels that receive divine influence: "*Hokhmah* (wisdom) is not called *Hokhmah* in its own right, but because of the Wise One who fills it from His source. And [*Binah*—understanding] is not called *Binah* in its own right, but because of the Understanding One who fills it with Himself" (6).

Here we have a fundamental change in attitude toward the nature of the *sefirot* and their relationship to their hidden source. They do not constitute the revealed God, complementing the existence of the hidden God, but they are vessels in the hands of an artisan, who fills them or empties them, constructs them or breaks them, all in accordance with his own desire. "And if the artisan breaks these vessels that he has prepared, the waters return to the source, and the vessels are left broken, dry without water"; "all is in His power, to take out of the vessels or to pour influence into them, or to take out, according to His will; and there is no god above him, that can add to or subtract from Him" (6). Even their formation by means of emanation is thrown into doubt, and it would appear from most of his statements that the author was trying to establish them as created forces.[54]

This considerable change in the evaluation of the *sefirot* is also noticeable in the effect it has on religious life, that is to say, on the relationship between man and his Creator. In the preceding sections I have shown in some detail how far removed *En-Sof* is from prayer, and even from spiritual concentration. The *sefirot* alone could be the objective when man tried to turn directly to God. But this is not the case with the material we are dealing with here. Naturally, the intention in performing the *mizvot* is focused on the inner life in the world of the *sefirot*, but it is not impossible for man to link himself directly with the supreme God, and in a number of liturgical passages found in these books one turns to the First Cause by using such phrases as "Master of the worlds" (*ribbon ha-olamim*).[55] The petitioner asks the supreme God to act in and through the *sefirot*.[56] In many places the author turns to the First Cause with the term "Thou" (*attah*), while in the main body of the Zohar this term is unusable even for *Keter*, who is called "He" (*hu*), and, obviously, there is no term at all that can be applied to *En-Sof* itself.

As to the essence of the *sefirot*, they are consequently outside the realm of the divine, for the unique divine being is the "Cause of causes." But nevertheless the *sefirot* are also quite separated from the lower worlds, and are raised above all existence that is not divine. They have acquired this intermediate status because the First Cause is immanent in them. God acts through the *sefirot*, not in His transcendental capacity, but by causing His radiance to dwell within the sefirotic system, and by spreading His influence there. Since the First Cause cnstructed the system, "for He made the image of the chariot of supernal man (the system of the *sefirot*), He descends there, and is called, in that image, *Yod He Vav He*, so that He might be recognized in all aspects."[57] Government of the worlds is enacted by the descent, as it were, of God among the *sefirot*. The presence of the First Cause in the *sefirot* penetrates their being from within, and surrounds them on every side: "You are in every *sefirah*, through its length and breadth, above and below, and between each *sefirah*, and in the density of each *sefirah*."[58]

From this point of view the world of the *sefirot* is compared to the organic structure of soul and body. The *sefirot* are like the limbs of the body, through which the divine soul works: "Through these names [of the *sefirot*] the Master of the world extends Himself, and He rules by them, receives His titles from them, conceals Himself in them, and dwells within them, like the soul and the limbs of the body"(5). The divine influence pours life into the *sefirot*: "Master of the worlds, You are the Cause of causes, the First Cause, who water the tree (the system of the *sefirot*) with a spring, and this spring is like the soul to the body, for it is the life of the body"(4). Like the soul in the body the single, infinite, and unchanging divine essence is revealed and acts within plurality, limitation, and change by means of the *sefirot*, without any alteration within the divine nature itself (7).[59]

The structure of the world of the *sefirot* is like a single and indivisible unit of "essence and vessels," and so it has a characteristic of the divine realm, even according to the concept of the *Raya Mehemna*. The sefirotic system is like "the portrait of God," for there the hidden essence of God dons form and image, which can be apprehended in prophetic vision and rational thought.[60] The immanence of the divine essence means that the mystery of the unity of God must of necessity apply to the *sefirot* as well, and any thoughts of plurality in their regard were considered blasphemous, even though they do not manifest in their nature a perfect unity. "Since You are within, whoever separates one of the ten from its fellow is thought of as making a separation in You"(4).

In short: there is no duality here between the hidden and the revealed God. The complexities of the transition from the hidden to the revealed domain, and the difficulties of the relationships between the two domains, have both been removed. The First Cause and the sefirotic system constitute two facets of existence of the one and only God: transcendent existence above the *sefirot*, and immanent existence within them, this latter being the existence of God as Creator and Guide. It is possible that, in conformity with this approach, a new meaning is propounded here for the term *azilut* (emanation). It does not signify the way in which the *sefirot* came into being. Their existence is "by way of *azilut*," by the essence of God extending itself to, and dwelling within them, through an immanence both inseparable and continuous.[61]

[3] The idea of immanence within the system of the *sefirot*, which gives them something of the character of divinity, is an indication of the major difference between the approach of the *Raya Mehemna* and the attitude of most Jewish philosophers; and it is this too that conveys the specific kabbalistic flavor of this idea of God. Were it not for this idea the *sefirot* would not differ fundamentally from "the separate intelligences" or other intermediate stages that in the view of the philosophers come between God and the world.

However, according to the author of the *Raya Mehemna* and the *Tikkunei ha-Zohar*, this immanence is not limited to the upper realms. On the contrary, he stresses time and again that the self-extending divine essence encompasses and penetrates every area of existence. "It is He that binds all the chariots of the angels, and binds them together; and He supports the upper and the lower worlds. And were He to remove Himself from them they would have neither sustenance, knowledge, or life. There is no place where He is not, above without end, and below without limit" (7). There is no place free of divinity, and it is the foundation of unity and unification among the separate non-divine forces. Even the combination of the four elements of matter is effected by the divinity that dwells within them. "He encompasses all worlds, and none but He surrounds them on every side, above and below and in the four corners of the globe, and none may go beyond His domain. He fills all worlds, and no other fills them . . . . He binds and joins the species with one another, above and below, and there is no juncture of the four elements except [by] the Holy One, blessed be He, existing among them" (3).[62]

This view of an all-embracing immanence seems to destroy the division between the divine "*sefirot* of emanation" and the lower regions. The latter are arranged in the form of three worlds (creation, formation, and making— *beriyah*, *yezirah*, *asiyah*), each of which contains ten *sefirot* or forces.[63] Consequently, the need arose to fix distinct boundaries between these different systems. In the main passage dealing with this problem we read: "In the ten *sefirot* of emanation the King is there; He and His essence are one there; He and His life are one there. This is not the case with the ten *sefirot* of *beriyah*, for they and their life are not one; they and their essence are not one. And the supreme Cause of all illumines the ten *sefirot* of emanation and the ten [*sefirot*] of *beriyah*, and illumines the ten companies of angels [*yezirah*] and the ten spheres of the firmament [*asiyah*], and He does not change in any place."[64] The divine essence is equally present in all realms, but the attachment of the essence to the garments varies according to their nature and status. In the world of emanation a unity exists between the essence and the *sefirot*, while in the other worlds they are in a state of separation. In a description quoted in the continuation of this passage, a different image is used for this distinction: "In the *sefirot* of emanation there is the actual likeness of the King; in the *sefirot* of *beriyah*, the seal of the King; in the *sefirot* of *yezirah*, and among the angels, who are the *Ḥayyot* [creatures], an impression of the seal in wax." Immanent divinity is reflected in all worlds, but the degree of brightness or opacity of the mirrors determines the nature of the image. This means that fundamentally, when all is said and done, the distinction between the world of emanation and the other worlds is simply one of degree, for by nature the *sefirot* of emanation are also distinguished from God, while, on the other hand, the self-extending divine essence dwells, without alteration, even among the lower regions.

The position of the author of the main body of the Zohar on this question is almost exactly the opposite. In his view the *sefirot* of emanation are of the actual essence of God, and there exists a fundamental difference in nature between them and the lower regions. This difference is brought out by the use of terms like *alma di-yihuda* (the world of unity) and *alma di-peruda* (the world of separation).[65] The *sefirot* of emanation form a unique, unified whole, attached to their hidden source, whereas all other beings are separated from the Godhead and from one another. There is no place here for the concept of immanence outside the system of the *sefirot*.[66] Even with regard to the world of the angels it is said that "the Holy One, blessed be He, is there, and is not [there]. He is there now, but when they wish to look upon and know Him, He removes Himself from them, and is not to be seen" (*Influence and Direction*, 11).

It is true that we do find, even in the Zohar itself, signs of the desire to bridge the gulf between God and the worlds. But this desire is actually fulfilled in the

Raya Mehemna and the *Tikkunei ha-Zohar* in the obscure image of the chain of emanation, stretching from *En-Sof* to the lowest realms of existence. The links in this chain are joined together and interlocked like the kernel and its shell; that is, the top of the chain is pure kernel, and the bottom of the chain is nothing but shell, and each intermediate link is the kernel of the one below it, and the shell of the one above it. "All consists of an inner kernel, with several shells covering the kernel; and the whole world [is constructed] according to this pattern, above and below: from the mysterious beginning of the highest point down to the lowest of all levels, it is all one within the other, and one within the other, so that we find that one [level] is the shell of another, and this other the shell of another . . . . And even though it is only garment it becomes the kernel of another level" (*The Forces of Uncleanness*, 11). The continuity of the chain is expressed more forcibly in another passage: "And so all is embraced and contained, one in the other, and interwoven one with the other, so that they are embraced within this world, which is the last, outermost, shell" (ibid., 13).[67]

So it looks as if we have reached some surprising conclusions. In the doctrine of the impersonal, emanating God, propounded by the Zohar, we find an obvious disinclination to posit a divine immanence penetrating all areas of existence. But in the concept of the personalist God, advocated by the *Raya Mehemna*, a concept that adversely affects the theory of emanation, we have seen that the idea of an all-embracing immanence is an important element. Apparently, however, this paradox merely reflects the inner tension that existed among the different streams of kabbalah between the theistic and the pantheistic tendencies, which was nearly always resolved by some kind of compromise. The denial of personality in God, and the theory of emanation, contained ideas that might tend toward a type of pantheism, and so the Zohar puts a brake on this movement toward pantheism by removing the possibility of immanence. The author of the *Raya Mehemna*, on the other hand, tried to prevent the severance of the worlds from God that is implicit in the personalist concept, and he therefore introduced and stressed the idea of immanence.[68]

NOTES

1. On the teaching of the German *hasidim* on the perception of God, see J. Dan, *Torat ha-sod shel Hasidut Ashkenaz* (Jerusalem, 1968), pp. 84–183.
2. Kabbalistic teaching does naturally have many points of contact with the mystical trends mentioned above, but even here one should not see the kabbalah as a continuation of *hekhalot* mysticism. Its sources are to be found in other spiritual strata, as later chapters will show.
3. Zohar III, 152a. [See below, *Torah*, 3.]
4. Zohar II, 247b. And see *Zohar Hadash, Shir ha-Shirim*, 70d.
5. *Guide for the Perplexed*, III. [Friedlander trans.]
6. One ought to note that in philosophy too perception is spoken of as the receiving of influence from "the Active Intellect." But there it is associated with intellectual perception, and the influence of "the Active Intellect" is not a process that contrasts with logical or empirical knowledge, but leads indeed to its perfection.
7. See also *Sefirot*, 35.
8. I. Tishby, ed. *Perush ha-Aggadot le-Rabbi Azriel* (Jerusalem, 1945), p. 15.
9. *Sefer Yezirah* I, 8. The kabbalists explained this passage with reference to *Keter* as

well, the nearest in degree of concealment to *En-Sof*, as will be seen later in *En-Sof and Keter*, below, p. 242.

10. In Rabbi Meir ibn Gabbai, *Derekh Emunah* (Berlin, 1850), 4a.

11. Beginning of chap. 7.

12. See, e.g., III, 130a.

13. E.g., I, 21a: "There is no mark of recognition in *En-Sof* at all. No question can touch it, and there is no idea that thought can contemplate."

14. Sect. 33. See G. Scholem, *Reshit ha-Kabbalah* (Jerusalem, 1948), pp. 63, 104–7.

15. *Perush Eser Sefirot*, in *Derekh Emunah*, 4a.

16. Consistent with this, Rabbi Moses de Leon does use causal terms in describing *Keter*, the first *sefirah*. See *Sefer Shekel ha-Kodesh* (1911), pp. 6–7.

17. The growth of the *sefirot* doctrine from contact with the remnants of Gnosis was proved and analyzed at length by G. Scholem in his *Reshit ha-Kabbalah*, pp. 26–36.

18. A very close approximation to this dualism can be seen in the Zoharic teaching concerning *sitra ahra* (the other side), but even here the kabbalists stopped short of absolute dualism. See below, introduction to *The Forces of Uncleanness*.

19. Judah Halevi, *Kuzari* IV, 16.

20. See G. Scholem, *Major Trends in Jewish Mysticism* (New York, 1946), p. 13. In the same spirit, which suited his own particular vein of thought, Rabbi Moses Cordovero already understood and defined the background of the dualism of *En-Sof* and the sefirotic system: "Now that we have demonstrated the numerical significance of the *sefirot*, we must ask whether they are rationally necessary, or not. And we must answer that they are necessary for a number of reasons. The first is that, since we believe in divine providence, and even in His providence concerning particulars, we are forced to say that His providence is exercised by means of the *sefirot*, for the incorporeal Oneness, the Cause of causes, is devoid of all change or attribute, such as, "wise," "righteous," "hearing," or the other epithets of which the philosophers have stripped Him; and similarly with bodily and physical character-istics, such as "And the Lord came down," "the ears of the Lord," "the hand of the Lord," "the eyes of the Lord," and similar expressions that occur in Scripture, and that refer to some limitation or corporeality, or those which refer to certain qualities . . . and so it is for this reason—namely, that we should not contradict the principles of our belief in the incorporeal Oneness, in this completely abstract being devoid of any quality that might necessitate corporeality or physical substance, while we are bound to believe also in His providence, for this too is one of the principles of the religion—that it is necessary for us to believe in the *sefirot*, so that the principles of our belief should not contradict one another." (*Pardes Rimmonim*, I, 8.)

21. G. Scholem, "Te'udah Hadashah le-Toledot Reshit ha-Kabbalah," *Sefer Bialik* (1934), pp. 148, 151.

22. As in *Sefer Yezirah* I, 7.

23. *Sefer Ma'arekhet ha-Elohut*, chap. 3.

24. Zohar, III, 288a.

25. This idea occurs at other points in the Zohar in connection with plurality and differentiation in the world of the *sefirot* (II, 176a; III, 141b). See also G. Scholem, *Major Trends in Jewish Mysticism*, pp. 223–25, 402, n. 66.

26. A good example of this double aspect of the mystery of the unity can be found in a passage of the Zohar (II, 216a–216b): "'Hear, O Israel'—here are included the woman and her husband, and since they are comprised together in one unit, we must now unify the limbs, and join together the two tabernacles as one throughout the limbs, with the purpose of ascending into conjunction with *En-Sof*, for all conjoins there, in order to be one single unit, the upper and the lower worlds." Here we have the depiction of three stages; two in the realm of the *sefirot*—the union of the woman with her husband, i.e., the union of *Malkhut* and *Tiferet*, and the unification

of the limbs, which are the other *sefirot*—while the third is the attachment of the *sefirot* to *En-Sof*.

27. G. Scholem, "Te'udah Ḥadashah," pp. 148–49.

28. A remarkable illustration of this is afforded by the following dialogue: Rabbi Isaac bar Sheshet asks, "How can you kabbalists turn your devotion in one blessing to one particular *sefirah*, and in another blessing to another *sefirah*? And, furthermore, are the *sefirot* really divine that a man can pray to them?" In the reply that one kabbalist gives, the *sefirot* appear as real intermediaries, to whom one does not pray directly at all: "This is the manner of prayer, which is always directed to the First Cause, but one concentrates one's thought on bringing divine influence down upon the *sefirah* that is connected with the object of one's petition." (Ribash, *Responsa*, no. 157.) However, this reply conforms only with those who regard the *sefirot* as attributes, or vessels, distinct from the essence of God—an idea treated below in section e.

29. The movement of the *sefirot* upward to *En-Sof* is described often in kabbalistic literature of the early period, and allusions to it can also be found in the Zohar, particularly in connection with the mystery of the sacrifices. See, for example, II, 219b, 259b, 268b, and below, *Sefirot*, 6.

30. G. Scholem, "Der Begriff der Kawwana in der alten Kabbala," *MGWJ* (1934), p. 497, and see there the interpretation of the passage, and also the analysis and explanation of statements from other kabbalists.

31. II, 260b.

32. II, 213b. See also II, 144a, 244b.

33. I discuss this idea below, pp. 269 ff.

34. See Rabbi Moses Cordovero, *Pardes Rimmonim*, III.

35. This idea, mentioned in Rabbi Isaac the Blind's commentary to the *Sefer Yezirah*, is expressed very fully in the writings of Rabbi Asher ben David, and it would appear that Rabbi Azriel of Gerona was also inclined toward it. See G. Scholem, *Reshit ha-Kabbalah*, pp. 109–10.

36. See G. Scholem, "Seridei Sifro shel R. Shem Tov Ibn Gaon al Yesodot Torat ha-Sefirot," *Kiryat Sefer*, 8, pp. 398ff.

37. These two factors are not expressly stated in the writings of the kabbalists, but they are implied by them. It is to be noted that similar motives are to be found in Rabbi Solomon ibn Gabirol's doctrine of the Will (see J. Guttmann; *Philosophies of Judaism* [1964], pp. 100–102), and this approach was no doubt formulated by those kabbalists who used Gabirol's ideas. See G. Scholem, "Ikvotav shel Gabirol ba-Kabbalah," *Me'assef Sofrei Erez Yisrael* (1940), pp. 171–74.

38. See Rabbi Meir ibn Gabbai, *Sefer Avodat ha-Kodesh*, I, chap. 3; Moses Cordovero, *Pardes Rimmonim*, III.

39. Zohar III, 288b (*Idra Zuta*).

40. *Zohar Ḥadash*, beginning of *Va-ethanan*.

41. However, it is possible that the reference here is to *Ḥokhmah*. Cf. Zohar I, 29a.

42. There would appear to be an opposite view of *Keter* in Zohar III, 269a: "Supernal *Keter* comprises all, and is not included in the number." But the meaning here apparently is that it is not included among those that are emanated, although it is thought of as the first *sefirah*. This approach is stated more clearly in I, 31b: "[*Ḥokhmah*] is second in the enumeration [of the *sefirot*], but is called 'beginning,' because although the hidden, supernal *Keter* is the first [in the enumeration of the *sefirot*], it is not included in the number [of those that are emanated], and so the second (*Ḥokhmah*) becomes the beginning." See *Pardes Rimmonim*, II, 3. Cordovero is forced, for the sake of consistency in his own view of the matter, to interpret this passage to mean that *Keter* is first both in the enumeration of the *sefirot* and also in the order of emanation.

43. In two places (*Sefirot*, 14, and III, 291a [*Idra Zuta*]) *Da'at* is mentioned as a higher

emanation, active in *Tiferet*, and we may deduce therefore that the author was
familiar with the *Da'at* theory. But even in these passages he does not give it the role
of a substitute *sefirah*.

44. *Sefer Shekel ha-Kodesh*, p. 25. Cf. Zohar II, 90a: "That which is hidden and has no
beginning we call 'it' (*Keter*)." Rabbi Moses de Leon's other remarks concerning
Keter (ibid., pp. 6, 23–24, 110–11) are consistent with the attitude that I have
demonstrated by collecting and analyzing the various statements in the Zohar.

45. This kind of thing misled several kabbalists into thinking that the Zohar taught that
En-Sof and *Keter* were identical.

46. In the other parts of the Zohar, however, *Ze'ir Anpin* appears sometimes to be clearly
identified with *Tiferet*.

47. Zohar III, 288b (*Idra Zuta*). See *Sefirot*, 12.

48. Zohar, III, 291b.

49. Since this term is also applied to the upper *sefirot*, in that they are the "cause" of the
lower *sefirot*, more extraordinary "causative" titles are sometimes given to the head
itself of the *sefirot*. See 2.

50. "Which is *En-Sof*, and higher than all the *sefirot*" (*Shekhinah*, 11); "Since [the lower
sefirot] depend on *Keter*, they are called ["water"] that has no end, for *Keter* is called
En-Sof ('no end')" (III, 258a [*Raya Mehemna*]).

51. An attempt to make a positive use of the expression *En-Sof* is to be found as well in
the main body of the Zohar, when it uses the term for the nine lights that shine in the
divine thought, i.e., in *Hokhmah* (*Sefirot*, 6. There is another version in *Zohar Hadash*,
Bereshit, beginning of *Sitrei Otiot*), but there the usage is connected precisely with the
concealed aspect of the lights, and with their desire to be united with the hidden
God.

52. The tetragrammaton, which was thought to indicate the divine essence.

53. Zohar II, 42b (*Raya Mehemna*).

54. It is true that they are called *sefirot azilut* in contrast to the lower forces, but it is
possible that, as we shall show later, *azilut* here has a different meaning from the
usual "emanation." D. H. Joel tried to prove, in his *Die Religionsphilosophie des Sohar*
(Leipzig, 1849), that the Zohar does not teach the theory of emanation, and that its
picture of God is perfectly in line with traditional Jewish theology. He is right to
some extent, as far as the attitude I am discussing here is concerned. But the point is
that this attitude does not represent the true and specifically kabbalistic viewpoint.
Furthermore, even the attitude here contradicts Joel on another matter, the
question of immanence, which I shall deal with in the next section. Joel tried to
divest Zoharic doctrine of any belief in divine immanence.

55. See 4, and Zohar III, 99b (*Raya Mehemna*).

56. Cf. above, pp. 234–5.

57. II, 42b (*Raya Mehemna*).

58. III, 109b (*Raya Mehemna*).

59. There are, of course, in the main body of the Zohar, comparisons of the *sefirot* to
limbs of the body, and to garments. And in a few places we even find the soul and
body image (see *Sefirot*, 35; Zohar I, 103b; III, 152a). But there the images and the
theistic expressions are not fundamental, because those matters which are compared
to limbs and to garments belong intrinsically to the divine realm. Furthermore, the
comparison with the activity of the soul is not applied to the emergence of *En-Sof*
from its concealment and its self-revelation through the processes of creation. For
the different views on the question of "essence and vessels," see *Pardes Rimmonim*, IV.

60. See 7; Zohar II, 42b; III, 222b (*Raya Mehemna*).

61. One cannot give a precise answer to this problem; there is also a case for regarding
azilut here as the usual "emanation." Rabbi Menahem Recanati, whose attitude to
the concept of the *sefirot* was similar to that of the *Raya Mehemna*, interprets the term

azilut quite clearly as extension of the divine essence, but in his view the *sefirot* were not created either, but "sparked forth" (*hitnozezu*): "Just as the soul clothes itself with the body, so with the Creator, may He be blessed—from His great light these vessels spark forth, and the sages call them *sefirot*. And the extension of the First Cause in these vessels, is called *azilut*". (*Pardes Rimmonim*, IV, 1.)

62. It seems to me that in his concept of divine immanence the author of the *Raya Mehemna* and the *Tikkunei ha-Zohar* was influenced by the theological writings of the German *hasidim*. The influence of German hasidism can be seen most clearly in the almost exactly parallel way in which the idea of immanence is expressed. A good example of this is the passage I have already quoted ("He encompasses all worlds, and none but He surrounds them on every side, above and below and in the four corners of the globe, and none may go beyond His domain. He fills all worlds, and no other fills them. . . ."). This echoes the verses of the Hymn of Unity for the third day: "You encompass all, and fill all, and, being all, You exist in all. There is none above You, and none below You, none outside You, and none between You . . . and none within is separated from You, and there is no place devoid of You" (*Shirei ha-Yihud ve-ha-Kavod*, ed. A. M. Habermann (Jerusalem, 1948), p. 26). Compare also the famous statement, "there is no place devoid of Him, above or below" (*Tikkunei ha-Zohar, Tikkun* no. 57). There are of course parallels to this in the sayings of the rabbis, e.g., "there is no place on earth devoid of the *Shekhinah*" (*Bemidbar Rabbah* 12: 4; see also *Shemot Rabbah* 2: 9, etc). But the phraseology used in the first passage demonstrates the connection with the theological literature of the German *hasidim*. See J. Dan, *Torat ha-Sod shel Hasidut Ashkenaz* (Jerusalem, 1968), pp. 174–83, and elsewhere in the chapter *Torat ha-Kavod*, pp. 104–70. In manuscripts of German hasidic theological texts there are a number of expressions that are very close indeed to descriptions of immanence in the *Raya Mehemna* and the *Tikkunei ha-Zohar*. It would be useful to make a careful comparison between the writings of this anonymous Spanish kabbalist and German source material, both on this particular point and on other matters.

63. See G. Scholem, "Le-Heker Kabbalat R. Yizhak ha-Kohen," *Tarbiz* 3; 55–58.

64. Preface to the *Tikkunei ha-Zohar*, 3b.

65. See G. Scholem, op. cit., pp. 37–39.

66. It goes without saying that the presence of the *Shekhinah* in the different worlds is frequently mentioned in the Zohar, but not the self-extension of the divine essence. See Rabbi Moses de Leon, *Sefer Shekel ha-Kodesh*, p. 92.

67. Cf. the description of the chain by which the soul is linked to *En-Sof* (Zohar II, 142b). See G. Scholem, *Major Trends in Jewish Mysticism*, pp. 221–25. A similar view of the combination and interlocking of the elements is to be found in the writings of Philo, who attributes this procedure to the Logos who dwells in the realm of the elements. See M. Stein, *Philon ha-Alexandroni* (Warsaw, 1937), p. 216.

68. See J. Abelson, *The Immanence of God in Rabbinical Literature* (1912). This book sets out to prove that the typical rabbinic concept of God consists of a mixture of the personalist idea and the theory of immanence. But the mixture in the *Raya Mehemna* is fundamentally different, for one cannot compare the self-extension of the essence of God with the presence in the world of the *Shekhinah*. And there are also significant differences, in the subject matter we are dealing with, in the idea of the personal God.

EN-SOF AND THE WORLD OF EMANATION

1. EN-SOF AND AYIN

(Zohar II, 239a)

Rabbi Eleazar asked Rabbi Simeon: We know that the whole-offering is connected to the Holy of Holies[1] so that it may be illumined. To what heights does the attachment of the will[2] of the priest, the Levites, and Israel extend?

He said: We have already taught that it extends to En-Sof,[3] for all attachment, unification, and completion is to be secreted in that secret which is not perceived or known, and which contains the will of all wills. En-Sof cannot be known, and does not produce end or beginning like the primal Ayin (nothing), which does bring forth beginning and end.[4] What is beginning? The supernal point,[5] which is the beginning of all, concealed and resting within thought,[6] and producing end[7] that is called "The end of the matter" (Ecclesiastes 12: 13). But there are no end, no wills, no lights, no luminaries in En-Sof.[8] All these luminaries and lights depend on it for their existence,[9] but they are not in a position to perceive.[10] That which knows, but does not know, is none but the Supernal Will, the secret of all secrets, Ayin.[11] And when the supernal point and the world to come[12] ascend they know only the scent, like someone who inhales a scent, and is perfumed by it.

[1] The whole-offering symbolizes the Shekhinah, and it ascends to Binah, which in the world of the sefirot is the Holy of Holies.

[2] The attachment of the human will to God by the concentrated intention of the person bringing the offering.

[3] This intention reaches the source of all wills.

[4] The concealed essence of En-Sof does not reveal itself in the sefirot as "beginning" or "end." The sefirot are the self-extension of Keter, which is also called Ayin Kadmon (primal nothing). This is also beyond the boundary of perception; but the perceptible sefirot have emanated from it. [5] Hokhmah, the beginning of revelation.

[6] It can be dimly perceived by thought, for it is the divine Thought, the source of thought in the lower worlds.

[7] Malkhut, which marks the final stage in the structure of the sefirotic world.

[8] There is no differentiation within En-Sof. Its nature is uniformly one, from every point of view.

[9] The sefirot, which are the lights of the Godhead, are maintained by the influence that descends from En-Sof.

[10] En-Sof is concealed, even from the perception of the sefirot.

[11] Only Keter, the supernal will, has knowledge, a faint knowledge, of the nature of En-Sof. [12] Binah.

2. CAUSE ABOVE ALL CAUSES

(Zohar I, 22b, *Tikkunei ha-Zohar*)

Rabbi Simeon began again by quoting: "See now that I, even I, am He, and there is no god with Me . . ." (Deuteronomy 32: 39).

Companions, listen to ancient things that it is my desire to reveal, since permission has been granted from on high. What is the significance of "See now that I, even I, am He"? This is the cause over and above all the highest things.[13] That which is called "the cause of causes"[14] is the cause of the [known] causes, for not one of these causes performs any act without obtaining permission from the cause that is above it, as I have explained above[15] on [the verse] "Let us make man" (Genesis 1: 26). "Let us make" indicates two, for one said to that which was above it "Let us make," and it could do nothing without the express permission of the one above it, and the one above it could do nothing without first obtaining advice from its fellow. But that which is called "cause above all causes,"[16] above which there is nothing higher, and below which there is nothing of equal stature, as it is said, "To whom then will you compare Me, that I should be equal? says the Holy One" (Isaiah 40: 25)—said, "See now that I, even I, am He, and there is no god with Me" from whom it should take advice, as was the case when "God said, Let us make man."

All the companions arose and said: Master, give us permission to speak in this place. Did you not explain earlier,[17] that the cause of causes said to *Keter*, "Let us make man"?

He said to them: Let your ears hear what your mouth speaks. Have I not just told you that there is that which is called "the cause of causes," and this is not the same as that which is called "cause above all causes," for "cause above all causes" has no companion from which it can take advice, for it is single, preceding all, with no partner, and it is for this reason that it says, "See now that I, even I, am He, and there is no god with Me," from whom it should take advice; for it has no companion, no partner, and no number. There does exist a shared unity, as with male and female, of whom it is said, "for one I called him" (Isaiah 51: 2).[18]

---

[13] *En-Sof.*

[14] *Hokhmah* or *Binah*, the source of the *sefirot* that are active in directing the world.

[15] At the beginning of the section (22a) he explains that the mother says to the father "Let us make man."   [16] *En-Sof.*

[17] This explanation is at the beginning of the section. It is missing in the main body of the Zohar but may be found in *Zohar Hadash, Tikkunim,* 114c–114d.

[18] The verse refers to Abraham and Sarah, who are here called "one." [This is a literal rendering of the verse. It is usually translated "when he (i.e., Abraham) was but one I called him."]

But this is one without number, and without companion, and it says therefore, "there is no god with Me."

They all arose and prostrated themselves before him, and said: Happy is the man who is united with his master in the revelation of hidden mysteries, which are not revealed [even] to the holy angels.

3. EN-SOF BEYOND ALL PERCEPTION

(Zohar III, 225a, *Raya Mehemna*)

He understands all, but there is none that understands Him. He is not called by the name *Yod*, *He*, *Vav*, *He*, nor by any other name, except when His light extends itself upon them.[19] And when He removes Himself from them, He has no name of His own at all.

"That which is exceedingly deep, who can find it?" (Ecclesiastes 7: 24). No light can look upon Him without becoming dark. Even the supernal *Keter*, whose light is the strongest of all the levels, and of all the hosts of Heaven, both the upper and the lower realms, is alluded to in "He made darkness His hiding-place";[20] while of *Ḥokhmah* and *Binah* it is said "Clouds and thick darkness surround Him" (Psalm 97: 2). This is even truer of the remaining *sefirot*, and even truer of the *Ḥayyot*, and even truer of the elements, which are dead bodies.

He encompasses all worlds, and none but He surrounds them on every side, above and below and in the four corners of the globe, and none may go beyond His domain. He fills all worlds, and no other fills them. He gives life to them, and there is no other god above Him to give Him life. This is the meaning of "You give life to them all" (Nehemiah 9: 6), and of this Daniel spoke: "All the inhabitants of the earth are reputed as nothing; and He does according to His will in the host of heaven" (Daniel 4: 32). He binds and joins the species with one another, above and below, and there is no juncture of the four elements except [by] the Holy One, blessed be He, existing among them.

4. THE CONDUCT OF THE WORLD THROUGH THE SEFIROT

(*Tikkunei ha-Ẓohar*, Second Preface, 17a–17b)

Elijah began and said: Master of the worlds, You are one but not in number;[21] You are the highest of the high, the secret of all secrets; You

[19] The names are titles given to the *sefirot*, and when the light of the essence of *En-Sof* is spread over them, these names may be applied to Him as well.

[20] Psalm 18: 12. When *Keter* wishes to apprehend the "hiding-place" of *En-Sof*, it appears as darkness, while *Ḥokhmah* and *Binah* are obscured like clouds and thick darkness.

[21] The unity of *En-Sof* is not a numerical unity; it cannot be followed by a second. In this respect *En-Sof* is differentiated from the *sefirot*, each of which is one in a series of ten.

are altogether beyond the reach of thought. You are He that produced ten *tikkunim*, which we call ten *sefirot*, so that through them You might guide the secret worlds that are not revealed, and the worlds that are revealed. And through them You are concealed[22] from mankind, and You bind them and unite them. Since You are within, whoever separates one of the ten from its fellow is thought of as making a separation in You.[23]

These ten *sefirot* follow the order in which they are one long, one short, and one intermediate.[24] You are the one who guides them, and there is no one to guide You, neither above, nor below, nor on any side. You have prepared garments for them,[25] from which the souls fly to the children of men.[26] Several bodies have You prepared for them, which are called "body" in respect of the garments that cover them. And they are named, in this arrangement,[27] as fellows: *Ḥesed*—right arm; *Gevurah*—left arm; *Tiferet*—torso; *Nezaḥ* and *Hod*—two legs; *Yesod*—the completion of the body, the sign of the holy covenant;[28] *Malkhut*—mouth,[29] which we call the oral Torah. The brain is *Ḥokhmah*, the inner thought; *Binah* is the heart, of which it is said "the heart understands."[30] Of these two it is written, "The hidden things belong to the Lord, our God" (Deuteronomy 29: 28). The supernal *Keter* is the crown of royalty (*malkhut*),[31] of which it is said, "It declares the end from the beginning"

---

[22] The *sefirot* are stages in the revelation of *En-Sof*, which clothes itself in them. But they also serve as a covering that conceals its essence, since were it not for this covering the lower regions would not have the power to apprehend it at all.

[23] The light of *En-Sof* in the *sefirot* maintains their unity. Consequently, whoever assigns to any one of the *sefirot* an existence that is separate from, and independent of, the whole unified system denies, as it were, the unity of *En-Sof* itself.

[24] The *sefirot* are arranged according to a system in which there are two extreme points, *Ḥesed* and *Din*, and an intermediate point, *Raḥamim*, where the two extremes meet. The parts of this harmonious triad are regarded as "long," "short," and "intermediate."

[25] The *sefirot* of the worlds of *beriyah*, *yezirah*, and *asiyah* [see above p. 250] are the garments of the divine *sefirot* of the world of emanation. The *sefirot* of each of these worlds are looked upon as the body of those below them, and the garment of those above them.

[26] The souls descend in a chain through the worlds of *beriyah*, *yezirah* and *asiyah*, and according to the author of the *Tikkunei ha-Zohar*, the lower parts of the soul actually originate in these worlds. [See below, pp. 713–14.]

[27] According to the structure of the human body.

[28] [I.e. the covenant of circumcision.]

[29] The mystery of speech, and therefore called the oral Torah, in contrast to *Tiferet*, which is the written Torah. It is possible that the reference here is to the mouth of the covenant, through which the divine influence descends.

[30] B.T. *Berakhot* 61a. [*Ha-lev mevin*. Both *mevin* and *binah* come from the same verbal root.]

[31] By this designation the last *sefirah* is connected with the first, through the mystical idea of "their end is fastened into their beginning." Hence the application to it of the scriptural phrase "it declares the end from the beginning."

(Isaiah 46: 10), and it is the headpiece of the *tefillin*.[32] Inwardly it is *Yod, He, Vav, He*, which is the way of emanation.[33] It is the watering-place of the tree, with its arms and its boughs, like water that waters the tree, and it grows because of the watering.[34]

Master of the worlds, You are the Cause of causes, the First Cause, who water the tree with a spring, and this spring is like the soul to the body, for it is like the life of the body. In You there is no image, and no likeness of what is within, or of what is without.[35] You created heaven and earth, and You have produced from them sun and moon and stars and planets, and, in the earth, trees and grasses and the Garden of Eden and wild beasts and birds and fish and men, so that through them the upper realms might be known, and how the upper and the lower realms are governed, and how the upper and lower realms might be distinguished.[36]

There is none that knows anything of You, and besides You there is no singleness and no unity in the upper or the lower worlds, and You are acknowledged as Lord over all. As for all the *sefirot*, each one has a known name, and the angels are designated by them,[37] but You have no known name, for You fill all names, and You are the perfect completion of them all. And when You remove Yourself from them, all the names are left like a body without a soul.

You are wise but not with a known wisdom; You understand but not with a known understanding.[38] You have no known place, except that which tells the children of men of Your strength and power, and shows them how the world is conducted with Justice and Mercy,[39] which are righteousness and law, in accordance with the deeds of the children of men. Justice is *Gevurah*; law—the central pillar;[40] righteousness—holy *Malkhut*; scales of righteousness—the two pedestals of truth;[41] a

---

[32] The strap that surrounds the brain, which is *Hokhmah*.

[33] The innermost part of *Keter* is the tetragrammaton, fully spelled out—*Yod, He, Vav, He*—i.e., ten letters in all, signifying the ten *sefirot*, which receive influence from the light of *En-Sof*, which illumines the inner core of *Keter*.

[34] The inner light of *Keter* waters *Tiferet*, which is the tree of emanation, and the lower *sefirot*, which are the arms and boughs of the tree.

[35] *En-Sof* lacks all likeness, not only of the nondivine substances (what is without) but also of the spiritual image of the *sefirot* (what is within).

[36] Contemplation of the creation in the lower world leads to a knowledge of how God governs the upper and lower realms, and to a recognition of their respective natures.

[37] At times the angels are designated by names reserved normally for the *sefirot*, which act through their power and mediation.

[38] The wisdom and understanding of *En-Sof* are essential to its nature, and not separate powers. The *sefirot Hokhmah* (Wisdom) and *Binah* (Understanding) are so called because the essential wisdom and understanding of *En-Sof* work through them.

[39] The *sefirot*, which have a precise and defined nature, and which seem to delimit space, are no more than a revelation to mankind of the forces that control the world. But one must not assign various separate attributes to *En-Sof* itself.

[40] *Tiferet.*   [41] *Nezah* and *Hod.*

righteous measure[42]—the sign of the covenant.[43] It is all to show how the world is conducted; not that You have a known righteousness which is Justice, nor a known law which is Mercy, nor any of these attributes at all.

5. SOUL AND BODY

(Zohar III, 275b–285a. *Raya Mehemna*)

You must know that He is called "wise," with every kind of wisdom, and "discerning," with every kind of discernment, and "merciful," with every kind of mercy, and "powerful," with every kind of power, and "counsellor," with every kind of counsel, and "righteous," with every kind of righteousness, and "sovereign," with every kind of sovereignty, *ad infinitum*, beyond the reach of thought. And at all these levels,[44] in one He is called "Merciful One," and in another "Judge," and so at all levels *ad infinitum*.

If this is so, is there then a difference between "Merciful One" and "Judge"?[45] No, because before He created the world He was designated at all these levels for the sake of the creatures who were yet to be created, for were it not for the creatures in the world why should He be called "Merciful One" and "Judge"? It was only for the sake of the creatures that were to be. Consequently, all the names are designations of His, relating to His acts. It was in this way that He created in His image the soul, which is given a name in accordance with its activities in the various parts of the body, which is called the "small world." Just as the Master of the world deals with every creature and every generation according to their acts, so does the soul according to the deeds of every part of the body. For the sake of that part of the body with which a man fulfills a commandment, the soul is called, in respect to it, "compassion," "love," "grace," and "mercy." And for the sake of that part of the body with which a man commits a transgression, the soul is called, in respect to it, "justice," "anger," and "ire." But apart from the body, what could possibly be the object of compassion or cruelty? In the same way, the Master of the world, before He created the world, and before He created His creatures—for what purpose could He have been called "merciful and gracious" or "Judge"? All His names are merely designations, and He is given them only for the sake of the creatures in the world.

[42] [Lit. "a righteous *hin*"—a measure of wheat. See Leviticus 19: 36.]

[43] *Yesod.*

[44] Among the *sefirot*, which are the attributes of the Godhead.

[45] The different names of the attributes seem to imply some kind of change or mutation within *En-Sof*. But these differences are not to be applied to *En-Sof* itself, but to its activity by means of the *sefirot*, which are the controlling forces. Furthermore, these names for *En-Sof* did not originate at the creation of the world. Before the creation *En-Sof* was designated by them, in preparation for what was to be.

Consequently, when a generation is good He is called, in respect to them, *Yod, He, Vav, He,* with the attribute of mercy; and when a generation is wicked He is called, in respect to them, *Adonai,* with the attribute of justice; to every generation, and to every man, according to his attributes; not that He has any attribute, or known name, like the *sefirot,* for every *sefirah* has a known name, an attribute, a limit, and an area.[46] Through these names the Master of the world extends Himself, and He rules by them, receives His titles from them, conceals Himself in them, and dwells within them, like the soul with the limbs of the body. And just as the Master of the worlds has no known name, and no known place, but His dominion extends on every side, so too the soul has no known name, and no known place in the body, but its dominion extends on every side, and there is no part empty of it. Therefore one should not assign it a single place, for were that so its dominion would be lacking in other parts of the body. And one should not call it by a single name, or two, or three, saying that it is "wise" or "discerning," or that it has knowledge, and nothing else, for if we do this we deprive it of the other levels. How much more is this true of the Master of the world—one should not assign to Him a known place, or give Him names or make a duality or a trinity of Him through them, like the level of the chariot,[47] of which it is said, "They shall call you thrice holy"[48]; for all the levels of all His chariots are threefold; for example, "The patriarchs are the chariot" (*Bereshit Rabbah* 47: 8), and they are the likeness of a lion, an ox, and an eagle, which form the chariot for man, as it is said, "As for the likeness of their faces, they had the face of a man" (Ezekiel 1: 10), and on the female side they rule over man, and the female is their chariot,[49] and so it is said of them, "They shall call you thrice holy." Similarly, the letters that are the faces of the creatures (*Ḥayyot*) are also threefold, as, for example, *yod-he-vav, he-vav-yod, vav-he-yod.*[50] The fourth *he*[51] [is referred to in] "They shall call you thrice holy." It is the completion of them all, for with them it completes the name *Yod-He-Vav-He.* But the Master of all—one should not make of Him a trinity, either by names or

[46] The nature of every *sefirah* is fixed and prescribed, according to the function that it performs.

[47] The *sefirot Ḥesed, Gevurah,* and *Tiferet,* which symbolize the patriarchs, constitute, together with *Malkhut,* the heavenly chariot, and they are the faces of the creatures (*Ḥayyot*) that Ezekiel saw in the chariot.

[48] A phrase from the "sanctification" of the Sabbath afternoon liturgy.

[49] From the male aspect in the Godhead, the likeness of man in the chariot is *Ḥokhmah,* the supernal father, and the three creatures serve as its chariot. But from the female aspect the likeness of man is *Malkhut,* which serves as the chariot for the creatures.

[50] The first three letters of the tetragrammaton *Yod-He-Vav-He* are included in various combinations in every creature.

[51] I.e., the last *he* of the tetragrammaton, which is the fourth letter of the name, and represents *Malkhut.*

by letters. He is called by all the names, but He has no known name. But every single name testifies to Him.

The name *Adonai*[52] (Lord) testifies to Him, in that He is Lord of all the worlds, and there is no one that knows [His worlds]. There are men who inherit three hundred and ten worlds. This is the meaning of "that I may cause those who love me to inherit substance"[53] according to the "something from nothing" level they have attained,[54] and this is the supernal *Ḥokhmah*. There are men who inherit only one world, according to their own level, as the teaching goes: "Every righteous man has a world of his own."[55] Thus every member of the house of Israel inherits worlds according to his level in the realms above. But the Master of the worlds has no worlds, in the numerical sense. He is rather the Lord of all the worlds, and the name *Adonai* testifies to Him. Similarly, [the name] *Yod-He-Vav-He*[56]—on Him depend all existing things,[57] and He and all existing things that belong to Him testify that the Master of the world existed before all existing things, exists in every existing thing, and will exist after every existing thing, and this is the mystery to which all existing things testify concerning Him: He was, He is, and He will be. The name *El*[58] testifies to the Master of all, to the fact that no name, being, or level has power, let alone the other lower creatures, and this is the import of "they are reputed as nothing, and He does according to His will in the host of heaven" (Daniel 4: 32). *Elohim*[59] testifies to His Godhead, that He is God, and God of gods, and that He is God above all, and that there is no god above Him. *Zevaot*[60] testifies to Him, as it is written "And He does according to His will [*khe-mizbeyeh*] in the host of heaven." *Shaddai*[61] testifies to Him, that when He said to the world "Enough! [*dai*]," it stayed within its limits, and expanded no further. And so it was with water, wind, and fire.[62] And, in the same way, every existing thing and every name testifies to Him, to the fact that, since He was single and alone before He created the world, there was no need[63] for Him to be given these names, or other titles, such as "merciful and gracious, long-suffering," and so on, "Judge," "powerful," "strong," and many other such. He is given all these names and titles for the sake of

---

[52] *Malkhut*.

[53] Proverbs 8: 21. The subject of the sentence is "Wisdom." *Yesh*, "substance," has a numerical value of 310.

[54] [*Yesh me-ayin* "something from nothing."] *Ḥokhmah* (Wisdom) is the beginning of substance that emanates from *Keter*, which is seen in its aspect of *Ayin* (Nothing).

[55] *Midrash Tehillim*, end of chapter 34.   [56] *Tiferet*.

[57] [*Havayah*, "existing thing," is an anagram of the tetragrammaton.]

[58] *Hesed. El* is understood here in its meaning of force, or power.   [59] *Gevurah*.

[60] *Nezah* and *Hod*. The name is interpreted as if derived from the Aramaic *zvi*, "will."

[61] *Yesod*.

[62] The elements, whose activity was limited by the power of the name *Shaddai*.

[63] [Lit., what need was there . . . ?]

all the worlds and their creatures, so that His dominion over them may be demonstrated.

And so with the soul: He compared her to Himself because of her dominion over all parts of the body; not that she is like Him in nature, for He created her, and there is no god above Him that created Him. Moreover, many changes, accidents, and causes can be assigned to the soul, which is not the case with the Master of all. Therefore she is like Him in her dominion over all the parts of the body, but not in any other way.

6. ESSENCE AND VESSELS

(Zohar II, 42b–43a, *Raya Mehemna*)

Woe to him who compares Him[64] to any attribute, even to those attributes which He has, let alone to mankind "whose foundation is in the dust" (Job 4: 19), and who wither and pass away. But the image we have of Him accords simply with His dominion over that particular attribute, and even over all creatures; but above that attribute, once He has removed Himself from it, He has no attribute, no image, and no form.[65] It is like the sea. The waters that come from the sea cannot be grasped, nor do they have form. But when the waters of the sea spread themselves over a vessel, which is the earth, an image is formed, and we can then make a calculation, as follows: the source of the sea is one; a spring comes from it as it spreads in the vessel, in a circle, which is *yod*; and so we have the source—one; and [together with] the spring that comes from it—two. After this, He makes a huge vessel, like someone digging a great pit that fills with the water that comes from the spring. This vessel is called "sea," and is the third vessel. And this huge vessel is split into seven vessels, like long vessels. Thus the waters from the sea are spread out into seven streams. And so we have a source, and a spring, and a sea, and seven streams, making ten. And if the artisan were to break the vessels that he has prepared, the waters would return to the source, and there would be left broken vessels, dry and waterless. Thus the Cause of causes makes ten *sefirot* and calls *Keter* "source," and there is no limit there to the outpouring of its light, and so He calls Himself "*En-Sof*."[66] But He has no image or form, and there is no vessel there with which to grasp Him, or to gain any knowledge of Him. Consequently, they said of Him, "Do not enquire into what is too wonderful for you, and do not probe into what is concealed from you."[67]

[64] I.e., *En-Sof*.

[65] It is only when the light of *En-Sof* extends itself over the divine attributes, and over the created beings, in order to rule over them and guide them, that we can attribute to it image and form, suited to the particular attribute in which it is active.

[66] The title *En-Sof*, "without end," signifies the infinite outpouring in *Keter*.

[67] B.T. *Ḥagigah* 13a, in the name of Ben Sira.

After this He makes a tiny vessel,[68] which is *yod*, and it is filled with Him, and He calls it a "spring spouting wisdom," and He calls Himself within it "wise," and the vessel He calls *Ḥokhmah* (Wisdom). After this He makes a large vessel and calls it "sea," and calls it *Binah* (Understanding), and calls Himself within it "understanding." He is wise in His own right, and understanding in His own right,[69] but *Ḥokhmah* is not called *Ḥokhmah* in its own right, but because of the Wise One who fills it from His source. And [*Binah*] is not called *Binah* in its own right, but because of the Understanding One who fills it with Himself, for were He to remove Himself from it, it would be left dry. This is the significance of "The waters fail from the sea, and the river is drained dry" (Job 14: 11). Subsequently, "He will smite it into seven streams" (Isaiah 11: 15); and He makes the seven precious vessels, and calls them: *Gedulah* (Greatness), *Gevurah* (Power), *Tiferet* (Beauty), *Neẓaḥ* (Eternity), *Hod* (Majesty), *Yesod* (Foundation), *Malkhut* (Kingdom). And He calls Himself: "great" in *Gedulah*, "loving" in *Ḥesed*, "powerful" in *Gevurah*, "beautiful" in *Tiferet*, "victorious in battle"[70] in the everlasting *Neẓaḥ*, and in *Hod* He names Himself "the glory of our Creator," and in *Yesod* He names Himself "righteous." As for *Yesod*, everything depends on it, all vessels and all worlds. And in *Malkhut* He names Himself "king." To Him belong "the greatness, the power, the beauty, the victory, and the glory, for 'all' is in the heavens"[71]—which is righteous[72]—and to Him belongs the kingdom, which is *Malkhut*. All is in His power, to take out of the vessels or to pour influence into them, or to take out, according to His will; and there is no god above Him, that can add to or subtract from Him.

7. ACTS OF *EN-SOF*

(*Zohar Ḥadash, Yitro*, ed. Venice, 55b–55d)

He brings everything from potentiality into actuality, and He varies His deeds, but there is no variety in Him. It is He that puts the *sefirot* in order, and there are among the *sefirot* great, intermediate, and small,[73] each one in its place in the order, but there is no order in Him. He created everything with *Binah*, and there is none that created Him. He is a designer, and designed everything with *Tiferet*, but He has no design or

---

[68] *Ḥokhmah* is called "a tiny vessel" because of its deeply hidden nature.

[69] *En-Sof* is not wise and understanding because of the *sefirot Ḥokhmah* and *Binah*, but the *sefirot* gain these titles because they themselves are filled with *En-Sof*'s own wisdom and understanding.

[70] [*Neẓaḥ* has the meaning of "victory" as well as "eternity."]

[71] 1 Chronicles 29: 11. [The complete verse in the standard translation is "Thine, O Lord, is the greatness, and the power, and the glory, and the victory, and the majesty; for all that is in the heaven and in the earth is Thine; Thine is the Kingdom, O Lord, and Thou art exalted as head above all."]

[72] *Yesod* is called *Kol* (all).   [73] *Ḥesed, Raḥamim*, and *Din*.

designer. He formed everything with *Malkhut*, but there is none that formed Him. Since He is within these ten *sefirot*, He created, designed, and formed everything with them. There He placed His unity, so that they might recognize Him there. And whoever separates one *sefirah* from its fellow among these ten *sefirot* that are called *Yod, He, Vav, He*, makes, as it were, a separation within Him. It is He that unites *Yod* with *He*, *Vav* with *He*, and they are called *Yod, He, Vav, He* only because of Him;[74] similarly with [the letters of] *Adonai*, and *Ehyeh*,[75] and *Elohim*; but, as soon as He removes Himself from there, He has no known name. It is He that binds all the chariots of the angels, and binds them together; and He supports the upper and the lower worlds. And were He to remove Himself from them they would have neither sustenance, knowledge, or life.

There is no place where He is not, above without end, and below without limit, and on every side there is no god but He. But despite the fact that He is in every place, He did not place His "creation," "formation," and "making"[76] in the Throne, nor among the angels, nor in the heavens, nor in the earth, nor in the sea, nor in any created being in the world, so that all creatures might recognize Him in the *sefirot*. Furthermore, all creatures [were created through them], some by means of "creation," some by means of "formation," and some by means of "making." And as for the *sefirot*, although He created, formed, and made everything through them, the names *beriyah, yezirah*, and *asiyah* do not apply to them, as they do to the lower worlds, but rather are they the way of emanation. Consequently, the "crown," "wisdom," "understanding," and "knowledge" of other created beings are not akin to them.[77] This is the import of "To whom then will you liken Me, that I should be equal? says the Holy One" (Isaiah 40: 25)—on the same pattern as the Torah, of which it is said "She is more precious than rubies; and all the things that you can desire are not to be compared to her" (Proverbs 3: 15). And He creates, forms, and makes everything.

Even though He is known to mankind through the ten *sefirot*, which are supernal *Keter, Ḥokhmah, Binah*, and so on, it is said of Him that He is wise, but not with a known wisdom; understanding, but not with a

[74] The letters are combined to form the names of God only when the light of *En-Sof* exists among them, and joins them together.

[75] [A name of God derived from the phrase "I am that I am (*Ehyeh asher ehyeh*) . . . 'I am' has sent you" (Exodus 3: 14).]

[76] In the system of worlds, the world of the *sefirot* is emanation, the world of the Throne is "creation" (*beriyah*), the world of the angels is "formation" (*yezirah*), the world of physical nature (heavens, earth, and sea) is "making" (*asiyah*). However, there are also aspects of *beriyah, yezirah*, and *asiyah* among the *sefirot*, namely, *Binah, Tiferet*, and *Malkhut*, as has already been explained above.

[77] *Keter, Ḥokhmah, Binah*, and *Da'at*. Even in the lower worlds of creation, formation, and making, there are arrangements of the ten *sefirot*, but they are not like the divine *sefirot*.

known understanding; loving, but not with a known love; powerful, but not with a known power. He is beauty in every place, but not in a known place; He is majesty and glory in every place, but not in a known place; He is righteous, but not in a known place; He is sovereign, but not with a known sovereignty; He is one, but not in number, like the one that amounts to thirteen attributes.[78] And even though He is not outside anything, He sustains the upper and the lower worlds, and sustains all the worlds, *ad infinitum*, and without limit, and there is no one who sustains Him. All thoughts weary themselves when thinking of Him, and not one of them knows how to perceive Him; and even Solomon, of whom it is said "he was wiser than all men" (1 Kings 5: 11), sought to perceive Him in thought, but could not; and so he said, "I said: I will get wisdom; but it was far from me" (Ecclesiastes 7: 23).

Whoever He gives life to, with *Yod, He, Vav, He,*[79] cannot be slain. And whoever He puts to death, with *Adonai,*[80] cannot be given life. And even though these letters contain death and life, the life and death that they contain come only from Him. They possess no relationship or unification except with respect to Him. The name is not pronounced perfectly except through Him, and it brings no deed into actuality except through Him. And all the foreign powers, which come from "the other side," are in His control,[81] to do with them as He wishes; and of them it is said, "All the inhabitants of the earth are reputed as nothing; and He does according to His will in the host of heaven" (Daniel 4: 32). And there is no one who can stay His hand, and say to Him, "What are You doing?"

He grasps all thoughts, but no thought can know Him. And He had no need to depict a place, so that one might think of Him, or know Him, were it not for the sake of mankind;[82] for their thought cannot perceive Him in every place, for He has worlds even above the *sefirot*, as innumerable as the hairs on one's head. But since they know how to call upon Him in a particular place, He prescribed *sefirot* for them, so that they might recognize Him through them, for they are connected with the upper and the lower worlds, and He created with them all created beings, that they might recognize Him through them.

---

[78] *Keter*, which contains the thirteen attributes of mercy, and is therefore "one in number."   [79] With the attribute of mercy.   [80] With the attribute of justice.

[81] Even the powers of "the other side" are not in complete control of themselves, but fulfill His wishes.

[82] From His own point of view there was no need to limit His attributes within the *sefirot*, which have, as it were, spatial boundaries. He designed the system of the *sefirot* only that mankind might use them in order to perceive Him.

SECTION II. *SEFIROT*

INTRODUCTION

a. The Nature and Function of the *Sefirot*

[1] The God who reveals Himself through His attributes and powers is depicted in a system of ten *sefirot*. The term *sefirot*, and also the numerical division into ten, are taken from the *Sefer Yezirah*, an early mystical work, composed, at the very latest, in the sixth century. There we read of the "ten *sefirot* of nothingness (*belimah*)." But the reference there is to the primary numbers, which together with the twenty-two letters of the Hebrew alphabet form the basic elements of existence, whereas in kabbalistic doctrine a totally different meaning is given to this ancient term.

Just as no use is made of the term *kabbalah* in the Zohar, so there is hardly any mention of *sefirot*, apart from in the later sections. Instead we have a whole string of names: "levels," "powers," "sides" or "areas" (*sitrin*), "worlds," "firmaments," "pillars," "lights," "colors," "days," "gates," "streams," "garments," "crowns," and others. Each term designates a particular facet of the nature or work of the *sefirot*.

The list of names of the *sefirot* themselves is even more varied, as we shall see. However, we do find, even at the very beginning of the kabbalah's development, some more or less fixed terms that are accepted as the main designations of the *sefirot*. These are: *Keter Elyon, Ḥokhmah, Binah, Ḥesed, Gevurah, Tiferet, Nezaḥ, Hod, Yesod, Malkhut*.[1] These names are already used by the early kabbalists as commonly accepted terms. This is true also of the Zohar, even though at times later names are more frequently used, particularly with regard to certain *sefirot*. For example, instead of *Keter*, some kabbalists prefer the term *rum ma'alah* ("the highest point above"); *Ḥesed* is often called *Gedulah* (Greatness); *Gevurah* is called *Din* (Judgment) or *Paḥad* (Fear); and *Tiferet* is called *Raḥamim* (Mercy).

Most of these terms were not selected for their intrinsic worth, nor were they originally arranged in a unified systematic order to indicate the nature of the *sefirot*. This is particularly obvious in the choice of the names of the seven lower *sefirot*, six of which were based on 1 Chronicles 29: 11: "Yours, O Lord, is the greatness and the power, and the beauty, and the victory,[2] and the majesty. . . . Yours is the kingdom." That is to say, that the origin of these names was exegetical, and not intrinsic to the subject in hand. Therefore, in their original form they are basically terms of praise and glorification, which do not say a great deal about the nature of the individual *sefirot*. This is true also of the term *Keter Elyon*. It indicates the eminence of the first *sefirah* in its relationship both to *En-Sof*, as the most supreme crown of the King, and to the other *sefirot*, in its character as the crown of crowns; as the Zohar puts it: "*Keter Elyon* above, with which all the crowns and diadems are crowned."[3] But this term does not even hint at a definition of the essential nature of the first *sefirah*, and it has no intrinsic connection with the names of the second and third *sefirot* (*Hokhmah* and *Binah*). But, if we introduce certain specific variations, that is, if we change *Keter* into *Razon* (Will) and *Tiferet* into *Rahamim* (Mercy)—names frequently found in the Zohar—and if we use, as was customary, *Hesed* (Love) instead of *Gedulah*, then we have a much more useful arrangement.

[2] The first *sefirah* is the primeval divine Will,[4] "the Will of wills," the source of all volitional impulses, the power of the initial awakening within the Godhead. This inapprehensible will "that cannot ever be known or grasped, the most recondite head in the world above" (6), is not directed toward any specific object. It is will in general without any separate, defined components— pure will, which acts on itself, and has no reference to the world outside itself. Looked at in this way, the first *sefirah* is called *Ehyeh* ("I shall be," or "I am"); that is to say, the source of all being, without there being postulated any specific being within itself, for "it includes everthing, because, since the paths are hidden and are not separable, and are gathered together in one place, it is called *Ehyeh* . . . it comprises everything, a generality with no particular"[5] (19).

The origin of actual existence is in the *sefirah Hokhmah*, which is the divine Thought. In actual fact, however, even in *Hokhmah* there is no revelation, nor any paticularization or separation of individual beings. It is consequently called *Mahashavah Setumah* (hidden Thought): "Thought is the beginning of all, and in that it is thought it is internal, secret, and unknowable" (7). But it contains the general material for the construction of the worlds, and all existing things are faintly and secretly adumbrated there: "He made all the designs there; He did all the engravings there" (11). In this sense, the school of Rabbi Isaac the Blind called it "Wisdom which encompasses all" or "The primeval being that encompasses all."

This inapprehensible material reaches the stage of revelation and substance in the third *sefirah*, *Binah*. Here existing things are separated and differentiated, and the faint sketches that are to be found in *Hokhmah*, and which have no independent existence, are here crystallized and given a life of their own: "When the Holy One, blessed be He, wished to create the world he looked at Thought (*Mahashavah*), the secret of the Torah, and He drew sketches. But it could not survive until He created repentance [*Binah*] . . . and there the letters were sketched and formed by engraving. When this had been created He looked at the palace [*Binah*] and sketched designs of the whole world before Him" (*The Account of Creation*, 4).

From the designs in *Binah* emanate and are revealed the seven lower *sefirot*, which constitute the structure of the world of emanation, and whose main characteristics are comprised in the names of three attributes: *Hesed* (Love), *Din* (Judgment), and *Rahamim* (Mercy)—also known as the *sefirot Gedulah, Gevurah,* and *Tiferet*. The three following *sefirot*—*Nezah, Hod*, and *Yesod*—are, when looked at in this way, only branches, or offshoots, of these attributes. And the last *sefirah* receives influence from these three, and acts under their direction.[6]

Through the attribute of *Hesed* is revealed the absolute goodness of God, which pours out light and an infinite torrent of blessing, like a river that bursts its banks and floods through every dam and dyke. The attribute of *Din* represents the strength and power of God's wrath, which tends to work against *Hesed*, and to stop up the source of its flow. These two extremes meet and intermingle in the attribute of *Raḥamim*, which forms a bridge between the stringency of Judgment and the pleasantness of Love.

Were it not for the mediation of *Raḥamim*, which balances and reconciles the two opposing forces, there would be perpetual tension and conflict between *Ḥesed* and *Din*, and the worlds would not be able to survive. When *Din* has the upper hand in the conflict, it arouses the force of destruction and kindles the flames of Gehinnom: "When the left [*Din*] was aroused, conflict was aroused, and in this conflict the fire of wrath was dominant, and from this conflict emerged Gehinnom, and Gehinnom was aroused on the left and clove [to it]" (*The Account of Creation*, 16). Similarly, the total domination of *Ḥesed* also has a harmful effect on the elements that sustain the worlds, for without *Din* the road toward righteousness and moral excellence would be perverted. Only through a reconciliation of these opposites in *Raḥamim* are continued existence and righteous conduct assured.

The force that acts directly in this balanced way is the last *sefirah*, which is situated at the lower extremity of the world of emanation, and at the top of the nondivine worlds. It brings to fulfillment the activity of the various attributes, and so it is called *Malkhut*, for the sovereignty of God is revealed there in the totality of His attributes.

[3] In this symbolic system the *sefirot* are seen as spiritual forces, as attributes of the soul, or as means of activity within the Godhead, that is to say, as revelations of the hidden God, both to Himself and to that which is other than He. The fundamental element in this revelation is His emergence from the depths of limitless infinity. The *sefirot* become specified, limited areas within the Godhead, not, of course, limited in the sense of tangible objects, but as displaying a spiritual pattern of categories, both of content and of character. This specific kind of divine limitation evidenced by the *sefirot* is described, by a number of paradoxical statements, in the writings of Rabbi Azriel of Gerona: "For *En-Sof* is a wholeness that lacks nothing, and it has power in a limitless area, and the limited area that is emanated from it to everything that exists are the *sefirot*, which have the power to act both in completeness and in incompleteness. And had it not produced a limited area for them we should not have recognized that it had the power to produce a limited area."[7] "And even though these things [i.e., the *sefirot*] have size and measure, and are ten in number, the measure that they have is without end."[8]

In the Zohar a particular force is mentioned called *bozina di-kardinuta* (spark of blackness) or *kav ha-midah* (the standard of measure), which fixes size and measurement in the *sefirot*. *Kav ha-midah* is emanated from *En-Sof*, and acts within the limits of the first *sefirah*. There it promotes and designs colors in secret, and as a result of this activity "the colors are painted below" (1). The activities of *kav ha-midah* are dealt with at length in a separate section.[9] According to the descriptions given there the *bozina di-kardinuta* is hidden within the Will (*Keter*) after it leaves the domain of *En-Sof*. As the Will extends itself, it brings into play the concealed beings that dwell within the Will, and initiates the process of emanation. After this it acts under the guise of *kav ha-midah*. Here is part of the description of this activity. "This is the measuring-line of the mystery of faith [i.e., the world of the *sefirot*], *kav ha-midah*: there is length and breadth in the measuring, depth and height in the measuring, circle and rectangle in the measuring—the measuring line encompasses all. All the lights and all the mysteries neither ascend, nor descend, nor extend themselves, except by means of this measuring line, apart from the veritably uppermost regions [*En-Sof* and *Keter*] where there is no measure . . . and He calculates and measures everything with one measuring line, beginning at the top, where measure begins, down to the end of the levels of faith." The *sefirot* depend for their existence on the activities of *kav ha-midah*. It is their finite nature that distinguishes them from *En-Sof* and *Keter*, for it establishes a contrast between the revealed nature of the emanated beings and the inaccessibility of the Emanator.

It is clear from the passage just quoted that the *sefirot*, which are finite and measurable, are not, however, static objects, like fixed, solid rungs on the ladder of the progressive revelation of the divine attributes. They are, on the contrary, dynamic forces, ascending and descending, and extending themselves within the area of the Godhead. This dynamism is found both in their hidden existence, which is oriented upward toward *En-Sof*, and also in their association with the lower world, as forces of creation and direction of the universe. They are in continuous motion, involved in innumerable processes of interweaving, interlinking, and union. Even their order changes as a result of their internal movement, and "their end is fastened into their beginning." The lower *sefirot* elevate themselves in their yearning to return and cleave to their source, and the upper *sefirot* move downward in order to give sustenance to the lower, and to transmit divine influence to the worlds below.

An ever-flowing torrent passes without cease through the world of emanation; it wells up from the hidden Source and comes down through the *sefirot* to *Malkhut*. From there the flow descends to the lower worlds, influencing the way in which they conduct themselves. Images of the fountain, the river, streams, and the sea are all used in portraying the *sefirot* in this particular context. From the depths of the first *sefirah* the fountain of *Hokhmah* that is called "Eden" bursts forth. The great upper river of *Binah* flows from there, and it branches out into the streams of the *sefirot*. The streams meet and mingle in *Yesod*, which is the lower river chaneling the waters of the divine flow to the sea of *Malkhut* (22; 23; and elsewhere).[10] The lower *sefirot* are connected with one another by channels, and in the upper *sefirot*, which are sources of the flow, there are ranks of spiritual beings that arrange the collection and transference of the flow: thirteen attributes of mercy in *Keter*, described in the anthropomorphic style of the *Idrot* as thirteen locks in the beard of the Holy, Ancient One; thirty-two paths of *Hokhmah*; and fifty gates of *Binah*.

[4] The *sefirot* are revealed in the world through their activities of creation and guidance. But, more than this, their very nature and their interrelationships can be perceived by the lower regions, to a larger or smaller extent, depending on their place in the order of emanation.[11] They are like gates or doors, and we can pass through them in order to gain a knowledge of the mystery of the Godhead. The entry commences with the lowest *sefirah*, which is the first gate, the nearest to the lower regions. "It is like an exalted king, who is high, hidden and concealed, and who has made gates for himself, one upon the other, and at the end of all the gates he has made one particular gate, with a number of locks, a number of doors, and a number of palaces. He says: Whoever

desires to enter into my presence, this gate shall be the first [that leads] to me; and whoever enters by this gate shall enter" (*Shekhinah*, 9).[12]

Entry into the gates of the *sefirot* is effected through the practice of prayer and the commandments with the correct devotion and intention. But how can man possibly find his way to the locked gates, and where can he find the key that will open them? In other words, how is it possible for man to reach the stage of contemplating the *sefirot* before observing the hidden secrets in the divine realm, through the ascent of the soul and the correct devotion of the mind? The teaching of the Zohar provides us with two answers to this question.

One answer states that the *sefirot* are revealed by means of the heavenly influence that is present in the worlds. The *sefirot* themselves dwell in the heights and cannot be known, but the influence that flows from them turns the whole of creation into a mirror that reflects the life of the Godhead. It is this idea that is apparently expressed in a homiletical interpretation of Psalm 19: " 'Their line is gone out through all the earth'—although (the *sefirot*) are mysteries of heaven that cannot be known to the worlds, their influence and effect pour down and extend to the lower world, and as a result of this extension we, in this world, can have perfect faith, and all the inhabitants of the world can ponder upon the mystery of faith of the Holy One, blessed be He, in those levels, as if they had been revealed, and were not hidden and concealed."[13] The worlds are garments for the divine light and influence that are active in them,[14] and from their midst a glimpse may be had of the mystery of the Godhead.

The second answer is bound up with one of the basic principles of kabbalistic teaching, which recurs time and time again in the Zohar: the worlds, with all the beings they contain, and especially man, are constructed on the pattern of the *sefirot*, "according to the form that is above." The *sefirot* are the divine master-copy of nondivine existence, both in general and in particular. "He made the lower world on the pattern of the upper world, and they complement each other, forming one whole, in a single unity."[15] "He made this world to match the world above, and whatever exists above has its counterpart below" (*The Account of Creation*, 5).[16] "The designs for all the worlds were sketched within the *sefirot* and served as patterns for the Creation" (ibid., 4). Consequently, contemplation of the created world leads to the revelation of the divine model that is reflected there, and the locked gates of the world of emanation are opened for man to pass through. The connection between a perception of a model and a grasp of the mystery of the *sefirot* is particularly evident when we come to a knowledge of the structure of the soul: "When you examine the levels you will find the mystery of wisdom in this matter [i.e, in the structure of the different parts of the soul], and everything is wisdom, that you might perceive in this way matters that are sealed."[17]

b. The Process of Emanation

[1] The process of emanation, that is, the way in which motion begins at the source and continues from stage to stage, is understood in two senses in the main body of the Zohar: (a) the formation of the *sefirot* through the emanatory process; and (b) the descent of the divine influence in order to sustain both the *sefirot* and the worlds. In the *Raya Mehemna* and the *Tikkunei ha-Zohar* it is understood in yet a third way: the self-extension of the divine essence in the

sefirot and the worlds. The term "emanation" (*azilut*) is actually mentioned only in the later parts of the Zohar.[18] Instead we have a whole succession of different terms: "extension" or "prolongation," "dissemination" or "expansion," "flow," "radiation," "illumination," and so on. These terms show that the Zohar when describing emanation uses the two most common images in all emanatory systems: the shining and radiation of light, and the flowing of water from the source.

The identification of the emanatory process with the absolute perfection and indissoluble unity of God creates a serious difficulty, which the early kabbalists labored hard to solve. On the face of it, the doctrine of emanation splits up the unity of the divine being, and spoils its perfection, by allowing parts of it to be hived off and to be reconstituted outside the domain of the Godhead. In an attempt to ward off this charge of inconsistency, the kabbalah of the Gerona school, especially in the writings of Rabbi Azriel, compared emanation to the lighting of one candle from another, where the first candle, although providing light for the second, loses no light of its own. In this way Rabbi Azriel contrasts the process of emanation with the act of birth: "There is a distinction between procreation and emanation . . . for in the world above there is neither diminution nor growth, and if there is emanation and growth from the holy spirit it is simply like the lighting of a candle from a candle that is already lit; for even if myriads upon myriads of candles were lit from it, its own light would not diminish owing to the power inherent in it."[19] A similar account occurs in the *Tikkunei ha-Zohar*:[20] "When He created the world with the attribute of *reshit* (beginning), He descended upon it, but there was no diminution above, and similarly with every *sefirah*; like someone lighting a candle from a candle,[21] where there is no diminution in the first one, nor in the second, *ad infinitum*, without end."

This image raises another problem. Should one see the formation of the *sefirot* as a dynamic expansion of the divine power, or as an emanation in substance of the divine being? The simile of the candle is very well suited to the expansion of power, which does not cause any diminution in the source. It is an image that does a great deal to explain the process by which influence flows down from the Emanator—a process that has a dynamism of its own. But it does not remove the difficulties we encounter if we posit an emanator of substance. These difficulties are not all that serious if we are dealing with the expansion of the divine being into nondivine substances, and nondivine areas, provided that there is no change or alteration in the being that is expanded. And this, in fact, is the case with the theory of immanence advocated by the author of the *Tikkunei ha-Zohar*, who uses the image of the candle quite openly in connection with the expansion of the divine being;[22] for, according to this view, the actual flame that kindles is not different, or divided from, the light of the first candle: the differences that do exist are purely on the side of the second candle. But, if we say that the *sefirot* are emanated in substance from the divine being, then we are necessarily attributing alteration and change to the essence of the divine being, and emanation then is not at all like the lighting of one candle from another. On the other hand, the view that the *sefirot* are part of the divine being—and this is the view of the author of the Zohar—makes it very difficult for anyone to maintain that they are *not* emanated in substance from that being.

The kabbalists found a way out of this difficulty by saying that the *sefirot* had their roots in the domain of the Emanator. And so, in accord with this view, they explained emanation as the uncovering of preexistent roots, or as a transference from the unknown to the known. The divine essence does not expand, nor does it suffer any change whatsoever, but the living entities concealed within it are gradually revealed through the various stages of the process of emanation. So we see that the *sefirot* have always existed and the only change that has occurred is their emergence into an active state. Or, in the language of the Gerona kabbalists, "the beings existed, but the emanation was new." It is in this sense that they depict emanation as the uprooting of plants from one place and resiting them elsewhere,[23] that is, the transference of the *sefirot* from one area to another. This idea occurs several times in the Zohar: "'the buds'—these are the plants that the Holy One, blessed be He, uproots, and replants in another place, and they grow like a plant when it is in flower."[24]

In a particular circle of thirteenth-century anonymous kabbalists, who appended the names of ancient authorities or of completely fictitious people to their writings, we find the view expressed that in the realm of *En-Sof* itself there exist three primeval lights. These three lights are particular to *En-Sof*, and integral to it, with the specific characteristics of "name, substance, and root of roots"; and they constitute the hidden being of the first three *sefirot*,[25] and the source from which they were drawn. There is no mention of this view either in the writings of the Gerona school or in the Zohar. The existence of the hidden beings has its beginning in *Keter*, and is more openly revealed in *Hokhmah* and *Binah*. They are called "plants" (*neti'ot*), "engravings" (*gilufim*), or "sketches" (*rishumim*). The process of emanation begins with the movement of germination and growth in the tiny plants, which are inside the supernal Will.[26] In *Hokhmah* "six great, supernal extremities are engraved, from which all derives" (10). This refers to the existence of the six *sefirot* from *Hesed* to *Yesod*. And the emergence of *Binah* from *Hokhmah* took place "when supernal *Hokhmah* provoked movement in its engravings" (*Influence and Direction*, 6). After the emanation of *Binah* "six sketches were embroidered as a decoration in it" (18), and from them the lower *sefirot* emanated.

The concept of *En-Sof* as a hidden, transcendent God, who can be apprehended only in a negative way, prevented these kabbalists from introducing preexistent beings into its domain. *En-Sof* takes no direct part in the process of emanation, neither as emanator, nor as source of those that are emanated. Only the engraving of beings in *Keter* can be attributed to it: "At the very beginning the king made engravings in the supernal purity [i.e., *Keter*]" (1). This engraving is an event that took place before emanation started, and when the time came for the movement from the known to the unknown, the process began of "uprooting and resiting the plants."

[2] The description of the sefirotic chain is one of the central themes in the Zohar, and it constantly recurs, but there are only a few passages where all the links in the chain from *Keter* to *Malkhut* are accounted for. Nor is there any logical consistency in the way in which the sequence of emanation is fixed. There hardly exists a single account of a continuous chain of emanation that includes the total number of the *sefirot* in a causative sequence, i.e., *Hokhmah* emanating from *Keter*, and *Binah* from *Hokhmah*, and *Hesed* from *Binah*, and so

on, without various gaps, and combinations, and intermediary stages, and the like. On the contrary, from one passage to another, and sometimes within the same passage itself, there are differences and contradictions, great or small, in the description of the order of emanation, both with regard to the symbols that are used, and also in the way that they are associated with one another. It is obvious that in this area, as in others, there is no firmly established systematic framework. The picture of the growth and structure of the world of emanation continually changes in order to accommodate the different aspects that are revealed to the kabbalist as a result of his contemplation of the *sefirot*. From this wide range of views I shall select just those which seem to be the most important.

At the highest stage, the transition from *Keter* to *Hokhmah* is usually depicted as a straightforward extension. But in a few passages we find descriptions of incidents that occur within *Keter* as if in preparation for the beginning of emanation. Once the hidden beings have been engraved in the splendor of *Keter*, which encompasses *En-Sof* in the shape of primeval air, there sparks forth within it from the mystery of *En-Sof* the *bozina di-kardinuta* (the spark of blackness), a powerful light, which because of its hidden nature is like pitch darkness. This is destined to serve as the *kav ha-midah* (the standard of measure) in the world of emanation. The "spark," just like hylic matter, has no character or form when it first appears. It is only when it starts to become active that its remarkable characteristics are discernible. A fountain bursts forth within the "spark," from which subsequently the individual aspects of the whole sefirotic system flow. The force of the torrent that flows from the fountain makes a hairline crack in the surface of the primeval air, and through this aperture "a single point shines, sealed, supernal [the *sefirah Hokhmah*] . . . the first word of all" (1). Similar incidents before the emanation of *Hokhmah* are described, with different imagery, as the reaction of the self-extension of the Will (*Keter*) to the power of the "spark of blackness," and as the growth of tiny plants within the Will as a result of the outpouring of the different facets of the "spark."[27]

We can detect in these passages an expansion of the process whereby *Hokhmah* emanated from *Keter* through a chain of intermediate occurrences. But nevertheless the continuous nature of the operation was sustained without a break. This is not the case, however, with another version, which is based on the old midrashic idea that the Holy One, blessed be He, "used to create worlds and destroy them, until He created those we have."[28] The worlds that were destroyed were, according to the Zohar, earlier emanations that were emanated from the Holy, Ancient One (*Keter*) before the system of the *sefirot* from *Hokhmah* downward was established. These earlier emanations, which were not viable and were therefore annulled, are called "kings," referring to "the kings of Edom that died," to which an allusion is found in Genesis 36: 31: "And these are the kings that reigned in the land of Edom, before there reigned any king over the children of Israel." They are depicted as designs that were woven into a curtain that the Holy, Ancient One spread out before him, and which became indistinct;[29] or as sparks that fly off the blacksmith's hammer and immediately become extinguished.[30] The reason for the destruction of the worlds, or for the death of the kings, is put like this: judgments at that time were severe, because they had not yet been constituted into that perfectly balanced system in which love, judgment, and mercy are intermingled. The balanced system is symbolized by a pair of scales (*matkala*)[31] or by an image of man, constructed in the form of perfect harmony, which holds opposite forces in balance through the union of male and female. ". . . And all the worlds were destroyed. For what reason? Because Man had not yet been prepared; for the preparation of Man in his image comprises all, and all can live in him. And since this preparation of Man did not exist, they were not able to survive or live, and were annulled" (12).[32] It was only after the unsuccessful emanations had been annulled and hidden that the process of permanent emanation began, and in the system from *Ḥokhmah* down to *Malkhut* a balanced equilibrium was established, and the complete, perfect image of man was designed.

The transition from *Ḥokhmah* to *Binah* is also portrayed occasionally as an intricate and complex process. *Ḥokhmah* is emanated from *Keter* in the shape of hidden Thought being sparked off from the concealed Will, which is attached to *En-Sof*. But it still yearns to return to its source, and to cling to Will. However, a curtain has been drawn, a partition has been erected between Thought and Will, so that the essential being of Thought should not suffer any damage and the process of emanation be interrupted. Nevertheless, a fine ray of supernal light has been drawn down through the curtain because of the strength of Thought's yearning, and this light has caused a secret illumination within Thought itself. As a result of the contact between the light of the curtain and the illumination of Thought, nine sparks fly out; they are called nine palaces, the molds of the *sefirot* within Thought. They too seek to ascend and to return to the realm of Will and *En-Sof*, and so they are given *in toto* the name of *En-Sof*.[33] However, once the sparks have appeared, Thought directs its attention downward and emanates *Binah* (6). This means that at this stage emanation does not occur as a free and direct manifestation of an impulse derived from an outpouring or an expansion, but as the result of an unfulfilled desire to return to the source.

The six *sefirot* below *Binah* are usually depicted as a group of forces connected with, and centered around *Tiferet*, the central pillar. The word *bereshit* ("in the beginning") is taken as referring to the way in which they emerged from *Binah*, as if it were two words *bara shit* ("He created six"), the "six" being "the six extremes that extend from the supernal mystery through the extension that He created from the primal point" (1). Together they constitute a kind of tree, with *Tiferet* as the trunk and the other *sefirot* as branches. Or they can be symbolized by the shape of the human body, with *Tiferet* as the torso, and the other *sefirot* as the limbs. They are denoted also by the letter *vav*. Its vertical form represents *Tiferet*, while its numerical connotation (six) represents them all together (18, and elsewhere). Sometimes it is only the three upper ones (*Ḥesed, Gevurah, Tiferet*) that are referred to, in the guise of the three patriarchs, while the three lower ones (*Nezaḥ, Hod, Yesod* are taken together as their sons or their messengers. In this way it is said of their emanation that they emerged from *Binah* as a single voice (*Tiferet*) that comprised the three of them: "This spirit (*Binah*) extended itself and brought forth a voice, comprised of fire, water, and wind [*Gevurah, Ḥesed*, and *Tiferet*], which were north, south, and east. This voice comprised all the other powers" (7). The image of the heard voice alludes to revelation on the part of *Binah*, which is in the hidden domain of the first three *sefirot* (23).

There are two main explanations of the way in which *Malkhut* was emanated. One of its characteristics is that of the female clinging to the male, and in this connection it is said that it was emanated as one with *Tiferet*, on the same level, like a body with two faces. It was then separated from *Tiferet* and descended to the bottom of the sefirotic order. "This concealed one [*Binah*] produced the earth [*Malkhut*], but it was included together with heaven [*Tiferet*], and they emerged together, attached to one another back to back . . . when the earth turned to dwell in its place and was separated from heaven's back, it was desolate, and despaired of ever clinging to heaven as it had at the beginning, for it saw heaven shining bright while it was obscured in darkness. But then supernal light went out over it, and illumined it, and it returned to its place to look upon heaven face to face, and then the earth was pacified, and became suffused with incense" (29).[34] *Tiferet* and *Malkhut* are symbolized by the sun and the moon, and the descent of *Malkhut* is called "the diminution of the moon."[35] This is derived from the *aggadah* (B.T. *Ḥullin* 60b), according to which the two luminaries were originally equal in size. But the moon complained to God and said "Can two kings make use of one crown?" God replied, "Go, and make yourself smaller."

However, another characteristic of *Malkhut* is that of gentle judgment, and in this context the Zohar see its source in *Gevurah*, the measure of strict judgment. "The left [*Gevurah*] flamed strongly and exuded odor. Throughout all levels it exuded odor, and from the fiery flame it produced the female, the moon" (2).

The order of emanation is bound up with the integral connection that exists between the *sefirot* themselves. This is the case not only with the specific connection between *Malkhut* and *Gevurah*, but in the much wider area of the whole sefirotic system. From this point of view we have to see the process of emanation as a chain of events running along three parallel lines: the line on the right, or the line of Love, where *Ḥesed* is emanated from *Ḥokhmah*, and *Neẓaḥ* from *Ḥesed*; the line on the left, or the line of Judgment, where *Gevurah* emanated from *Binah*, and *Hod* from *Gevurah*; and the line in the middle, or the line of Mercy, which comprises the chain of *Keter*, *Tiferet*, and *Yesod*. This concept, which is of great importance in kabbalistic doctrine, especially in the later period,[36] does not appear in a definite crystallized form in the Zohar. There are, however, references to it in several places. Sometimes it is said quite plainly: "*Ḥokhmah* is the sum of all, and supernal *Ḥesed* emerges from *Ḥokhmah*; *Gevurah*, which is strict Judgment, emerges from *Binah*" (20).[37] This idea recurs several times[38] in a more obscure form, and especially with reference to *Binah* as the source of Judgment, which is quite common. The emergence of *Yesod* from *Tiferet* is also mentioned in many passages (2, and elsewhere).

In this context the link between *Tiferet* and *Keter* is of special significance. *Tiferet* is not emanated directly from *Keter*, but contact between them is maintained by means of *Da'at* (Knowledge), which is a continuation of *Keter*, and becomes the inner core of *Tiferet*. In the Zohar there are only a few references to this idea, but they are perfectly clear. *Da'at* is called "that which proceeded from the depth of the well." It unites *Ḥokhmah* with *Binah* and dwells in the head of *Ze'ir Anpin*, whose main feature is *Tiferet*, "and from there it proceeded and entered the body, and filled all the chambers and entrances of the body. This is the meaning of 'By knowledge are the chambers filled'"

(13).[39] In the vicinity of this passage we find a clear differentiation between *Da'at* as a title given to *Tiferet* itself, and the supernal *Da'at*, of which it is said: "Another *Da'at* is not revealed, for [*Keter*] concealed a path within it and is included in it."[40] We see, therefore, that although the Zohar does not accept the view that *Keter* should not be included in the number of the *sefirot*, and that *Da'at* is needed to make the number up to ten, it nevertheless brings *Da'at* into the system as a third brain in the head of *Ze'ir Anpin*, and as an intermediate link in the middle line, which stretches from *Keter* to *Yesod*.

[3] The mystery of the act of creation forms a permanent and all-embracing framework for the symbolism of the various links in the chain of the *sefirot*. The process of creation of the lower worlds parallels and reflects the process of divine emanation. Consequently, the section of the Torah in Genesis dealing with the creation has a double meaning. Literally, it describes the creation of the world, and mystically, it describes the process of emanation; as Nachmanides put it:[41] "Truthfully speaking,[41a] Scripture speaks of the lower worlds, and alludes to the upper worlds." This double meaning is explained and emphasized in the Zohar[42] as well: "The act of creation also [occurred] in these two places, one act above, and one act below, and it is for this reason that the Torah begins with the lettet *bet*.[43] The act of creation below is like a copy of that above. This [i.e., the emanatory force] made the upper world, and this [i.e., the creative force] made the lower world."

The process of emanation is contained within the opening verses of Genesis, if one knows how to uncover the mystery to which they allude. In the light of the mystical interpretation, which is revealed and dealt with at length in the Zohar, these verses take on a completely different meaning. Let us take as a striking example of this the audacious interpretation of the first three words:[44] "With this *reshit* the sealed one, that is not known, created this palace. This palace is called *elohim*, and the mystical reference to this is '*Bereshit bara elohim*'" (1). In other words, by means of the *sefirah Hokhmah*, which is called *reshit* (beginning),[45] because it is the beginning of emanation, the hidden emanator, who cannot be mentioned by name because of his complete concealment, emanated the *sefirah Binah*, which appears in its aspect of a palace, called *elohim*.[46] The result is that *elohim* in this verse is not the Creator, but the created. But the creation that is the subject of the verse is not what it literally appears to be. It refers to emanation, as is quite plainly stated in the continuation of the passage: "'*bara*'—extension from the point on high [i.e., *Hokhmah*]."

There is on the face of it an absolute contradiction between this interpretation and another passage that we find in the Zohar: "When the Holy One, blessed be He, created His world, He created them from nothing (*ayin*), and brought them into actuality, and made substance out of them; and you find the word *bara* used always of something that He created from nothing, and brought into actuality" (*The Account of Creation*, 9).[47] Now even if this refers to the lower worlds, for according to some kabbalists they were actually created *ex nihilo* and not through emanation, this would still not remove the contradiction with the interpretation given above, since it says here that *bara* "always" refers to creation from nothing.

It is this apparent contradiction that compels us to investigate the deeper meaning of the idea of divine emanation as a mystical element in the act of creation. The term "creation of something from nothing" is actually applicable to the formation of the *sefirot*; but just as the word "creation" has basically a different meaning when seen through the mirror of kabbalah, so likewise the terms "something" (*yesh*) and "nothing" (*ayin*). These terms originate in the speculative thought of the Jewish philosophers, but then take on a new form and become mystical symbols. *Ayin* denotes the first *sefirah*, preexistent and concealed, the source of the *sefirot*; and *Yesh* is a title given to the second *sefirah*, the beginning of emanation. So we find that in the mystical interpretation of creation, "creation of something from nothing" means the emergence of *Hokhmah* from *Keter*, i.e., the first stage in the process of emanation.[48]

What is the significance of this divine *Ayin* (nothing), which according to the definition of one kabbalist is "more substantive (*yesh*) than all the substances in the world"?[49] Why is the most exalted point in the world of the *sefirot* called "Nothing"? In the Zohar the name is cited several times as a well-known term,[50] but without any explanation. The kabbalist, whom we have just quoted, explains the name as indicating absolute unparalleled simplicity: "Since it is simple, such that all simple things are compound compared with its simplicity, it is called, in contrast to them, 'Nothing'." Rabbi Moses de Leon quotes the view, found among other kabbalists as well, that "Nothing" indicates that its existence is beyond the limit of perception: "And it is therefore called 'Nothing', that is to say, there is no one who can understand it, and if you were to ask: Is there not here something that man can think about? The answer is 'Nothing'; for whatever we may say, 'Nothing' is something concealed, that no one can grasp."[51] It is in this sense that, in the kabbalah of Gerona, *Keter* is called "the cessation of thought" (*afisat ha-mahashavah*), that is to say, it is like nonexistence, nothing, with regard to thought, which cannot attain it.

However, there is a more basic, fundamental significance in this image, bound up with the ontological status, the real essence, of the first *sefirah*. It occupies a position between two radically different types of being, between the inapprehensible secrecy of *En-Sof* and the beginning of the manifestation of the emanatory powers, which act and reveal themselves in creation, between "the light that does not exist in light"[52] and the luminaries that kindle and give light to others. In its role as preexistent Will *Keter* forms the bridge for the transition from *En-Sof* to emanation, but, on the other hand, in its capacity as "Nothing," it reflects the yawning gulf that exists between these two quite separate areas of existence. In this latter capacity it appears in mystical contemplation as a cessation on both sides: the cessation of *En-Sof* in relation to what is below it, and the cessation of creation and emanation in relation to what is above them. *En-Sof* has this quality of absolute concealment because at the limit of its being it ceases to exist, as it were. At the same time, when the *sefirot*, having a strong desire to return to their source, begin to ascend, they gradually peter out and vanish as they reach the outer limit of their goal. In this connection *Keter* is given names of an even more surprising and audacious character. In the kabbalah of the Gerona school they call it "Darkness," a being in which all light vanishes and is extinguished, but nevertheless it is the source of all the lights of emanation and creation. Rabbi Joseph ben Shalom Ashkenazi, the author of the commentary to the *Sefer Yezirah* ascribed to Rabbi Abraham ben David,[53] calls the first *sefirah* "Annihilation" (*Hefsed*). In his view any change in nature in the life of a being, "which is the stripping of form and its annihilation," comes from the power of "Nothing," which is supernal *Keter*, called "Annihilation."[54] This means that the cessation of being in the divine "Nothing," in the transition from *En-Sof* to emanation, is reflected in every metamorphosis at the point of transition from one form to another. Similar to the term "Annihilation" is the interpretation given to the words "Destruction and death" in Job 28: 22 by Rabbi Ezra:[55] "The cessation, from which comes the emanation of all beings."

It is true that this new mystical meaning for the phrase "creation of something from nothing," as the breaking away of the substance of emanation from the area of the divine nothingness, is not clearly stated in the main body of the Zohar, and the expression itself is not used in direct connection with the process of emanation. But the subject is alluded to at a number of points, for example: "Actual Eden [*Hokhmah*] is called 'father', because this Eden originates from the place called 'Nothing'."[56] That is to say, *Hokhmah* is seen here as the father of emanation and the beginning of existence, since its source is absolute nothingness, beyond any category of existence.

The most important symbol that represents *Hokhmah* as the beginning of substantive being is that of the point. "When the most secret of secrets sought to be revealed, He made, first of all, a single point, and this became Thought" (11). At first, there was no actual existence in this primal point, but everything was compressed within it, as Rabbi Moses de Leon wrote:[57] "The beginning of existence is the mystery of the hidden point, which is called *Hokhmah*, the primal, hidden one, and this is the mystery of the point of Thought. . . . This is the beginning of all, and the beginning of all things, and from a single point you can draw out all things. Understand that when the hidden, concealed thing feels impelled to bring forth its own existence, it produces at first something like the point of a needle, and subsequently it brings forth everything from there. In the same way, He, may His name be blessed, brought forth at first from the hidden, concealed thing the ray of a single hidden, concealed point, and from it He drew out His existence, through the rays of the mysteries, from a secret and hidden emanation. And consider that when this emanation was emanated from Nothing, all things and all levels depended on Thought." Just as a line is drawn from a geometrical point and one can then make designs with it, so the stream of emanation extends in a straight line from the point of *Hokhmah* to the structure of the upper world (3).

The next stage is the erection of the palace of *Binah*: "Then 'the beginning' [the point of *Hokhmah*] extended itself and made a palace for itself, for glory and praise" (1). The symbol of the palace serves two purposes: *Binah* is, at the beginning, a glorious palace for the point of *Hokhmah*, which extends itself and gradually unfolds its own compressed essence; but, as the process goes on and the beings of the lower *sefirot* are designed within *Binah*, the palace becomes a storehouse and, later on, a home for the *sefirot*, which become crystallized and so have an independent existence. This process is described as the product of sowing the seed of emanation, symbolized by spiritual letters and vowel-points flowing down from *Hokhmah* to *Binah* (ibid.). Through this image of the sowing, and reception, of the seed, the palace becomes the mother's womb, on analogy with the view of *Hokhmah* and *Binah* as the father and mother of the lower *sefirot*. This symbolism is extremely common in the Zohar. It occurs in another form in connection with the palace: the union of *Hokhmah* with *Binah*, for the actual purpose of emanating the *sefirot*, is depicted as opening the lock on the palace gates. "On these gates [of the palace of *Binah*] there is a lock, which has a narrow place where the key [of *Hokhmah*] may be inserted. It reacts only to the action of the key, and none but the key knows of it. And concerning this mystery [it is said], 'With *Reshit* (beginning) God created' " (10).

Following the father-mother symbolism, the lower *sefirot* are represented as being within *Binah* like an embryo in a mother's womb, and, as the process of emanation continues, they are emanated through the mystery of birth[58] as seven children. Alternatively, they appear as son and daughter, if we consider the six extremities as one unit in the shape of *Tiferet*, and together with it the image of *Malkhut*, which is the daughter (16). Parallel with this anthropomorphic symbolism, which describes the formation of the *sefirot* in terms of pregnancy, birth, and the establishment of a family in the realm of the divine, we have another set of symbols, taken from the creation of the world, which describe the lower *sefirot* as parts of the structure of the divine cosmos that is formed from within the supernal palace of the preexistent point. Consequently, they are called *sefirot ha-binyan* (the *sefirot* of structure, or the *sefirot* of building). The Zohar contains a large number of different cosmic symbols, all of which go to make up this particular image, and so we shall have to content ourselves with but a selection of them, and give just the general outlines.

As a result of an interpretation of the first verse of Genesis, the lower *sefirot* are thought of as heaven and earth. Heaven is *Tiferet*, which comprises and unites within itself the six extremities (the *sefirot* from *Hesed* to *Yesod*), while earth is *Malkhut* (29). Just as the earth is watered and fructified by the blessing of rain that comes from heaven, so *Malkhut*, the female force, receives a stream of influence from *Tiferet*, the male force. This is the basic implication also in applying to *Tiferet* and *Malkhut* the symbols of sun and moon. The moon has no light to give of its own, but whatever light it has it receives from the rays of the sun. The hosts of heaven provide symbols of a much wider and all-embracing character. The seven *sefirot* are seven firmaments, above which is *Binah*, the supernal firmament (21; 22). Or, put in another way, the *sefirot* are the seven stars that shine in the supernal firmament of *Binah* (23).[59]

The three chief *sefirot*, *Hesed*, *Gevurah*, and *Tiferet*, are the light, darkness, and firmament that occur in the first chapter of Genesis (2). The light and the darkness stand for the contrast between love and judgment, while the firmament, which is the area where light and darkness meet and interchange in the hours of twilight, represents the way in which these opposing powers are tempered and mixed together in mercy. Similar ideas are expressed through the symbols of the elements or the points of the compass. *Hesed* and *Gevurah* are water and fire—the water of divine influence and blessing, and the fire that burns and destroys—and they come together in wind.[60] The fourth element, dust, is *Malkhut*, the supernal earth.[61] When we come to the points of the compass, *Hesed* is the south, where there is an abundance of light; *Gevurah* is the north, where there is no light; *Tiferet* is the east, the bridge between north and south and the place where the sun rises, the sun being a symbol of *Tiferet*; and *Malkhut* is the west, which receives light from the setting sun just as *Malkhut* receives influence from *Tiferet*.

As I conclude this discussion of the cosmic symbols I must deal with one specific arrangement, in which the *sefirot* are not depicted as divine elements in the creation of the world, but as the actual days of creation, either "supernal days" (*yomin ila'in*)[62] or "primeval days" (*yomin kadma'in*).[63] The acts of each one of the days of creation manifest the nature and power of one of the days in the upper world, which are parallel to the days in the lower world. To fit in with the days of creation, the order of the days in the upper world is that in which the *sefirot* emanated, not their final positional order. Thus the fourth day is not *Nezah*, but *Malkhut*, which emanated with *Tiferet* and so is placed after the third day. And the Sabbath is *Yesod*, not *Malkhut*.[64] These symbols are a clear reflection of the common ground that exists between the processes of emanation and creation. Each stage in the unfolding of the divine powers contains, unbeknown, whatever is to be revealed later in the corresponding stage of creation.

c. The Paths of Symbolism

[1] During this explanation of some of the specific aspects of the world of emanation, we have already encountered a very wide and varied range of symbols relating to the *sefirot*. But the symbols whose nature and content I have touched upon so far are only a small part of the great wealth of symbols that are to be found in kabbalistic literature, particular in the Zohar, and that help to form the language and thought patterns there. To the reader who is unskilled in mystical teaching the language of the kabbalists seems to be an unintelligible, mysterious tongue, or even at times an inarticulate babble. This is because it is saturated with symbolic elements that are usually employed without any explanation at all. Words that refer to objects and events in normal life are joined together and interwoven in such a way that, when looked at literally, they form a strange and confused picture. Only if you hold the key to the symbolic meaning will you be able to grasp the real purport of the most common words.

By far the most important storehouse of kabbalistic symbolism is the Torah. When the kabbalist comes to assess the Torah's fundamental nature, its hidden mystery, he does not see it as a collection of commandments, statutes, and ordinances, of ethical pronouncements and accounts of historical events, all proceeding from the mouth of God. It is for him a massive treasury of divine forces and divine lights that have donned the form of letters and words and so revealed themselves in the book of the Torah.[65] "We also possess a true tradition," writes Nachmanides,[66] "that the whole Torah consists of the names of the Holy One, blessed be He ... and it would appear that the Torah that was written in black fire on white fire was as we have described it: the script was continuous with no breaks between the words, and one could read it either according to the divine names, or in the way that we do in order to understand the Torah and the commandments. And it was given to Moses, our teacher, according to the reading of the commandments, but the reading of the names was transmitted to him orally." The method of reading the law and the commandments that was given to Moses on Mt. Sinai was consequently only one of the combinations formed by weaving together the sacred names, which

shine forth in the Torah in innumerable combinations, all reflecting the divine.
Another image used depicts the inner nature of the Torah as the organic
structure formed by parts and limbs in the mystery of the shape of supernal Man
in the divine realm.[67] Even the commandments are not what they seem to be; in
their true nature they are the actualization, in the world, of the divine mystery.
Therefore, "he who subtracts even one commandment of the Torah diminishes,
as it were, the image of faith, for they are all joints and limbs in the image of
[supernal] Man and, consequently, they all go to make up the mystery of the
unification [of God's name]."[68] Hence we arrive at the crucial and unambi-
guous conclusion that the Torah is identical with God: "The commandments
form a single entity, and they depend upon the celestial Chariot, each one
fulfilling its own particular function. Every commandment depends upon one
specific part of the Chariot. This being so, the Holy One, blessed be He, is not
one particular area divorced from the Torah, and the Torah is not outside Him,
nor is He something outside the Torah. It is for this reason that the kabbalists
say that the Holy One, blessed be His name, is the Torah."[69]

In view of this it is no surprise to find that every word, indeed every letter, in
the Torah becomes in kabbalah symbolic of the *sefirot*. "In the Torah are all the
celestial and sealed mysteries which it is impossible to grasp. In the Torah are
all those celestial things that are revealed and are not revealed. In the Torah are
all the things of the upper world and the lower world; all the things of this world,
and all the things of the world to come are in the Torah."[70] The Torah is
compared to a beautiful girl, who is closely confined in her palace and is seen by
no one except her beloved, who yearns for her, and walks up and down near the
palace. But, at first, she does not speak, even with him, except through a
curtain, and then through a veil. At last, but only "when he has become
accustomed to her, she reveals herself to him face to face, and speaks to him
about all her hidden mysteries, and all the hidden paths that have lain
concealed in her heart from ancient times."[71] The ability to lift the veil that is
spread over the face of the Torah, and to uncover the divine being that peeps
through the mantle made of symbols, is the exalted stage reached by "the sons of
the palace," and their unique reward.

But the symbolist version of the kabbalah is not confined to the Torah alone.
The world and all that it contains is saturated with divine influence, and
constructed on a celestial pattern,[72] and is therefore a most appropriate
symbolic mirror of the divine life. The hidden light is obscured by a much
thicker curtain in the real world than it is in the Torah, but, even so, "those who
have sharp eyes" have the special ability to penetrate this curtain, and see in
every object, in every situation, in every event, a ray of the concealed splendor
of God. The whole of nondivine existence is a great storehouse, as it were, full of
symbols of the divine.

[2] From what has been said so far, we can already see that the mystical
symbol in kabbalistic doctrine is fundamentally different from the allegorical
allusions in philosophical discourse.[73] What they have in common is that the
philosophers also make use of images and figures, particularly when explaining
the secrets of the Torah, in order to indicate the nature, situation, and activity
of the divine being, spiritual substances, and cosmic forces. In philosophical
usage, however, the figure is purely metaphorical. That is to say, it has no

integral connection with the object that it represents. It denotes something that is really quite foreign to it, and is substituted for that object for literary or stylistic effect. When a particular word appears in an allegorical context, it becomes divorced from the object to which it usually refers, is emptied of its original meaning, in order to provide temporary accommodation for another meaning. There will be some accidental connection, by analogy or association, between the two meanings, but no more than that, just like the connection between a metaphor and the object of the metaphor. It is the accidental connection that determines the choice of a particular object to fulfill a particular allegorical role. This is not the case with a mystical symbol. There exists a permanent, integral relationship between the symbol and the thing symbolized, for a symbol has its symbolic character impressed upon it from the very beginning of its existence. Consequently, symbolic usage does not divorce the symbolic significance from the actual object utilized. On the contrary, by disclosing the symbolic relationship it has with the hidden divine being, one reveals the real nature of the object, in all its perfection. In mystical symbolism one does not exchange one meaning for another, but one adds to the common, revealed meaning a revelation of its own internal hidden mystery.

There is another fundamental distinction between a mystic symbol and an allegorical image. This involves the different nature of the matter alluded to. One uses allegorical expressions in order to make it easier for people to understand speculative ideas or incorporeal beings by giving them a tangible form. The subject matter can also be expressed directly by using conceptual terms, but by employing images it can be grasped by people who are not used to thinking speculatively. But the subject matter of mystical symbolism, such as the divine life in the world of emanation, which is reflected in the kabbalistic system of symbols, cannot be expressed directly at all. The nature of mystical perception is defined by the Zohar as follows: "'And the perceivers shall shine' (Daniel 12: 3). Who are the perceivers? It is the wise man who, of himself, looks upon things that cannot be expressed orally—these are called 'the perceivers'" (5). In other words, the kabbalist "perceiver" is the man whose eye is sharp enough to see the hidden beings in their entirety in the symbolic mirror of the Torah and of the ordinary visible world.

A good example of the contrast that exists between the content of an image and the content of a symbol is provided by the differing attitudes toward the corporeal terms used in the Torah. The philosophers, especially Maimonides, spent an enormous amount of energy explaining that these terms were tangible images of intangible ideas. For example, phrases such as "the hand of the Lord," "the face of the Lord," "the eyes of the Lord," were intended in their view to give tangible expression to God's power, existence, and providence. The names of objects that exist in the created world are being used metaphorically, in a nonliteral sense, in order to describe God; and there is no intrinsic connection whatsoever between their own normal meaning and the object of which they are an image. Indeed, according to the philosophers who have the ability to think in abstract terms, these tangible images are quite superfluous. It is only because of the masses, whose power of thought is limited, and restricted to corporeal things, that "the Torah speaks in the language of the people."[74] In contrast to this, the kabbalists see in the whole structure of the human body, and in all its individual parts, sublime symbols that reflect in their very own nature spiritual beings that actually exist in the realm of the divine. More than this, the original being, the earliest existence of hands, face, and eyes, and so on, occurred in the spiritual image of the divine Primordial Man (*Adam Kadmon*), and the corporeal objects indicated by these terms are nothing but faint shadows or reflections of supernal beings. Therefore the Torah uses these anthropomorphic expressions not in order to make things more comprehensible to the masses, but, on the contrary, in order to give the mystics an insight into the symbolic secret that they contain—a secret that, but for its corporeal garb, could not be revealed at all.

We can see here another way of differentiating the religious standpoint that is bound up with the symbolistic approach of the kabbalah. The imagery of kabbalistic symbolism contrasts not only with the allegorical imagery of philosophy, but also, by its very nature, with the imagery of myth. Myth presents the divine as a fundamental cosmic force, or as a material object, or in the guise of a number of gods having human form. But all this is intrinsically different from the imagery of kabbalah, although it appears to be similar. Believers in myth do not see their corporeal forms and images as symbols of spiritual substances, as the symbolists of kabbalah do, but, for them, the image and that which is denoted by the image are one and the same. In other words, that which exists in the life of nature and the life of man is basically identical with divine existence. They would, at most, make a distinction of degree between the divine, on the one hand, and the manifestation of the divine in nature, on the other. For example, light and fire, which are part of the divine, are the actual light and fire as we know them in physical terms, except that the power of the former is greater than all the light and fire in the world. Similarly, divine man is differentiated by size, strength, and power from all terrestrial men.

The kabbalists were aware of the fact that their own symbolism seemed to be very close to myth, and they issued strict prohibitions, and wrote very vehemently, against the tendency to interpret the symbols of the *sefirot* in mythical, corporeal terms. Rabbi Joseph Gikatilla, a contemporary of the author of the Zohar, writes:[75] "All these matters that we read in the Torah, such as 'hand', and 'foot,' and 'ear,' and 'eye,' and all other such things—what are they? Know and believe that, even though all these matters demonstrate, and testify to His greatness and His truth, there is no creature that can know or understand the nature of the thing called 'hand' or 'foot' or 'ear' and the like. And even though we are made in the image and likeness [of God], do not think for a moment that 'eye' is in the form of a real eye, or that 'hand' is in the form of a real hand. But these are innermost and most recondite matters in the real existence of God, may He be blessed. From them the source and the flow go out to all existing things, through the decree of God, may He be blessed. But the nature of 'hand' is not like the nature of a hand, and their shape is not the same, as it is said (Isaiah 40: 25): 'To whom then will you liken Me, that I should be equal?' Know and understand that between Him and us there is no likeness as to substance and shape, but the forms of the limbs that we have denote that they are made in the likeness of signs that indicate secret, celestial matters, which the mind cannot know except through a kind of reminder. For example, we may write 'Reuben ben Jacob.' Now, neither the letters nor the shape of 'Reuben ben Jacob' are actually his form, shape, or being, but a reminder that the 'Reuben ben Jacob' written here is a sign that represents the substance and shape that is commonly called 'Reuben ben Jacob.'" And so we find in the Zohar that, before a discussion of the anthropomorphic symbols in the *Idra Rabba*, a warning is put in the mouth of Rabbi Simeon ben Yohai: "Cursed be the man that makes a graven or molten image, the work of the hands of the craftsman, and that sets it up in secret" (*Events and Personalities*, 12). In other words, to take the symbols literally as denoting the actual essence of God is considered to be a form of idolatry.

[3] However, the relationship of kabbalistic symbolism to myth is not so simple and uncomplicated as would at first appear from categorical statements such as these. One can be absolutely sure, of course, that all kabbalists, out of religious conviction, would associate themselves with any expression of serious opposition to myth, because of their fidelity to traditional Jewish religious principles. Consequently, there is no kabbalistic movement that does not resist, either explicitly, or by using phrases like "so to speak" or "as it were," a mythical interpretation of symbols of the divine. Nevertheless, because of certain unconscious emotional and visionary drives, affecting the very depths of the human spirit and demanding some kind of expression, there were a number of leading figures in kabbalah, from various periods in its history, who were not altogether consistent in their anti-mythical standpoint. When we look at the history of kabbalah with this in mind, we see that there was a deep rift that divided the Jewish mystical world into two opposing camps, which, in the process of time, became interlocked and welded together. Those kabbalists that were of a speculative turn of mind, such as Rabbi Azriel of Gerona, and other disciples of Rabbi Isaac the Blind in Spain, and Rabbi Moses Cordovero in Safed, omitted myth completely from their universe of discourse, and at times actively opposed mythical tendencies. In contrast to them, we find extremely important kabbalists, for whom the emotional attraction of myth was so strong that they cultivated it and expressed it in their teachings, despite their outward protestations; and they consequently obliterated the boundaries between symbolism and myth. The greatest kabbalists in this category were the author of the Zohar in Spain, and Rabbi Isaac Luria (the *Ari*) in Safed. Let me give a few examples from the Zohar of symbolic material, where the mythical element is uppermost and most easily seen.[76]

If we compare the description of *Adam Kadmon* (Primordial Man) in the Zohar with the parallel description in the writings of the school of Rabbi Isaac the Blind, we notice a very big difference. In the latter we find careful, recondite allusions, in which we can feel the anxiety to preserve the purely symbolic character of the representation of God in a bodily image. But in the Zohar we have long and detailed descriptions, which occur again and again, squeezing the maximum effect out of the anthropomorphic symbols. We can sense the absolute delight and satisfaction that the author of the Zohar must have felt when he depicted God, without any theological qualms or reservations, just as He appeared to him in his vision. This is particularly striking in the *Idrot*, where the human faces of the various levels in the divine domain are drawn in the finest detail, so that we get peculiar and minute descriptions of the cavities in the skull, the hairs on the head, the curls in the beard. Not for nothing does the *Idra Rabba* begin with a trenchant warning against assigning human attributes to God, for the mythical drive runs riot here and needs to be restrained, and, from the point of view of pure religious conviction, ought to be condemned.

In the whole array of anthropomorphic symbols special importance is given to sexual symbolism, which portrays the life of the divine in the context of a male-female relationship. The sexual terms indicate, according to the symbolic interpretation, the processes whereby divine influence flows, and is received, in the world of emanation. The same *sefirah* that is described as "female" in relation to the source above it of the influence that it has, is also thought of as "male" in relation to that which is below it. "Although this king [*Binah*] is supernal king, it is nevertheless female in relation to the supernal point [*Hokhmah*], which is concealed from all. And even though it is female, it is male in relation to the lower king [*Tiferet*]."[77] However, this aspect is not fundamental to the very rich and varied sexual symbolism of the Zohar, which I shall deal with in more detail in the following section. In the vision of the divine life and the control of the worlds that appears in the mirror of male/female union and separation, which has a central place in the theosophy of the Zohar, we see a reflection of the myth about the gods as celestial forces of fertility and procreation that is commonly found in different forms in the religions of the ancient world. When we come to the *sefirah Yesod*, which is symbolized by the penis, we even hear echoes of ancient phallus worship.[78]

We can also see the transition from pure symbolism to a mythical view of things in the use made of personality symbols, that is to say, in the way in which the *sefirot* are given the names of patriarchs and of leaders of the people in the distant past. These symbols are arranged in a definite order: Abraham, Isaac, and Jacob represent *Hesed*, *Gevurah*, and *Tiferet*; Moses and Aaron represent *Nezah* and *Hod*; Joseph represents *Yesod*, and David *Malkhut*. In its aspect as a female force *Malkhut* is also symbolized by the figures of famous women, for example, the matriarchs, particularly Rachel, and also Miriam and Esther. There are no personality symbols for the upper *sefirot*, except that *Binah*, the supernal mother, is sometimes symbolized by Leah. These symbols are bound up with the special characteristics that these figures displayed, either in their own personal histories, in the stories associated with them in scriptural exegesis, or in the *aggadot* of the rabbis. For example, Abraham symbolizes *Hesed* because of the loving-kindness he showed; the "Fear" of Isaac (see Genesis 31: 42) represents *Gevurah*, and his love for Esau symbolizes the close relationship that exists between the aspect of "Judgment" (*Din*) that is in *Gevurah*, and the "other side"; Jacob, who is called "a perfect man",[79] symbolizes *Tiferet*, which brings the opposing forces of Love and Judgment to a perfect resolution. *Nezah* and *Hod*, which appear as twins and serve together as the source of prophecy, are symbolized by Moses, the father of prophecy, and by Aaron, his brother. Joseph the righteous, the preserver of chastity, symbolizes *Yesod*, which is the sign of the covenant [of circumcision] in the realms above. King David symbolizes *Malkhut*, in its aspect of sovereignty, and also because, according to the *aggadah*,[80] his life was not his own: he took some years from the life of Adam; in the same way, *Malkhut* has no light of its own but takes its light from *Tiferet*. The personalities that serve as symbols were in their life-time the representatives and embodiments of the *sefirot* symbolized, and gained a clear perception of them. So far the relationships between them remain within the realm of symbolism. But in many passages we find allusions to a very different kind of relationship: the personality used as a symbol is raised, either during his lifetime or after his death, to the level of the *sefirah* that he symbolizes. Allusions of this kind are found mainly in connection with Jacob, who symbolizes *Tiferet*, and with Moses, who reaches Jacob's level and even higher. They both fulfill the role of *Tiferet* as the consort of the *Shekhinah* in the mystery of the divine union, Moses serving in this capacity during his lifetime, while Jacob is granted that role after his death. "Jacob called her [i.e., the *Shekhinah*] 'angel' when he was about to depart from the world. Why? Because at that moment he took possession of her in order to rule [over her]. Moses in his lifetime, Jacob after he departed from the world; Moses in body, Jacob in spirit. Blessed was the portion of Moses" (*Events and Personalities*, 21). In the continuation of this passage we read about the moment of Jacob's death: "he now sets his house in order, and ascends to his level, because the conjunction [i.e., sexual union] occurred with Jacob; the body became attached to the necessary place, and the two arms with it."[81] Here we can see the process of transition from a normal symbolic state to an identification of symbol with the thing symbolized, and this leads almost to the deification of the most outstanding men. The mythical character of all this is especially striking in that the apotheosis actually takes place in the mystery of sexual union in the divine realm.

Last, I can cite as an example the material dealing with "the death of the kings" or "the destruction of the worlds," which I have already discussed in another connection.[82] A mythical note can be detected in the very idea that, before the world of emanation was established in its present form, the Emanator had tried unsuccessfully to emanate other beings which had not survived. Of course, one could try to avoid this difficulty by saying that the images of death and destruction are only symbols for a spiritual movement in the divine thought. That is to say that the kings that died, and the worlds that were destroyed were not actual, existing things that were first emanated and then dispensed with, but only the possibilities of being, which entered the divine thought but never emerged into actuality because they could not be utilized in constructing and establishing the worlds.[83] Most of the passages in the Zohar that deal with this subject, however, show, either by their style or through their content, that this is not something that can be explained merely in a symbolic-speculative way. On the contrary, when we put together various hints and allusions, we see their obviously mythical character, and that in the most crucial passages the author tried to conceal this fact.

It is said at one point[84] that the worlds that were destroyed consisted of three hundred and twenty sparks that came from the *bozina di-kardinuta* (spark of blackness), and they "flared, and shone, and went out immediately." Elsewhere[85] it says, without any reference to the destruction of the worlds, that by these sparks the divine thought was cleansed of dross. This means that at the very beginning there was in the divine thought a kind of dross, so to speak—that is, the root of evil nestling there and producing blemished worlds. It was only after these worlds had been destroyed and the evil had been rooted out from the divine thought that it could establish worlds that would be well-ordered.[86] One must assume that the strange and mysterious passage[87] dealing with the image of man in emanation, constructed by three hundred and twenty-five sparks from the *bozina di-kardinuta*, also refers to the mystery of the destruction of earlier worlds. There it is said that the man had the character of stern judgments, and that the forces of uncleanness streamed from the hairs of his head, where the sparks of the *bozina di-kardinuta* were to be found, and this image could be purified only by the removal of the hairs. Purification by the removal of hairs is a more concrete image for cleansing the divine thought of dross, and the meaning is apparently the same.[88] This view of the destruction of the worlds clarifies an obscue reference in a passage that depicts the forces of "the other side" as monsters living in their rivers. We read there that when the great monster entered the first river "it immediately became full, and overflowed, and extinguished the sparks, which had been gathered together in the worlds that had been destroyed earlier" (*The Powers of Uncleanness*, 17). How did the sparks get into the realm of "the other side"? According to the passages quoted, it was like this: the sparks contained the root of evil, and they were therefore dispersed, like dross, to the abode of evil.[89]

So we see that, hidden in the idea of the destruction of the worlds, there are grains of a daring myth about the way in which the Godhead is cleansed of the root of evil that it contains, before the system of the *sefirot* can be established. This idea became the basis of the more elaborate and far-reaching myth of the mystery of *zimzum* (contraction) and the breaking of the vessels in Lurianic kabbalah.[90]

d. An Array of Symbols[91]

[1. Lights, Colors, and Darkness.] The basic and most commonly used symbol in the Zohar is, as its name implies, that of light and splendor. It appears in every section of the book and in the treatment of every subject.[92] Every link in the chain of the *sefirot* is depicted as a new sparking forth of light; the descent of divine influence is a torrent of light; and the whole world of emanation is a sea of brilliant splendor. Even the acts of Will and Thought within the Godhead are frequently portrayed as hidden flashes of light, and a common simile is that the divine forces act "like a hammer striking sparks." The *sefirot* are called "lights" or "mirrors," and even *En-Sof* and *Keter*, to whom the designation of light is not really suited, because they are absolutely concealed, are nevertheless described as beings that give forth rays of light. *En-Sof* is called, paradoxically, "light that does not exist in light,"[93] and *Keter* is designated as "innermost light" or "the supernal, concealed, luminary,"[94] and so on. The seven lower *sefirot* are comprised within four lights, three representing *Hesed*, *Gevurah*, and *Tiferet*, which also include *Nezah*, *Hod*, and *Yesod*, and the fourth representing *Malkhut*. "Come and see. There are four lights. Three of them are sealed, and one is revealed: a light that shines; a light of splendor that shines like the splendor of the heavens in its purity; a light of purple that receives all the lights; a light that does not shine but gazes at these and receives them, and these lights appear in it as in a crystal ball against the sun" (5).[95] Thus both the source and the end of the sefirotic system shine, but they are lights that are not really lights: the source (*En-Sof*) is "a light that does not exist in light," because it is so concealed, and the end (*Malkhut*) is "a light that does not shine," because it has no independent light of its own.

An important fact follows from this view of the *sefirot* as mirrors of light: they reflect one another. This means that each *sefirah* comprises nine others, and reflects the whole system. The internal reflection in the divine attributes maintains unity of content and identity of nature within the large number of variations to be found there. This idea, which was later much elaborated by Rabbi Moses Cordovero, is already found in the school of Rabbi Isaac the Blind, and it is touched upon in a few passages in the Zohar as well. For example, it is said that on the Day of Atonement "all the celestial levels [the *sefirot*] come, one after the other, to rest by the moon [*Malkhut*], and to give it light. And each one of them shares in the mystery of ten, so that it amounts to one hundred, and when it stands in the mystery of one hundred, then everything is one."[96]

Differentiation among the lights of emanation is effected by their being colored by the *kav ha-midah* (the standard of measure), which acts from the domain of the first *sefirah*. There was no color there at all, before the activity of the *kav ha-midah*: "No white, no black, no red, no yellow, no color at all" (1). However, in many passages, *Keter* itself is accorded the color white. In its aspect of *Atika Kadisha* it is called "the white head," and the supernal whiteness that it contains symbolizes the purity of love and the perfection of mercy, in contrast to the redness of judgment that glows in *Ze'ir Anpin* (14). This whiteness is "white within white, and white that comprises all white" (*Influence and Direction*, 7); that is to say that it is the source of every variety of whiteness; and the luminaries in the world of emanation are kindled from it, and as they are kindled so it acts through three shades of whiteness (ibid.).

The colors most commonly found in the Zohar are those of *Ḥesed*, *Gevurah*, and *Tiferet*—white, red, and yellow. White and red symbolize the contrast between love and judgment, and yellow is meant to be a mixture of the two. The symbols of silver and gold,[97] and water and fire, for *Ḥesed* and *Gevurah* are also part of the mystic significance of these colors. *Malkhut* is symbolized by the color blue, because it is the colour of the sea into which the rivers are emptied, and the word "blue" (*tekhelet*) alludes to the fact that it comprises all (*khol*) colors. In the same sense, it is depicted as the celestial rainbow, which is clothed in the colors white, red, and yellow (*The Natural World*, 11). In their own domain, the colors of *Ḥesed*, *Gevurah*, and *Tiferet* are called "concealed, radiant colors," that is, their brightness is dim when seen from below, but they are radiant in themselves. When, however, they shine in the rainbow of *Malkhut* they are called "visible colors that are not radiant" (5), because their radiance is darkened when they are revealed.

A different account of the connection between the colors and the *sefirot* is supplied by the mystic symbol of the range of colors in the flame of a burning lamp. The lamp and the wick represent ordinary material existence; the blue-black light at the tip of the wick symbolizes *Malkhut*; the white light that provides illumination represents *Tiferet*; and *Binah* is reflected in the concealed light of the "halo" that surrounds the flame. The interplay of colors in the lower part of the light—which is sometimes blue and sometimes blackish, and sometimes contains a trace of red—signifies the fluctuations in the nature of

Malkhut, which depend on its situation relative to the other *sefirot*. When it is in harmonious association with the upper *sefirot*, it is blue, which comprises all the colors. When Judgment is the dominant factor in it, it contains a flash of red. And when it is divorced from the *sefirot* it turns black; that is, it lacks light, and becomes dark. Whiteness signifies in *Tiferet* its normal nature as the attribute of Mercy; and the hidden light that surrounds the flame symbolizes *Binah*, which is concealed from the sight of the *sefirot* that are below it, but includes them and embraces them as a mother embraces her children (4). Another passage (*The Powers of Uncleanness*, 6) describes the connection of the blue in *Malkhut* to red and black differently. The original redness is the strict judgment that is in *Gevurah*. When the rays of its splendor are projected downwards this redness is divided into two: the brighter portion produces blue in *Malkhut* in the guise of lenient judgment, while the dimmer portion produces blackness in "the other side," which is "a red color (derived) from utter filth, and because of this utter filth it became black, and all was poured out from supernal redness."

The color black is the color of darkness, which in kabbalistic symbolism has four different meanings. Primordial darkness is *Keter*, which has a black appearance, either because of the depth of its concealment or because of its blinding brightness.[98] *Gevurah* is called "darkness" because of the dark nature of Judgment, which obscures the light of Mercy. However, it is not actual obscurity but a powerful fire in which all the colors blaze forth and are revealed according to the strength of Judgment's activity. But when the attribute of Judgment is a source that nourishes the forces of "the other side," which is envisaged as the darkness of the annihilating abyss that desires to swallow up and extinguish the light, *Gevurah* appears as a darkened fire. "Darkness is a black fire, strong in color, a red fire, strong in appearance, a green fire, strong in shape, a white fire, a color that comprises all. Darkness is the strong fire in all fire, and this is that which gives strength to *tohu* ["the other side"]. Darkness is fire, but it is darkened fire only when it gives strength to *tohu* . . . when it looks kindly upon evil, and then it is called 'darkness', because it dwells with it in order to give it strength" (*The Powers of Uncleanness*, 5).[99] *Malkhut* is symbolized by the darkness of night, in two respects: first, because of the strong connection that exists between it and the darkness of Judgment in *Gevurah*, and second, because it has no light of its own;[100] that is to say, darkness is not attributed to it as a positive force but as an absence of light.

[2. The Mystery of Language, Torah, and Names.] The processes involved in the production of speech, expressed by word enunciation, are often cited in the Zohar as symbols of the chain of the *sefirot*. The initial movement occurs within concealed Thought, that is, in the *sefirah Ḥokhmah*, as a result of an impulse from the Will (*Keter*). When Thought has become crystallized in its hidden domain, it extends itself and seeks a means of self-expression. It first of all extends into *Binah*, in the form of breath being expelled in the throat. At this stage Thought is like an internal, inaudible, voice. In other words, the voice has already emerged within the depths of the soul, but it has not yet moved from a concealed to a revealed state. In the next stage, at the emanation of *Tiferet*, which comprises six extremities, the audible voice breaks through. By the various tonalities of the voice hidden Thought is revealed in outward expression, but the revelation is not yet complete because it still lacks that particularity of content which accompanies enunciation of speech. This next step is effected by the emanation of *Malkhut*, which is the mystery of divine speech. So in this process of the revelation of language we have two hidden stages—Thought, and the internal voice; and two revealed stages—the audible voice, and speech. Parallel to this, we have two male/female pairs in the world of emanation: father and mother (*Ḥokhmah* and *Binah*), and the king and the consort (*Tiferet* and *Malkhut*).[101] From another point of view, however, this process indicates the unity of the *sefirot*, for every stage is part of the expansion of Thought, and all the stages are concerned with the same basic material. "If you examine the levels [you will see] that it is Thought, understanding, voice, and speech, and it is all one, and Thought is the beginning of all, and there is no division; but it is all one, and all connected, for it is actual Thought connected with *Ayin*, and it is forever inseparable" (7).

This actual process is symbolized again by the different levels at which the Torah exists and develops in the divine realm. According to the *aggadah*,[102] a primordial spiritual Torah existed two thousand years before the creation of the world, and it was used as a kind of blueprint for the creation. This spiritual Torah symbolizes in the Zohar the divine Thought itself.[103] This Torah contains no letters at all, but it is the origin of the spiritual letters, which flow down from it as the seed of emanation, and which are given shape in *Binah*.[104] The letters become crystallized as emanation proceeds from *Binah*; and from a combination of the letters the written Torah is constructed in *Tiferet*.[105] The content of the written Torah, which is hidden and sealed, is made manifest in the oral Torah in *Malkhut*.[106] The relationship between the written Torah and the oral Torah is similar to that between voice and speech. Just as voice is a prerequisite of speech, and there can be no speech without voice, so the oral Torah can exist only on the basis of the written Torah; and just as the content of Thought, which is comprised within the voice, remains incomprehensible without the enunciation of speech, so the words of the written Torah need clarification by the oral Torah. This is the relationship of "the universal that needs the particular, and the particular that needs the universal" (7). The unity of the *sefirot* can also be seen in this account, for we are dealing here not with any intrinsic novelty or change, but with stages in the development of the divine Torah. This unity, in fact, is given additional strength, because both the beginning and the end of the chain, that is, *Ḥokhmah* and *Malkhut*, are identical in nature, in that one is upper, and the other lower, Wisdom. The primordial Torah is the wisdom of Thought, which comprises everything, and which is creative and formative simply by its own thought process: this is designated "the wisdom of God." The oral Torah, on the other hand, is the wisdom of conduct, which enlightens and guides every particular, and reveals the kingdom of God: this is called "the wisdom of Solomon."[107]

The divine Torah is, in its entirety, one sacred name, of which it is said "it is His name, and His name is it."[108] In other words, the description of the sefirotic chain in terms of the development of the Torah means that the concealed Emanator, Who can be given no name, gives Himself a name through His emanation. This single, all-inclusive name separates out into its individual elements; and so the Torah can be seen as a great storehouse of the names of God in different combinations,[109] all of which designate specific forces of emanation. In this storehouse there is a range of ten names, which must not be obliterated, for they enjoy the highest degree of sanctity, and these ten are applied particularly to the ten *sefirot*.[110] The names in the order of the *sefirot* are: *Ehyeh, Yah, YHVH* with the vocalization of *Elohim, El, Elohim, YHVH, YHVH Zeva'ot, Elohim Zeva'ot*,[111] *Shaddai, Adonai*. There are a very large number of interpretations of these names in the Zohar, and in the other kabbalistic texts, and I can give only a few brief indications of them here. *Ehyeh* signifies *Keter* as the source of emanation, which is prepared and about to come into being, but without there being any actual existence within *Keter*.[112] *Yah* refers to the continuous attachment of *Ḥokhmah* (father), the point symbolized by the letter *yod*, to *Binah* (mother), the palace symbolized by the letter *he*. *YHVH*, vocalized like *Elohim*, shows that *Binah* in itself is Mercy, but the roots of Judgment are planted within it, and it emanates the judgment that is contained within *Gevurah*. *El*, whose letters form the beginning of the name *Elohim*, points to the unification of the opposing forces of Love and Judgment in the life of God.[113] *Elohim* and *YHVH* are already known in aggadic midrash as representing the attributes of Judgment and Mercy. *Zeva'ot* alludes to the outpouring of forces that flow from *Nezah* and *Hod*, on the pattern of the twin sources of semen in the male.[114] *Shaddai* indicates *Yesod* as a channel for the transmission of the divine influence, which provides all the worlds with sufficient (*dai*) for their needs. *Adonai* refers to the mastery that is revealed in *Malkhut* as the power that governs the world.

The name *Elohim* is often used for three *sefirot* jointly: *Binah, Gevurah*, and *Malkhut*.[115] Thus, for example, *Elohim* in the biblical story of creation refers to *Binah*, and in other places *Binah* is called *Elohim Ḥayyim* (living God). The attribution of the name *Elohim*, which really belongs to *Gevurah*, to *Binah* and *Malkhut* can be explained quite simply by the fact that the two latter are connected with the attribute of Judgment: *Binah* is the source of Judgment, and *Malkhut* acts with the power of Judgment through its nature as the attribute of lenient judgment. However, we find in the Zohar, in connection with *Binah*, another symbolic explanation, which gives a profound significance to the way in which the name *Elohim* is made up. *Binah* belongs in essence to the hidden domain of the first three *sefirot*. From this point of view, it has no name that can refer to either its activity or its manifestation. It is called simply *Mi* (who?). This name indicates that it exists at a level that can be contemplated by posing a question as to its nature. But since this contemplation must be interrupted during the descent from one stage to another, it becomes clear that the mystery is not revealed, and the question remains unanswered. "The hidden, primordial entity, called *Mi*, can be the object of a question. When man asks, and strives to contemplate and to know from level to level, to the very last level—when he reaches that point [*Malkhut*]—*Mah* (what?), what do you know, what can you contemplate, for what have you striven? Behold, everything is concealed as at the first."[116] Only when the whole structure of emanation has been designed within *Binah*, and only when *Binah*, like a mother with her children, has emanated the lower *sefirot*, which are called *Eleh* (these), because they come within the boundary of perception—only then can it be given a name. This name is *Elohim*, which occurs in the biblical creation story, and whose letters designate the conjunction of *Mi* and *Eleh*. It designates, in other words, the way in which *Binah* moves from the secrecy of the unanswerable question in order to reveal itself as the originator of creation (11).

YHVH is the name of the essence upon which all divine names and titles depend, because it signifies the living essence of the revealed God. It is therefore assigned to the central *sefirah, Tiferet,* called *Ha-kadosh barukh hu* (the Holy One, blessed be He), to which all the other *sefirot* are joined, like branches to the trunk of a tree. This name also has a wider significance in that it designates *Ze'ir Anpin,* which comprises the whole of emanation from *Hokhmah* to *Malkhut.* In other words, it signifies the revealed God in His full stature, in contrast to *Atika Kadisha (Keter)* which is not revealed at all.[117] The letters of the name are additionally used to indicate the various stages of emanation, from the beginning to the end: *yod* is *Hokhmah,* the first *he* is *Binah, vav* is *Tiferet,* which includes the six extremities; and the last *he* is *Malkhut.*[118] Even *Keter,* which has no letter of its own, is designated by the tip of the letter *yod.*[119]

In connection with this particular type of symbolism, which is quite common, we ought to look at the assignation of the same letter (*he*) to both *Binah* and *Malkhut,* and at the significance of the last *he* of the tetragrammaton as a symbol of *Malkhut. Binah* and *Malkhut* are on parallel levels, one concealed, and the other revealed; they are both female, both mothers, an upper *Shekhinah* and a lower *Shekhinah.*[120] *Binah* is called "the concealed world," while, in contrast, *Malkhut* is "the revealed world," and they are symbolized by the two sisters Leah and Rachel.[121] The activity of *Binah* occurs in the upper realms, among the forces of emanation, and it gives life to, and supports them. This activity is continued and completed by the activity of *Malkhut* in the lower realms, among the forces of creation, and they are nourished by its influence and committed to its care. It is this reciprocity which is indicated by both *Binah* and *Malkhut* having the same letter. However, while the letter *he* belongs to *Binah* as a right, and is attached to it always, the letter that *Malkhut* ought really to have, in view of its basic nature, is *dalet,* which would indicate its relative poverty (*dalut*), in that it has no light of its own. Nevertheless, when it receives influence from the upper realms by being linked into the system of the *sefirot,* and particularly through its intercourse with *Tiferet,* it is symbolized by the last *he* of the tetragrammaton, which, because of its proximity in the alphabet to the next letter, *vav,* indicates the flow of blessing which descends into it through the mystery of intercourse.[122]

[3. *Adam Kadmon.*] I have already had to touch upon anthropomorphic symbols in the Zohar several times, and have shown how common and important they are. There are some extraordinary descriptions of the figure of Man. It is portrayed as a most perfect and exalted image, which from several points of view constitutes the overall symbolic framework of the sefirotic system.[123] The God who reveals Himself in the world of emanation is "the supernal man" or "primordial man" (*Adam Kadmon*),[124] and it was only after the construction of the image of man had been finally determined that perfection was achieved in the Godhead. "The image was perfected that comprises all images, the image that comprises all names . . . when the crowns and the diadems were joined together, then it was the perfection of all, for the image of man is the image of the upper and the lower worlds that are comprised within it, and since this image comprises the upper and lower worlds the *Atika*

Kadisha established its attributes, and the attribute of *Ze'ir Anpin* was in this image and this attribute."[125] Man below is created in both body and soul[126] in the image of man above, but his likeness is only a pale imitation of the divine model. "The image [of man below] that seems in its characteristics to be like this image [of man above] is not this image, but something like this image."[127] The true, original man is within the Godhead, and corporeal man reflects him in the way he is constructed.

Adam Kadmon's shape is depicted schematically, and the most common way of doing this is to arrange the exterior parts of the human anatomy in such a way as to correspond with the lower *sefirot* from *Ḥesed* downward, and to portray the exterior or interior parts of the head as representing the three upper *sefirot*. The second preface of the *Tikkunei ha-Zohar* gives this type of picture in its entirety: "*Ḥesed*—right arm; *Gevurah*—left arm; *Tiferet*—torso; *Nezaḥ* and *Hod*—two legs; *Yesod*—the completion of the body, the sign of the holy covenant; *Malkhut*—mouth. . . . The brain is *Hokhmah*, the inner thought; *Binah* is the heart. . . . The supernal *Keter* is the crown of royalty . . . and it is the headpiece of the *tefillin*" (*En-Sof*, 4). This scheme, with a few differences, is frequently presented, or referred to, in the main body of the Zohar as well, and most of the limbs are already mentioned in the *Sefer ha-Bahir*.[128] The main differences are that the upper *sefirot* are usually symbolized by three heads, or three brains; while *Malkhut* is not included at all in the anatomical system, but appears separately as an image of the female.[129] *Nezaḥ* and *Hod* are portrayed symbolically by the two kidneys, or the two testicles, as well as by two legs.

However, anthropomorphic symbolism in the Zohar is not confined to this system. On the contrary, there is hardly one part of the human body, whether external or internal, that is not pressed into service for symbolic purposes. Sometimes a minute anatomical analysis is offered in order to symbolize the Godhead; the parts of the skull, the hair, facial features, and the beard are especially subject to detailed exposition.[130] The *Sifra di-Zeniuta*, *Idra Rabba*, and *Idra Zuta*, as well as many passages in the *Raya Mehemna* and the *Tikkunei ha-Zohar*, are packed tight with this kind of material. This is not the place to go into a detailed explanation of these symbols, but as an example I shall deal with the symbolic significance of three internal organs that go to make up a comprehensive system of their own: the brain, the heart, and the liver. The brain is *Hokhmah*, and this includes *Binah* as well; the heart is *Tiferet*, the middle *sefirah*, with its six dependent offshoots; and the liver is *Malkhut*. The principal passage that describes these symbols explains the activity and the interrelationship of these organs in the upper world by comparing them to the organs in the lower world: "There are three rulers above, through whom the Holy One, blessed be He, is known, and they are His honored mystery, and these are they: the brain, the heart, and the liver. They act in an opposite way to this world. In the world above, the brain receives first, and it then supplies the heart; the heart receives, and supplies the liver; and after this the liver provides a portion to all the sources below, to each according to his due. In the world below, the liver receives first, and it subsequently brings everything to the heart, and the heart receives the best of the food. When it has taken, and strengthened itself, it gives of that very strength and delight that it has received to the brain, and it activates it; and then the liver shares food out again to all the sources of the body."[131] When, however, man approaches God, through the sacrifices, for example, or through the fulfillment of the commandments, there is a perfect parallel between the terrestrial and the celestial organs. The impulsion from below comes, first of all, to the liver in the realms above (*Malkhut*). From there, it passes to the heart (*Tiferet*), and thence to the brain (*Hokhmah*). There it causes the source of influence to open, and the influence descends to the lower worlds by way of the liver.

The ten *sefirot* in their entirety are included in the image of man, according to the system most commonly used, but the principal part of the image is *Tiferet*,[132] symbolized by the torso, from which the head and the other limbs branch out. However, when the *sefirot* are divided between *Atika Kadisha* (*Keter*) and *Ze'ir Anpin* (comprising the *sefirot* from *Hokhmah* to *Malkhut*),[133] the whole image consists of *Ze'ir Anpin*,[134] whereas *Atika Kadisha* is merely a head, or three heads, without a body. In this description *Da'at* is brought in as a third brain in the head of *Ze'ir Anpin*, in order to complement *Hokhmah* and *Binah* (13). So in the world of emanation we have the image of a single man,[135] apart from the last *sefirah*, the female, which is an image on its own. But the *Adam Kadmon* of the sefirotic system is not the only "man" in the upper regions. The ranks of nondivine beings, like the forces of the Chariot and the angels, are also constructed in the image of man. "There are several levels above, different from one another, and from level to level there is the mystic symbol of man. The Holy One, blessed be He, has made the levels that are of one kind into an image of one body, so that they make up the mystic symbol of man. And we have learned that on the second day of Creation, when Gehinnom was created, a body was made in the mystic symbol of man, and the limbs were officers [i.e., angels], who drew near to the fire and died, and returned as at the beginning" (*The Activity of "The Other Side"*, 1). It is also stated quite explicitly that the "camps" of the *Shekhinah* were constructed in the shape of a body with limbs.[136]

In later sections, in the *Raya Mehemna* and the *Tikkunei ha-Zohar*, we find a fundamentally different view of the subject under discussion, and we come across a new terminology, which is used in a confusing and illogical way. But the basic meaning is sufficiently clear. The new element here is principally that, in addition to the image of man that comprises the whole system of the *sefirot*, every individual *sefirah* constitutes an image of man, each one being formed in the likeness of the man above it. "What does 'in His image' mean? . . . The higher *Shekhinah* [*Binah*] is the image of supernal man, which is *Hokhmah*, and the lower *Shekhinah* [*Malkhut*] is the image of the man that is the central pillar [*Tiferet*]. Furthermore, the central pillar [is made] in the likeness of *Keter*, and this is the man of creation (*beriyah*); and the man of formation (*yezirah*) is righteous [*Yesod*] in the likeness of *Hokhmah* . . . and the lower *Shekhinah*, the man of making (*asiyah*), is the image of the upper *Shekhinah* . . . each *sefirah* is called 'man,' and the lower *Shekhinah* 'the image of man.'"[137] New terms appear here: "man of creation," "man of formation" and "man of making." But they do not refer to the world-system of creation, formation and making,[138] which, according to this particular kabbalist, are three worlds below the level of emanation. They are, instead, names of *sefirot* in the world of emanation. In this passage they are assigned to *Tiferet*, *Yesod*, and *Malkhut*, but elsewhere[139] it is said that the three upper *sefirot* are given these names, on a higher plane. In other words, the triad of creation, formation, and making does not refer to inner content, but to a structural framework. This division, however, also appears on a much lower level, in the physical body of man in the lower world, in the shape of the tripartite nature of the soul, namely, *neshamah*, *ruah*, and *nefesh*, which correspond to the world of thought, of speech, and of action. There are, therefore, in man's psychic constitution three spiritual images: the man of creation, the man of formation, and the man of making.[140] The man of creation, who occupies the highest place in this scheme, that is, *Keter*, is called "primordial man preceding all preexistents."[141] And so the image of man within the Godhead is broken up in a most extraordinary way, and the terminology that sought to differentiate it from the nondivine images is completely blurred. In one passage, however, this kabbalist also emphasizes the unity and the uniqueness of the divine image when compared with other images: "There is a man in the likeness of the Holy One, blessed be He, which is His emanation, and this is *YHVH*. It has no creation, formation, or making, but emanation."[142] This means that, even in his view, the system of the *sefirot* can be depicted, in an all-embracing way, in a single, unique image, differentiated even by name from all other images, in that it is seen as the man of emanation.[143]

[4. Male and Female.] The image of supernal man, which is composed of the *sefirot* from *Keter*, or *Hokhmah*, to *Yesod*, is a male image, and it comprises the active divine forces from which influence flows. Side by side with this we have the last *sefirah* as the image of the female, that is, as the passive force which receives the influence. But it must not be regarded as a second "man." It is rather the completion of the male image, for the perfection of man, in the world below and in the world above, consists in the harmonious partnership of male and female; and where there is male without female, man is throught to be defective, only half a body, as it were. We are given a taste of this ideal unity of male and female in the description of how they were first created with two faces, that is to say, they were physically attached to one another all the time. This unity involved those powers which were especially characterized by the male element, namely, the *sefirot Tiferet* and *Yesod*, symbolized respectively by the torso, and by the sign of the covenant of circumcision. On this level the most common terms for the male and the female are: "the Holy One, blessed be He" and "the *Shekhinah*"; and "the king" and "the consort."

However, male and female appear not only as the embodiment of the sefirotic system, and as the perfection of the image or the completion of the structure, but they also appear at the head of the system. *Hokhmah* and *Binah* in the overall picture of the image of man are portrayed as parts of the head of the male. But they also exist in their own right as a pair, male and female, having the role of father (*abba*) and mother (*imma*), although they do not constitute specific images of man.[144] By arranging the higher powers on the pattern of a male/female relationship, the foundation was laid for establishing the structure of emanation, and for balancing the whole system around the twofold image of male and female. "This *Hokhmah*, which includes everything, when it emerged from, and was illuminated by, *Atika Kadisha*, was illuminated in no other way except as male and female; for this *Hokhmah* extended itself and brought forth *Binah* from itself, and so there existed male and female. *Hokhmah* father, *Binah* mother, *Ḥokhmah* and *Binah* were equally weighed, male and female, and because of them everything survives as male and female, for were it not so they would not survive" (16).

Ḥokhmah and *Binah* are the sources of the lower *sefirot*, which were formed in *Binah*'s womb, and emanated from it through the mystery of birth. From this point of view, their relationship to the second male/female pair in the Godhead is like that of parents to a son and daughter. They shower their children with gifts and blessings, adorn them with crowns, and radiate light and splendor upon them. The father is fonder of the daughter, while the mother favors the son.[145] The father's love for the daughter is so disproportionate that it provokes jealousy in the mother: "The father's continual desire is solely for the daughter, because she is the only daughter among six sons, and he has shared out portions, gifts, and presents to the six sons, but to her he has apportioned nothing, and she has no inheritance at all. But despite this he watches over her with more love and longing than over anyone else. In his love he calls her 'daughter'; this is not enough for him and he calls her 'sister'; this is not enough for him, and he calls her 'mother'. . . . Therefore, the supernal world [mother] says to her [to the daughter]: 'Is it a small matter that you have taken away my husband?' (Genesis 30: 15) for all his love is centred on you."[146] The love of the father and mother, and the illumination they afford, assist the union of the son with the daughter,[147] which in this sense is described as the union of brother and sister.[148]

Looked at in another way, in the context of the union between male and female, there is a very close parallel between the activity of the two pairs. The *sefirot* are formed by the union of *abba* and *imma*, which is also the source of their sustenance. From the union of the king with the consort the souls are born,[149] and from this union the lower worlds receive the influence that keeps them alive. In other words, *Ḥokhmah* and *Binah* are father and mother to the forces of emanation, while *Tiferet* and *Malkhut* are father and mother to the forces of creation. There is, however, an important difference in the relationships of the two pairs. *Abba* and *imma* are in a state of uninterrupted union, while the Holy One, blessed be He, and the *Shekhinah* are not attached to one another continuously, but come together from time to time after periods of separation. "The first *he* [*imma*] is not called 'bride,' but the second *he* [*Shekhinah*] is called 'bride' at certain times, for on many occasions the male does not unite with her, but leaves her. Of such a time it is written 'And you shall not approach a woman in her menstrual uncleanness' (Leviticus 18: 19). When the female has become clean, and the male wishes to unite with her, then she is called 'bride', for she comes as a real bride. But as for *imma*, the delight of both of them [*abba* and *imma*] is never interrupted. They go out together, they dwell together; they are not separated, they do not leave one another."[150] During the time of separation the consort is like a menstruating woman, as it were, and her subsequent intercourse with the king is prompted by a powerful urge. Their union, therefore, is always like the first contact between bridegroom and bride, and they are called "lovers" (*dodim*). This is not the case, however, with the union between *abba* and *imma*, who are called simply "friends" (*re'im*). "Those who desire one another, and are not perpetually [together], are called 'lovers', while those that are perpetually [together], and are never out of each other's sight, and never parted from each other, are called 'friends' . . . the latter through the delight of continuous unity, the former through temporary desire."[151]

This distinction demonstrates the nature and the special meaning of the symbolic portrayal of these *sefirot* as male and female pairs. *Hokhmah* and *Binah* represent the archetype of the founders of the family, who have a harmonious and peaceful existence together, enjoying a normal, very close, relationship, with a lasting, mutual sympathy, while their ambitions, through and through, are focused on the upbringing of the children and the welfare of the family. *Binah*, in particular, portrays the characteristics of the perfect matriarch. She is frequently depicted as a mother caring for her young, or as a nurse providing milk.[152] In contrast to this, *Tiferet* and *Malkhut* present the supernal image of a pair of intermittent lovers, caught up in the entanglements of desire. Here the mystery of male and female is the apotheosis of lovers' passion, with all its different moods and vicissitudes, its exultation and its despair, its radiance and its darkness, its pleasure and its pain, the delight of union and the burden of separation. Verses from the Song of Songs are interpreted mystically to refer to this type of love.

Descriptions of the act of intercourse itself, and also of the emotions and movements connected with it, are both common and frank in the Zohar. The actual physiological process of the flow of semen from its higher source in the brain, according to traditional medieval theory, and its transmission to the female by the channel of *Yesod* through different parts of the body, is a topic that recurs again and again and is described in detail in a number of different ways.[153] The first movement in the embrace that precedes intercourse is the raising of the male's left arm, that is to say, the kindling of the flame from the fire of *Gevurah*, and placing it beneath the head of the female, in order to arouse her and to kindle her love. When the flame of the first arousal has abated, the right arm rises to embrace her and to fondle her with the gentleness and love of *Hesed*. "'The Lord has made bare His holy arm' (Isaiah 52: 10). This is one arm upon which salvation depends, upon which vengeance depends, upon which redemption depends. Why? In order to raise the Assembly of Israel [the *Shekhinah*] from the dust, and to bring her to him, in order that they might be united together. And when this [arm] is aroused to meet her, how much fear there is in the world until he lays the arm beneath her head, in order to be at one with her, as it is said 'His left hand under my head, etc.' (Song of Songs 2: 6). Then judgment is quieted, and sins are forgiven. After this, the right hand comes to embrace. Then joy dwells in the world, and all faces shine. After this, she is united [with him] in body, and then all is called 'one,' without separation."[154] The role of the attribute of Judgment in the first stages of arousal can be explained as being parallel to the first incitement to sexual intercourse in man, which derives from the evil inclination.[155]

While activity in intercourse itself is the function of the male, it is the female which provides the stimulus for desire leading to intercourse. When she "arouses delight in Him first, and draws Him to her with great love and desire" (32), then the union is complete and all the worlds are saturated with the influence of love. But when the stimulus comes from the male side, and the desire of the female is aroused only subsequently, then Judgment is dominant both in the act of union and in the worlds. The female desires a kiss, which is "the cleaving of spirit to spirit," so that there should be no separation between her and the male.[156] The activity of the supernal female in the matter of desire raises a problem: "Everywhere the male pursues the female and arouses love in her, but here we find that she arouses love, and pursues him. And in the eyes of the world the female gains no credit for pursuing the male" (35). The answer is that the desire of the female for the male in the realms above is prompted by the feeling of love for her that is experienced by the souls of the righteous in the world below. And since the source and origin of the souls of the righteous is to be found in *Tiferet*, which has a male character, we see that "the male arouses his affection and love for the female, and then the female is connected in love to the male" (ibid.). This means that the male, in the world above, and the souls of the righteous are united in their love for the *Shekhinah*. This idea is used here to explain how the two aspects of the male work together in a complementary fashion in order to arouse desire in the female. The same idea appears in a much more extraordinary form in order to explain the arousal of desire in the supernal male. The attachment of the *Shekhinah* to the righteous makes the male in the higher world jealous, and kindles his desire. "When is the desire of the male for the female aroused? When he is jealous of her. Come and see the mystery of the matter. When there is a righteous man in the world, from the very beginning the *Shekhinah* does not leave him, and her desire is for him. Then the love-desire for her in the world above is like the desire of the male for the female when he is jealous of her; and so 'I will establish my covenant with you' (Genesis 6: 18): desire is aroused because of you."[157] Therefore the righteous are, as it were, competitors with the supernal male for the love of the *Shekhinah*, and they assist thereby the work of divine union.

In connection with the yearning of the *Shekhinah* when she is alone and separated from her lover, there are two beautiful ideas that deserve notice. One is introduced as an interpretation of Song of Songs 8: 6, "Set me as a seal upon your heart, as a seal upon your arm." The *Shekhinah* beseeches the male that, even when they are separated and far from one another, the memory of her should not leave him, but that her image should be impressed on his heart just as a seal is impressed on wax. "When the Assembly of Israel [i.e., the *Shekhinah*] is closely attached to her husband, she says, 'Set me as a seal.' When the seal is attached to the necessary place it leaves a complete image of itself; even if the seal then goes elsewhere, and does not remain but is removed from there, it leaves a complete image of itself, which stays there. And so the Assembly of Israel says: since I have been closely attached to you, my complete image is impressed on you, for, even if I go elsewhere, you will find my image impressed on you, and you will remember me."[158] The second idea describes her anguish "because of the thrust of love that she cannot bear" (*Events and Personalities*, 21). The pains of love destroy her beauty and reduce her image "until nothing can be seen of her but the tiniest point" (ibid.). In this condition she leaves her retinue and remains alone with her grief, and they roar because of their longing for her. The sound of their roaring arouses the male-king and then "her much-beloved leaves his palace with many gifts and many offerings, with perfumes and spices, and comes to her, and finds her black and tiny, with no image or beauty at all" (ibid.). She gains new strength through the joy of meeting her lover and through the pleasures of love, and her beauty is restored and becomes resplendent once more. Sensuous, erotic nuances like these provide a kind of musical accompaniment to the more sensual descriptions that are such a striking feature of the mystical symbolism of sexual intercourse in the Zohar.

NOTES

1. [These terms may be translated in order as follows:
   Keter Elyon supernal crown
   Hokhmah wisdom
   Binah understanding, or intelligence
   Hesed love
   Gevurah power
   Tiferet beauty
   Nezah eternity, or endurance
   Hod majesty
   Yesod foundation
   Malkhut kingdom, or sovereignty.]

2. [See n. 70 on p. 266.]

3. III, 288b (*Idra Zuta*).

4. On this point there is a difference of opinion at the very beginning of the kabbalistic period. In the *Sefer ha-Bahir*, and also in the writings of Rabbi Isaac the Blind, and his faithful pupil, Rabbi Ezra of Gerona, the first *sefirah* is called *Mahashavah* (Thought) or *Mahashavah Tehorah* (pure Thought). But Rabbi Isaac's other pupils, particularly Rabbi Azriel of Gerona, gave the name *Mahashavah* to *Hokhmah*, and *Keter* they called *Razon* (Will). Rabbi Azriel gives a number of different indications of the nature of *Razon*, e.g., "*Razon*, which nothing preceded," "*Razon* comprises everything," "*Razon*, beyond which there is nothing," and so on. See I. Tishby, ed. *Perush ha-Aggadot le-Rabbi Azriel*, p. 133 (Index to the names of the *sefirot*); G. Scholem, *Reshit ha-Kabbalah*, pp. 140–41.

   In the *Tikkunei ha-Zohar* also, *Keter* is called *Mahashavah*, just as we find it in the writings of the early kabbalists. See end of *Tikkun* 19, end of *Tikkun* 22, and elsewhere.

5. We do, in fact, find some passages that speak of beings within the Will, but their independent existence begins only when the Will extends itself.

6. Actually, when considered independently, it follows its own nature and tends toward *Din*, and is called "the mild attribute of Judgment." See the introduction to the section on the *Shekhinah*, pp. 371–73.

7. *Perush Eser Sefirot*, 3a. Compare Rabbi Solomon Ibn Gabirol on the divine will, in his *Sefer Mekor Hayyim* [*Fons Vitae*] (Jerusalem, 1926) chap. 3, p. 57: "The will, which is the power that creates these elements, is limited as to its activity, but limitless as to its nature. Hence, its activity is limited."

8. *Perush Sefer Yezirah* (attributed in printed editions to Nachmanides), chap. 1, p. 5.

9. *Zohar Hadash, parashah Va-ethanan.*

10. See also the introduction to the section *Influence and Direction*, and the Zoharic passages there.

11. The first *sefirah* is beyond the limit of perception, and even the second cannot be understood except as the beginning of existence in the world of emanation (1). Contemplation of the actual essence begins with *Binah*, but only as a form of interrogation, in its aspect of *Mi* (Who?), without any clear response (Zohar I, 30a).

12. See also *Shekhinah*, 10.

13. Zohar II, 137a. But this passage is not altogether clear, and it is possible that the allusion is to the influence of the upper *sefirot* upon the lower *sefirot*.
14. See Zohar III, 152a.
15. Zohar I, 38a.
16. See also *The Account of Creation*, 10; and *The Activity of "The Other Side"*, 1.
17. Zohar I, 83b [See below, p. 732.]
18. However, in the *Midrash ha-Ne'elam* the term is used a few times, particularly in its verbal form, both in Hebrew and in Aramaic. See *The Account of Creation*, 12, 15, and elsewhere.
19. *Perush ha-Aggadot le-Rabbi Azriel*, p. 118.
20. *Tikkun* 19.
21. This simile is also to be found in a similar sense, among the neo-Pythagoreans, in connection with spiritual perception, which is granted to man as a gift from God, without causing any diminution in the source, "like someone lighting a candle from a candle." See E. Hoffmann's essay in *Die Geschichte der Philosophie* (Berlin, 1925), p. 239.
22. His intention is quite clear from the sentence: "[The Cause of causes] descended upon [the *sefirah*], but there was no diminution above." Hence one can say with complete certainty that the author does not think of emanation as being the formation of the *sefirot*, but as being the expansion of the divine essence within the *sefirot*.
23. See Rabbi Ezra's *Commentary to the Song of Songs* (Altona, printed in the name of Nachmanides), 23b. The image is taken from *Bereshit Rabbah* 15: 1.
24. III, 4b. See also I, 35b; *Zohar Hadash*, beginning of *Va-ethanan*.
25. See Rabbi Moses Cordovero, *Sefer Pardes Rimmonim*, pt. 11, chaps. 1–4; G. Scholem, *Reshit ha-Kabbalah*, pp. 171–74.
26. *Zohar Hadash*, ibid.
27. See below, p. 310.
28. *Bereshit Rabbah* 3: 9.
29. Zohar III, 128a (*Idra Rabba*).
30. Ibid., 292b (*Idra Zuta*).
31. Zohar II, 176b (beginning of *Sifra di-Zeniuta*).
32. See also Zohar III, 142a (*Idra Rabba*).
33. Similar ideas are touched upon, in a variant form, in a passage that deals with nine points, that appear "in the mystery of the letter *yod*, the supernal, secret point [*Hokhmah*] . . . and they are called *En-Sof*" (*Zohar Hadash*, beginning of *Bereshit*, *Sitrei Otiot*).
34. See also 1 and 19.
35. See *Shekhinah*, 13; Zohar I, 20a.
36. See Rabbi Moses Cordovero, *Pardes Rimmonim*, pt. 5, chaps. 3ff.
37. Cf. Zohar II, 64a–64b.
38. See 2, 19, and 35.
39. See also 15.
40. Zohar III, 291a (*Idra Zuta*).
41. *Commentary to the Pentateuch*, Genesis 1: 1.
41a. [Literally, "according to the way of truth"—a semi-technical phrase introducing a mystical interpretation.]
42. I, 240b.
43. [The numerical significance of *bet* is two.]
44. [*Bereshit bara elohim*, traditionally rendered "In the beginning God created."]
45. [The Hebrew letter *bet* is a preposition meaning "in, by, or with." And so the translation "by means of the beginning" is grammatically feasible.]
46. This interpretation is found in the teaching of the early kabbalists and does not originate with the Zohar. See, for example, *Sefer Ma'arekhet ha-Elohut*, chap. 7.

47. This passage, which occurs in the *Midrash ha-Ne'elam*, is based on Nachmanides (on Genesis 1: 1): "The Holy One, blessed be He, created all created things from absolute nothingness, and we have in the holy tongue no other expression for the creation of something from nothing except the word *bara*." See below, p. 554. See also Maimonides, *Guide for the Perplexed* II, 30; III, 10.

48. See G. Scholem, *Major Trends in Jewish Mysticism*, pp. 25, 217-18.

49. G. Scholem, "Sefer *Masoret ha-Berit* le-R. David ben R. Avraham ha-Lavan," *Kovez al Yad* (Jerusalem, 1936), p. 31.

50. See *En-Sof*, 1; below, 6 and 19.

51. *Sefer Shekel ha-Kodesh*, p. 7. And see also ibid., pp. 23-24.

52. *Zohar Hadash*, beginning of *Va-ethanan*.

53. See G. Scholem, *Perakim le-Toledot Sifrut ha-Kabbalah* (1931), pp. 2-18.

54. Preface to the Commentary on *Sefer Yezirah* (Warsaw), p. 5. And see G. Scholem, *Major Trends in Jewish Mysticism*, pp. 217-18.

55. *Commentary to Song of Songs*, ascribed to Nachmanides, third preface.

56. Zohar II, 90a. See *En-Sof*, 5 (*Raya Mehemna*). There *Hokhmah* is called "something from nothing" (*yesh me-ayin*).

57. *Sefer Shekel ha-Kodesh*, pp. 25-26.

58. See below, 1 and 19.

59. See also *Influence and Direction*, 3.

60. See *Powers of Uncleanness*, 5; and *The Account of Creation*, 3.

61. See Zohar II, 23b-24b; Rabbi Moses de Leon, *Sefer Shekel ha-Kodesh*, pp. 118-22.

62. See below, 10.

63. See Zohar III, 134b.

64. See *Events and Personalities*, 19; and *The Powers of Uncleanness*, 6.

65. See Zohar III, 152a [below, p. 1126]; G. Scholem, *Perakim*, pp. 111-15.

66. Preface to his *Commentary to the Pentateuch*.

67. See Zohar I, 134b; [below, pp. 1123-24]; *Perush ha-Aggadot le-Rabbi Azriel*, pp. 37-39.

68. Zohar II, 162b.

69. Rabbi Menahem Recanati, *Sefer Ta'amei ha-Mizvot* (Basle 1581), 3a.

70. Zohar I, 134b [below, p. 1124].

71. *Events and Personalities*, 20 (end). It would seem that the comparison of the Torah to a beautiful girl, and in particular the words that immediately precede this comparison, namely, that the Torah "is revealed for a moment and then immediately hidden," show the influence of Maimonides, who in the preface to his *Guide for the Perplexed* uses the image of a flash of lightning. This is glossed in the *Sitrei Torah* as something "that shows itself, gleams, and disappears."

72. See above, p. 273.

73. This distinction was explained by G. Scholem in *Major Trends in Jewish Mysticism*, pp. 25-28. See also W. R. Inge, *Christian Mysticism* (London, 1918), pp. 250-56.

74. See *The Guide for the Perplexed*, part 1, chap. 26.

75. *Sefer Sha'arei Orah* (Warsaw, 1883), p. 4. The *Sefer Shi'ur Komah* (Warsaw, 1883) by Rabbi Moses Cordovero is entirely devoted to removing corporeality from the symbols of the *sefirot*; see particularly pp. 126-27.

76. For the significance of the revival of myth in kabbalah, see G. Scholem, *Major Trends in Jewish Mysticism*, pp. 34-37; "Kabbala und Mythus," *Eranos Jahrbuch* 17 (1949): 287-334.

77. Zohar II, 3a.

78. See G. Scholem, ibid., pp. 222-25.

79. [Genesis 25: 27, often translated "a quiet man."]

80. *Bemidbar Rabbah* 14: 24.

81. See Zohar I, 21b-22a.

82. See above, p. 276.
83. This, in fact, is the explanation offered by Rabbi Moses Cordovero. See *Sefer Shi'ur Komah*, pp. 130–31.
84. Zohar III, 292b (*Idra Zuta*).
85. Zohar II, 254b.
86. It is possible that the reason given for the destruction of the worlds before *Atika Kadisha* "prepared His attributes" (12) alludes to the process of clearing out the dross.
87. Zohar III, 48b–49a.
88. It is true that the latter passage deals with events during one of the stages in the process of emanation: the transition, apparently, from *Binah* to *Gevurah*. But this fact does not contradict the view that the reference here is to the destruction of the worlds. In a passage by Rabbi Isaac Hacohen on the emanation of the left-hand side, which was, it seems, known to the author of the Zohar, the destruction of the worlds is depicted as an event precisely at this stage of emanation. See G. Scholem, "Kabbalot R. Ya'akov ve-R. Yizhak benei R. Ya'akov ha-Kohen," *Mad'ei ha-Yahadut* 2 (1927): 194.
89. In Zohar I, 223b, we find also a clear reference to the fact that the kings that died belonged to the realm of the husks. There it says that the kings of Edom that died are called "sons of the East," and it is explained earlier in the same passage that the wisdom of the sons of the East lay in their knowledge of "the lower crowns," i.e., the *sefirot* of "the other side."
90. See I. Tishby, *Torat ha-Ra ve-ha-Kelipah be-Kabbalat ha-Ari* (1942), pp. 41–43, 47–49, 52–59.
91. In this section I describe briefly groups of the more important symbols that have not been fully explained so far, or that have not been mentioned at all.
92. For the meaning and importance of light images in religious and philosophical thought, see Clemens Bäumker, *Witelo* (1908), pp. 357–514.
93. *Zohar Hadash*, beginning of *Va-ethanan*.
94. Zohar III, 291b.
95. Cf. Rabbi Moses de Leon, *Sefer Shekel ha-Kodesh*, pp. 123–24.
96. Zohar II, 185b. See also I, 123a; II, 127a.
97. See *Angels*, 11.
98. See *Shekhinah*, 1.
99. See also *The Powers of Uncleanness*, 6.
100. See below, 2 and 29.
101. See Zohar I, 50b.
102. *Midrash Tehillim* 90: 12.
103. See *The Account of Creation*, 4.
104. See 1; Zohar I, 156b (*Sitrei Torah*).
105. See 2; and cf. Zohar III, 290a.
106. See 28. There it would appear that *Hokhmah* is called "Written Torah," but this is not usual.
107. See 23; Zohar I, 145a, 248b; Rabbi Moses de Leon, *Sefer Shekel ha-Kodesh*, p. 26.
108. See *Perush ha-Aggadot le-Rabbi Azriel*, p. 37.
109. See above, pp. 283f.
110. See Zohar III, 10b–11b; *Sefer Shekel ha-Kodesh*, pp. 125–30; Rabbi Moses Cordovero, *Sefer Pardes Rimmonim*, pt. 20.
111. In the Zohar *Zeva'ot* is usually used on its own as a joint name for *Nezah* and *Hod*.
112. See 1 and 19.
113. See 2.
114. See Zohar III, 296a.
115. See 19.

116. Zohar I, 1b.
117. See Zohar II, 64b; III, 158b.
118. See 18; 19; Zohar I, 162a (*Sitrei Torah*).
119. See 17; Zohar III, 267b.
120. See 24; 25.
121. See Zohar I, 158a–158b; II, 29b.
122. See 4.
123. On the doctrine of primordial man in Gnosis and in other religions, see W. Bousset, *Hauptprobleme der Gnosis* (1907), chap. 4, pp. 160ff.
124. The Hebrew term *Adam Kadmon* occurs only in the later strata of the Zohar, as I shall explain below.
125. Zohar III, 141a–141b (*Idra Rabba*), and see below, 12.
126. See Zohar I, 140a; Rabbi Moses de Leon, *Sefer ha-Nefesh ha-Ḥakhamah*, pt. 1. It is explained at several points in the Zohar (I, 83a–83b [see below, pp. 731–32]; 206a; II, 142a–142b) that *Malkhut*, *Tiferet*, and *Binah* are akin to the three parts of the human soul, namely, *nefesh*, *ruaḥ*, and *neshamah*.
127. Zohar III, 141a–141b (*Idra Rabba*).
128. See secs. 36, 55.
129. See below, pp. 298ff.
130. See 13, 14, 15; *Influence and Direction*, 7.
131. Zohar II, 153a. In another passage (III, 224a–224b) [*Body and Soul*, 8] these organs are given a different symbolic meaning: the brain and the heart represent *Tiferet* and *Malkhut*; the liver and the lobe of the liver represent Samael and Lilith.
132. See Zohar II, 169b, 180b.
133. See above, pp. 245f.
134. See Zohar III, 139b, 141b (*Idra Rabba*).
135. However, in one important passage (Zohar II, 167a–167b), which is very obscure and needs special explanation, reference is made, in the main body of the Zohar, to two images of man in the world of emanation, "first man" (*adam kedama'ah*) and "second man" (*adam tinyana*).
136. See Zohar II, 142a–142b.
137. *Zohar Ḥadash*, *Tikkunim* 114c–114d.
138. [See above, p. 250.]
139. *Tikkunei ha-Zohar*, *Tikkun* 70, 120a–120b. See also ibid., end of *Tikkun* 19.
140. *Zohar Ḥadash*, *Yitro*, 34b.
141. See the passages referred to in nn. 137 and 139.
142. *Tikkunei ha-Zohar*, end of *Tikkun* 67, 98b.
143. In the Zohar too (I, 22b, which belongs to the *Tikkunim*) there is a distinction between the man of emanation and the man of creation, but it looks as if both are placed within the realm of the *sefirot*, although the significance of the distinction is not clear.
144. See Zohar I, 246b. It is explained there that, although *Binah* is female, it must be regarded as male as well, since it is also the head of the body of the male image.
145. See Zohar II, 145b; III, 100b, 258a (*Raya Mehemna*).
146. Zohar I, 156b (*Sitrei Torah*).
147. See 34; Zohar III, 100b.
148. See Zohar III, 7b. [See below, pp. 1368–69]
149. See Zohar I, 209a; II, 223b.
150. Zohar III, 290b (*Idra Zuta*). See also III, 77b.
151. Ibid., 4a.
152. See, for example, Zohar III, 290b–291a (*Idra Zuta*), and below, 15.
153. See, for example, Zohar I, 162a–162b; II, 128b–129a; III, 247a–247b, 296a–296b (*Idra Zuta*).

154. Zohar III, 214b. See below, 35.

155. Zohar I, 49b.

156. See 33; Zohar II, 124b.

157. Zohar I, 66b. ["Covenant" is a word specifically used for the covenant of circumcision.]

158. Zohar II, 114a. See below, 35.

SEFIROT

1. THE PROCESS OF EMANATION

(Zohar I, 15a–15b)

"In the beginning" (Genesis 1: 1)—At the very beginning the king[1] made engravings[2] in the supernal purity.[3] A spark of blackness[4] emerged in the sealed within the sealed,[5] from the mystery of *En-Sof*, a mist within matter,[6] implanted in a ring,[7] no white, no black, no red, no yellow, no color at all.[8] When he measured with the standard of measure,[9] he made colors to provide light. Within the spark, in the innermost part, emerged a source, from which the colors are painted below,[10] and it is sealed among the sealed things of the mystery of *En-Sof*. It penetrated, but did not penetrate, its air;[11] it was not known at all,[12] until from the pressure of its penetration a single point shone, sealed, supernal. Beyond this point nothing is known,[13] and so it is called *reshit* (beginning): the first word of all.[14]

---

[1] *En-Sof*, which is here called "king," began to arouse itself in order to emanate and develop its hidden powers.

[2] He impressed a tenuous and concealed existence upon the powers that were later to be revealed and to act within the system of the *sefirot*.

[3] Nothing is said of the origin of this celestial radiance, which surrounds and envelops *En-Sof*. It is the first *sefirah* which, according to the Zohar, is preexistent with *En-Sof*.

[4] *Bozina di-kardinuta*, the sparking of light from *En-Sof*. This spark is described as "darkened," because it is so concealed.

[5] The supernal purity.

[6] The spark that shines out in the hidden domain, in which as yet there are no forms, is compared to a mist that rises within hylic matter.

[7] The spark is surrounded and enclosed by the ring of the supernal purity.

[8] There are no forms there that can be depicted, or that can shine, with different colors.

[9] The spark of blackness is the standard of measure. Its function is to give size and limitation to the forces that are to be revealed in the world of emanation, so that they might act as standards that govern the divine control of the world. The radiation of colors in the world above is the beginning of this measuring.

[10] From the source that emerges in the spark, the colors flow through to the array of the *sefirot*.

[11] The primordial air is a symbol of the first *sefirah*, and the source flows within it, internally. The strength of the flow makes a very fine "fracture" in the primordial air, and the pressure forces the first point through this opening. This point is the second *sefirah*.

[12] The source is not revealed outside the domain of the primordial air.

[13] The point is the first stage in the revelation of the divine, and the final limit of perception from the world below.

[14] The first of the ten words by which the world was created (B.T. *Megillah* 21b).

"And they that are wise shall shine as the brightness (*zohar*) of the firmament; and they that turn the many to righteousness as the stars for ever and ever" (Daniel 12: 3). *Zohar*, sealed among the sealed things, made contact with its air, which touched, but did not touch, the point.[15] Then the "beginning" (*reshit*) extended itself and made a palace[16] for itself, for glory and praise. There it sowed the holy seed[17] in order to beget offspring for the benefit of the world. This mystery is [in the verse] "the holy seed shall be its stock" (Isaiah 6: 13). *Zohar*, which sowed seed in its own honor like the seed of the silk [worm], [that makes] fine purple fabric, is the one that covers itself within, and makes a palace for itself, which brings praise to it, and benefit to all. With this *reshit* the sealed one, which is not known, created this palace. This palace is called *Elohim*, and this mystery is [in the verse] *Bereshit bara Elohim* (Genesis 1: 1).[18] *Zohar* is that from which all the words were created, through the mystery of the expansion of the point of this concealed brightness. Since the word *bara* (He created) is used here, it is not surprising that it is written "And God created man in His image" (Genesis 1: 27).[19]

Zohar—this mystery is [in the word] *bereshit*: that which precedes all,[20] whose name is *Ehyeh*, a sacred name engraved in its extremities,[21] *Elohim* engraved in the crown,[22] *Asher*[23]—a hidden and concealed palace, the beginning of the mystery of *reshit*[24]—*Asher*, the head (*rosh*)[25] that emerges from *reshit*. And when, after this, point and palace were established together, then *bereshit* comprised the supernal *reshit*[26]

---

[15] The point that emerges from the air has only slight contact with it. The concealed "brightness" (*zohar*) within stimulates the point into activity by making contact with the air.

[16] The third *sefirah*, constructed through the expansion of the point, for which it serves as a dwelling and a palace.

[17] The palace is the supernal mother, and the point is the father, which produces the seed of emanation that is sown in the palace.

[18] [To be translated here: "with *reshit* it created *Elohim*."] *En-Sof*, which is not mentioned explicitly in the Torah but only hinted at, created, by means of *reshit*, the third *sefirah*, called *Elohim*.

[19] Some maintain that the word *bara* signifies creation *ex nihilo*. If this is so it is difficult to see how the word can be used of the creation of the third *sefirah*, which was created from another substance (*Keter* = *Ayin*, which means "nothing"; *Hokhmah* = *Yesh*, which means "substance"). The answer is that the use of the verb *bara* in the verse dealing with creation of man proves that it is not used solely of creation *ex nihilo*.

[20] *Keter*, which precedes even the first point.

[21] In the limits of its being.

[22] The name *Elohim* is assigned to the palace (*Binah*), but it also represents the last *sefirah* (*Malkhut*), which is called "crown."

[23] The second word in the phrase *ehyeh asher ehyeh* ("I am who I am"—Exodus 3: 14).

[24] The beginning of the expansion from *reshit*.

[25] *Asher* is an anagram of *rosh*, which is the beginning of the word *reshit*.

[26] The point and the palace, which together constitute the beginning (*reshit*) of the lower *sefirot*.

according to the way of wisdom;[27] for subsequently the form of the palace was changed, and it was called "a house" (*bayit*), the supernal point was called "head" (*rosh*), comprised, one in the other, in the mystery of the word *bereshit*,[28] when all [was] together in one unit before there was habitation in the house. When the seed was sown in order to prepare for habitation, then it was called *Elohim*,[29] hidden and concealed.[30] *Zohar*—hidden and stored away, until building [began] within it,[31] in order to produce offspring, and the house stood as the process of "the holy seed" gathered momentum.[32] But before it was impregnated, and before the process of habitation began, it was not called *Elohim*, but everything was comprised within the generality of *bereshit*. Once it was established in the name of *Elohim*, then it produced the offspring from the seed that was sown in it. What was this seed? Engraved letters,[33] the mystery of the Torah, which emerged from that point.[34] The point sowed the seed of three vowels[35] in the palace: *holem*, *shurek*, *hirek*, and they were comprised, one within the other,[36] and became a single mystery: a voice that emerged in a single combination. When it emerged, its partner[37] emerged with it, which comprised all the letters,[38] as it is written: *et ha-shamayim* ("the heavens")—the voice and its partner.[39] This voice, which is "the heavens", is the last *ehyeh*. *Zohar*—which comprises all the letters and all the colors in the way [that

---

[27] According to the mystical significance of the letters of the word *bereshit*.

[28] *Bereshit* is composed of the letters of *bayit* and *rosh*.

[29] When the palace received the seed and started to become active, it acquired a name of its own. But before this its name was included in the word *bereshit*, which is the basic name of the point.

[30] The name *Elohim* denotes a number of *sefirot*. In this *sefirah* it is concealed, because it is usually called *YHVH*, with the vocalization of *Elohim*.

[31] The palace was concealed until the process started within it of building the lower *sefirot*. Perhaps the original Aramaic ought to be rendered: "until children were formed within it." This translation would suit better the image of seed, pregnancy, and birth.

[32] The formation process, which began by the seed spreading through the house.

[33] The spiritual letters engraved in the light of the Godhead. They are the mystic representation of the divine structure of the Torah.

[34] The supernal Torah was emanated from the point, which is also the divine Thought.

[35] One (*holem*) is placed above a letter, one (*shurek*) in the middle of a letter, and one (*hirek*) below a letter.

[36] The seed comprises both letters and vowel-points. They are brought together, and form the voice, which is the *sefirah Tiferet*, also called "the written Torah."

[37] The *Shekhinah*, i.e., the *sefirah Malkhut*, which is the mystic symbol of speech, also called "the oral Torah."

[38] In the word *et*, which is its symbol, and which is a combination of two letters, *alef* and *tav*, the first and last letters of the Hebrew alphabet.

[39] *Tiferet*, called *shamayim*, and *Malkhut*, called *et*.

we have explained] so far, *YHVH Elohenu YHVH*[40]—these are three
levels that represent this supernal mystery.[41]

Bereshit bara Elohim ("In the beginning God created"). *Bereshit*—a
primeval mystery;[42] *bara*—a concealed mystery,[43] from which all
extends; *Elohim*—a mystery that supports all below.[44] *Et ha-shamayim*
("the heavens")—in order not to separate male and female, which are
united together.[45] *Et*—when He took all these letters, [*et*] comprised all
the letters, beginning and end. Subsequently, the letter *he* was added[46]
in order to combine the letters with the *he*, and it was called *attah*
("you"), and of this it is said, "You gave life to them all" (Nehemiah 9:
6). *Et*—the mystery of *Adonai*, and thus is it called;[47] *ha-shamayim*—this is
YHVH, the higher mystery.[48] *Ve-et*—the arrangement of male and
female; *ve-et*—the mystery of *va-YHVH*,[49] and all is one. *Ha-arez*—this is
Elohim, on the pattern of the upper world,[50] so as to make fruits and
herbs. This name is included in three places,[51] and thence the name
extends on several sides.[52]

Thus far the secret of the innermost mystery, which He engraved,
built, and sustained[53] in a concealed way, through the mystery of one

[40] The three divine names in the first verse of the *Shema* (Deuteronomy 6: 4), which
contains the mystery of the unity of God.

[41] The mystic symbol of these three names parallels the mystical connotation of *ehyeh
asher ehyeh*.

[42] The sparking forth of the first point.

[43] An allusion to the hidden source of emanation.

[44] *Binah* is the main support of the lower *sefirot*, to which it gives birth.

[45] *Tiferet* and *Malkhut* are, mystically speaking, male and female within the
Godhead, and they emerged united together, a single entity with two faces. Whoever
separates them destroys the unity of the Godhead.

[46] *Malkhut* is symbolized by the second *he* of the divine name, *YHVH* (*Yod-He-
Vav-He*). This symbol signifies the unity of the upper *sefirot*, from which it receives
influence, so that it can nourish and support the lower worlds. The addition of "*he*"
changes *et* into *attah*.

[47] *Adonai*, the name given specifically to *Malkhut*, is pronounced exactly as written. It
is revealed in its entirety.

[48] *Tiferet*, which occupies a higher position than *Malkhut*.

[49] According to the midrash (*Bereshit Rabbah* 51: 3): "Wherever the phrase 'and the
Lord' (*va-YHVH*) occurs, it implies He and His court." The Zohar takes "He and His
court" to mean *Tiferet* and *Malkhut*. [*Ve-et* is a continuation of Genesis 1: 1—*ve-et ha-arez*
(and the earth).]

[50] On the pattern of *Binah*, which is also called *Elohim*. The activity of *Malkhut* in the
lower worlds parallels the activity of *Binah* in the world of the *sefirot*.

[51] Three *sefirot* are given the name *Elohim*: *Binah*, *Gevurah*, and *Malkhut*.

[52] Even nondivine substances, both in the sacred and the profane domain, are given
the name *Elohim* in the Bible (e.g., angels, judges, idols. Cf. *elohim aherim*—"other gods").

[53] The engraving of the hidden beings, the "building" of the point and the palace,
and the sustaining of the lower *sefirot*—all this is contained in the first verse of the creation
story, according to its mystical interpretation.

verse. From now on:[54] *bereshit—bara shit* ["He created six"],[55] "from the one end of heaven unto the other" (Deuteronomy 4: 32) the six extremes that extend from the supernal mystery[56] through the extension that He created from the primal point; *bara*—extension from the point on high. And here was engraved the mystery of the forty-two-lettered name.[57]

"And they that are wise shall shine . . ." like the musical accents.[58] The letters and vowel-points follow them in their singing, and move at their behest, like an army at the behest of the king. The letters are the body, and the vowel-points are the spirit. All of them in their travels follow the accents, and stand in their place. When the singing of the accents moves, the letters and the vowel-points move after them, and when it stops, they do not move but remain in their stations.

"And they that are wise shall shine . . ."—letters and vowel-points; "as the brightness"—the singing of the accents; "of the firmament"—the extension of the singing, like those which prolong[59] and continue the singing; "and they that turn the many to righteousness"—these are the pauses among the accents,[60] which stop their travels, as a result of which speech is heard. "Shall shine"—that is, the letters and the vowel-points, and they will shine together on their travels, in a concealed mystery, on a journey by hidden paths. All extends from this.[61]

2. THE CHAIN OF THE *SEFIROT*

(Zohar I, 16b–17a)

"And God said: Let there be light. And there was light" (Genesis 1: 3). From here we can begin to find hidden [mysteries], how the world was created in detail.[62] Before this it was described in general,[63] and it is

[54] A further explanation of the mystery.

[55] The six *sefirot* from *Ḥesed* to *Binah* are called the six "extremities," i.e., the four points of the compass, the realm above and the realm below. In the middle stands *Tiferet*, called *shamayim* (heaven).

[56] The hidden source.

[57] The name that is constructed from the first forty-two Hebrew letters of the Bible between the *beth* of *bereshit* and the *beth* of *va-vohu* inclusive [i.e., between "In the beginning" and "and void"].

[58] The cantillation of the accents, which clarifies the meaning of the words, is like a shining light that illumines the way for the letters and the vowel-points.

[59] The accents that serve to prolong the note. They are like the firmament, which is stretched out above the earth.

[60] The accents that interrupt the flow of the notes. These accents fix the enunciation of speech, and they are called "they that turn the many to righteousness," because they establish the correct phrasing of the words.

[61] The combination of letters and vowel-points that follow the cantillation of the accents symbolizes the process of emanation.

[62] Through the emanation of the seven lower *sefirot*.

[63] The first verses describe the emanation of the upper *sefirot*, which contain all the *sefirot*.

given later in general once more;[64] so that we have a generality, a particularity, and a generality.[65] Up to this point, all depended on the air,[66] in the mystery of *En-Sof*. When the force[67] spread through the supernal palace.[68] [which is] the mystery of *Elohim*, it is described in terms of speech:[69] "And God said." For in the preceding [verses] no actual "saying" is specified. And even though *bereshit* is a "saying",[70] "and He said" is not written in connection with it. *Va-yomer* (And He said)—an object of inquiry and knowledge.[71] *Va-yomer*—a power that was raised, and the raising was in silence, from the mystery of *En-Sof* through the mystery of Thought.[72] "And God said"—now it begot that palace that was conceived from the holy seed, and it begot silence, and [the voice of] the newborn[73] was heard outside. That which begot it begot it in silence, so that it could not be heard at all. When that which emerged emerged from it, a voice was formed that was heard outside.

"Let there be light" (*yehi or*)—all that emerged through this mystery emerged. *Yehi*—[this refers] to the mystery of father and mother [74] which is *yah*,[75] and it subsequently relates to the primal point,[76] in order to be the beginning of the extension of another thing: "light."

"And there was light" (*va-yehi or*)—the light that had already existed. This light is a sealed mystery: the expansion that extended itself and burst through from the secret mystery of the hidden supernal air.[77] First of all, [the expansion] burst through,[78] and produced a single hidden point from its own mystery, for thus did *En-Sof* burst out of its air and

---

[64] In the second chapter of Genesis a general picture of the creation is given again.

[65] According to the *gemara* (B.T. *Baba Kamma* 63a): "[Where you have] a generality, a particularity, and a generality, you interpret in the light of the particularity." That is to say, that one should understand the emanation of the upper *sefirot* in the light of the process that is continued in the lower *sefirot*.

[66] On *Keter*, which is the primal air, that was split when *Hokhmah* was emanated.

[67] The seed of *Hokhmah*.   [68] In *Binah*.

[69] [Lit., "saying is written therein."] Before this there was thought, but not speech.

[70] The first of the ten "sayings" with which the world was created.

[71] *Binah* is the first *sefirah* about whose nature one can inquire, and of which one can gain some knowledge.

[72] Even though there is some manifestation of "saying" in *Binah*, it still belongs to the hidden realms and it was emanated silently from *En-Sof*, by means of *Hokhmah*, which is Thought. The "saying" is in the heart, and *Binah* is a kind of unheard, inner voice. The word *va-yomer* here is interpreted in the sense of "lifting up," as in Deuteronomy 26: 17–18: "You have exalted (*he-emarta*) the Lord . . . and the Lord has exalted you (*he-emirkhah*)."

[73] The son, *Tiferet*, which is the heard voice.   [74] *Hokhmah* and *Binah*.

[75] *Yod* and *he*, the first two letters of the tetragrammaton *YHVH*.

[76] The second *yod* in the word *yehi* relates to *Hokhmah*, the primal point, through which *Hesed*, the primal light, comes into being.

[77] The light is the expansion of air, as it goes on to explain.

[78] The initial expansion was the emergence of the point of *Hokhmah* through the split in the air.

reveal a single point: *yod*. Once that *yod* had extended itself, whatever remained of the mystery of the hidden air was light.[79] When the first point, *yod*, was discovered by it, it then appeared upon it,[80] touching but not touching. Once it had extended itself it emerged as the light, a remnant of the air, "the light that had already existed."[81] This [light] existed; it emerged, and removed itself, and was hidden,[82] and one single point of it remained,[83] and it has continuous contact,[84] in a secret way, with this point, touching and not touching, illuminating it by means of the primal point,[85] which had emerged from it. Therefore all hangs together; it illuminates on this side and on that.[86] When it ascends everything ascends and is incorporated with it,[87] and it reaches, and is concealed in, the place of *En-Sof*, and all is made one.

This point of light is "Light",[88] and it expanded, and seven letters of the alphabet[89] shone in it, but they did not solidify, and they were moist. Then darkness[90] emerged, and another seven letters of the alphabet emerged, and they did not solidify, and remained moist. The firmament[91] emerged, and dissipated the division[92] between the two sides, and another eight letters emerged in it, making twenty-two in all. The seven letters on this side, and the seven letters on that side drew together, and were all engraved in the firmament, and they stayed moist. The firmament solidified, and the letters solidified, and they assumed their different shapes, and the Torah was engraved[93] there in order to give light to the realms outside.

[79] If you take the letter *yod* away from the word *avir* (air), you are left with *or* (light).

[80] The light, which is a remnant of air, hovers over the point, and lightly touches it.

[81] This light extends itself again, and this extension is "the light that had already existed" (*Bereshit Rabbah* 3: 2), for even before this extension it existed as light after the point had emerged.

[82] The extension of the light, which was a remnant of the air, returns to its source, to the realm of *Keter*.

[83] This point is the point of *Ḥesed*.

[84] The supernal light, which removes and conceals its expansion, is in continuous, secret contact with the point that it leaves behind.

[85] The contact is effected by means of *Hokhmah*, the primal point, that emerged from the supernal light when it was still contained within the mystery of air.

[86] The supernal light illuminates both points.

[87] When the supernal light ascends and conceals itself, all the *sefirot* return with it to their hidden source.

[88] The *sefirah* *Ḥesed* (Love).

[89] The spiritual letters are the seed of *Hokhmah*, and their combination creates the divine Torah in the world of emanation. While there is division between Love and Judgment the letters do not solidify, and they cannot be combined.

[90] *Gevurah* (Might, the *sefirah* of Judgment).   [91] *Tiferet*.

[92] *Tiferet*, which is Mercy, holds the balance between Love and Judgment, and removes the conflict between them.

[93] *Tiferet* is the mystic symbol of the written Torah, and from there the light of the Torah shines upon the regions below.

"Let there be light," which is *Elgadol* (great God),[94] is the mystery that emerged from the primal air.[95] "And there was"—the mystery of darkness,[96] called *Elohim*. "Light"—where the left is included with the right,[97] and then, from the mystery of *El*, *Elohim* is made; right is included with left, and left with right.

"And God saw the light that it was good"—this is the central pillar.[98] *Ki tov* ("that it was good") illumines the regions above and the regions below, and all the remaining extremities,[99] through the mystery of *YHVH*, the name that holds together all the extremities.

"And God divided. . . ." He broke up the controversy so that all should be perfect.

"And God called. . . ." What does "and He called" mean? He called and summoned[100] the perfect light, which stands in the center, to produce a light, which is the foundation (*Yesod*) of the world, and upon which worlds rest. And from that perfect light, the central pillar, there was drawn forth, from the right side,[101] *Yesod*, the life of the worlds, which is "day."

"And the darkness He called 'night' "—He called and summoned that from the side of darkness there should be produced a female, the moon, which rules by night and is called "night," the mystery of *Adonai*, "Lord (*Adon*) of all the earth" (Joshua 3: 11).

The right entered the perfect pillar that is in the center, which comprises the mystery of the left,[102] and ascended aloft to the primal point, and it took and seized hold of the power of the three vowel-points: *holem, shurek, hirek*, which are the holy seed—for there is no seed sown except through this mystery—and all was joined together[103] through the central pillar, and it produced the foundation (*Yesod*) of the world, and it is, therefore, called "all" (*Kol*), for it holds all through the light of

[94] The name *El* is particular to *Hesed*, which is also called *Gedulah* (greatness).

[95] *Hesed* emanated from the light of *Keter*, by the process that has already been described.

[96] The word *va-yehi* ("and there was") signifies darkness and judgment, according to the rabbinic statement (B.T. *Megillah* 10b): "wherever *va-yehi* is used, there is always a reference to trouble."

[97] In the use of the word "light," for the second time in the verse, there is an allusion to the intermingling of Judgment with Love, and then the name *Elohim*, particular to *Gevurah*, signifies the intermingling of Love with Judgment, because of the inclusion of the letters of *El* in the name *Elohim*.   [98] *Tiferet*.

[99] The *sefirot* from *Hesed* downward, in the middle of which stands *Tiferet*.

[100] The word *va-yikra* ("And He called") is a summons that day, which is *Yesod*, should be emanated from the perfect light, *Tiferet*. Similarly, He "calls," i.e., summons, night, *Malkhut*, from the darkness, which is *Gevurah*.

[101] *Yesod* is emanated from *Tiferet*, with the aid of *Hesed*.

[102] *Tiferet* mingles within itself the attribute of Judgment.

[103] *Hesed*, which brings with it the seed of *Hokhmah*, is joined once more to *Tiferet*, and this union brings about the emanation of *Yesod*, which is the channel by which the seed is transmitted to the realms below.

desire.[104] The left flamed strongly[105] and exuded odor. Throughout all levels it exuded odor, and from the fiery flame it produced the female, the moon; and this flame was darkened, because it came from darkness. And these two sides[106] produced these two levels,[107] one male and one female.

Yesod took hold of the central pillar through the additional light that it contains, for when this central pillar was perfected, and it made perfect peace throughout the extremities, an additional amount of light was immediately accorded it from above, and from all the extremities in an all-inclusive joy, and from this addition of joy the foundation of the worlds emerged, and it was called *Musaf* (addition). All the hosts[108] emerged from here into the realms below, and holy spirits, and souls,[109] through the mystery of *YHVH Zevaot, El Elohei ha-ruḥot* ("God, the God of the spirits"—Numbers 16: 22). Night, *Adon kol ha-arez* ("Lord of all the earth") is from the left side, from that Darkness. And since the desire of Darkness was to be included with the right, and its strength was weakened,[110] Night spread out from it. When Night began to spread out, and before the act was completed, Darkness entered, and was included with the right, and the right took hold of it and Night was left in want.[111] And just as it was the desire of Darkness to be included with Light, so it was the desire of Night to be included with Day. Darkness lacks Light and so it produced a level in want and without its own light. Darkness does not illumine unless it is included with Light. Night, which came from it, does not illumine unless it is included with Day. Night's lack cannot be made up except through *Musaf* (addition). What was added here was subtracted there. In *Musaf* there is the mystery of the supernal point, and the mystery of the central pillar[112] with all the extremities, and, therefore, two letters[113] were added to it, and from Night these two letters were subtracted, and so we have *kara* (He called). It is written *va-yikra* (And [God] called), and then *vav* and *yod* are

---

[104] Desire for intercourse, in which all the *sefirot* are involved.

[105] From the flame of Judgment, which draws power from all the *sefirot*, *Malkhut*, the female, is emanated.

[106] Right and left.   [107] *Yesod* and *Malkhut*.   [108] Angels.

[109] Souls are born from the union of *Yesod* with *Malkhut*.

[110] The desire of Judgment to be connected with Love weakens its strength. Because of this weakness *Malkhut* spreads out from it in the guise of lenient Judgment.

[111] *Malkhut* lacks two things: its attribute of Judgment is faulty because it was emanated when its source, strict Judgment, was weakened; and it has no light of its own, because it was emanated from Darkness.

[112] *Yesod* includes the seed of *Ḥokhmah*, and the power of *Tiferet*, from which *Yesod* is emanated.

[113] In the description of the emanation of *Yesod* two letters are added to the word *kara* (He called), namely, *vav* and *yod*, which are *Tiferet* and *Ḥokhmah*, making the word *va-yikra* (And He called). But these two letters are missing when the emanation of *Malkhut* is described, and it is written simply *kara*. [See n. 100 above.]

subtracted, and it is then written *kara laylah* (He called "night"). Here is the mystery of the seventy-two-lettered name,[114] the engraving of the supernal *Keter*.[115]

3. STRAIGHT LINE

(Zohar I, 18a)

"And God said: Let the waters be gathered" (Genesis 1: 9)[116]—by means of a line,[117] so that it should be by a straight path, for all emerged, while still hidden, from the mystery of the primal point,[118] until it reached and entered the supernal palace.[119] From there it went forth in a straight line to the remaining levels, until it came to "one place," which brought all together into the totality of male and female. And what was this? The life of the worlds.[120] "The waters"—that came forth from above, from the upper letter *he*.[121] "Under the heaven"—small *vav*,[122] which explains the letter *vav*:[123] one is heaven, and one is "under the heaven." Then "let the dry land appear"—this is the lower *he*.[124] This is revealed, and all the remainder is concealed, and from this latter one may perceive this hidden wisdom.[125] "Into one place"—for here is the bond of unity of the upper world.[126]

[114] The seventy-two-lettered name [of God] is made up of three verses of Exodus 14: 19–21, each of which begins with the letters *vav-yod*. Or possibly the Zohar assigns the seventy-two-lettered name to the *sefirot*, *Ḥesed*, *Gevurah*, and *Tiferet*, whose emanation is described in the verses that have been interpreted above.

[115] The name is engraved by *Keter*.

[116] The complete verse reads: "And God said: Let the waters under the heaven be gathered together into one place, and let the dry land appear. And it was so."

[117] The word *yikkavu* (let them be gathered together) is taken as referring to the descent of emanatory influence in a straight line (*kav*).

[118] *Hokhmah*.

[119] *Binah*.

[120] *Yesod*, through whom the *sefirot* are joined together through the union of male and female.

[121] *Binah*, the first *he* in the name *YHVH*, and this is alluded to here by the *he* in the word *ha-mayim* (the waters).

[122] *Yesod*, included with, and joined to, *Tiferet*, which is large *vav*, and called "heaven."

[123] The name *vav* contains the letter *vav* twice, signifying the two *sefirot*: *Tiferet* and *Yesod*.

[124] *Malkhut*, which in itself is "dry," for its influence comes entirely from the other *sefirot*.

[125] From a contemplation of *Malkhut*, which is the most revealed *sefirah*, one may perceive the hidden *sefirot*.

[126] *Yesod* is called "one place," for in it are united all the *sefirot* down to *Malkhut*.

4. THE UNIFICATION OF THE *SEFIROT* THROUGH THE MYSTERY OF THE LIGHT OF THE LAMP

(Zohar I, 50b–51b)

Rabbi Simeon began by saying: There are two verses[127] written: "For the Lord your God is a devouring fire" (Deuteronomy 4: 24), and it is also written there, "And you that cleave to the Lord your God are alive, all of you, to-day" (ibid., 4). We have reconciled these verses in several places, and the companions have an understanding of them. Come and see. "For the Lord your God is a devouring fire,"—this matter has already been clarified among the companions: there is a fire that devours fire.[128] It devours it and consumes it, for there is a fire stronger than fire, and we have explained it. But come and see. Whoever wishes to understand the wisdom of the holy unification, let him look at the flame that rises from a glowing coal, or from a burning lamp, for the flame rises only when it takes hold of some coarse matter. Come and see. In the rising flame there are two lights: one is a radiant white light,[129] and one is a light that contains black or blue.[130] The white light is above, and ascends in a direct line, and beneath it is the blue or black light, which is a throne for the white, and the white light rests upon it, and they are connected together, forming one whole, and the black light, or [that which has] blue color, is the throne of glory for the white. And this is the mystic significance of the blue.[131] And this blue-black throne is joined to something else, below it, so that it can burn, and it stimulates it[132] to grasp the white light. This blue-black [light] sometimes changes to red,[133] but the white light above it never changes, for it is always white. However, the blue changes to these colors: sometimes blue or black, and sometimes red. This [light] is connected on two sides. It is connected above to the white light, and it is connected below to what is beneath it, to what has been prepared for it, so that it might illuminate and grasp it. This [light] devours continuously, and consumes whatever is placed beneath it; for the blue light consumes and

---

[127] There is an apparent contradiction between the two verses, because if God is a "consuming fire," how can one "cleave" to Him? Cf. B.T. *Yoma* 21b.

[128] *Malkhut*, which is the attribute of Judgment, is nourished by the fire of the angels, and it consumes the fire of the husks.   [129] Representing *Tiferet*.

[130] *Malkhut* in itself is dark, and has no light. But when it receives influence from the *sefirot* it becomes blue, which is compounded of all the colors.

[131] Both on the fringes (*zizit*) [which a Jew wears] and in the tabernacle, its role being to disperse the husks.

[132] The lower regions, upon which *Malkhut* rests, stimulate it to unite with *Tiferet*.

[133] When *Malkhut* receives influence from the *sefirah Gevurah*, which is strict Judgment.

devours whatever is attached to it below, whatever it rests upon, since it is its habit to consume and devour; for the destruction of all, the death of all,[134] depends upon it, and therefore it devours whatever is attached to it below. [But] the white light, which rests upon it, does not devour or consume at all, and its light does not change. Concerning this, Moses said "For the Lord your God is a devouring fire," really devouring, devouring and consuming whatever rests beneath it. That is why he said "the Lord your God," and not "our God," because Moses was [linked] to the white light above,[135] which does not consume, and does not devour.

Come and see. The only stimulus that causes the blue light to burn and grasp the white light is that which comes from Israel, who cleave to it below. Come and see. Although it is the way of this blue-black flame to consume whatever is attached to it beneath, Israel, who do cleave to it beneath, survive as they are. This is the meaning of "And you that cleave to the Lord your God are alive,"—"to the Lord your God" not "our God," to the blue-black light that devours and consumes whatever is attached to it beneath; and yet you who cleave to it survive, as it is written "alive, all of you, to-day." Above the white light rests a concealed light,[136] which encompasses it. Here is a supernal mystery, and you will find all in the ascending flame: the wisdom of the upper realms is in it.

Rabbi Pinhas came and kissed him. He said: Blessed be the Merciful One, who summoned me here.

They went with Rabbi Pinhas for three miles. Rabbi Simeon and the companions turned. Rabbi Simeon said: What we have said is a wise mystery concerning the holy unification, for the last *He* of the holy name is the blue-black light, that is joined to *Yod-He-Vav*, which is the radiant white light. Come and see. Sometimes the blue light is *dalet*, and sometimes *he*, but when Israel do not cleave to it below, in order to make it burn and take hold of the white light, it is *dalet*, and when they stimulate it to unite itself with the white light it is called *he*.[137] How do we know this? It is written "If there be a damsel that is a virgin . . ." (Deuteronomy 22: 23). It is written *na'ar* without a *he*.[138] For what reason? Because she has not been united with a male, and wherever male and female do not exist *he* is also absent. It has departed thence, and she

---

[134] *Malkhut* is called "The Tree of Death," especially when it is separated from *Tiferet*.

[135] Moses was at the level of *Tiferet*.

[136] The halo round the light represents *Binah*, the mother of the *sefirot*, and the source of their nourishment.

[137] When *Malkhut* is poor and weak, with no influence from above, it is symbolized by the letter *dalet* [Hebrew *dal* = poor, weak]. When it is rich, through its union with *Tiferet* and the other *sefirot*, it is the last *He* of YHVH.

[138] [Damsel is *na'arah*, with *he* as the last letter, but in this verse it is written *na'ar*.]

is left *"dalet."* Whenever she is joined to the radiant white light she is called *he*, for then everything is united together. She cleaves to the white light, and Israel cleave to her, and they remain beneath her, to make her burn, and then all is one.

This too is the mystical significance of sacrifice, for the rising smoke stimulates the blue light to burn, and when it burns it joins with the white light, and the flame burns as a single unity. And since it is the manner of the blue light to consume and devour what is attached to it beneath, so, when the will exists and the flame burns in single union,[139] then it is written: "Then the fire of the Lord fell, and consumed the burnt-offering . . ." (1 Kings 18: 38)—then it is known that the lamp burns in a single union and in a single bond: the blue light clings to the white light, and they are one. [Then] it consumes the portions and offerings beneath it, for it consumes [the offerings] beneath it only when it burns, and is joined to the white light; and then there is peace in all the worlds, and all is bound together in a single unity. And when the blue light has finished consuming [the offerings] beneath it, the priests, the Levites, and Israel cleave to it beneath:[140] some in joyful song, some with a willing heart, and others in prayer, and the flame burns above them, and the lights cleave to one another, and illumine the worlds, and the upper and lower realms are blessed, and then: "And you that cleave to the Lord your God are alive, all of you, to-day." "And you"—it need have said simply "you." But the "and" serves to add the portions and the offerings, which cleave to it and are devoured and consumed, while you who cleave to it, to the blue-black devouring light, you survive, as it is written "alive, all of you, to-day."

It is taught: "It is good to dream about any color, except blue" (B.T. *Berakhot* 57b), because it devours and consumes continuously,[141] and it is a tree that contains death, and it rests upon the lower world, and, because everything remains beneath it, it devours and consumes. You might object, and say that it also rests in the heavens above, and yet there are several powers above,[142] all of which survive. [But] come and see. All those in the world above are comprised within this blue light,[143] but with the lower realms it is not so: they are coarse matter, which [the light] stands and rests upon, and so it devours and consumes them. And

---

[139] The "devouring" of the sacrifice is not a destruction that derives from the side of Judgment, but the binding of the upper and lower worlds at the moment of intercourse.

[140] The stimulus that comes from the bringing of the sacrificial offerings makes possible the attachment of Israel to the fire of the *Shekhinah*.

[141] Death and destruction have dominion in this world, because it is governed by *Malkhut*.

[142] The hosts of Heaven, and the angels.

[143] They are spiritual and closer to the *Shekhinah*, and so they are not burned by the flame.

there is nothing in the world that does not perish, because the blue light
consumes whatever it stands upon.

5. COLORS AND LIGHTS

(Zohar II, 23a–23b)

Rabbi Simeon was seated one day with Rabbi Eleazar, his son, and
Rabbi Abba.

Rabbi Eleazar said: This verse that is written, "And I appeared to
Abraham, to Isaac, and to Jacob . . ." (Exodus 6: 3)—why does it say
"and I appeared"? It should have said "and I spoke."

He said to him: Eleazar, my son, it is a supernal mystery. Come and
see. There are colors that are seen, and colors that are not seen, and both
of them are a supernal mystery of faith, which people do not know and
cannot contemplate. Man was not granted these [colors] that are seen,
until the patriarchs came and understood them. And concerning this it is
written "and I appeared," for they saw the revealed colors. What are the
revealed colors? Those of *El Shaddai*,[144] which are colors in a supernal
vision, and they can be seen. As for the colors in the higher realm,[145]
which are sealed and not seen, no man has understood them except
Moses. And of this it is written "but by My name *YHVH* I did not make
Myself known to them"—I was not revealed to them in the most exalted
colors. You might think that the patriarchs knew nothing of them
[whatsoever], but they did have some knowledge because of those that
were revealed.[146]

It is written "And the perceivers shall shine as the brightness of the
firmament; and they that turn the many to righteousness as the stars for
ever and ever" (Daniel 12: 3). "And the perceivers shall shine"—who
are the perceivers? It is the wise man who, of himself, looks upon things
that cannot be expressed orally—these are called "the perceivers."
"Shall shine as the brightness of the firmament"—what is the firmament? This is the firmament of Moses,[147] who stands in the middle, and
his brightness is concealed and not revealed. And he stands above the
firmament that does not illumine,[148] in which colors may be seen, and
these colors, even though they are seen, do not shine with the brightness
of the concealed colors.

---

[144] *Malkhut*. Exodus 6: 3 reads "And I appeared to Abraham, to Isaac, and to Jacob,
as *El Shaddai* (God Almighty); but by My name *YHVH* I did not make Myself known to
them."

[145] The colors of *Ḥesed*, *Gevurah*, and *Tiferet*, to which the tetragrammaton is
particularly applied.

[146] The patriarchs did not perceive their real nature, as Moses did, but they gained
some knowledge of them because their power and activity were revealed through
Malkhut.   [147] *Tiferet*, at whose level Moses was privileged enough to stand.

[148] *Malkhut*, which has no light of its own.

Come and see. There are four lights. Three of them are sealed and one is revealed: a light that shines;[149] a light of splendor[150] that shines like the splendor of the heavens in its purity; a light of purple[151] that receives all the lights; a light that does not shine[152] but gazes at these and receives them, and these lights appear in it, as in a crystal ball against the sun. These three that we mentioned are sealed, and stand above the one that is revealed. And this is the mystical significance of the eye. Come and see. Three revealed colors[153] are traced in the eye, and none of them is radiant, because they are in a light that does not shine. And these are patterned after the sealed [colors] that stand above them.[154] And these are the ones that appeared to the patriarchs, that they might know the sealed, radiant ones by means of those which are not radiant. And those which are radiant but are sealed were revealed to Moses in his firmament. And they stand above the colors that are seen in the eye. And the mystery of this [can be seen thus]: close your eye[155] and move your head in a circle, and the shining, radiant colors will be revealed. One is not permitted to see them except with one's eyes closed, because they are supernal and sealed, and stand above the visible colors that are not radiant. Concerning this we read that Moses was granted the privilege of the "shining mirror" (B.T. *Yevamot* 49b) that stands above the [mirror] that does not shine.[156] The rest of mankind [see] the mirror that does not shine. The patriarchs saw, by means of the revealed colors, those which are sealed, which stand above those which do not shine. Concerning this it is written, "And I appeared to Abraham, to Isaac, and to Jacob, as *El Shaddaï*"—in the colors that are seen. "But by My name *YHVH* I did not make Myself known to them"—these are the upper colors, the sealed, radiant ones, which Moses was granted the privilege of seeing. And this is the mystery of the closed and open eye: the closed eye sees the shining mirror, and the open eye sees the mirror that does not shine. Therefore "And I appeared"—the mirror that does not shine, but which is revealed, is described in terms of vision; but the shining mirror, which is concealed, is described in terms of knowledge, as it is written "I did not make Myself known."

Rabbi Eleazar and Rabbi Abba came and kissed his hands.

Rabbi Abba wept and said: Alas, for the time when you depart from

---

[149] *Ḥesed.*   [150] *Gevurah.*

[151] *Tiferet*, which mixes the other two lights within itself.   [152] *Malkhut.*

[153] The white and the colors in the eye-ball. These colors do not shine in the open eye, and they are a manifestation of the colors in *Malkhut.*

[154] In the eye also there are sealed colors, upon which the revealed colors are modeled.

[155] With the eyes closed, one sees, as it were, the colors of the rainbow, and these are the sealed colors.

[156] The two mirrors are *Tiferet* and *Malkhut.*

the world, and the world will be orphaned of you. Who will be able to illumine the words of Torah?

6. THE LIGHTS OF THOUGHT

(Zohar I, 65a)

Rabbi Simeon said: I raise my hands to the realms above in prayer. When the supernal will[157] in the highest realms rests upon the will that cannot ever be known or grasped,[158] the most recondite head[159] in the world above—and this head produced what it produced,[160] which is not known, and illumined what it illumined, and all in secrecy—the desire of the supernal thought[161] is to pursue it and be illumined by it. A curtain is spread,[162] and from this curtain, through the pursuit of the supernal thought, it touches but does not touch,[163] until the curtain illumines what it illumines, and then the supernal thought shines with a secret illumination, unknown, and the thought is unknown. Then the illumination of the thought that is not known strikes against the light of the curtain that stands [there], reflecting light from that which is not known, revealed, or perceptible, and then the illumination of the thought that is not known strikes against the light of the curtain, and they shine together, and nine palaces are made.[164] The palaces are neither lights, nor spirits, nor souls,[165] and no one can fathom them.[166] The desire of all nine lights,[167] all of which exist in thought, which is numerically one of them,[168] is to pursue them[169] while they exist in thought, and they cannot be grasped or known. And these do not grasp either will or supernal thought;[170] they perceive and do not perceive them. In these are preserved all the mysteries of faith. And all these

[157] *En-Sof*, called "supernal will" here to distinguish it from *Keter*, which is simply "will."   [158] *Keter*.

[159] *Keter*, the white head. It is called "recondite head" in contrast to *Hokhmah*, which also appears as a "head," but not so concealed as *Keter*.

[160] It emanates *Hokhmah*, which is thought.

[161] *Hokhmah* yearns to cleave to its source, *Keter*, and to receive light from it at the moment when *En-Sof* rests upon *Keter*.

[162] Between *Keter* and *Hokhmah*.

[163] The light of *Keter* shines very faintly through the curtain.

[164] The conjunction of the light of the curtain with the light of thought produces nine palaces, which are the hidden essences of the nine *sefirot*, from *Hokhmah* downwards.

[165] In their hidden essence they are different from the *sefirot*, which are actually designated as lights, spirits, and souls.

[166] No one can understand their real nature.

[167] The author here calls the palaces "lights," on analogy, having first made the point that they are different from the *sefirot*.

[168] The palaces are nine in number, including *Hokhmah*, which is one of the nine in the enumeration of the *sefirot*.

[169] The palaces also yearn to cleave to their sources, thought and will.

[170] They do not grasp the nature of will or thought.

lights, from the mystery of supernal thought downward, are all called *En-Sof*.[171] Thus far do the lights reach and do not reach,[172] and they are not known. Here there is no will and no thought.[173]

When thought shines, and the source of its illumination is not known, then it is clothed and sealed within understanding (*Binah*), and shines upon whom it shines, and one penetrates the other, until they are all comprised together.[174] And through the mystery of the sacrificial offering, as it ascends, all are bound together and illumine one another.[175] Then they all share in the process of ascent, and thought is crowned in *En-Sof*. The illumination[176] from which supernal thought derives its light is called *Ayin* (Nothing), and from it it derives its being and life, and it shines upon what it shines, and all rests upon this.

7. THOUGHT, VOICE, AND SPEECH—I

(Zohar I, 246b)

"Naphtali is a hind sent forth. He gives beautiful words" (Genesis 49: 21). And it is written "Your speaking is comely" (Song of Songs 4: 3)—for the voice governs speech,[177] and there is no voice without speech, and this voice is sent forth from a profound place[178] in the realms above, and it is sent from its presence in order to govern speech, for there is no voice without speech, and no speech without voice, and this is the universal that needs the particular, and the particular that needs the universal.[179] And this voice comes from the south[180] and governs the west,[181] possessing two sides. This is why it is written "and of Naphtali he said . . . Possess the west and the south" (Deuteronomy 33:

[171] The totality of the hidden lights, which continually seek to return to their source, is designated *En-Sof*.

[172] The region of the lights stretches to this point, and their illumination is not revealed or perceptible.

[173] These lights are neither *Keter* nor *Ḥokhmah*. It is possible, however, that the reference here is to will and thought in the realms below, that cannot ascend in perception to this region.

[174] When the lights of thought spark forth, the process of emanation begins. *Ḥokhmah* builds the palace of *Binah*, and is concealed within it through the mystic symbol of supernal intercourse between "father" and "mother," in order to emanate the remaining *sefirot*.

[175] The offering brings together and unites the *sefirot*, and through their unification they ascend with thought to *En-Sof*.   [176] *Keter*, which is called *Ayin*.

[177] *Tiferet* governs *Malkhut*. There is no complete revelation in *Tiferet*, which is like a voice without proper syllabic division, while *Malkhut* is like the enunciation of speech, which is praised in the quotation from the Song of Songs.

[178] From *Binah*, which is like the breath of air as it is expelled from the lungs, which produces the voice.

[179] *Tiferet* is the universal and *Malkhut* the particular.

[180] From *Ḥesed*. *Tiferet* acts on *Malkhut* through the power of *Ḥesed*, which is the right [south] arm.   [181] *Malkhut*.

23). Above, male, and below, female;[182] therefore "Naphtali is a hind sent forth"—female below; and likewise male above, since it is written "He gives beautiful words." It is written "he gives," not "she gives."

Come and see. Thought[183] is the beginning of all, and in that it is thought it is internal, secret, and unknowable. When this thought extended farther it came to a place where spirit[184] dwelt, and when it reached this place it was called *Binah* (understanding), and this is not so secret as the preceding, even though it is also secret. This spirit extended itself and brought forth a voice, comprised of fire, water, and wind,[185] which were north, south and east. This voice comprised all the other powers. And this voice governs speech, and produces a word in its correct form, since the voice was sent forth from the place of the spirit, and came to govern the word, to produce correct words. And if you examine the levels [you will see] that it is thought, understanding, voice, and speech, and it is all one, and thought is the beginning of all, and there is no division; but it is all one, and all connected, for it is actual thought connected with *Ayin*,[186] and it is forever inseparable. And this is [the meaning of] "The Lord shall be one, and His name one" (Zechariah 14: 9).

8. THOUGHT, VOICE, AND SPEECH—II

(Zohar I, 74a)

Rabbi Simeon said: How precious are the words of Torah! Happy is he who studies them, and knows how to walk in the way of truth!

"The house, when it was being built . . ." (1 Kings 6: 7)[187]—When it arose in the will of the Holy One, blessed be He, to act gloriously[188] in His own honor the desire arose from thought[189] to extend itself, and it extended itself from the place where thought is concealed, which is unknowable, until it spread and settled in the throat,[190] the place that gushes continuously[191] through the mystery that is the breath of life, and then, once this thought had extended itself and settled in this place, thought was called "living God (*Elohim hayyim*)," as it is written, "He is

---

[182] Naphtali symbolizes both *Tiferet* and *Malkhut* together. So it is written "he gives" in the masculine, and also "a hind sent forth" in the feminine. In its male role it determines speech, described as "beautiful words."   [183] *Hokhmah.*

[184] *Binah*, which is called "the spirit of God [*ruah Elohim*]."

[185] *Gevurah*, *Hesed*, and *Tiferet*, which are also north, south, and east. These three *sefirot* are intermingled and included in *Tiferet*, which is the voice.

[186] With *Keter*. All the *sefirot* from *Malkhut* to *Keter* constitute one single system.

[187] The complete verse reads: "The house, when it was being built, was built of stone perfected at the quarry; and there was neither hammer nor axe nor any tool of iron heard in the house, while it was being built."

[188] To build the world of emanation.   [189] *Hokhmah.*

[190] *Binah*, the source of the voice.   [191] *Binah* is an ever-flowing stream.

the living God" (Jeremiah 10: 10). It wished to extend itself again, and be revealed, and thence emerged fire, wind, and water,[192] collected together, and then Jacob[193] emerged, a perfect man, and he was the voice that went forth and was heard. Henceforward, thought, which was concealed and silent, was heard openly. This thought extended itself yet farther in order to be revealed, and the voice struck and knocked against the lips, and then speech[194] went forth, which perfected all, and revealed all. This means that everything is this concealed thought, which was within, and all is one.[195] When this self-extension reached, and became, speech, through the power of the voice, then "the house . . . was being built." It is not written "when it was built" but "when it was being built"—at various intervals.[196]

"Stone perfected," as it has been explained, for it is written "the crown with which his [i.e., Solomon's] mother has crowned him"[197] (Song of Songs 3: 11). "Journey"[198]—since it emerged from inside, and rested, and journeyed outward; it emerged from the higher realms, and rested, and journeyed to the lower realms. "And there was neither hammer nor axe nor any tool of iron heard"—these are the remaining lower levels,[199] all of which depend on it, but they are not heard, nor are they received within,[200] when it ascends in order to be reunited in the realms above and to be nourished there. This is [the meaning of] "when it was being built."[201] And then, while it is being nourished, they all exist in joy; they are nourished and filled with blessing, and then all the worlds are united in a single mystery, in a single unity, and there is no division among the worlds at all. After they have, each one of them, taken their portion, they all separate and spread out to their appointed regions.

9. THOUGHT AND UNDERSTANDING

(*Zohar Ḥadash, Yitro,* 33b; *Tikkunei ha-Zohar*)

The soul is [derived] from the side of *Binah* (understanding), and above it dwells thought, which has no end; and in it[202] there is no image, no

[192] *Gevurah, Tiferet,* and *Ḥesed.*   [193] *Tiferet.*   [194] *Malkhut.*

[195] This description demonstrates the essential unity of the *sefirot,* for all the *sefirot* are parts of the self-extension of thought.

[196] The "building" is constructed stage by stage.

[197] "Perfected" in Hebrew here is *shelemah.* This is read by our author as *shelomoh* (Solomon)—hence "stone of Solomon," for *Malkhut* (sovereignty, kingship) is called *even* (stone), and it is alluded to here by the crown of King Solomon.

[198] [Heb. *massa,* translated as "quarry" in the verse cited.]

[199] The lower worlds, including the husks.

[200] They are nourished by *Malkhut,* and bound to it, when it is in its place, but they do not accompany it when it ascends in order to be reunited with the upper *sefirot.*

[201] The "building" is continually being renewed by the unification of the *sefirot.*

[202] In *Binah.*

form, and no likeness, because it is the world to come.[203] In it there is no body and no likeness, as the masters of the Mishnah taught (B.T. *Berakhot* 17a): In the world to come there is no body, no corporeality. The soul clothes itself with a throne,[204] which is man,[205] and with his four spirits. There[206] it is said "You saw no manner of form" (Deuteronomy 4: 15), and of this it is said, "The eye has not seen a God beside You" (Isaiah 64: 3). It was through this thought that all the prophets delineated[207] all the images and all the forms that were below it, but above it no form can be perceived at all. In it they were unable to perceive any form or color, let alone above it.

10. GATES

(Zohar I, 3b–4a)

"*Bereshit* (In the beginning)", Rabbi Yudai said: What does "with (*be*)*reshit*" mean? With wisdom (*Hokhmah*). This is the wisdom upon which the world relies, in order to enter the supernal hidden mysteries. And here the six great supernal extremities are engraved, from which all derives,[208] for from them six fountains and streams are made so that they might be poured into the great sea. This is the meaning of *bara shit* (He created six). They were created from here. Who created them? He who is not mentioned,[209] that hidden one who is unknowable.

Rabbi Hiyya and Rabbi Jose were walking along, and when they came to a certain field Rabbi Hiyya said to Rabbi Jose: What you said concerning "He created six" is certainly true, for there are six celestial days in the Torah,[210] not more: the others are sealed. But I have seen it said in the secrets of the Torah as follows: The holy hidden one[211] made an engraving in the midst of a certain secret thing,[212] perforated by an inserted point.[213] He engraved this engraving, and hid it, like someone

[203] *Binah* is the source of souls, and the most exalted place of their delight.

[204] When it descends into a body.

[205] The image of man in the created world, which is the world of the throne.

[206] This apparently refers to *Binah*.

[207] The divine thought delineates prophetic visions in the lower *sefirot*.

[208] *Hokhmah* is the source of the *sefirot* and the six extremities, i.e., the *sefirot* from *Hesed* to *Yesod* are engraved within it in their higher, hidden being. From there they are emanated, and they become fountains and streams in order to transmit the divine influence to *Malkhut*, which is the great sea.

[209] The supernal emanator, *Keter* or *En-Sof*, who engraved the *sefirot* in *Hokhmah*, and emanated them from there, is not explicitly mentioned, but is alluded to in the word *bara* (He created).

[210] The divine Torah, *Tiferet*, comprises only six extremities.

[211] *Hokhmah*, apparently.   [212] *Binah*.

[213] *Hokhmah*, which is the primal point, is inserted in *Binah*, through intercourse.

who hides everything behind a key,[214] and this key hid everything in a palace.[215] And even though everything is hidden in the palace, the whole thing depends principally upon the key, the key that shuts and opens. In this palace there are hidden treasures, in ever greater quantity. In this palace there are gates, made in a mysterious way, and they are fifty in number. They are engraved toward the four extremities, and they are forty-nine in number.[216] One gate has no extremity, and it is not known whether it is above or below. Consequently, this gate is hidden. On these gates there is a lock,[217] which has a narrow place where the key may be inserted. It reacts only to the action of the key, and none but the key knows of it. And concerning this mystery [it is said]: "*Bereshit* God created." *Bereshit* is the key through which everything is concealed, and it shuts and opens, and six gates are comprised[218] within the key that shuts and opens. And when it shuts these gates and comprises them within itself, then it is in truth written concerning this: "*Bereshit*"—a word revealed in a word concealed,[219] and, in any event, *bara* is a word concealed. It shuts and does not open.

Rabbi Jose said: It is indeed so, and we have heard the holy luminary say so, that *bara* is a word concealed, that it shuts and does not open, and that, while it was shut in the word *bara*, the world[220] did not come into being or exist, and that *tohu* (waste)[221] covered everything, and that while *tohu* reigned, the world did not come into being or exist. When did the key open gates, and the time come for it to have intercourse and beget offspring? When Abraham came,[222] as it is written "These are the generations of the heaven and the earth, when they were created (*be-hibara'am*)" (Genesis 2: 4). And we have learned: *be-avraham* (with Abraham).[223] And because everything was concealed in the word *bara*, the letters turned to intercourse, and the pillar emerged that begot

[214] The male symbol in *Hokhmah*, the key that shuts and opens the palace of *Binah*, in intercourse.

[215] It introduced into *Binah* the seed of emanation.

[216] The forty-nine gates of *Binah* are revealed through the *sefirot*, which represent the four points of the compass (*Hesed* = south; *Gevurah* = north; *Tiferet* = east; *Malkhut* = west). But the fiftieth gate remains completely hidden, and was not revealed even to Moses (see B.T. *Nedarim* 38a). [217] The female symbol in *Binah*.

[218] The six *sefirot* that are comprised within *Hokhmah*, and emanated from it. Before their emanation they are like closed gates.

[219] *Bereshit* is split up into two words: *bara shit* (He created six). The first word is concealed and represents the situation before the emanation of the *sefirot*, and the second word is revealed, for it shows the "birth" of the six *sefirot*.

[220] The lower *sefirot*, which are the forces that construct and guide the worlds.

[221] *Hokhmah*, which is like hylic matter in the realm of the divine, i.e., potentiality, which comprises everything, but which has not yet emerged into actuality.

[222] When *Hesed* was emanated, which is Abraham's attribute, and the first of the six "extremities."

[223] *Bereshit Rabbah* 12: 8. [*Be-hibara'am* is an anagram of *be-avraham*.]

generations—*ever* (penis), the sacred foundation[224] upon which the world rests. When the *ever* was inscribed by the word *bara*, the supernal hidden One inscribed something else for the sake of His name and His glory, and this is the mystery of *Mi bara eleh*[225] (Who created these?—Isaiah 40: 26), and, similarly, the holy name, which is to be blessed,[226] namely, *mah* (what?) was inscribed. He produced *ever* from *bara*, and He inscribed *eleh* at one end, and *ever* at the other end[227]—the holy concealed One[228]—*eleh* exists, *ever* exists. When this was completed the other was completed.[229] He engraved a *he* on the *ever*, and a *yod* on the *eleh*; the letters were stimulated to complete this end and that end, and then He produced *mem*. He took one for this end, and one for that end, and the holy name was completed, and *Elohim* was formed. Likewise the name of *Avraham* [was completed]. When this was completed, the other was completed. There are some who say that the Holy One, blessed be He, took *mi* and applied it to *eleh*, and so *Elohim* was formed, and that the Holy One, blessed be He, took *mah* and applied it to *ever*, and so *Avraham* was formed,[230] and then He produced generations, and the complete name emerged, which did not exist previously. This is the significance of "These are the generations of the heaven and the earth, when they were created." They all remained in a state of suspension, until the name of Abraham was created. When the name of Abraham was completed, the holy name was completed. This is the significance of ". . . in the day that the Lord God (*Elohim*) made earth and heaven" (Genesis 2: 4).

[224] The first three letters of the name *avraham* are the same as those of *bara* (he created), but in the form that may also be read *ever* (penis), which symbolizes the *sefirah Yesod*, the force of procreation.

[225] *Binah*, called *Mi*, emanated the lower *sefirot*, called *Eleh*. The terms *mi* and *eleh*, which signify the revelation of the *sefirot* through emanation, parallel the process of revelation from *bara* to *ever*.

[226] *Malkhut*, called *Mah*, is also inscribed in the name *Avraham*, [the last two letters of which can form the Hebrew word *mah*].

[227] In the verse "These are the generations of the heaven and the earth when they were created," both terms are inscribed. *Eleh* (these) is the first word, and the letters of *ever* are to be found in the last word—*be-hibara'am*.

[228] The subject of the sentence.

[229] When the letters *he* and *mem* were added to *ever*, thus completing the name *Avraham*, the letters *yod* and *mem* were added to *eleh*, thus completing the name *Elohim*.

[230] According to this interpretation, the completion of the name *Elohim*, a name given to *Binah* in connection with the creation of the world, signifies the union of *Binah*, the supernal mother, with the *sefirot* to which she gave birth. The completion of the name *Avraham* signifies the union of the *sefirot* by means of *Yesod*, which is *ever*, with *Malkhut*, the lower mother, called *Mah*, in order to produce and create the lower worlds.

11. *MI-ELEH-ELOHIM*

(Zohar I, 2a)

When the most secret of secrets[231] sought to be revealed, He made, first of all, a single point,[232] and this became thought. He made all the designs there;[233] He did all the engravings there, and He engraved within the hidden holy luminary[234] an engraving of a hidden design,[235] [which was] the holy of holies, a deep construction that emerged from thought and was called *Mi*, the beginning of the construction. It existed and did not exist,[236] deep and secret; it was called by no other name but *Mi*.[237] It[238] sought to be revealed and to acquire a name, and it clothed itself[239] with a precious, radiant garment, and created *Eleh*,[240] and *Eleh* became a name.[241] The letters joined one another, and it[242] was completed through the name *Elohim*. Before it created *Eleh*, it did not have the name *Elohim*.[243] And those who sinned with the calf said, in connection with this mystery: "These (*Eleh*) are your gods, O Israel" (Exodus 32: 8).[244] And just as *Mi* is conjoined with *Eleh*, so the name is continually conjoined,[245] and through this mystery the world is sustained.[246]

[231] *En-Sof* or *Keter*.
[232] *Hokhmah*, which is the divine thought, and the beginning of emanation, because *Keter* is preexistent in the same way as *En-Sof*.
[233] The *sefirot* were designed and engraved in the divine thought, in secret, before their emergence into actuality through the process of emanation.
[234] *Hokhmah*.
[235] *Binah*, the beginning of the construction of the seven lower *sefirot*.
[236] It had a precarious, hidden existence.
[237] Before the lower *sefirot* were produced by *Binah* it was not specifically called *Elohim*, but simply *Mi* (Who?), which designates its concealed nature, for it could be perceived only as the subject matter of a question.
[238] I.e., *Binah*.
[239] *Binah* clothed itself in the light of *Hokhmah*.
[240] It emanated the more accessible *sefirot*, whom it is possible to describe, and these are called *Eleh*.
[241] The designation *Eleh* became the name *Elohim* by the addition of the two letters of *Mi*.
[242] *Binah*.
[243] Only when the *sefirot* were emanated, and *Binah* became the "mother of children," was it known by the name *Elohim*.
[244] Their sin consisted in the fact that they separated the lower *sefirot* from their source, and ascribed actual divinity to those that are called *Eleh*.
[245] Just as the name *Elohim* is a composite name, so it acts in a composite way, for *Malkhut* and *Gevurah* are also called *Elohim*, and so are angels and judges.
[246] Through the mystery of the combination of *Mi* with *Eleh*.

12. THE DEATH OF THE KINGS

(Zohar III, 135a–135b, *Idra Rabba*)

It is taught in the *Sifra di-Zeniuta*:[247] Before the *Atika Atikin*[248] prepared His attributes,[249] He constructed kings, inscribed kings, and conjectured kings,[250] but they could not survive,[251] so that after a time He concealed them. This is [the meaning of] the verse "And these are the kings that reigned in the land of Edom" (Genesis 36: 31). "In the land of Edom"—in the place where all the judgments exist.[252] None [of the kings] could survive until the white head,[253] *Atika Atikin*, was prepared. When He was prepared, He prepared all the attributes below; He prepared all the attributes of the upper and lower worlds. Hence we learn that unless the leader of the people is prepared first, his people are not prepared; but if he is prepared, all are prepared; and if he is not prepared first, the people cannot be prepared. How do we know this? From the Ancient of Days, because while He was yet unprepared as to His attributes, all these that had to be prepared remained unprepared, and all the worlds were destroyed.[254] This is [the meaning of] the verse: "And Bela the son of Beor reigned in Edom" (ibid., 32). "He reigned in Edom"—this is a weighty mystery: the place where all the judgments are accumulated and suspended.[255] "Bela the son of Beor"[256]—it is taught: he is the harsh verdict, the most powerful of all, through whom thousands upon thousands of yelling and lamenting ones are gathered together. "And the name of his city was Dinhabah" (ibid.). What is Dinhabah? It signifies "Give judgment (*din havah*),"[257] as it says "The horseleech has two daughters: Give, give" (Proverbs 30: 15). When [King Bela] attempted to live there, he did not survive, he could not survive, and all the worlds were destroyed. For what reason? Because

[247] This statement does not occur in the version of the *Sifra di-Zeniuta* that we have, but the sentiment expressed can be found at the beginning (Zohar II, 176b).

[248] *Keter.*

[249] Before He arrayed His attributes into a system by mingling *Hesed, Din*, and *Rahamim* (Love, Judgment, and Mercy).

[250] He attempted to set up the structure of emanation.

[251] Because they were judgments without mercy.

[252] [One of the root meanings of *Edom* is "red "] which is the color of strict judgment.

[253] *Keter*, symbolized by perfect whiteness, pure mercy without any admixture of judgment.

[254] According to the rabbinic statement in *Bereshit Rabbah* 3: 9, that the Holy One, blessed be He, "created worlds and destroyed them, before He created these."

[255] From there they emerge and begin their activity.

[256] The Hebrew word *bela* signifies "destruction," and the whole name is like that of Balaam, son of Beor, who is on "the other side."

[257] He tries continually to impose the rule of strict judgment and the torments of Gehinnom upon the world, and the verse from Proverbs is interpreted in this way (see B.T. *Avodah Zarah* 17a).

Man had not yet been prepared;[258] for the preparation of Man in his image comprises all, and all can live in him. And since this preparation of Man did not exist, they were not able to survive or live, and were annulled. Can you really believe that they were annulled? Surely they are all comprised within Man?[259] Yes, they were annulled, and were removed from the [earlier] preparation, until the preparation of the image of Man came into being. When that image came they were all comprised [in it], and assumed another existence. Some of them were sweet; some of them were both sweet and not sweet; and some of them were not sweet at all.[260] And if you say that it is written "And he died . . . and he died . . ."[261] and [this means] that they were completely annulled, this is not really the case, for whoever descends from the first stage of his existence is referred to as if he had died, as it is said "the king of Egypt died" (Exodus 2: 23),[262] because he descended from the first stage of his existence. And when Man was prepared they were given other names, and they were sweetened through him with continued life, and they remained in their places. They were all given names different from their earlier ones, except for him of whom it is written "and his wife's name was Mehetabel, the daughter of Matred, the daughter of Me-Zahab" (Genesis 36: 39). For what reason? Because they were not annulled as the others were, for they were male and female,[263] like the palm tree that is both male and female as it grows. Therefore, since they were both male and female, death is not mentioned in connection with them as it is with the others, and they survived. But they did not really live until the image of Man was prepared. When the image of man was prepared they resumed another existence, and lived.

---

[258] The system of emanation had not yet been prepared in the image of supernal Man, which constitutes a harmonious structure by balancing the opposing forces. In the idea of the image of Man even the forces of destruction of "the other side" are able to survive.

[259] Once the image of Man had been prepared, all the forces that were not able to exist before existed in it.

[260] The *sefirot* on the right-hand side and in the middle were absolutely sweet; the *sefirot* on the left-hand side were both sweet and not sweet; the forces of "the other side" were not sweet at all.

[261] Genesis 36: 33–39. Each verse begins with "And he died."

[262] According to a rabbinic interpretation, the king of Egypt did not actually die, but was smitten with leprosy (*Shemot Rabbah* 1: 41).

[263] A balancing of opposites occurs through the partnership of male and female, and so these forces, which are given the names of kings of Edom, Hadar and Mehetabel, were not annulled; but they were not able, nevertheless, to take their places until the system of emanation was prepared through the image of Man. Hadar and Mehetabel symbolize, apparently, *Tiferet* and *Malkhut*.

13. *ATIKA KADISHA* AND *ZE'IR ANPIN*

(Zohar III, 289b–290a, *Idra Zuta*)

This *Atika Kadisha*,[264] the secret of secrets, because it is the supreme head of the upper worlds, is referred to only as a single head without a body,[265] in order to sustain all, and it is secret, hidden, and concealed from all. Its attributes were prepared[266] in the brain that is concealed from all, and it spread forth, and when all was prepared the supernal *Hesed*[267] emerged. And the supernal *Hesed* spread forth and was prepared, and all was comprised within this concealed brain. When this whiteness[268] was prepared in this light, that which knocked, knocked[269] against this brain, and it became radiant, and another brain[270] was suspended [and came down] from the precious source, and it spread forth and illuminated thirty-two paths. When the light of the precious source was kindled,[271] three supernal heads were illuminated—two heads and one that comprised them—and they depend upon the source and are included with it. Henceforth, the beauty of the beard began to reveal itself, and this is the hidden source, and they were prepared.[272] Just as there are three crowned heads in *Atika Kadisha*, so everything consists of three heads.[273] When they[274] are kindled they all depend upon one another through the three heads, one on each side,[275] and one that comprises them.

[264] [The Holy, Ancient One], the hidden area of *En-Sof* and *Keter*, which is depicted as three heads: the unknown head, which is *En-Sof*; the supernal head, *Keter*, attached to *En-Sof*; and the concealed brain, the aspect of *Hokhmah* which is in *Keter*, from which the *sefirah Hokhmah* is emanated. Here, first of all, we are concerned with the second head, the *sefirah Keter*, from which flow channels of influence bearing the thirteen attributes of Mercy, symbolically portrayed as a beard with thirteen curls. This beard is also called the precious source, or the hidden source from which influence flows, and upon which everything depends.

[265] *En-Sof*, because of its great concealment, has no name or title. Nor has *Keter* any specific letter assigned to it from the tetragrammaton. It is alluded to only by the point of the *yod* (the first letter), which is a sort of head without a body. The *yod* itself is a symbol of *Hokhmah*.

[266] In the third head, the concealed brain, where the self-extension of *Keter* began.

[267] *Hesed* (Love), which is in the thirteen attributes of Mercy (*Rahamim*) that belong to *Keter*.   [268] The supernal *Hesed*.

[269] *En-Sof* stimulated the concealed brain to begin the process of emanation.

[270] *Hokhmah*, which is emanated from the concealed brain through the source. The thirty-two paths then emerge from *Hokhmah*.

[271] When the light of *Hokhmah* radiated from the source, the three heads of *Atika Kadisha* all shone, and they were included with it, the three heads being *Keter*, the concealed brain, and *En-Sof*, which comprises the other two.

[272] When emanation appeared the hidden heads were prepared, and they acted as the sources of emanation.

[273] Emanation is constructed entirely round the triangle of *Hesed*, *Din*, and *Rahamim*.

[274] I.e., the *sefirot*.   [275] Right and left.

And if you say: Who is *Atika Kadisha*? come and see. Beyond the heights above there is that which is not known, is not recognized, and is not described,[276] and it comprises everything, and two heads are comprised in it. And everything is prepared thus. And [*Atika Kadisha*] is not in number, or in thought, or in calculation, but in the devotion of the heart.[277] Of this it is said, "I said: I will take heed to my ways, that I sin not with my tongue" (Psalm 39: 2).

The place where the beginning commences[278] from *Atika Kadisha*, which is illuminated[279] from the source, is the light of *Hokhmah*, which spreads out into thirty-two directions and emerges from the concealed brain, from the light that is in it. That which *Atika Kadisha* illuminated first of all is its illumination, the beginning of that which was to be revealed, and it became three heads,[280] and one head comprised them all.[281] These three spread out to *Ze'ir Anpin*,[282] and all is illuminated through these.

Hokhmah was engraved and produced a river,[283] which welled up and emerged in order to water the garden,[284] and it entered the head of *Ze'ir Anpin*, and became a brain, and from there it proceeded and surged through the whole body[285] and watered all the plants.[286] This is [the meaning of] the verse "And a river went out of Eden to water the garden" (Genesis 2: 10). *Hokhmah* was again engraved,[287] and it proceeded and entered the head of *Ze'ir Anpin*, and became another brain by means of the light that proceeded from it. These two processes were engraved and joined together by means of that which proceeded from the depth of the well,[288] as it is written, "By His knowledge the

[276] *En-Sof*, the concealed head, which is not alluded to even by the smallest mark, like the point of the *yod*.

[277] Only through the devotion of the heart is it possible to approach *En-Sof*, but not through intellectual perception or through the words of prayer. Whoever prays to *En-Sof* commits a sin, and this is the significance of "that I sin not with my tongue."

[278] The beginning of the appearance of emanation.

[279] The place where the beginning commenced was illuminated from the source.

[280] Three heads came into being, as the process of emanation extended from *Hokhmah*, namely, *Hokhmah*, *Binah*, and *Da'at*.

[281] The three of them were comprised under one head.

[282] The whole structure of emanation from *Hokhmah* downwards is called *Ze'ir Anpin* (Short Countenance), in contradistinction to the realm of *Atika Kadisha*, which is called *Arikh Anpin* (Long Countenance). The main element in *Ze'ir Anpin* is *Tiferet*, which is at the centre of the *sefirot*. [See G. Scholem, *Major Trends*, p. 270, for his rendering of *Ze'ir Anpin* as "The Impatient" and of *Arikh Anpin* as "The Long-Suffering."]

[283] *Binah*. [284] The world of emanation. [285] *Tiferet*. [286] The *sefirot*.

[287] The light of *Hokhmah* itself became a brain in the image of *Ze'ir Anpin*.

[288] *Hokhmah* and *Binah* are joined together in intercourse by means of *Da'at* (Knowledge), which proceeds from *Keter*, the depth of the well. *Da'at* is the extension of the light of *Keter*, and plays a balancing role in the intermingling of the triad—*Hokhmah*, *Binah*, and *Da'at*. *Hokhmah* and *Binah* are the depths that are broken, so that they may produce emanation by the intercourse that takes place by means of *Da'at*.

depths were broken" (Proverbs 3: 20), and it entered the head of *Ze'ir Anpin*[289] and became another brain, and from there it proceeded and entered the body, and filled all the chambers and entrances of the body. This is [the meaning of] the verse "By knowledge are the chambers filled" (Proverbs 24: 4). And these illumine the light of the supernal, concealed brain, which radiates through the source. They all depend upon one another, and they are all connected one with the other, one with the other so that it may be seen that all is one, and all is *Atika*, and nothing is separated from it at all. These three lights illuminate three others, called "fathers,"[290] and these illumine "sons,"[291] and everything shines from one place. When this *Atika*, the Will of wills, reveals itself,[292] everything shines, and everything experiences perfect joy.

14. THE WHITE HEAD AND THE STRONG SKULL

(Zohar III, 135b, *Idra Rabba*)

It is taught: When it became the intention of the white head[293] to act gloriously for the sake of its own honor,[294] it prepared, and established, and produced from the spark of blackness[295] a single ray,[296] and this spread out in three hundred and seventy directions. The spark remained, and the revolving pure air[297] began to emerge and blew upon it. Then a single, strong skull[298] was prepared, and it came forth, and extended in four directions.[299] The spark was enveloped, grasped, and contained within the pure air. Do you really think that [it was actually contained] within it?[300] No, it was concealed in it,[301] and so this skull

---

[289] *Da'at* also becomes a brain in the head of *Ze'ir Anpin*, and it becomes the third head.

[290] *Hesed, Gevurah,* and *Tiferet,* the second triad in *Zeir Anpin*.

[291] *Nezah, Hod,* and *Yesod,* the third triad.

[292] The shining of the light of *Atika*, which is absolute Mercy, spreads joy throughout *Ze'ir Anpin*, which constitutes the world of Judgment, in contradistinction to *Atika*.

[293] *Keter,* which is all Mercy.

[294] I.e., to establish the world of emanation, so that its glory might be revealed.

[295] A spark (*bozina di-kardinuta*) from the light of *En-Sof* that shines in *Keter*. It is also called *kav ha-midah* (the line of measurement), because it sets the limits and boundaries for the *sefirot*.

[296] *Hokhmah,* the first point of emanation.

[297] From *Keter,* which is seen as the primal air that surrounds *En-Sof*.

[298] *Binah,* which is one of the three "heads" (*Hokhmah, Binah,* and *Da'at*), in the system of emanation.

[299] From *Binah* are emanated the *sefirot* which correspond to the four points of the compass (*Hesed* = south; *Gevurah* = north; *Tiferet* = east; *Malkhut* = west).

[300] For if this were so, the specific nature of the spark of *Hokhmah* would be lost in the air of *Keter*.

[301] The spark was concealed in the air, and from this association the skull (*Binah*) drew strength which enabled it to emanate the lower *sefirot*.

extended toward the extremities.[302] This air is the secret of secrets of the Ancient of Days.[303]. By means of the spirit[304] concealed in this skull, fire[305] extended on one side and air[306] on one side, and pure air remained above it[307] on this side and pure fire[308] on that. What is [the purpose of] this fire?[309] It is not real fire; but the spark that is contained within the pure air illuminates two hundred and seventy worlds, and judgment exists at its side,[310] and therefore this skull is called "the strong skull."[311]

In this skull there reside ninety million worlds, which journey forth and depend upon it. Into this skull drips dew from the white head, which remains full of it.[312] And because of this dew, which is shaken down from its head, the dead will come to life again. This is the dew that comprises two colors: when it is in the white head, there is whiteness[313] in it, which comprises all the colors; but when it resides in the head of *Ze'ir Anpin*,[314] redness[315] can be seen in it, like white crystal, in which both white and red may be seen. Therefore it is written, "And many of those that sleep in the dust of the earth shall awake, some to everlasting life, and some to reproaches and everlasting abhorrence" (Daniel 12: 2). "To everlasting life"—because they deserve that whiteness, which comes from the Ancient of Days, the *Arikh Anpin*.[316] "To reproaches and everlasting abhorrence"—because they deserve the redness of the *Ze'ir Anpin*. And all is contained in this dew. This is [the meaning of] the verse "Your dew is as the dew of lights" (Isaiah 26: 19)—"lights"; hence, two. And this dew that drips drips every day into the apple orchard,[317] in the form of colors, white and red.

15. THE COUNTENANCE OF THE KING

(Zohar II, 122b–123a)

It is taught in the *Mystery of Mysteries*: The king's head is arranged

---

[302] The four points of the compass.   [303] *Keter.*

[304] I.e., the air of *Keter.*   [305] *Gevurah.*

[306] *Hesed.*   [307] Above the air of *Hesed.*   [308] Above the fire of *Gevurah.*

[309] What is the reason for the pure fire that is above *Gevurah*, for there is no judgment in the upper *sefirot?*

[310] *Binah*, that is emanated from *Hokhmah*, is Mercy as to its own essence, but the roots of Judgment are implanted in it, since it is the source of the strict judgment of *Gevurah.*

[311] The "strength" alludes to the power of Judgment.

[312] The white head is always full of the dew of influence, even though the dew drips down from it.

[313] The supernal Love, which comprises all manifestations of love.

[314] Which comprises the whole structure of emanation at the top of which is the skull of *Binah.*   [315] The color of Judgment.   [316] *Keter.*

[317] *Malkhut*, that receives influence from *Hesed, Gevurah*, and *Tiferet*, which are called "apples." And from *Malkhut* the dew of influence descends to the lower worlds.

according to *Ḥesed* and *Gevurah*.[318] Hairs are suspended from this head, waves upon waves, which are all an extension,[319] and which serve to support the upper and the lower worlds: princes of princes, masters of truth, masters of balance,[320] masters of howling, masters of screaming, masters of judgment, masters of mercy, meanings of Torah, and secrets of Torah, cleannesses and uncleannesses—all of them are called "hairs of the king," that is to say, the extension that proceeds from the holy king, and it all descends from *Atika Kadisha*.[321]

The forehead of the king is the visitation of the wicked. When they are called to account because of their deeds, and when their sins are revealed, then it is called "the forehead of the king," that is to say, *Gevurah*.[322] It strengthens itself with its judgments, and extends itself to its extremities.[323] And this differs from the forehead of *Atika Kadisha*, which is called *Razon* ("will," or "pleasure").[324]

The eyes of the king are the supervision of all, the supervision of the upper and the lower worlds, and all the masters of supervision[325] are called thus. There are [different] colors joined together in the eyes, and all the masters of the supervision of the king are given the names of these colors, each one according to its way; all are called by the names of the colors of the eye. When the supervision of the king appears, the colors are stimulated.

The eyebrows are called "the place," which assigns supervision to all the colors, the masters of supervision. These eyebrows, in relation to the lower regions, are eyebrows of supervision [that derive] from the river that extends and emerges, and [they are] the place which brings [influence] from that river in order to bathe in the whiteness of *Atika*, in the milk that flows from the mother;[326] for when *Gevurah* extends itself,

[318] *Ze'ir Anpin* is the structure of emanation from *Ḥokhmah* down to *Malkhut*. In the center of this structure is *Tiferet*. The head of *Ze'ir Anpin* consists of *Ḥokhmah* and *Binah*, and they are here designated by those qualities which emanated from them, namely, *Ḥesed* (Love) and *Gevurah* (Power or Might).

[319] The extension of the powers that are active in the world.

[320] Powers that are held in balance, which do not tend either toward Mercy or toward Judgment. They weigh human actions in a just balance.

[321] From *Keter*, which in its aspect of *Arikh Anpin* is above *Ze'ir Anpin*, and from which *Ze'ir Anpin* receives its flow of divine influence.

[322] The Zohar apparently here interprets *mezah* (forehead) as if it were derived from *nezah* (victory).

[323] Judgment, contained within the forehead, spreads out on all sides in order to punish the wicked.

[324] The revelation of the forehead in *Atika Kadisha* indicates the ascendancy of Mercy and the forgiveness of sins.

[325] All the powers of supervision are called "the eyes of the king," and they are categorized differently on the pattern of the various colors in the eye.

[326] The eyebrows are channels through which the stream of supervision flows from *Binah*, which is called "river" and "mother." This flow of supervision is *Rahamim* (Mercy), and it is like mother's milk, which flows from the whiteness of *Atika Kadisha*.

and the eyes shine with a red color, *Atika Kadisha* illumines its own whiteness, and it shines in the mother, and she is filled with milk and suckles everything, and all the eyes bathe in the mother's milk, which flows forth perpetually. This is [the meaning of] Scripture: "Bathing in milk" (Song of Songs 5: 12)—in the milk of the mother, which flows forth perpetually, without cease.

The nose of the holy king is the focal point of the countenance.[327] When the forces of power extend themselves and are gathered together, they are the nose of the holy king,[328] and these powers depend upon the single *Gevurah* and emerge from there. When the judgments are aroused and come from their borders, they are tempered only by the smoke of the altar, and then it is written: "And the Lord smelled the sweet savour" (Genesis 8: 21). The nose of *Atika* is different, since it does not need [the sweet savor], because the nose of *Atika* is called "long-suffering" in every respect; the light of the concealed wisdom[329] is called his "nose." And this is "praise" as it is written "My praise will I show you" (Isaiah 48: 9),[330] and King David was inspired by this: "Praise of David" (Psalm 145: 1).

The ears of the king: when the desire is there and the mother gives suck, and the light of *Atika Kadisha* is kindled, then the light of the two brains and the light of the father and mother are aroused[331]—all of these are called "the brains of the king," and they shine together, and when they shine together they are called "the ears of the king," for Israel's prayers are received, and then the movement begins toward good and evil, and by this movement the winged creatures[332] are aroused who receive the sounds in the world, and all of them are called "the ears of the king."

The face of the king: the light of the father and mother and their

This happens when the redness of Judgment shines in the eyes of the king, and the supernal Mercy is aroused in order to temper Judgment.

[327] The most noticeable feature of the countenance (see B.T. *Yevamot* 120b).

[328] The nose contains the powers of Judgment (*Din*). The Hebrew word for "nose" (*af*) means "anger" as well.

[329] The aspect of *Hokhmah*, which is contained in *Keter*, and from which the *sefirah Hokhmah* emanates. The concealed Wisdom is absolute Mercy. ["Long-suffering" is a translation of *arikh anpin* which also means "long countenance" or "long nose."]

[330] The usual translation of this verse is "For My name's sake will I defer My anger (*api*) and for My praise will I refrain for you, so that I shall not cut you off." [The root of the Hebrew word for "refrain" here is *hatam*, from which *hotem* (nose) is also derived.] The nose of *Atika Kadisha* is called "praise," and the verse is interpreted here as follows: the "nose" that acts on your behalf will not be the angry "nose" of *Ze'ir Anpin*, but the long-suffering one, which is "My praise."

[331] The light of the brains in the head of the king contains the illumination of *Hokhmah* and *Binah*, which are called "father" and "mother," and these latter are the head itself.   [332] The angels.

self-extension,[333] which illumine, encompass, and shine in the head of the king, and then, through them, testimony is given concerning the king.[334]

The beard of the king is the most important of all. Supernal *Hesed* and *Gevurah* commence from the head.[335] The light of the father and mother is divided, the light of the father into three lights, and that of the mother into two, making five in all. *Hesed* and *Gevurah* are [comprised] in one light, making six. *Hesed* subsequently crowned itself and shone with two shining lights, making eight, and *Gevurah* was illuminated with one, making nine. And when all the lights are joined together they are called "the beard of the king," and then it was written: "The Lord will go forth as a mighty man. He will arouse jealousy like a man of war . . ." (Isaiah 42: 13).

The lips of the king: thus is it taught: When the illumination of the father was kindled it shone in three lights. From one light supernal *Hesed* shone; from one light the illumination called "the brain of the king"[336] was kindled; and one light was suspended until the illumination of the mother was kindled, and when this was kindled it shone in five lights. In what way was it kindled? From a path, hidden and concealed, to which the father clove—as it is written: "The path that no bird of prey knows . . ." (Job 28: 7)—just as the male cleaves to the female. And she was impregnated and produced five lights, and from these five lights fifty great gates of lights were engraved.[337] They are fifty in number. Corresponding to them are the forty-nine clean facets and the forty-nine unclean facets of the Torah,[338] with one left over. And when this one, which is kindled in everything, is joined together with the suspended [light] of the father,[339] and when they dwell together in the king, they are called "the lips of the king," and consequently he utters words of truth.

The mouth depends on them,[340] the opening of the mouth. What is

[333] The light of knowledge (*Da'at*), which is the third brain.

[334] These lights, which constitute the face of the king, serve as witnesses to the nature of the king (according to B.T. *Yevamot* 120a: Evidence may not be given except from the face together with the nose . . .).

[335] In the king's beard there are nine features (curls), which are described in detail in the *Idrot*. According to the description here the features of the beard are branches of *Hesed* and *Gevurah* (which spread out from the head, i.e., from *Hokhmah* and *Binah*) and of the light of the father and mother, which is the face of the king.

[336] The first brain, derived from *Hokhmah*.

[337] The path is the female characteristic of *Binah*, by which intercourse is effected with *Hokhmah*. As a result of this intercourse five lights are produced, each one of which branches out into ten, thus making the fifty gates of *Binah*.

[338] Through which the Torah may be interpreted.

[339] The light of the fiftieth gate, which is the ineffable light of *Binah*, together with the third light of the father constitute the lips of the king.

[340] I.e. on the lips.

the mouth? It is nothing less than concealed *Da'at* (knowledge) in the mouth of the king, and it is called "the extension of *Tiferet*,"[341] by which all the treasures and all the colors are supported, as it is written: "And by knowledge (*da'at*) are the chambers filled" (Proverbs 24: 4). This *Da'at* is concealed in the mother,[342] and fills all the chambers and entrances, and when the light that is in it is aroused and emerges then it is called "the mouth of the Lord." And when the lips, which are the two lights of the father and mother, are summoned to the light of *Da'at*, they join themselves together, and words are then uttered with truth, with wisdom, with discernment, and with knowledge, and then all the words of the Holy One, blessed be He, are uttered with these. These three shine and penetrate inwardly, and are crowned as one. And when they are joined together with one crown they are called "his palate is sweet" (Song of Songs 5: 16), and they are the palate of the king, and are called "the sweetness of the king," and concerning this it is written: "Taste and see that the Lord is good" (Psalm 34: 9).

16. FATHER AND MOTHER, SON AND DAUGHTER

(Zohar III, 290a; *Idra Zuta*)

Rabbi Simeon raised his hands and rejoiced.

He said: It is surely the time to reveal [mysteries], and everything may be interpreted at this time. It is taught: When *Atika Kadisha*,[343] the mystery of all mysteries, sought to prepare itself,[344] it prepared everything in the form of male and female. Once male and female had been included, they existed in no other way except as male and female. This *Hokhmah*, which includes everything, when it emerged from, and was illuminated by, *Atika Kadisha*, was illuminated in no other way except as male and female;[345] for this *Hokhmah* extended itself and brought forth *Binah* from itself, and so there existed male and female. *Hokhmah* father, *Binah* mother, *Hokhmah* and *Binah* were equally weighed,[346] male and female, and because of them everything survives as male and female, for were it not so they would not survive. This beginning was the father of all, the father of all fathers.[347] They[348] were

---

[341] *Da'at* is a supernal emanation, holding the balance between *Hokhmah* and *Binah*. It stands on the line that joins *Keter* with *Tiferet*, and it maintains the contact between them. Hence it is called "the extension of *Tiferet*." The illumination of *Da'at* in *Tiferet* is the mouth of the king.

[342] Perhaps the meaning here is that intercourse between *Hokhmah* and *Binah* was effected by means of *Da'at*.   [343] *Keter*.

[344] By revealing itself in emanation.

[345] When *Hokhmah* was emanated it already contained *Binah*, the female, within itself, and this emerged later.

[346] Male and female balanced each other.

[347] *Hesed*, *Gevurah*, and *Tiferet*.   [348] I.e., *Hokhmah* and *Binah*.

joined together and they illumined one another. When they joined
together they produced offspring, and faith[349] extended itself.

In the *aggadah* of the school of Rav Yeva Sava it is taught: What is
Binah? When they are joined together, *yod* and *he*,[350] she becomes
pregnant and produces a son,[351] and gives birth, and so she is called
Binah,[352] son and *yod he*: they are joined together and the son is within
them. The perfection of everything exists in the way they are arranged; it
is all-inclusive: father and mother, son and daughter.[353]

These matters were not meant to be revealed except to the supreme
holy ones, who have entered and emerged,[354] and who know the paths
of the Holy One, blessed be He, and who do not deviate either to the left
or to the right, as it is written, "For the ways of the Lord are right, and
the just do walk in them . . ." (Hosea 14: 10). Happy is the portion of the
man who is privileged to know His paths, and who does not deviate from
or go astray in them, for these matters are concealed and the supreme
holy ones are illumined by them, like one who is illumined by the light of
a lamp.[355] These matters were not transmitted except to him who has
entered and emerged, for he who has not entered and emerged—it were
better for him had he not been created. Thus is it revealed before *Atika
Kadisha*, the mystery of all mysteries, that these matters illumine my
heart in the fullness of love and fear of the Holy One, blessed be He. And
as for these sons of mine here, I know that they have entered and
emerged, and have been illumined by these things, [but] not by all of
them. But now they shall be illumined to perfection, as is right. Happy is
my portion with them in this world.

17. THE LETTER *YOD*

(Zohar III, 10b)

The *yod* of the holy name[356] is tied with three knots.[357] Therefore this
yod has one point above, one point below, and one in the middle, since
there are three knots tied in it. One point is above, supernal *Keter*, the
highest of the high, the head of all heads, and it stands above all. One
point is in the middle, and this is another head,[358] since there are three
heads and each one of them is a head in its own right; and so the middle

---

[349] The world of emanation.

[350] The first two letters of the tetragrammaton, representing *Hokhmah* and *Binah*.

[351] *Tiferet*.

[352] [*Yod, he*, plus the letters of *ben* ("son"), make the word *Binah*.]

[353] *Tiferet* and *Malkhut*.

[354] Who have entered the garden of *kabbalah* in peace, and emerged in peace.

[355] Even the supreme holy ones perceive these matters, as if they were illumined by
the light of a lamp, and not more clearly than that.

[356] The tetragrammaton, *yod-he-vav-he*.

[357] *Keter, Hokhmah*, and *Binah*, which are the three "heads."   [358] *Hokhmah*.

point is another head that emerges from the point above, and it is head of all the other heads in the construction of the holy name, and this head is concealed from all. Another head is below,[359] the head that waters the garden,[360] a water spring, from which all the plants[361] quench their thirst. This is the *yod* with three knots. It is therefore called a "chain," like a chain that is interlinked, and all is one.

18. THE LETTERS *YOD, HE, VAV*

(Zohar II, 126b–127a)

Rabbi Simeon said: We have already learned that when the Holy One, blessed be He, created the world, He made engravings of the mysteries of faith[362] inside the radiances in the supernal mysteries; He engraved above, and He engraved below, and all was in a single mystery, in the mystery of the engravings of the holy name, *Yod-He-Vav-He*, which rules through its letters above and below, and through this mystery the worlds were completed, the upper world[363] and the lower world.[364] The upper world was completed through the mystery of the letter *yod*, the supernal point,[365] the first, that emerged from the hidden and concealed,[366] which is unknown and unknowable, and completely beyond knowledge, the supreme mystery of *En-Sof*. And from this secret a single ray[367] shone forth, slender and concealed, which contained within itself the sum of all the lights. And in the concealed ray there knocked that which had not knocked, and there shone that which had not shone, and then it produced a single ray,[368] which was pleasure for pleasure,[369] and it took delight [in it] and the slender concealed ray was hidden within this ray. As for the ray that is pleasure for pleasure, concealed, six sketches were embroidered as a decoration in it, which were known only to the slender light when it had entered in order to be hidden, pleasure in pleasure shining with illumination. And this ray,[370] which emerged from the slender ray, was awesome, and terrible, and powerful in the extreme.[371] It extended itself and a world was made,[372] illuminating all the worlds, a secret world, completely unknown, and in it there dwell sixty million,

---

[359] *Binah.*   [360] The world of emanation.   [361] The *sefirot.*

[362] He engraved the *sefirot*, which are "the mysteries of faith."

[363] The upper *sefirot*, especially *Hokhmah* and *Binah.*

[364] The lower *sefirot*, from *Hesed* downward, especially *Tiferet* and *Malkhut.*

[365] *Hokhmah.*   [366] *Keter*, which is attached to *En-Sof.*

[367] *Hokhmah*, which contains all the *sefirot.*   [368] *Hokhmah* produced *Binah.*

[369] *Hokhmah*, which is *eden* (pleasure), takes pleasure in *Binah* through the mystery of intercourse.   [370] *Binah.*

[371] The roots of Judgment are contained within it.

[372] The *sefirot*, which were like an embryo in its mother's womb, grew and caused *Binah* to expand. At this stage they were still concealed, and were thought of as the hosts, sixty million in number, in the hidden world of *Binah.*

who are inhabitants on high, celestial camps and hosts. And when it had produced them and they were completed as one, then an immediate union [was formed],[373] and they are the mystery of the letter *vav*, which was united with that secret world.

19. NAMES OF GOD

(Zohar III, 65a–65b)

Rabbi Eleazar was sitting before Rabbi Simeon, his father. He said to him: We have learned that [the name] *Elohim* always signifies Judgment, [but] there are times when *YHVH* is pronounced *Elohim*, as, for example, in "Lord, God" (*Adonai Elohim*—Genesis 15: 2, and frequently). Why is it pronounced *Elohim*, since [these] letters[374] always signify Mercy?

He said to him: It is written thus in Scripture, namely, "Know this day, and lay it to your heart that *YHVH* is *Elohim*" (Deuteronomy 4: 39); and it is written "*YHVH* is *Elohim*" (1 Kings 18: 39).

This I know, he said, that where there is Judgment there is Mercy, and that sometimes where there is Mercy there is Judgment.[375]

He said to him: Come and see that such is the case. *YHVH* always signifies Mercy, but when the wicked turn Mercy into Judgment,[376] then it is written *YHVH*, but we pronounce it *Elohim*. But come and see the secret of the matter. There are three levels,[377] and each level is independent, even though they are all one, and all bound together as one, and not separated from one another.[378] Come and see. All the plants[379] and all the lights, all of them, shine forth, and receive light, moisture, and blessing from the river[380] that wells up and flows out, in which all is comprised,[381] and that contains the sum of all.[382] This river is called "the mother" of the garden,[383] and she is above the garden,

---

[373] The six *sefirot* taken together are the letter *vav* [which has the numerical value of six]. When they are joined to the letters *yod*, *he*, which are *Hokhmah* and *Binah*, they constitute together the divine name *yod*, *he*, *vav*.   [374] [I.e., *YHVH*.]

[375] In the Godhead, cruel, unadulterated Judgment does not exist but is tempered with mercy; and sometimes the attribute of Mercy is combined with the activity of Judgment. But this is no answer to the question of why *YHVH*, which is specifically connected with Mercy, should be vocalized *Elohim*, which is associated particularly with Judgment.

[376] The deeds of the wicked turn Mercy into Judgment, and this necessitates that the tetragrammaton itself be changed, so that it is vocalized *Elohim*.

[377] *Binah*, *Gevurah*, and *Malkhut*, all three of which are called *Elohim*.

[378] Each *sefirah* exists in its own right, but the fact that they all share the same name points to their intrinsic unity.   [379] The *sefirot*.   [380] *Binah*.

[381] All the lower *sefirot* are contained within it before they emanate.

[382] At the time of the unification [of the Name] the *sefirot* return to their source and are comprised in it.   [383] The world of emanation.

because Eden is joined with her and does not part from her.[384] Consequently, all the fountains emerge and flow forth, and provide water on all sides, and they open doors[385] in her, and so Mercy is derived from her, and [doors of] Mercy are opened in her. And since they call her "mother," female, *Gevurah* and Judgment emerge from her.[386] She is called "Mercy" in her own right, but Judgments are aroused from her side, and so [the name *YHVH*] is written as Mercy, but vocalized as Judgment: the consonants [indicate] Mercy, but Judgment is at her side, thus: *YEHOVIH*.[387] This is the first level.

Second level: another level emerges from, and is aroused by, the first, and it is called *Gevurah*. And this is called *Elohim*, with the actual letters of the name, and it is one of the beginnings of *Ze'ir Anpin*, and is attached to it.[388] Because they are attached to one another it is written "The Lord, He is God" (*YHVH hu ha-Elohim*), for *YHVH* is *Elohim* in these actual letters, and it is one. This is the second level.

Third level: *Zedek*[389] (Righteousness), the last crown, that [which is] the court of the King. And it is taught: *Adonai*; thus is it written, and thus is it pronounced. The Assembly of Israel[390] is given this name, and this name[391] is completed in this place.

These are three levels, called by the names of Judgment, and all are bound together inseparably, as we have explained.

He said to him: If it please my father, behold, I have heard [an explanation of] the scriptural phrase "I am that I am (*ehyeh asher ehyeh*)" (Exodus 3: 14), and I do not understand it.

He said to him: Eleazar, my son, the companions have explained it. Behold, everything is bound together in one thing, and the mystery of the thing is *Ehyeh*. It includes everything,[392] because, since the paths are hidden[393] and are not separable, and are gathered together in one

[384] *Binah* is called "mother" and "a flowing river," because *Hokhmah*, which is called "Eden," is united with her and impregnates her with the seed of emanation.

[385] The fifty gates of *Binah*.

[386] According to her own nature, she is Mercy, the source of influence, but in her role as the female, relative to *Hokhmah*, the roots of Judgment are implanted within her, and the *sefirah*, *Gevurah*, strict Judgment, emanates from her.

[387] [The combination *YEHOVIH* is pronounced "*Elohim*."]

[388] *Ze'ir Anpin* comprises the *sefirot*, whose head consists of *Hokhmah* and *Binah*, with *Tiferet* at the center. From the point of view of *Tiferet*, who is referred to specifically by the name *YHVH*, *Gevurah* is one of the beginnings of the image of *Ze'ir Anpin*, and so it is written "*YHVH* is *Elohim*," for *Gevurah* is contained within *Ze'ir Anpin*, whose principal constituent is *YHVH*.

[389] *Malkhut*, lenient Judgment.   [390] Of the higher world, *Malkhut*.

[391] The name *Elohim*, which is completed in *Malkhut*, for *Malkhut* is also called *Elohim* from time to time, because its origin is in *Gevurah*.

[392] *Keter*, in which everything is comprised in perfect concealment. The name *Ehyeh* when applied to *Keter* signifies the hidden universal being, completely unrevealed.

[393] The paths of *Hokhmah* had not yet been opened, nor had they yet branched out in order to act as channels of the divine influence.

place, it is called *Ehyeh*, the sum of all, hidden and not revealed. Once the beginning[394] had emerged from it, and the river [395] became impregnated, so that it could produce everything, then it was called *asher ehyeh*, that is to say "therefore I shall be,"[396]—I shall be [there] to produce and beget everything. *Ehyeh* (I am), that is to say, now I comprise everything, a generality with no particular; *asher ehyeh* (therefore I shall be)—for the mother shall become pregnant and shall produce all the particular things, in order to reveal the supernal name.[397]

Subsequently, Moses wanted to know the exact details of the matter and this was explained by "*Ehyeh*"[398] where it is not written "*asher ehyeh*." And we find in the book of King Solomon: *asher*—through being attached to pleasure,[399] the palace existed in an exalted association as it is said "Happy am I (*be-oshri*), for my daughters call me happy (*ishruni*)" (Genesis 30: 13). "*Ehyeh*," that is, about to beget in the future. Come and see how [the Holy One, blessed be He] came down from one level to the next in order to reveal the mystery of the holy name, and to show Moses the bond of faith. First of all, "*Ehyeh*," the sum of all, the hidden one, that is not revealed at all, as I have said. And a sign of this is "I was with Him, as a nursling . . .,"[400] and it is written "Man does not know the price of it. . . ."[401] After this He[402] brought forth the mystery of the supernal beginning, the commencement of all,[403] and this river, the supernal mother,[404] became pregnant, and was due to produce offspring, and He said "*asher ehyeh*," that is, about to beget and to arrange everything. And then He started to beget, and so it is not written *asher* but simply *ehyeh*, that is to say, "now let everything emerge and be perfectly arranged." When everything had emerged and been arranged, every single thing in its place, He left everything[405] and said "*YHVH*"[406]—this is the particular, and this is actual existence. At that moment Moses knew the mystery of the holy name, the secret and the revealed,[407] and perceived

---

[394] *Hokhmah*, the beginning of emanation.   [395] *Binah*.

[396] The word *asher* gives the reason why emanation was to be revealed in the future from *Binah*, namely, that it had been impregnated by *Hokhmah*.

[397] *YHVH*, whose letters comprise the whole system of emanation.

[398] Exodus 3: 14 in the phrase "'I am' (*Ehyeh*) sent me to you."

[399] Through the attachment of *Binah*, the palace, to *Hokhmah* in intercourse. The pleasure of this intercourse is alluded to in the word *asher*, which is here connected with a verbal root meaning "pleasure, bliss."

[400] Proverbs 8: 30. *Hokhmah* (Wisdom) says here "*ehyeh ezlo*," I was with Him, i.e., with the concealed, *Keter*.

[401] Job 28: 13. The preceding lines are "But wisdom, where shall it be found? And where is the place of understanding?" One cannot know the worth of *Hokhmah*, since one cannot gain a perception of the hidden source, *Ayin*, which is *Keter*.

[402] I.e., *Keter*.   [403] *Hokhmah*.   [404] *Binah*.

[405] He left the name *Ehyeh* altogether.

[406] Exodus 3: 15: "Thus shall you say to the children of Israel: *YHVH*, the God of your fathers . . . has sent me to you."   [407] The names *Ehyeh* and *YHVH*.

that which no other human being has perceived. Blessed is his portion!

Rabbi Eleazar came and kissed his hands.

He said to him: Eleazar, my son, henceforth take care that you write the holy name[408] as it should be written,[409] for whoever does not know how to write the holy name as it should be written, and to tie the knot of faith, binding one with the other in order to unify the holy name, is designated by the verse: "Because he has despised the word of the Lord, and has broken His commandment, that soul shall be utterly cut off . . ." (Numbers 15: 31)—even if he omits only one level or one knot from one of the letters. Come and see. *Yod* at the beginning is the sum of all,[410] concealed on all sides; the paths are not open; the sum of male and female;[411] the upper point of the *yod* indicating *Ayin*.[412] After this [we have] the *yod* that brings out the river that flows forth and emerges from it, and becomes pregnant by it, [and that is] *he*. Of this it is written "A river was going out of Eden" (Genesis 2: 10). It says "was going out," not "went out."[413] Consequently, it did not wish to separate from it. Therefore, it is written "My love" (Song of Songs 1: 9 and elsewhere). If you object and say that it is written "river," in the singular, and yet we have three[414]—yes, that is really so. *Yod* produces three, and in those three everything is contained. *Yod* produces in front of itself the river and two children,[415] whom the mother suckles, for she conceived them and bore them. Then we have *he* like this: *he*, together with the children that are below the father and the mother. When [the mother] had borne, she produced a son and placed him in front of her, and so it is necessary to write *vav*. This [son] inherits the patrimony of the father and the mother, and inherits two portions, and from him the daughter takes her nourishment, and so it is necessary to write after this *vav-he* together. Just as the first *he* [is written] *yod-he* together without disjunction, so also *vav-he* are together without disjunction.

So we have explained these matters, and these words ascend to another place. Happy is the portion of the righteous, who know the supernal mysteries of the holy King, and who are worthy enough to give thanks to Him. This is [the meaning of] the verse "Surely the righteous shall give thanks to Your name; the upright shall dwell in Your presence" (Psalm 140: 14).

[408] In the scrolls of the Torah, *tefillin* (phylacteries), and *mezuzot*.

[409] I.e., with proper concentration on the mystical significance of the name.

[410] The letter *yod*, at its beginning, i.e., at its topmost point, signifies *Keter*, which comprises everything, without particularization or differentiation.

[411] There is no separation of the male and female aspects in *Keter*.   [412] I.e., *Keter*.

[413] [The Hebrew uses the continuous form, not the perfect tense]. *Binah* cleaves to *Hokhmah* even after it has emanated from it.

[414] After the letter *yod* there are three more letters in the tetragrammaton.

[415] *Tiferet* and *Malkhut*.

20. PATRIARCHS

(Zohar II, 175b)

It is taught: Rabbi Simeon said: "And the middle bar in the midst of the boards, which shall pass through from end to end" (Exodus 26: 28)—this is Jacob,[416] the perfect, holy one, as we have explained, since it is written "Jacob was a complete man, dwelling in tents" (Genesis 25: 27). It is not written "dwelling in a tent," but "dwelling in tents," that is, two,[417] for he grasped both one and the other. So here also it is written "And the middle bar in the midst of the boards, which shall pass through from end to end," for he grasped both one and the other. For we have learned: What does "*ish tam*"[418] mean? As the [Aramaic] translation has it, "complete," complete in everything, complete on both sides, that of *Atika Kadisha*, and that of *Ze'ir Anpin*;[419] the completion of the supernal *Ḥesed*, and the supernal *Gevurah*,[420] completing both one and the other.

Rabbi Simeon said: We have seen that *Hokhmah* is the sum of all,[421] that supernal *Ḥesed* emerges from *Hokhmah*, and that *Gevurah*, which is strict Judgment, emerges from *Binah*. Jacob completes both sides. The patriarchs[422] are the sum of all,[423] and Jacob is the sum of the patriarchs.[424]

It is taught: *Hokhmah* broke out along its paths and brought a wind to the sea,[425] and the waters were gathered to one place, and the fifty gates of *Binah* were opened. From these paths ten crowns[426] emerged with shining rays, and twenty-two paths remained. The wind burst out down these paths, and the fifty gates of *Binah* were opened, and twenty-two

---

[416] A symbol of *Tiferet*, the attribute of Mercy, which holds the balance between Love and Judgment, and, therefore, the middle bar, joining both ends.

[417] *Ḥesed* and *Gevurah*.

[418] [Variously translated "perfect," "complete," "whole," or "quiet man."]

[419] *Atika Kadisha* is *Keter*, and *Ze'ir Anpin* is the system of the *sefirot* from *Hokhmah* down to *Malkhut*. *Tiferet* is the *sefirah* in the middle of *Ze'ir Anpin*, and in this position it is in a direct line with *Keter*, and so it provides the connecting link between *Atika Kadisha* and *Ze'ir Anpin*.

[420] Since it holds the balance between them.

[421] Before they were separated from one another in the process of emanation, all the *sefirot* had a common existence within *Hokhmah*.

[422] *Ḥesed, Gevurah*, and *Tiferet*.

[423] All the attributes are comprised in the triad of Love, Judgment, and Mercy.

[424] Mercy is an admixture of Love and Judgment. Consequently, the three attributes are comprised within *Tiferet*, which is Mercy.

[425] *Hokhmah* caused movement along its thirty-two paths, and through them emanated a torrent of influence, which was collected together, and from this *Binah*, the supernal sea, was formed.

[426] The system of the ten *sefirot* was established.

[letters] were engraved[427] on the fifty gates of the Jubilee,[428] and [the gates] were crowned with the seventy-two letters[429] of the holy name. These[430] were opened on every side, and were crowned with the twenty-two crowns of Mercy[431] contained within the Ancient of Days,[432] that gives light to them, to each one on every side. The fifty engravings were crowned with the forty-two sacred letters of the holy name[433] with which heaven and earth were created, and eight gates were engraved with their engravings, and these are the eight letters of Mercy, as it is written "*YHVH YHVH* God, merciful and gracious" (Exodus 34: 6), which emerged from *Atika Kadisha* to *Ze'ir* and were united with these holy crowns, the supernal and exalted *Hokhmah* and *Binah*.[434] Supernal *Hesed* emerged from this side, and the Judgment of *Gevurah* from the other side. The merit of Jacob came and completed them both, and united them, for he is the supernal perfection.

21. FIRMAMENTS

(Zohar II, 164b–165a)

Rabbi Hiyya began by quoting "[He] covers Himself with light as with a garment, stretching out the heavens like a curtain" (Psalm 104: 2). They have interpreted this verse [to mean] that when the Holy One, blessed be He, created the world, He wrapped Himself in the primal light,[435] and with it created the heavens[436] (*Bereshit Rabbah* 3: 4). Come and see. Light and darkness[437] were not together, light being on the right side, and darkness on the left side. What did the Holy One, blessed be He, do? He combined them[438] and created the heavens from them. What are the heavens? Fire and water. He combined them, and made peace between them. When He had brought them together, and

---

[427] The letters of the alphabet were spiritually engraved in *Binah*, which contained the source of the sacred letters.   [428] I.e., *Binah*.

[429] The seventy-two-lettered name of God is comprised in three verses, namely, Exodus 14: 19–21. It was formed in *Binah* from the twenty-two basic letters and the fifty gates.   [430] I.e., the twenty-two letters.

[431] Thirteen attributes of Mercy belonging to *Atika Kadisha* (Exodus 34: 6–7) and nine attributes of *Ze'ir Anpin* (Numbers 14: 18).

[432] The attributes of *Ze'ir Anpin* are also contained within *Atika Kadisha*.

[433] There are fifty engravings to match the fifty gates of *Binah*, namely, the forty-two-lettered name, which consists basically of the initial letters of the prayer *ana ba-koah*, but which can also be represented by the first forty-two letters of Genesis, which form the name derived from the account of Creation, together with the eight letters of the two tetragrammata at the beginning of the thirteen attributes of Mercy.

[434] The eight letters of Mercy, which pour down from *Atika Kadisha*, are joined to *Hokhmah* and *Binah*, which are at the head of *Ze'ir Anpin*.   [435] *Hesed*.   [436] *Tiferet*.

[437] *Hesed* and *Gevurah*, which are also fire and water. [The Hebrew word *shamayim* (heavens) is derived homiletically from *esh* (fire) and *mayim* (water).]

[438] *Tiferet* is an admixture of *Hesed* and *Gevurah*.

stretched them out like a curtain, He stretched them and made of them a letter *vav*,[439] and this is called *yeriah* (curtain). "Curtains," for behold, from this letter an illumination spread forth, and curtains were made.[440] This is [the meaning of] the verse, "And you shall make the tabernacle with ten curtains" (Exodus 26: 1). And seven firmaments[441] are stretched out, concealed in the celestial treasury, as they have explained, and one firmament[442] stands above them. There is no color in this firmament,[443] and it has no place in revelation, and only by discernment can one seek to understand it. This firmament is concealed and gives light to all of them,[444] and causes them to move in the way which is suited to each one of them. From this firmament and beyond no one can know or see; and it is incumbent upon man to stop his mouth from speaking and from seeking to understand with discernment. Whoever seeks to understand will recoil, for no one can know. There are ten curtains, which are ten firmaments. And what are they? The curtains of the tabernacle that are ten in number, and they can be known by the wise in heart. Whoever knows them can seek to understand the great wisdom and the mysteries of the world,[445] and can seek to understand the world above, the place that each one attains, apart from the two that stand to the right and to the left, for they are concealed with the *Shekhinah*.[446]

22. FIRMAMENTS, STREAMS, AND SEA

(Zohar I, 85b–86a)

Rabbi Jose began by quoting: "Who has raised up from the east, summoning righteousness to attend him" (Isaiah 41: 2). This verse has been explained by the companions, but this verse is concerned with wisdom's mystery, for we have learned: The Holy One, blessed be He, made seven firmaments[447] in the realms above, and they are all worthy enough to know the glory of the Holy One, blessed be He, and they are all prepared to demonstrate the mystery of the supernal faith. Come and see. There is an upper firmament,[448] concealed, that is higher than these

[439] In the tetragrammaton. This letter symbolizes *Tiferet*.
[440] The *Shekhinah* is referred to here as "the tabernacle." Ten forces are engendered in the world of the Chariot from the illumination of *Tiferet*, and these match the ten *sefirot*.
[441] Seven *sefirot* from *Ḥesed* to *Malkhut*.   [442] *Binah*.
[443] *Binah* is completely beyond pictorial perception.
[444] *Binah* illuminates and governs all the *sefirot*.
[445] Whoever can perceive the ten powers that are below the *Shekhinah* can through them seek to understand, depending on his own spiritual stature, the *sefirot* which are parallel to them.
[446] In this perception it is not possible to gain a direct understanding of *Nezaḥ* and *Hod*, which stand above the *Shekhinah*, to the right and left, because they are attached to the *Shekhinah*, and concealed with her in the mystery of intercourse.
[447] The *sefirot* from *Ḥesed* downwards.   [448] *Binah*.

seven, and this is the firmament that guides them and sheds light upon them all. And it is unknowable, but [only] an object of enquiry,[449] for it is not known, since it is concealed and profound, and all are dumbfounded by it. It is therefore called *Mi* (who?), as they have explained, since it is written "From the womb of *Mi* (who) came the ice" (Job 38: 29),[450] and it has been clarified already. This is the upper firmament that stands above all these seven. And there is a lower firmament[451] that is beneath them all, and it does not shed light, and because it is lower and does not shed light the firmament that is above them is joined with it.[452]

The two letters of the upper firmament called *Mi* are contained within it, and it is called *Yam* (sea),[453] because all the other firmaments become streams, and enter it, and then it is the supernal sea, and produces fruits and fish, according to their species.[454] And concerning this David said, "Yonder sea, great and wide; therein are creeping things innumerable, living creatures both small and great" (Psalm 104: 25). And concerning this it is written, "Who has raised up from the east, summoning righteousness to attend him". "Who has raised up from the east"—this is Abraham; "summoning righteousness to attend him"—this is Sarah.[455] Another interpretation:[456] "summoning righteousness to attend him . . ."—this is the lowest of all the firmaments that became a sea. "He gives nations before him"[457]—who? The lowest firmament that we have mentioned, that which takes vengeance[458] and overthrows enemies. It was this that occasioned David to utter praise, "You have made my enemies turn their back upon me, and I have cut off those that hated me" (Psalm 18: 41).

[449] The highest point of human perception is *Binah*, but only questions can be asked about it, without any reply. And it is therefore called *Mi* (who?).

[450] [Usually translated "From whose womb did the ice come?"]. "Ice" here is probably a reference to *Tiferet*, the central point of the *sefirot* which emanated from *Binah*, because the verse continues "And the hoar-frost of heaven, *Mi* (who?) begot it," and "heaven" is a term used for *Tiferet*.

[451] *Malkhut*, which has no light of its own.

[452] *Malkhut*, the receptive power, is joined with *Binah*, the source of divine influence. The two *sefirot* are parallel in a number of ways. They are both female, both mothers, and both symbols of the *Shekhinah*.

[453] The Hebrew letters of the word *Mi*, i.e., *m,y*, a designation of *Binah*, are reversed in the name for *Malkhut*, forming the word *yam* (sea).

[454] *Malkhut* produces and sustains all the powers and worlds in the lower realms.

[455] This interpretation, taken from B.T. *Baba Batra* 15a, is quoted incidentally, and is then developed in terms more relevant to the context.

[456] *Binah*, which is called *Mi*, emanated *Malkhut*, called *Zedek* (righteousness), from *Tiferet*, called *Mizrah* (east).

[457] The continuation of the verse in Isaiah.

[458] *Malkhut* is the attribute of Judgment that punishes the wicked and wreaks vengeance on the nations.

23. THE STREETS OF THE RIVER

(Zohar I, 141a–141b)

"And he moved from there and dug another well . . ." (Genesis 26: 22).
Rabbi Hiyya began by quoting: "And the Lord will guide you
continually (*tamid*), and satisfy your soul in drought (*zahzahot*), and
strengthen your bones . . ." (Isaiah 58: 11). They have interpreted this
verse, and it has been clarified. But those who possess faith have
strengthened themselves with this verse, and have received assurance
from it concerning the world to come. "The Lord will guide you
continually"—in this world, and in the world to come. "The Lord will
guide you." Seeing that it says "The Lord will guide you," what need is
there for "continually?" But this is the offering at twilight,[459] which is
supported by the arm of Isaac,[460] and this is the portion in the world to
come.[461] Whence do we know this? From David, as it is written "He
guides me in the paths of righteousness (*zedek*)[462] for His name's sake"
(Psalm 23: 3).

"And satisfy your soul with *zahzahot*." This is the resplendent
mirror,[463] from which the souls all derive pleasure by looking at and
enjoying it. "And strengthen your bones." The beginning and end of
this verse are not consistent. If the soul of the righteous is to bathe in the
joy of celestial bliss, what can "strengthen your bones" mean?[464] But
they have already explained it. This is the resurrection of the dead, for
the Holy One, blessed be He, will give life to the dead, and restore man's
bones to their primal condition, in a perfect body, and the soul will add
light from the resplendent mirror, in order to shine with the body, in
perfect existence, as it should be. Consequently, it is written "and you
shall be like a watered garden" (continuation of Isaiah 58: 11). What
does "like a watered garden" mean? Its upper waters will never cease to
all eternity, and this garden is watered by it and is saturated by it
continually.[465] "And like a spring of water [whose waters fail not]"

[459] [*Tamid* (continually) is also the name for the daily sacrificial offering.] Here it
refers to *Malkhut*, which has the characteristic of night.
[460] *Malkhut* is supported by influence from *Gevurah*, represented by Isaac.
[461] *Malkhut* is the abode of souls that are worthy enough to ascend to the divine
realm.
[462] *Zedek* is *Malkhut* and the phrase "He guides me" shows that "The Lord will guide
you" in the Isaiah quotation also refers to *Malkhut*.
[463] *Tiferet*, whose radiance gives joy to the souls when they are in *Malkhut*. [*Zahzahot*,
translated above as "drought," is connected with a verbal root meaning "sparkle, light,
radiance."]
[464] If the verse deals with the joy of souls in the world to come, why does it then go on
to talk of "strengthening the bones," which implies physical sustenance?
[465] The garden is *Malkhut*, which receives influence from *Yesod*, which is the river
whose waters never cease. The soul, which receives light from *Malkhut* and from *Tiferet*,
is compared both to the garden and to the river.

(ibid.). This is the river that flows out from Eden, whose waters never cease.

Come and see. "A well of living waters" (Genesis 26: 19). This is the supernal mystery within the mystery of faith, the well in which there is "a spring of water," and this is the well[466] that is filled by that "spring of water."[467] They are two levels, which are really one, male and female as one, as is fitting. Come and see. The "spring of water" and the well are one,[468] and the whole is called "well," for it is the source that enters and never ceases, and the well is filled, and whoever looks upon this well looks upon the supernal mystery of faith.[469] And this is the sign of the patriarchs, who labored to dig water-wells within the supernal mystery,[470] and one must not make a division between the source and the well, for all is one.

"And he called its name *Reḥovot*" (Genesis 26: 22). This is an allusion to the fact that his children would in the future work and repair the well, as was fitting, through the mystery of the sacrifices and offerings, as, for example, "And He put him into the garden of Eden to work it and to keep it" (Genesis 2: 15).[471] These are the sacrifices and the offerings, and because of this its springs spread out on every side, as it is said, "Let your springs be dispersed outward, and courses of water in the streets (*reḥovot*)" (Proverbs 5: 15). Therefore "he called its name *Reḥovot*."

Rabbi Simeon began by quoting: "Wisdom cries aloud outside; she utters her voice in the streets" (Proverbs 1: 20). This verse is a supernal mystery. What does "Wisdom (*ḥokhmot*)"[472] mean? It means supernal Wisdom, and lesser Wisdom,[473] which is comprised within the supernal and resides there. "She cried aloud outside." Come and see. Supernal *Hokhmah* is the most recondite of all, and it is not revealed, as it is said "Man does not know its worth . . ." (Job 28: 13). And when it extends itself in order to shed light, it illumines the mystery of the world to come,[474] and the world to come is created from it, as we have learned: the world to come was created with a *yod*[475] (B.T. *Menaḥot* 29b), and this *Hokhmah* is hidden there, and they are one. And while it is situated in its entirety in the mystery of the world to come, as we have said, it sheds light joyfully, and it is all in silence,[476] for it is never heard outside. Once

---

[466] *Malkhut.*   [467] *Yesod.*   [468] Through intercourse.

[469] *Malkhut* is the door through which one may gain a perception of the whole world of emanation.

[470] The digging of wells by the patriarchs is a symbol of the unification of the well with the source in the realms above.

[471] Adam was also commanded to bring offerings in order to help in the process of unification.   [472] [*Hokhmot* literally means "wisdoms."]

[473] *Malkhut*, contained within *Hokhmah*, its supernal source.   [474] *Binah.*

[475] The letter *yod* of the tetragrammaton symbolizes *Hokhmah.*

[476] The light of *Hokhmah* and *Binah* is concealed, and is not revealed "outside," in the conduct of the world.

more it seeks to extend itself, and from that place there emerge fire and water and wind,[477] as it has been explained, and a single sound is formed,[478] which travels outside and is heard, as it has been explained. Then from that point onward it is "outside," for inside it was silent, and was never heard, but now that the mystery is heard it is called "outside." At this point man must prepare [himself] through his deeds, and inquire.[479] "In the streets (rehovot)." What is rehovot? This is the firmament,[480] in which are all the shining stars,[481] and it is the source whose waters do not cease, as it is said "And a river goes out of Eden to water the garden" (Genesis 2: 10), and this is rehovot, and there "she utters her voice," the upper and the lower,[482] and all is one. It is for this reason that Solomon said "Prepare your work outside, and make it fit for yourself in the field . . ." (Proverbs 24: 27). "Prepare . . . outside," as it has been explained, as it is written "[Wisdom] cries aloud outside," for from that point forward there is work to prepare, and things to question, as it is written "For ask now of the days past . . . from one end of heaven to the other" (Deuteronomy 4: 32). "And make it fit for yourself in the field." This is "the field[483] which the Lord has blessed" (Genesis 27: 27). And when man has gained knowledge of Wisdom's mystery, and prepared himself with its help, what is written subsequently? "Afterward build your house" (continuation of Proverbs 24: 27). This is man's soul in his body, which will be prepared, so that he will be perfect man.[484] Therefore, when Isaac had dug and made a well in peace,[485] he called that peace Rehovot,[486] and all was as it should be. Happy are the righteous, whose deeds are used by God to sustain the world, as it is written "For the upright shall dwell in the land" (Proverbs 2: 21). They shall cause the land to dwell,[487] and they have explained it previously.

24. THE JUBILEE AND THE YEAR OF RELEASE

(Zohar II, 183a)

Rabbi Eleazar began by quoting: "Yea, the bird has found a house, and the swallow a nest for herself, where she may lay her young; Your

[477] Gevurah, Hesed, and Tiferet.

[478] The sound is Tiferet, which comprises Gevurah and Hesed.

[479] The performance of the commandments and the worship of God must be dedicated to this area, and it is this area which provides the opportunity for investigating and understanding the nature of the sefirot.   [480] Yesod.   [481] The sefirot.

[482] The two "wisdoms" meet in Yesod, the upper by pouring influence into it and the lower by receiving influence from it.   [483] Malkhut.

[484] Through a perception of the divine Wisdom, man acquires perfection.

[485] There was no dispute about it.

[486] According to this interpretation he gave the name Rehovot to peace (i.e., Yesod) and not to the well (Malkhut).

[487] [Yishkenu (they shall dwell) is read as yashkinu (they shall cause to dwell).] They will cause Malkhut, called erez (land), to dwell in union with Yesod.

altars . . ." (Psalm 84: 4). "Yea, the bird has found a house,"—these are
the birds of heaven, some of whom put their nests outside, and some of
whom put their nests inside, like the swallow (*deror*), which is a bird that
places its dwelling in any man's house, and is not afraid. Why is this?
Because they all call him "*deror.*" What is *deror*? Freedom, as it is said
"you shall proclaim freedom (*deror*)" (Leviticus 25: 10), the Aramaic
translation of which is *heru* (freedom). This then is the bird of freedom,
for after it has made its nest in the house and produced young, its nest
[remains] in the house for fifty days,[488] and after this they separate from
each other, and this is the bird that is *deror*, freedom. Come and see what
is written: "You shall hallow the fiftieth year, and proclaim freedom in
the land" (ibid.). Thence[489] freedom goes out to all, and since freedom
emerges from it, the Torah[490] that [also] emerges from it is called
"freedom." It is consequently written "graven (*harut*) upon the tablets"
(Exodus 32: 16). Do not read *harut*, but *herut* (freedom), and this is the
Torah that is called "freedom," for that which the supernal One
brought forth on this day is called "freedom," and it is freedom for all.
And this day is the upper freedom, for there is a lower freedom[491] and an
upper freedom. An upper *he*, and a lower *he*;[492] an upper freedom, and a
lower freedom; the year of release [493] and the Jubilee; they are as one.

25. THE HILLS OF THE WORLD

(Zohar II, 22a)

Rabbi Abba began by quoting: "Trust in the Lord for ever, for the Lord
is God, Rock of worlds" (Isaiah 26: 4). "Trust in the Lord." All the
world's inhabitants need to strengthen themselves through the Holy
One, blessed be He, and to place their trust in Him. If this is so, what is
the meaning of "for ever" (*adei ad*)?[494] This is [to ensure] that man's
strength should be in the place[495] where the sustenance and binding of
all is situated, and this is called "*ad*," and they have already interpreted
it, as it is said "In the morning he consumes *ad*" (Genesis 49: 27).[496]
This *ad* is the place that holds together all the extremities, from one end

[488] So matching the Jubilee year (the year of freedom), which occurs every fiftieth
year.
[489] From *Binah*, which contains fifty gates and is called "Jubilee." *Binah* is the source
of all release and redemption.
[490] *Tiferet*, the written Torah, emanates from *Binah*.
[491] *Malkhut*, which receives the characteristic of freedom from *Binah*.
[492] The two letters *he* in the tetragrammaton.
[493] [Every seventh year.] *Malkhut* is the seventh *sefirah* below *Hesed*.
[494] Which seems to imply a limitation. [Literally "as far as *ad*."]
[495] *Tiferet*, where all the *sefirot* are interlinked and united, and particularly those from
Hesed downward.
[496] [*Ad* here is usually translated "prey."] *Tiferet* has the characteristic of day.
[Perhaps we ought to render "in the morning it is *ad* that consumes."]

to the other, so that they should be sustained and bound together with an immovable knot.

And this *ad* is the object of the desire of all, as it is said "*ad* is the desire of the hills of the world" (Genesis 49: 26).[497] What are "the hills of the world?" They are two mothers,[498] females, the Jubilee and the year of release, and they are called "world," as it is said "from world to world (*min ha-olam ve-ad ha-olam*)" (Psalm 106: 48), and their desire is toward *ad*, since he is the sustainer of all the extremities. The desire of the Jubilee toward *ad*[499] is to crown him and to spread blessings upon him, and to pour sweet fountains over him. This is [the meaning of] the verse "Go forth, O daughters of Zion, and gaze upon King Solomon, even upon the crown with which his mother has crowned him" (Song of Songs 3: 11). The desire of the year of release[500] is to be blessed and illumined by him. This *ad* is indeed "the desire of the hills of the world." Therefore "trust in the Lord, as far as *ad*," because upward of that point there is an area that is secret and concealed, that cannot be perceived, a place from which the worlds emerged and were formed. This is the significance of "for the Lord is God, Rock of worlds,"[501] and it is a hidden and concealed place. Consequently, "Trust in the Lord, as far as *ad*"—up to this point every man is permitted to contemplate it, but from this point onward man is not permitted to contemplate it, for it is concealed from all. And who is this? *Yah YHVH*, for from there all the worlds were formed, and there is no one who can understand that place.

26. THE TREE OF LIFE AND THE TREE OF KNOWLEDGE—I

(Zohar III, 239a–239b)

It is written "The eye has not seen a God beside You, who works for him that waits for Him" (Isaiah 64: 3). "Who works." Surely it ought to be "who have worked?" "That waits for Him." It ought to have said "for You." However, there is a place on high[502] that moves outwards and kindles all the lights on every side, and it is called "the world to come," and from it a tree[503] emerges in order to be nourished and prepared. This tree is exalted and honored above all the other trees, and they have

---

[497] [Usually translated: "Unto the utmost bound of the everlasting hills." *Olam* can mean both "world" and "eternity."] [498] *Binah* and *Malkhut*.

[499] *Binah*, the mother, yearns to shower divine influence upon her son, *Tiferet*.

[500] *Malkhut* yearns to be blessed by *Tiferet* through intercourse.

[501] "Lord God" (Heb. *Yah YHVH*) signifies *Ḥokhmah* and *Binah*, and "Rock" (*zur*) is connected here with "to form" (*zayyer*). [The verse reads, literally, "in the Lord God, Rock of worlds."]

[502] *Binah* is called "the world to come" because of the influence that extends and comes from it without cease to the *sefirot* that have been emanated from it.

[503] *Tiferet*, the Tree of Life.

already explained this. This world to come, which extends outward, cares for this tree all the time, watering it and preparing it through its work, crowning it with crowns, never at any time withholding its streams from it. Faith depends on this tree:[504] it is more to be found in this tree than in any other tree; everything is sustained by it. For this reason it is written "whatsoever (the) God does it shall be forever" (Ecclesiastes 3: 14)—there is no doubt that He was, He is, and He will be—"nothing can be added to it, nor any thing taken from it" (ibid.). Therefore it is written in the Torah, "You shall not add to it, nor subtract from it" (Deuteronomy 13: 1), for this tree is [the tree] of the Torah, and this place is cared for by God always. God, without qualification,[505] is *Gevurah*, infinite and unsearchable,[506] as it is said "His discernment is past finding out" (Isaiah 40: 28)—*ha-Elohim*, not *Elohim*. Therefore "He worked," "He works," continually,[507] like a source whose waters never fail. Therefore it is written "*Ha-Elohim* has so worked that man should fear before Him" (Ecclesiastes 3: 14). He prepared this tree perfectly, for it takes hold of every side above and below, so that they might fear before Him, and never exchange Him for something strange.

Rabbi Abba said: You have said well, without a doubt, but we must look at the matter again. At first we have "He works," and after this "And *ha-Elohim* worked." What is the difference between them? "He works" means, to be sure, that He prepares this tree, whose waters never fail. But after this "He worked." What does "He worked" mean? It means that *ha-Elohim* made another tree[508] below it, and it does not say of this "He works"[509] because He made this lower tree and prepared it, so that whoever enters[510] into the upper tree should not do so without

---

[504] The system of the *sefirot*, which is the mystery of faith, depends on, and is linked with, *Tiferet*, and so the basis of faith in the unification is to be found in *Tiferet* too.

[505] *Ha-Elohim*, with the definite article [in the verse from Ecclesiastes].

[506] The name *Elohim* is particular to *Gevurah*, but *ha-Elohim* is *Binah*, which contains *Gevurah*, because it is the source of Judgment, but it emanates from the hidden realm of *En-Sof* and *Keter*, which is called *En-Ḥeker* (Unsearchable).

[507] At the end of the verse cited next it says "He worked," signifying the emanation of *Tiferet* by *Binah*, but at the beginning of the verse, cited earlier, the present tense is used "He works" [translated above as "does"]. This alludes to the outpouring of divine influence, which continues unceasingly. Hence the interpretation of "who works for him that waits for Him" is that *Binah* bestows influence continuously on *Tiferet*.

[508] Rabbi Abba explains the end of the verse as referring to *Malkhut*, which is the Tree of Knowledge.

[509] With *Malkhut* it does not use the present tense as with *Tiferet*, because *Binah* did no more than emanate it. It does not receive a continuous flow of influence, and even the influence that does reach it comes by way of *Tiferet*.

[510] *Malkhut* is the gate by which one enters the mystery of the divine, whose basis is in *Tiferet*. With the aspect of Judgment that it contains it repulses and punishes those who seek to enter without being sufficiently worthy.

permission, but would find the lower tree [in his way], and then he would be afraid to enter unless he were first found to be worthy enough. Come and see. This is the doorkeeper, and it is for this reason that it is called "keeper of Israel" (Psalm 121: 4).[511] This lower tree is satiated and nourished by the upper tree. And so it is not written "He works" but "He worked." For what reason? So that the inhabitants of the world should fear before Him, and not approach Him, apart from those who are worthy enough to approach, and no one else; and also so that men should keep to the paths of the Torah, and not turn to the right or the left.

27. THE TREE OF LIFE AND THE TREE OF KNOWLEDGE—II

(Zohar I, 35a)

Rabbi Abba said: Why is it written "the tree of life in the midst of the garden, and the tree of the knowledge of good [and evil]" (Genesis 2: 9)? The Tree of Life.[512] We have already learned that it is a journey of five hundred years[513] (*Bereshit Rabbah* 15: 7), and all the waters of creation[514] separate in different directions beneath it. The Tree of Life is actually in the middle of the garden, and it gathers all the waters of creation and they separate beneath it, for the river[515] that extends and emerges encompasses the garden and enters it, and thence[516] the waters separate in several directions.[517] The garden receives all, and after this [the waters] emerge from it and separate into several streams[518] below, as it is said, "They give drink to every beast of the field" (Psalm 104: 11). Just as [the waters] emerge from that supernal world[519] and water the high mountains[520] of pure balsam, so, subsequently, when they come to the Tree of Life, they separate beneath it in every direction as is required. "The Tree of the Knowledge[521] of Good and Evil." Why is it so called? This tree is not in the middle, and what does "knowledge of good and evil" mean?[522] Since it draws its nourishment from two extremes,[523] and knows them as one who feeds on sweet and bitter, and since it draws its nourishment from two extremes, and knows them and

---

[511] It "keeps" the way to *Tiferet*, which is called "Israel."   [512] *Tiferet*.

[513] The five *sefirot* from *Tiferet* to *Malkhut*.

[514] The influence from *Hokhmah* and *Binah*.

[515] *Yesod*, which is below *Tiferet*, transmits influence to *Malkhut*, which is the garden.

[516] From *Yesod*.   [517] Within *Malkhut*.

[518] Into the camps of the *Shekhinah*, and the lower worlds.   [519] *Binah*.

[520] The *sefirot* from *Hesed* to *Yesod*.   [521] *Malkhut*.

[522] There are two questions. The first, apparently, refers to Genesis 3: 3, where the Tree of Knowledge is described as "the tree that is in the midst of the garden," although we know it was not in the middle of the garden. The second concerns the meaning of "knowledge of good and evil."   [523] From *Hesed* and *Gevurah*.

dwells among them, it is called "good and evil." And all the plants[524] gather around it, and other celestial plants[525] are attached to it, and they are called "cedars of Lebanon [which He has planted]" (Psalm 104: 16). What are these "cedars of Lebanon?" They are the six supernal days,[526] the six days of creation.

28. THE WRITTEN TORAH AND THE ORAL TORAH

(Zohar II, 200a)

"And a book of remembrance was written [before Him, for them that feared the Lord, and thought upon His name]" (Malachi 3: 16). What is this? There is a book above,[527] and there is a book below.[528] "Remembrance" is the sign of the holy covenant,[529] which receives and retains all life in the realms above. "A book of remembrance"—two levels that are one,[530] and a mystic symbol of this is "the name *YHVH*"[531] (Genesis 16: 13, and often): "name" is one, *YHVH* is one, and the whole is a single unity; for there is a name, and there is a name: a name above,[532] which is inscribed by that which is not known and not susceptible to knowledge at all, and this is called the "supernal point"; a name below,[533] which is called *shem* (name), "from one end of heaven (*shamayim*) to the other end of heaven" (Deuteronomy 4: 32), because the end of the heavens is called "remembrance," and this name is the "lower point," a name for that "remembrance" which is the end of the heavens and receives all life in the realms above, and this is the end of heavens below, and its name is the "lower point." This point is a book that is susceptible to calculation,[534] which is [the force of] "and thought

[524] It would appear that the reference here is to the "shoots" of influence that are produced by *Hesed* and *Gevurah*.

[525] The *sefirot* from *Hesod* to *Yesod*, to which *Malkhut* is linked. The Tree of Knowledge is therefore described as being "in the midst of the garden," because it is attached to all the plants of the garden.

[526] The six *sefirot* from *Hesed* to *Yesod*, which are the forces of creation and divine guidance, are the six supernal days of creation.

[527] Judging by the context, this is the supernal book, the written Torah, which symbolizes *Hokhmah*. Usually, the written Torah is *Tiferet*, and *Hokhmah* is the Torah that is concealed within the divine thought, and that came into being two thousand years before the creation of the world. [528] *Malkhut*.

[529] *Yesod*. *Zikkaron* (remembrance) is here connected with *zakhar* (male).

[530] *Malkhut* and *Yesod*, connected together.

[531] *Malkhut* and *Tiferet*, which are also taken together.

[532] *Hokhmah*, which is the name inscribed and engraved by the concealed *Keter* and *En-Sof*.

[533] *Malkhut* is the name given to the six *sefirot* from *Hesed* to *Yesod*, which are the extreme limits of *Tiferet*, called *shamayim* (heavens), and it is a name especially assigned to *Yesod*, which is the lower end of the heavens.

[534] *Malkhut* is revealed, and therefore like something that can be counted [Heb. *hashav* means "think" and "count"], in contrast to the supernal book which is concealed.

upon His name." The book we have mentioned and the name are one thing on every side.[535] Since this point is situated in the middle,[536] it is above all those which are attached to it.[537] Six extremities[538] are attached to the supernal book that is above them, and six extremities[539] are attached to the lower book that is above them, and so [we have] an upper book and a lower book, and the whole is called "Torah." What is the difference between one and the other? The upper book is the written Torah, because it is sealed and exists only in writing (bi-ktav), for there is the place where it is to be revealed to the realms below. And where is that? The world to come.[540] The lower book is the Torah, which is called the oral Torah (Torah she-be-al peh). What is al-peh (lit., on mouth)? These are the chariots below, upon which it stands. And since they are not included in the writing above,[541] they are called al-peh. And this Torah stands al-peh, since it is written "and from thence it was parted and became four heads" (Genesis 2: 10).[542] Although the upper Torah stands above, it is not called al-ktav (on ktav) but bi-ktav (in ktav), for it stands in ktav (lit., in writing), and a palace[543] is made for this "writing," and it stands within this palace, and conceals itself there, and so it is called "Torah in ktav," and not "Torah on ktav," But the lower Torah stands upon its chariots, and is called "al peh," for it stands upon them. And because they[544] are not allowed within,[545] in the "writing," they do not constitute a palace for this point, as for the upper point. And because it stands above them it is called "Terumah."[546]

29. HEAVEN AND EARTH, DAY AND NIGHT

(Zohar I, 30b–31a)

"In the beginning God created" (Genesis 1: 1)—the mystic significance of "from the beginning (reshit) of your dough you shall set apart a cake for an offering" (Numbers 15: 20). The [letter] bet [of be-reshit (in the

---

[535] Both in content and number, since the numerical equivalent of both sefer (book) and shem (name) is 340.

[536] Malkhut here has its aspect of Zion, which is at the center.

[537] The palaces and the lower worlds.

[538] From Hesed to Yesod, whose source is Hokhmah.

[539] Six palaces that are below Malkhut.

[540] Binah is called ktav (writing) in relation to Hokhmah, because in Binah the emanation of Hokhmah is revealed.   [541] The divine emanation.

[542] Malkhut is above the chariots, which emerge from it, and constitute the world of separation that is outside the divine realm. This is alluded to in the verse from Genesis.

[543] Binah is the palace of Hokhmah, in the symbolism of intercourse.

[544] I.e., the chariots.   [545] Within divine emanation.

[546] [Lit., "that which is raised aloft," hence "an offering."]

beginning)] is the house (*bet*) of the world,[547] which is watered by the river that enters it, the mystic significance of the verse "a river goes out from Eden to water the garden" (Genesis 2: 10). This river gathers everything from the supernal depth,[548] its waters never ceasing, in order to water the garden.[549] This supernal depth, the first *bet*,[550] "*be-resh-it*"—the letters are concealed within it by means of a narrow path hidden within it. From this depth two forces[551] emerged: "the heavens" (continuation of Genesis 1: 1). It is not written "heavens," but "the heavens,"[552] from that depth which is concealed from all. "And the earth"—this concealed one[553] produced the earth, but it was included together with heaven, and they emerged together, attached to one another back to back.[554] When the beginning (*reshit*) of all was illuminated, heaven took it, and put it in its place,[555] as it is written "and the earth (*ve-et ha-arez*)." The *vav* included the letters that are *et*.[556] When the earth turned to dwell in its place and was separated from heaven's back, it was desolate, and despaired[557] of ever clinging to heaven as it had at the beginning, for it saw heaven shining bright while it was obscured in darkness. But then supernal light went out over it and illumined it, and it returned to its place[558] to look upon heaven face to face, and then the earth was pacified, and became suffused with incense.

The light went forth[559] on the right side, and the darkness on the left side, and He then divided them, so that they might look upon each other. This is [the significance of] the verse "And God divided the light

[547] *Malkhut*, which receives influence from *Yesod*, called "river." In this sense, the letter *bet* in the word *be-reshit* refers to the link between *Malkhut*, which is the lower Wisdom, and the supernal Wisdom.

[548] *Binah*, which is the supernal river.   [549] *Malkhut*.

[550] The letter *bet* also refers to *Binah*, the supernal *Shekhinah*, and as a result of its union with *reshit* (= *Hokhmah*) the seed of emanation is poured into it, which takes the form of spiritual letters within it.

[551] *Tiferet* and *Malkhut*, which are "heaven" and "earth."

[552] The definite article (the letter *he*) designates *Binah*, which is the first *he* in the tetragrammaton.   [553] *Binah*.

[554] *Malkhut* at that time did not have a separate existence of its own, but was attached to *Tiferet*, back to back.

[555] When *Hokhmah* ("*reshit*") received additional light from *Keter*, it poured more light on *Tiferet* ("heaven"), and with this power *Tiferet* took *Malkhut* from its back and put it in its proper place in the system of emanation.

[556] All the spiritual letters from *alef* to *tav*, designated by the word *et*, were contained by this process in *Tiferet*, which is the letter *vav* of the tetragrammaton. Through the power of these letters *Malkhut* ("earth") was given an independent existence.

[557] Lit., "waste and void," derived from Genesis 1: 2.

[558] *Malkhut* rejoined *Tiferet*, but whereas the earlier union was back to back, this union was face to face.

[559] This reverts to the beginning of the emanation of *Tiferet* and *Malkhut*. The light is *Tiferet*, day, and it is called "light" because it was emanated on the side of *Hesed* (the right side), and *Hesed* is "light." Darkness is *Malkhut*, night, and it is called "darkness' because it emanated on the side of *Gevurah* (the left side), and *Gevurah* is "darkness."

from the darkness" (Genesis 1: 4). You may ask whether this was a real division.[560] No. Day came from the side of light, which is the right side, and night from the side of darkness, which is the left side, and when they emerged together He divided them, and the division was along their backs, so that they could look upon one another face to face, and cleave to one another, so that all should be one. And he was called "day,"[561] and He called him "day," and she was called "night," as it is written "And God called the light 'day,' and the darkness He called 'night'" (Genesis 1: 5), because darkness takes hold of her,[562] and she has no light of her own. And although she comes from the side of fire, which is darkness, she remains darkened until she is illumined from the side of light.[563] Day illumines night, but night does not shine until that time of which it is written "the night shall shine as the day; the darkness shall be as the light" (Psalm 139: 12).

30. ZION AND JERUSALEM

(Zohar I, 186a)

Rabbi Judah began by quoting: "The Lord thundered in the heavens, and the Most High gave forth His voice; hailstones and coals of fire" (Psalm 18: 14). Come and see. When the Holy One, blessed be He, created the world, He prepared for it seven pillars[564] upon which it was to stand, and these pillars all rest upon one single pillar,[565] and they have already explained it, for it is written "Wisdom has built her house; she has hewn out her seven pillars" (Proverbs 9: 1), and they all stand at one level, called "the righteous, foundation (yesod) of the world" (Proverbs 10: 25). When the world was created, it was created from that place,[566] which is the perfection and completion of the world, for it is the single point of the world, and the center of all. And what is it? Zion, as it is written "A Psalm of Asaph. God, God, the Lord has spoken, and called the earth, from the rising of the sun to its setting" (Psalm 50: 1). From which place? From Zion, as it is written "Out of Zion, the perfection of beauty, has God shined forth" (Psalm 50: 2), from the place that is the limit of the perfection of complete faith, as it should be. Zion is the strength and the point of the whole world, and from that place the whole world was made and completed, and from it the whole world is nourished.

Come and see. "The Lord thundered in the heavens, and the Most

---

[560] A complete separation.   [561] In accordance with his nature.

[562] Gevurah takes hold of Malkhut.

[563] Although the essence of Gevurah, called "darkness," is the fire of Judgment, this fire does not give light to Malkhut, which is linked to it. Malkhut remains darkened, until it receives light from Tiferet.   [564] The sefirot from Hesed to Malkhut.

[565] Yesod.   [566] From Yesod, which is called "Zion."

SEFIROT

363

High gave forth His voice. . . ." Since it says "The Lord thundered in the heavens," what need has it to say "and the Most High gave forth His voice"? But here we have a mystery of faith. When I say that Zion is the perfection and beauty of the world, and the world is nourished by it,[567] there are really two levels,[568] namely, Zion and Jerusalem. One is Judgment[569] and one is Mercy,[570] and both are one,[571] Judgment on one side, Mercy on the other. From the uppermost realms[572] emerges a voice that is heard.[573] After this voice has emerged and is heard, judgments emerge,[574] and the paths of Judgment and Mercy go forth and separate from each other there. "And the Lord thundered in the heavens"—this is the court (lit., judgment house) in *Raḥamim* (Mercy).[575] "And the Most High,"[576]—even though it is not discovered[577] or known, once the voice emerges everything is there, Judgment and Mercy, and this is [the import of] the verse "And the Most High gave forth His voice." As soon as "He gives forth His voice" there are "hailstones and coals of fire": water and fire.[578]

31. THE HOLY ONE, BLESSED BE HE, AND THE ASSEMBLY OF ISRAEL

(Zohar III, 74a)

Rabbi Hiyya began by quoting: "As an apple among the trees of the wood, so is my beloved among the sons" (Song of Songs 2: 3). The companions have explained this verse. But how beloved is the Assembly of Israel[579] to the Holy One, blessed be He,[580] when she praises Him like this. One must consider why she chooses an apple with which to praise Him, and not something else, not with colors, or with scent, or with taste. Indeed, since it is written "apple," she actually praises Him with all of these: with colors, with scent, and with taste. Just as an apple is a cure for everything, so the Holy One, blessed be He, is a cure for everything. Just as there are colors in an apple, as we have explained, so there are wonderful colors in the Holy One, blessed be He. Just as an apple has a more delicate scent than any other tree, so it is written of the

[567] The implied difficulty is this: how can one say that the world is nourished by *Yesod*, when the conduct of the world is in the hands of *Malkhut?*

[568] *Yesod* and *Malkhut*, which are Zion and Jerusalem. [569] *Malkhut*. [570] *Yesod*.

[571] In the mystic symbol of intercourse. [572] From *Binah*.

[573] *Tiferet*, in which is revealed the mystery of the Godhead; in contrast to *Binah*, which is a voice that is not heard.

[574] Below *Binah* judgments are revealed, and *Tiferet* is composed of both *Ḥesed* (Love) and *Din* (Judgment).

[575] "And He thundered" signifies the activity of Judgment, but the name *YHVH* (Lord) signifies Mercy. [576] *Binah*.

[577] The existence of *Binah* is concealed.

[578] *Ḥesed* and *Gevurah*, both contained within *Tiferet*.

[579] *Malkhut*. [580] *Tiferet*.

Holy One, blessed be He, "His fragrance is as Lebanon" (Hosea 14: 7). Just as the apple has a sweet taste, so it is written of the Holy One, blessed be He, "His mouth is most sweet" (Song of Songs 5: 16). And the Holy One, blessed be He, praises the Assembly of Israel by comparing her with a rose,[581] and we have already explained the reasons why [He compared her] with a rose,[582] and it is clear.

Rabbi Judah said: When the righteous increase in the world the Assembly of Israel exudes a sweet perfume, and she is blessed by the Holy King, and her face shines. But when the wicked increase in the world the Assembly of Israel does not exude sweet perfumes, so to speak, and she tastes of the bitter "other side." Then is it written, "He has cast down earth from heaven[583] [the beauty (tiferet) of Israel]" (Lamentations 2: 1), and her face is darkened.

32. THE AROUSAL OF LOVE

(Zohar III, 45a–45b)

Come and see. When the dawn breaks, all the wielders of judgment[584] are humbled and disappear, and the Assembly of Israel converses with the Holy One, blessed be He. That hour is a favorable hour for all, and the King extends to her and to all those who are with her a scepter[585] with a thread of Love, so that she might be in unison with the holy King, and this has already been explained.

Come and see. When the Holy One, blessed be He, is with the Assembly of Israel,[586] on those occasions when He is with her, and she arouses delight in Him first and draws Him to her with great love and desire, then she is filled from the right side,[587] and there exist large crowds on the right side throughout all the worlds. But when the Holy One, blessed be he, arouses love and delight first, and she is aroused afterward, and not at the same time that He is aroused, then all is on the female side,[588] and the left[589] is aroused, and large crowds exist and are aroused on the left side throughout all the worlds.

33. THE MYSTERY OF THE KISS

(Zohar II, 146a–146b)

Another interpretation: "Let him kiss me with the kisses of his mouth"

[581] "As a rose among thorns, so is my love among the daughters" (Song of Songs 2: 2).
[582] Just as there is both red and white in the rose, and it is "among thorns," so there is Judgment and Mercy in *Malkhut* from the viewpoint of the *sefirot*, and it is surrounded by "husks." [583] *Malkhut*, called "earth," is dismissed from *Tiferet*, called "heaven."
[584] The powers of "the other side."   [585] [Cf. Esther 4: 11.]
[586] In sexual union.   [587] I.e., from the side of *Hesed* (Love).
[588] I.e., on the side of *Din* (Judgment).   [599] *Gevurah*, strict Judgment.

(Song of Songs 1: 2). What did King Solomon mean by introducing words of love between the upper world and the lower world,[590] and by beginning the praise of love, which he has introduced between them, with "let him kiss me"? They have already given an explanation for this, and it is that inseparable love of spirit for spirit can be [expressed] only by a kiss, and a kiss is with the mouth, for that is the source and outlet of the spirit. And when they kiss one another, the spirits cling to each other, and they are one, and then love is one.

In the Book of the Ancient Rav Hamnuna Sava, he says on this verse: The kiss of love extends into four spirits,[591] and the four spirits cling together, and they are within the mystery of faith,[592] and they ascend by four letters,[593] and these are the letters upon which the Holy Name depends, and upon which the upper and the lower realms depend, and upon which the praise in the Song of Songs depends. And which are they? *Alef, he, bet, he.* They are the supernal chariot, and they are the companionship, unison, and wholeness of all. These letters are four spirits; they are the spirits of love and delight, for all the limbs of the body are without any pain at all. There are four spirits in the kiss, and each one of them is comprised within its companion. And since one spirit is comprised within another,[594] and this other is comprised within the former the two spirits become one, and then the four are wholly joined together in one single unison, flowing into one another and being contained within one another. And when they spread abroad[595] a single fruit is made from these four spirits, one spirit comprised of four spirits, and this ascends and splits firmaments until it ascends and dwells by a palace called "the palace of love," a palace upon which all love depends, and this spirit is similarly called "Love." And when this spirit ascends, it stimulates the palace to unite with that which is above.

34. INTERCOURSE

(Zohar III, 61b–62a)

Come and see. It is written, "And a river goes out from Eden to water the garden" (Genesis 2: 10). This river[596] spreads out toward its sides when

[590] I.e., between *Tiferet* and *Malkhut.*

[591] The male spirit coalesces with the female spirit, and the female with the male, and so we have four altogether. [Heb. *ruaḥ* (spirit) also means "direction," and "breath," thus offering a play on words.]

[592] This process concerning the kiss in the lower world has its prototype in the mystery of the Godhead.

[593] The four letters of *ahavah* (love), namely, *alef, he, bet, he,* which are parallel to the letters of the tetragrammaton (*yod, he, vav, he*).

[594] We have here an explanation of the process whereby the spirits of the kiss came into being, as mentioned above.

[595] The spirit of Love is engendered by the spirits of the kiss, and this stimulates love in the celestial world.   [596] *Binah,* the mother.

Eden[597] has intercourse with it in perfect union, through the path that is not known[598] either above or below, as it is said, "the path that no bird of prey knows" (Job 28: 7), and they remain contented, for they do not separate one from the other. Then fountains and streams go forth and crown the holy soul[599] with all the crowns, and then it is written, "the crown with which his mother has crowned him" (Song of Songs 3: 11). At that moment the son comes into the inheritance of his father and mother, and he enjoys that delight and luxuriates [in it].

And it is taught: When the supernal King[600] sits among the royal luxuries, [crowned] with his crowns, then it is written "While the king sits at his table, my spikenard sends forth its fragrance" (Song of Songs 1: 12). This is *Yesod*, which produces blessings so that the Holy King may have intercourse with the consort.[601] Then blessings are given throughout all the worlds, and the upper and lower realms are blessed.

35. LOVE AND JEALOUSY

(Zohar I, 244b–245b)

Rabbi Eleazar and Rabbi Abba found refuge in the cave at Lydda, which they entered because of the heat of the sun, for they were on a journey.

Rabbi Abba said: This cave is crowned with words of Torah.

Rabbi Eleazar began by quoting: 'Set me as a seal upon your heart, as a seal upon your arm; [for love is strong as death, jealousy is hard as Sheol] its flashes are flashes of fire, a flame of the Lord" (Song of Songs 8: 6). We have already discussed this verse, but one night I was standing before my father, and I heard him say that the only way in which the desire and yearning of the Assembly of Israel[602] for the Holy One, blessed be he,[603] reach fulfilment is through the souls of the righteous, for they stimulate the flow of the lower waters toward the upper, and at that moment the fulfilment of desire and yearning [is accomplished] through one union, which bears fruit.

Come and see. After they have clung one to the other, and she has received her desire, she says "Set me as a seal upon your heart." Why "as a seal"? When a seal is affixed to a certain place, even after it is taken away again a mark is left there, which is permanent; its whole shape and image remain behind. So the Assembly of Israel says: Behold, I have been attached to you. And now, even though I have become separated from you and have gone into exile, "set me as a seal upon your heart," so that my entire image shall be in you, like the seal, whose image is left behind in its entirety at the place where it was affixed.

"For love is strong as death"—it is as strong as the separation of the

---

[597] *Hokhmah*, the father.   [598] The female element in *Binah*.
[599] *Tiferet*.   [600] *Tiferet*.   [601] *Malkhut*.   [602] *Malkhut*.   [603] *Tiferet*.

spirit from the body. For we have learned: When the time comes for a man to depart from the world, and he sees what he sees, the spirit moves through every part of the body, following all its convolutions, like someone who sets out to sea without oars, going up and down, without any peace. And it goes and asks leave of every part of the body,[604] and [no time] is more violent than the day when the spirit separates from the body. So the love of the Assembly of Israel for the Holy One, blessed be He, is strong, just as death is strong when the spirit seeks to separate from the body.

"Jealousy is hard as Sheol." A lover who is not jealous—his love is not love. When he becomes jealous, his love is complete. Hence we learn that a man needs to be jealous of his wife, so that he may bind himself to her in perfect love, for as a result he will not glance at another woman. What does "hard as Sheol" mean? Just as it is hard for the wicked to contemplate descending there, so with jealousy: it is hard for the lover who is jealous to separate from his love. Another interpretation: "Jealousy is hard as Sheol." When they take the wicked down to Sheol they recount to them their sins. In the same way the jealous man investigates his own sin,[605] and ponders on many deeds, and then he is bound in the knot of love.

"Its flashes are flashes of fire, a flame of the Lord." What is "a flame of the Lord"? This is the flame that burns and emerges from *shofar* (ram's horn),[606] which arouses and enflames. And what is this?[607] The left;[608] this is [the significance of] the verse "his left hand is under my head" (Song of Songs 2: 6). This it is that enflames the flame of love that the Assembly of Israel feels for the Holy One, blessed be he. Consequently, "Many waters cannot quench love" (Song of Songs 8: 7), for when the right[609] comes, which is [called] "waters," it makes love burn even more, and does not quench the flame of the left, as it is said "His right hand embraces me" (continuation of Song of Songs 2: 6). This is [the significance of] the verse "Many waters cannot quench love," and everything follows in the same way.

While they were sitting there, they heard the voice of Rabbi Simeon, who was traveling with Rabbi Judah and Rabbi Isaac. As he approached the cave, Rabbi Eleazar and Rabbi Abba came out.

Rabbi Simeon said: I saw from the walls of the cave that the *Shekhinah* was here.

They sat down.

Rabbi Simeon said: What have you been discussing?

Rabbi Abba replied: The love of the Assembly of Israel for the Holy

---

[604] It asks permission to leave the body.
[605] He afflicts himself by considering his own inadequacies.
[606] *Binah.*   [607] I.e., the flame.   [608] *Gevurah.*   [609] *Ḥesed.*

One, blessed be He, and Rabbi Eleazar was applying the verse "Set me as a seal upon your heart" to the Assembly of Israel.

He said to him: Eleazar, have you looked upon the supernal love, and the knot of affection?

Rabbi Simeon was silent for a while.

He said: Silence is good in every place, but not silence in matters of Torah. A treasure is in safe keeping with me, and I do not want you to be deprived of it. It is an exalted matter, and I found it in the Book of Rav Hamnuna Sava.

Come and see. Everywhere the male pursues the female and arouses love in her, but here we find that she arouses love, and pursues him. And in the eyes of the world the female gains no credit for pursuing the male. But this is a hidden matter, and an exalted matter from the king's treasure-house. Come and see. There are three souls, and they ascend[610] by known celestial degrees, and, although they are three, they are really four.[611] One: the supernal soul[612] that cannot be grasped, and the treasurer[613] of the supernal court[614] is not affected by her,[615] even less so the lower [treasurer].[616] She is the soul of souls, and she is concealed and unknowable, and they all[617] depend on her. She enwraps herself with an envelopment of crystal light,[618] shining within,[619] and she drops jewels, drop by drop,[620] and they are all connected together like the connections of the limbs in a single body, and she enters into the midst of them,[621] and demonstrates her activity through them; she and they are one, and there is no division between them. This supernal soul is the most concealed of all.

Another soul is the female[622] that conceals herself among her hosts,[623] and she is their soul, and from them comes the unity of the body,[624] so that she might demonstrate [her] work through them to the whole world, like the body, which is the tool of the soul, with which she does her work. And they are modeled on the hidden connections[625] of the realms above.

---

[610] Their place is in the realms above.

[611] The second soul, *Malkhut*, also contains *Tiferet*, thus making four altogether.

[612] *En-Sof*.   [613] *Hokhmah*, apparently.   [614] *Binah*.

[615] He has no perception of the nature of *En-Sof*.

[616] *Yesod*, the treasurer of *Malkhut*, which is the lower court.   [617] All the *sefirot*.

[618] Before emanation begins *En-Sof* wraps itself in the primal light of *Keter*, called "crystal light," because it has no color.

[619] *Keter* is a kind of halo around *En-Sof*.

[620] *En-Sof* emanates the *sefirot*.

[621] *En-Sof* dwells among the *sefirot*, and works by using them as intermediaries.

[622] *Malkhut*.   [623] The powers of the chariot, and the angels.

[624] In their unity they constitute, as it were, the body of the *Shekhinah*, which acts as her instrument in the conduct of the world.

[625] The *sefirot*, which can also be seen as parts of the one body in the world of emanation.

Another soul[626] is the souls of the righteous below. The souls of the righteous come from the celestial souls, from the soul of the female, and the soul of the male.[627] Therefore the souls of the righteous are more exalted than all the hosts and camps[628] of the world above.

You might object by saying that if they are so exalted by reason of the two extremities,[629] why do they come down into the world,[630] and why do they go up from it?[631] [There is a parable] of a certain king who had a son. He sent him to a village so that he might be brought up and reared there until he came of age, and so that they might teach him the customs of the royal palace. The king heard that his son had grown up and had come of age. What did he do out of love for his son? He sent the consort, his mother, for him, and brought him into his palace and rejoiced in him every day. In the same way, the Holy One, blessed be He, had a son by the consort, and who was he? The holy supernal soul. He sent him to a village, to this world, so that he might grow up there, and so that they might teach him the customs of the royal palace.[632] When the king knew that his son had come of age in the village, and that the time had come to bring him into his palace, what did he do out of love for his son? He sent the consort for him and brought him into his palace. The soul does not go up from this world until the consort comes for it, and leads it to the palace of the king, and there it dwells forever. But despite all this, it is the way of the world that when the prince leaves them the villagers weep. But there was a clever man there who said: "Why do you weep? He is a prince, and it is not right that he should dwell among us any longer, but rather in his father's palace." In the same way Moses, who was a clever man, saw that the villagers were weeping, and he said on this subject, "You are the children of the Lord your God; you shall not cut yourselves" (Deuteronomy 14: 1). Come and see. If the righteous all knew this they would be glad when the day came for them to leave this world. This is the very greatest honor: that the consort should come for them, to lead them to the royal palace, so that the king might rejoice in them every day; for the Holy One, blessed be He, takes delight only in the souls of the righteous.

Come and see. The arousal of the love that the Assembly of Israel has for the Holy One, blessed be He, is caused by the souls of the righteous in

[626] The third soul, which is really the fourth. [See n. 610, above.]

[627] They are emanated through the intercourse of *Tiferet* with *Malkhut*, which together constitute the second soul.

[628] For they are created [not emanated].   [629] *Tiferet* and *Malkhut*.

[630] Existence in the terrestrial world would be degrading for them.

[631] And if you were to reply that existence in this world is, on the contrary, an honor for them, why do they leave this world?

[632] The purpose of the soul's descent into the world is to learn Torah and to perfect itself through the fulfillment of the commandments and good deeds. When it has acquired this perfection, it returns to the upper world.

the world below, because they come from the side of the king, from the male side, and this arousal comes to the female from the male side, and then love is aroused; for the male arouses his affection and love for the female, and then the female is connected in love to the male.[633] It is like this: the yearning of the female to cast up the lower waters toward the upper waters is [accomplished] only through the souls of the righteous.

Happy are the righteous, in this world and in the world to come, for upon them depend the upper and the lower realms. Therefore it is written, without qualification, "The righteous is the foundation (yesod) of the world" (Proverbs 10: 25). The mystery of all is that the righteous is the foundation of the world above,[634] and the foundation of the world below,[635] and the Assembly of Israel is comprised of the righteous above and the righteous below. The righteous at one extreme, and the righteous at the other extreme, inherit her. This is [the meaning of] the verse: "The righteous shall inherit the land" (Psalm 37: 29). They shall really inherit "the land."[636]

---

[633] The arousal is from the male side by means of the souls of the righteous, which are emanated from the male side. The difficulty at the beginning is therefore resolved. In the world of the sefirot too, it is the male that pursues the female.

[634] The sefirah Yesod, which is called "righteous," is the male element.

[635] The righteous man in this world, who cleaves to the Shekhinah.

[636] "The land" (ha-arez) is Malkhut.

SECTION III. *SHEKHINAH*

INTRODUCTION

a. The Character and Situation of the *Shekhinah*

The last *sefirah* assumes a special character in the sefirotic system. It is represented as the passive female who receives and transmits the influence which descends from the active male forces. A central feature of the Zohar is the description of the essential nature of this *sefirah*, and its multifarious ramifications. Once all the different veils of kabbalistic symbolism have been lifted, the many facets of this *sefirah* become apparent.[1] Its particular characteristic is that it has no light or definite color of its own, but, on the other hand, precisely because of this, it acts as a mirror for every light and colour. The different nuances of color, the rays of light, and the shadows that they cast, flicker unceasingly within the *sefirah*, and, because of this continuous stream of transformations, it is depicted as representing the variegated nature of the divine world.

It is true, of course, that with the other *sefirot* also we find a rich and varied number of symbols used to represent them, but in their case this wide variety is basically nothing more than a manifestation of the different aspects of their single fixed nature that are visible to the contemplation of the mystic. With the last *sefirah* it is quite different, because the changes and the variations take place within its own nature, and affect its position within the system. There are a large number of symbols that specifically depict this unstable quality in the nature of the *sefirah*. It is called *shoshanah* (lily) "because she changes (*ishtaniat*) from color to color, and varies (*shaniat*) her colors" (3); before intercourse "she is green like a rose whose leaves are green," and after intercourse "she is red, with white colors" (ibid.). In contrast to *Tiferet*, which is symbolized by the unchanging white flame of the lamp, *Malkhut* is represented by the lower part of the flame, which is constantly changing color. "This blue-black [light] sometimes changes to red, but the white light above it never changes, for it is always white. However, the blue changes to these colors: sometimes blue or black, and sometimes red" (*Sefirot*, 4). *Tiferet*, which is the Tree of Life, "never changes or turns," but *Malkhut* is represented by the Tree of Knowledge of Good and Evil "which changes and turns from color to color, from good to evil, and from evil to good . . . and it is consequently called 'the sword that turns,' that turns from one side to the other, from good to evil, from Mercy to Judgment, from peace to war; it turns through everything."[2]

Because of its position in the world of emanation, we can trace the origin of these fluctuations to the changing relationships that it has with the *sefirot*. When it is in the situation of intercourse it experiences perfect unity with *Tiferet* and *Yesod*, which are the male forces, and it imbibes from them a stream of Mercy, which is their attribute. In this situation it is also very close to *Ḥesed* and *Gevurah*, and *Nezaḥ* and *Hod*, which are respectively the arms and legs of the male, and it receives from them the flow of Love and Judgment, and consequently it comprises all the "colors." Sometimes, however, its union with all the *sefirot*, pouring out their influence, is not perfect, and then one or other of their attributes becomes dominant. When it is sated with the flow of Love, it bestows abundant blessing on the lower worlds, and then it appears to them as a male force discharging its influence. But when Judgment has the upper hand then it is like a pregnant female, whose goodness is shut up and confined within her. "And this [*Malkhut*] is an angel, sometimes male and sometimes female. That is to say, that when it prepares blessings for the world it is male, and it is called 'male'; as a male prepares blessings for the female, so it prepares blessings for the world. But when it stands in judgment on the world then it is called 'female' . . . . Consequently, it is written 'the flaming sword that turned every way' (Genesis 3: 24): there are angels sent out into the world who turn into several colors, sometimes females, sometimes males, sometimes Judgment, sometimes Mercy, and all are [comprised] in one color. So this angel [appears] in many colors, and all the colors of the world are in this place . . . and because all these colors are in it, it is also ruler of the whole world."[3]

Malkhut's activity as ruler of the world, alluded to at the end of this passage, presents us with a completely new view of its status. It is now seen as being outside the system of the *sefirot*, and in this position it undergoes further changes. In relation to the upper world it is the last link in the chain of emanation, acting as a receptacle for the supernal flow of influence, and representing the extreme limit of the divine being. In relation to the lower world, however, it is the very beginning and highest point, assuming the role of mother and ruler of the world. When looked at in this way, it is presented as a parallel force to the three upper *sefirot*, and it is given their names. Like the first *sefirah*, which stands at the head of the divine order of things as supernal *Keter*, it is called "*atarah*" (crown), for all the worlds are crowned by it. In the writings of the Gerona kabbalists it is also called "*razon*" (will). *Keter* is the hidden Will, preceding Thought, stimulating it, and setting it in motion; and *Malkhut* is the will that puts into practice the ideas that occur within Thought. In relation to the second *sefirah*, *Hokhmah*, the creative wisdom of Thought, *Malkhut* is called "the lower *Hokhmah*," that is, the wisdom of practical affairs and government. Both of them are envisaged as a point: *Hokhmah* as the very first point in the development of the forces of emanation, and *Malkhut* as the topmost point of the worlds, where the whole of non-divine existence is concentrated before it spreads outward. The parallel with *Binah* is mainly one of femininity and motherhood: the upper mother and the lower mother. But the importance of the connection here is further enhanced by the use of the name "*Shekhinah*," which is applied to both of them: an upper *Shekhinah* and a lower *Shekhinah*. The parallel in this case proceeds from lower to upper. The name "*Shekhinah*" is assigned first to *Malkhut*, and from there it is transferred to *Binah*. In aggadic literature the *Shekhinah* is the divine presence, existing and active in the world and among the people of Israel. It is identified in kabbalistic doctrine with the last *sefirah* in its capacity as the ruler of the world, and as "the Assembly of Israel" in the realms above, a designation reserved exclusively for *Malkhut*. Now, since the activity of *Binah* in the upper worlds is similar to the activity of *Malkhut* in the lower worlds, it is also called the "upper *Shekhinah*." We see revealed in the image of the *Shekhinah* the features of *Malkhut* as it turns away from its place, and from its links with the sefirotic system, toward nondivine existence. The *Shekhinah* becomes here a broad curtain embroidered with a number of specific symbols, which I shall later discuss in more detail.

I have so far mentioned two positions in connection with *Malkhut*: first, its position in the scheme of emanation, and, second, its position at the head of the created world, and also within it. But it has a third position, and this completes the many-faceted character of this *sefirah*. This position is its relationship to *sitra ahra* ("the other side"), the domain of the evil powers.[4] The husks, the powers of uncleanness, burst out of the darkness of the deep in their desire to get near the realm of holiness and feed on it, and they lie in ambush near the *Shekhinah*. In this situation it is "like a lily among thorns," and it needs special protection to prevent it from being pierced by the thorns. The relationship that it has with its evil neighbors undergoes many vicissitudes. Sometimes it has the upper hand and it subdues and dominates the husks, but at others the power of "the other side" prevails, and the serpent breaches the walls of the sanctuary and overcomes the *Shekhinah*, as I shall describe below.

And so the *Shekhinah* is placed in, and connected very strongly to, the three systems which, in kabbalistic teaching, constitute the totality of existence: the system of the *sefirot*, the system of the worlds, and the system of the husks. Several symbols—that of the sea, for example—serve to illustrate the fluctuations in its character and situation as it comes into contact with each particular system. In the sefirotic system, it is the great sea, which receives the torrents of influence that flow into it. In its activity as ruler of the worlds, the sea nourishes the worlds with its waters, whose taste changes from sweet to bitter and from bitter to sweet, depending on the nature of the characteristic, Love or Judgment, that is dominant at the time. But when "the other side" subjugates the *Shekhinah*, the waters of the sea turn into "waters of cursing" (Numbers 5: 22), which bring a curse upon the world. "Come and see. A number of sweet streams enter this holy sea, but because it is the judgment of the world its waters are bitter, for the death of all the world's inhabitants is contained therein. But, although they are bitter, when they begin to spread forth they become sweet. Sometimes the waters of the sea are bitter, and sometimes it is a sea that swallows up all the other waters, and it is called 'the congealed sea,' and it swallows up all the others and draws them into itself, and they do not trickle out. Sometimes [the sources of] the waters are opened, and there flows forth from the sea whatever proceeds towards the lower worlds. And this sea is sustained in many different ways. 'The waters of cursing'—when the serpent comes and spews out venom, they are 'the waters of cursing.' "[5]

b. Cutting and Separation

The large number of changes that take place in the nature of the *Shekhinah*, and all the different relationships that it has, raise the problem of its unification with the other *sefirot*. I have already discussed, in another connection, the difficulties and complexities that arise in the kabbalistic concept of the divine unity as a result of the dualism of *En-Sof* and the sefirotic system on the one hand, and the plurality of the *sefirot* on the other. And I described this concept as one of dynamic unity.[6] But does not this view of the *Shekhinah* imply the complete disintegration of this unity? Does not the fact that this divine force is joined at times, either voluntarily or by compulsion, with nondivine forces remove the very foundation of the idea of unity?

The kabbalists undoubtedly saw the point of this question, and understood the theological peril involved. In their mystical speculation on the nature of sin, they saw as "the root of rebellion" and as the denial of the main principle of faith the concept of the *Shekhinah* as a separate independent power, divorced from the system of the *sefirot*. On the other hand, they did not deny the possibility of such a divorce. The basis of unification in mystical terms is the mystery of intercourse between the *Shekhinah* and her "husband," *Tiferet*; that is to say, her inseparable connection with the sefirotic system.[7] And man's religious task is to sustain this unification through devotion in prayer and the fulfillment of the commandments. Only through concentration on this unification is man both able and permitted to draw near to the *Shekhinah* and to serve her in divine worship, and then she becomes a window through which the divine light may shine, a channel for the transmission of influence to the lower worlds, and a gate through which the soul may enter the divine realm. The *Shekhinah*'s rule over the world and her association with cosmic forces are both effected through the mystery of the unification, without her being separated from the system of the *sefirot*. Her radiance spreads out and settles on the world, and her power is active in it, but at the same time she dwells in her place in the world of emanation and is to be found in the upper realms, like the sun, which is fixed in the heavens but spreads its light upon the earth. "Thus have we learned: When the sun shines it is in the heavens, but its power and its strength rule throughout the earth. And so 'the whole earth is full of his glory' (Isaiah 6: 3) . . . . Come and see. There is the *Shekhinah* below and the *Shekhinah* above. The *Shekhinah* is above in the twelve regions of the holy chariots and among the twelve supernal *ḥayyot* (creatures); the *Shekhinah* is below among the twelve holy tribes. Thus the *Shekhinah* above and below is comprised together, and everything is united at one and the same time" (23).[8] But if man isolates the *Shekhinah* in his own thought, and wishes to cleave to her, and worship her on her own in her capacity as a ruler of the world, and therefore very near to the lower worlds, he damages the divine unity and is like an idolater. "If he who brings an offering to this name [i.e., to the *Shekhinah*] is denounced thus in the Torah: 'He that sacrifices to the gods . . . shall be utterly destroyed' (Exodus 22: 19), the man who changes its specific name should be denounced even more harshly."[9]

Such a thought, which disqualifies an act of worship, and which to the mystic is the fundamental sin, is called "cutting the shoots," after a well-known phrase in the *aggadah* concerning the four scholars who entered Paradise: "the 'Other' cut the shoots."[10] The "shoots" are the *sefirot*, which are planted in the garden of the world of emanation, and the sin of "cutting," which was committed even by Elisha ben Abuyah (the "Other"), is the separation of the *sefirot* from one another in mystic contemplation, and particularly the severance of the *Shekhinah* from the sefirotic system. This was also the sin of Adam, described in the Bible as eating the fruit of the Tree of Knowledge, and it is in connection with Adam's sin that the mystery of this "cutting" is explained in the Zohar.[11]

The Tree of Knowledge is the *Shekhinah*, and the prohibition of eating from it really means that it is prohibited to cleave to her with the intention of separating her. But Adam did separate the Tree of Knowledge from the Tree of Life, which is *Tiferet*. In other words, in his thought he destroyed the divine unity.

The consequences of the sin of "cutting" are not restricted to the punishment that the sinner brings upon himself. This sin has an effect upon the upper worlds and does real harm to the *Shekhinah*. The thought of separation causes the forces in the Godhead actually to separate; the links that connect the *Shekhinah* to *Tiferet*, and to the other *sefirot* are severed, and the channels of influence are stopped up. The state of separation that results from the sin is depicted by using a number of different symbols. In terms of the male-female image, the *Shekhinah* is like a forlorn and forsaken woman. In the linguistic symbolism of voice and speech (*Tiferet* and the *Shekhinah*) the consequence of the "cutting" is a dumbness caused by the separation of speech from voice; that is, the "cutting" compels the *Shekhinah* to be silent in her solitude.[12] The most important and most profound symbol in this connection is that of the Tree of Death. The Tree of Knowledge contains the death-force, which is not revealed while it remains united with the Tree of Life; but once Knowledge is divorced from Life the Tree of Knowledge becomes the Tree of Death. This is the mystery of death, which is decreed for the world at the instigation of the serpent. " 'From every tree of the garden you may freely eat' (Genesis 2: 16); He allowed him everything [even the Tree of Knowledge], that he might eat them together in unity. . . . But this tree [the Tree of Knowledge] is the Tree of Death. . . . Whoever takes it on its own dies, for he takes a deadly potion in that he separates it from Life. Consequently, 'on the day that you eat of it you shall surely die', because he will have separated the shoots."[13]

In this connection the symbol of the Tree of Death[14] is used in two senses. In one sense, death signifies the kindling of the fire of Judgment, and the dominant power of anger, in the *Shekhinah*. When she is active in the mystery of unification, all the attributes are comprised and intermingled within her, and sometimes she has a favorable inclination toward Love. But in actual essence she is much more closely connected with *Gevurah*, which is strict Judgment, and consequently she is called "the attribute of lenient Judgment." Therefore when she is in the position of complete separation, and removed from the influence of the *sefirot*, the power of Judgment that is within her becomes dominant, and bursts forth in all its strength and fury. Then she acts like a raging and devouring fire, casting terror upon the world and its inhabitants. "There is no one in the world who can abide with her [i.e., the *Shekhinah*] unless he can arouse this 'good' [*Yesod*] toward her. . . . And if you cannot arouse this 'good' to meet her, keep far away from her and do not go near her; do not go into the raging fiery furnace. And if you do go near her, do so in fear, like someone who is fearful of death, for the fire is raging and is burning the world with its flames."[15]

The Tree of Death symbolizes, in another sense, the complete separation of the *Shekhinah* from the forces of holiness, and her union with "the other side," which by its very nature seeks to act as a force of death and destruction. The most desirable situation would be for the *Shekhinah* to be specifically united in intercourse with *Tiferet*, and to be linked thereby, through the power of the influence that she receives in intercourse, to the forces of the Chariot and the angels that are below it. She would thus be preserved from any union or close contact with "the other side." Adam's sin of "cutting" threw the situation of the *Shekhinah* into complete disarray, and overturned the whole system. "And this is the sin; namely, that the primordial serpent promoted a union below [with "the other side"] and a separation above [in the system of the *sefirot*], and therefore brought certain consequences upon the world, for the separation should have been below, and the union above. And the black light [the *Shekhinah*] should be united above in a single union, and be united subsequently in its unification with its entourage. And [one needs] to separate it from the evil side."[16] This is the most serious consequence of the sin of "cutting." The *Shekhinah* becomes, as it were, a demonic force, a partner of "the other side." Whoever cleaves to her in this situation attracts to himself the spirit of idolatry, of bloodshed, and of sexual immorality.[17] A fundamental change takes place in the character of the sacred female in the divine realm, and verses from Proverbs and Ecclesiastes[18] dealing with the "strange" and evil woman are interpreted with specific reference to her.[19]

c. The Attribute of Judgment and its Relationship to "the Other Side"

The connection of the dominance of Judgment in the *Shekhinah* with its union with "the other side," in the symbol of the Tree of Death, requires me to clarify still further the relationship between divine Judgment and "the other side," and I shall deal with this in a later section. But here I need to say a little about this with specific reference to the *Shekhinah*.

We must distinguish a number of different stages in the activity of the *Shekhinah* as the attribute of Judgment. Its relationship with "the other side" changes from one stage to the other, and even undergoes a complete dialectic reversal. When it rules over the world, it acts as the heavenly court, and it manifests the attribute of Judgment through its role as the righteous judge; that is to say, by limiting the hitherto unlimited flow of Love, and by giving rewards and punishments to match its demands for righteousness and virtue: "for Righteousness [the *Shekhinah*] reveals the supernal *Gevurah* and the rule of the Holy One, blessed be He; and [the Holy One, blessed be He] has given Righteousness dominion over all the worlds, so that it might manage them and put them in order, as is fitting" (7). When the world is in its ordered state, and is no longer subject, through its iniquities, to the side of guilt, the *Shekhinah* ceases to act in this role with the flame of strict Judgment. On the contrary, the strict Judgment of *Gevurah*, which the mortals of this world could not possibly survive because of its enormous power, becomes weaker and more lenient within the *Shekhinah*, and reaches the lower worlds in sweetness. "If [*Gevurah*] were to arouse Judgment against this world [the inhabitants of] the world would not be able to bear it, for no one can bear that mighty supernal fire except the lower fire [the *Shekhinah*], which is a fire that bears fire. But just as this world is the lowest of all worlds, so all its judgments come from [the *Shekhinah*, called] 'the lower world,' for it is the God-judge, and it is called 'the heavenly Judgment on this world.' "[20]

There are many forces, depicted as armed military companies, that surround the *Shekhinah*, and precede it, and act as its messengers in order to sustain the rule of righteousness in the world (8). When the wicked are to be punished, it also makes use of the powers of "the other side," in order to maintain the supremacy of divine righteousness. "When Righteousness arouses itself through its judgments, a number of noonday destructions arouse themselves, on the right hand and on the left hand, and a number of rods emerge from them, rods of fire, rods of hot coals, rods of flame; all of them emerge and are aroused in the world, and scourge mankind" (*The Activity of "the Other Side"*, 8). Even when the source of the *Shekhinah*'s influence is stopped up by the forces of "the other side," when they are like a stone on the mouth of a well, they still act at its behest in order to preserve the line of strict justice. "Subsequently, 'they put the stone back'—at the behest of the well, that they might stand before it and demand justice for the world, so that the world might conduct itself in justice. And this is necessary, for the world can endure only through justice, so that everything may exist in truth and righteousness" (4). Here we have then one aspect of the relationship between the attribute of Judgment and "the other side"—a master-servant relationship. The forces of evil are subject to the rule of the *Shekhinah*, and are active in the world as her ministers, performing her will.

"The other side," however, is not content with this dependent role, and tries to break the yoke of the *Shekhinah* and rule over her. He lies in wait at the *Shekhinah*'s door ("sin couches at the door"—Genesis 4: 7),[21] looking for the appropriate moment to seize and subdue her. He is mainly intent on interrupting the sacred intercourse of male and female within the Godhead, so that the male force in him, which is designated sometimes as Samael and at other times as the serpent, can take hold of the *Shekhinah* as she becomes separated from her husband, and have intercourse with her. The sins of Israel increase his power, and he seeks with their help to put his plans into practice. The *Shekhinah* finds herself in great peril, and a struggle begins between her and "the other side." In this struggle the fire of strict Judgment is kindled within the Godhead, and the *Shekhinah* is filled with sacred fury. With the power of this flaming Judgment she acts like an avenging sword, and she repels and crushes the rebel slave, who is seeking to profane her glory. "*Het* [i.e., sin, 'the other side'] lies very close to her. The tribes do not contain these letters, because they come from the side of holiness on high, but the letters do remain close to her. . . . When this tree [the *Shekhinah*] is victorious, the good side seizes 'the other side' completely, and subjugates it" (*Events and Personalities*, 21). The victory of the *Shekhinah* over "the other side" is revealed below in the vengeance that she takes on the nations, who are the representatives in the world of the powers of uncleanness. "Come and see. When the Holy One, blessed be He, wishes to take vengeance upon the idolatrous nations, the left [*Gevurah*] is aroused, and the moon [the *Shekhinah*] is filled with blood from that side. Then the wells and the streams below, all those of the left side, flow with blood."[22] The *Shekhinah* in her struggle comes into contact with the serpent, but she remains clean and undefiled, and, as a token of her purity, she is examined before divine intercourse is renewed, on the pattern of the examination of the adulteress. "The holy land [i.e., the *Shekhinah*] was under the authority of the Holy One, blessed be He, and no alien authority had access there. How could the holy land be examined [to see] if she had remained faithful, and was not united with any alien authority? By bringing an offering of barley, on the pattern of the suspected adulteress" (*Events and Personalities*, 21).[23]

On this view of the struggle between holiness and uncleanness, the power of Judgment and "the other side" have a distinctly hostile relationship to one another. The dominance of Judgment in the *Shekhinah* leads to the destruction of evil. But in the portrayal of the examination of the *Shekhinah* as a suspected adulteress, we can already see another possibility, namely, that the *Shekhinah*'s power of resistance in the struggle may be too feeble, and she may eventually be united with "the other side." We come back here to the point from which we started, in our explanation of the symbol of the Tree of Death. The existence of the *Shekhinah* in the sefirotic system depends on deeds performed in the lower worlds. And when they adversely affect her through the sin of "cutting," or when the world is inclined toward the side of guilt because of the multiplicity of its sins and the dominance of evil in Israel, then the power of "the other side" gains the ascendancy, and is able to subjugate the *Shekhinah*; and the fury of Judgment, which burns in her in this situation, is liable to become subservient to "the other side" and to be used by it as a means of death and destruction. "But when the wicked increase in the world, the Assembly of Israel [the *Shekhinah*] does not exude sweet perfumes, so to speak, and she tastes of the bitter "other side" . . . and her face is darkened" (*Sefirot*, 31). The male force in "the other side" succeeds in having intercourse with her and defiling her. "This serpent is the left arm of the spirit of uncleanness, and his rider [Samael] takes hold of it, and he approaches the moon [the *Shekhinah*] and attracts her into the close association of plucking [i.e., intercourse], and she becomes defiled."[24] While she is subject to "the other side" she is thought of as a menstruant with regard to her "proper" husband, and he keeps aloof from her. "When the powerful serpent of the realms above arouses himself because of the sins of the world, and dwells and unites with the female [the *Shekhinah*] and casts his filth upon her, the male [*Tiferet*] leaves her, because she has been defiled, and she is called 'unclean,' and it is not proper for the male to approach her, for it would be woeful for him to be defiled with her at a time when she is unclean. . . . Woe to him who approaches her at that time, for whoever approaches her causes a defect to be seen in the realms above."[25] Whoever cleaves to the *Shekhinah* during her uncleanness imbibes from her the poison of death, because she is at that time in union with "the other side", and she nourishes his forces through her role as mother of the husks. "And all of them [including the powers of uncleanness] depend upon this mother [the *Shekhinah*], the holy mother, and they cling to her. When do they cling to her? When this mother is nourished by 'the other side' [i.e., is in intercourse with the male], and the Temple is defiled, and the powerful serpent begins to reveal himself, then the kid [i.e., the husks] feeds on its mother's milk, and the judgments [of 'the other side'] are aroused."[26]

To sum up: There are three ways in which the power of Judgment in the *Shekhinah* is revealed in the world, and in each one we see a different relationship between the *Shekhinah* and "the other side." First of all, we have the Judgment of justice, which promotes the rule of righteousness and virtue in order to sustain the world, and here the forces of "the other side" act as its henchmen. Second, we have the Judgment of vengeance, which acts in order to protect the *Shekhinah* and to rescue her from her tormentors, and it has weapons that it can use in its battle against the husks. Third, we have the Judgment of fury, which is aroused because of the sins of the world, and is a reaction to the harm that has been done to the *Shekhinah*. This last Judgment becomes a destructive power that helps to destroy the world, when "the other side" wins its battle with the forces of holiness. It is in this particular aspect of Judgment that the *Shekhinah* becomes divorced from the sefirotic system and is joined to the system of the husks; and the seeds of destruction, which are concealed in the very nature of the attribute of Judgment, germinate and produce the Tree of Death of "the other side."

d. The Mother of the World and the Assembly of Israel

This aspect of fury, which we have seen in the *Shekhinah* as the attribute of Judgment, casts fear and trembling on the world, and death and destruction are also implicit in it. When it is joined with "the other side" then it assumes a demonic character. But it also has completely opposite features, bright and resplendent, which are revealed in its role as the all-merciful mother[27] who showers kindness and love upon all, and particularly on the people Israel, who owe their origin to her, and who continue to look to her for succor.

As the center of the world, and the source of its birth and continued existence, the *Shekhinah* is symbolized by the foundation-stone, which is placed in the middle of the world. "When the Holy One, blessed be He, created the world, He threw down a precious stone from beneath the throne of His glory, and it sank into the deep. One edge (lit., head) of the stone became lodged in the deeps, and another in the realms above. And there was another edge, a supernal one, a single point [i.e. the *Shekhinah*], which is in the middle of the world, and the world expanded from there, to the right and to the left, and upon all sides, and it is sustained by this central point" (*The Account of Creation*, 7). The world receives from this stone its flow of blessing. "Why is [the stone] called *shetiyah* (foundation)? First, because from it the world was founded (*ashtil*); and second, *shetiyah* is *shat yah* (the Lord placed), for the Holy One, blessed be He, placed it so that the world might receive blessing from it" (ibid., 8). In a very similar symbolic description we find its position vis-à-vis the worlds represented by the central point of a circle, on which the whole circle depends.[28]

The mercifulness of the *Shekhinah*, and her devoted sustenance of the worlds and the created beings who are entrusted to her care, are emphasized in many passages in the Zohar. Here are two of the more noteworthy examples of these symbolic-aggadic descriptions. The *Shekhinah* is called "the redeeming angel," because she acts as the divine agent in the world whose task it is to support the children of her household. "She is called 'an angel' when she is a messenger from above and receives glorious light from the supernal mirror, for then father and mother [*Hokhmah* and *Binah*] bless her, and say to her, 'Go, my daughter, and keep your house. Look after your house. This is what you shall do to your house: go and feed them. Go, for the world below is waiting for you. The members of your household expect food from you. You have all that is necessary to provide for them'" (*Events and Personalities*, 21). On the basis of rabbinic parables concerning the hind, she is described as a merciful hind, who occupies herself with providing food for the other animals. "It is a particular animal, a merciful one, than whom there is none more merciful among all the animals of the world; for when time presses, and she needs food both for herself and for all the animals, she goes far away on a distant journey and comes back bringing food. And she has no desire to eat until she has returned to her place. Why? So that the other animals may assemble near her and she can distribute the food. When she returns all the other animals assemble near her, and she stands in the middle and distributes [food] to each one of them. . . . And she is satisfied by the food that she distributes, as if she had eaten more than any one else" (5).

The most common personality symbol used to designate the role of the *Shekhinah* as ruler of the world is that of queen or consort. Out of his great love and devotion to her the king entrusts to her all the powers with which to rule the world (8). The creatures (*Ḥayyot*) of the chariot, the wheels (*Ofannim*), and the angels make up her retinue in the royal court. They dwell in the upper palaces, ministering to her, and executing her wishes. The queen-symbol is assigned to her both in her actions of Judgment and in her actions of Mercy, depending on the deeds of the lower worlds. In the descriptions of the normal method of ruling the world, we find that great emphasis is placed on the gentleness and grace of the queen, and on the adoration and complete trust of her servants. All the dwellers on high praise and glorify her, and yearn to take shelter in her shadow and to benefit from the radiance of her glory. Her maidens and the members of her entourage assist her when she adorns herself before intercourse with her husband. "And the maidens who stand with her adorn and beautify themselves with finery, one behind her, one in front of her, one on this side, and one on that, and she stands in the middle, and the Sanhedrin of seventy-two stand in their semi-circular court in order to make a circle around the moon [the *Shekhinah*], [so that] the consort might adorn herself for her husband" (14). The reciprocal love relationship that exists between the ruler and her subjects becomes evident when she suffers the distress of being separated from her husband, when "she makes herself extremely small, because of the thrust of love that she cannot bear, until nothing can be seen of her but the tiniest point." Then she has not the power to supply the needs of her servants, and with great grief "she envelops herself straightaway with all her hosts and her companies, and she says 'I am black' . . . meaning 'I have no room to bring you in under my wings'. . . . Therefore 'Do not look upon me' [meaning] 'Do not look at me at all, because I am a tiny point.' " The diminution of the adored queen and her self-conceal-ment plunge her deserted servants into gloom and dismay, and in their distress "they roar like mighty lions." Their roaring arouses the king, who draws the long-suffering queen toward him in love. "When she has been restored and rendered beautiful in her image, as at the beginning, they and all the remaining hosts stand, ready to listen to what she says, and she stands like a king among his troops" (*Events and Personalities*, 21). This moving description presents a beautiful picture of the queen as a merciful and much-loved mother.

However, the height of maternal perfection is revealed in the *Shekhinah's* connection with Israel. Whereas the other nations of the world are not subject to the rule and providence of the *Shekhinah* directly, but only through guardian angels specifically appointed for them, Israel is the most precious son, the most cherished child, with whom the supernal mother occupies herself directly, and whose destiny is her chief cause of concern. " 'My dove, my undefiled is but one.

She is the only one of her mother.' This is the holy *Shekhinah*, emerging from the protective vessels, the light of light, illuminating all, and she is called 'mother.' This is what the Holy One, blessed be He, did on earth. He scattered all the peoples on every side, and appointed guardian angels over them . . . and He took as His own portion the Assembly of Israel . . . and He called her 'My dove, my undefiled, [who] is but one. She is the only one of her mother.' This is the *Shekhinah* of His glory, which He caused to dwell among them, unique, and reserved for her alone" (*Events and Personalities*, 2). The male and female elements in the Godhead are father and mother to Israel, and not only to the nation as a whole, but to every individual, because the holy souls of the Jewish people are produced by intercourse in the upper realms, and they fly down to the world from the *Shekhinah*. The strong ties that exist between these *sefirot* and Israel are represented by symbols of a specifically nationalistic character. *Tiferet* is called "the old man Israel," and the *Shekhinah* "the Assembly of Israel." *Yesod* and *Malkhut* are Zion and Jerusalem. And, in another guise, the female quality of the *Shekhinah*, the mystery of the womb, is symbolized by the designation "Zion," or "Holy of Holies." The name "Assembly of Israel" (*knesset yisrael*), which frequently occurs as the usual title of the *Shekhinah*, signifies the divine essence of the people Israel concentrated in the *Shekhinah*. It is even because of Israel that the *Shekhinah* dwells in the world. When the Temple was still standing, and Israel dwelt in its land, the *Shekhinah* also resided there in the Holy of Holies, like a chaste woman who does not go out of the door of her house. And when Israel went into exile, she went with them into the lands of the other nations in order to protect them. " 'In the covert of the cliff"—this is the place that is called 'the Holy of Holies,' the heart of the entire world. And so it is written 'In the covert of the cliff.' Since the *Shekhinah* secluded herself there, like a woman who is faithful to her husband, not venturing outside the house . . . so the Assembly of Israel did not live anywhere except in its place, in the seclusion of that level, apart from the days of exile when it is in the lands of the dispersion. And because it is in exile the other peoples enjoy prosperity and tranquillity" (24).[29] The *Shekhinah* bestows her influence upon Israel alone, but through them the whole world is nourished by the residue of this influence. "When the Temple was still standing, Israel would perform their rites, and bring offerings and sacrifices. And the *Shekhinah* rested upon them in the Temple, like a mother hovering over her children, and all faces were resplendent with light, so that there was blessing both above and below. And there was not a single day without blessings and joys, and Israel dwelt securely in the land, and the whole world was nourished because of them" (16). The tribes of Israel are the *Shekhinah*'s chariots in the world, and they match the twelve chariots that she has in the realms above. "There is another arrangement below, the arrangement of the bride [the *Shekhinah*] that Solomon mentioned in the Song of Songs . . . and this arrangement is with twelve tribes, who are below her, and they are the arrangement of her body . . . for this sea [the *Shekhinah*] is arranged with the number twelve in both worlds, twelve above, the chariots of the appointed ones [i.e., the angels] . . . and below, the twelve tribes."[30] Mother and children dwell together, and they depend upon one another. Israel can exist only beneath the wings of the *Shekhinah*, and she likewise cannot fulfill her role completely without the love of her children.

e. The Exile of the *Shekhinah*

The bonds that the *Shekhinah* has with Israel in her role as the divine mother of the nation, and as "the Assembly of Israel" in the realms above, are expressed even more emphatically in the development of the idea of the exile of the *Shekhinah*, which originated in rabbinic *aggadah*.[31] "Come and see how beloved Israel are to the Holy One, blessed be He, for wherever they are exiled the *Shekhinah* is with them ... and when they are redeemed in the future the *Shekhinah* will again be with them, as it is said 'And the Lord, your God, will return with your captivity' (Deuteronomy 30: 3). It does not say 'He will bring back,' but 'He will return,'[32] meaning that the Holy One, blessed be He, will return with them from their places of exile."[33] The rabbis intended, by this concept, to stress the eternal love that the Holy One, blessed be He, has for Israel. He is faithful to the covenant that He made with His chosen people, even when they rebel against Him through their transgressions. And as a sign of His love He joins them in their sufferings and their wanderings in the lands of their exile. In kabbalistic literature, and especially in the Zohar, this idea is equated with the new mystical and mythical concept of the *Shekhinah* as the female force in the Godhead, and as the supernal mother of Israel. The whole topic, with its various nuances, is bound up with the complex network of relationships between the female *Shekhinah* and the *sefirot*, the lower worlds, and "the other side." The Zohar usually describes the exile of the *Shekhinah* by means of parables and aggadic stories, and the absence of logical consistency here is quite striking. Different, and sometimes opposing, motifs are all jumbled together, and on occasions they are intermingled in one and the same passage. For the sake of clarity, I shall try to separate out and analyze the various themes.

According to one version, the mother-*Shekhinah* goes into exile quite willingly, out of love and pity for her exiled children. She cannot forsake them in their time of trouble, and she tries to bear the burden of defeat and subjection with them, in order to strengthen and protect them, and to hasten their final redemption. When the Temple, which was her abode, was destroyed, she bewailed and lamented this terrible catastrophe. "When the Temple was destroyed the *Shekhinah* came and went up to all those places where she used to dwell at first, and she would weep for her home and for Israel, who had gone into exile, and for all the righteous and the pious ones who used to be there and had perished" (16). She is symbolized by Rachel, the mother of the nation, weeping for her children. "Whenever Israel go into exile she weeps for them, for she is their mother."[34] When she saw that the Holy One, blessed be He, had departed from Israel, and had decreed that they should go into exile, she left her husband, and joined her children in exile. "It is like the king who was angry with his son, and for a punishment decreed that he should go far away from him to a distant land. The consort heard of this and said, 'Since my son has gone to a distant land, and the king has expelled him from his palace, I shall not forsake him. Either we both return to the royal palace, or we both live together in another land.' "[35] She takes it upon herself to protect the nations while she is in their lands, so that Israel who are dispersed there may also be protected. " 'They made me keeper of the vineyards,' so that I might go into exile to keep the other peoples, for Israel's sake. 'But my own vineyard I have not kept,' for I am not able to keep them as I did at the beginning. Before, I kept my own vineyard, and the other vineyards were kept as a result, but now I keep the other vineyards, so that my own vineyard among them should be kept" (25). We see here that in the exile of the *Shekhinah* there is no implication of dismissal or divorce, and in one particular passage this fact is clearly emphasized: "And if you say 'She is in exile, and she has been divorced,' this is not the case. She actually went into exile in order to live with Israel and to protect them, but she was not divorced."[36]

A similar viewpoint can be seen in another version, according to which the Holy One, blessed be He, leaves the *Shekhinah* with Israel as a surety that He will fulfill the covenant that exists between them, that He will never forsake them, and that He will come and redeem them. In other words, the exile of the *Shekhinah* is due not to the mother's pity but to the continuing love of the father. "Even though the Holy One, blessed be He, has gone far away from us, He has left a surety with us, and we take care of His greatest treasure. Whoever wants His surety—let him come and dwell with us. Therefore 'I will set My tabernacle among you'—I shall put My surety in your hands, so that I may dwell with you. And even though Israel are now in exile, they have the surety of the Holy One, blessed be He, and they will never forsake it" (27). This means that the male force in the Godhead has imposed upon himself a separation from the female for the good of Israel. And when his desire for the distant consort is too strong to bear, he comes and is revealed, for her sake, in the synagogues and schools of the exile. "Happy are Israel, because their merit is such that they have been given this surety from the supernal King; for, even though they are in exile, the Holy One, blessed be He, comes on the New Moons, and Sabbaths, and Festivals, to take care of them, and to look at the surety that they hold for Him, for it is an object He cherishes. . . . When the desire of the Holy One, blessed be He, for the consort and for Israel is aroused, He climbs mountains, descends cliffs, and mounts walls in order to look at and care for them through the lattices in the wall. When He sees them, He begins to weep. This is [the meaning of] the verse 'My beloved is like a gazelle, or a young hart,' because He leaps from wall to mountain, and from mountain to wall. 'Behold, he stands behind our wall' (Song of Songs 2: 9)—in the synagogues, and in the schools."[37] The *Shekhinah* in exile is like a beautiful bride who lives in the street of the tanners, and were it not for the great desire that the Holy One, blessed be He, has for her, He would not enter such a despicable place. "It is like a man who was in love with a woman who lived in the street of the tanners. If she had not been there, he would never have set foot in the place; but because she was there it seemed to him like the street of the spice merchants, where all the finest perfumes in the world could be found" (28).

In these two versions, despite the basic differences in the nature and image of the *Shekhinah*, we can detect far-reaching and intricate variations on the old, original theme of the *aggadah*. But an absolutely different note is struck in the descriptions of the exile of the *Shekhinah* as the rejection of the consort, or the supernal mother.[38] It is said of her, in her role as the heavenly Assembly of Israel, "The Holy One, blessed be He, does not overthrow a nation, until He first overthrows its guardian angel."[39] The *Shekhinah* is thus dislodged from her throne, and dismissed from her home, when the time comes for the destruction of the Temple and the exile of Israel. "When the Holy One, blessed be He, wished to destroy His house below, and the holy land below, He first put aside the holy land above [the *Shekhinah*], and made her come down from the level where she took nourishment from the sacred heavens [*Tiferet*], and afterward He destroyed the one below" (17). The *Shekhinah* is like Israel's guardian angel, and her destiny is bound up with the destiny of the people assigned to her charge. Their joint fate is particularly evident when she is seen as the mother of the nation. The child's upbringing is a duty imposed upon the mother, and she becomes responsible for his actions. If the child sins and goes astray, she shares his guilt and is punished with him. "Come and see. Whenever Israel go far away from the king's palace, the consort, so to speak, goes away with them. For what reason? Because the consort did not give the son instruction by chastising him—for the king does not chastise his son but leaves everything to the consort: the management of the palace, the chastisement of the child, and his upbringing in the true way that leads to the king . . . and the mystery of this is in the verse 'For your transgressions was your mother put away,' 'Your mother' is the Assembly of Israel" (26). And so the *Shekhinah* is forcibly dismissed, as it were, and exile is decreed for her, which she must suffer with Israel. "Sometimes [the son] sins, as at the beginning. What does the king do? He dismisses him, and his mother with him, from the palace. He says, 'You will both go, and you will both suffer exile and chastisement there.' "[40] The rejected *Shekhinah* is plunged into the great anguish of separation; the outpouring of influence from the supernal realm is taken away from her; she is as if struck dumb, and without any strength. "It is written 'I was dumb with silence, I held my peace, had no comfort' (Psalm 39: 3). 'I was dumb with silence'—this verse is spoken in exile by the Assembly of Israel [the *Shekhinah*]. For what reason? Because the voice [*Tiferet*] governs speech [the *Shekhinah*], and when she is in exile the voice is separated from her, and no word is heard . . . for she is dumb in exile, and silent, with no voice."[41] This is the mystical explanation for the cessation of prophecy in exile: the divine speech is dumb.[42] In this situation the unity of the tetragrammaton is destroyed, for the last letter, *he*, which symbolizes the *Shekhinah*, is detached from the other letters.[43] To add insult to injury, the king invites the servant-girl, Lilith, to take the place of the rejected consort, and cohabits with her (18);[44] that is to say, the *Shekhinah* suffers absolute wretchedness and impoverishment while the flow of blessing of the male is given to the female element in "the other side."

The connection with "the other side" brings us to the last aspect of the idea of the *Shekhinah*'s exile. According to several passages in the Zohar, the main cause of her exile was not her rejection by the king, but her capture by "the other side," who, because of Israel's sins, was in the ascendant when the Temple was destroyed. "All the [inhabitants of the] upper and the lower regions wept over her [i.e., the *Shekhinah*], and went into mourning. For what reason? Because 'the other side' had control of her, for he was in control of the holy land" (19). The transfer of the captive *Shekhinah* to the domain of "the other side" causes the nations to exercise power over Israel in the world below. "When Israel sinned, and defiled the land, they immediately forced the *Shekhinah*, as it were, to leave her place, and she drew near to another place [i.e., to "the other side"], and then the other peoples became dominant, and permission to rule was granted them" (24). The subjection of the *Shekhinah* to "the other side," because of the sins of Israel, which was discussed at length in section c above, is the esoteric mystical reason for the exile of the *Shekhinah*. The exile in the realms above means that the divine being is thrown into disorder, the channels of influence are blocked, and the luminaries are damaged, because the *Shekhinah* is separated from the sefirotic system and becomes joined to "the other side." Israel's exile in the lands of the nations is a development parallel to the event taking place in the upper worlds.

This concept of the exile of the *Shekhinah*, which is mentioned many times in the Zohar without its ever being clearly defined, assumes far greater importance in the kabbalistic doctrine of a later age. Lurianic kabbalah, which places the themes of exile and redemption at the very center of its speculation on the "war" between the Godhead and "the other side," seized upon this concept of the *Shekhinah*'s exile and made it the cornerstone of the immense mythical structure that it was later to erect.

NOTES

1. See A. E. Waite, *The Holy Kabbala* (1929), pp. 341ff. The author, a Christian, made a large number of errors in his interpretation of the symbols because he did not have sufficient knowledge of the sources, but, despite this, the material he collected is of considerable interest, as are some of his specific interpretations. See also G. Scholem, "Zur Entwicklungsgeschichte der kabbalistischen Konzeption der Schechinah," *Eranos-Jahrbuch* 21 (1952); 45–107; R. Patai, *The Hebrew Goddess* (1967), pp. 186–206.
2. Zohar I, 221b.
3. Ibid., 232a.
4. I shall deal with the nature and activity of "the other side" in a later section. Here we are concerned only with its relationship to the *Shekhinah*.
5. Zohar III, 125a.
6. See above, pp. 238–40.
7. See Zohar I, 12a and elsewhere.
8. See Rabbi Moses de Leon, *Sefer Shekel ha-Kodesh*, pp. 91–93. With regard to the twelve camps of the *Shekhinah*, which are led by the four angels of the *Shekhinah*, there is an almost parallel passage in the gnostic *Book of Baruch*. There it is stated that the angels of "*Edem*" (the female image in the divine powers, parallel to the *Shekhinah* in the Zohar; the word is a combination of "*Eden*" and "*Adamah*" (Earth); it is also called "Israel") were twelve in number at first, and were subsequently divided into four groups, and these are the four rivers that flow out of the Garden of Eden, according to Genesis 2: 10: "and from thence it was divided, and became four heads." This verse is interpreted several times in the Zohar with reference to the angels of the *Shekhinah*. See below p. 559, nn. 14, 33. See also *Seder Gan Eden* (in Jellinek's *Bet ha-Midrash*, III, p. 138), which is part of the Zoharic literature (see above, p. 123, n. 578). On the gnostic *Book of Baruch* in general, see W. Schultz, *Dokumente der Gnosis* (Jena, 1910), pp. 24–34, 237; H. Leisegang, *Die Gnosis* (Leipzig, 1924), pp. 156–68; H. Jonas, *Gnosis und spätantiker Geist* (Göttingen, 1934), 1: 335–341. On angels and the rivers of the Garden of Eden, see in particular Schultz, pp. 24–26, 32; Leisegang, pp. 158–60, 166–68. We can also draw other interesting parallels, including some dealing with "the mystery of intercourse," between the

Zohar and the gnostic *Book of Baruch*, the remains of which are preserved in Hippolytus, and which belongs to "Judaised" gnostic movements. (Some of the other parallels are noted below on pp. 398 and 474.) It is not impossible that echoes of gnostic mythology in the *Book of Baruch* found their way into the Zohar by way of Christian theological writings, or from undiscovered sources.

9. *Zohar Hadash, Bereshit*, 18c, *Midrash ha-Ne'elam.*

10. B.T. *Hagigah* 14b. See *Bereshit Rabbah*, 19: 4 (in connection with the sin of Adam).

11. See Zohar I, 12a–12b, 35b–36a, 221a–221b.

12. See ibid., 36a.

13. Ibid., 35b.

14. This picture of the Tree of Death, whose use in the Zohar as a symbol of the demonic aspect of the *Shekhinah* is being discussed here, may be found in a work that antedates the Zohar, the *Seder Eliyahu Rabba* (ed. Friedmann, p. 24). G. Scholem has drawn attention to this in his *Von der mystischen Gestalt der Gottheit* (Zürich, 1962), p. 296, n. 88.

15. Zohar III, 110b.

16. Zohar I, 12b.

17. See ibid., 36a.

18. "Her feet go down to death; her steps take hold on Sheol" (Proverbs 5: 5); "I find the woman more bitter than death" (Ecclesiastes 7: 26).

19. Zohar I, 35b. Once Adam was pardoned and forgiven, the *Shekhinah* was released from her subjection to "the other side." But, as a result of the first sin, she continues to act as the Tree of Death in its first sense, i.e., as a power of Judgment, restraining and diminishing the flow of Love in the flood of life. This is the mystical significance of the advent of death and destruction in the world consequent upon the actions of the serpent. "It [the *Shekhinah*] is a tree that contains death, and it rests upon the lower world, and, because everything remains beneath it, it devours and consumes. . . . And there is nothing in the world that does not perish, because the blue light [the *Shekhinah*] consumes whatever it stands upon" (*Sefirot*, 4).

20. Zohar II, 186a.

21. See Zohar II, 219b.

22. Zohar II, 29a.

23. See also below, 6.

24. Zohar I, 64a.

25. Zohar III, 79a.

26. Zohar II, 125a.

27. On this dual image of the divine mother in different mythological systems, see *Eranos Jahrbuch* (1938), "Vorträge über Gestalt und Kult der 'Grossen Mutter'." As to the death force in her, see in particular pp. 45–46, 126–28, 175ff., 411–12.

28. Zohar I, 229a.

29. See also 23.

30. Zohar I, 241a–241b.

31. See J. Abelson, *The Immanence of God in Rabbinical Literature*, pp. 126–33.

32. [The usual translation of the verse is, in fact, "The Lord your God will turn your captivity," but the Hebrew actually uses the indicative *ve-shav* (He will return) and not the causative *ve-heshiv* (He will cause to return).]

33. B.T. *Megillah* 29a. There are various versions of this idea, which occurs very frequently in rabbinic midrash.

34. Zohar II, 29b.

35. Zohar III, 297b.

36. Zohar II, 216b.

37. Zohar III, 114b.

38. The source of this new idea of the exile of the *Shekhinah* can be traced to the *Sefer*

ha-Bahir, which applies rabbinic statements concerning the terrestrial Assembly of Israel, to "the Assembly of Israel" in the realms above. See G. Scholem, *Reshit ha-Kabbalah* (Jerusalem, 1948), p. 34.

39. *Shemot Rabbah*, 21: 5.
40. Zohar II, 189a.
41. Zohar I, 36a.
42. See Zohar II, 25b–26a.
43. See 26; Zohar III, 77b.
44. See also Zohar I, 122a–122b.

SHEKHINAH

1. THE HOUSE OF THE WORLD

(Zohar I, 172a–172b)

Rabbi Hiyya began by quoting: "A Song of Ascents; of Solomon. If the Lord does not build the house . . . if the Lord does not keep the city . . ." (Psalm 127: 1). Come and see. When the Holy One, blessed be He, desired to create the world, He brought a mist out of the spark of blackness,[1] and it began to shine from the midst of the darkness, and it remained aloft,[2] and it came downward.[3] This darkness shone and sparkled with one hundred narrow-broad pathways,[4] and the house[5] of the world was made. The house is in the middle of everything,[6] and there are a great many doors and rooms all round it, exalted, holy places, where the birds of heaven[7] nest, each one according to its kind. In the middle of it there grows a great and powerful tree,[8] with an abundance of branches and fruit, containing food for all. This tree goes up to the clouds of heaven and is hidden among three mountains.[9] It emerges from beneath these three mountains, stretching upward and descending downward. The house is saturated by it, and it conceals inside it[10] a number of supernal treasures that cannot be known. In this way the house is built and perfected. The tree is revealed by day and hidden by night, and the house rules by night and is hidden by day.[11]

When darkness[12] enters and is connected to it, and it is in the ascendant, and all the doors[13] are closed[14] on every side, then a number of spirits[15] fly immediately into the air, desiring to know and to enter it,

---

[1] The *bozina di-kardinuta*, a spark that shines in the domain of *Keter*, which is thought of as "darkness," because of its utter seclusion. From this spark the process of emanation begins, which is depicted here as the rising of a mist in the darkness.

[2] The actual mist remains in the upper, concealed domain.

[3] Its power acts outside the supernal domain in order to establish the system of the *sefirot*.

[4] With the ten *sefirot*, each of which comprises ten. The upper *sefirot* are like narrow paths, and the lower *sefirot* are like long and broad ways.   [5] *Malkhut*.

[6] The *sefirot* encompass *Malkhut* from above, and the worlds encompass it from below.

[7] The angels.   [8] *Tiferet*, the Tree of Life.

[9] *Keter, Hokhmah,* and *Binah*.   [10] Through intercourse.

[11] *Tiferet* has the characteristics of day, and *Malkhut* the characteristics of night.

[12] *Gevurah*, which is connected to *Malkhut*, pouring into it strict Judgment at the beginning of the night.

[13] The gates of Mercy and the channels of influence.

[14] Because of the domination of the husks.

[15] The forces of "the other side."

and they come in among the birds,[16] and they gather information[17] [from them], and they move about and see what they see, until the darkness that is connected to it is aroused, and produces a flame,[18] and smites with all the mighty hammers, opening doors and splitting rocks. The flame ascends and descends, and it smites the world, and voices are aroused above and below. A herald ascends at once and joins himself to the air, and makes a proclamation. The air emerges from the pillar of cloud from the inner altar,[19] and as it emerges it spreads out toward the four corners of the world. A thousand thousands[20] stand on [this] side, which is the left, and a myriad of myriads stand on [that] side, which is the right, and the herald stands at his station, crying with all his might and making a proclamation. How many there are then who prepare song and offer worship! Two doors are opened, one on the south side and one on the north side.[21] The house ascends and takes up its position, and joins itself to both realms,[22] and songs are sung and praises rise. That which enters[23] enters immediately in silence,[24] and the house shines with six lights[25] that cast radiance on every side. And streams of spices emerge[26] and all the beasts of the field[27] are refreshed, as it is said, "They give drink to every beast of the field; the wild asses quench their thirst . . ." (Psalm 104: 11), and they sing until the break of day. When the day breaks, the stars and the planets, the heavens and their hosts, all utter praises, and break out into song, as it is said, "When the morning stars sang together, and all the sons of God shouted for joy" (Job 38: 7).

Come and see. "If the Lord does not build the house, its builders labor in vain; if the Lord does not keep the city the guardian watches in vain." "If the Lord. . . ." This is the supernal king,[28] who is building this house all the time, and beautifying it. When? When the devotions[29] and acts of worship rise from below, as they should. "If the Lord does not keep the city." When? When night falls, and armed spirits[30] settle, and wander through the world, and the doors are closed, and [the city] is guarded from every side, so that the uncircumcised and the unclean should not approach it,[31] as it is said, "The uncircumcised and the unclean shall no

---

[16] The angels.   [17] The spirits obtain information from the angels.

[18] At midnight a flame emerges from *Gevurah*, who drives away the husks.

[19] This is *Binah*, apparently. Most of the symbols here have parallels in the sacrificial worship of the Temple, but their precise significance is not clear.   [20] Angels.

[21] Doors through which influence might descend from *Hesed* and *Gevurah*.

[22] *Hesed* and *Gevurah*, which arouse love between *Malkhut* and *Tiferet*.

[23] *Tiferet* by means of *Yesod*.   [24] In intercourse.

[25] With the six *sefirot* from *Hesed* to *Yesod*.   [26] From *Malkhut*.

[27] The angels.   [28] *Tiferet*.

[29] The *kavvanot*, the correct intentions with which prayer and the commandments should be performed.   [30] The forces of "the other side."

[31] The Holy One, blessed be He, protects *Malkhut* from the husks, so that they should not defile her.

longer come into you" (Isaiah 52: 1); for the Holy One, blessed be He, will drive them out of the world. Who is uncircumcised, and who is unclean? All is one. The uncircumcised and the unclean is the one by whom Adam and his wife were seduced, the one whom they followed, thus bringing death to the whole world. He is the one who defiles the house, until the Holy One, blessed be He, drives him out of the world. Consequently, it is true that "If the Lord does not keep the city, [the guardian watches] in vain."[32]

2. A LILY

(Zohar I, 1a)

Rabbi Hezekiah began by quoting: "As a lily among thorns" (Song of Songs 2: 2). Who is the lily? It is the Assembly of Israel.[33] Just as the lily, which is among thorns, contains both red and white, so the Assembly of Israel contains both Judgment and Mercy. Just as the lily has thirteen leaves, so the Assembly of Israel has thirteen attributes of Mercy, which encompass it on every side. From the moment that "God" is mentioned here, He brought forth thirteen words with which to surround the Assembly of Israel, and to protect her, and then [the name] is mentioned again.[34] Why is it mentioned a second time? In order to produce the five strong leaves that surround the lily,[35] and these five are called "salvations,"[36] and they are five gates.[37] And concerning this mystery it is written "I will lift up the cup of salvations" (Psalm 116: 13). This is the cup of benediction.[38] The cup of benediction has to be [held] by five fingers, and not more, like the lily, which rests on five strong leaves, like five fingers. This lily[39] is the cup of benediction.

3. A ROSE AND A LILY

(Zohar I, 221a)

Rabbi Simeon began by quoting: "I am a rose of Sharon, a lily of the valleys" (Song of Songs 2: 1). How beloved is the Assembly of Israel[40] to

[32] The angels who guard the *Shekhinah* cannot protect her if the Holy One, blessed be He, Himself, does not guard her.
[33] *Malkhut*, who dwells near the husks, which are the thorns.
[34] The name *"Elohim"* (God) in the story of Creation (Genesis 1: 1) is *Binah*. The thirteen words that intervene between the first mention of *"Elohim"* and the second (in Genesis 1: 2) represent the thirteen attributes of Mercy, which emerged from *Binah* in order to surround *Malkhut*.
[35] From the second mention of the name to the third mention there are five words, and they represent the five *sefirot* from *Ḥesed* to *Hod* (*Yesod* being included with *Tiferet*) that emanate from *Binah*, and bring the flow of influence down to *Malkhut*.
[36] Because of the influence that brings salvation to *Malkhut*.
[37] Through which one may enter into the mystery of the Godhead.
[38] At the grace after meals.   [39] *Malkhut*.   [40] *Malkhut*.

the Holy One, blessed be He,[41] for the Holy One, blessed be He, praises
her, and she praises Him, without ceasing, and she summons a great
many to utter praise and song without cease to the Holy One, blessed be
He. Blessed is the portion of Israel, which they take hold of, the lot of the
sacred portion, as it is written "For the portion of the Lord is His people,
[Jacob the lot of His inheritance]" (Deuteronomy 32: 9).

"I am a rose of Sharon"—this is the Assembly of Israel, which stands
in radiant beauty in the Garden of Eden.[42] "*Sharon*"—because she sings
to (*sharah*), and praises the supernal king. Another interpretation: "I am
a rose of Sharon," for she wishes to be refreshed by being watered by the
deep river,[43] the source of rivers,[44] as it is written "And the parched
land shall become a pool" (Isaiah 35: 7). "A lily of the valleys," because
she stands in the depth of everything.[45] What are these "valleys"? [It is]
similar to the verse, "Out of the depths I cry to you, O Lord" (Psalm
130: 1).[46] "A rose of Sharon"—a rose from that watering-place, [from
which] the rivers go forth without cease for ever. "A lily of the
valleys"—a lily from that place called "the depth of everything,"
enclosed on all sides.

Come and see. At first[47] she is green like a rose, whose leaves are
green; afterward "a lily" (*shoshanah*), she is red with white colors.[48]
Shoshanah, with six leaves;[49] *shoshanah*, because she changes (*ishtaniat*)
from color to color, and varies (*shaniat*) her colors. "A lily"—first a rose;
when she wishes to unite with the king, she is called "rose"; after she has
become united with him, with the king, with those kisses, she is called
"lily," since it is written "His lips are as lilies" (Song of Songs 5: 13). "A
lily of the valleys," for she changes her colors, sometimes for good,
sometimes for evil, sometimes for Mercy, sometimes for Judgment.

4. A WELL

(Zohar I, 151b–152a, *Sitrei Torah*)

"And he looked, and behold a well in the field, and, behold, three flocks
of sheep lying there by it" (Genesis 29: 2). "Well" is the level of "The

---

[41] *Tiferet.*   [42] In the world of emanation.

[43] Here "*Sharon*" is derived from *sharah*, in its meaning "to soak, water." *Malkhut*,
which in itself is dry, seeks the flow of influence from *Binah*.

[44] The source of the *sefirot*, which are rivers transmitting the divine influence.

[45] In *Ḥokhmah*. *Malkhut*, the lower Wisdom, is connected with the upper Wisdom,
which is here designated as "depths." [Heb. *amakim* means "valleys, depths."]

[46] This alludes to an interpretation of this verse found elsewhere in the Zohar (II,
63b; III, 265b), which imposes upon a person when praying the obligation to
concentrate on drawing down the flow of blessing from the depths of *Ḥokhmah*.

[47] Before intercourse.

[48] The Judgment in her is sweetened with the influence of Mercy.

[49] The six *sefirot* from *Ḥesed* to *Yesod*. [Heb. *shesh* means "six".]

Lord of all the earth" (Joshua 3: 11 and 13); "in the field"—a field of sacred apples;[50] "three flocks of sheep"—three supernal, sacred levels, ranged above the well, and they are *Nezah*, *Hod*, and the foundation of the world (*Yesod*). They bring down water from above and fill the well, because the source, the foundation of the world, when he resides in the well,[51] produces fruit, and gushes continuously, and the well is filled by him. When she is filled, then, to be sure, "out of that well they watered the flocks" (Genesis 29: 2)—these are all the crowds and the holy companies, all of whom drink and refresh themselves from the well, as befits each one of them. "And the stone at the well's mouth was great" (ibid.). This is the stone over which men stumble, a stone of stumbling and a rock of offense,[52] which is always at the mouth of the well, [that is,] at her behest, when she demands justice for the whole world, so that nourishment and goodness might not descend to the world.[53] "And all the flocks were gathered there" (ibid., 3). It does not say "the flocks were gathered there," but "all the flocks," holy companies above, and holy companies below, those above with songs and praises, and these below with prayers and supplications, both together immediately "rolled the stone from the mouth of the well"; they rolled it and removed it from the region of holiness, and she removed herself from Judgment.[54] At once "they watered the sheep"; the celestial angels received [influence] above, and Israel received [it] below. Subsequently, "they put the stone back, [at the mouth of the well, in its place]" at the behest of the well, that they might stand before it[55] and demand justice for the world, so that the world might conduct itself in justice. And this is necessary, for the world can endure only through justice, so that everything may exist in truth and righteousness.

5. A HIND

(Zohar III, 249a–249b)

Rabbi Abba began by quoting: "As a hart craves for the water brooks, so my soul craves for you, O God" (Psalm 42: 2). They have clarified this

---

[50] *Malkhut* is both "a well" and "a field." It is a well when it is already filled with divine influence and governs the worlds. It is a field when it is receiving influence from *Ḥesed*, *Gevurah*, and *Tiferet*, which are called "apples," because of their various hues.

[51] In intercourse.

[52] [Cf. Isaiah 8: 14.] These are the husks, which make men stumble in sin and which serve as the agents of *Malkhut*, when she governs the world with the attribute of Judgment.

[53] So that no more influence than is actually required should descend.

[54] *Malkhut* departed from the attribute of Judgment, and for a while the channels of Mercy were opened.

[55] *Malkhut* commands the husks to resume their stations, and to serve her.

verse.[56] It is written here "hart" (*ayal*), and it is written elsewhere "hind" (*ayelet*),[57] because there is a male and there is a female, and even though there is both male and female,[58] it is all one. This hart is called "a male," and it is also called "a female," since it is written "as a hart craves (*ta'arog*)" and not "*ya'arog*,"[59] but it is all one. "The hind of the dawn" (Psalm 22: 1). What is "the hind of the dawn"? It is a particular animal, a merciful one, than whom there is none more merciful among the animals of the world; for when time presses,[60] and she needs food both for herself and for all the animals, she goes far away[61] on a distant journey, and comes back bringing food. And she has no desire to eat until she has returned to her place. Why? So that the other animals may assemble near her and she can distribute the food. When she returns all the other animals assemble near her, and she stands in the middle, and distributes [food] to each one of them. A sign for this is "She rises while it is yet night, and gives food to her household" (Proverbs 31: 15). And she is satisfied by the food that she distributes, as if she had eaten more than any one else. And, when the morning comes, called "the dawn," it brings to her the pains of exile,[62] and she is therefore called "the hind of the dawn," because of the blackness of the morning, when she experiences pains like a woman in childbirth.[63] This is [the meaning of] the verse "As a woman with child, that draws near to the time of her delivery, is in pain, and cries out in her pains . . ." (Isaiah 26: 17).

When does she distribute [the food] to them? When the morning is about to dawn; while it is still night, and darkness reigns, and day is about to break,[64] as it is said "She rises while it is yet night, and gives food to her household. . . ." When the morning shines forth they are all sated with her food. At once a voice is awakened in the middle of the firmament. It cries out loudly and says: "You, who are near,[65] come in

[56] See *Midrash Tehillim*, beginning of chap. 42. This statement is based on rabbinic *aggadot* concerning the hind (ibid., chap. 22: 14; B.T. *Baba Batra*, 16b), which the Zohar sees as symbolic of the *Shekhinah*. The mystical significance of this aggadic description is not clear in every detail.

[57] Psalm 22: 1, *Ayelet ha-shaḥar* (the hind of the dawn).

[58] *Tiferet* and *Malkhut*, which are united as one in the mystery of intercourse. Therefore, in this verse, although it refers mystically to *Malkhut*, it calls her *ayal* (hart), in the masculine.

[59] [*Ta'arog* = she craves. One would expect *ya'arog* = he craves.]

[60] When she needs the flow of influence both for herself and for the worlds that are nourished through her.   [61] She ascends to the upper *sefirot*.

[62] A reference is made here, apparently, *en passant*, to the dawn of redemption. Before this dawn breaks "the pains of the Messiah" will come, and the *Shekhinah* who dwells with Israel in exile must bear them as well as they.

[63] She is to give birth to the redemption and to the souls of the Messiahs.

[64] *Malkhut* reigns at night-time, for she represents night. At that time she prepares the influence that she received from the *sefirot*, when she went up to them during the day, and she then distributes it before daybreak.   [65] The forces of holiness.

to your places; you, who are far away,[66] leave; let each one of you be gathered to his proper place." When the sun shines each one of them is gathered to his place. This is [the significance of] the verse, "The sun rises, they are gathered . . ." (Psalm 104: 22). She goes in the day, and is revealed at night, and makes her distribution in the morning, and she is therefore called "the hind of the dawn." After this, she summons her strength like a warrior, and goes, and she is called "a hart."

Where does she go? She goes sixty leagues[67] from the place from which she started, and she enters the mount of darkness.[68] [As soon as] she enters the mount of darkness a tortuous snake[69] is prepared for her, and it follows her, and she goes up from there to the mount of light.[70] When she arrives there, the Holy One, blessed be He, summons for her another snake, which comes out, and they attack one another and she is saved.[71] She then takes food from there, and returns to her place at midnight. From midnight onward she begins to distribute [the food] until the darkness before the morning disappears. When the day dawns she goes and is no longer seen, as we have explained.

When the world needs rain,[72] all the other animals assemble near her, and she goes up to the top of a high mountain, and, bowing her head between her knees, she utters lowing sounds, one after the other, and the Holy One, blessed be He, hears her voice, and is filled with Mercy, and takes pity on the world. She comes down from the top of the mountain, and runs and conceals herself, and all the other animals run after her, but they do not find her. This is [the significance of] the verse, "As a hart craves for the water brooks." What does "for the water brooks" mean? For the water brooks[73] that have dried up, and for which the world really thirsts: these are the ones she "craves."

When she is pregnant, she is closed up.[74] When the time comes for her to give birth, she lows, and utters cries, cry after cry, as many as seventy cries, which match the number of words in "May the Lord answer you in the day of trouble" (Psalm 20), which is the song sung by this pregnant one. The Holy One, blessed be He, hears her, and goes to her aid. He immediately brings forth a great snake[75] from among the mountains of darkness,[76] and it comes through the hills, its mouth licking the dust. It

[66] The husks. [67] She ascends to the six *sefirot*, each one of which comprises ten.

[68] *Gevurah*, strict Judgment.

[69] The force of "the other side," which is nourished by the attribute of Judgment. [Cf. Isaiah 27: 1]. [70] *Ḥesed*.

[71] The Holy One, blessed be He, incites the forces of "the other side" against one another, in order to rescue *Malkhut* from the first serpent that had pursued her.

[72] The flow of divine influence.

[73] The "water brooks" are *Nezah* and *Hod*. See Zohar III, 68a.

[74] She cannot produce the flow of divine influence, because sins are dominant in the world, and "the other side" has stopped up the channels.

[75] "The other side" bites the *Shekhinah*, receiving in this way a portion of sanctity, and then it moves away from the door of the *Shekhinah*. [76] The home of the husks.

draws near to the hind, and bites her twice at the appropriate place. The first time, blood[77] comes out, and it licks it up. The second time, water[78] comes out, and all the animals in the mountains drink, and she is opened and gives birth. You have an indication of this in "He smote the rock with his rod twice" (Numbers 20: 11); and it is written "and the congregation drank, and their cattle" (ibid.). At that very time, when the Holy One, blessed be He, took pity upon the young of this animal,[79] what is written? "The voice of the Lord makes the hinds calve, and strips the forests bare . . ." (Psalm 29: 9). "The voice of the Lord makes the hinds calve"—those pains and travails awaken seventy voices. And then immediately "He strips the forests bare," in order to bring the snake through, and so that the animal might be revealed among them,[80] and go on her way. "And in His temple [all say: 'Glory']" (ibid.). What does "in His temple" mean? In the temple[81] of the Holy One, blessed be He, all the crowds open their mouths and say "Glory." What glory? "Blessed be the glory of the Lord from His place" (Ezekiel 3: 12).

6. A WOMAN OF WORTH

(Zohar III, 97a, *Raya Mehemna*)

"And he shall wave the sheaf . . ." (Leviticus 23: 11). This is the commandment to bring the offering of the sheaf. This offering [is to be effected] entirely by close attachment,[82] above and below, the consort and her children going together. Israel offer this sheaf in their purity, and the sheaf is taken from the barley,[83] and it is offered in order to promote love between the wife and her husband. The woman who plays the harlot[84] moves away from them, because she cannot exist by her side. The woman of worth[85] comes near, and approaches the High Priest,[86] and she is certainly pure: "[And if the woman is not defiled, but is clean,] then she shall be cleared and shall conceive seed" (Numbers 5: 28), and she gives additional strength and love to her husband. The woman who plays the harlot flees from the sanctuary, so as not to come near it, for if she were to come near it at the very time when the woman of worth was examining herself, she would perish from the world. So she

[77] Which provides nourishment for the snake.
[78] I.e., influence for the lower worlds.   [79] The *Shekhinah*.
[80] Among those who are thirsting for the flow of divine influence.
[81] In the *Shekhinah*, which is also called "the glory of the Lord."
[82] Through the sheaf-offering the *Shekhinah* is cleansed from contact with the husks. When it is offered, Israel become attached to the *Shekhinah*, and the *Shekhinah* becomes attached to *Tiferet*, her "husband."
[83] Like the offering in "the law of jealousy" (Numbers, chap. 5), the purity of the *Shekhinah* being examined through the sheaf-offering.
[84] Lilith, the female element in "the other side."   [85] The *Shekhinah*.
[86] *Ḥesed*, who is the High Priest among the *sefirot*.

has no desire to come near to the sanctuary, and she flees from it, and Israel are left in their purity, with no foreign admixture, in respect to the mystery of faith.[87] This recondite mystery is that of two sisters,[88] and when one caught the scent of the examination of the other "her belly became swollen, and her thigh fell away" (Numbers 5: 27), for the examination of the woman of worth is a fatal potion for the woman who plays the harlot. This, therefore, is the counsel that the Holy One, blessed be He, gave to His children; that they should bring this offering for the sake of the woman of worth, so that the woman who plays the harlot should flee from her, and Israel should be left without any foreign admixture. Happy are they in this world, and in the world to come!

7. *ZEDEK* (RIGHTEOUSNESS)

(Zohar II, 139b–140a)

[Rabbi Simeon] began by quoting: "Who (*mi*) has raised up from the east . . ." (Isaiah 41:2). They have already explained this verse, and it has been clarified, but it is a mystery of wisdom. *Mi* is the mystery of the supernal world,[89] for thence emerged the beginning of the revelation of the mystery of faith,[90] and we have already explained it. Furthermore; *Mi*, the most recondite secret,[91] which is unknowable and completely unrevealed, revealed its glory, so that they might recognize it, from the place that is called "the east,"[92] for thence came the beginning of the whole mystery of faith and the revelation of light. Subsequently, "*Zedek* (Righteousness) he calls to his feet" (ibid.),[93] for Righteousness reveals the supernal *Gevurah* and the rule of the Holy One, blessed be He; and [the Holy One, blessed be He] has given Righteousness dominion over all the world, so that it might manage them and put them in order, as is fitting. "He sets nations before him, and makes him rule over kings" (ibid.), for all the kings in the world are subject to this Righteousness, as it is said "And He will judge the world with Righteousness, [He will minister judgment to the peoples with equity]" (Psalm 9: 9). Further-more: "Righteousness he calls to his feet"—who calls to whom? It is Righteousness that calls without cease to the resplendent mirror;[94] it is

[87] The world of emanation. "The other side" removes itself from Israel as well, and they stand in purity before the Godhead.
[88] The story is of two sisters. One of them was defiled, and she sent her pure sister to be examined in her stead. When the defiled one kissed her sister on her return from the examination, she scented "the water of cursing" and died (*Tanhuma, Naso,* 6).
[89] *Binah.* [90] The *sefirot* emanated from *Binah,* particularly *Tiferet* and *Malkhut.*
[91] Apparently, *Keter.*
[92] This is usually *Tiferet,* but perhaps here it refers to *Hokhmah.*
[93] [Usually translated "At whose steps victory attends."] *Zedek* is *Malkhut,* the attribute of lenient Judgment, in which is revealed the force of strict Judgment from *Gevurah.* [94] *Tiferet.*

never silent. And Righteousness stands perpetually at its feet,[95] and it does not move from there, calling, never silent. This is [the significance of] the verse: "O God, do not keep silence; do not hold Your peace, and be not still, O God" (Psalm 83: 2).

8. THE AGENT OF THE HOLY ONE, BLESSED BE HE

(Zohar II, 50b–51a)

Rabbi Abba said: How many thousands, how many myriads of sacred camps does the Holy One, blessed be He, have; masters of exalted countenances, masters of eyes, masters of weaponry, masters of howling, masters of yelling, masters of Mercy, masters of Judgment. Above them He has appointed the consort[96] to minister to Him in the palace. The consort also has armed camps, to match them.[97] The armed camps exist with sixty countenances, and they all surround her, girded with swords. Multitudes go out, and multitudes come in; with six wings they fly throughout the world. Each one of them is preceded by coals of flaming fire; he is clothed with blazing fire and, on his back, the flame of the sword that casts its flames throughout the world so as to put a protection in front of her. This is [the meaning of] the verse "and the flaming sword that turned every way, to guard the way to the Tree of Life" (Genesis 3: 24). Who is "the way to the Tree of Life"? It is the great consort; she is the way to that great and powerful tree, the Tree of Life,[98] as it is written "Behold, it is the litter of Solomon;[99] sixty mighty men surround it, of the mighty men of Israel" (Song of Songs 3: 7)—the supernal Israel—"all girded with the sword" (ibid., 8).

When the consort moves, they all move with her, as it is said "And the angel of God moved" (Exodus 14: 19). Is she really called "the angel of God"? Rabbi Abba said: Yes. Come and see. Rabbi Simeon said as follows: The Holy One, blessed be He, established before Him a holy palace[100]—a supernal palace, a holy city—a supernal city, called "Jerusalem," the holy city. Whoever wishes to enter into the presence of the king[101] may do so only from this holy city. [Thence] the path leads to the king, for the path from there is prepared. This is [the meaning of] the verse "This is the gate of the Lord; the righteous shall enter into it" (Psalm 118: 20). Every mission that the king wishes [to send] comes from the house of the consort; and every mission from the lower world to the

[95] *Malkhut* stands near *Nezaḥ* and *Hod* who are, as it were, the two legs of *Tiferet*.

[96] The *Shekhinah*.

[97] The description of the angels of the *Shekhinah* as angels of destruction is paralleled in the Gnostic *Book of Baruch*. See W. Schultz, *Dokumente der Gnosis*, pp. 25–26. And see above p. 385, n. 8.

[98] *Tiferet*, which represents the "Israel" of the celestial world.

[99] The litter of Solomon, who is the celestial Israel, is interpreted here to refer to the consort.　　[100] The *Shekhinah*.　　[101] *Tiferet*.

king enters the house of the consort first, and then comes to the king. So it is that the consort is the agent for all, from the upper world to the lower world, and from the lower world to the upper world, and consequently she is the agent for all. This is [the meaning of] the verse, "And the angel of God, who went before the camp of Israel"—the supernal Israel—"moved [and went behind them]" (Exodus 14: 19). "The angel of God" is the one referred to in "And the Lord went before them . . ." (Exodus 13: 21) and this is [alluded to in] "that they might go by day and by night" (ibid.),[102] as they have explained. But is it really an honorable thing for the king that the consort should go, and wage war, and act as an agent? A comparison, however, may be drawn with a certain king who made love to a noble consort. The king considered her to be more glorious than all the other consorts in the world. He said: They are all like servants compared with my consort. She is superior to them all. What shall I do for her? My entire household shall be put into her charge. The king issued a proclamation: Henceforth, all the king's affairs shall be entrusted to the consort. What did he do? The king put into her care his complete armory, all his troops, all the royal jewels, all the royal treasuries. He said: Henceforth, whoever needs to speak with me cannot do so unless he tells the consort first. In the same way, the Holy One, blessed be He, out of His great love and affection for the Assembly of Israel,[103] put everything into her control. He said: All the others are worthless compared with her.

9. GATE

(Zohar I, 7b)

"In the beginning." Rabbi Hiyya began by quoting "The fear of the Lord[104] is the beginning of wisdom; a good understanding have all they that practise them; His praise endures for ever" (Psalm 111: 10). "The beginning of wisdom"—this verse should have said "The fear of the Lord is the end of wisdom," because the fear of the Lord really is the end of wisdom.[105] However, it is the beginning in that it provides entry to the level of the supernal wisdom. This is [the significance of] the verse "Open for me the gates of righteousness" (Psalm 118: 19), "This is the gate of the Lord" (ibid., 20).[106] This is certain, because if one does not

---

[102] "And the Lord" is seen here as pertaining to the *Shekhinah*, who is engaged on a mission for *Tiferet*. This is in accord with the rabbinic statement (*Bereshit Rabbah* 51: 3) that "wherever 'and the Lord' occurs, it signifies the Lord and His court." The phrase "by day and by night" indicates that the *Shekhinah* works with the aid of both *Ḥesed* and *Gevurah*.   [103] The *Shekhinah*.

[104] *Malkhut*, whose main element is Judgment, and which is therefore called "Fear."

[105] *Malkhut* is the lower *Ḥokhmah* (Wisdom).

[106] He brings proof that *Malkhut*, which is called "Righteousness," is also referred to as "Gate," because through *Malkhut* one may enter into the mystery of the Godhead, as far as supernal *Ḥokhmah*.

enter through this gate, one cannot gain entry to the worlds. It is like an exalted king,[107] who is high, hidden and concealed, and who has made gates[108] for himself, one upon the other,[109] and at the end of all the gates he has made one particular gate,[110] with a number of locks, a number of doors, and a number of palaces.[111] He says: Whoever desires to enter into my presence, this gate shall be the first [that leads] to me; and whoever enters by this gate shall enter. So here, the first gate to the supernal wisdom is "the fear of the Lord," and this is the "beginning—two": two that are joined together, two points, one hidden and concealed, and one manifest.[112] Since there is no separation between them, they are called "beginning"—one, and not two; whoever takes one takes the other,[113] and it is all one, for He is one, and His name is one, as it is written "For it is You alone whose name is the Lord" (Psalm 83: 19).

10. THE DOOR OF THE TENT

(Zohar I, 103b)

Rabbi Simeon said: "Her husband is known in the gates" (Proverbs 31: 23). What are these gates? It is similar to the verse "Lift up your heads, gates; and be lifted up, everlasting doors" (Psalm 24: 7), for through these gates, which are the higher levels,[114] the Holy One, blessed be He,[115] is known, and in no other way is it possible to cleave to Him.

Come and see. Man's soul can be known only through the organs of the body, which are the levels that perform the work of the soul. Consequently, it is both known and unknown. In the same way, the Holy One, blessed be He, is both known and unknown, because He is the soul's soul, the spirit's spirit, hidden and concealed from all. But through these gates, which are the doors of the soul, the Holy One, blessed be He, may be known.

Come and see. The door has a door, and the level has a level, and through them the glory of the Holy One, blessed be He, is known. "The door of the tent" (Genesis 18: 10)—this is the door of Righteousness,[116] as it is said "Open for me the gates of righteousness; [I will enter into

---

[107] *Hokhmah.*   [108] *Sefirot.*   [109] I.e., one above the other.   [110] *Malkhut.*

[111] The camps of the *Shekhinah*, the chariots and the palaces through which one must pass in order to reach *Malkhut.*

[112] The word *bereshit* (in the beginning) alludes to both *Hokhmah* and *Malkhut* (the letter *bet* symbolizing *Malkhut*, because it is the home—*bet*—of the world). *Hokhmah* and *Malkhut* are the two points that are connected with each other. [*Bet* also signifies the number two.]

[113] When one reaches *Malkhut*, it is as if one had already reached supernal *Hokhmah* as well, because the sefirotic system is the world of unification, and supernal *Hokhmah* is reflected in the lower *Hokhmah.*

[114] The *sefirot*, through which the hidden *En-Sof* is revealed.

[115] *En-Sof.*   [116] *Zedek*, i.e., *Malkhut.*

them, I will give thanks to the Lord. This is the gate of the Lord; the righteous shall enter into it]" (Psalm 118: 19–20). This is the first door to be entered, and through this door all the other supernal doors[117] may be seen. Whoever attains a knowledge of this, attains a knowledge of both this and all the other doors, because they all envelop it. But at the present time, when this door is not known, because Israel is in exile, all the doors have departed from it, and [Israel] cannot know it or cleave to it. But when Israel emerges from exile all the upper levels will envelop it, as they should, and then the inhabitants of the world will know supernal, glorious wisdom, such as they had not known previously, as it is written "And the spirit of the Lord shall rest upon it, the spirit of wisdom and understanding, the spirit of counsel and might, the spirit of knowledge and of the fear of the Lord" (Isaiah 11: 2)—they will all[118] envelop this lower door, which is the door of the tent, and they will all envelop the King Messiah, so that he may judge the world, as it is written "And with righteousness shall he judge the poor . . ." (Isaiah 11: 4).

Consequently, when Abraham was given the message, it was this level that spoke,[119] as it has been explained, as it is written "And it said: I will certainly return to you, when the season comes round" (Genesis 18: 10). "And it said"—it does not say who it was. It was "the door of the tent." Therefore "and Sarah heard" this level that was speaking with him, and she had never heard this before, as it is written "And Sarah heard the door of the tent"[120] giving him a message, and saying "I will certainly return to you, when the season comes round, and Sarah, your wife, shall have a son."

11. A CONTINUAL BURNT-OFFERING

(Zohar III, 256b, *Raya Mehemna*)

"A continual burnt-offering"[121] (Numbers 28: 6, and elsewhere). This is the *Shekhinah* that rises to the upper regions through this level,[122] as it is said of it "Evening and morning, every day, continually, and they say twice, in love, 'Hear, O Israel.'"[123] She rises through the central pillar, which is continually with her, without any separation [between them] whatsoever. Where does she rise to? To the place from which she was hewn, which is *En-Sof*, and higher than all the *sefirot*. Consequently, they

---

[117] The *sefirot*.   [118] All the *sefirot* referred to in this verse.

[119] It was "the door of the tent," i.e., *Malkhut*, that gave him the message.

[120] [This is a literal translation of Genesis 18: 10.]

[121] [Heb. *olat tamid*. *Olah* (burnt-offering) means literally "that which rises."]

[122] Through *Tiferet*, which is called "*tamid*" (continual). This is referred to in the line quoted, "every day continually," for *Tiferet* is also called "*yom*" (day), and it is the central pillar.

[123] A quotation from the prayer, the *Musaf Kedushah*. Cf. *Tanna de-Ve Eliyahu Rabba*, end of chap. 21.

have taught: the burnt-offering rises entirely to the Highest.[124] And
when she rises, all the *sefirot* attach themselves to her, and rise with her.
And what is this ascent of hers? It is "for a sweet savor" (Numbers 28: 6),
in order to place a good scent before the Lord. Subsequently, it is said of
her "And [Aaron] came down from offering the sin-offering, and the
burnt-offering" (Leviticus 9: 22); she descends full of atonement for the
sins of Israel. See, her ascent was through the central pillar, and her
descent was also that way, and all her hosts [with her].[125] It is, therefore,
called "a ladder," by which all the beings ascend and descend, and they
depend upon [the name] *YHVH*.

12. MOON

(Zohar I, 199a)

Rabbi Judah said: When the Holy One, blessed be He, created the
moon,[126] He would look upon her continually, as it is written, "the eyes
of the Lord, your God, are continually upon her" (Deuteronomy 11:
12). His concern for her is continuous. And it is written "Then did He see
her [and declare her; He established her, and also searched her out]"
(Job 28: 27), for the sun[127] is illumined through His concern for her.[128]
"He declared her (*va-yesapperah*)." What does *va-yesapperah* mean? It is
similar to "Its stones are a place of sapphire (*sappir*)" (Job 28: 6).[129] "He
established her (*hekhinah*)," for she dwells in her place (*mekhonah*) among
the twelve regions,[130] divided among seventy guardian angels;[131] He
has established her among the seven supernal pillars,[132] so that she
might be illumined, and dwell in her fullness. "He also searched her out"
in order to care for her continually, at every moment, without any
interruption whatsoever. After this He gave man a warning, and said
"And He said to man: Behold, the fear of the Lord, that is wisdom; and
to depart from evil is understanding" (Job 28: 28), for she is crowned
with the lower worlds, that they might fear and know the Holy One,
blessed be He, through her.[133] "And to depart from evil is understand-

---

[124] B.T. *Hagigah* 6a.

[125] The hosts of the *Shekhinah* also ascend and descend with her [cf. Genesis 28: 12]
and they are called "beings" (*havayot*), because they obtained their existence from, and
are linked to, the name *YHVH*.   [126] *Malkhut*.   [127] *Tiferet*.

[128] The light of *Tiferet* grows stronger because of His concern for *Malkhut*.

[129] Hence *va-yesapperah* may be rendered here "He bejeweled her" or "He beautified
her."

[130] The camps of the *Shekhinah*.

[131] The guardian angels of the seventy nations, which govern by virtue of the
influence that they receive from *Malkhut*.

[132] The seven *sefirot* that are above *Malkhut*.

[133] The good deeds performed by mankind crown her, and of her it is said "the fear of
the Lord, that is wisdom"—for if they fear her, and honor her as they should, she will
open a door to the perception of the divine.

ing"—the separation of the dross, which should not be brought when one approaches her,[134] and then understanding comes into being, giving one knowledge and perception of the glory of the supernal King.

13. THE DIMINUTION OF THE MOON

(Zohar I, 181a–181b)

[Rabbi Simeon] began by quoting: "Behold, my servant shall become wise. He shall be exalted and lifted up, and shall be very high" (Isaiah 52: 13). Happy is the portion of the righteous, to whom the Holy One, blessed be He, reveals the ways of the Torah, so that they might walk in them. Come and see. This verse is an exalted mystery. "Behold, my servant shall become wise"—they have [already] explained it. But come and see. When the Holy One, blessed be He, created the world, He made the moon[135] and diminished its light, for it has none of its own at all, and because it made itself smaller, it had to receive its light from the sun, and from the power of the supernal luminaries. When the Temple was still standing, Israel would busy themselves with offerings and sacrifices and other forms of worship, practiced by the priests, the Levites, and the Israelites, in order to forge links and kindle lights. But once the Temple was destroyed the light darkened, and the moon was not illuminated by the sun; the sun departed from it, and it was not illuminated; and there has not been a single day when it has not been subject to curses, pains, and torments, as has been explained. And what is written concerning the time to come[136] when the moon will be illuminated? "Behold, my servant shall become wise"—it refers to the moon. "Behold, my servant shall become wise"—this is the mystery of faith. "Behold, he shall become wise," for an impulse shall occur toward the realms above, like someone who smells a scent and comes to bestir himself and investigate.[137] "He shall be exalted" on the side of the light[138] that is higher than all lights. "He shall be exalted," as it is said, "And therefore will He be exalted, that He may have mercy upon you" (Isaiah 30: 18). "And lifted up" on the side of Abraham; "and shall be high" on the side of Isaac; "very" on the side of Jacob.[139] And despite the fact that they have explained it [in another way], it is all one in the mystery of wisdom. At that time, the Holy One, blessed be He, [will stimulate] a supernal impulse in order to give light to it, to the moon, as is fitting, as it is said,

[134] By removing the husks from *Malkhut*, man acquires understanding with which to perceive the higher realms.

[135] *Malkhut*, which receives light from *Tiferet*, the sun.

[136] The days of the Messiah.

[137] *Malkhut* will gain strength from the influence that descends from above.

[138] The higher *sefirot*, which are *Raḥamim* (Mercy).

[139] Abraham, Isaac, and Jacob represent *Ḥesed*, *Gevurah*, and *Tiferet*.

"the light of the moon shall be as the light of the sun, and the light of the sun shall be sevenfold, as the light of seven days" (Isaiah 30: 26).

14. THE SHAPE OF THE MOON

(Zohar Ḥadash, Bereshit, 5a, Sitrei Otiot)

The form of the letters in the sacred mystery: the lower *he*[140] that we have mentioned, the symbol of the Temple, the moon, when it is in the ascendant, and beautifies itself for the sun, in order to receive light from it, these beloved crowns stand opposite each other. And the maidens who stand with her adorn and beautify themselves with finery, one behind her, one in front of her, one on this side, and one on that, and she stands in the middle, and the Sanhedrin[141] of seventy-two stand in their semicircular court in order to make a circle round the moon, [so that] the consort might adorn herself for her husband. And she is in this form: כ, a half-moon, with a point[142] in the center, for it is the point that receives light from the sun, in order to provide the whole body with light. This mystery [is alluded to] in the point that is situated in half of the eye, for everything depends for its existence on the point that stands in the center, which receives all the light to illumine the whole eye. The moon[143] is illuminated only from this single point, which is situated and sealed in the center, even though it cannot actually be seen in the moon. Come and see. Every circle that exists is constructed from a single point that stands in the center. Consequently, with the circle of the moon, the whole is constructed from the single point that is sealed within it, in its center. And this point, which stands in the center, receives all the light, and illumines the body, and it is all illuminated.

15. STATES OF THE MOON

(Zohar III, 248b, Raya Mehamna)

"And in your new moons" (Numbers 28: 11). The sages of the Mishnah said[144] that when they used to sanctify the new moons at the behest of the court they would light flares on the mountaintops; and they used to say: If you see [the moon] like this, sanctify it. Sometimes the moon had this shape: ∪, with its horns facing upward.[145] Sometimes it would be facing downward in this shape: ∩. Sometimes it would be facing toward

---

[140] The *Shekhinah*.

[141] Angels in the palaces of the *Shekhinah*, who administer Judgment.

[142] The point of Zion, the mystical symbol of the womb.   [143] *Malkhut*.

[144] B.T. *Rosh Hashanah* 22b; 20a.

[145] The interpretation seems to be as follows: the four points of the compass, in the order given here, are *Tiferet*, *Yesod*, *Ḥesed*, and *Gevurah*. "Upward" and "downward" are *Neẓaḥ* and *Hod*. *Malkhut* (the moon) faces these *sefirot*, in order to receive influence from them.

the East, like this: C. And sometimes toward the West, like this: כ.
Sometimes toward the South, and sometimes toward the North. In this
way it faces the six extremities, which are comprised in *Tiferet*, which is
[the letter] *vav*,[146] [and they are]: *Gedulah, Gevurah, Tiferet, Nezah, Hod,*
and *Yesod*. The point that pours forth influence upon it from within is
Hokhmah, and the thread that surrounds it is *Keter*.[147] This point is
sometimes a crown, and sometimes a throne upon which to sit, and
sometimes a stool for the feet.[148] Why is it called "moon (*levanah*)"?
Because of the white-heat (*libbun*) of the law, which is within; "glorious is
the daughter of the king within" (Psalm 45: 14), and she is made white
by the fire of *Binah*, which descends upon her.[149] The mystery of this
[may be seen in] "Though your sins be as scarlet, they shall be as white
as snow" (Isaiah 1: 18). Whereas she used to be *Adonai*, red Judgment in
Gevurah, where *Binah* is, [now] she is made white on the side of *Hesed*,
where *Hokhmah* is, and she reverts [to being] *YHVH*.[150] What
transforms her from Judgment to Mercy? The perfectly righteous; for
the moon is on the side of the Tree of Knowledge of Good and Evil,[151]
but its bark is darkened. "If it is a dark spot,"[152] [refers to] the
maidservant, the evil inclination "and if it is not lower than the skin, but
is dim," then it has nothing of its own, but the thread illuminates it,[153]
and accompanies it in the night which is exile; but it will leave it in the
day that is the world to come,[154] when "to you that fear My name the
sun of righteousness shall arise with healing in its wings" (Malachi 3:
20). But the moon of the Tree of Life,[155] this point that is within, is like a

---

[146] [The letter *vav* has the numerical equivalent of 6.]

[147] The central point in the circle of the moon, which is the mystical symbol of the
womb in *Malkhut*, and from which the light issues forth, emanates from *Hokhmah*. And
the thread of *Keter* surrounds it.

[148] When *Malkhut* ascends, the point serves as a crown for *Tiferet*, and when it
remains in its place it is like a throne or a footstool.

[149] The essential nature of *Malkhut* is Judgment; but just as the *halakhah* (the law) is
made in the heat of argument, so *Malkhut* is also made white (*levanah*), in its point, when
it is refined in the fire of *Binah*. *Binah* is the source of Judgment, but through the strength
of its fire *Malkhut* is linked to *Hesed*, which is emanated from *Hokhmah*.

[150] In her role of Judgment she is called *Adonai*, but once she is linked with *Hesed* and
Rahamim (Love and Mercy) she becomes the last letter *H* of the tetragrammaton.

[151] *Malkhut* has in essence a close connection with evil, and the darkened husks, the
evil inclination, and Lilith surround her.

[152] This is a misquotation. The verse (Leviticus 13: 21) reads "if there be no white
hairs in it, and if it is not lower than the skin, but is dim. . . ."

[153] She has no light of her own, but a narrow thread illumines her from *Tiferet*, and
with its aid she guides the world in exile.

[154] In the time to come the world will be guided by *Tiferet*, the sun, and then the
thread of light will depart from *Malkhut*, which will be united with *Tiferet*.

[155] In the inner point, where the mystery of love is to be found, *Malkhut*, after her
"whitening" in the Tree of Life, is bound to *Tiferet*; and then influence flows at this point
without interruption.

never-ceasing fountain, of which it is written "like a spring of water, whose waters do not fail" (Isaiah 58: 11), and it is called "a hind of love" on the side of *Hesed*. This is [the significance of] the verse "I have loved you with an everlasting love; therefore with affection have I drawn you" (Jeremiah 31: 3). And it has two horns of light,[156] like this: ∪. Sometimes "one is higher than the other" (Daniel 8: 3), like this: ∪; and sometimes they are equal, like this: ∪.

16. THE DESTRUCTION OF THE TEMPLE
(Zohar I, 202b–203a)

Rabbi Hezekiah began by quoting: "The burden concerning the valley of vision. What ails you now, that you have gone up entirely to the roofs?" (Isaiah 22: 1). Come and see. They have interpreted this to mean that, when the Temple was destroyed, all the priests went up to the roofs of the Temple, with their keys in their hands, and said "Up till now we have been Your treasurers. From this point on, take what is Yours."[157] But come and see: "the valley of vision" is the *Shekhinah*, who was in the Temple. All the world's inhabitants would suck the milk of prophecy from her. Even though the prophets all prophesied from another place,[158] they would actually suck their prophecy from her,[159] and so she is called "the valley of vision." "Vision"—they have already explained that it is the vision of all the supernal colors.[160] "What ails you now, that you have gone up entirely to the roofs?" When the Temple was destroyed the *Shekhinah* came and went up to all those places where she used to dwell at first, and she would weep for her home and for Israel, who had gone into exile, and for all the righteous and the pious ones who used to be there and had perished. How do we know this? Because it is written "Thus says the Lord: A voice is heard in Ramah, lamentation and bitter weeping, Rachel weeping for her children" (Jeremiah 31: 15). And it has already been explained that at that time the Holy One, blessed be He, questioned the *Shekhinah*, and said to her "What ails you now, that you have gone up entirely to the roofs?" What is the point of "entirely"? Is not "you have gone up" sufficient? What does "entirely" mean? It is meant to include all the hosts, and all the other chariots, all of whom lamented the destruction of the Temple with her. And so we have "What ails you now?" And she said to Him: My children are in exile, and the Temple is burnt, and so why should I remain here? And yet You have said "You that are full of uproar, a

[156] *Nezah* and *Hod*, which provide her with influence, sometimes in equal measure, and sometimes with one providing more than the other.

[157] See B.T. *Ta'anit* 29a.

[158] The source of prophecy is in *Nezah* and *Hod*.

[159] The *Shekhinah* was the channel through which prophecy was transmitted.

[160] The *sefirot*, which are the supernal colors, are all reflected in her.

tumultuous city, a joyous town, your slain are not slain with the sword, nor dead in battle" (Isaiah 22: 2); "Therefore I said: Look away from me, I will weep bitterly . . ." (ibid., 4). They have already explained that the Holy One, blessed be He, said to her "Thus says the Lord: Refrain your voice from weeping, and your eyes from tears . . ." (Jeremiah 31: 16).

Now come and see. From the day that the Temple was destroyed there has not been a single day without curses. When the Temple was still standing, Israel would perform their rites, and bring offerings and sacrifices. And the *Shekhinah* rested upon them in the Temple, like a mother hovering over her children, and all faces were resplendent with light, so that there was blessing both above and below. And there was not a single day without blessings and joys, and Israel dwelt securely in the land, and the whole world was nourished because of them. Now that the Temple is destroyed, and the *Shekhinah* is with them in exile, there is not a single day without curses, and the world is cursed, and there is no joy to be found, above or below. But in time to come the Holy One, blessed be He, will raise the Assembly of Israel from the dust, as it has been explained, in order to make the world rejoice in everything, as it has been said, "I will bring them to My holy mountain, and make them rejoice in My house of prayer . . ." (Isaiah 56: 7); and it is written, "They shall come with weeping, and with supplications will I lead them" (Jeremiah 31: 9). As it was at the beginning, where it is written "She weeps grievously in the night, and her tears are on her cheeks" (Lamentations 1: 2), so subsequently they shall return in tears, as it is written, "They shall come with weeping. . . ."

17. THE CASTING-DOWN OF THE *SHEKHINAH*

(Zohar II, 175a)

It is taught: "Happy are you, O earth, when your king is a free man" (Ecclesiastes 10: 17). What is "earth"? Earth without qualification;[161] for it is taught: What is the meaning of the verse "He cast down from heaven to earth the beauty of Israel" (Lamentations 2: 1)? This "earth" is a mystery among the crowns of the holy King, and it is mentioned in the verse "on the day that the Lord God made heaven and earth" (Genesis 2: 4). Whatever food and nourishment this "earth" obtained it drew from the place called "heaven."[162] The "earth" drew nourishment from no other place except from the sacred perfection called "heaven." When the Holy One, blessed be He, wished to destroy His house below, and the holy land below, He first put aside the holy land

---

[161] *Malkhut.*

[162] *Tiferet.* The verse quoted from Genesis refers, according to this interpretation, to the emanation of *Tiferet* and *Malkhut* by *Ḥokhmah* and *Binah.*

above, and made her come down from the level where she took nourishment from the sacred heavens, and afterward He destroyed the one below. This is [the meaning of] the verse "He cast down from heaven to earth"—at first—and afterward "He did not remember His footstool" (Lamentations 2: 1); for it is taught: These are the ways of the Holy One, blessed be He. When He wishes to judge the world, He passes judgment on the world above first, and then He establishes [His judgment] in the world below, as it is written "The Lord will punish the host of the high heaven on high" and afterward "the kings of the earth upon the earth" (Isaiah 24: 21).

18. THE DISMISSAL OF THE QUEEN

(Zohar III, 69a)

It is taught: One day the companions were traveling with Rabbi Simeon. Rabbi Simeon said: We see that all these peoples are higher, and Israel is the lowest of them all. Why is this? Because the King[163] has dismissed the consort[164] from His presence and brought in a maidservant in her place, as it is said, "For three things the earth quakes. . . . For a servant when he reigns. . . . And for a servant-girl that is heir to her mistress" (Proverbs 30: 21–23). Who is the servant-girl? She is the foreign crown,[165] whose firstborn the Holy One, blessed be He, slew in Egypt, as it is written, "even unto the firstborn of the servant-girl that is behind the mill" (Exodus 11: 5). At first she lived behind the mill, and now this servant-girl is heir to her mistress.

Rabbi Simeon wept, and said: A king without a consort is not called "king." Where is the glory of a king who cleaves to a servant-girl, to the maidservant of the consort? The secret of the matter [is] that in time to come a voice will bring news to the consort, and say: "Rejoice greatly, O daughter of Zion; shout, O daughter of Jerusalem; look, your king comes to you; righteous and victorious is he" (Zechariah 9: 9). That is to say, that the victorious one is righteous,[166] for up till now he had ridden[167] in a place that was not his, in a foreign place, and had nourished it. And it is written, concerning this, "Lowly, and riding upon an ass" (ibid.); he was "lowly" at first, "and riding upon an ass," as we have explained— they are the lower crowns of the idolatrous peoples, whose firstborn the Holy One, blessed be He, slew in Egypt. This is [the significance of] the verse "and all the first-born of beasts" (Exodus 11: 5); we have already explained these things. "Righteous and victorious is he," so to speak. He is certainly victorious over all, for up to this time the Righteous One had

163 *Tiferet.*   164 The *Shekhinah*, who is the guiding spirit of Israel.
165 Lilith, the dominant female on "the other side." The nations rule through the power that she has.   166 I.e., *Yesod.*   167 In intercourse.

lived without Righteousness.[168] But now that they are united together as one, "righteous and victorious is he," for he does not dwell with "the other side."

19. THE MOURNING OF THE HOLY ONE, BLESSED BE HE, AND THE ANGELS

(Zohar I, 210a–210b)

Rabbi Hiyya began by quoting: "Rejoice with Jerusalem, and be glad with her, all you that love her; rejoice for joy with her . . ." (Isaiah 66: 10). Come and see. When the Temple was destroyed, and the sins [of Israel] began to take effect, and Israel were exiled from the land, the Holy One, blessed be He, departed to the higher realms, and He did not look upon the destruction of the Temple, or upon His people who had gone into exile. And the *Shekhinah* went into exile with them. When He came down, He looked upon His house that had been burned; He looked for His people, and they had gone into exile; He inquired for the consort, and she had been sent away. Immediately, "In that day the Lord, the God of hosts, proclaimed weeping, and lamentation, and baldness, and girding with sackcloth" (Isaiah 22: 12). And of her also, what is written? "Lament like a virgin girded with sackcloth for the husband of her youth" (Joel 1: 8), as it is said: "because he is not" (Jeremiah 31: 15),[169] for he had left her, and there was a separation [between them]. Even the heavens and earth went wholly into mourning, as it is written, "I clothe the heavens with blackness, and I make sackcloth their covering" (Isaiah 50: 3). All the angels above went into mourning for her, as it is written, "Behold the Arielim cry openly, and the angels of peace weep bitterly" (Isaiah 33: 7). Sun and moon went into mourning, and their light became dark, as it is written, "The sun was darkened [as it rose, and the moon did not cause her light to shine]" (Isaiah 13: 10). And all the upper and the lower realms wept for her, and went into mourning. Why was this? Because "the other side" had control of her, because it had control of the holy land.

20. SEPARATION

(Zohar I, 182a)

"As many were appalled at you—so marred was his visage unlike that of a man, and his form unlike that of the sons of men" (Isaiah 52: 14). Come and see. It has already been explained that when the Temple was destroyed, and the *Shekhinah* went into exile into the lands of the nations,

---

[168] *Zedek*, i.e., the *Shekhinah*.

[169] [This phrase is usually translated "for they are not" in order to fit the context (q.v.); but it is literally a third-person-singular form.]

it is written "Behold the Arielim cry openly, and the angels of peace weep bitterly" (Isaiah 33: 7). They all wept over this, and composed dirges and lamentations, and all for the *Shekhinah* who had been exiled from her place. And just as she suffered a change from her earlier state, so too her husband:[170] his light no longer shone, and he was changed from what he was before, as it is written, "The sun was darkened as it rose" (Isaiah 13: 10), and of this it is written, "so marred was his visage unlike that of a man." Another interpretation: "So marred was his visage unlike that of a man"—it refers to the servant,[171] whose countenance and form were changed from what they were before. Another interpretation: "So marred was his visage unlike that of a man"—as it is said "I clothe the heavens with blackness, and I make sackcloth their covering" (Isaiah 50: 3), for from the day that the Temple was destroyed the heavens[172] did not shine with their customary light. The secret of the matter is that blessings reside only in the place where male and female are together, and they have explained it, as it is said "male and female He created them, and blessed them" (Genesis 5: 2), and so "marred was his visage unlike that of a man." And this too may be compared with "The righteous[173] perishes" (Isaiah 57: 1). The passive is not used, but the active, "perishes,"[174] for blessings reside only in the place where male and female are together, as it has been explained.

21. IN EXILE

(Zohar III, 17a–17b)

In the Book of Rav Hamnuna Sava it says: Whenever the Assembly of Israel[175] is with the Holy One, blessed be He,[176] the Holy One, blessed be He, is, as it were, in perfection, and He sustains Himself with the flow that comes from the nourishing milk of the supernal mother,[177] and with that nourishment which He imbibes He gives all the others drink, and nourishes them. And we have learned that Rabbi Simeon said: Whenever the Assembly of Israel is with the Holy One, blessed be He, the Holy One, blessed be He, is in perfection, in joy; blessings rest upon Him, and go forth from Him to all the others. And whenever the Assembly of Israel is not with the Holy One, blessed be He, blessings are withheld, so to speak, from Him, and from all the others. The secret of the matter is that whenever male and female are not [together] blessings

---

[170] *Tiferet*, which is the sun.

[171] Metatron, who ministers to the *Shekhinah*.

[172] *Tiferet*. According to this interpretation, it was not only the light that *Tiferet* cast downward that was darkened, but also the light that came to *Tiferet* from the higher realms.   [173] *Yesod*.

[174] The flow of influence, which used to descend to the male, has ceased.

[175] The *Shekhinah*.   [176] *Tiferet*.   [177] *Binah*.

do not rest upon Him. And because of this, the Holy One, blessed be He, groans and weeps, as it is said, "He roars mightily over His habitation" (Jeremiah 25: 30). What does He say? "Alas, that I have destroyed My house, and burned My temple. . . ."[178]

When the Assembly of Israel went into exile she said to Him: "Tell me, you whom my soul loves" (Song of Songs 1: 7f.), you, who are the beloved of my soul, you in whom is all the love of my soul, "how do you feed," how do you nourish yourself from the depths of the unceasing river?[179] How do you nourish yourself from the illumination of the supernal Eden?[180] "How do you cause [your flocks] to rest at noon," how do you nourish all the others,[181] who are continuously watered by you? I used to be nourished by you every day, and watered, and I would water all the lower worlds, and Israel would be nourished through me, but now "why should I be like one that veils herself," how can I enshroud myself without blessings, when there is need of these blessings, and yet I do not have any? "Beside the flocks of your companions"— how can I stand beside them, and not feed them, or nourish them? "The flocks of your companions"—these are Israel, the children of the patriarchs, who are the holy Chariot on high.[182] The Holy One, blessed be He, said to her: Leave my [distress], for my [distress] is too secret a thing to be disclosed. But "if you do not know," yourself, this is [my] advice to you. "You most beautiful of women," as it is said, "Behold, you are beautiful, my love" (Song of Songs 1: 15), "Go out and follow in the footsteps of the flock"—these are the righteous, who are trampled under foot, and who give you the power to sustain yourself. "And feed your kids by the tents of the shepherds"—these are the little children in their teacher's house, by whom the world is sustained, and who give strength to the Assembly of Israel in exile. "The tents of the righteous"—these are the houses of their teachers, the place of the house of study, where the Torah may always be found.

22. LONGING

(Zohar III, 42a–42b)

Rabbi Eleazar began by quoting: "By night on my bed I sought [him whom my soul loves. I sought him but I did not find him]" (Song of

[178] B.T. *Berakhot* 3a: "Alas, for My children, whose sins have caused Me to destroy My house, and burn My temple, and exile them among the nations of the world."
[179] From *Binah*, the source of influence. [180] *Hokhmah.*
[181] *Tarbiz* ("you cause to rest") is here interpreted in the sense of pouring water out for the flock. And *zohorayim* ("noon," a dual form) refers to the *sefirot* and the other celestial hosts who depend on the flow of influence from above.
[182] Israel are called "your companions" because of the patriarchs, who are the symbols of *Ḥesed, Gevurah*, and *Tiferet*, which form the supernal Chariot.

Songs 3: 1). "On (al) my bed"[183]—it ought to have said "in my bed."
What is the significance of al mishkavi? The Assembly of Israel[184] spoke
to the Holy One, blessed be He,[185] and petitioned Him concerning the
exile, because she dwelt among the other nations with her children, and
lay in the dust. And because she dwelt in a foreign, unclean, land, she
said "concerning my dwelling" I petition, because I dwell in exile.
Therefore, "I sought him whom my soul loves," that He might bring me
out of [exile]. "I sought him but I did not find him," because it is not His
custom to cohabit with me anywhere except in His palace. "[I sought
him, but I could not find him;] I called him, but he did not answer me"
(Song of Songs 5: 6)—because I dwell among other peoples, and His
children alone hear His voice, as it is written "Did ever a people hear the
voice of God . . ." (Deuteronomy 4: 33)?

    Rabbi Isaac said: "By night on my bed." The Assembly of Israel said:
Concerning my bed I pleaded with Him, that He might lie with me, and
give me pleasure, and bless me with perfect delight; for we have learned
that, as a result of the King's cohabitation with the Assembly of Israel,
large numbers of the righteous come into their sacred inheritance, and a
multitude of blessings are bestowed on the world.

23. THE *SHEKHINAH*, ABOVE AND BELOW

(Zohar I, 159b–160a)

Rabbi Hiyya began by quoting: "And I have also heard the groaning of
the children of Israel, whom the Egyptians keep in bondage; and I have
remembered My covenant" (Exodus 6: 5). "And I have remembered"—this is *zekhirah* (remembering), because it is in the realms above
that this planet, which is above in the male (*zakhar*),[186] is joined to
pekidah (visitation), which is in exile below, in the female.[187] Likewise:
"And God remembered Rachel" (Genesis 30: 22), as it is said "And I
have remembered My covenant."[188]

    Come and see. It is written "I have surely visited you" (Exodus 3: 16).
What is the significance of "I have surely visited"? "Visitation" applies
to the female, and at that time she was in exile, and yet she says "I have

[183] [*Al* means "on, above, concerning." *Al mishkavi* can be translated both "on my
bed" and, as below, "concerning my dwelling."]
[184] The *Shekhinah*.   [185] *Tiferet.*
[186] The essence of redemption comes from the male side, *Tiferet*, through which *Keter*,
called "planet," works. Therefore the announcement of redemption contains a reference
to *zekhirah*, which denotes both "remembrance" and the male element.
[187] *Pekidah* ("visitation") comes from the female side, the *Shekhinah*, which is in exile,
and which acts through the power of the male.
[188] Children also depend on "the planet," which works through the male (*zakhar*),
and so we have "And He remembered (*va-yizkor*)." [The context concerns Rachel's
having children.]

surely visited"? But one must meditate on this, and here we have a secret of wisdom. If she was in exile how could she appear to Moses, and how could she say "I have surely visited"? Thus have we learned: When the sun shines it is in the heavens, but its power and its strength rule throughout the earth. And so "the whole earth is full of his glory" (Isaiah 6: 3). When the Temple was still standing "the whole earth was full of his glory," namely, the holy land. But now that Israel are in exile, she is in the realms above,[189] and the strength encompasses Israel, in order to protect them, even though they are in another land. And come and see. There is the *Shekhinah* below, and the *Shekhinah* above. The *Shekhinah* is above in the twelve regions of the holy chariots, and among the twelve supernal *hayyot* (creatures); the *Shekhinah* is below among the twelve holy tribes. Thus the *Shekhinah* above and below is comprised together, and everything is united at one and the same time. Therefore when Israel is in exile she is in disorder below;[190] and she is also in disorder above because she is in disorder below. And this is [the significance of] her being in exile with Israel; she shares their exile.[191] How can she be restored?[192] It may be compared to a king whose son has died. What does he do? He dismantles his bed in mourning for his son. And he does not make up his bed, but takes thorns and thistles, and puts them beneath the bed, and lies upon it. And so with the Holy One, blessed be He. When Israel went into exile, and the Temple was destroyed, He took thorns and thistles, and put them beneath Him. This is [the meaning of] the verse, "And the angel of the Lord appeared to him in a flame of fire out of the midst of a bush" (Exodus 3: 2), because Israel were in exile.[193]

"I have surely visited you." How can one "visit" and what can he do to that which is not under his authority?[194] But *pakod* from above, and *pakadti* from below.[195] Why is this? Because the "remembering"

[189] The *Shekhinah* herself is not in exile. She resides in her place in the realms above. But her strength and her concern accompany Israel in exile.

[190] Because the arrangement of the tribes has been thrown into disarray, and this is a model of the way in which the camps of the *Shekhinah* are arranged in the realms above.

[191] Even in her place on high she suffers, when Israel are in exile.

[192] During the exile.

[193] The answer, apparently, is that even in exile there is a revelation of the *Shekhinah*, and this is her "restoration." But she is plunged in grief because she is forced to reveal herself among the husks, i.e., the thorns, and this is symbolized by the vision of the burning bush. It is possible, however, that the point of the story is that even in exile she may be restored through intercourse, but not through perfect intercourse, and this is depicted by the idea of lying on thorns.

[194] Redemption will not derive from *Malkhut*, but from a higher source, especially after the power of *Malkhut* has been weakened by exile.

[195] [*Pakod pakadti* is the Hebrew original, with emphatic duplication of the verb, of "I have surely visited."] The duplication of the verb shows that the announcement of redemption comes actually from the male side [*zakhar*], and for this reason it says *va-ezkor*

happened first, as it is written "I have remembered My covenant."
Since it is written "I have remembered," remembering (*zekhirah*) was
promised her, and so it is written later "I have surely visited," for a sign
had already been given before. So it was with Sarah,[196] where it is
written, "And the Lord visited Sarah" (Genesis 23: 1). But with Rachel,
where "remembering" is not mentioned previously, it does not speak of
"visiting" but "remembering,"[197] and it is all through the male
(*zekhirah*), through the mystery of the planet.[198]

24. IN THE LAND OF ISRAEL AND OUTSIDE THE LAND

(Zohar I, 84b–85a)

Rabbi Abba began by quoting: "But Jonah arose to flee to Tarshish
from the presence of the Lord" (Jonah 1: 3). Woe to the man who tries to
hide himself from the Holy One, blessed be He, of whom it is written "Do
I not fill heaven and earth, says the Lord?" (Jeremiah 23: 24). And yet
he tried to flee from Him? However, it is written, "O my dove (*yonati*) in
the clefts of the rock, in the covert of the cliff" (Song of Songs 2: 14).
"My dove"—this is the Assembly of Israel;[199] "in the clefts of the
rock"—this is Jerusalem, which is the highest point in the whole world:
just as the rock is higher and stronger than anything else, so Jerusalem is
higher and stronger than anything else. "In the covert of the cliff"—this
is the place that is called "the Holy of Holies," the heart of the entire
world. And so it is written "In the covert of the cliff." Since the *Shekhinah*
secluded herself there, like a woman who is faithful to her husband, not
venturing outside the house, as it is written "Your wife shall be as a
fruitful vine, in the innermost parts of your house" (Psalm 128: 3), so the
Assembly of Israel did not live anywhere except in its place, in the
seclusion of that level, apart from the days of exile, when it is in the lands
of the dispersion. And because it is in exile, the other peoples enjoy
prosperity and tranquillity.

Come and see. When Israel dwelt in the Holy Land, everything was
ordered as it should be, and the throne was in perfection over them, and
they engaged in worship [in the Temple], which split the world's
atmospheres. The worship ascended above, to its place, because Israel,
alone in the earth, was prepared for worship. Consequently, the other
peoples, the idolaters, were kept at a distance, for they had no power

("I have remembered.") And only by using the power of the male is the *Shekhinah* able to
say: "I have visited."

[196] The announcement to Sarah also uses the term "visit," because the promise had
already been given to Abraham, and this announcement was from the male side.

[197] "And God remembered Rachel" (Genesis 30: 22).

[198] Through the mystery of the activity of *Keter* in the male.   [199] The *Shekhinah*.

over [Israel] as they have now, because they were nourished only by the last drops.[200] You might object, and say that we know that there were several kings ruling in the world when the Temple was still standing. But come and see. During the era of the First Temple, before Israel defiled the land, the other peoples, the idolaters, did not rule, but they were nourished only by the last drops, and this gave them their power, which was not very great. When Israel sinned and defiled the land, they immediately forced the *Shekhinah*, as it were, to leave her place, and she drew near to another place,[201] and then the other peoples began to rule, and permission to rule was granted them. Come and see. No other ruler[202] has been appointed for the land of Israel except the Holy One, blessed be He, alone. But when Israel sinned, and fell to offering incense to other gods in the midst of the land, then the *Shekhinah* was expelled, as it were, from her place, and they continued to offer incense and to link other gods with the *Shekhinah*, and then the power to rule was given to them, for incense helps to forge a link.[203] Then the other peoples began to rule, and the prophets ceased, and none of the supernal levels[204] ruled over the land. And the rule of the other peoples was not taken away, because they had drawn the *Shekhinah* toward them. Consequently, with the Second Temple, power was not taken away from the other peoples, not to speak of the time when the *Shekhinah* was exiled among the other peoples, to a place where the other guardian angels have authority; for all of them draw nourishment from the *Shekhinah*, who has come near to them. Therefore, when Israel dwelt in their land, and were engaged in the worship of God, the *Shekhinah* acted chastely among them, and did not leave the house and show herself outside. Consequently, all the prophets who lived at that time received their prophecy only in her place, as we have said. It was for this reason that Jonah wanted to flee outside the Holy Land, so that prophecy might not be revealed to him, and so that he would not have to go on the mission of the Holy One, blessed be He. If you object and say that we know that the *Shekhinah* was revealed in Babylon, which is outside [the land of Israel], we can reconcile it in this way. It is written "[the word of the Lord] came expressly" (Ezekiel 1: 3)—something happened that had not happened[205] before, since the building of the Temple, and this prophecy was of a unique kind, necessary for that particular time. And it is written "by the river Kevar" (ibid.)—the river that already (*kevar*) existed from the time that the world was created, and the *Shekhinah* is revealed by it

[200] By the remains of the flow of influence that descended upon Israel.
[201] To the domain of "the other side."   [202] Guardian angel.
[203] When incense is offered to God a unifying link is effected among the *sefirot*. When they offered incense to the pagan gods this served to link the *Shekhinah* with "the other side."   [204] The *sefirot*.
[205] [This interpretation is based on the repetition of the verb in the Hebrew original of "came expressly," namely, *hayoh hayah*.]

continuously,[206] as it is written "And a river went out of Eden to water the garden; and from thence it was parted [and became four heads]" (Genesis 2: 10), and this [river] was one of them, and there the *Shekhinah* was revealed, at the precise moment when Israel needed her in their tribulation. But at other times she is not revealed. Therefore Jonah left the Holy Land and fled, in order that the *Shekhinah* should not rest upon him or reveal herself to him. This is [the meaning of] the verse "from the presence of the Lord," since it is also written, "For the men knew that he was fleeing from the presence of the Lord" (Jonah 1: 10).

25. THE DARKENED LIGHT

(Zohar III, 45b)

Rabbi Judah began by quoting: "You may not look upon me, because I am blackened, because the sun has tanned me" (Song of Songs 1: 6). This verse has been explained. But when the moon[207] hid herself in exile, she said "You may not look upon me." Not that this was a command, not to look at her, but since she saw how Israel yearned to look at the light, she said "You may not look upon me"—you are not able to see me—it is impossible to see me. Why is this? Because "I am blackened"—because I am in darkness. Why does it say "*sheharhoret* (blackened)"? It should have said *shehorah*.[208] But there are two darknesses. One is because "the sun has tanned me," because the sun has withdrawn its light from me and does not look on me,[209] and the other is caused by the fact that "my mother's sons burned in anger against me." *Sheshzafatni* (it has tanned me)? It should have said *shezafatni*. But there is an allusion here to the number six,[210] for when the sun shines, it shines with six lights, and when it removes itself, the whole six are removed with it. "My mother's sons"—these are they that come from the side of strict Judgment.[211] "They burned in anger against me," as it is said "My throat burns" (Psalm 69: 4). This is [the significance of] the verse "To our very necks we are pursued" (Lamentations 5: 5), for when Israel went into exile, they went with their hands tied behind their backs, and millstones round their necks, and they could not open their mouths. "They made me keeper of the vineyards," so that I might go

---

[206] At its source in the Garden of Eden. [207] The *Shekhinah*.

[208] [The common word for "black." *Sheharhoret* is an intensive form.]

[209] The sun (*Tiferet*) has left the moon (the *Shekhinah*) in darkness, by removing its light.

[210] The first syllable of *sheshzafatni* refers to the number six (*shesh*), i.e., to the six *sefirot* from whom the *Shekhinah* receives influence by means of *Tiferet*. When the latter departs, their light departs also.

[211] The husks, who originate in *Gevurah*, are called "my mother's sons," because the *Shekhinah* also emanated from *Gevurah*. In exile they harass the *Shekhinah*, and make her dumb.

into exile to keep the other peoples, for Israel's sake. "But my own vineyard I have not kept," for I am not able to keep them as I did at the beginning. Before, I kept my own vineyards, and the other vineyards were kept as a result, but now I keep the other vineyards, so that my own vineyard among them should be kept.[212]

26. JOY AND SORROW

(Zohar III, 74a–75a)

Rabbi Eleazar was seated before his father. He said to him: Whenever there is intercession in the world it involves the consort,[213] and whenever there is accusation in the world it involves the consort. Why is this?

He said to him: It is like a king who had a son by a certain consort. Whenever the son performed the king's will, the king would make his home with the consort. But whenever the son did not perform the king's will, the king would forsake his home and the consort. So it is with the Holy One, blessed be He, and the Assembly of Israel.[214] Whenever Israel perform the will of the Holy One, blessed be He, the Holy One, blessed be He, makes His home with the Assembly of Israel. But whenever Israel do not perform the will of the Holy One, blessed be He, the Holy One, blessed be He, does not make His home with the Assembly of Israel. Why is this? Because Israel is the firstborn of the Holy One, blessed be He, as it is written "Israel is my son, my firstborn" (Exodus 4: 22). The mother is the Assembly of Israel, as it is written "Do not forsake the teaching of your mother" (Proverbs 1: 8). Come and see. Whenever Israel go far away from the king's palace, the consort, so to speak, goes away with them. For what reason? Because the consort did not give the son instruction by chastising him; for the king does not chastise his son, but leaves everything to the consort: the management of the palace, the chastisement of the child, and his upbringing in the true way that leads to the king. The mystery of the matter is in the verse "The words of King Lemuel; the burden with which his mother corrected him" (Proverbs 31: 1). This is Bathsheba, and it has already been explained.[215] It is written "The proverbs of Solomon. A wise son makes a father glad; but a foolish son is the grief of his mother" (Proverbs 10: 1)—he really is "the grief of his mother." See what is written, "A wise son makes a father glad," when the son walks in the correct way, and is

[212] When Israel dwelt in their own land they received influence directly from the *Shekhinah*, and the other nations were nourished by the remnants of that influence. In exile, however, the influence is given to the guardian angels of the nations, and Israel receives a restricted amount from them.   [213] The *Shekhinah*.

[214] *Tiferet* and the *Shekhinah*.

[215] Bathsheba (lit., "the daughter of seven") is the *Shekhinah*, who comprises seven *sefirot*.

wise. "He makes a father glad"—this is the holy king[216] above. He "makes a father glad," without any qualification. If the son follows a crooked path, what is written? "A foolish son is the grief of his mother"—his mother, but not his father. And the mystery of this is in the verse, "For your transgressions was your mother put away" (Isaiah 50: 1). "Your mother" is the Assembly of Israel.

Come and see. The Holy One, blessed be He, has never experienced such joy as on the day when Solomon attained wisdom, and uttered the Song of Songs. Then the consort's countenance shone, and the king came and established his home with her. This is [the meaning of] the verse: "And Solomon's wisdom[217] excelled . . ." (1 Kings 5: 10). What does "excelled" mean? It means that the consort's beauty increased, and she excelled with her levels[218] all the other levels, because the king had made his home with her. Why was this so? Because she had presented the world with this wise son, and when she brought forth Solomon she brought forth the whole of Israel,[219] and they were all of very high degree, righteous like Solomon, so that the Holy One, blessed be He, rejoiced in them, and they in Him. On the very day that Solomon completed the house below, the consort prepared a home for the king, and they set up house together, and her face shone with perfect joy. Then there was joy for all, above and below. Why was this so? Because it is written "The burden with which his mother corrected him," for she dealt with him as the king desired. And when this son, as I have said, does not conduct himself as the king desires, then all are naked,[220] nakedness on all sides, for the king separates from the consort, and the consort leaves his palace, and so all are naked. Is there not "nakedness" when the king is without the consort and the consort without the king? It is for this reason that it is written "The nakedness of your father, and the nakedness of your mother, you shall not uncover; she is your mother" (Leviticus 18: 7). She is certainly your mother, and dwells with you. Therefore "you shall not uncover her nakedness" (ibid.).

Rabbi Simeon clasped his hands, and wept, and said: Woe, if I speak, and reveal the mystery, and woe, if I do not speak, for then the companions would be deprived of it. "Ah (*ahah*) Lord God, will You make a full end of the remnant of Israel?" (Ezekiel 11: 13). What is the significance of "*ahah*" and "will You make a full end"? But this is the mystery of the matter: When the lower [letter] *he*[221] is dismissed from the king's palace, the other *he*, the upper one,[222] withholds blessing

---

[216] *Tiferet.*   [217] The *Shekhinah*, the lower Wisdom.

[218] The angels, who were there to serve her, were more numerous.

[219] All Solomon's contemporaries.

[220] The mystery of "the uncovering of the nakedness" of the father and mother consists in Israel, through its sins, compelling the *Shekhinah* to depart from her husband.

[221] The *Shekhinah*, the second *he* of the tetragrammaton *YHVH.*

[222] *Binah*, the first *he*, which is the source of influence.

because of her, and then it is written "*Ahah*, will You make a full end?" since, just as this *he* is deprived of blessings, so the other *he* withholds them from all.[223] What is the reason? Because blessings are to be found only where male and female are together. Concerning this it is written "The Lord roars from on high, and utters His voice from His holy habitation. He roars mightily because of His dwelling" (Jeremiah 25: 30)—His real dwelling, that is, the consort. It is certainly so. And what does He say? "Alas that I have destroyed my house . . ."[224] "My house"—cohabitation with the consort. This is indeed [signified by] "The nakedness of your father, and the nakedness of your mother, you shall not uncover" for on all sides it is nakedness.[225] And then "The heavens are clothed in blackness, and sackcloth is made their covering" (Isaiah 50: 3),[226] for the gathering-place of the blessings of the rivers' sources, which used to flow and provide water as was fitting, is sealed.

We have learned: When the king is separated from the consort and blessings are not to be found, he is called *VY*. Why *VY*? It has been taught: The head of *Yesod* is *Y*, because *Yesod* is small *V*, and the Holy One, blessed be He, is large *V*, the upper one,[227] and so it is written *VV*,[228] two *vavim* together, and the head of *Yesod* is *Y*. When the consort departs from the king, and blessings are withheld from the king, and intercourse does not exist at the head of *Yesod*, the upper *V* takes the head of *Yesod*, which is *Y*, and draws it toward itself, and then it is *VY*: woe (*vy*) for all, for the upper and the lower realms. Concerning this we have learned (cf. B.T. *Sotah* 48a): Since Jerusalem was destroyed, blessings are not to be found in the world, and there is not a day that does not have its curses, for blessings are withheld every day.

He said to him: If this is so, what is the difference between *AVY* and *HVY*?[229]

He said to him: Since the matter depends on repentance, and they do not repent, the upper *H*[230] takes, and draws toward itself, *V* and *Y*, because they do not repent, and then it is called *HVY*. *AVY*—when the king departs farther and farther toward the higher regions, and the children of men cry out and he does not care for them, and that supernal *Ehyeh*,[231] the concealed one, draws up toward itself *V* and *Y*, so that their

---

[223] The full destruction comes as a result of the two letters *he*, indicated in the word *ahah*.   [224] B.T. *Berakhot* 3a. [See above p. 411.]

[225] On the side of *Tiferet*, and on the side of *Malkhut*.

[226] The verse is not quoted accurately. The original reads, "I clothe the heavens with blackness, and I make sackcloth their covering."

[227] *Tiferet* is symbolized by the letter *vav* (*V*) of *YHVH*, and *Yesod* that is connected with it is called "small *vav*." [The letter *yod* is shaped like a small *vav*.]

[228] The name of the letter *vav* has two *vavim*.

[229] [Both words, pronounced respectively *Oy*, and *Hoy*, mean "Woe."]

[230] *Binah*, which is called "Repentance" (*Teshuvah*).

[231] *Keter*, symbolized by the letter *alef* (i.e., *A*).

prayer should not be received, then it is called *AVY*; for the *alef* draws up toward itself *V* and *Y*, and then repentance is not to be found. Therefore the *H* departs from these letters, for the matter does not depend on repentance, for, to be sure, when the sins of the world grew very numerous, and repentance was suspended, and they had no desire for it, then the *H* departed, and the *A* drew the *V* and the *Y* up toward it, and it was called *AVY*. When the Temple was destroyed, and repentance departed, they immediately cried out and said "Woe (*AVY—oy*) unto us! for the day turns" (Jeremiah 6: 4). What is the meaning of "the day turns"? This is the supernal day, called "repentance," which departed and passed away, and is not to be found, the day whose well-known [custom] it is to stretch out its right hand to receive the wicked [who repent]. And now it has turned, and is not to be found. Therefore they say "*oy* (*AVY*)" and not "*hoy* (*HVY*)." "For the shadows of the evening are stretched out" (ibid.), for authority has been given to the guardian angels, appointed over the rest of the peoples, to rule over them.

It has been taught: *V* ascended[232] to the upper regions, and the palace was burned, the people went into exile, the consort was dismissed, and the Temple was destroyed. Subsequently, when *V* came down to his place he looked at his house, and found it destroyed, sought the consort and found that she had departed and gone away, saw the palace and found it burned, sought the people and found it in exile, saw the blessings of the deep rivers, which used to flow, and found them stopped up, and then immediately it is written "And in that day did the Lord, the God of hosts, decree weeping, lamentation, baldness, and girding with sack-cloth" (Isaiah 22: 12). And then "The heavens were clothed with blackness." Then *V* and *Y* began to flow, each toward the other,[233] and supernal *H* stretched forth its sources toward "the other side," and blessings were not to be found, for male and female were not there, and they did not dwell together. Then "He roars mightily because of His dwelling."

Rabbi Simeon wept, and Rabbi Eleazar wept. Rabbi Eleazar said: Weeping has penetrated my heart on the one side, and joy is in my heart on the other, for I have heard things that I had not heard before. How happy is my portion!

27. SURETY

(Zohar III, 114a)

"And I will set My tabernacle (*mishkani*) among you" (Leviticus 26: 11). "And I will set My tabernacle"—this is the *Shekhinah*: "*mishkani*," My

[232] It has gone up to *Keter*, so that the latter becomes *AVY*.

[233] The flow of influence from the male does not descend to the female, but an internal flow takes place from *Tiferet* to *Yesod*, and from *Yesod* to *Tiferet*.

surety,[234] since it was taken as surety,[235] because of the sins of Israel, and so *"mishkani"* [means] "My surety," without a doubt.[236] It is like a man who was fond of someone. He said to him: "My love for you is so great that I should like to live with you." [The other] said: "How do I know that you will continue to live with me?" He took the most precious thing in his house and brought it to him. He said: "Look, you now have this surety, that I shall never leave you." In the same way, the Holy One, blessed be He, wanted to dwell with Israel. What did He do? He took the most precious thing He had, and brought it down to Israel. He said to them: "Israel, look, you now have My surety, for I shall never leave you." And even though the Holy One, blessed be He, has gone far away from us, He has left a surety with us, and we take care of His greatest treasure. Whoever wants His surety—let him come and dwell with us. Therefore, "I will set My tabernacle among you"—I shall put My surety in your hands, so that I might dwell with you. And even though Israel are now in exile, they have the surety of the Holy One, blessed be He, and they will never forsake it.

"And My soul shall not abhor you" (ibid.). It is like a man who loved his companion, and wanted to live with him. What did he do? He took his bed, and brought it to his house. He said: "Look, my bed is in your house, for I shall not go away from you, from your bed, or from your possessions." In the same way, the Holy One, blessed be He, said "I will set My tabernacle among you, and My soul shall not abhor you. Look, My bed is in your house. Since My bed is with you, you will know that I shall not leave you, and therefore, My soul shall not abhor you."

28. IN THE STREET OF THE TANNERS

(Zohar III, 115b)

Rabbi Hiyya said: I have heard a new interpretation that Rabbi Eleazar said: "I will not reject them, nor will I abhor them, to destroy them utterly" (Leviticus 26: 44). Should it not have said "I will not smite them, nor will I slay them, to destroy them utterly"? Yet [it says] "I will not reject them, nor will I abhor them." Whoever hates another person is rejected by him, and abhorred by him. But in this case, "I will not reject them, nor will I abhor them." Why is this? Because My soul's beloved is among them, and for her sake they are all loved by Me. It is

[234] [There is a play on words here between *mishkani* (my tabernacle) and *mashkoni* (my surety).]

[235] The *Shekhinah* has gone into exile to the lands of the other nations, because of the sins of Israel.

[236] Both at the time of the Temple's existence, and in exile, the *Shekhinah* dwells with Israel, as a kind of pledge, that the Holy One, blessed be He, will never forsake His people.

written *le-khalotam* (to destroy them), without the letter *vav*:[237] for her
sake I will not reject them, nor will I abhor them, for she is the beloved of
my soul; my love is with her. It is like a man who was in love with a
woman who lived in the street of the tanners. If she had not been there,
he would never have set foot in the place; but because she was there it
seemed to him like the street of the spice merchants, where all the finest
perfumes in the world could be found. So here "Yet for all that, when
they are in the land of their enemies" (ibid.), which is the street of the
tanners, "I will not reject them, nor will I abhor them." Why?
"*Le-khalatam*," because of their bride, whom I love; for it is the beloved of
My soul who dwells there, and to Me it is like all the finest perfumes in
the world, because of the bride that is with them.

[237] [So that it can also be read *le-khalatam* (for their bride)], i.e., the *Shekhinah*, the
bride of the Holy One, blessed be He.

SECTION IV. INFLUENCE AND DIRECTION

INTRODUCTION

a. Dynamic Direction

The question of the direction and providence of God as it affects the world and mankind was a crucial problem in medieval religious thought, especially in the twelfth and thirteenth centuries; that is, in the formative period of the kabbalah, and at the time when the *Sefer ha-Bahir* was being written. The traditional Jewish view, both biblical and rabbinic, was that religious faith involved the absolute subordination of the world and its inhabitants to the perpetual and all-encompassing direction of God, and to the providence that He exercised over every individual, in the detailed assignment of reward and punishment. During the Middle Ages, however, the religious attitude of the Jews was deeply influenced by widespread philosophical ideas that saw God solely as the First Cause, and removed Him from any involvement in the ordinary process of events either in animate or inanimate life. Most Jewish philosophers strongly opposed this point of view, and tried to maintain and substantiate the traditional Jewish concept. But, as a result of the controversies that they had with non-Jewish philosophers, they made certain concessions and imposed a large number of restrictions as to the nature and extent of divine direction. The most extreme among them, together with their disciples, were even inclined to deny God's providence over individuals, and to reject the possibility of miracles as being contrary to the laws of nature. Kabbalistic teaching propounded a completely opposite view, and stressed as much as it could the necessity for absolute faith in direction and providence from the realms above. The Zohar contains a fierce polemic against those who deny divine providence, and who substitute chance as an important factor in the affairs of the world and in the destiny of mankind. "The fools who neither know nor study wisdom say that this world proceeds by chance, and that the Holy One, blessed be He, has no concern for them, but 'that which befalls[1] the sons of men befalls beasts; even one thing befalls them...' (Ecclesiastes 3: 19). But when Solomon saw these fools who say such things, he called them 'beasts,' for they make themselves into real beasts, who say such things.... May these beasts, these fools, breathe their last, they who are of such little faith. Woe to them, woe to their souls! It were better for them if they had not come into the world."[2] These words were clearly aimed at the traces of atheism that began to appear in the attitudes of contemporary philosophizers.

The great change that took place in kabbalah with regard to the concept of the Godhead involved also a basic alteration in the idea of the nature of providence and divine direction of the world. The simple and wholehearted theistic faith of early Judaism saw in the divine conduct of the world the work of a Lord and Creator, all-mighty and all-powerful, who dwelt in the heavens above, and who kept His worldly domain in order, scrutinizing the lives of His servant-creatures. In His direction of the world, God acted for good or ill with perfect justice, as He thought fit, or beyond the demands of strict justice, as He Himself determined, and these acts were put into effect like royal edicts, or as elements of moral instruction and as the manifestations of love shown by a father or a teacher. In this relationship there is no direct contact between the ruler and the ruled, and the influence of the lower world is restricted to a plea for mercy and compassion.[3] Now, in kabbalistic literature, including the Zohar, we do, of course, find descriptions and accounts that present a similar view. This is particularly noticeable in the picture of the *Shekhinah*. I have already shown in the previous introduction how the *Shekhinah* is given the character of a personal ruler in her role as the consort or supernal mother. She is active in the direction and maintenance of the world, distributing reward and punishment by means of her agents and messengers. But in actual fact, the method of direction, which the kabbalists had in mind, is absolutely different from the method envisaged in the traditional concept. The system of the *sefirot*, in which, according to kabbalistic teaching, the Godhead is depicted in the role of a personal deity manifesting Himself in the creation and direction of the world, is a system of dynamic beings; and the activity that comes from them is thought of as the realization of forces hidden within them, which then flow down in the form of a specific influence. The actual nature of the influence, as well as its greater or lesser extent, or its cessation altogether, which determine the way in which the worlds are directed, all depend on the situation of the *sefirot*—that is, on the relationships within the Godhead of the powers of Love and Judgment, on their combination, intermingling, or separation, as explained in earlier introductions.[4] This situation continually changes, and the forces come down on the side of punishment or favor, depending on the vagaries of activity in the lower world. These changes, however, are not merely the result of strict justice or exact calculation, nor are they simply the manifestations of an autocratic will, as the traditional concept of divine direction would have them; for the influence of the lower worlds is also considered to have a dynamism of its own. The intentions and acts of man also bring certain forces into play. His good deeds form a positive, constructive, beneficent force, and his bad deeds engender a negative, destructive, maleficent force. These forces flow upward, and as "a stimulation from below" (*itaruta diltata*) they affect the balance in the interrelationships of the divine powers. The force of good deeds increases the power of Love, and the force of bad deeds increases the power of Judgment. Therefore man is a partner with God in the conduct of the world, and the actual work of direction is a result of the cross-influence of the upper and lower forces.

   The dynamic nature of the divine control of the world and the interrelationships that exist between the upper and the lower worlds are nowhere more clearly seen than in the activity of the *Shekhinah*. She is represented by a number of different symbols, such as "the female," "the sea," "the field," "the garden," and so on, in all of which she appears as a receptacle for the flow of supernal influence. One may therefore describe her as a kind of storehouse of divine powers. In her direction of the world she activates the forces that are stored up within her, and distributes them in the form of life and sustenance to the realms below. It is in this dynamic activity that we see the true meaning of the concept in the Zohar of the *Shekhinah* as the ruler of the world. Both aspects of her activity, namely, the storing of the divine powers and their subsequent activation, are depicted, for example, in the paradoxical image of the transformation of a garden into a fountain. "There is one garden (the *Shekhinah*) below them (i.e., below the upper *sefirot*), and this garden is protected on all sides. Below this garden are other gardens (i.e., the worlds) that produce their species of fruit. And this garden changes and becomes a fountain that waters them" (*Events and Personalities*, 4). The watering of the gardens, that is to say, the distribution of the heavenly powers, depends on the forces that proceed from actions in the lower world, which also reach the *Shekhinah* in the first instance, and are stored up within her. In the preceding introduction[5] I dealt at length with the way in which the power of Judgment increased in the *Shekhinah* as a result of the sins of mankind, and we saw this as a process whereby the negative power gained ascendancy over the positive power in the conduct of the world. Sometimes, when there is a diminution in worldly virtue there is a consequent diminution in the flow of Love, or a complete cessation. "When all [the supernal influence] that she (the *Shekhinah*) has gathered has reached her, she stores it, and shuts it up, and restricts it, so that it does not descend and illumine, except like a kind of dew, drop by drop, little by little. Why is this? Because there is no faith below, except, as it is said 'Here a little, there a little' (Isaiah 28: 13); a little virtue, a little illumination of dew, measure for measure; for were it not for the [small amount of] faith in the world, she would discharge [the influence] on every side, without any hindrance, and she would rejoice, and then they would give her (i.e., from above) many presents and gifts, one upon the other, and they would not hinder her in any way. But it is the lower realms that hinder them (i.e., the upper powers), and they hinder her, and then she is 'closed up.' "[6] Another account states that the sea of the *Shekhinah* either fills with the waters of influence or dries up, depending on the state of virtue or sin in the world. " 'For He has founded it upon the seas, and established it upon the floods' (Psalm 24: 2). These are the seven pillars (the *sefirot*) upon which she stands, and they fill her. . . . How is she filled with them? When the righteous increase in the world then the land (the *Shekhinah*) produces fruit, and is filled with everything. But when the wicked increase in the world, then it is written 'The waters disappear from the sea' (Job 14: 11). . . . This is the holy land, of which we have spoken, which is watered by watering from on high."[7] This change, which the *Shekhinah* suffers because of the influence of the lower worlds, and which establishes the way in which the world is run, is also described through the images of the well and the pit: when virtue increases she becomes a well of living waters, bubbling over with the supernal flow and with the influence of the souls of the righteous. But when sins increase, she is like an empty pit.[8]

The flow of influence that directs the world is symbolized by a number of different liquids, such as water, rain, dew, oil, wine, and so on. Its highest source is in the first *sefirah*, and it descends by way of the other *sefirot* when it is stimulated by the realms below. "What is 'the precious oil'? It is the oil of the holy anointing, which flows and emerges from *Atika Kadisha* (*Keter*), and exists in the supernal river (*Binah*), and which nourishes the children in order to kindle lights. This oil flows in the head of the king, and from his head to the splendor of the sacred beard, and from there it flows into all the precious garments with which the king clothes himself. . . . And come and see: This precious oil was not ready [to descend] until the worship below [in the Temple] ascended, and they encountered one another"(1). The chief roles in the dynamic process of activating and using the divine powers are assigned to two *sefirot: Binah* (the upper river) and *Yesod* (the lower river). They work as parallel forces, *Binah* directing the *sefirot* that are below it, and *Yesod* directing the worlds by means of the *Shekhinah*(3).[9] The mystery of *Yesod*'s dynamism is expressed in sexual symbols. The main symbol for the flow of influence is that of the semen, which originates in the brain, flows through various parts of the body, and manifests itself as a fertilizing power in the male genital organ, which serves as a symbol of *Yesod* in the figure of primordial man (*Adam Kadmon*). "For the righteous (i.e., *Yesod*) takes all and possesses everything together, and all blessings are contained within him. He discharges blessings from the head above, and every part of the body is ready to discharge blessings into him, and then he becomes 'a river going out of Eden.' What is 'Eden'? Whenever all the parts of the body are brought together in a single bond, enjoying pleasure and delight from the head, above and below, and when because of this pleasure and delight they all discharge into him, then he becomes a flowing river going out of real Eden"(2).[10] Male and female, *Yesod* and *Malkhut*, which are both channel and storehouse of the divine powers, constitute one entity like the unity of the source and the well (*Sefirot*, 23). This unity is destroyed during exile, when the female is taken away from the male, as a result of the sins of the world. Then the direction of the world is impaired, because the channel of influence is sealed and the dynamic forces cannot act in the lower realms. Only remnants of the influence, which had previously been sown in the garden of the *Shekhinah*, exist in order to sustain the world(13). Were it not for these remnants the world would turn into chaos, for it is the flow of the divine forces that basically controls and sustains it.

b. The Tension and Balancing of Opposites

A fundamental element in what I have called the "dynamic" concept of the divine direction of the world is the continual tension that exists in the life of the Godhead, in the activity of the lower realms, and in the way in which the world is controlled. The whole of existence is subject to the extreme tension of direct opposites: the leniency of Love or Mercy and the harshness of Judgment, virtues and vices, good and evil, God and "the other side," the forces of construction and the forces of destruction. The nature and balancing of these opposites, upon which the proper direction and maintenance of the world depend, are described in the Zohar in various ways.

As already explained, the *sefirot* are divided into two main areas, depicted as *Atika Kadisha* and *Ze'ir Anpin*;[11] that is, on the one side, *Keter* in close association with *En-Sof*, and, on the other, the totality of the forces of emanation from *Hokhmah* to *Malkhut*. *Ze'ir Anpin* is portrayed as the force of Judgment, keeping an account of sin, punishing and destroying the wicked, while *Atika Kadisha* is the force of absolute Mercy, a restraining influence on Judgment, and sustaining the world with a more lenient form of Judgment. "When the Ancient of ancients (*Atika de-atikin*), the Will of wills, is revealed, all the lights called by this name shine and Mercy exists throughout. But when the most secret of secrets is not revealed and these lights do not shine, then judgments are aroused, and it turns into Judgment. Who causes this Judgment? The Will of wills that is not revealed [because of the power of sin], and, consequently, the wicked turn Mercy into Judgment."[12] The interrelationships of these powers and their activity in the conduct of the world are depicted by using the images of the physical features of *Adam Kadmon*. The eyes of *Atika Kadisha* are like a single eye, because they look down upon the world with absolute Mercy, with no admixture of Judgment(7). The forehead of *Ze'ir Anpin* manifests itself in the visitation of iniquity, and when it appears it threatens the whole world with the terror of Judgment. It is only when the forehead of *Atika Kadisha* reveals itself in Mercy that the power of Judgment can be restrained. "The forehead of the skull (of *Ze'ir Anpin*) is the keenest of scrutinies, and reveals itself only when the wicked have to be visited, and when their deeds need to be examined. And it is taught: When this forehead is revealed all the prosecutors are aroused, and the whole world is given over to Judgment. But when the prayers of Israel rise up before the Ancient of Days, and he wishes to have mercy upon his children, he reveals the forehead of the Will of wills, and it illumines [the forehead of] *Ze'ir Anpin*, and Judgment is quieted"(9). The nose of *Ze'ir Anpin* breathes out black and red smoke, for the forces of destruction, which are called "anger," "ire," and "destroyer," are contained within it, and only the nose of *Atika Kadisha* can prevent the smoke of strict Judgment from rising. "It is taught: The nose (of *Ze'ir Anpin*) is small, and when the smoke begins to emerge it comes out hurriedly, and becomes Judgment. And who prevents the nose from producing smoke? The nose of *Atika Kadisha*, which is called 'the longest nose' of all."[13] According to these and similar accounts, the essence of *Ze'ir Anpin*, which comprises the powers that direct the world, consists mainly of Judgment (*Din*) with only a small element of Mercy (*Rahamim*), and were it not for the softening of Judgment and the illumination of Mercy on the part of *Atika Kadisha*, the sins of mankind would lead to the destruction of the world. The balancing of forces here, which assures the survival of the world, arises from the relationships between the divine powers that govern the lower realms, and the higher force that directs and supervises these powers.

This scheme is one of two opposing powers, Judgment and Mercy, with the former subject to the latter, which is above it in the emanatory system. That is to say, we have here two competing forces of unequal weight, without any real conflict between them, and it must be said that this does not represent the fundamental viewpoint of the Zohar. The basic and more frequently occurring idea is that the world of emanation is built up on a threefold pattern: two completely opposite extremes with a force in the middle that holds the balance between them. "Just as there are three crowned heads in *Atika Kadisha*, so everything consists of three heads. When they (i.e., the *sefirot*) are kindled, they all depend upon one another through the three heads, one on each side, and one that comprises them" (*Sefirot*, 13). There are no opposites in *Atika Kadisha* itself, but the triad that is to be found there serves as a supernal pattern for the structure of the forces of emanation. The first triad, where the existence and intermingling of opposites are beyond the reach of perception, is that of *Hokhmah*, *Binah*, and *Da'at*, and this branches out into the chief central triad of *Hesed*, *Gevurah*, and *Tiferet*, which comprise the attributes of Love, Judgment, and Mercy. The last triad consists of *Neẓaḥ*, *Hod*, and *Yesod*, which are subdivisions of these attributes, while *Malkhut*, by virtue of its position, represents the totality of all the attributes. Love and Judgment are two fiercely hostile forces in this system, each trying to overthrow and annihilate the other. A compromise has to be effected in this struggle by the attribute of Mercy, whose natural role is to moderate extremes and to mix them together in a single whole. When Love and Judgment come into contact and are mingled together in Mercy, the hostile tension that is part of their very nature becomes "a conflict of love and affection and the preservation of the world."[14] In this state they are balanced in perfect harmony, and the world is directed as it should be. The opposing powers work together in harness, complementing one another. The balancing of the two powers does not, however, destroy the tension between them, and the danger of rupture is always present. Any deterioration in the way the lower worlds conduct themselves is liable to have a bad effect on the normal direction of the world by the upper realms, and then the opposing forces return to their hostile and divisive attitude, increasing the power of Judgment to an abnormal degree and bringing retribution on the world. "Each of the supernal crowns (the *sefirot*) of the holy king contains Mercy in Judgment, and Judgment in Mercy, but the wicked turn Mercy into Judgment."[15] This conflict, which arises when the peace and concord in the mingling of Love and Judgment are disrupted, stokes the fires of Gehinnom;[16] that is, it gives added power to "the other side," who is not an opponent with the ability to act positively in a harmonious relationship, but a cruel and implacable enemy, whose main and consistent purpose is to destroy.[17]

The preservation of the world, therefore, depends on the mingling and moderation of opposing forces. The foundations of life and of ordered direction in the world are like "mountains suspended by a hair," liable to fall at any moment. "When the Holy One, blessed be He, created the world, He made the heavens of fire and water (Judgment and Love), mixed together, but they did not congeal. Later they congealed, and stood through a supernal spirit (Mercy). Thence He established the world that it might stand upon pillars, and those pillars stand only because of that spirit. When the spirit departs they all totter and shake, and the world trembles" (*The Account of Creation*, 6). Only a single step separates the conflict of harmonious love, which sustains the world, from the conflict of divisive hatred, which plunges the world into destruction and disaster. Herein lies the tremendous responsibility of mankind, for it is man that has the wherewithal to harmonize the opposing powers and to effect a balance between them, and it is his actions that can turn the scale toward innocence or guilt. The consequences of man's actions are not confined to the reward or punishment that might come to him personally, for there is a kind of collective responsibility. The actions of individuals are combined together, and it is their total influence that determines the way in which the whole world is governed. "When the Holy One, blessed be He, increases Love in the world [because of the preponderance of human virtue], man should walk in the streets and show himself to everyone, for when the goodness of the Holy One, blessed be He, resides in the world, it resides in everything, and He does good to all and increases it in the world. . .[but] when Judgment hangs over the world [because of the preponderance of human sin], man should not show himself in the street, or walk about alone in the world, for when Judgment resides in the world, it hovers over everything and whoever meets it and comes into contact with it is judged by that Judgment."[18] Man's involvement in the direction of the world, which is one of the basic tenets of kabbalistic doctrine, imposes upon him a very heavy responsibility. He has continually to see himself as part of the complex of the opposing forces in the Godhead and in the cosmos, and it is part of his task to help to moderate the extremes, and so to bring peace to the Godhead and to the world. On the other hand, he must beware of increasing the power of the opposing forces, and so feeding the fire of a destructive conflict.

NOTES

1. [Heb. *mikreh*, used in medieval Heb. for "chance."]
2. Zohar III, 157b.
3. This very general account obviously does not exhaust all the various nuances of earlier Jewish ideas on the subject. We have, for example, a different view expressed in the aggadic concept of the *Shekhinah*, and of the influence that the righteous have on God's actions. These ideas are very similar to kabbalistic teaching and they could in fact have influenced it, but they do not constitute part of the fundamental Jewish attitude in earlier times. With regard to the *Shekhinah* in this connection, see Abelson, *The Immanence of God*, pp. 12ff. However, in my view, because of his apologetic tendencies, the author goes too far in presenting the idea of the *Shekhinah* in rabbinic literature as definite proof that belief in divine immanence, in the wider sense, was a principal feature of rabbinic Judaism. However, discussion of this question lies outside my particular brief.
4. See above, pp. 270–71; 371–73; 376.
5. See above, pp. 376–79.
6. Zohar III, 197a. ["Closed up" is a reference to the "closing up" of the womb in Genesis 20: 18.]
7. Zohar I, 67a.
8. See Zohar I, 60a–60b; III, 266a–266b.
9. See also 4 and 5.
10. [Heb. *Eden* means "pleasure."]
11. *Atika Kadisha* is the head without the body, and *Ze'ir Anpin* is the whole of primordial man. See above, pp. 245–46, 297.
12. Zohar III, 137b (*Idra Rabba*).
13. Ibid., 137b–138a. [*Erekh apayim*, translated here "the longest nose," is the traditional "long-suffering." *Apayim* is the dual form of *af*, meaning both "nose" and "anger."]
14. Zohar I, 17b.
15. Zohar III, 30b.
16. Zohar I, 17a–17b; see *The Account of Creation*, 16.
17. In the introductions that follow I shall deal with the conflicts between "the other side" and the divine powers, and with his role in the direction of the world.
18. Zohar III, 54a–54b. See also *The Activity of "the Other Side"*, 12. Even though these passages do not state explicitly that the rule of Love and Judgment, or of Good and Evil, is connected with deeds in the lower worlds, we may deduce that such is the author's intention. But, even if we assume that he is referring solely to activity in the upper world, there is no doubt that the influence that the lower worlds have in establishing relationships among the divine powers, and in determining the conduct of the entire world, is a common theme in the Zohar.

INFLUENCE AND DIRECTION

1. INFLUENCE FROM *ATIKA KADISHA*

(Zohar III, 7b–8a)

"It is like the precious oil upon the head, [coming down upon the beard, even Aaron's beard, that comes down upon the collar of his garments]" (Psalm 133: 2). What is "the precious oil"? It is the oil of the holy anointing,[1] which flows and emerges from *Atika Kadisha*,[2] exists in the supernal river,[3] and nourishes the children[4] in order to kindle lights. This oil flows in the head of the king,[5] and from his head to the splendor of the sacred beard,[6] and from there it flows into all the precious garments[7] with which the king clothes himself. This is [the significance of] the phrase: "that comes down upon the collar of his garments"— through his attributes.[8] And these are the crowns of the king, upon which is the holy name. Come and see: All the influence and all the joy of the worlds descend, for the purpose of blessing, only through these sacred crowns, which are the name of the holy king.[9] Consequently, "that comes down *al pi midotav*"—through his ways,[10] as it is said "through Aaron and his sons shall it be" (Numbers 4: 27). Similarly, through his ways it descends and flows upon all the worlds [so that] blessings may exist for all. And come and see: This precious oil was not ready [to descend] until the worship below [in the Temple] ascended, and they encountered one another. This is the meaning of "Oil and incense rejoice the heart" (Proverbs 27: 9), oil downward and incense upward, and then there is joy for all.

2. THE UPPER MOTHER AND THE LOWER MOTHER

(Zohar I, 247b)

"The blessings of your father[11] are mightier than the blessings of my

---

[1] The influence from *Hokhmah*, which is called "*kodesh*" (holiness).
[2] *Keter.*   [3] *Binah.*   [4] The lower *sefirot.*
[5] In *Atika Kadisha*, which is the highest point in the system of emanation.
[6] The curls in the beard of *Atika Kadisha* symbolize the thirteen attributes of Mercy, which serve as channels for the transmission of influence.   [7] The *sefirot.*
[8] [The Heb. original for "upon the collar of his garments" is *al pi midotav*, which may also be translated in later Hebrew "through his attributes."]
[9] All the *sefirot* are comprised in the divine name *YHVH.*
[10] The ways through which he governs the world [*midotav* also means "his characteristics, attributes, methods, ways"].
[11] [The reference is to Jacob, father of Joseph.]

progenitors" (Genesis 49: 26). "The blessings of your father are" really "mightier," because Jacob is a river of praise for all, far more so than the other patriarchs, for he was perfect in everything, and he gave all to Joseph. Why was this? Because it was right that it should be so, for the righteous[12] takes all, and possesses everything together, and all blessings are contained within him. He discharges blessings from the head above, and every part of the body is ready to discharge blessings into him, and then he becomes "a river going out of Eden." What is "Eden"? Whenever all the parts of the body are brought together in a single bond, enjoying pleasure and delight from the head, above and below, and when because of this pleasure and delight they all discharge into him, then he becomes a flowing river going out of real Eden.[13] Furthermore, "out of Eden" [means that] out of the supernal Wisdom flows all,[14] that it might be extended [to the realms below], and it becomes a river that goes on until it reaches this level, and then everything is [surrounded] by blessings, and all is one. "Unto (ad) the desire of the hills of the world" (Genesis 49: 26). This ad[15] (unto) is the desire of the hills of the world. What are they? Two females, one above and one below,[16] each one of whom is called "a world." The desire of every part of the body is in those two mothers: desire for the child from the upper mother, and a desire to be united in the lower mother. And the desire of all is one, and therefore they are all as they should be. "They shall be on the head of Joseph . . ." (ibid.), so that the level of the righteous one may be blessed, and so that he may take all, as is fitting.

3. FEEDING THE UPPER AND THE LOWER WORLDS

(Zohar I, 162b)

It is written, "And God set them in the firmament of the heaven" (Genesis 1: 17). This is the righteous one.[17] Even though it is said "the firmament of the heaven" [it means] the actual firmament of heaven that is the final completion of the body.[18] Come and see. There are two

[12] *Yesod*, which is Joseph, while Jacob is *Tiferet*.

[13] Out of sensual pleasure. [*Eden* literally means "pleasure."]

[14] The semen of *Yesod* comes from *Hokhmah* (Wisdom), which is called "Eden," and which is here the brain.

[15] *Ad* is here *Yesod*. [Literally, we could translate the Hebrew: "unto is the desire. . . ." The traditional translations of this verse are, of course, quite different].

[16] *Binah* and *Malkhut*. Both of them desire *Yesod*. *Binah* wishes to pour influence into *Yesod*, and *Malkhut* wishes to be united with him. Looked at in another way, all the *sefirot*, which are like the different parts of the body, have a desire for *Binah* and *Malkhut*.

[17] *Yesod*.

[18] It would seem that both "firmament" and "heaven" are symbols of *Tiferet*, but the combination "the firmament of the heaven" designates *Yesod*, which is an extension of *Tiferet*.

firmaments,[19] the beginning and the completion, one patterned on the other. The beginning is the eighth firmament, in which are deposited all the lesser and greater stars,[20] and this is the upper firmament, the concealed one, which sustains all and from which all proceeds, and this is the eighth [counting] from bottom[21] to top, the beginning that produces all. Similarly, there is also the eighth firmament [counting] from top[22] to bottom, in which are deposited all the stars, the lights and luminaries, and it bears all and is the completion of all. Just as the eighth firmament, which is the beginning of all, holds all the lights in dependence, and bears them, and they go forth from it, so too this eighth firmament holds all the lights in dependence, and bears them, and they go forth from it to all the worlds.[23] The beginning and the completion are of the same pattern, and therefore it is a flowing river that goes forth,[24] and its waters never cease; everything is so that the completion shall be like the beginning. Consequently, "God set them in the firmament of the heaven." Why? "To give light upon the earth"[25] (ibid.). And although everything has previously been explained,[26] they are of the same pattern, and this is the explanation of the matter. What is the difference between them? One sustains and nourishes the upper world, in which it is, and all the upper extremities, and the other sustains and nourishes the lower world[27] and all the lower extremities.[28] You might question what this upper world is,[29] since the upper eighth firmament, the concealed one, is the upper world and is called such, for there are two worlds,[30] as has been explained. [The answer is] that it is the upper world, but that all those which proceed from it[31] are [also] called by its name, and those which proceed from the lower world are called by *its* name, and both the one and the other are united. Blessed is He for ever, and throughout the worlds.

4. BLESSING

(Zohar I, 208b)

"And Joseph could not restrain himself [before all those that stood by him; and he cried out: Take everybody away from me. And there was no one with him, when Joseph made himself known to his brothers]" (Genesis 45: 1-2). Rabbi Hezekiah began by quoting: "A Song of

---

[19] *Binah* and *Yesod*.   [20] The *sefirot*.   [21] From *Malkhut*.   [22] From *Hokhmah*.

[23] *Yesod* absorbs the influence of the *sefirot* and then transmits it to the realms below.

[24] *Binah* and *Yesod* may both be regarded as a river.

[25] I.e., to give light to *Malkhut*, which is called "earth."

[26] In a different fashion.   [27] *Malkhut*.

[28] The palaces and chariots of *Malkhut*.

[29] *Binah* is itself the upper world. How then can it be said to sustain the upper world?

[30] *Binah* and *Malkhut*.

[31] The *sefirot* from *Hesed* to *Yesod* are also called "the upper world."

Degrees. To you I raise my eyes, you who dwell in the heavens" (Psalm
123: 1). They have interpreted this verse, and it has been explained. But
come and see. "To you I raise my eyes," and it is written, "I raise my
eyes to the hills" (Psalm 121: 1). But one is above[32] and the other is
below.[33] "I raise my eyes to the hills"—this is above, in order to draw
blessings down from the upper to the lower world from those supernal
hills,[34] in order to draw blessings down from them to the Assembly of
Israel,[35] who receive blessings from them. "To you I raise my eyes"—in
order to look expectantly for the blessings that descend from there[36] to
the lower regions; "You who dwell in the heavens," for all strength, and
power, and sustenance are in the heavens,[37] because when the Jubilee[38]
opens the fountains of all these gates[39] they all exist in the heavens, and
when the heavens receive the lights that emerge from the Jubilee they
feed and water the Assembly of Israel by means of a righteous one.[40]
And when he is aroused by her, how many are they[41] that stand on every
side in order to be refreshed and blessed from there, as it is said, "The
young lions roar after their prey, and seek their food from God" (Psalm
104: 21). Then she ascends into the mystery of mysteries,[42] as is fitting,
and receives pleasure from her husband, as is proper, when they are
alone,[43] as it is said "there was no one with him," for it is written "Take
everybody away from me." And after she has received pleasure from her
husband they are all refreshed and nourished, as it is said "They give
drink to every beast of the field; the wild asses quench their thirst"
(Psalm 104: 11).

5. RIGHTEOUSNESS

(Zohar I, 208a–208b)

"And Joseph could not restrain himself before all those that stood by
him. . ." (Genesis 45: 1). Rabbi Hiyya began by quoting: "He has
scattered; he has given to the needy; his righteousness endures for ever;
his horn shall be exalted in honor" (Psalm 112: 9). Come and see. The
Holy One, blessed be He, created the world, and put man in charge of it,
so that he might be king over all. And man became diversified into
several types in the world. Some were righteous, and some wicked; some
were foolish, and some wise; and they were all preserved in the world:

[32] The *Shekhinah* faces the upper regions in order to attract to herself the divine
influence.
[33] The lower regions face the *Shekhinah* in order to receive influence from her.
[34] The *sefirot* from *Ḥesed* to *Yesod*.   [35] To the *Shekhinah*.   [36] From the *Shekhinah*.
[37] The *Shekhinah*'s existence depends on *Tiferet*, which is called "heavens."
[38] *Binah*.   [39] The fifty gates of *Binah*.   [40] *Yesod*.   [41] The lower realms.
[42] Into the mystery of intercourse.
[43] When the time for intercourse comes, the *Shekhinah* leaves her entourage.

rich and poor, so that they could all benefit one another.[44] The righteous could benefit the wicked, the wise could benefit the foolish, the rich could benefit the poor, for in this way man earns eternal life, and becomes bound to the Tree of Life. Furthermore, the righteousness that he performs lasts for ever, as it is written, "his righteousness endures for ever."

"He has scattered; he has given to the needy." Rabbi Eleazar said: When the Holy One, Blessed be He, created the world, He established it on a single pillar, and "Righteous" is its name, and this righteous one is the foundation (*Yesod*) of the world. He waters and feeds all, as it is written "And a river goes out of Eden to water the garden, and from there it is parted and becomes four heads" (Genesis 2: 10). "From there it is parted." What does "it is parted" mean? The garden[45] receives all the food and drink from the river,[46] and afterward the drink is scattered to the four corners of the world. How many are they[47] who wait to be refreshed and nourished from there, as it is said, "The eyes of all wait for you, and you give them their food in due season" (Psalm 145: 15). Consequently, "He has scattered; he has given to the needy." This [refers to] the righteous one.[48] "His righteousness endures for ever"— this is the Assembly of Israel,[49] for by this means she exists through the mystery of peace,[50] with a complete existence. "The wicked shall see and be angry" (Psalm 112: 10). This is the kingdom of the idolaters.[51] Come and see. The kingdom of heaven is the Temple that sustains all the needy beneath the *Shekhinah*, and this righteous one is called "the disburser of charity,"[52] who has compassion on all and feeds them, as it is written, "he has scattered; he has given to the needy." Consequently, disbursers of charity receive a reward matching [that of] all those who give charity.

Come and see. "And Joseph could not restrain himself before all those that stood." These are they who stand [and wait] to be fed and refreshed by him. "And there was no one with him when Joseph made himself known to his brothers." "With him" refers to the Assembly of Israel. "His brothers" are the other chariot-hosts,[53] of whom it is written "For the sake of my brothers and my companions" (Psalm 122: 8).

---

[44] The righteous bring the wicked back in repentance: the wise teach the foolish, and the rich maintain the poor.   [45] *Malkhut.*   [46] *Yesod.*

[47] The lower realms.   [48] *Yesod.*   [49] *Malkhut.*

[50] Through intercourse with *Yesod*, who is called "Peace."

[51] The nations are angry because they do not share in the influence resulting from the intercourse.

[52] [*Zedakah* ("charity") also means "righteousness."]

[53] The camps of the *Shekhinah*, who participate in the influence resulting from the intercourse. This latter is indicated by the verb "made himself known," which is connected here with "And the man knew Eve, his wife" (Genesis 4: 1).

6. WATERING

(Zohar III, 181a)

Rabbi Simeon began by quoting: "Who sends forth springs into the streams ... they give drink to every beast of the field" (Psalm 104: 11–12). King David uttered these verses through the holy spirit, and one must ponder on them. Come and see. When supernal *Hokhmah* provoked movement in its engravings,[54] even though it is secluded on every side, an opening was made, and a river[55] poured out of it, filling the supernal gates.[56] Just as a fountain or a water source fills a mighty stream, and from thence sources of rivers extend and flow on every side, so here: through one narrow channel[57] that is not known, that great river emerges and gushes forth, and from thence sources and streams extend,[58] and they are filled with it. This is [the meaning of] the verse "Who sends forth springs into the streams." These are the holy, supernal rivers[59] of pure balsam. And they are all saturated as one with the flowing of the holy, supernal stream, which gushes forth. After this "they give drink to every beast of the field (*sadai*)." This is [the significance of] the verse "and from thence it was parted and became four heads" (Genesis 2: 10); these four heads are the beasts of *sadai*, the sum of all the camps and all the hosts that are comprised with them. *Sadai*: do not pronounce it *sadai*, but *Shaddai* (the Almighty), for he receives and completes the name from the foundation (*Yesod*) of the world.[60] "The wild asses quench their thirst" (Psalm 104: 11). These are they of whom it is written "and the wheels (*ofannim*) were lifted up beside them, for the spirit of the beast was in the wheels" (Ezekiel 1: 20). Who is "the beast"? These "beasts of the field" are few in number, and each one of them is assigned to one of the four points of the compass, and this particular one is called "beast,"[61] and there are wheels beside each one of them and they move only through the spirit of the particular beast that moves above them. When these are saturated by the supernal "watering," all the remaining hosts[62] drink and are saturated, and they strengthen their roots, and become interdependent at known levels. This is the [meaning

[54] *Hokhmah* stimulates movement in the designs of the *sefirot*, which are engraved in it, and which have a concealed existence there before the process of emanation.

[55] *Binah.* [56] The fifty gates of *Binah.* [57] The channel of *Hokhmah.*

[58] The seven lower *sefirot* and their channels of influence. [59] These same *sefirot.*

[60] The beasts of the Chariot are called "the beasts of the field" (*sadai*), because at their head stands Metatron, who controls them, and he is called *Shaddai*. This name is also given to the *sefirah*, *Yesod*, from whom Metatron receives his power of control (Metatron is equivalent to *Shaddai* in *gematria*).

[61] Metatron is the supernal beast, through whose spirit the other beasts and the wheels move. Perhaps, however, the reference here is to *Malkhut*, which controls all the forces in the Chariot.

[62] The angels, which are "the birds of heaven."

of the] verse "Beside them dwell the birds of heaven. . ." (Psalm 104: 12). "He waters the mountains from his upper chambers" (Psalm 104: 13). These are the remaining upper levels.[63] And after all this "the earth is full of the fruit of your works" (ibid.)—the earth below, and all the worlds together rejoice and are blessed.

7. THE EYES OF THE LORD

(Zohar III, 129b; Idra Rabba)

The eyes of the white head[64] are different from other eyes. The eye has no lid, and the eye has no brows. Why is this? It is written, "Behold, He neither slumbers, nor sleeps, the protector of Israel" (Psalm 121: 4)—the Israel of the upper world;[65] and it is written "your eyes are open" (Jeremiah 32: 19). And it is taught: Whatever happens in Mercy, the eye has no lid [there], and the eye has no brows. How much more is this true of the white head, which needs no protection.

Rabbi Simeon said to Rabbi Abba: To what does this refer?

He said to him: To the fish in the sea, whose eyes have no lids, whose eyes have no brows, for they do not sleep and do not need a protection for the eye. How much more is this true of the Most Ancient One.[66] He needs no protection, especially since he supervises everything, nourishes everything, and does not sleep. This is [the significance of] the verse "Behold, He neither slumbers, nor sleeps, the protector of Israel"—the Israel of the upper world.

It is written "Behold the eye of the Lord is toward those who fear Him" (Psalm 33: 18). And it is written "the eyes of the Lord run to and fro through the whole earth" (Zechariah 4: 10). There is no contradiction here. One refers to *Ze'ir Anpin*[67] and the other to *Arikh Anpin*.[68] Nevertheless, there are two eyes that become one,[69] an eye that is white within white, and white that comprises all white.[70]

The first white shines, and ascends and descends in order to be

---

[63] The upper dwellings in the worlds that are above the earth.

[64] *Keter*, which is all Mercy, and is depicted as *Arikh Anpin* (lit., long countenance), in contrast to *Ze'ir Anpin* (lit., short countenance, i.e., the pattern of emanation from Ḥokhmah downward), which contains Judgment.

[65] *Tiferet*, which *Keter* protects from the husks.   [66] *Keter*.

[67] Of him it is said that his eyes "run to and fro through the whole earth," because he keeps an eye on the wicked as well, in order to punish them with Judgment.

[68] *Keter*, which contains no Judgment, looks after "those who fear," for they deserve Mercy.

[69] Of *Keter* it is said "the eye of the Lord," in the singular, because its two eyes are really one, there being no differentiation between right and left, i.e., between Love and Judgment.

[70] In the supernal eye there are three kinds of whiteness, which act in different areas in the world of emanation.

comprised, for it is bound up in a bond.[71] It is taught: This white struck and kindled three lights,[72] called "majesty," "beauty," and "joy,"[73] and they shine joyfully in perfection.

The second white shines, and ascends and descends, and it strikes and kindles three other lights, called "*Nezaḥ*", "*Hesed*", and "*Tiferet*", and they shine joyfully in perfection.

The third white sparkles and shines, and descends and ascends, and emerges from the seclusion of the brain,[74] and it strikes the middle, seventh, light[75] and produces a way to the lower heart,[76] and all the lights below[77] are kindled.

8. DIRECTION ON WEEKDAYS AND ON THE SABBATH

(Zohar I, 75a–75b)

Rabbi Simeon began by quoting: "So says the Lord God: The gate of the inner court that faces east shall be shut the six working days; but on the sabbath it shall be opened, and on the day of the new moon it shall be opened" (Ezekiel 46: 1). One needs to ponder upon this verse, and it is a mystery as has been explained. "It shall be shut the six working days"—why? These are the weekdays[78] when this gate shall be shut, so that the profane shall not be used with the holy.[79] "But on the sabbath it shall be opened, and on the day of the new moon it shall be opened," for then the holy is used with the holy,[80] and then the moon is illumined so that it may be joined with the sun.

Come and see. This gate is not open on the six weekdays, because on weekdays the lower world[81] is nourished, and on these six weekdays [the husks] rule over the world, except for the land of Israel; and they rule because the gate is closed. But "on the sabbath . . . and on the day of the new moon" they all depart and they no longer rule, because this gate is [then] opened, and the world is nourished in joy from there, and the

[71] When it is active in the world of emanation, the white of *Keter* is comprised within the *sefirot*, and is bound up in the bond of the *sefirot*. [72] *Sefirot*.

[73] From the context it would seem that the three are *Hod*, *Gevurah*, and *Yesod*.

[74] In the white head there is a concealed and unknowable brain, which is the source of emanation.

[75] This refers, apparently, to *Yesod*, which is the seventh, counting from *Binah*, and is situated on the middle line, below *Tiferet*.

[76] It opens the channel of influence from *Yesod* to *Malkhut*, which is the lower heart.

[77] The lower powers, which receive influence from *Malkhut*.

[78] I.e., the husks that rule on weekdays. Alternatively, they represent Metatron and his hosts, by whom the world is directed on weekdays.

[79] *Malkhut*, the gate of the world of emanation, is closed, and does not pour down influence, so that the husks cannot gain control of her.

[80] The intercourse of *Malkhut* with *Tiferet*, i.e., of the moon with the sun.

[81] The domain of the husks.

world is not committed to a foreign power. You might ask whether the six weekdays rule entirely on their own.[82] Come and see. "That faces east"—before they rise in order to rule,[83] he looks down upon the world continually. But [the gate] is not opened, to allow the world to gain nourishment from the holy, except on the sabbath and on the day of the new moon. And all the days are connected with the sabbath, and nourished from there,[84] because on the sabbath-day all the gates are opened, and there is rest for all, for the upper and the lower worlds.

9. ACCEPTABLE TIME

(Zohar III, 136a–136b; *Idra Rabba*)

The forehead of the skull[85] is the keenest of scrutinies,[86] and reveals itself only when the wicked have to be visited, and when their deeds need to be examined. And it is taught: When this forehead is revealed, all the prosecutors are aroused, and the whole world is given over to Judgment. But when the prayers of Israel rise up before the Ancient of Days,[87] and he wishes to have mercy upon his children, he reveals the forehead of the Will of wills,[88] and it illumines [the forehead of] *Ze'ir Anpin*, and Judgment is quieted.

On this forehead[89] there emerges a single hair,[90] which spreads from the brain,[91] which produces five gates,[92] and as it spreads the forehead is formed that scrutinizes the wicked of the world, those who are not ashamed of their deeds. This is the meaning of the verse "You had the forehead of a harlot; you refused to be ashamed" (Jeremiah 3: 3). It is taught: The hair does not remain in this place on the forehead,[93] for it reveals itself to those who are impudent in their iniquities.

[82] Without any divine providence at all in the world.
[83] "East" (Heb. *kadim*) is connected here with *kodem* ("before"). The husks are subject to divine supervision.
[84] The influence that exists on weekdays is merely a remnant of the influence that descends on the sabbath.
[85] The forehead of *Ze'ir Anpin* (i.e., the system of emanation from *Hokhmah* downward). Its skull is *Binah*.
[86] [More literally, "the providence of providence."] This skull scrutinizes men's deeds, and since its essential characteristic is that of Judgment, it reveals itself only when the wicked have to be punished. [87] *Keter*, which is Mercy, entirely.
[88] *Keter*. This designation indicates basically the forehead of providence that belongs to *Keter*. [89] Of *Ze'ir Anpin*.
[90] Hairs symbolize strict Judgment, or even "the other side," whose powers are called *se'irim* ("goats") [connected with the root *se'ar* ("hair")].
[91] From the brain of the skull, from *Binah*.
[92] Which branch out into the fifty gates of *Binah*.
[93] This means, judging from the context, that the hair does not remain in the place where it grew, on the forehead of *Ze'ir Anpin*, but it spreads farther in order to reveal Judgment to the wicked. But in a parallel passage (III, 129b) the same expression occurs, and there it means that there is no hair at all on the forehead of *Keter*.

When the Holy One, Blessed be He, stirs Himself in order to take delight in the righteous, the countenance of the Ancient of Days illumines the countenance of *Ze'ir Anpin*, and his forehead is revealed, and shines on this [other] forehead. Then it is called "an acceptable time"[94] (Psalm 69: 14). And whenever Judgment is suspended,[95] and the forehead of *Ze'ir Anpin* is revealed, the forehead of the Ancient of ancients is revealed, and Judgment is quieted and is not enacted.

It is taught: This forehead spreads into two hundred thousand of the reddest rednesses,[96] which are comprised and included in it. And when the forehead of *Ze'ir Anpin* is revealed, they all have the power to destroy, but when the forehead of the Will of wills is revealed, which shines upon this [other] forehead, they are all quieted.

10. ATONEMENT FOR SIN

(Zohar I, 206b)

"For behold, the kings [assembled themselves]" (Psalm 48: 5). Rabbi Judah said: The mystery of faith is here, for when the Will is there, and the bond is crowned as one,[97] then the two worlds[98] are bound together, and are assembled together, one to open the treasury, and the other to gather and to enter it. Then, "behold, the kings assembled themselves"—two sacred worlds, the upper world and the lower world. "They passed over together." The mystery of the matter [is] that when they were joined together "they passed over together"; for all the sins of the world do not pass over in order to be forgiven until [the two worlds] are joined together, as it is written "that passes over iniquity" (Micah 7: 18). Consequently "they passed over together"—the sins passed over and were forgiven because at that time all countenances shone, and all sins were passed over.

11. THE PRESENCE OF GOD IN THE WORLDS

(Zohar III, 159a)

The Holy One, blessed be He,[99] has three worlds, and He is hidden within them. The first world [is] that supernal world concealed from all,[100] which cannot be seen, and cannot be known, except by Him, who

---

[94] [Lit., "time of will."] This refers particularly to the time of the afternoon prayer on the sabbath, for on weekdays it is the time of strict Judgment.

[95] In preparation for action.

[96] The powers of Judgment, including the forces of destruction of "the other side."

[97] The *sefirot* are united when the revelation takes place of the Mercy that is in *Keter*, which is the Will.

[98] The male world, and *Yesod*, in particular, which pours out influence, and the female world, i.e., *Malkhut*, which receives influence.   [99] *En-Sof.*

[100] *Keter*, concealed even from the perception of the *sefirot*.

is hidden within it. The second world, which is connected to the one above it,[101] is the one from which the Holy One, Blessed be He, is known, as it is written "Open for me the gates of righteousness" (Psalm 118: 19), "This is the gate of the Lord" (ibid., v. 20). The third world[102] [is] the world that is below them, where separation exists.[103] This is the world where the angels on high dwell, and the Holy One, Blessed be He, is there, and is not [there]. He is there now, but when they wish to look upon and know Him, He removes Himself from them, and is not to be seen, so that they all enquire "Where is the place of His glory?"[104] "Blessed be the glory of the Lord from His place" (Ezekiel 3: 12). This is the world where He has no continuous presence.

12. THE CONCEALED LIGHT

(Zohar II, 148b–149a)

It is written "And God said, Let there be light. And there was light" (Genesis 1: 3). Rabbi Jose said: This light is concealed and stored up for the righteous in the world to come, as they have explained, as it is written, "Light is sown for the righteous" (Psalm 97: 11)—for the really righteous, without qualification.[105] And this light has no role in the world, except on the first day; and then it was concealed, and no longer used.

Rabbi Judah said: Had it not been concealed from everything, the world could not have endured a single moment. But it was concealed, and sown, like the seed that produces offspring, seeds and fruit,[106] and by it the world is sustained. And not a day passes without something emerging from it into the world, and sustaining everything, for by it the Holy One, blessed be He, nourishes the world. Wherever they study the Torah at night, a single ray[107] comes from the concealed light and stretches out to those that study. This is the meaning of the verse "By day the Lord will command His love, and in the night His song will be with me" (Psalm 42: 9), and they have already interpreted this. What is written about the day that the tabernacle was erected below? "And Moses was unable to enter the tent of meeting because the cloud dwelt upon it" (Exodus 40: 35). What is the cloud? A single ray it was that came from the side of the primal light, that emerged in the joy of the

[101] The world of the *sefirot*, from *Hokhmah* downward, and particularly *Malkhut*, which is called *Zedek* (Righteousness). It is the gateway to the perception of the mystery of the Godhead.   [102] The world of the Chariot.

[103] Separation from the Godhead.

[104] A quotation from the *Kedushah* of the *Musaf* (Additional) Service.

[105] For every righteous individual.

[106] Even though it is concealed, it is active by sending down influence through *Yesod*, which is the supernal Righteous One. It therefore acts like the seed concealed in the ground.   [107] A ray of Love.

bride,[108] when she entered the tabernacle below. And from that day it was not revealed, but it serves its purpose in the world, and every day it renews the work of creation.

13. THE PRIMAL LIGHT

(Zohar II, 166b–167a)

The Holy One, blessed be He, sowed this light[109] in the Garden of Eden,[110] and He arranged it in rows[111] with the help of the Righteous One,[112] who is the gardener in the Garden. And he took this light, and sowed it as a seed of truth, and arranged it in rows in the Garden, and it sprouted and grew and produced fruit, by which the world is nourished. This is the meaning of the verse "Light is sown for the righteous. . ." (Psalm 97: 11). And it is written "The garden causes the things that are sown in it to spring forth" (Isaiah 61: 11). What are "the things that are sown in it"? These are the sowings of the primal light, which is always sown. Now it brings forth and produces fruit, and now it is sown as at the beginning.[113] Before the world eats this fruit, the seed produces and gives fruit, and does not rest. Consequently, all the worlds are nourished through the supply of the gardener, who is called the Righteous One, and who never rests or ceases, except when Israel is in exile.

You might object that it is written, concerning the time of the exile, "The waters fail from the sea, and the river is drained dry" (Job 14: 11). How then can it produce offspring? But it is written "sown"—it is continually sown. From the time that the river[114] ceases, the gardener does not enter the Garden.[115] But the light, which is continually sown, produces fruit, and it is sown of itself, as at the beginning,[116] and it does not rest at all, like a garden that goes on producing, and some of the seed falls in its place, and it continues to produce by itself, as at the first. You might say that the offspring and the fruit are the same as when the gardener is there. But it is not so. On the other hand, the seed is never absent.

14. THE RENEWAL OF THE WORK OF CREATION

(Zohar I, 207a)

Another interpretation: "The Lord by wisdom founded the earth"

[108] The *Shekhinah*.

[109] The outpouring of the primal light, which is Love (*Ḥesed*).   [110] *Malkhut*.

[111] The outpouring of influence is divided into various types in *Malkhut*, depending on the needs of the lower world.   [112] *Yesod*.

[113] Even after it has produced fruit, it continues to be sown and goes on producing.

[114] The flow of influence. [115] There is no intercourse between *Yesod* and *Malkhut*.

[116] The earlier sowing remains active, even when *Yesod* and *Malkhut* are separated, and it produces, as it were, wild fruit.

(Proverbs 3: 19). The upper world[117] was created only from Wisdom, and the lower world was created only from Wisdom,[118] and they all emerged from the upper Wisdom and from the lower Wisdom. "By understanding He established the heavens" (ibid.) "Established." What does "established" mean?[119] He goes on establishing [them] every day, and does not cease.[120] They were not arranged at one particular time, but He arranges them daily. This is the mystery of the verse, "The heavens are not clean in His sight" (Job 15: 15). Do you imagine that this is meant to be derogatory of the heavens? No, it is to the heavens' credit that, because of the great love and pleasure that the Holy One, blessed be He, feels for them, and their preciousness in His sight, they are still not arranged as they should be, even though He arranges them every day; for great is the love He bears them, and He wishes to shine upon them continuously, without cease, for in this way does the world to come[121] produce lights that shine every day, continuously, without ceasing, in order to grant them perpetual illumination. Consequently, "They are not clean in His sight." It is not written merely "they are not clean," but "they are not clean in His sight." And so "By understanding is He establishing the heavens." What are "the heavens"? This is the mystery of the patriarchs, and the mystery of the patriarchs is Jacob, who represents the sum of them,[122] for Jacob is the praise of the patriarchs, and he is there to shed light upon the world. And because he ascends into the world to come,[123] a beautiful branch comes from him, and all the lights emerge from him, together with complete satiety and anointing oil with which to illumine the earth.[124] Who is this? It is Joseph the Righteous,[125] who provides satiety for the whole world, and the world is nourished by him. Therefore, whatever the Holy One, blessed be He, does in the world is all done through the supernal mystery,[126] and all is as it should be.

[117] *Binah*, which is the upper earth, was emanated from the upper *Hokhmah*.

[118] The actual earth was created by means of *Malkhut*, which is the lower *Hokhmah*.

[119] [Unlike the previous verb "founded," which is in the perfect tense, the Hebrew for "established" (*konen*) is, strictly speaking, a present participle, and indicates therefore a continuous action.]

[120] The actual heavens do not depend solely on their creation at the beginning, but they are renewed daily through the divine influence that descends from *Binah*.

[121] *Binah*.

[122] Here he gives the mystical interpretation of "He established the heavens." The heavens are *Tiferet*, symbolized by Jacob, the totality of the patriarchs, and *Tiferet* is sustained by *Binah* ("understanding").

[123] *Tiferet* is concealed in its source, *Binah*.

[124] Both *Malkhut* and the actual earth. [125] *Yesod*.

[126] The lower heavens and earth are parallel to the upper, and similarly with Jacob and Joseph.